# TELLINGS AND TEXTS

# Tellings and Texts

## Music, Literature and Performance in North India

*Edited by Francesca Orsini*
*and Katherine Butler Schofield*

OpenBook Publishers

http://www.openbookpublishers.com



All external links were active on 22/09/2015 and archived via the Internet Archive Wayback Machine: https://archive.org/web/

Digital material and resources associated with this volume are available at http://www.openbookpublishers.com/isbn/9781783741021#resources

ISBN Paperback: 978-1-78374-102-1
ISBN Hardback: 978-1-78374-103-8
ISBN Digital (PDF): 978-1-78374-104-5
ISBN Digital ebook (epub): 978-1-78374-105-2
ISBN Digital ebook (mobi): 9978-1-78374-106-9
DOI: 10.11647/OBP.0062

King's College London has generously contributed to the publication of this volume.

Cover image: Late eighteenth-century miniature by Mir Kalan Khan (Awadh, c.1775). Photo by Pernille Klemp. © The David Collection, Copenhagen. Inventory no. 50/1981. All rights reserved.

Cover design by Heidi Coburn.

All paper used by Open Book Publishers is SFI (Sustainable Forestry Initiative) and PEFC (Programme for the Endorsement of Forest Certification Schemes) Certified.

Printed in the United Kingdom and United States by Lightning Source for Open Book Publishers

*To Aditya's memory, once again*

# Contents

7. Did Surdas Perform the *Bhāgavata-purāṇa?* 209
*John Stratton Hawley*

8. Text, Orality, and Performance in Newar Devotional Music 231
*Richard Widdess*

**III. Written Clues about Performed Texts**

9. Listening for the Context: Tuning in to the Reception of *Riti* Poetry 249
*Allison Busch*

10. Reading the Acts and Lives of Performers in Mughal Persian Texts 283
*Sunil Sharma*

11. Persian Poets on the Streets: The Lore of Indo-Persian Poetic Circles in Late Mughal India 303
*Stefano Pellò*

12. Texts and Tellings: *Kathas* in the Fifteenth and Sixteenth Centuries 327
*Francesca Orsini*

13. A Curious King, a Psychic Leper, and the Workings of *Karma*: Bajid's Entertaining Narratives 359
*Imre Bangha*

**IV. Musical Knowledge and Aesthetics**

14. *Raga* in the Early Sixteenth Century 385
*Allyn Miner*

15. Learning to Taste the Emotions: The Mughal *Rasika* 407
*Katherine Butler Schofield*

16. Patterns of Composition in the Seventeenth-Century Bengali Literature of Arakan 423
*Thibaut d'Hubert*

17. The Musical Lives of Texts: Rhythms and Communal Relationships among the Nizamis and Some of Their Neighbours in South and West Asia 445
*Richard K. Wolf*

Glossary 485
Bibliography 493
Index 535

# Acknowledgements

This volume brings together the papers presented at the third and final conference of the AHRC-funded project "North Indian Literary Culture and History from a Multilingual Perspective: 1450-1650", which Francesca ran at the School of Oriental and African Studies (SOAS) between 2006-2009 and in which Katherine was intimately involved from start to finish. The conference was initially entitled "Tellings, Not Texts", but over the course of the three days it became clear that texts were very much involved in many of the performance forms and traditions we were discussing, hence the change of title. (The first conference volume, *After Timur Left*, came out in 2014 from Oxford University Press, New Delhi, co-edited by Francesca and Samira Sheikh.) We would first of all like to thank the AHRC for its generous support. The conference, which took place on 8-10 June 2009, benefited from a British Academy conference support grant, for which we are also grateful, as we are to the European Research Council which supported Katherine's contributions in the latter stages. We would like here to heartily thank all the contributors for their patience and good humour as we asked for more and more changes. We thank Alessandra Tosi for her enthusiasm and welcome, and Dr David Lunn for careful copy-editing. Our dear friend Aditya Behl helped plan the conference and was supposed to come, but was in the end too ill to travel. He died, tragically young, two months later. We would like to dedicate the volume to him, for he remains in our thoughts and in our love.

FO and KBS

London and Cambridge, July 2015

# Note on Transliteration

A volume of this kind inevitably has a large number of transliterated words in several languages. To make the text readable without sacrificing its scholarly appeal, we have chosen to use diacritical marks for book titles and direct quotations, and to keep them to a minimum elsewhere; in some instances, notably where metrical considerations are important, they are used more extensively. For Devanagari, the transliteration used follows R.S. McGregor, *The Oxford Hindi-English Dictionary* (New Delhi: Oxford University Press, 1993), with the exception that nasalised vowels are transliterated with a ṃ instead of ṁ. For Persian words, we have slightly adapted existing systems as below. In spite of our efforts, we have not achieved complete consistency.

| | | | | | |
|---|---|---|---|---|---|
| ا A | ب B | پ P | ت T | ث S̱ | |
| ج J | چ CH | ح Ḥ | خ KH | | |
| د D | ذ Ẕ | ر R | ز Z | ژ ZH | |
| س S | ش SH | ص Ṣ | ض Ż | | |
| ط Ṭ | ظ Ẓ | ع ʻ | غ GH | ف F | ق Q |
| ک K | گ G | ل L | م M | ن N | |

و W,V, Ū (O only if specified as *majhul*) ہ H

ی Y, Ī (E only if specified as *majhul*)

short vowels: a, i, u

# Note on Dating Systems

This volume necessarily makes reference to four discrete calendrical systems.

Where otherwise unmarked, we use the Common/Christian Era (Anno Domini), denoted "CE".

The Islamic calendar (denoted "AH": Anno Hegirae, or Hijri year), commenced in the year 622 CE. A lunar calendar, it does not correspond directly to the Gregorian Calendar, and the year 2015 CE is 1436-37 AH.

The Vikram Samvat calendar, denoted "VS", is between 56-57 years ahead of the Common Era, thus 2015 CE covers 2071-72 VS.

Finally, the Banggabda or Bengali Calendar, denoted "BA", is between 593-94 years behind the Common Era, thus 2015 CE is 1421-22 BA.

Both VS and BA are solar calendars, but do not begin in January, so there is no precise overlap with CE.

# List of Illustrations


5.1 (L) Jnaneshwari Stamp, issued in 1990 to commemorate the 700th anniversary of the composition of the *Jñāneśvarī*; (R) "Saint Dnyaneshwar" stamp, issued in 1997 in memory of Jnaneswhar/ Jnandev. Public Domain. 171

5.2 Namdev Performing a *Kirtan*, folio from a nineteenth-century publication of Mahipati's eighteenth-century biography [1890]. Public Domain. 173

5.3 Four typical *badas* or "notebooks" in the collection of the Bhandarkar Oriental Research Institute. Author's photograph, CC BY. 175

5.4 Transcript of a *kirtan* from a Marathi *bada*, c. eighteenth century. Bhandarkar Oriental Research Institute. Author's photograph, CC BY. 178

5.5 A representative page from Lohiya, K. 1997. *Kirtan mārga darśikā* (Pune: Sharada Sahitya), pp. 194-95. All rights reserved. 179

5.6 (L) section is taken from the *Śrī Nāmdev gāthā* (1970), p. 343; (R) is taken from the *Bhaktavijay* 1996 [1762], pp. 164-65. Image by the author, CC BY. 181

8.1 *Dapha* group performing in Suryamarhi Square, Bhaktapur. September 2007. Author's photograph, CC BY. 233

8.2 Raga Lalit. Bhaktapur, early seventeenth century. Photograph by Gert-Matthias Wegner, CC BY. 235

8.3 *Dapha* group performing at the Taleju temple, Kathmandu, in 1664. Detail of a painting now in the Collège de France, Paris. Author's sketch, CC BY. 237

8.4 *Ganamani*. Dattatreya Navadapha songbook, song no. 63 (fol. 20r-20v). Public Domain. 239

8.5 One side of the Bhairav Navadapha group performing on the first day of Biskah, Tahmarhi Square, Bhaktapur. The chariot of Bhairav is visible behind the singers. April 2003. Author's photograph, CC BY. 244

# Notes on Contributors

**Muzaffar Alam** is George V. Bobrinskoy Professor in South Asian Languages and Civilizations at the University of Chicago. He is the author of, among others, *The Crisis of Empire in Mughal North India* (1986) and *The Languages of Political Islam in India: c.1200-1800* (2004); and, with Sanjay Subrahmanyam, of *Writing the Mughal World: Studies on Culture and Politics* (2011).

**Imre Bangha** is Associate Professor of Hindi at the University of Oxford. He studied Indology in Budapest and holds a PhD in Hindi from Visva-Bharati. His publications include English, Hindi, and Hungarian books and articles on Brajbhasha and other forms of early Hindi with special focus on the poetic works of Anandghan, Thakur, Vishnudas, Tulsidas, Kabir, and Bajid, as well as on Rekhta literature in the Nagari script.

**Amy Bard** teaches Urdu and Hindi language and literature at Harvard University. In addition to her work on Shi'i religiosity, Bard's current projects include translating contemporary memoirs and autobiographical fiction from Hindi and Urdu to English.

**Allison Busch** is Associate Professor in the Department of Middle Eastern, South Asian, and African Studies at Columbia University. Her expertise is in Hindi literature, and she also has a special interest in Mughal-period court culture. Her recent monograph *Poetry of Kings* came out from Oxford University Press in 2011. Professor Busch is the editor (with Thomas de Bruijn) of *Culture and Circulation: Literature in Motion in Early Modern India* (2014), a collection of essays that explores relationships across literary languages in South Asia. One ongoing research project concerns the historical poetry produced in Rajput kingdoms during the heyday of Mughal rule. She is also working (with the art historian Molly Aitken) on a book about aesthetic representations of the Indian heroine across the arts.

**John E. Cort** is Professor of Asian and Comparative Religions at Denison University in Granville, Ohio. He is the author of *Jains in the World: Religious Values and Ideology in India* (2001), *Framing the Jina: Narratives of Icons and Idols in Jain History* (2010), and, with Lawrence A. Babb and Michael W. Meister, *Desert Temples: Sacred Centers of Rajasthan in Historical, Art-Historical and Social Contexts* (2008), as well as many articles on the Jains and on religion and culture in western India. He has edited *Open Boundaries: Jain Communities and Cultures in Indian History* (1998) and, with Andrea Luithle-Hardenberg and Leslie C. Orr, the forthcoming *Cooperation and Competition, Conflict and Contribution: The Jain Community, British Expansion, and Jainological Scholarship, 1800-1950.*

**Thibaut d'Hubert** is assistant professor at the University of Chicago where he teaches Bengali language and literature in the Department of South Asian Languages and Civilizations. His main field of research is the literary history of Bengal. His research interests include Indic and Persian poetics, the editing of premodern Bengali texts, the study of scribal practices, South Asian traditional hermeneutics, and the history of translation. He is currently working on a book project on the Bengali poet Alaol (fl.1651-1671) and the formation of vernacular Muslim literatures around the Bay of Bengal (c. sixteenth–seventeenth centuries). With Alexandre Papas (CNRS/CETOBAC, Paris), he is preparing a handbook on the reception of the works of the Persian polymath of Herat 'Abd al-Rahman Jami (1414-1492) based on material presented by various scholars during two conferences held in Chicago (2012) and Paris (2013).

**John Stratton Hawley**—informally, Jack—is Professor of Religion at Barnard College, Columbia University. Two books in which he has long been involved have recently appeared from Harvard University Press: *Sur's Ocean: Poems from the Early Tradition* (with Kenneth E. Bryant), one of the initial volumes in the Murty Classical Library of India, and *A Storm of Songs: India and the Idea of the Bhakti Movement.*

**Monika Horstmann** (a.k.a. Monika Boehm-Tettelbach) retired as Head of the Department of Modern South Asian Languages and Literatures, South Asia Institute, Heidelberg University. Her research focuses on early modern North Indian literatures and religious movements and on the interface between religion and politics. Recent books include *Der Zusammenhang der Welt* (2009) and *Jaipur 1778: The Making of a King* (2013), and a volume co-edited with Heidi R.M. Pauwels, *Indian Satire in the Period of First Modernity* (2012).

**Pasha M. Khan** is Chair in Urdu Language and Culture and an Assistant Professor at the Institute of Islamic Studies, McGill University. Among other subjects, he has written about the *shahr-āshob* genre of Urdu poetry (in *Nationalism in the Vernacular*, ed. by Shobna Nijhawan, 2009), and on the line between history and romance in the *Shahnamah* (*Indian Economic and Social History Review*, 2012). At present he is working on a book tentatively entitled *The Broken Spell*, which deals with the the art of storytelling (*dāstān-go'ī*), the lives of storytellers, and the relationship between between Urdu/Persian stories and histories in India from the beginning of the Mughal era to the twentieth century.

**Allyn Miner** is a Lecturer in the Department of South Asia Studies at the University of Pennsylvania, where she teaches sitar performance and courses on music and dance. She has a PhD in Musicology from Banaras Hindu University and a PhD in Sanskrit from the University of Pennsylvania. Her research interests centre on Hindi, Urdu, and Sanskrit texts related to music and the social history of music in various periods in North India. Her book *Sitar and Sarod in the 18th and 19th Centuries* (1997) is a standard reference work on the history of the sitar. Her translation of the *Saṅgītopaniṣatsāroddhāra* examines developments in music theory in fourteenth-century Gujarat.

**Christian Lee Novetzke** is Professor of South Asia Studies, Comparative Religion, and International Studies at the Jackson School of International Studies at the University of Washington, Seattle. His work explores the histories, cultures, and religions of South Asia from the medieval period to the modern and contemporary. Novetzke's work includes three books: *Religion and Public Memory* (2008 and 2009); *The Quotidian Revolution: Vernacularization, Religion, and Everyday Life in Premodern India* (2017); and *Amar Akbar Anthony: Bollywood, Brotherhood, and the Nation*, written with Andy Rotman and William Elison (2016).

**Francesca Orsini** is Professor of Hindi and South Asian Literature at the School of Oriental and African Studies, University of London. Her research spans modern and contemporary Hindi literature (*The Hindi Public Sphere:*

*Language and Literature in the Age of Nationalism*, 2002), cultural history (she edited *Love in South Asia: A Cultural History*, 2006), popular literature and the history of the book (*Print and Pleasure: The Genres of Commercial Publishing in Nineteenth-century North India*, 2009), and multilingual literary history (*Hindi and Urdu Before the Divide*, 2010; *After Timur Left: Culture and Circulation in Fifteenth-century North India*, co-edited with S. Sheikh, 2014).

**Stefano Pellò** is Lecturer in Persian and Indo-Persian studies at the University "Ca' Foscari" of Venice, and has been Visiting Lecturer at the School of Oriental and African Studies in London and at Columbia University, New York. His main research area is currently the diffusion and reception of Persian linguistic and literary culture in and beyond South Asia, and the related cosmopolitan processes of cultural and aesthetic interaction, particularly in the poetic sphere. He has also published studies on the traditional Persian philological and rhetorical disciplines and works as a literary translator. Among his main publications are *Tutiyān-e Hind*, a book on the history of Persian grammatical writings (*Dabistan-i Parsi: Una grammatica persiana del XIX secolo*, 2003), and the first Italian complete annotated translation of the *Divan of Hafez of Shiraz* (2005).

**Katherine Butler Schofield** (née Brown) is a historian of music in Mughal India and the colonial Indian Ocean. Working largely with Persian sources for Hindustani music c.1570-1860, she has established music as central to Mughal technologies of sovereignty and selfhood, identified classicisation processes at work in early modern Indian arts, examined the role of connoisseurship in nourishing male friendships, told tales about ill-fated courtesans and overweening *ustads*, and traced the lineage of the chief musicians to the Mughal emperors from Akbar to Bahadur Shah Zafar. Her current European Research Council project, "Musical Transitions to European Colonialism in the Eastern Indian Ocean" (2011-2015), investigates the ways in which the musical field was transformed in India and the Malay world c.1750-1900 as pre-colonial polities gave way to colonial regimes. As part of this project she is co-writing a book, *Hindustani Music Between Empires: Alternative Histories*.

**Sunil Sharma** is Professor of Persianate and Comparative Literature at Boston University. He received his PhD from the University of Chicago. He is the author of two monographs: *Persian Poetry at the Indian Frontier: Mas'ūd Sa'd Salmān of Lahore* (2000) and *Amir Khusraw: The Poet of Sultans* *and Sufis* (2005); two collaborative works: *Atiya's Journeys: A Muslim Woman from Colonial Bombay to Edwardian Britain* (2010) and *In the Bazaar of Love: The Selected Poetry of Amir Khusrau* (2011); and co-editor of two volumes of essays: *Necklace of the Pleiades: Studies in Persian Literature Presented to Heshmat Moayyad on his 80th Birthday* (2007) and *On the Wonders of Land and Sea: Persianate Travel Writing* (2013). He has written numerous articles and co-curated several exhibitions at Harvard University. His research interests are in the areas of Persianate literary and visual cultures, translation, and travel writing.

**Richard Widdess** is Professor of Musicology in the Department of Music, School of Oriental and African Studies, University of London. His research and teaching focus on the classical and religious musical traditions of South Asia, with reference to history, theory, ethnography, music analysis, and cognition. He has written three books on South Asian music: on *The Rāgas of Early Indian Music* (1995), tracing evidence for the development of the *raga* concept to c.1250; *Dhrupad* (with Ritwik Sanyal, 2004), on the oldest style of North Indian classical singing; and *Dāphā: Sacred Singing in a South Asian City* (2013), a study of the music of temple singing groups in Bhaktapur, Nepal. His current research addresses the cognitive and cultural significance of musical structure in contexts of orality.

**Richard K. Wolf** is Professor of Music and South Asian Studies at Harvard University. His books and articles consider musical and social issues of language, emotion, poetics, time, space, and religious experience. Wolf also performs concerts internationally on the South Indian *vīṇā*. In recent years his field investigations have expanded from South Asia to Central and West Asia. His most recent single-authored book, *The Voice in the Drum: Music, Language and Emotion in Islamicate South Asia* (2014), is a hybrid ethnomusicological study written in the form of a novel.

# Introduction

*Francesca Orsini and Katherine Butler Schofield*

*Khwāndan*: To read, to recite [...] to sing.[1]

What would an auditory history of South Asia sound like? As we walk down a city street or a neighbourhood lane in contemporary India, loudspeakers hanging from electricity poles spread the tune of a choral *bhajan* or amateur singing at a ritual wake, while few neighbourhoods are out of aural reach of an *azan*, the call to prayer. Public spaces are routinely occupied by religious processions with drums, marriage processions with *band baja*, or political demonstrations with loud slogans and public speeches. Every town has public spaces—a *maidan*, *lila* ground, *karbala*, or park—where religious performances and "programmes", fairs (*melas*), and political rallies regularly attract visitors and broadcast their activities through their lively noises. Amidst the cacophony of traffic sounds—extra-loud car horns, shrill cycle-rickshaw bells, the deeper grumble of buses and trucks—people's mobile ringtones advertise their musical taste: Punjabi beats, melodious *ghazals*, or the latest Bombay dance number. Several times a day, when your own mobile rings and you pick up, a jingle or a verse addresses you for no apparent reason. This soundscape is not static and unchanging. On the Delhi metro, the bilingual warnings "*metro paridhan ko ganda karna ek dandaniy apradh hai*"

1 Francis Joseph Steingass, *A Comprehensive Persian-English Dictionary* (London: Routledge & Kegan Paul, 1892), p. 481. In Indo-Persian literature, *khwānanda* was the most commonly used word for a professional singer. Whether a *khwānanda* was a singer, a reader, or a reciter can only be understood from context.

 http://dx.doi.org/10.11647/OBP.0062.18

and "mind the gap" have replaced the scratchy audio cassettes on buses as accompaniments on one's daily journey through the city, while fewer autorickshaws seem to ride with their radio on full-blast.

South Asia's visual culture has been the object of much study in recent years, from calendar art to photography, from truck art to political statuary. Yet it would be hard to deny that making sound and hearing or listening to music, songs, speeches, sermons, and stories have been equally constitutive of South Asian social and cultural history until the present day.[2] But how has the mosaic of sounds, voices, and tellings changed over time? More fundamentally, how can we even write the history of sound at all, given that its nature is ephemeral: over in a moment, gone forever, and never fully captured in words on a page?

This volume explores the interconnected histories of singing, storytelling, and oral performance in early modern and contemporary North India (and Pakistan), in an attempt to restore the auditory realm to the literary and cultural history of South Asia. It does not aim at comprehensive coverage—there is no essay that deals with the rich performance traditions of Punjab, for example[3]—but presents strategically identified case studies that show different uses of texts in performance, give an idea of the wide range of performance practices, and highlight the significant circulation of aesthetic concepts and ideas about the beneficial effects of music, singing, and storytelling.

In the past two decades, an interest in what has been labelled acoustic or auditory history—the history not just of "music" but of historical soundworlds in their broadest possible sense—has begun to emerge in the study of Western music. This new move has received considerable stimulus from parallel work in ethnomusicology on contemporary soundscapes,[4] research that has been foundational in the

---

2 The list of studies of contemporary South Asian soundworlds—musical, literary, and ritual performances—would in itself take hours to recite. As Stuart Blackburn and Joyce Burkhalter Flueckinger noted of *Oral Epics in India*, "[w]hen Milman Parry went to the Balkans in search of oral epics in the 1930s, he had problems locating singers; for researchers in South Asia today, the problem is not where to find oral epics, but which ones to study"; 'Introduction', *Oral Epics in India* (Berkeley: University of California Press, 1989), p. 1.

3 These have been abundantly studied, from Richard C. Temple's classic *Legends of the Panjâb* (1884) to Michael Nijhawan's recent study of *dhadhi* singers in *Dhadi Darbar: Religion, Violence, and the Performance of Sikh History* (New Delhi: Oxford University Press, 2006).

4 The "soundscape" concept ultimately derives from Canadian composer R. Murray Schafer's 1977 monograph *The Soundscape: Our Sonic Environment and the Tuning of the*

new interdiscipline of sound studies or "acoustemology", which takes in fields as diverse as geography, anthropology, environmental science, and music.[5]

While most scholarship on acoustic history and auditory cultures has been restricted to the period of recorded sound (the late nineteenth through the twenty-first centuries), Emma Dillon's magisterial 2012 monograph *The Sense of Sound* definitively turns musicology's attention to the European medieval past and to the difficult task of disinterring auditory history, and the history of music as it was sounded and embodied, from its textual traces.[6] Although such a task is made easier by the existence of detailed musical notation for European music that allows some sense of sounded reality to echo in the present, Dillon's methodology offers much of relevance to our quest to understand the acoustic and somatic lives of North Indian texts. Historians, too, have recently turned to the auditory, with Mark Smith's pioneering volume *Hearing History* opening our ears to the sounds of early modern Europe and America.[7] Typically, though, the pre-twentieth-century acoustic histories of other literate cultures so far remain largely untold. The recent works of Gary Tomlinson and Barbara Andaya, on the soundscapes of the pre-colonial Aztec and Malay worlds respectively, thus provide stimulating foils for us, with their insistence that sound was heard and understood differently in earlier cultural contexts and that sonic power and song were of vital significance and signification to Southeast Asian and American polities.[8]

---

*World* (New York: Knopf), but was then more famously taken up by Arjun Appadurai in his 1990 article 'Disjuncture and Difference in the Global Cultural Economy', *Public Culture* 2.2 (1990), 1-24.

5 For an excellent review of these influential developments in ethnomusicology and sound studies, see David W. Samuels et al., 'Soundscapes: Towards a Sounded Anthropology', *Annual Review of Anthropology* 39 (2010), 329-45. The term "acoustemology" is a coinage of ethnomusicologist Steven Feld; e.g. 'Waterfalls of Song: An Acoustemology of Place Resounding in Bosavi, Papua New Guinea', in *Senses of Place*, ed. by Steven Feld and Keith Basso (Santa Fe: School of American Research Press, 1996), pp. 91-135.

6 Emma Dillon, *The Sense of Sound: Musical Meaning in France, 1260-1330* (New York: Oxford University Press, 2012).

7 Mark M. Smith, ed., *Hearing History: A Reader* (Athens, GA: University of Georgia Press, 2004).

8 Gary Tomlinson, *The Singing of the New World: Indigenous Voice in the Era of European Contact* (Cambridge: Cambridge University Press, 2009); Barbara Watson Andaya, 'Distant Drums and Thunderous Cannon: Authority in Traditional Malay Society', *International Journal of Asia Pacific Studies* 7.2 (2011), 19-35.

In this volume, therefore, we undertake a task that has not, to our knowledge, been attempted before for the literary cultures of North India.[9] We seek to theorise the deep interdependencies of written text, sound, performer, audience, and meaning that the case studies in this volume make audible, in a situation where in most cases we no longer possess nor can ever recover the soundedness of the texts with which we work (see Schofield in this volume). By and large, texts that were once recited, sung, danced, and enacted have been territory ceded to scholars of literature and religion, who have generally acknowledged their aural and performative dimensions but gone little further.[10] The aural domain, in turn, has been relegated to ethnomusicologists studying the highly exclusive soundworld of North Indian art music.[11] And the very few ethnomusicologists who have brought tools of sonic analysis to bear on the textual archive have restricted their studies to instrumental genres and *raga* examples, whose mnemonic notation systems have been easier to translate, if only partially, into sound.[12] Perhaps concerned that their literary understanding might be found wanting, or perhaps because of the sheer inaudibility of most historical texts, music historians have steered clear of explaining how poems subtitled with *raga* and *tala* names might have sounded, or what other sonic hints might tell us about the lives of North Indian texts as they circulated as sounded and embodied entities in a resonant world.

In any case, the overwhelming majority of ethnomusicologists study the present, not the past: music, singing, and storytelling in North India have primarily been the domain of anthropologists of music and scholars of orality, who rarely view the living traditions they study as part of a cultural and literary field that can be mapped historically. This is the connection that this book aims to make: the contemporary ethnographies

9 Though the last chapter, 'Hierarchies of Response', of Aditya Behl's posthumously published monograph is typically prescient; *Love's Subtle Magic: An Indian Islamic Literary Tradition, 1379-1545* (New York: Oxford University Press, 2012b).

10 An exception is Christian Novetzke's *Religion and Public Memory: A Cultural History of Saint Namdev in India* (New York: Columbia University Press, 2008).

11 Most recently, see the important collection of essays *Hindustani Music: Thirteenth to Twentieth Centuries*, ed. by Joep Bor, Françoise "Nalini" Delvoye, Emmie te Nijenhuis, and Jane Harvey (New Delhi: Manohar, 2010).

12 See e.g. Allyn Miner, *Sitar and Sarod in the 18th and 19th Centuries* (New Delhi: Motilal Banarsidass, 1997); and D. Richard Widdess, *The Ragas of Early Indian Music: Modes, Melodies and Musical Notations from the Gupta Period to c.1250* (Oxford: Clarendon, 1995).

by Amy Bard, Christian Novetzke, Richard Widdess, and Richard Wolf show what uses—sometimes startling and counter-intuitive ones—words, texts, and books are put to in contemporary formal and informal performance practices, and the subtle nuances of tone, emphasis, and effect that each performance brings. They show the textual scholars what they are missing and suggest exciting possibilities. Conversely, the essays by textual scholars and music historians reveal that even texts, when examined in this light, turn out to provide a surprising amount of clues about what Stefano Pellò calls the pre-textual and con-textual life of poetry, sermons, and stories: the anecdotes, gossip, and discussions that accompanied and explained how certain texts came into being (Cort, Pellò, Sharma); the correct knowledge that was required in order to understand and appreciate sophisticated oral performances (Hawley, Khan, d'Hubert); the performance needed to bring the texts we have to life (Horstmann, Novetzke, Busch, Bangha, Orsini). Through a number of recurring key words like *raga* (musical mode), *rasa* (juice, sentiment), *rasika* (connoisseur), and *bhava* (emotion), these essays also show how aesthetic and/or spiritual cultivation and understanding were crucial to the listening of music and tales in the early modern period. Such words were part of a code that straddled the multilingual poetic, musical, and visual arts—though declined with subtle differences in the courtly, sufi, and *bhakti* (devotion) contexts where songs and tales circulated (see particularly Miner, d'Hubert, Schofield, and Busch).[13]

## Oral-literate, Multilingual, and Intermedial

General accounts of orality in South Asia typically begin with the oral-mnemonic tradition of Vedic and post-Vedic knowledge (the *Upanishads*, Panini's grammar, etc.). But as Sheldon Pollock has pointed out, this much touted orality, while undoubtedly and bedazzingly true, has too often been taken as emblematic of a general Indian "indifference" to writing. The cultural premium on memorised knowledge (*kanthastha* or "held in the throat", as Pollock reminds us) "left indelible traces in secular written culture". And "from the moment writing was invented

13 Persian and Persianate intellectuals, the essays by Schofield and d'Hubert show us, consciously translated Indic aesthetic terminology and set up equivalences with Perso-Arabic terms, like *vacana* with *sukhan* (as "speech"), or *rasa* with *zauq* and *lazzat* (as "taste" or "pleasure").

*literary* culture, the culture of kavya, became indissolubly connected to writing, so much so that the history of the one becomes unintelligible without taking into account the history of the other".[14] Similarly, Richard Widdess has noted that although there has been perhaps an even stronger emphasis placed on the superiority of oral-aural modes of transmission in Indian musical discourse, "many systems of 'oral notation' exist, and have existed since ancient times. These systems use solmization or other mnemonic syllables, and are primarily recited or sung, although they can also be written down"—and have been used to notate musical examples in written treatises since the Gupta period.[15] Like Pollock, Stuart Blackburn notes of South India that even the early Sangam corpus of Tamil poetry (third century CE, but edited and anthologised only in the eighth) valorises *both* orality *and* writing: "Many of the poems are presented as if spoken or sung by bards, while, on the other hand, many give prominence to the role of the poet-scholar (*pulavar*)".[16] Both Blackburn and Pollock note the endurance of practices of orality in South Asia "as both fact and ideal" well into the modern period, and their persistence into the present day is particularly obvious in their continuing predominance in music pedagogy.[17] Christian Novetzke notes that pre-modern sants and performers in Maharashtra lived in a milieu where literacy was a fairly ordinary and widespread skill. Yet the public culture of *bhakti* and the logic of performance meant that, though literate, *kirtankars* would still privilege orality. In fact, as he puts it, the *kirtankar* "might be considered an intermediary between text and orality" (p. 180).

Velcheru Narayana Rao coined the very useful term "oral-literate" to describe *pandits*, poets, and storytellers who operate within a culture that is both orally transmitted and literate at the same time—and this is a term that applies in different ways to almost *all* the people, cases,

14 Sheldon Pollock, 'Literary Culture and Manuscript Culture in Precolonial India', in *Literary Cultures and the Material Book*, ed. by Simon Eliot, Andrew Nash, and Ian Willison (London: British Library, 2007), pp. 79, 80.

15 Widdess (1995), p. 87. Solmization is a system of attributing a distinct syllable to each note in a musical scale; key examples include European sol-fa (do re mi fa so la ti) and Indian *sargam* (sa re ga ma pa dha ni).

16 S. Blackburn, *Print, Folklore, and Nationalism in Colonial South India* (New Delhi: Permanent Black, 2006), 'Introduction', p. 20.

17 Pollock (2007), p. 78; Huib Schippers, 'The Guru Recontextualized? Perspectives on Learning North Indian Classical Music in Shifting Contexts for Professional Training', *Asian Music* 38.1 (2007), 123-38.

and genres presented in this volume: from preachers to *kirtankars*, from poets to musicians, from musical treatises to song-poems, from poetry manuals to *tazkiras* that record the gossip around poets, from early modern tales to the contemporary *niyaz kahani* pamphlets of Amy Bard's essay. Perhaps the most surprising group that qualify as oral-literate are musicians; the consensus modern view that Hindustani *ustads* were illiterate is belied by a series of treatises and song collections written by hereditary musicians and their disciples from Mughal times down to the present day, demonstrating literacy in Sanskrit, Persian, Brajbhasha, and Urdu.[18] Indeed most of the essays prefer to use the term performative rather than oral, in order to stress that sight, gesture, and sound were all involved.[19] About *qissa* storytelling, for example, Pasha M. Khan notes that the seventeenth-century manual

> *Ṭirāz al-akhbār* makes it clear to us that the term "*qissa-khwan*" does not convey the full range and force of the storyteller's activities. Impressive as it seems that storytellers like Fakhr al-Zamani recited and improvised the interminable *Dāstān-i Amīr Ḥamza* from memory, they did not *simply* read them, but performed them. In his description of the presentation of the *qissa*, Fakhr al-Zamani prescribes not only modulations of the voice, but gestures and postures for the storyteller. (Khan, p. 198)

The same is true of many of the performance practices covered in this book: singing, poetic recitation, and storytelling. Conversely, the mere physical *presence* of a book during a performance—even if it is not consulted—may work symbolically as an authorising gesture, as Widdess shows in his essay.

Methodologically, however, although scholars of literature and religion concerned with the past are aware of the all-important oral dimension of performance, and ethnomusicologists and scholars of orality recognise that the living traditions they study are part of cultural and literary fields that have much longer histories, by and large it is

---

18 See, for example, Ras Baras Khan's 1698 treatise, the *Shams al-aṣvāt*, trans. by Mehrdad Fallahzadeh (Uppsala: Acta Universitatis Upsaliensis, 2012); Khushhal Khan "Anup"'s Braj and Persian *Rāg darshan* (Brajbhasha (1800): University of Pennsylvania Rare Book and Manuscript Library, Lawrence J Schoenberg Collection, LJS 63; Persian (1808): Government Oriental Manuscripts Library, University of Madras, D1024 P Ms); and Karamatullah Khan's *Isrār-e karāmat* (Allahabad: Janaki Press, 1908).

19 In other words, we are using the terms performative and performativity not in the sense bequeathed to us by J.L. Austin via Judith Butler, but rather following their more general usage in ethnomusicology and performance studies.

difficult for one person to have the technical training to do both. The documents we have from the past—written texts, manuscripts, visual images, and written descriptions—often bear only scant traces of their oral-performative contexts, or else describe them in terms that are minimal or opaque, as in the musical notation of *ragas* or attempts to describe aesthetic experience. Conversely, current performance traditions that have been orally transmitted, especially the further we move from institutional centres, often bear only oblique traces of their history.[20] We will come back to the relationship between texts/books and orality below.

Trying to reconstruct the oral-performative history of early modern North India, as this book tries to do, presents additional challenges. While certain aspects have been well studied—*bhakti* sayings, songs, and performances; the circulation of songs and singers in devotional circles and across North Indian courts (especially the Mughal imperial court); sufi romances in Hindavi[21]—others remain unclear. Texts of the time often contain lively religious discussions, *goshtis*, and repartees, but what relationship do those iconic representations bear to real events and/or practices? Numerous musical treatises contain notated *raga* examples, but what do these actually tell us about how the *ragas* sounded in performance? Many texts that suggest concurrent oral-performative practices such as Puranas or sufi *malfuzat*, or that were explicitly offered to patrons, were written or copied in the high languages of Persian and Sanskrit—does this mean they reflect speech practices, or rather protocols of writing? Much path-breaking work is currently being done on Sanskrit-Persian interactions in the Mughal period,[22] and questions like "did the Mughals (or sufis) really know Sanskrit?", or "did they really speak in Persian?", regularly arise. While the answers necessarily

---

20 See e.g. James Caron, 'Reading the Power of Printed Orality in Afghanistan: Popular Pashto Literature as Historical Evidence and Public Intervention', *Journal of Social History* 45.1 (2011), 172.

21 On *bhakti*, see e.g. Rupert Snell, *The Eighty-four Hymns of Hita Harivaṃśa: an Edition of the Caurāsī Pada* (Delhi: Motilal Banarsidass, 1991). On songs and singers, see Françoise "Nalini" Delvoye, 'Collections of Lyrics in Hindustani Music: The Case of Dhrupad' and the bibliography she gives, in Bor et al. (2010), pp. 141-58, and more generally part I of that volume, 'The Formative Period', pp. 35-194. On Hindavi sufi romances, see the work of Aditya Behl, and especially *Love's Subtle Magic*.

22 See Audrey Truschke, 'Cosmopolitan Encounters: Sanskrit and Persian at the Mughal Court' (PhD dissertation, Columbia University, 2012), http://hdl.handle.net/10022/AC:P:12951; see also Busch and Schofield in this volume.

vary according to the educational capital and background of patrons and audiences, we must recognise that the multiple diglossia of the time means that texts written in the high languages existed in an oral context that was vernacular and multilingual.

To state it more clearly, we begin from the premise that the linguistic economy of North India can be described as one of "multiple diglossias",[23] with several high languages—Arabic, Persian, Sanskrit—and a general spoken vernacular (what we call here Hindavi) that was variously written in the Persian, Kaithi, or Devanagari scripts. We intentionally use the term Hindavi, which was the term (together with Hindi and Hindui) employed for North Indian vernaculars in Persian sources, in order to avoid the split history of Hindi and Urdu that has dominated modern scholarship and language consciousness.[24] A concurrent premise is that language and script were a function of written transmission and the competence of patrons and copyists: script was not intrinsic to a language, and the script and language of writing did not necessarily reproduce the language of oral performance or exchange. The protocols of high language meant that discussions in Hindavi between a sufi *pir* and his disciples would be written down in Persian, or that the Hindavi song-poems composed by Persian literati were referred to but not included in Persian-language histories and anthologies.[25]

Once we are aware of these premises, we begin to see that texts that appear to exist in separate domains sealed by boundaries of script and literacy could and did circulate thanks to oral transmission, translation, exposition, and memorisation. We also see that at times the texts are

---

23 See María Angeles Gallego, 'The Languages of Medieval Iberia and their Religious Dimension', *Medieval Encounters* 9.1 (2003): 107-39.

24 We consider Hindavi here as synonymous with *bhakha*. Though modern scholarship distinguishes between Western and Eastern Hindi, and between Avadhi, Brajbhasha, Khari Boli (Hindi and Urdu), etc., it is our contention—supported by the wide circulation of texts like the "Avadhi" *Candāyan* in Delhi and of Kabir's poems or Gwaliyari *dhrupad* all over North India—that vernacular (or *bhakha*, "language", as vernacular sources call it) literary forms travelled easily and widely at this time within a unified language domain. True, terms like "eastern" (*purbi*) and "of Gwalior" (*gwaliyari*) were also sometimes used in this period, but it was only at the end of sixteenth century that Brajbhasha emerged as a separate, specific (partly) codified literary vernacular; see Allison Busch, *Poetry of Kings: The Classical Hindi Literature of Mughal India* (New York: Oxford University Press, 2011).

25 For Hindavi and the written protocols of Persian, see Francesca Orsini, 'Traces of a Multilingual World: Hindavi in Persian Texts', in *After Timur Left: Culture and Circulation in Fifteenth-century North India*, ed. by F. Orsini and S. Sheikh (New Delhi: Oxford University Press, 2014), pp. 403-36.

themselves translations of oral vernacular tellings/performances. Thus Jack Hawley's essay on Surdas's reworking of a passage from the Sanskrit *Bhāgavata-purāṇa* shows us that the Brajbhasha poet-singer Surdas, traditionally memorialised as being blind, knew the Sanskrit canonical text well enough to riff on it and could expect his audience to understand his game.[26] His quasi-contemporary, the poet Alam, declared that "since few listen to this tale in Sanskrit, I have bound [this tale] together in *chaupais* in *bhakha*".[27] Does he mean that he knew the Sanskrit versions of the tale? The case of 'Abd al-Rahman Chishti's *Mir'āt al-makhlūqāt*, analysed in Muzaffar Alam's essay, is even more intriguing: the Persian text purports to be a translation of a Sanskrit Purana and its author declares and cites evidence of his knowledge of Sanskrit and of the text. The aim is to render public something that the keepers of the original text—the Brahmins—have tried to keep secret, i.e. that Shiva himself predicted the advent of Adam and the Prophet Muhammad and the takeover of India by their descendants, who intermarried with the local population. The text faithfully reproduces in Persian the generic conventions of the Purana—the chain of narrators, the explanation of past and future events, etc.—but what is the relationship of this text to orality? Were 'Abd al-Rahman or his readers familiar with the Sanskrit text and/or oral expositions of the *Bhaviṣya-purāṇa*; did he sermonise on it; and if so in which language?

Several essays in this volume seek to tease out the oral-performative dimension of written texts and genres, particularly those in the high languages or whose accessibility is uncertain. Taken together, the contributions of Busch, Schofield, Sharma, and Khan show that texts that have come down to us as part of separate and sophisticated traditions—Brajbhasha *riti* poetry, Hindustani music theory and song lyrics, and Persian poetry and storytelling—were all consumed by the same people at the Mughal court. Thus, while seeking to understand the logic internal to the formation and transmission of each archive (courtly and *madrasa* Persian, Jain, courtly *bhakha*, *bhakti*, sufi), it has been crucial for us to also question their limits and exclusions, and to place them within the larger

---

26 Already in his 1984 book *Sūrdas: Poet, Singer, Saint* (Seattle: University of Washington Press, and Delhi: Oxford University Press), Hawley argued that Surdas's blindness should be taken metaphorically, and expressed doubts about his illiteracy, too.

27 Alam, *Ālamkr̥t Mādhavānal Kāmakandalā*, ed. by Rajkumari Misra (Allahabad: Ratnakumari Svadhyay Sansthan, 1982), 6.5, p. 5, see Orsini in this volume.

framework of orature and oral transmission.[28] An approach sensitive to oral circulation and performance highlights the dynamics through which these connections took place. The result is a map of a richer and more densely interconnected cultural and social world.

Of course there is a way in which music in particular has long been viewed as constitutive of premodern India's "composite culture", the aesthetic glue that held the otherwise fractious/centripetal polity together. While parallel religious nationalisms have positioned Hindu (and Jain) and Muslim communities as inevitably hostile and barely reconciled, the discourse of "composite culture" has upheld music and painting as evidence that Hindus and Muslims had been friends and had cultivated similar tastes.[29] In this discourse, music or *bhakti* and sufi religions are held up selectively as special cases of "synthesis", representing a "bridge" that connected what are still perceived as separate communities, each with their own traditions. In the process, music, *bhakti*, and sufism get extracted from their social histories and charged with a mysterious agent-less intentionality that obscures the messy and much larger-scale social processes of conscious mixing and intentional borrowing by thoughtful and knowledgeable men and women that historically must have occurred to produce any kind of "composite".[30] In contradistinction, while our evidence shows much circulation and translation of music and song genres, singers and performers, stories, and even aesthetic categories, we see these as normal products of a culturally diverse and multilingual polity—a regular multilingualism—with multilayered, distinct, yet interlocking contexts: courtly, urban, ritual/devotional, rural. The evidence also leads us away

28 The term "orature" was coined by the Ugandan linguist Pio Zirimu but has been given broader scope by Ngugi wa Thiong'o, e.g. in his 'Notes towards a Performance Theory of Orature', *Performance Research* 12.3 (2007), 4-7.

29 On the genealogy of the concept of "composite culture" to refer to Hindu-Muslim interactions over the *longue durée*, see Kathryn Hansen, 'Who Wants to be a Cosmopolitan? Readings from the Composite Culture', *Indian Economic and Social History Review* 47.3 (2010), 291-308.

30 On the inadequacy of the terms "synthesis", "influence", and "composite" to describe the processes of appropriation between Indian and West Asian musicians that forged Hindustani music, see Katherine Butler Brown [Schofield], 'Evidence of Indo-Persian Musical Synthesis? The *Tanbur* and *Rudra Vina* in Seventeenth-century Indo-Persian Treatises', *Journal of the Indian Musicological Society* 36-7 (2006), 89-103. On the need to consider traditional culture-producers' intelligence and intent in creating art works, see Molly Emma Aitken's ground-breaking monograph on Rajput court painters, *The Intelligence of Tradition in Rajput Court Painting* (New Haven: Yale, 2010).

from the idea of the "composite" to thinking in terms of individuals actively appropriating across cultural and linguistic thresholds and between media (from poetry to musical sound to painting, etc.) to produce a widely shared early modern aesthetic of borrowing and reuse that revelled in virtuosity, brilliance, and multilayered depth and richness.[31]

## Spaces of Performance and Performers

A major advantage of a multilingual and intermedial approach to orality and performance traditions is that it allows us to explore literary culture beyond the court, to understand the links between forms and performers outside and within the court, and to examine the dynamics of classicisation and popularisation. It also allows us to attend to the oral-performative aspects of poetic culture and wit, so obviously valued as cultural assets (see Pellò in this volume), and to consider the performers who enacted/produced these verbal forms, their social position, their self-presentation, and their own mobility.

Ever since Françoise "Nalini" Delvoye's pioneering studies of *dhrupad* texts in Persian sources, of the circulation of songs and of song-poets (*vaggeyakar*) from the court of Gwalior to that of the Sultan of Gujarat and thence to Akbar's court and sub-imperial centres, and of the relationships between Tansen, Swami Haridas in Vrindaban, and Muhammad Ghaus Gwaliori, we have been alerted to the intense circulation of songs, musicians, and musical knowledge between courtly and devotional/ritual domains.[32] The striking flexibility in song themes and "retooling" of song texts as well as poems, so that a ruler's name could be substituted by another, or by the name of Krishna, were a direct consequence of this circulation, as Busch reminds us in her essay.

The essays in this volume cover a wide range of performance spaces and domains. Sharma, Busch, Khan, and Schofield explore the culture of poetic, musical, and storytelling performances at the Mughal court

31 For a fine example of this aesthetic in action, see Aitken's chapter on Rajput paintings of Layla and Majnun; (2010), pp. 155-209.

32 See e.g. Françoise "Nalini" Delvoye, 'Indo-Persian Accounts on Music Patronage in the Sultanate of Gujarat', in *The Making of Indo-Persian Culture*, ed. by Muzaffar Alam, Françoise "Nalini" Delvoye, and Marc Gaborieau (Delhi: Manohar and Centre de Sciences Humaines, 2000), pp. 253-80.

from Akbar's reign to Muhammad Shah's. Sharma's essay, for instance, details the kinds of Persian poetic and prose texts that were recited and discussed at the Mughal court, and notes that "in the Mughal context storytelling, poetic recitation, and discussion also functioned as a form of re-enacting and validating the canon in the face of new literary developments and challenges, especially when it came to poetry" (p. 288). He notes that Emperor Akbar preferred literary gatherings that involved storytelling to poetry recitations (*musha'iras*), whereas his son and successor Jahangir was fond of listening to and discussing Persian poetry, particularly the *ghazal*, during long night gatherings. He also observes that Emperor Shah Jahan was particularly interested in literary works concerned with contemporary history, while Aurangzeb 'Alamgir was especially fond of Jalaluddin Rumi's *Maṡnavī*. Sharma points out that during Shah Jahan's period (r.1628-1656), many Persian poets at court wrote short topical poems in *masnavi* form to be recited at court, suggesting that "these poems gradually replaced the ceremonial *qasida* as the traditional poetic form to mark formal occasions" (p. 292). As far as the performance of the *ghazal* is concerned, anecdotes show a certain overlap between courtly and sufi practices by the sixteenth century, and *khayal*, now known only as a genre of classical music, enjoyed a dual existence in both the *dargah* and the *darbar* from its sixteenth-century appearance until at least the time of Muhammad Shah (r.1719-1748).[33]

Allyn Miner's essay shows how much of that musical knowledge was already cultivated at pre-Mughal courts such as the Sharqi court in Jaunpur, and how the musical knowledge codified there and in other apparently peripheral locations such as Rewa[34] circulated among three different kinds of constituencies: one made of connoisseurs and music specialists who wanted to learn the specific qualities of each *raga*; another constituted by those who only wanted the basic vocabulary and took pleasure in the imaginative aspects of *raga* visualisation; and a third one made of practitioners and religious devotees who employed a more restricted range of *ragas* for ritual singing.

33 Katherine Butler Brown [Schofield], 'The Origins and Early Development of Khayal', in Bor et al. (2010), pp. 159-96.

34 Apparently being the operative word here; it is worth noting that Tansen was employed at Rewa immediately before his services were requisitioned by Akbar, so the Raja was clearly a patron of considerable discrimination.

Several essays tackle performance texts and traditions at regional courts (Miner, Busch, d'Hubert, Orsini). Orsini's traces the emergence of *kathas* or tales for local courts such as the Baghela of "Amarpur" in the wake of epic and Puranic retellings. Allison Busch's pathbreaking work has shown how *riti* poets like Keshavdas, working in the small court in Orchha, created a new literary culture in the early sixteenth century by carefully studying Sanskrit models and reproducing them in the vernacular.[35] She has also shown how, in the wake of political alliances between local rulers like the Bundelas of Orchha and Mughal princes, this literary culture spread into the heart of the Mughal imperial court and found ready patronage not only in the imperial entourage, but also among its ministers (like Todar Mal, whom Alam also mentioned in admiring terms in his 1582 *Mādhavānal Kāmakandalā*) and Rajput *mansabdar*s, and who in their home territories developed their own sub-imperial courtly cultures and employed their own array of poets, genealogists, and storytellers.[36] In her essay for this volume Busch focuses on the oral and performative dimensions of this literary culture in the form of memorising verses and rules as a necessary preparation for extempore poetic performances, of the retooling of verses by itinerant poets for successive patrons, and on the functions of poetry at these courts, including the performance of martial poetry on the battlefield itself, with the expressed aim of enthusing the warriors. Nor should we forget that these local rulers were also major patrons of ritual and devotional performances and sponsored a whole range of temples, monasteries (*maths*), and festivals.[37] A particularly interesting case is that of the sophisticated seventeenth-century poet Alaol, the subject of Thibaut d'Hubert's contribution, whose Bengali narrative poems/romances were informed by Persian, Sanskrit, and Hindavi poetics and literary models. The case of Alaol points to a kind of cosmopolitanism that was directly produced by the confluence of multilingual literary traditions, translated into the local literary language for a small but heterogeneous court in Arakan (now Myanmar). Widdess's essay also touches on the circulation of North Indian musical and literary culture

35 Busch (2011).

36 Catherine Asher and Cynthia Talbot, *India Before Europe* (Cambridge: Cambridge University Press, 2006); Aitken (2010).

37 See Monika Thiel-Horstmann, *In Favour of Govinddevjī: Historical Documents Relating to a Deity of Vrindaban and Eastern Rajasthan* (Delhi: Indira Gandhi National Centre for the Arts in association with Manohar Publishers and Distributors, 1999).

at the Malla court in Nepal. Not only did *sangitashastra* texts circulate there, but it is also here that some of the earliest manuscripts are to be found. He further notes that some of the Malla kings' *dapha* compositions are present in contemporary *dapha* songbooks—a tantalising "tenuous textual continuity can thus be demonstrated between the early seventeenth-century palace context and twenty-first-century farmers' music" (p. 234)—while the wonderful detail in his Figure 8.3 shows how non-courtly genres and performers were visualised in a hierarchical spatial fashion.

Several other essays focus on urban spaces and activities among a range of merchant, service, professional, and artisanal groups. Stefano Pellò shows how *tazkiras* of poets written in Persian from the eighteenth and nineteenth centuries focus on the activities and the professionalisation of contemporary poets and their disciples outside the court, in the urban spaces of Delhi and Lucknow, and in doing so eulogise and canonise them. But these texts also display keen interest in humbler and more marginal figures in the urban landscape such as madmen, opium-addicts, jesters, and street performers. John Cort's essay focuses on the parallel world of Jain laymen in Mughal Agra, who met regularly in a temple courtyard and constituted themselves into debating circles that produced newly-authoritative doctrinal and liturgical texts and virtually emptied the figure of the *bhattarak* of authority.[38] This was a process of vernacularisation of knowledge that happened independently of royal initiatives or patronage, the fruits of which are still part of Jain ritual practices today. Novetzke's essay on *kirtan* performances and Widdess's on *dapha* both straddle premodern texts and contemporary performances and include urban ritual performances among artisanal/subaltern groups, while Richard Wolf's takes us to the diasporic urban streets of Karachi for rhythmically sophisticated perfomances of Nizami drumming.

With the essays by Horstmann, Novetzke, Hawley, Bangha, and Alam we are taken to spaces that range from small-town (*qasba*) sufi establishments and villages, *maths*, and festivals (*mahotsav*) where Dadupanthi *acharyas* would deliver their sermons.[39] The great circulation of Surdas's songs

38 The term *bhattarak* (*bhaṭṭaraka*) indicates the head of Digambara Jain institutions, responsible for managing endowments, running the institutions, and training scholars, as well as for maintaining libraries and presiding over installation ceremonies; see Cort in this volume.

39 As Novetzke puts it: "for the professional performer appearances at the Pune *darbar*

and Bajid's *arilla* verses, and of manuscripts with Bajid's short, humorous tales, points to a popular realm of religious, entertaining, and instructive performance that would definitely include Novetzke's *kirtans*, which nowadays usually comprise "a story from the life of a sant that goes along with the song, and usually other songs or texts are brought in that can range from Sanskritic philosophy to sufi mysticism to the wisdom of political leaders and popular adages and sayings of unknown provenance in any language, including English" (p. 171). That Bajid's manuscripts are also held in royal libraries like the Pothikhana in Jaipur alerts us to the fact that, just as there is a sophisticated oral knowledge that does not depend on literacy (Hawley, Wolf), so elite tastes could and did include popular genres. Conversely, the career of the early-seventeenth-century Iranian *émigré* storyteller Fakhr al-Zamani shows the remarkable mobility from urban to courtly spaces of both performer and genre. "If Fakhr al-Zamani's progress is any indication, *qissas* that began at the 'popular' level could, given a chance and perhaps with some stylistic alterations, eventually be performed in the courts of nobles and preserved as manuscripts in their libraries", notes Khan (p. 192). And while his gestural style of storytelling recalls the figure of the *naqqal*, a professional actor who conveyed "a story with words and actions, attempting to *embody* the narrative and its characters", Khan reminds us that *naqqals* were lower on the scale of professions than *qissa-khwan*,[40] and Fakhr al-Zamani never used the word *naqqali* for what he did (Khan, p. 198).

## Contemporary Ethnography and History

Because of the challenges outlined above, we considered it to be vital to bring ethnomusicologists and scholars of contemporary performance practices into conversation with the more historically-oriented among us. We do not wish to suggest naively that contemporary performances

---

were few. The regular terrain of the *kirtankar* consisted of the many village centres, pilgrimage networks, and holy sites that dotted the Deccan" (p. 176).

40 *Naqqals* in both Dargah Quli Khan's *Muraqqa'-i Dehlī* (c.1740) and Wajid 'Ali Shah's *Bānī* (1877) were street performers of equivalent status to (and in personnel possibly substantially overlapping with) *bhands* and *bhagats*; Ibbetson thought *naqqal* and *bhand* were synonymous. Dargah Quli Khan, *Muraqqa'-e Dehli*, trans. by Chander Shekhar and Shama Mitra Chenoy (Delhi: Deputy, 1989), p. 99; Wajid 'Ali Shah, *Bānī* (Lucknow: Sangit Natak Akademi, 1987), pp. 115-16; and Denzil Ibbetson and Edward Maclagan, *A Glossary of the Tribes and Castes of the Punjab and North-West Frontier Province* (Lahore: Superintendent, Govt. Printing, 1911), pp. 156-57.

reflect past practices. But what their study reveals holds great imaginative power for historical work. For example, contemporary ethnographies show us a consistent combination of recitation of oral/written text with extempore exposition (*arthav* or, in *raga* performance, *vistar*) right across the genres and contexts we are looking at.[41] For the earliest tales, the text is indeed all we have; but were any of these tales—particularly those rich in ritual, technical, or esoteric meanings—accompanied by exposition? It seems likely, particularly in cases where the length of the stanzas and the narrative "density" in extant copies vary.[42] There are, for instance, obvious markers of ritual beginning in most of our texts—but how much richer is Philip Lutgendorf's description of *kathavachaks* (called Vyasas in this instance) taking their seat after worshipping the seat and garlanding the book, etc., in *katha* performances of the *Rāmcaritmānas*![43] Christian Novetzke makes the useful distinction between "didactic *kirtan*" (which includes a wide range of modes, as we shall see) and "ecstatic *kirtan*" on the basis of the protocols of sitting and standing. In the ecstatic "Varkari *kirtan*" everyone stands and dances, whereas in the other forms of *kirtan* only the performer (*kirtankar*) stands while the audience sits, though the audience still participates in many ways, "singing along with the songs, finishing well known verses along with the *kirtankar*, sometimes interacting with the *kirtankar*, and so on" (p. 172).

In many cases, all we have for past musical performances are musical treatises or manuscripts with song texts. Mukund Lath and Winand Callewaert have argued that the form in which the song-texts are collected and ordered in a manuscript can tell us whether it was a singer's own workmanlike collection or a systematisation, e.g. for ritual purposes, though Miner in this volume suggests that the very presence of a *raga* in *bhakti* texts indicates, at the very least, "that the original compiler or composers moved in or were connected with court or temple circles" (p. 399). Christian Novetzke has made a crucial distinction between formal *pothis* and informal *badas* (more on which below). In the case of the book used in *dapha*

41 Of the specialists who still recite narrative texts (*panchalis*) in Bengal, d'Hubert notes that the names they are called by—*kathak*, *pathak*, or *gayen*—each stress one aspect of their style of recitation: "the two first terms refer to a musically tuned reading cum commentary, and the second more specifically to singing" (pp. 427-28).

42 For interpolations that appear to be the result of storytellers' intervention, see Orsini in this volume.

43 Philip Lutgendorf, *The Life of a Text: Performing the Rāmcaritmānas of Tulsidas* (Berkeley: University of California Press, 1991), pp. 182-85.

performances, we could muse over the meaning and interpretation of the song texts, were Richard Widdess not to tell us that in *dapha* performance sound and key words and effort are much more important than the text.

We can imagine Bajid's short and entertaining tales retold in intimate familial contexts, and similar *qissas* were printed in chapbook forms not dissimilar from the *niyaz kahanis* that Amy Bard writes about. But while Bajid's mock subversion of the moral ending puzzles us, Bard gives us a rich account of the various ways in which tellers and listeners interpret the *kahanis* and relate them to their own life experiences. Both Bajid's irreverent stories and Amy Bard's contemporary formal and informal miracle tales show an informal relationship between written texts and orality. One intriguing notion she puts forward concerns the different quality of listening in formal and informal *niyaz kahanis*—reading them is perceived as hardly efficacious. Although both types of *mo'jizat* emphasise listening, formal *kahanis* efface narrators, are less "personal", less interactive, and more listening-oriented. In casual *mo'jizat*, which speak to local, familial needs with clear geographical anchoring, listeners are likely to "talk back". (Though why Osho was so keen on Bajid and what use he made of his verses and tales remains an intriguing question!)

## Books and Performance

The conference from which this volume draws was originally entitled "Tellings, Not Texts", but one participant pointed out that "Tellings *and* Texts" was a more appropriate title, since texts—in their material form as books—were often present in the performances we talked about. What roles do texts play in performance, we asked, and what is the relationship between them? Which way does the directionality go—from text to performance or from performance/oral exposition to text? Here, too, early modern North India shows a great range of possibilities and choices.

At one end of the spectrum, we see a great deal of interest in books as material objects. Already at North Indian Sultanate courts illustrated manuscripts (and illuminated Qur'ans) were valued and copied in Persianate and Indic styles and provide a tantalising glimpse of the circulation of shared tastes among elites that impacted, for example, upon Jain book-copying and book-dedicating practices.[44] It is surely not by chance that the earliest illustrated manuscripts of the Sanskrit *Bhāgavata-purāṇa* also appeared in this period. The dazzling and profuse production of the imperial Mughal workshop (*karkhana*) has tended to absorb most scholarly attention, and we still await a comprehensive picture of illustrated book production in this period that devotes parallel and equal consideration to non-imperial manuscripts and book circulation.

Among the religious groups of the period, too, we find a striking investment in books. The most obvious example is that of the *pothis* (compilations) of the early Sikh gurus. Guru Nanak himself, who "believed that he had been assigned by God the vocation of singing his praises [...] and that his hymns were the result of direct communication from God", nonetheless urged writing God's name as a devotional act. This has been taken as an implicit hint towards the fact that already in his lifetime disciples wrote down his hymns in a *pothi*.[45] As G.S. Mann points out, Guru Nanak referred explicitly to the role of the Qur'an in Muslim devotional life and must have been familiar with the practice common in sufi *khanqahs* of placing the Qur'an in the open to allow for full access.[46] Having a *pothi* became crucial to the authority claims of his descendants and disciples at their various seats (*gaddis*). Textual history shows that the early *pothis* were subsequently added to, though much emphasis has traditionally been placed within the Sikh tradition on the singularity and unbroken continuity of the *Guru Granth*—whose status is very much that of a sacred text, to be read, recited, and sung to *raga* but also worshipped in private and public rituals.

The Sikhs were not the only sant group who invested in writing, compiling, and copying books. Dadu Dayal's disciples also compiled his utterances (*vani*) together with those of other sants (*panch-vani*), as well as enormous and literally comprehensive compilations (lit. *sarvangi*). They also wrote the first biographies/hagiographies (*parchais*

44 See Éloïse Brac de la Perrière, *L'art du livre dans l'Inde des sultanats* (Paris: Presses de l'Université Paris-Sorbonne, 2008), and Preeti Khosla's PhD dissertation on 'The Visual Languages of the North Indian Styles of Book Paintings during the Sultanate Period (1411-1525)' (School of Oriental and African Studies, London, 2014).

45 Gurinder Singh Mann, *The Making of Sikh Scriptures* (New Delhi: Oxford University Press, 2001), p. 10. Jack Hawley also reminds us of Guru Nanak's dislike for the proliferation of mercenary and beggarly performers (p. 211).

46 Mann (2001), p. 12.

and *bhaktamals*) in the vernacular in North India, and the manuals for sermons that Monika Horstmann writes about.[47] She notes that, especially from the eighteenth century, "the wealth of manuscripts often of great length and calligraphic quality indicate that the patrons of these were men—and occasionally women—of considerable means" (p. 45). These developments form a striking parallel to the already existing but growing production in sufi circles of compilations of sayings (*malfuzat*) and biographical dictionaries (*tazkiras*) devoted to one's master—a sure way of placing him on the map. Another related phenomenon concerns the considerable growth in the eighteenth and early nineteenth centuries of writing about and by elite lineages of musicians, especially *kalawants* and those with lineal connections to Delhi. Far from confirming the "illiterate *ustad*" stereotype we have inherited from nationalist musicologists,[48] the later Mughal period saw major professional musicians and socially prominent amateurs writing their own names into history in the form of two kinds of books: *tazkiras* and song collections[49] in Persian and Hindavi.[50] This oral-literate field of musical knowledge transmission probably developed in part as a way of ensuring the longevity of lineages and the preservation of lineal musical property threatened in the eighteenth century by increased economic migration away from traditional centres of familial oral transmission. The evidence of lineages of hereditary performers who, alongside

---

47 For Dadu-panthi biographies, see e.g. Jangopal, *The Hindī Biography of Dādū Dayāl*, ed. and trans. by Winand M. Callewaert (Delhi: Motilal Banarsidass, 1988); for Dadu-panthi compendia, see Winand M. Callewaert, *The Sarvāṅgī of Gopāldās: A 17th Century Anthology of Bhakti Literature* (New Delhi: Manohar Publications, 1993), and W.M. Callewaert and Bart Op de Beeck, *Nirguṇa Bhakti Sāgara = Devotional Hindī Literature: A Critical Edition of the Pañc-Vāṇī or Five Works of Dādū, Kābir, Nāmdev, Raidās, Hardās with the Hindī Songs of Gorakhnāth and Sundardās*, 2 vols (New Delhi: Manohar Publications, 1991).

48 See e.g. Janaki Bakhle on V.N. Bhatkhande's condemnation of Muslim *ustads* as ignorant and illiterate, in *Two Men and Music: Nationalism in the Making of an Indian Classical Tradition* (New York: Oxford University Press, 2005), pp. 109-13, 120-23.

49 The history of song collections in South Asia is patently much older and more extensive (see Busch and Bangha in this volume); but before this eighteenth-century flurry of activity, collections of the courtly repertoire that forms the basis of what is now called Hindustani music (*dhrupad, khayal, tappa*, etc.) are significantly rarer than, say, *bhakti* collections.

50 For bibliographical details of many of these texts, see the database SHAMSA: Sources for the History and Analysis of Music/Dance in South Asia, held at King's College London. At the time of writing it holds information on all known major writings (300+ sources) on North Indian music c.1700-1900 written in Persian, Hindavi, English, and modern Hindi, Urdu, and Bengali.

oral transmission, simultaneously contributed to the written lineage of Indo-Persianate musical knowledge furthermore underlines the central importance of community and *silsila*, or what Indrani Chatterjee calls "monastic governmentality", in sustaining written as well as oral knowledge systems in early modern India.[51]

In this period we thus see a marked expansion of textuality—not just in Persian and Sanskrit, but also in the vernaculars—to new groups and new genres, often as the writing down of oral genres, if not whole performances. As Bangha points out, until the sixteenth century only

> Puranic, epic and historical narratives and Sufi romances—composed normally in the *doha-chaupai* metre, conveying important religious or political messages, and usually of a performative nature—[...] had been deemed worthy of being committed to writing in the vernacular. Towards the end of the sixteeenth century, instead, books began to appear in Brajbhasha that were composed in order to be read and studied and not primarily to be performed (see Busch in this volume). This is also the time when we can spot the beginning of an ever-increasing activity to commit to writing Hindi songs that have so far been transmitted in oral performance. (p. 359)

About Bengali *mangalkabya*s, d'Hubert notes that the poet is typically represented but as the conduit of the Goddess's wish to tell the story. The ritual act by which he grabs a flywhisk marks not only the beginning of the performance but also the moment in which he remembers the text: "in terms of representation of the literary activity, it is not only that performance is the main way to share the content of a written text; rather it means that no text is ever able to come to existence without a setting of ritual performance" (p. 428).

Courtly literary culture, Busch reminds us, was very much a *written* literary culture—she quotes a description of the court of Bir Singh Deo Bundela by Keshavdas in which "there sat countless writers writing, hundreds, and thousands of them" (p. 254). While her essay painstakingly teases out the performative elements and qualities of the poetic, historical, martial texts, and manuals written by Brajbhasha *riti* poets, she is also keen to stress that this "*riti* corpus was underwritten first and foremost by a *textual* engagement with the Sanskrit past". Sunil Sharma points out that while history records that Akbar had Persian

51 On the centrality of lineage to political formation and knowledge production in South Asia, see Indrani Chatterjee, 'Monastic Governmentality, Colonial Misogyny, and Postcolonial Amnesia in South Asia', *History of the Present* 3.1 (2013), 57-98.

classics like the *Shāhnāma* and the *Gulistān* read out in court and these works were meant to be read aloud in sections, "their orality was accompanied by an equal value placed on these works as books, and it was usually through the copying and use of manuscripts of these texts that they were transmitted with the seals of the members of the royal family and nobility" (p. 288).

Inside and outside the court, the Puranas (which both Muzaffar Alam and Jack Hawley touch upon) present a tantalising case. While Puranas remained written in Sanskrit in North India and the *Bhāgavata-purāṇa* attracted important Sanskrit commentaries by the main Vaishnava *acharyas*, Hawley reminds us that the *Bhāgavata-purāṇa* was performed in a number of ways both in Sanskrit and in the vernacular: through recitation; reading and exposition involving sermons and songs; or in rituals (*yajnas*). Indeed, the *Bhāgavata māhātmya* manuscripts that began to appear at the turn of the eighteenth century expressed the need to regulate these performances. In their different ways, both 'Abd al-Rahman Chishti's Persian Purana and Surdas's "song commentary" are evidence of this culture of Puranas circulating between writing and performance.[52]

By comparison, John Cort's essay explores the process by which Jain hymns in Sanskrit (*stotras*) were skilfully translated by Banarsidas and his circle in Agra in the early seventeenth century. (As he points out, they chose to translate not Jain scriptures, but ritual texts.) The written translation was itself the result of oral debates, and in turn it became the subject of further debates. Yet "no one wanted to *read* a *kirtan* or an *abhang*, after all—they wanted to see it, hear it, and experience it displayed before them", as Novetzke forcefully argues. Perhaps the most unexpected arguments about the directionality between performance and text and the role of texts in performance come from his essay and Widdess's. By contrasting the *bada* (notebook) of *kirtan* performers—"loosely organised and often hastily constructed with lots of margin corrections, lines crossed out, and other emendations"—with the orderly *pothi* (book) of theologians and institutional figures, Novetzke argues that *badas* represent the logic of *kirtan* performance. His argument is worth quoting in full:

---

52 Vernacular translations of the *Bhāgavata-purāṇa*, particularly of books X and XI, also proliferated from the sixteenth century onwards; see R.S. McGregor, *Hindi Literature from its Beginnings to the Nineteenth Century* (Wiesbaden: Harrassowitz, 1984), pp. 96-97.

> [The *bada*] is a format that privileges performance. Text here is submitted to the demands of performance. The text is a tool, a means and not an end. Furthermore, its role is not preservation—it may function as an archive, but its composition is not intended to ossify a text and convey it into the future as a fixed form. Instead, the text is dynamic, meant to trigger and prompt a performance, existing as a kind of outline of a *kirtan*, but containing no narrative, typological, or historical logic independent of performance. In other words, it cannot stand alone, as can a *pothi* or a fixed, complete composition. (p. 179)[53]

As the archetypal *kirtankar*, Namdev expresses suspicion of books and scriptures and expresses a theory of practice in which devotion "is on display, through the body and voice, and never on paper". "Despite the rather impressive rate of literacy among the Marathi sants", Novetzke argues, "the logic of practice of Varkari religious expression has been oral, or rather performative, and not written". *Kirtan* is the performance of devotion and is central to *bhakti* practice because it is public and open to all.

Monika Horstmann likewise makes the case that the thematic and musical arrangement of sant *vanis*, and the fact that all these texts are used as manuals by preachers, means that "there can be no doubt that the *Dādūvāṇī* originated from the redaction of sayings by, or used by, Dadu in live homiletic contexts" (p. 59). During Dadupanthi festive occasions today, preachers do not consult a prepared script but "may hold the open sacred scripture in front of them", though their sermons will draw upon material taken from a range of books. And if they are preaching about a verse in the scriptures they might read the verses out. "The live performance of a sermon is therefore oral in its fullest sense", she notes, "although it draws on memorised or printed material and perhaps on notes the preacher has taken while preparing for the task" (p. 36). The manuals that she and Khan write about can be viewed in a similar light—not as free-standing texts but as aids to performance. Indeed, she points out that notwithstanding the respect accorded to

53 He also points out the implications for collecting, archiving, preservation, and research: "Major archival institutions—such as university libraries, research centres, and other institutes—amid their many collections of *pothis* do not generally collect *badas*. Even the concern with which these notebooks are preserved today differs from the careful attention given to manuscripts—*badas* are alien to the teak-wood glass case, rarely have an index or catalogue citations, and generally rest in haphazard stacks or even piles in the closets of institutions and private collectors" (p. 175).

Mahant Pokhardas's spiritual stature, his sermons were acknowledged to be hard to enjoy since he read out the manual!

While Fakhr al-Zamani's seventeenth-century Persian manual on storytelling, the *Ṭirāz al-akhbār*, resembles the Dadupanthi sermon manuals in containing useful lists of terms, lexical aids, assorted sayings, and nutshell versions of longer stories, it seems closer to the *ritigranth* manuals (Busch) in operating as a proof, almost a certificate, of its author's own skills as a storyteller, and in elevating storytelling to an art that requires a manual. Khan notes that the text not only tells us much about the process of *qissa* performance but also shows us "one manner in which the *qissa* was defined or 'encoded'" (Khan, p. 186). In the case of the *qissa*, the manual's approach to genre as an assemblage of elements (Khan uses the term *bayaz* or scrapbook) that could and should be combined and recombined in new and attractive ways "undermines the very idea of monolithic genres", because if we look at the range of intertextual and extra-literary material that each *qissa-khwan* was supposed to have "in his throat", the range is stupendous and in fact crosses the line between mimetic and veracious genres that Fakhr al-Zamani otherwise subscribed to (p. 186). Each *qissa* performance was therefore something of an "intertextual tapestry" that "can only be comprehended as a complex of *multi-generic* intertexts that fall under the order of the master genre code of the *qissa*" (p. 205).

By contrast, in the Newar devotional singing (*dapha*) studied by Richard Widdess, the book containing the song-texts is important—but only as a ritual object. It is never consulted, and the boys who are taught the songs from it are not taught to *read* them. For singers and audience the texts only provide clues to meaning: "a word, name or phrase evokes a network of meanings and associations, which may in turn determine when and where the song is sung". What is important, he notes, is the performance, "which has its own meanings and values independently of the text: as religious exertion, as an expression of social identity, and as a component in urban ritual" (Widdess, p. 244). When he asked one group why they go to the trouble of singing the entire Sanskrit poem *Gītagovinda* in one all-night performance when they do not understand the words, "they explained that the *objective* is to sing all night. Therefore they *choose* to sing the *Gītagovinda*, because it takes that length of time" (p. 240).

# Beyond Text: Musical Sound and the Inexpressible

This, finally, leads us to the question of the limits of the verbal—what does music, what do singing or vocally heightened forms of recitation, add or do to a text that supersedes what a text can do alone? In considering this issue in particular, the insights of our contemporary ethnographic case studies have proven especially helpful.

Rhythmic patterns are sometimes inserted verbally in performance scenes within tales or poems (Orsini, Busch), and the notated non-lexical syllables of courtly *taranas* that were vocalised and embodied by drummers and dancers in performance are interlaced with Persian couplets in eighteenth-century song collections.[54] But in Richard Wolf's essay, drum syllables become a code unto themselves, speaking of the performers' mastery and enjoyment of skills recognised by each other and by those few in the audience—like Madhavanal with Kamakandala (Orsini)—who can understand their abstract relationships with verbal texts. And as Widdess concludes, cases like *dapha*, *khayal*, or the *marai kirtan* in Bengal suggest that "some South Asian musical forms escape such conventional categories as *orality* and *text*, but are better understood as *performance*: a process in which text may be present, in written and/ or oral form, but is subsumed by musical elaboration and the enactment of religious and social meanings" (p. 245). The presence of cosmic sound within the body is key for *bhakti* poets like Kabir, and for their contemporary performers like Prahlad Singh Tipania, who evoke the continuous inner sound, the subtle voice (*nada, jhini avaz*).[55]

For the period before recorded sound, the question of what music does that goes beyond text is more difficult to answer because we no longer have access to the object under discussion. Since Plato,[56] music in many cultures, past and present, has been used to deal with excess; to go beyond words, to express the inexpressible; to soothe, magnify, and charm the

54 See e.g. Sophia Plowden's song collection, Fitzwilliam Museum, Cambridge, MS 380.

55 For a sensitive and embodied discussion, see Linda Hess's forthcoming book, *Bodies of Song: Kabir Oral Traditions and Performative Worlds in North India* (New York: Oxford University Press), ch. 1.

56 Plato's theory of the "music of the spheres", which built upon Pythagoras, was a clear influence on Indo-Persian treatises on Hindustani music; see especially Shaikh 'Abdul Karim bin Shaikh Farid Ansari al-Qadiri, *Javāhir al-mūsīqāt-i Muḥammadī* (British Library, MS Or. 12,857).

emotions through the senses rather than the intellect. Because music's mode of communication is abstract, music's semantic and affective associations are more ambiguous than language, capable of expressing a greater depth and number of nuances, often simultaneously.[57] This is not to say that music's significations are endless: music always exists within a culturally specific net of meaning that determines its limits. What it does mean is that the very choice to recite or to sing, and in many of our cases the choice of *raga* in which to set a text, can both enrich and multiply the possible meanings of text—or conversely render a lyric less ambiguous by intimating one meaning among many.

What is more, the *raga* itself exists both as a specifically musical formula (a set of notes that need to be sung in particular orders and ways), *nadamaya*, and as an icon, *devatamaya*, that conveys a distinct mood and set of associations accompanied by specific instructions as to the correct time or season to stimulate those associations.[58] In the Mughal court, a clear "scientific" correlation was drawn between each of the seven notes of the Hindustani scale, the seven celestial bodies, and the four elements presiding over each, embedding *raga* firmly in the fields of Islamicate cosmology and Unani medicine.[59] But this was in large part an attempt to interpret in new terms why the Indic system associated each *raga* with particular iconographies, deities and *nayak-nayikas*, timings, and *rasa*. At the heart of both knowledge systems was an attempt to account for each *raga*'s effect on the listener, its *ta'sir*. This effect was not merely subjective, it was specific; and it was not merely affective, able to transport listeners into a state of meditation or restlessness or tearfulness, it was supernatural—it rearranged the natural world, whether that be a heart sickened by melancholy or a gathering rain cloud refusing to burst. Although the rational, "scientific" underpinnings of the explanation of *ta'sir* had attenuated by the nineteenth century, the

57 Dillon (2012), pp. 6-7, 16-43, especially on Augustine pp. 36-42; see also Laudan Nooshin, 'Prelude: Power and the Play of Music', in *Music and the Play of Power in the Middle East, North Africa and Central Asia*, ed. by L. Nooshin (Aldershot: Ashgate, 2009), pp. 1-32, especially 1-4 and 9-17; and Victor Jankélévitch, *Music and the Ineffable*, trans. by Carolyn Abbate (Princeton: Princeton University Press, 2003).

58 Discussion of Somanatha's *Rāgavibodha* (1609) in Harold Powers, 'Illustrated Inventories of Indian Rāgamāla Painting', *Journal of the American Oriental Society* 100.4 (1980), 473-93, especially pp. 473-75.

59 Katherine Butler Brown [Schofield], '*Rāga* Systems in Performance', in 'Hindustani Music in the Time of Aurangzeb' (PhD dissertation, School of Oriental and African Studies, London, 2003), pp. 177-225.

*Ma'dan al-mūsīqī* (1869) nonetheless describes in magical terms how the singer's command over *ta'sir* should work. The singer was in effect a necromancer (an *'amil*), and the melodic form of the *raga* was a magical formula (*'amal; du'a ba tarkib*) that, when voiced at the right cosmological time, would conjure up a spirit (a *muwakkal*) that would do his bidding. That spirit was the *ta'sir* of the *raga*.[60]

In other words, sound in and of itself was powerful—effective and affecting—and the silencing of this dimension to the texts with which we work is definitively a loss. We are not *'amils*, and cannot conjure up the inexpressible experience of sounds that have long passed into silence. But all our work in this volume is underpinned by the conviction that we must be constantly mindful of the fact that texts in North India were (and are) frequently experienced as live auditory entities with a fuller range of experiential possibilities than may be apparent on the surface of the page.

60 Munshi Muhammad Karam Imam Khan, *Ma'dan al-mūsīqī* (Lucknow: Hindustani Press, 1925), pp. 111-16.

# I. BETWEEN TEXTS AND PRACTICES

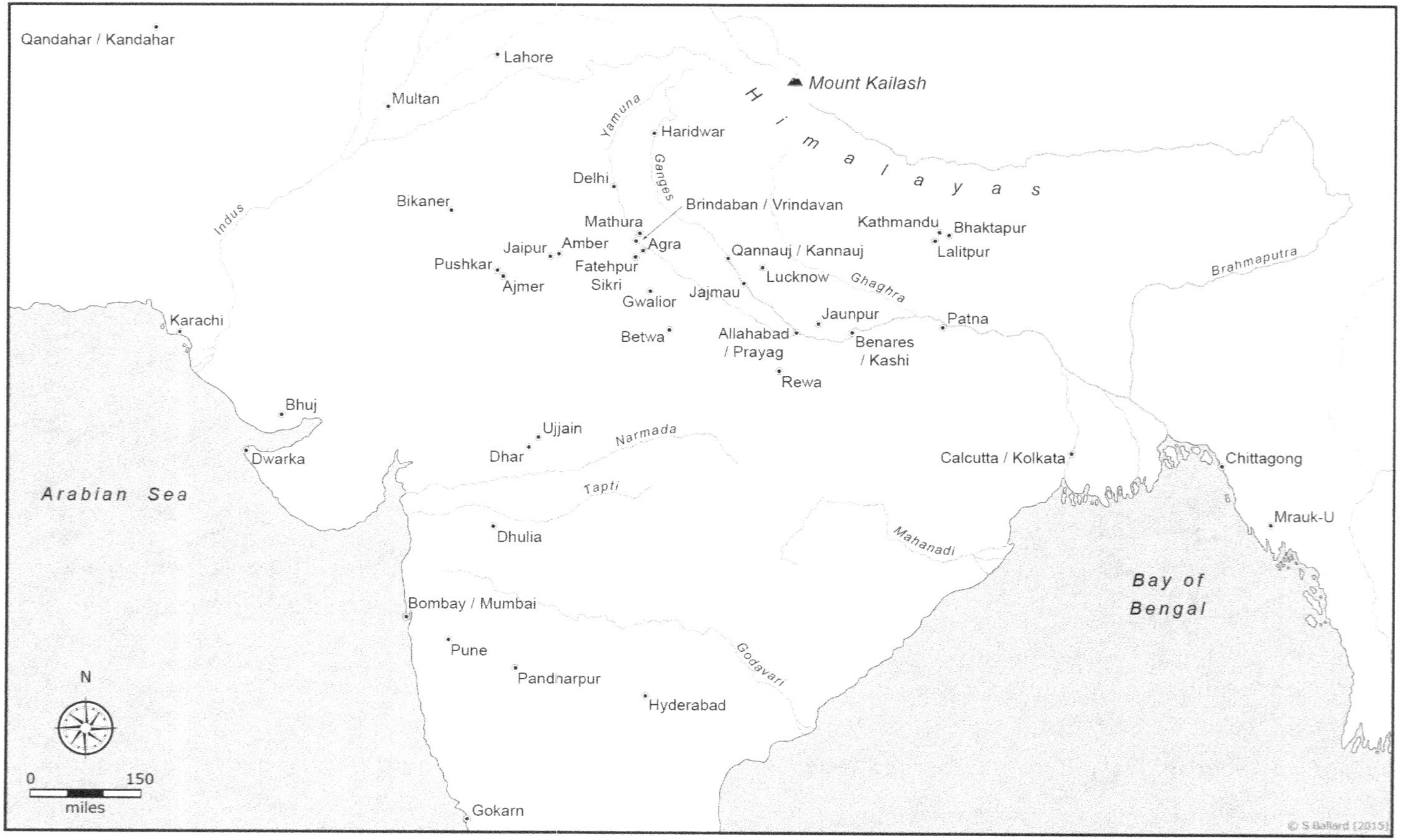


Northern India and region. Map by Sebastian Ballard, CC BY.

# 1. The Example in Dadupanthi Homiletics[1]

*Monika Horstmann*

India is rife with preaching. There is no city, no village where there are not on generous display flyers, posters, and banners announcing a *katha* or *pravachan*, the terms commonly used in North India for sermons.[2] Preachers may draw thousands of listeners; popular preachers and recorded sermons are marketed like any other celebrity or commodity; newspapers feature "spiritual columns"; special TV channels broadcast religious programmes featuring long homilies. Homiletic traditions vary widely by regional culture, sect, stylistics, duration, locale of performance, established or *ad hoc* relationship between preacher and audience, range of reach from local to global, involvement in, or abstention from, political involvement on the part of the preacher or his or her patrons, to name just a few of the numerous variables. Sermons

1 I wish to thank the organiser and participants of the workshop "Tellings, Not Texts: Singing, Story-tellings and Performance" for their stimulating interventions. I particularly acknowledge Francesca Orsini's suggestions, the correction Muzaffar Alam made of my earlier translation of the Persianate couplet below, and Sharad Chandra Ojha's communication on the Dadupanthi community of Andhi. All that may be useful in this article I owe to the gracious forthcomingness of the Dadupanthi community. I especially remember the late Acharya Swami Hariramji of Naraina and the late Mahant Pokhardasji of Gangadasji ki Poh. Among the living I express my special gratitude to Acharya Sv. Gopaldasji of Naraina and to Sukhdevdasji Maharaj of Gangadasji ki Poh for three decades of unflinching friendship and forebearance.

2 As a caveat it may be added that performances of widely different formats are named by these terms. My description of preaching in the Dadupanth, which already shows numerous variants, can therefore not be taken as representative of the genre *in toto*.

 http://dx.doi.org/10.11647/OBP.0062.01

may be published and in their printed version retain the properties of the live performance to varying degrees. And yet it is surprising that interest in the homiletic tools used by modern preachers has not been particularly vigorous.[3]

This chapter examines a single homiletic tool—the example—as it features in the Dadupanth. I will work my way through the topic by relating live performance to what texts, which started being written from the early seventeenth century, reveal about preaching and the role and function of example. The analytical expertise that comes from reasonable familiarity with the live homiletic performances that I have witnessed only in that sect accounts for such an approach. For the earlier period, we only have the bare texts, whereas for the contemporary period we have the same texts (and others in the same genre) and instances of their use. For this reason, in this essay I will consciously move back and forth between older texts and contemporary preachers, mindful that contemporary practices, while providing clues about how the synthetic texts would be expanded in homiletic performance, may not mirror older ones.

## The Dadupanth in its Cultural Region

The Dadupanth, named after its founder Dadu (1554-1603), took its origin in Rajasthan, where Dadu, as a young man with a religious vocation, had migrated from his home in Ahmedabad. The sect comprises male *sadhus* and female *sadhvis*, organised in numerous branches, on the one hand, and lay followers, on the other hand.[4] The Dadupanth belongs to the sant religion which favours interior worship of the monistically

3 Scholars have explored in great depth the homiletic and literary structures of Buddhist and Jain preaching that emerge in their canonical and other literature. By contrast, the resources of modern preachers have not attracted comparable scholarly interest; Kirin Narayan's *Storytellers, Saints, and Scoundrels: Folk Narrative in Hindu Religious Teaching* (Philadelphia: University of Pennsylvania Press, 1989), a quite self-referential account of the performance of folk-narrative in a religious context, does not touch upon homiletics. By comparison, other forms of oral religious narrative, mainly oral epics, have attracted great attention, e.g. John D. Smith, *The Epic of Pābūjī* (Cambridge: Cambridge University, 1991); *Śrī Devnārāyaṇ Kathā: An Oral Narrative of Marwar*, ed. by Aditya Malik (New Delhi: D.K. Printworld, 2003); and idem, *Nectar Gaze and Poison Breath: An Analysis and Translation of the Rajasthani Oral Narrative of Devnārāyaṇ* (New York: Oxford University Press, 2005).

4 Dadupanthi monastic lineages are not divided by gender. The head of a lineage may have both male and female disciples.

conceived divine over the orthodox *varnashrama* Hinduism with its rituals. Though predicated on interior religion, Dadupanthi worship, as much as other sant forms of religion, has an important public arena with rituals of its own, namely the *satsang* or congregation of devotees. Here faith is disseminated by the word, mainly in the form of devotional singing and preaching. The high points of communal religious life are formed by the *melas*, religious fairs, which also feature sumptuous communal feasting. Wealthy lay followers and some representatives of monastic lineages directly or indirectly meet the expenses for all these events. Preaching is one of the instruments that bond together celibate *sadhus* and lay followers. The sant *sadhu* or guru is a spiritual advisor and ideally should be an exemplar of monastic virtues. He thereby represents a type of religious specialist different from the officiating priest who, according to the orthodox *varnashrama dharma*, need not relate to the interior religious life of his clients. The particular symbiotic relationship between celibate *sadhus* and *sadhvis* and their lay followers favours a flourishing tradition of preaching. Lay followers sustain the celibate religious men and women in all their material needs, while these sustain the lay followers in their religious quest.[5] This is not to offer a monocausal explanation of the institution of preaching. Given their emphasis on the revealed word as authority, religious groups along the devotional (*bhakti*) spectrum generally feel the need for religious instruction and exegesis by discourse to give proof of that authority. A point against attributing the sole cause to the symbiosis between preachers and laymen could be made by pointing to the parallel institution of *katha* in the Sikh tradition, where the dichotomy between a celibate monkhood and lay followers is not typical, or to Vaishnava *kathakars*.[6]

Rajasthan being the homeland of the Dadupanth, the sect's profile in general and the art of the preachers in particular need to be contextualised in the religious culture of that region, for the sants—Dadupanthis and others—share features relevant to our topic with other religious groups

5 See further below. For the symbiotic relationship between monks and nuns on the one hand and lay followers on the other, see Monika Thiel-Horstmann, *Symbiotic Antinomy: The Social Organisation of a North Indian Sect* (Canberra: Faculty of Asian Studies, Australian National University, 1986).

6 The introduction of *katha* as an element of Sikh worship is attributed by the sectarian tradition to Bhai Mani Singh (1644-1734); Mandanjit Kaur, *The Golden Temple: Past and Present* (Amritsar: Department of Guru Nanak Studies, Guru Nanak Dev University, 1983), p. 96.

in their habitat. This habitat includes both Rajasthan and the more-or-less culturally and linguistically contiguous Gujarat, the adjacent regions up to Punjab in the North and down to Madhya Pradesh in the South-East, and Dadupanthi enclaves in Bengal and elsewhere. The inhabitants of this region acknowledged and addressed religious difference. This is perhaps best captured in the recurrent term "six *darshanas*" to indicate the totality of creeds in the region, which sants propagating their own creed used to express the idea that their thought was superior. The six creeds (not the six commonly understood doxographic systems usually indicated by that term) were by and large—for the stereotype is a shorthand term—all and sundry religions, and the term remained current into the twentieth century. In the common understanding of the sants, these creeds comprised, to say it in a verse by Dadu:

> *jogī jaṃgama sevaṛe, bauddha saṃnyāsī śekha*
> *ṣaddarśana Dādū rāma binā, sabai kapaṭa ke bhekha.* (33.1//7)[7]
>
> *Yogis, jangamas, sevaras* (Jains), Buddhists, *sanyasis* and *shaykhs*—
> Unless they have the name of Ram, the [proponents of the] six doctrines wear false religious costumes.

By the time of the sants, Buddhists had become a rare species, a sign of the antiquity of the stereotype. Its frequent usage nevertheless indicates the acute rivalry amongst religious groups. Preaching was naturally also a way in which rivals could score points. In the process, assimilation of homiletic practice took place.

In Rajasthan and for homiletic practice the Jains provided a powerful ancient model group. Whereas Dadupanthis rejected Jain doctrines, Jain practice made its impact on them and other sants.

The lifestyles found in the Dadupanthi *sadhu* and *sadhvi* order with its many branches vary. (The picture that I am giving here is rather one of the past, for the monkhood, including the small number of nuns, now counts a few hundred at the most.) In the early period of the sect the followers of Dadu were given to a peripatetic lifestyle. They observed the *ramat*, i.e. itinerancy in a group of followers. The master and his followers moved along routes that touched the villages of patrons and emerging places of worship and religious centres (*maths*) of *sadhus*.

7 Dadu, *Śrī Dādūvāṇī*, ed. with commentary by Swami Narayandas (Jaipur: Shri Dadu Dayalu Mahasabha, 2004, 6th edn), *Sakhi* 14.33, p. 296.

This lifestyle has not quite vanished, though it has become much less perceivable because the number of *sadhus* and *sadhvis* has dwindled. The branch of Dadupanthi *virakts* especially adhered to a peripatetic life, and a few of them continue to do so. With no fixed settlements they moved alone or in groups or clusters. The leaders of those clusters (*mandalis*) were called *mandaleshvars*. Due to the great mobility of *sadhus* and *sadhvis*, many religious centres of the Dadupanth (*maths*) remained as good as vacant outside of the festival season. There may have been there a *mahant* or his deputy with a small number of resident monks and disciples, and perhaps a staff of labourers, according to the local circumstances.[8] During religious festivals, however, temples and *maths* even today easily draw thousands of visitors.

Those festivals provide important occasions for preaching and may last several days, with sermons featuring every day. The other occasion for preaching is formed by the *chaumasa*, the four months of the rainy season, when *mahants* and their retinue and *virakts* (wandering *sadhus*) are invited either by other *maths* or families of lay followers to sojourn with them. In the golden past of the Dadupanth, that is up to the end of the nineteenth century, the arrival of monks and nuns and their guru-*mahant* used to be observed with great éclat and ritual propriety—by the various royal courts of Rajasthan, too. Now *chaumasas* are still occasions for the display of generous hospitality—for acting as a *chaumasa* host is still considered a highly meritorious act—but they take place in a much reduced format. During these four months, monks are supposed to preach regularly, ideally every day. The occasions of Dadupanthi preaching thereby obviously resemble those of the Jain tradition, where the rainy season is that of the *paryushana*, the season of regular sermons given by Jain monks or nuns. As is well known, the Jain community is also organised as a dyad of ascetics and lay followers (literally, "listeners" to the instruction imparted by ascetics), and the first archetypal event after the enlightenment of a Jain fordmaker is his *samavasarana*, the occasion and locale of his first sermon.

The ceremonial arrival of a Jain monk or nun in a place that can still be observed regularly in Rajasthan has its counterpart in that of

8 For the institution of the *math*, see Véronique Bouillier, 'Y'a-t-il des monastères dans l'Hindouisme? Quelques exemples shivaïtes', in *La Vie monastique dans le miroir de la parenté*, ed. by Adeline Herrou and Gisèle Krauskopff (Paris: L'Harmattan, 2009), pp. 25-35.

Dadupanthi *sadhus* and *sadhvis*. The Jain emphasis on written sacred texts and religious instruction of a congregation by *sadhus* or *sadhvis* has its counterpart in similar activities in the Dadupanth, and so does the injunction that the sacred texts have to be studied, which is called *svadhyaya* (lit. "self-study"), a precondition for any aspiring preacher. This study does not only cover the sacred scriptures, but also extends to other material which enables a preacher to compose a sermon, material comprising religious songs, verses, verse narratives of both sant and other provenance, mnemonic and other homiletic aids. The fruit of such study and instruction imparted to disciples in the art of preaching may be seen in the sparse analysed samples of sermons available.[9]

Dadupanthi sermons delivered in Hindi on the great festive occasions last between one hour and an hour and a half. According to what I have seen, a preacher does not consult a prepared script but may hold the open sacred scripture in front of him. If he preaches on a sequence of couplets from the sacred scripture, he may read these out as he proceeds in his discourse. This is not to claim that no preacher uses or ever used written scripts; numerous manuscripts show by their annotations in the margin that their users made exegetical notes. Dadu's disciple Bakhana, a resident of Naraina, has in his "Chapter on the Orator Without a Purpose" a couplet saying,

> On paper you find all their *prasangs* (contextualising examples), on paper you find the "Chapter of Remembrance",
> On paper you find the boundless light, but inside of them terrible darkness holds sway.[10]

The live performance of a sermon is therefore oral in its fullest sense, although it draws on memorised or printed material and perhaps on notes the preacher has taken while preparing for the task. Preaching during the *chaumasa* is mandatory for heads of religious institutions. The mandatory character of preaching is mentioned as enjoined upon monks in the *Panthpaddhati* by Jnandas, which may date to around the middle of the eighteenth century.[11]

---

9 To my knowledge only M. Thiel-Horstmann, 'Dadupanthi Sermons', in association with Tilak Raj Chopra, in *Living Texts from India*, ed. by M. Thiel-Horstmann, T.R. Chopra, and Richard K. Barz (Wiesbaden: Harrassowitz, 1989), pp. 141-83.

10 Bakhana, *Baṣanāṁ-vāṇī*, ed. by Bhajandas Swami with commentary by Brajendrakumar Singhal (Jaipur: Shri Swami Lakshmiram Trust, [n.d.]), p. 123 (*sakhi* 2).

11 Monika Horstmann, 'The Flow of Grace: Food and Feast in the Hagiography of the

I myself have not seen a disciple being actually trained for his job as a preacher. At the time of my research I was ignorant of the wide scope of issues that needed examination, but in part the missing evidence of homiletic training is also symptomatic of the structural change in the Dadupanth, where the number of *sadhus* has constantly dwindled since the earlier part of the twentieth century, and all the more during the last three decades that I have been watching the life of the sect.[12] Naturally this has resulted in a declining demand for homiletic pursuits.

Taken together, texts reaching down to the beginning of the sect as well as live experience and recorded homilies give an idea of the status and means of the art of preaching, though we are far from being able to trace changes that inevitably occurred in topics and homiletic strategies over the long period of four hundred years. Suffice it to mention that, to my limited knowledge, long hagiographic narratives such as those composed by Jangopal, or the narratives of Bajid discussed by Imre Bangha in this volume, do not feature in homilies as long extracts or full-length texts. Portions of Raghavdas's *Bhaktamāl* are however read out by preachers and may thus form the substitute of a homily. *Kathas* based on the *Bhāgavata-purāṇa* also enjoy popularity. The text, especially Book 11, which is relevant to ascetics, has always inspired sants to compose their own versions.[13]

Since the early anthologies of the Dadupanth that appeared not long after Dadu's death, Dadupanthi texts have featured, besides the sacred word of Dadu, compositions by other sants and non-sants, as well as texts that must be considered to have formed homiletic aids. These consist of lists of terms, of celestial bodies, lexical aids, assorted sayings, and nutshell versions of the Indian epics. When the Dadupanth adopted Sanskritic intellectual mores, texts on grammar or poetry also became popular.

---

Dadupanth', *Zeitschrift der Deutschen Morgenländischen Gesellschaft* 150 (2000), pp. 513-80: pp. 531 (st. 18), 535 (st. 62).

12 A *sadhu*, now in his early fifties and a walking treasure-house of religious and folk couplets and the narratives connected with these, told me that during his childhood (like most *sadhus* he had joined the monkhood as a child) and youth, there were held among the *sadhus* contests of reciting memorised *sakhis* (couplets) from the religious tradition. These exercises would certainly have been useful for aspiring preachers, though that particular *sadhu* received hardly any formal education, not to speak of the education required to be a preacher.

13 See, for example, Monika Horstmann, 'Caturdās's *Bhāṣā* Version of the Eleventh Book of the *Bhāgavatapurāṇa*', in *Transforming Tradition: Cultural Essays in Honour of Mukund Lath*, ed. by M. Horstmann (New Delhi: Aditya Prakashan, 2013), pp. 47-62.

Preaching is mentioned alongside devotional singing and communal feasting by Dadu's first hagiographer Jangopal as what Dadu himself practised when he came to the villages of his followers.[14] In 1660, Raghavdas wrote his hagiography *Bhaktamāl*. In this text he enumerated the fifty-two direct disciples of Dadu and many later disciples as well.[15] In the case of a good number of Dadu's direct disciples, he mentioned that they were talented orators. Raghavdas clearly distinguishes the various talents relating to the word and its performance, namely preaching, the composition of devotional songs and verses, and devotional singing. About Dadu's son and successor as head of the sect he says, "as an orator he resembled Vyasa Muni".[16] His rhetorical skills were complemented by his famed qualities as a singer, on which the hagiography elaborates. Raghavdas's account of two of Dadu's disciples, Rajjab and Jagjivandas, is especially relevant for the topic of example. Of Rajjab, a famous and prolific author, he enumerates all poetic and rhetoric accomplishments:

> ... in his *Sarvāṅgī* he told the essential truth, he compiled [in it] the poetry of all, *sakhis*, *sabads* (devotional songs), *kavittas*, not one of them without an example (*drishtant*), all the topical stories (*prastav*) in the world were standing before him in obeyance...[17]

In this quotation the term *prastav* needs to be noticed, which according to Swami Narayandas means *prasang*, the context and the topical narrative elaborating on the example (*drishtant*), to which we will presently turn.[18]

Of Jagjivandas, Raghavdas says:

> ... He was a great and accomplished pandit, the excellency of his knowledge is beyond description, his *vani* is vast, his examples (*drishtant*) in the form of *sakhis* are attractive...[19]

---

14 See Monika Horstmann, 'Dadupanthi Anthologies of the Eighteenth and Nineteenth Centuries', *Bhakti in Current Research, 2001-2003*, ed. by M. Horstmann (New Delhi: Manohar, 2006), pp. 173-75 with reference to primary sources.

15 Fifty-two is the canonical number of Dadu's direct disciples, probably conceived on the model of the fifty-two branches of *samnyasis* and Vaishnava Naga (warrior ascetic) branches. Raghavdas himself belonged to the first lineage of Dadupanthi Nagas.

16 Raghavdas, *Bhaktamāla* (*Caturdās kṛt ṭīkā sahit*), ed. by Agarchand Nahta (Jodhpur: Rajasthan Prachyavidya Pratishthan, 1965), *chhappai* 366.

17 *Raghavdas, Bhaktamāla* (Nahta, 1965), *chhappai* 378.

18 Raghavdas, *Bhaktamāla* (*Caturdās jī kṛt padya ṭīkā tathā* Bhaktacaritra prakāśikā *gadya ṭīka sahit*), ed. by Swami Narayandas (Jaipur: Shri Dadu Dayalu Mahasabha, [n.d.]), *chhappai* 493, commentary.

19 Raghavdas, *Bhaktamāla* (Nahta, 1965), *chhappai* 391.

Dayaldas is said to have been won over by a sermon given by Dadu, which he was able to repeat from memory word for word.[20] Kapil Muni administered to his audience "the nectar of immortality in the form of *kathas*, and Chainji loved performing sermons (*katha*) and praise (*kirtan*)".[21] All these references show that preaching was considered a constituent of worship and that the preachers had at their disposal as an homiletic tool the *drishtant* (example), completed by a prose narrative (*prastav*, or more commonly *prasang*[-*katha*], i.e. topic, narrative context).

As I turn to present-day homiletic practice, my observations span only three decades.[22] Thus any changes in homiletic tradition remain a vexingly elusive issue. Only a few factors of change can be hinted at. The Dadupanth developed a literary, aesthetic, and learned culture that was supported by patronage. To no small extent the Dadupanthi Nagas contributed to these achievements. When their military and ceremonial function at the court of Jaipur waned and their link with wealthy magnates and nobles slackened as a consequence of British Paramountcy, the Dadupanth sought to redress the decline of the tradition and the blatant lack of education among its *sadhus* that had become all too manifest, at least by the end of the nineteenth century. In 1928 the Dadu Mahavidyalay was founded in Jaipur expressly to redress this lack, and monks were encouraged to have young *sadhu*-disciples enrolled in this college for a formal education in Hindi and Sanskrit.[23]

The Dadu Mahavidyalay enjoyed for many years the reputation of being Jaipur's premier Sanskrit college. One of the three preachers whose

20 Raghavdas, *Bhaktamāla* (Narayandas, [n.d.]), *chhappai* 503.

21 Ibid., *chhappais* 528 and 571, respectively.

22 Some of this, dating from the early 1980s, has been documented (Thiel-Horstmann, 1989); some material recorded in 2005 at the halts of a Dadupanthi foot pilgrimage has been touched upon briefly in M. Horstmann, 'An Indian Sacred Journey', in *Prozessionen, Wallfahrten, Aufmärsche: Bewegung zwischen Religion und Politik in Europa und Asien seit dem Mittelalter*, ed. by J. Gengnagel, M. Horstmann, and G. Schwedler (Köln, Weimar, Wien: Böhlau, 2008), pp. 336-60. Some homiletic material, recorded at the workshop organised in 2004 at the Indira Gandhi National Centre for the Arts on the occasion of the fourth centenary of Dadu's death, still awaits analysis. Additional evidence is provided by recordings of the late Swami Hariramji's sermon at the Naraina mela of 1987 (anonymous, [n.d.]). Numerous performances I have attended over the years remained unrecorded.

23 The college exists to this day, but it is no longer a training college for *sadhus*. Run by the Dadupanth and under its headmaster Swami Bajarangdasji, who is also an alumnus of the Dadu Mahavidyalay, it is overwhelmingly staffed by non-Dadupanthi teachers. The college is also one of the richest repositories of Dadupanthi manuscripts.

sermons I examined,[24] the late nineteenth Acharya of the Dadupanth, Swami Hariram (1917-2001), was educated in both the traditional and college style, first during his childhood and early youth by his guru at the Dadudvara of Naraina, the headquarters of the sect, and then up to his late twenties at the Dadu Mahavidyalay, where he earned the degrees of Shastri in Grammar and of Kavyatirtha, before he passed an exam in Hindi literature from the University of Calcutta. His preparations for the exam of Shastri in Vedanta were interrupted in 1944 when he was made the *pujari* of Naraina.[25] The second preacher is Mandaleshwar[26] Haridas, who was trained in the traditional way by his guru. Haridas used to write poetry himself, and he is an acclaimed orator. He used to be *mahant* of Kacharoda near Phulera, but at one point resigned and took to peripatetic life. There has probably been no *mela* in the last thirty years that has not featured his sermons. The third preacher is the late Mahant Pokhardas (d.2008) of Gangaramji ki Poh (Nagaur District), who had been trained at the *math* by his guru Gangaramji and, though carefully fulfilling his homiletic duties, was not a preacher by vocation.

The touchstone of preaching is no doubt that it be both understood and enjoyed by the audience. Swami Hariramji's sermons were greatly praised by everyone, but some people would pass the comment: "He is very learned", in other words, a little hard to enjoy. Haridasji's sermons reach the heart of everyone. Pokhardasji's homilies were far from flamboyant, but they were devoutly listened to as the words of a beloved guru. As for the comprehensibility of sermons as a whole and the many quotations that occur in them and may be used as *drishtant* elaborated on by a prose narrative, every devotee understands them. Devotees are themselves often mines of quotations from the scriptures and oral sources. An incident of this, perhaps only striking to me, was a public recital of memorised couplets by Dadu, chanted from a dais with great gusto and at rapid pace to an enthusiastic audience, which lasted about twenty-five minutes. This took place during a stop in a foot pilgrimage in 2005. The performer was a local bus driver. This reminds one of the aforementioned competitions of reciting couplets memorised from the scripture, which a monk remembered having practised as a child-*sadhu*.

---

24 Thiel-Horstmann (1989).

25 Baldev Vamshi, *Smaraṇāñjali: Śrī 1008 Śrī Dādū sampradayācārya śrī svāmī Harirām jī mahārāj (1917-2001)* (New Delhi: Akhil Bharatiya Shri Dadu Sevak Samaj, 2002), pp. 5-6.

26 This title describes the head of a group of wandering *sadhus* (*virakt*). It does not necessarily indicate that its bearer really leads a peripatetic life.

## Examples

So far the term *drishtant* (*dṛṣṭānt*), "example", has been found to describe a verse quoted from the sacred words of Dadu, the compositions of other sants or by authors of the wider tradition inside and outside of the sant spectrum. The *drishtant* is usually elaborated through a *prasang*, "context", i.e. one or several contextualising verses pertinent to the topic of the sermon, and an ensuing narrative, which in its turn can be simply called either *prasang* or *prastav*. According to modern terminology, that narrative is called a *prasang-katha*. What has come down to us are, first of all, the sant or other poetic compositions, from which *drishtants* can be drawn. Second, special collections of *drishtants* have also come down to us, either by that name or under other rubrics, notably *phutkar* "miscellaneous". What was not transmitted in sectarian writing until well into the twentieth century were the prose narratives themselves. These were part of the oral tradition transmitted in the monastic milieu which formed a specialised domain within the floating oral tradition of the region concerned and beyond that region, for the oral tradition travelled with its transmitters and audiences, among whom transhumance, periodic migrancy, and other forms of mobility attributed to the circulation of tradition.

The Dadupanthi *exemplum* thereby partly differs from, and partly converges with, its medieval European counterpart, which has been the subject of intense research by scholars of both medieval and Renaissance literature and history. Since the late 1960s, the historical aspects of *exempla* have found special interest also among scholars of medieval history, since Jacques LeGoff in 1968 launched

> [u]n plan d'étude d'un genre littéraraire, les *exempla*, [...] qui devrait conduire à la connaissance précise des contes populaires du Moyen Age, l'*exemplum*, historiette à l'usage des prédicateurs, étant en general la transportations savant à l'usage du peuple d'un conte populaire sous-jacent.[27]

The medieval *exemplum* was thus defined as a narrative used by preachers, irrespective of its classical function or the function that it assumed when used by Renaissance intellectuals.[28] In medieval Europe, the *exemplum* as

27 Quoted by Jaques Berlioz, 'Les recherches en France sur les *exempla* médiévaux, 1968-1988', in *Exempel und Exempelsammlungen*, ed. by Walter Haug and Burghart Wachinger (Tübingen: Max Niemeyer, 1991), p. 289.

28 Medieval homiletic tools formed to no small extent the source for the development

a homiletic tool attained importance from the eleventh century onwards, when it flourished in monastic as well as urban milieux. This culminated in the period between 1220 and 1320, when after the Lateran Council of 1215 the Mendicant Orders oriented their attention especially to the laity. A new public, beyond the walls of monasteries, needed to be convinced of the religious message. Dadupanthi preachers have found themselves confronting the same task.

The study of the *exemplum* as narrative in European medieval preaching into the Renaissance has also shed light on its enormous variations. Basically, the purpose and function of example may well be captured in the words of Peter von Moos in his study of *exemplum* from antiquity to Renaissance:

> Exemplum is a set of events of real or imagined human life in the recent or distant past which, isolated *ad hoc* from its original context, is mostly narrated (in a *historia*) or just alluded to (*commemoratio*) with the pragmatic, strategic or theoretical intention of illustration, confirmation, stating and resolving of a problem, reflection and orientation.[29]

As for its variants, all kinds of literary types or fragments and quotations thereof may serve as *exemplum* in that sense. This prompted Burghart Wachinger to make a statement also applicable to the Dadupanthi case: "An example is that which serves as an example for something else. Only its function in context renders an example an example".[30]

---

of the tools of intellectuals of the Renaissance. For an overview, see *Les instruments de travail à la Renaissance*, ed. by Jean-François Gilmont and Alexandre Vanautgaerden (Turnhout: Brepols, 2010).

29 "Exemplum ist ein in pragmatischer, strategischer oder theoretischer Absicht zur Veranschaulichung, Bestätigung, Problemdarlegung und Problemlösung, zur Reflexion und Orientierung aus dem ursprünglichen Kontext *ad hoc* isolierter, meist (in einer *historia*) erzählter oder nur anspielend erwähnter (*commemoratio*) Ereigniszusammenhang aus dem wirklichen oder vorgestellten Leben naher und ferner Vergangenheit"; Peter von Moos, *Geschichte der Topik. Das rhetorische Exemplum von der Antike zur Neuzeit und der Historiae im "Polycraticus" Johanns von Salisbury* (Hildesheim: Georg Olms, 1988), p. xi (my translation).

30 Burghart Wachinger in *Kleinere Erzählformen im Mittelalter: Paderborner Colloquium 1987*, ed. by Klaus, L. Grubmüller, Peter Johnson, and Hans-Hugo Steinhoff (Paderborn: Schöningh, 1988), p. 230, n. 11, as quoted by Walter Haug, "Exempelsamlungen im narrativen Rahmen: Von 'Pañcatantra' zum 'Dekamerone'", in *Exempel und Exempelsammlungen*, ed. by Walter Haug and Burghart Wachinger (Tübingen: Niemeyer, 1991), p. 265 (my translation).

The narration may be complex, boxing additional examples and sub-narratives, or may shrink towards zero so that the example may be mentioned in a mere figure of speech which assumes that the listener or reader is aware of the narrative implied.[31]

In the Dadupanthi tradition, the narrative is an inherent but latent constituent of the verse *exemplum*. The *exemplum* triggers the narrative. This no doubt raises the question, to be addressed further on, if to any significant extent we can assume an established link between a particular verse example and the ensuing narrative.

The *drishtant* as a homiletic device is also found elsewhere in the Indian preaching tradition. In the late thirteenth century, soon after their founder Chakradhara's death (1278, according to the sectarian tradition) the Mahanubhavas made compilations of *drishtants*, extracted from Chakradhara's works and used for religious instruction. In this way they took care to preserve his original teachings.[32] Let it be repeated that in the Dadupanthi tradition *drishtant* is only one of the numerous homiletic instruments at the preacher's disposal. Lists of various items, names, yogic postures, lexical and many more aids—come down to us in Dadupanthi compilations—added to his tool-box.[33]

Whereas in Sanskrit poetics the *drishtanta* or "the aim or end of what is seen"[34] is a syntactic figure of speech which forms "the adjunction of a second situation which bears upon the same point as the first and where the purpose is entirely one of illustration",[35] this description is only one of the various descriptions applicable to the *drishtant* used for homiletic purposes. It enunciates a general truth A, which is exemplified by a proposition B (or the other way round), as in the following verse:

---

31 See Haug (1991), p. 267.

32 Shankar Gopal Tulpule, *Classical Marāṭhī Literature: From the Beginning to A.D. 1818* (Wiesbaden, Otto Harrassowitz, 1979), pp. 324-25.

33 For a lexical aid, see Garibdas's *Anabhay-prabodh*, discussed in Winand M. Callewaert, 'The Anabhay-prabodha of the Dadupanthi Garībdās', *Orientalia Lovanensia Periodica* 5 (1974) and 8 (1977), 163-85, 309-30. A related work is the *Sarb-bistār* (*Sarvavistāra*), which explains key-terms by appropriate stanzas (Naraina MS VS 1895). For a list of yogic postures and gestures, see the *Aṣṭ kumbhak das mudrā* in the same manuscript.

34 Monier Monier-Williams, *A Sanskrit-English Dictionary* (Oxford: Clarendon Press, 1956 ed.), s.v. *dṛṣṭānta*, pp. 491-92.

35 Edwin Gerow, *A Glossary of Indian Figures of Speech* (The Hague and Paris: Mouton, 1971), p. 199, with sub-categories on pp. 199-201; for a comparison with the figures of speech in Latin antiquity, see also Gero Jenner, *Die poetischen Figuren der Inder von Bhāmaha bis Mammaṭa* (Hamburg: Ludwig Appel Verlag, 1969).

> Absorbed in playing with cowries, a child fearfully holds his breath.
> Bakhana says: You will find the Lord, if in the same way you direct all your attention to His feet.[36]

The use of examples going beyond figures of speech is certainly well attested in literary history, though not necessarily by that term. Poetics would be a case in point, as for example Vishvanatha Kaviraja's *Sāhityadarpaṇa*, followed by Keshavdas in his *Rasikapriyā* and in the same author's *Kavipriyā* (see Busch in this volume). In these texts abstract definitions and tropes to be employed in poetry are illustrated through examples. The *Rasikapriyā*, though not the *Kavipriyā*, also provides narrative verses to illustrate the definition.

For the Dadupanthi tradition, we need to consider separately first the *drishtant* in the sense of a verse, mostly in the form of a couplet (*doha*) or a song or a portion thereof, and second the narrative (*prasang-katha*) in which the example is unfolded. Raghavdas's hagiography is perhaps the first Dadupanthi source to expressly mention the verse example and a subsequent narrative. In this connection he refers to Jagjivandas, who composed some 2,500 couplets and was famous for his elaboration of couplets in narratives.

From an early period onwards we indeed find in the Dadupanthi compilations of *sakhis* ("testimonies") by Jagjivandas grouped together, significantly often next to other *drishtant sakhis* or *sakhis* of the *phutkar* (miscellaneous) rubric, which in turn could also be arranged systematically by topics or authors or both categories.[37] An early occurrence dated 1676 CE is a manuscript which gives 109 of Jagjivandas's *sakhis*.[38] In any event,

---

36 Bakhana [n.d.] p. 101, *sakhi* 1. The commentator explains that the child is absorbed in his play and at the same time afraid that his parents may come and interrupt it.

37 The portion of that rubric can easily run into hundreds of *sakhis*. See for example MS 4 (undated) with 667 items plus another 210 *chands* of "*drishtants* etc." in Gopalnarayan Bahura and Lakshminarayn Goswami Diksit, *Vidyā-bhūṣaṇ-granth-saṅgrah-granth-sūcī*, ed. by Svargiy Purohit Harinanarayanji (Jodhpur: Rajasthan Prachya-vidya-pratishthan, henceforth *Vidyā-bhūṣaṇ*). A good number of voluminous manuscripts, pointing to the considerable wealth of the patron, come from Dadupanthi Naga lineages; see for example *Vidyā-bhūṣaṇ* MS 68 (undated, but according to the genealogy given in the colophon from about the end of the nineteenth century) with 107 *drishtant sakhis* by Jagjivan which follow 120 *drishtant sakhis* by Raghodas. A Naga manuscript, Naraina MS VS 1895 (*jyeṣṭha* b. 7), also a Naga manuscript, has first 46 folios and a little further down in the anthology 80 folios of just the *phutkar* (miscellaneous) type.

38 Dadu Mahavidyalay MS 2. W.M. Callewaert, who filmed the manuscript, gives no Vikrama date.

Jagjivandas's *drishtants* as well as those of Raghavdas form stock items in Dadupanthi anthologies, especially those rich in homiletic aids.

The wealth of manuscripts often of great length and calligraphic quality indicate that the patrons of these were men—and occasionally women—of considerable means. The anthologies reflect in many ways the homiletic requirements of their patrons. This points to the fortunes of the Dadupanth. From the late eighteenth century the Nagas especially accumulated great wealth, which was also spent on the production of exquisite manuscripts. A brief remark on that branch may not be out of place, since the text to be examined presently was composed by a Dadupanthi Naga. The Nagas, fighting monks, have a long history and in the period under review were attached to almost all major religious orders. The Dadupanthi Nagas cultivated Rajput ideals, also with respect to courtly taste for literature and the arts.[39] They regard as the progenitor of their lineages Sundardas, the son of Raja Jaitsi of Bikaner. Hapoji (Haridas), the sixth son of Raja Mansingh of Amer by a servant woman, joined those Nagas who were disciples of Dadu, though they may have resisted full institutional integration into the early Dadupanth. In their formative period these Nagas are not reported as warriors but as men cultivating literature. Famous among them is Raghavdas, the author of the *Bhaktamāl* (1660), who belonged to the same lineage as Hapoji. In pursuing the arts, the Nagas emulated the taste of the kings and court of Amer. In the latter part of the eighteenth century the Nagas became formally attached to the Kachhwaha court, now residing in Jaipur. In the early nineteenth century we find their leader Santoshdas also serving in the royal bodyguard.[40] Whereas they had previously engaged in fighting as a special contingent in the Jaipur army, between 1818 and 1857 they were deployed to quell civil rebellions of local Thakurs after Jaipur became a British protectorate. Their standing firmly by the side of the British in the revolt of 1857 earned them recognition. Towards the end of the nineteenth century, though still on the payroll of

39 On the Nagas, see James Hastings, 'Poets, Saints and Warriors: The Dadu Panth, Religious Change and Identity Formation in Jaipur State. Circa 1562-1860 CE' (PhD dissertation, University of Wisconsin-Madison, 2002), specifically pp. 176-77 for the Nagas, literature, and the arts.

40 *Dastūr komvār* (Jaipur, Rajasthan State Archives, Bikaner) 31, pp. 796-98 for the years VS 1863 and 1874. Santoshdas is mentioned as serving in front of the Chandra Mahal and in the Sukhnivas, the private wing and suite, respectively, of the royal palace. He acknowledged his subservience to the king by giving him *nazar* of a ceremonial shawl and *prasad*, which shows both his subservience to the king and his religious rank.

Jaipur State and enjoying land and revenue grants, they had lost most of their practical function. At the beginning of the twentieth century, the army of Jaipur was finally re-organised on modern principles and the Dadupanthi Nagas were disbanded, and apart from the *mahant* of Nivai, the head of all Nagas who retained the privilege of having his own chair in the *darbar*, and another Dadupanthi who retained the rank of one of the eleven *rajgurus* of the Jaipur king, all their privileges lapsed.[41] While the Nagas and the Dadupanth as a whole suffered by this change, and innumerable Dadupanthi institutions went to shambles, several members of the Naga elite established themselves in the professions, and some of their leaders had the considerable foresight to encourage their disciples to resign the monkhood and adjust to civil society.

What we can lay our hands on up to the early nineteenth century is only the overwhelmingly copious manuscript evidence of the *drishtant* tradition. The prose narratives attached to them remain as yet elusive, not to speak of the difficulty of determining how firmly the verse examples were connected with particular narratives. The evidence becomes more explicit with the year 1827 (VS 1884), when Champaram ceremonially completed his *Dr̥ṣṭānt-saṃgrah*.[42] In this work he adopted a structure either new or hitherto not recognised by students of Dadupanthi homiletics. Champaram still does not give us prose narratives, but he opens up an avenue leading to them. Champaram's work, published for the first time as late as 1984, became a recognised source for examples, recorded in scholarly works long before its publication, for C.P. Tripathi had used it in manuscript form for his 1909 edition of the *Dādūvāṇī*.

Champaram, who died in VS 1900 (c.1843 CE), was a Naga of the *akhara* of Giridhardas within the Udaipur Jamat, which was founded sometime before 1784.[43] He was quite a typical author for the literary

41 The rank of *rajguru* had been acquired by Jugaldas, who was a guru of the Sisodia wife of Jaisingh III and the mother of Ramsingh II. His descendant Gangadas, who died in 1970, still bore the title of *rajguru*; see Narayandas, *Dādū panth paricay*, 3 vols (Jaipur: Shri Dadu Dayalu Mahasabha, VS 2035-2036), Vol. 2, pp. 805, 807-08; and *Śrī Dādū mahāvidyālay rajat-jayantī granth*, ed. by Swami Surjandas (Jaipur: Shri Dadu Mahavidyalay Rajat-Jayanti Mahotsav Samiti, VS 2009), pp. 142-43.

42 Published in Narayandas, *Śrī dr̥ṣṭānt-sudhā-sindhu*. 6 vols (Jaipur: [n.p.], 2019 VS].

43 For Champaram's death, Narayandas (VS 2035-2036), Vol. 3, p. 94. The Udaipur(vati) Jamat is based in the Sikar district of Rajasthan. Its foundation is variously dated CE 1833 and even 1848; see Hastings (2002, p. 220) for references. Both these dates do not tally with the fact that the founder of that Jamat, Harikeshdas, died in 1784/

culture of the Nagas. Besides the *Dr̥ṣṭānt-saṃgrah*, he composed a work on prosody (*Prastārdīpak*) and the *Kṣīrārṇav*, which is among the largest anthologies compiled by Dadupanthis and to date unpublished. This work was completed ceremonially in 1840 at the main *mela* of the sect at Naraina and also includes Champaram's own verses. The *Dr̥ṣṭānt-saṃgrah* is a work of some consequence for the topic of homiletics. This is what the author says in it about himself and his work:

> Within my intellectual capacity, I have made exegesis in the form of examples,
> devotees must not blame me for what I have heard myself from my guru. (1)
>
> The words of Dadu Din Dayalu are an ocean,
> one cannot swim across, even the most excellent *pandits* get exhausted. (2)
>
> While *pandits* preach, they give many examples,
> I have not written down all of these, may all Sants pardon me for this. (3)
>
> My name is Champaram, I am the servant of all Sants,
> nobody should feel frustrated by listening to the book I have written. (4)
>
> In the year VS 1884, on the full moon day of Asoj,[44] in Rupnagar. (5)
>
> Herewith the *pada* part of the book called *Dr̥ṣṭānt-saṃgrah* is finished.
>
> The book *Dr̥ṣṭānt-saṃgrah* is complete with this. 449 *dohas*, 13 ancient *drishtants*. The total number of verses of the book is authenticated as 715.[45]

The "ancient *drishtants*" are examples in which the name of its author is given, such as Jagjivandas, Bakhana, and Raghavdas. All other examples, that is 436, are anonymous.

---

VS 1840 (Narayandas VS 2035-6, Vol. 3, p. 13). His grand-disciple was Giridhardas. Neither does the late date tally with the genealogy Champaram gives of himself, namely Vriddhanand (the mystical guru who, according to hagiography, appeared to Dadu twice in his life), Dadu, Sundardas (the elder, the alleged progenitor of the Dadupanthi Naga lineage), Prahlad, his two disciples Haridas (Hapoji) and Shyamdas, Chaturdas, Keval, Hridayram (who in VS 1750 caused a schism of the Dadupanth), Harikeshdas (d.1784), Prem, Ramjidas, Shukdev, Bhojandas, and finally Champaram himself. That late date seems to have been the result of a confusion of the foundation of the Udaipur Jamat with the merger of the Ramgarh Jamat with the Udaipur Jamat which took place in VS 1900 (c.1843 CE); see Narayandas (VS 2035-6), Vol. 3, p. 55.

44 This day marks the end of phase of the moon during which the Navaratra and Vijayadashami celebrations take place. These festivals relate especially to warriors, and hence to the Nagas.

45 The computation of the verses may be that of the scribe, not of Champaram himself.

Champaram follows exactly the sequence of the *sakhis* and *padas* as they occur in the various chapters of the *Dādūvāṇī* and complements each of the couplets or song verses of songs he selects with a *prasang* couplet. In this way a selection from the canonical scripture gets firmly linked with a verse establishing a context. He gives no prose narrative, though, for the preacher was supposed to provide it. The editor of Champaram's work, however, the most prolific Dadupanthi author and polyhistor of the twentieth century, Swami Narayandas, who was also first initiated as a Naga but at some point adopted the lifestyle of a solitary *virakt* in Pushkar, complemented the *prasangs* with prose narratives. The Swami, who was born in 1903 and died in the 1990s aged well over ninety, also compiled six volumes of *drishtants* (over 3000 of them) and a number of other works related to the genre.[46] In his edition of Champaram's work Narayandas points out that he heard Champaram's *drishtants* with the stories supplemented by himself from the then elderly Mandaleshwar Ramdas Dubal Dhaniyan,[47] who in turn had picked them up from the old monk Ramnivas. Narayandas does not give exact dates for these two men but says that the tradition he received can be estimated to span about three hundred years.[48] In any case, the oral tradition on which the narratives provided by Narayandas are based goes back to the period of Champaram himself.

In what follows I will discuss cases from Champaram's work and the prose narratives supplemented by Narayandas. I shall focus on one particular aspect that can be systematically captured best as an aspect of one of the seven characteristics proposed by John D. Lyons in his study of sixteenth- and seventeenth-century exemplarity. This is the characteristic of exteriority, which will here be further limited to an aspect which I propose to call territoriality. According to Lyons:

> Example is a way of gesturing outside the pure discourse of the speaker/writer toward support in a commonly accepted textual or referential world. As external to discourse, or as a unit of discourse separated from the unqualified enunciation of the speaker alone, example can be conceived as something that speaker and audience, writer and reader look toward as possible common ground. In this case example would be ouside the "inside"

46 Narayandas, *Śrī dṛṣṭānt-sudhā-sindhu*. 6 vols (Jaipur: [n.p.], [n.d.] [c.VS 2019]).

47 Narayandas (VS 2035-6), Vol. 2, p. 1000. He wrote a summary of Jagannath's *Guṇgañjnāmā*, one of the great Dadupanthi anthologies, and was renowned for his knowledge of *drishtants*.

48 Narayandas, *Śrīdādūvāṇī pravacan paddhati* (Jaipur: Shri Dadu Dayalu Mahasabha, VS 2040), p. 2.

> constituted by the discourse of direct assertion and would itself be a closed entity, which would present itself to be beheld by the public. Example is part of argumentation as a kind of evidence in the full Latin sense of *evidentia*, something capable of being seen, radiating its visibility outward (*ex + videre*). Although example is often associated with authority it differs from simple authoritarian assertion by appealing to something that diverts the audience from a direct affirmation and says "see for yourself".[49]

In the beginning of this essay I dwelt at some length on the cultural region and lifestyle of the Dadupanth. Through its *ramats* and by establishing footholds all over Rajasthan, the Dadupanth made a territorial claim that needed to be confirmed continuously by pointing to the roots that it had sunk in the region and, possibly, to the intimate link that the populace had with Dadu himself. I call this aspect "territoriality". We find that more often than not the *prasangs* and the narratives they triggered connect preacher and audience with particular topographically defined situations and characters. Thus narrative strengthens the sect's link with localities where followers of the sect live and helps forge and sustain territorial alliances.

## Case 1[50]

आज्ञा अपरंपार की, बसि अंबर भरतार।
हरे पटंबर पहर कर, धरती करे सिंगार॥३.१५७॥

*ājñā aparampāra kī, basi ambara bhartāra,*
*hare paṭambara pahara kara, dharati kare siṅgāra.*

If it is your will, Infinite One, reside in the sky, oh Lord,
Donning a green shawl, the earth will embellish herself. (3.157)

### Example:

आंधी गांवहि मांहि, रहे जू दादूदासजी।
वर्षा बरसी नांहि, कर विनती बर साइया॥३.१८॥

*āndhī gāṃvahi māṃhi, rahe jū Dādū Dāsajī,*
*varṣā barasī nāṃhi, kar vinati bar sāiyā.*

49 John D. Lyons, *Exemplum: The Rhetoric of Example in Early Modern France and Italy* (Princeton: Princeton University Press, 1989), p. 28.
50 Narayandas (VS 2040), pp. 82-83, Dadu's *sakhi* 3.157.

When Dadu Das stayed in the village of Andhi,
He asked the Lord for a boon [with the words]: "There is no rain!" (3.18)

The *sakhi* by Dadu is from the "*Virah kau aṅg*" ("The Chapter on Separation"). The couplets in that chapter express that the only way to experience the divine beloved is by suffering the pangs of separation from him. The lover thirsting for the sight of his beloved is absorbed in him. Consumed by the piercing pain of the arrow of separation, man is shattered and transformed. This is the note set by the couplet immediately preceding the one quoted above and which is the first of three *sakhis* which conclude the chapter on *viraha*, capturing the ultimate union of the *virahini* with her beloved with images of the rainy season. These *sakhis* can be read in two ways, as prayers for the *rasa* of union with the divine and for rain. The *prasang* dwells on the prayer for rain as it was uttered by Dadu when he stayed in Andhi. The generally valid prayer for release from spiritual and physical drought is transported to the topographically specific, to the village of Andhi (Jamva Ramgarh tahsil, Jaipur district). Andhi is a constituency of the Dadupanth founded in Dadu's own lifetime.

Narayandas adds to the example given by Champaram the story of how Dadu's disciples Purnadas and Tarachand, both Khandal Vaishyas from the Maharval *gotra*, were in the process of organising the master's *chaturmasa* in Andhi and how the whole village was in dispair and about to leave for Malwa because a drought had hit it. Due to Dadu's intercession, it started raining. The inhabitants of Andhi and the *chaturmasa* were saved.

Purnadas, the devout Mahajan disciple from Andhi, occurs already in the earliest hagiography by Jangopal.[51] Purnadas had invited Dadu to Andhi, and the large number of people who are reported by Jangopal to have gone there to see Dadu indicates that he stayed there for an extended period. There was also at least one more festival in Andhi organised by disciples of Dadu. Jangopal mentions eleven of these disciples by name, including Purnadas, though he does not refer to Tarachand.[52] This may point to the elaboration of the tradition of connecting that *sakhi* with Andhi by pointing to another individual of local importance.

How the tradition and its elaboration were formed we do not know in detail. However, we know about Andhi, a place where today about 100 families are Dadupanthis, about a tenth of the village population,

51 Jangopal, *The Hindī Biography of Dādū Dayāl* [Jangopāl's *Dādū-janma-līlā*], ed. by Winand M. Callewaert (Delhi: Motilal Banarsidass, 1988), 9.18.

52 Jangopal (1988), 14.28-30.

sixty of them Maharval Khandelvas. The Dadupanthis have four places (*ramshalas*) in Andhi, the oldest one said to have been the locale of Dadu's *chaturmasa*. It is a big complex, now in a state of disrepair, with interesting remains such as those of an aqueduct, something that points to the patronage the place must have enjoyed in the past. As one enquires about the Dadupanth from people in Andhi, it is the Meharval shopkeepers who are immediately forthcoming and show the visitor round the village, take him to their religious places, and point out the event of Dadu's *chaturmasa*.[53] The Dadupanthis of Andhi have maintained a distinctly local Dadupanthi identity, which they enact with enthusiasm and vigour. Today they are pillars of a relatively recent tradition of a Dadupanthi sacred journey, where they form a distinct local group.[54] The refreshed memory of their role at the formative stage of their sect encouraged them to invest in 1996 in a new *ramshala* though they are not well-off. They are emphasising their adherence to Dadu, although they realise that the festivals they celebrated in the past are no longer in vogue and also beyond their means.

This then is a case where tradition and its narrative as part of the community's memory have been crucial for the identity of a local caste group within the sect that seeks to assert its position in the vagaries of change.

## Case 2[55]

दादू निबरा ना रहै, ब्रह्म सरीखा होइ।
लै समाधि रस पीजिये, दादू जब लग दोइ॥४.३११॥

*Dādū nibarā nā rahai, brahma sarikhā hoi*
*lai samādhi rasa pījiye, Dādū jaba laga doi.*

Dadu, do not stop striving though you have become like *brahman*,
As long as there are two, drink the *rasa* of profound meditation leading to absorption. (4.311)

53 I am basing this on the report of my collaborator, Sharad Chandra Ojha, who made inquiries in Andhi in March 2004.

54 Horstmann (2008), pp. 353-54.

55 Narayandas (VS 2040), pp. 115-18. Dadu's *sakhis* 4.311-12, 317, and 331 (there are no intervening *sakhis* Champaram commented on). The numbering of Dadu's compositions is throughout that given by Swami Narayandas both in his edition of Champaram's work and that of the *Dādūvāṇī*; see *Śrī Dādūvāṇī*, ed. with commentary by Swami Narayandas (Jaipur: Shri Dadu Dayalu Mahasabha, 2004, 6th edn).

Example:

न्यारे ने हीरा लह्यो, फिर भी हेरत ठौ
बहुर्यों बूझी बादशाह, अब क्यों ढूंढत और॥४.२५॥

*nyāre ne hīrā lahyo, phira bhī herata ṭhaura*
*bahuryoṃ būjhi bādśāha, aba kyoṁ ḍhūṃḍhata aura.*

The man sifting dust for valuable matter had found some, yet still he went on searching the place,
The emperor asked once again: "Why do you now search again?" (4.25)

बेखुदखबर होशियार बाशद, खुदखबरपामाल।
बेकीमत मस्तानः गल्तान, नूर प्याले ख्याल॥४.३१२॥

*bekhudkhabara hoshiyāra bāshada, khudkhabara pāmāla,*
*bekīmata mastānaḥ galtāna, nūra pyāle khyāla.*

He who is forgetful of himself is wide attentive, he who is carefree is worthless,
Priceless is he who is drunk, wallowing in his desire for the cup of light. (4.312)

Example:

या साखी सुन औलिया, चल आया आमेर।
कथा करत गुरु देख के, मुड़ चालत लियो फेर॥४.२६॥

*yā sākhī suna auliyā, cala āyā Āmera,*
*kathā karata guru dekha ke, muṛa cālata liyo phera.*

Because the saint had heard this *sakhi*, he came to Amer,
Seeing the guru preaching, he turned and went back. (4.26)

दादू हरि रस पीवतां, कबहूं अरुचि न होइ।
पीवत प्यासा नित नवा, पीवणहारा सोइ॥४.३१७॥

*Dādū hari rasa pīvatāṃ, kabahūṃ aruci na hoi.*
*Pīvata pyāsā nita navā, pīvaṇahārā soi.*

Dadu, while drinking the juice of Hari he will never grow a dislike of it,
While drinking his thirst will be perpetually renewed: Such is the one who truly drinks. (4.317)

## Example:

वरुण मित्र किया जाट को, आना मेरे गेह।
गया तिसाया पीवत भया, अमृत कर अति नेह॥४.२७॥

*Varuṇa mitra kiyā jāṭa ko, ānā mere geha,*
*gayā tisāyā pīvata bhayā, amr̥ta kara ati neha.*

Varun befriended a Jat, [who said,] "Come to my house!"
He went because he was thirsty. Passionately fond of the nectar, he drank continuously. (4.27)

चिड़ी चंचु भर ले गई, नीर निघट नहिं जाइ।
ऐसा बासण ना किया, सब दरिया मांहि समाइ॥४.३३१॥

*ciṛī cañcu bhara le gaī, nīra nighaṭa nahiṃ jāi*
*aisā bāsaṇa nā kiyā, saba dariyā māṃhi samāi.*

The bird took a beakful [of water]. The water is not diminished by this.
No pitcher was made to contain all oceans. (4.331)

## Example:

गुरु दादू का दर्श कर, अक्बर किया संवाद।
साखि सुनाइ कबीर की, ब्रह्म सु अगम अगाध॥४.२८॥

*guru Dādū kā darśa kara, Akbara kiyā saṃvāda*
*sākhi sunāi Kabīra kī, brahma su agama agādha.*

Receiving Dadu, Akbar had a conversation with him.
Dadu recited a *sakhi* of Kabir [and said]:
"The Supreme Self is inaccessible and unfathomable". (4.28)

The *sakhis* come from the "*Paricay kau aṅg*" ("The Chapter on the Experience"). Within that chapter of 351 couplets, Champaram provides a *prasang* for twenty-eight of them. The quoted *prasangs* (25-28) thus stand last in that chapter of his commentary. Experiencing the divine is an act of applying oneself continuously and drinking with all one's senses the nectar that starts flowing when the soul realises union with the divine. The first *sakhi* of Case 2 is not topographically specific but has a humble man teach the emperor a lesson on persistence. The story supplemented by Narayandas has the emperor pass by a man sifting dust for something valuable. Commiserating with him, he slips a precious stone into the dust. The pauper duly finds it, but when the king passes by on some later occasion he sees the same man again sifting dust. The king asks him why he is doing so now that he is wealthy. The man answers that one does not give up a job in which there is such great profit. This narrative is not associated with Dadupanthi territoriality but asks the listener to judge the man's action by the standard of what any sensible person would do. The example links the notion of continuous meditation, which is remote from the lives of ordinary listeners, to their ordinary life-experience. It says: "It is only sensible to doggedly pursue a track which has been found to deliver infinite wealth".

The next *sakhi* depicts a man drunk on a potion of light. This is complemented by the example of the Muslim saint (*auliya*) who heard someone pronouncing this *sakhi* by Dadu. It struck the saint as the uttering of a mystic fully immersed in God and therefore lost to the world—Dadu must be the master whom he had been looking for! Accordingly, he went to visit Dadu in Amer (where Dadu had resided since c.1580). When the saint came to Amer he found Dadu preaching, that is, interacting with the world and not withdrawn from it in the state of mystic rapture. Appalled by this, he turned on his heels and returned from where he had come.

This is all that we can conclude from the example, which also has the function to authenticate the *sakhi* as Dadu's, for in the verse itself his name is not given. The narrative supplemented by Narayandas says that Dadu was on his way back to Amer from Fatehpur Sikri, where he had been received by Emperor Akbar. His return, then, must have been a triumphant one. The veracity of Dadu's interview with Akbar has been debated. It is said to have taken place in 1586. Dadu's residence in Amer lies at the foot of the structures preceding the royal palace of Amer, on land provided by the then-king Bhagavantdas, who is said to have been the mediator in the meeting of Dadu with the emperor. In 1585 a daughter of Bhagavantdas, Man Bai, was married to prince Salim, the later Emperor Jahangir. Dadu's meeting with Akbar figures in the earliest hagiography devoted to Dadu, by Jangopal, who wrote it not long after Dadu's death. It would have been embarrassing for a religious community to falsely claim that the king on whose land and under whose vigilant eye Dadu lived, had been instrumental in the meeting of their master with the emperor. I therefore see no reason to disavow the veracity of that meeting, although there are no other sources to support it. This is not surprising, for the meeting will not have had the same importance for the emperor that it had for Dadu's followers. A master who had received the emperor's attention, one who spoke in the parlance of a sufi saint—he it was who so deeply disappointed the *auliya*. Did Dadu then just pose as a mystic? A disciple was sent to prevail on the *auliya* to come back, and he agreed after some hesitation. Dadu found out what troubled him, and argued that unless he instructed his followers they would remain ignorant of the mystic state of which that *sakhi* was the expression. The example is interesting for bringing up a Muslim saint as interlocutor of Dadu. This is an apposite exegesis of that Persianate *sakhi* amidst a sequence of almost exclusively Hindi sayings in the latter part of the fourth chapter of *sakhis* in the *Dādūvāṇī*, and it once again brings home to the listener a grand moment in the history of the sect.

This is followed by a *sakhi* that expresses once again the bhakta's insatiable thirst for God and is complemented by an example introducing Varun and a Jat as interlocutors. The narrative elaborates that Varun, after all the god commanding the water, had come to the desert of Marwar and, suffering from hunger and thirst, was fed and given something to drink at the house of a Jat. Varun promised him that he would help him in times of need. When there was a drought, the Jat asked Varun to give him of his nectar to drink and drank insatiably. Here the territorial aspect is constituted by Marwar, where Jats are numerous. Jats form a major part of the Dadupanthi constituency. I will return to this presently.

Dadu's last *sakhi* in the sequence talks of the boundlessness of the ocean of *brahman*. Champaram's example points to the apposite saying of Kabir without quoting it, for he could expect every Dadupanthi preacher to be familiar with it. Its earliest Dadupanthi occurrence is in Jangopal's hagiography of Dadu:

तन मटकी मन मही प्रांण बिलोवणहार।
तत कबीरा ले गया औरंनि हूं आधार॥

*tana maṭakī mana mahī prāṃṇa bilovaṇahāra,*
*tata Kabīra le gayā auraṃni huṃ ādhāra.*

The body is a churn, the mind is the milk, breath churns it up.
Kabir took the essence with him to also support others.[56]

The story complementing this is also set in the context of Dadu's conversation with Akbar in Fatehpur Sikri. On that occasion Dadu reportedly quoted Kabir's couplet. The narrative confirms the link joining Kabir and Dadu, who saw himself, and was seen by his disciples, as a trustee of the spiritual bequest of Kabir. Kabir gives legitimation to Dadu, and at the same time, according to the sect, Dadu also enjoys a sovereignty that partly derived from the recognition Akbar had given him. Both the example and, in even more certain terms, the narrative place this in a topographic perspective.

Up to this stage, we have proceeded from verses by Dadu complemented by verse examples provided by Champaram and, then, by prose narratives provided by Champaram's editor, Swami Narayandas. This is an oral tradition now reduced to writing. The question to be asked is how far this tradition has remained oral in the sense of not relying on written sources as derived orality. Related to this question is one that I raised earlier in this essay, namely whether the link between the verses by Dadu and examples as given by Champaram can be considered as fairly stable. A third question, which is pretty futile to raise now given that the preaching tradition is seriously eroded, would have been whether the prose narratives provided by Narayandas represent a broadly shared tradition or vary from monastic lineage to monastic lineage, and whether they keep constantly absorbing folk narratives or are relatively frozen. New forms of religious communication have gained prominence over preaching. For example, hagiographical films on Dadu or other sants shown at *melas* and available also on DVD have become quite popular and draw undivided attention. They deserve attention also because their

56 *Dādū-janma-līlā*, see Callewaert (1988) 5.27, Winand Callewart's translation with minor modifications: Callewaert took *prāṃṇa* to mean "life-giver", whereas I take it in its literal sense and interpret the verse as referring to the yogic practice. Swami Narayandas adds a variant of the last quarter of Kabir's saying which makes it: "Kabir took the essence with him, while the world drinks the whey".

production involves new forms of patronage and aims at middle class target groups, who have had a strong impact on the recent, distinctly laical, development of the sect. Sectarian preachers can also hardly cope with performers boosted by the media and enjoying popularity with the urban middle class.

The *exempla* quoted under Case 2 and the stories relating to them do indeed form part of the surviving oral tradition. In 1985 I recorded the sermon of Mahant Pokhardasji of Gangaramji ki Poh. The sermon was on *sakhi* chapter four of the *Dādūvāṇī*, the "*Paricay kau aṅg*" ("The Chapter on Experience") to which the *exempla* quoted under Case 2 refer. Pokhardasji, like his guru Gangadasji, was a Jat, and his local followers were mainly Jats and Rajputs, including affluent followers from the professional classes of Jaipur and Jodhpur. In a region where the rivalry between the Jats and Rajputs is engrained, this is significant, especially because the *math* has served as a haven for Rajput widows who turned Dadupanthi nuns. It had been the charismatic Mahant Gangadasji who had supported these women and encouraged them in the face of initially fierce oppostion from the local Rajputs. As for Pokhardasji, he was not much conversant with Hindi, which he used only as the language for homilies. He felt really comfortable only with Marwari. His charisma was not that of an orator, but of a shepherd of his following which ranged, and continues to range under his successor, from village people to urban public service elites. What he had learnt, he had acquired from his guru Gangadasji. There is hardly a chance that he ever studied manuscripts, not to speak of doing so with the intent of looking for homiletic aids. When I recorded his sermon, Swami Narayandas's edition of Champaram's examples was barely a year old. Under the circumstances, the only channel of transmission of the examples given by Champaram he could access was the oral tradition that had come to him mainly through his guru and perhaps through preachers he may have listened to at religious functions.

Pokhardasji took recourse to a sermon pattern which is rhetorically not very sophisticated. It consists in the consecutive treatment of *sakhis*, in that case from the "*Paricay kau aṅg*". He commented on *sakhi* by *sakhi*. In this fashion Pokhardasji strung together *sakhis* 299 to 331 from that chapter, giving, apart from some variants, only the stories recorded by Narayandas. Not all the *sakhis* he built his homily on were ones Champaram had provided examples to, but those that had also occurred in Pokhardasji's sermon. He also used the very same *sakhi* by Kabir which had already been quoted by Jangopal in his hagiography and also by Narayandas. When giving the narratives supplementing the examples of Champaram, Narayandas often adds that one needs to consider not only that particular single *sakhi* for which Champaram provides an example but a whole cluster of *sakhis* from the relevant chapter.[57] In fact Champaram himself quite often proceeds by *sakhi* clusters. This is in accordance with the method Pokhardasji followed, whose homily covered an unbroken string of *sakhis* from that one chapter. All this points to a transmission of the *Dādūvāṇī* which was supported by the homiletic tradition that provided an internal structure, including clustering. The thematic *sakhi* chapters, and to some extent also the songs, the refrains or select stanzas of which are also used as topics for homilies, are thereby given a living body fashioned from (a) the citation from the *Dādūvāṇī*, (b) the example, and (c) a narrative. The link between a *sakhi*, or a verse from a song, and a particular example and narrative, which may at first sight appear idiosyncratic, thus seems to have been forged by an ongoing homiletic tradition.

As one tries to find access to the tradition, particular preferences of preachers and singers find an explanation. There is, for example, one very popular song by Dadu which has been often sung at the festivals of the Dadupanth of the last decades of the twentieth century by a distinguished singer from a Naga lineage, with other singers following suit.[58] The performance of that song by an expert singer provides for a deeply emotional experience. It was only by studying Champaram that I discovered that that song also represented an *exemplum* supplemented by the story of how the learned Jagjivandas became a Dadupanthi and the founder of the early Dadupanthi settlement at Dausa. Dausa is an ancient stronghold of the Kachwaha dynasty, and here the early Dadupanthi constituency that had formed around Jagjivandas was supported by merchant castes.[59] These patrons became momentous in a number of sectarian settlements which soon formed in Marwar, Shekhavati, and other regions. The Dausa Dadupanthis even now

57 See for example Narayandas (VS 2040), pp. 106 (3 *sakhis*), 118 (6 *sakhis*).

58 Song 193 ("*Raga* Ramkali"): *paṇḍita, rāma milai so kījai…*; Narayandas (VS 2040), p. 374.

59 The Dadupanthi settlement at Dausa was soon recognised by the ruling Kachhwaha house, a fact which is not mentioned by Swami Narayandas in his narrative, an author who knew it so well but whose objective here was to provide a narrative for religious instruction and not a lesson in history.

keep recollecting, re-living, and reminding their co-religionists of their role in the making of the sect, and also as sponsors of festivals and pilgrimages.[60] The ancient examples and stories have been instruments of self-assertion in the rapidly changing world of the merchant castes of that region. The role of the Dausa community in the history of the Dadupanth cannot be overestimated, and it is interesting to see how the story of the origin of their branch became linked to one of the songs of Dadu, the performance of which is able to raise great emotion. In this way territoriality is established, sustained, and mobilised by historical recollection, homily, and emotion.

The sectarian homiletic tradition of which I have spoken goes back to the formative stage of the sect. With its stories complementing the scriptural passages and *exempla*, however recently printed, this tradition sheds light on the transmission of the *Dādūvāṇī* itself and of similar text corpora. On the surface of it the *Dādūvāṇī* and many other *vanis* in the Dadupanthi tradition are thematically and musically arranged scriptures. *Per se* that canonical corpus tells us almost nothing about the way in which these texts were brought to life. However, given the fact that most of the huge collections of texts were similarly arranged by thematical chapters and also that all these texts represent manuals for preachers, there can be no doubt that the *Dādūvāṇī* originated from the redaction of sayings by, or used by, Dadu in live homiletic contexts. Again, what we have at our disposal are only those collected sayings, soon declared canonical, but not the examples that Dadu certainly gave and elaborated on through stories. The huge anthologies by Rajjab, Gopaldas, and others modified the system initially introduced by Dadu's amanuensis Mohandas Daftari when he edited the words of the master.[61] Whereas Mohandas had arranged the *sakhis* under thematic chapters and the songs by *ragas*, the anthologies, each of which comprises compositions of well over a hundred authors, became arranged exclusively by thematic chapters. In these chapters, couplets, songs, and all other compositions are found collected under the appropriate thematic headline. This system perfectly meets the requirement of preachers, and also reflects how soon the sectarian tradition answered their homiletic needs by bountifully producing the appropriate resources.

---

60 Horstmann (2008).

61 Horstmann (2005), pp. 164-69 with reference to primary sources.

# 2. Making it Vernacular in Agra: The Practice of Translation by Seventeenth-Century Jains[1]

*John E. Cort*

## Languages and Translation

In one sense, everyone "translates" all the time. Translation is simply the basic interpretive process of rendering external data into terms that "make sense" to a person. Even between two speakers of the same language, the process of trying to understand each other involves a mode of translation. Less ubiquitous, but still almost universal, is the process of translating between and among different languages. As long as there have been languages, people have had to cross the linguistic borders between them. Everyday functioning in polylingual social settings requires translation, the finding of rough and ready equivalencies and similarities of meaning across languages so that one can engage in both

1 This chapter is based on research funded by two Senior Short-Term Fellowships from the American Institute of Indian Studies, 1999-2000 and 2006-2007. All translations are mine, unless otherwise noted. In addition to the many comments from participants at the 2009 SOAS conference, I have benefitted from comments made in response to a presentation of a version of this essay on a panel entitled "Translation in South Asian History" at the Annual Meeting of the Association of Asian Studies, Philadelphia, 27 March 2010. In particular, I thank the following people for specific comments at the two occasions, and after reading earlier drafts: Imre Bangha, Allison Busch, Walter Hakala, Jack Hawley, Christian Novetzke, Deven Patel, and Gary Tubb. All errors of fact and interpretation are, of course, mine.

 http://dx.doi.org/10.11647/OBP.0062.02

necessary and casual communication with others. For some people, this process is elevated into a more consciously pursued practice. A person works carefully and painstakingly to bring a text in one language—a legal contract, a government document, a bill of lading, a poem—into a second language. Issues of accuracy and precision become more important. Greater control over both languages, the source and the target, becomes a concern. Training and experience in translation may be desirable skills on the part of the practitioner.

In some settings this practice of translation becomes a performance. The tour guide, the pilgrim priest, the simultaneous translator at a diplomatic conference, the person signing a speech or performance for hearing-impaired members of the audience—each is performing translation. The concept of performance can also be extended to the playful and painful rendering of a powerful hymn from a classical language understood by few into a vernacular tongue, so that everyone who hears or reads it can appreciate and experience its beauty and influence. If the concept of "practice" in translation emphasises the need for discipline and application, the concept of "performance" reminds us that translation can be a virtuoso act aimed at receiving the appreciation of an audience.

I advance these general observations about translation as everyday experience, as practice, and as performance, in order to provide a setting for the specific discussion that follows, in which I examine the practice and performance of translation by a handful of Digambar Jains in seventeenth-century North India. In addition to being poets and translators, the men in question were businessmen, government servants, and professional intellectuals. They engaged in translation as part of their day-to-day life in the polylingual metropoles of Mughal India. Due to their occupations and their interests, they also engaged in the more explicit and formal practice of translation. Because the particular texts that they translated were intended to reach and appeal to a target audience of their fellow Jains, they furthermore engaged in the performance of translation. To gain a fuller understanding of seventeenth-century North Indian literary and intellectual culture, therefore, it behooves us to pay attention to the widespread practice and performance of translation in this culture, a practice and performance that have hitherto been largely ignored by scholarship.

It is an obvious truism to say that India has always been multilingual. In this, India has been no different than any other culture, as the monolingual culture is an invention of the modern nation-state, aided by print-capitalism.[2] Languages and dialects (the difference between the two also largely an invention of nationalism) changed within short distances, so people inevitably needed to be able to shift language to speak to others whom they met in a regional market or on pilgrimage, when men left home for work, or in marriage negotiations. The languages of governance were often different from the local vernaculars. Religious languages—which we often term as "classical"—differed, often sharply, from the vernaculars. Literary languages also differed from the spoken vernaculars; the idea that literature should represent, if not be identical with, the spoken tongue is another creation of modernity (and literary high modernism). Commerce, military service, and religious mendicancy all generated their distinctive forms of linguistic communication.

As I said, there is nothing uniquely Indian about this. However, when one compares the cultural and intellectual attitudes to this multilingual condition in India to those found in the European and Mediterranean cultures that we loosely term as "Western", there is a striking difference. From the times of classical antiquity, and the first productions of Christian scripture in Greek and Latin as opposed to the earlier Hebrew and Aramaic, philosophers, theologians, and writers have thought long and hard about what it means "to translate" from one language into another.[3] One would think that a culture in which language itself (*vac*) has a sacred presence, and in which grammar rather than mathematics formed the foundation for logic, would have generated a tradition of inquiry into the meaning and possibility of translation. For most of Indian history, however, this has not been the case. This is evident in the *Hindī sāhitya koś* (*Dictionary of Hindi Literature*), edited by Dhirendra Varma (1963). In the first volume of this massive work, totaling 997 pages, which is a glossary of literary terms (*paribhashik shabdavali*), not a single entry is devoted to a discussion of translation per se.[4] This has continued into English-language scholarship. To cite just two influential recent examples, in neither of the massive volumes

2 Benedict Anderson, *Imagined Communities: Reflections on the Origin and Spread of Nationalism* (London: Verso, 2006, revised edn), pp. 67-82.

3 The best introduction to the philosophical and theological problems raised by multilinguality and translation remains George Steiner, *After Babel: Aspects of Language and Translation* (Oxford: Oxford University Press, 1992, 2nd edn).

4 *Hindī sāhitya koś*, ed. by Dhirendra Varma, 2 vols (Varanasi: Jnanmandal Limited, 1963).

by Sheldon Pollock on South Asian literary cultures, totalling some 1,600 pages, is translation a topic of analysis.[5]

In part this is a reflection of a broader cultural and academic devaluation of translation and translators, which has led to what Lawrence Venuti has called "the translator's invisibility".[6] Publishers often either omit the name of a translator, or bury it in fine print on the copyright page. Academic tenure and promotion committees place little if any weight on translation as evidence of "real" scholarly activity. This neglect extends into scholarship, as it is common to find detailed studies of important authors in which scant attention is paid to those author's translations. The major biography of Banarsidas, for example, devotes only about one page out of 332 to his two iconic translations.[7] Translation is not considered to be "original", and so it is often dismissed as unimportant, uncreative, and ultimately derivative and mechanical work.

There were some exceptions, of course, especially in the context of religious communities such as the Jains and Buddhists. They developed their own sacred languages, which acquired sacred status within the specific communities; but they then had to come to terms with the privileged status of Sanskrit in classical and medieval India as the pre-eminent language of all intellectual discourse. Many Buddhist texts such as the *Dhammapada* were translated from Pali into Sanskrit, and the famous Buddhist translation workshops in China indicate that the Buddhists had no ideological objection to translation. Further, the number of Sanskrit and Pali texts that were translated into Chinese multiple times indicates some level of concern for accuracy and faithfulness in translation.

We can see possible tensions over translation expressed in the story of the famous fourth- or fifth-century CE Shvetambar Jain monk Siddhasena Divakara.[8] He was a convert, from being a Brahmin to being a Jain monk,

5 *Literary Cultures in History: Reconstructions from South Asia* (Berkeley: University of California Press, 2003) and *The Language of the Gods in the World of Men* (Berkeley: University of California Press, 2006).

6 Lawrence Venuti, *The Translator's Invisibility: A History of Translation* (London: Routledge, 1995).

7 Ravindra Kumar Jain, *Kavivar Banārsīdās* (Varanasi: Bharatiya Jnanpith Prakashan, 1966). For iconic translation, see the next section.

8 Phyllis Granoff, 'The Biographies of Siddhasena: A Study in the Texture of Allusion and the Weaving of a Group-Image', *Journal of Indian Philosophy* 17 (1989): 329-84 and 18 (1990): 261-304; also 'Buddhaghoṣa's Penance and Siddhasena's Crime: Remarks on Some Buddhist and Jain Attitudes Towards the Language of Religious Texts', in *From*

and from Sanskrit to Prakrit, but was still enthralled by Sanskrit intellectual culture. He arrogantly offered to render the Jain scriptures, composed in Ardha-Magadhi Prakrit, into Sanskrit.[9] The other Jains were angered at the proposal. They said that Siddhasena was implying that the enlightened and omniscient Jinas, and their enlightened successors, had been incapable of writing Sanskrit. Siddhasena, in their opinion, was therefore implicitly doubting that very omniscience as well. The monks imposed a penance on Siddhasena, who had to wander incognito for many years—in other words, they rendered him symbolically speechless. This story does not deny the possibility of translation, but rather criticises an attempt to elevate Sanskrit to a position equal to Ardha-Magadhi. Granoff has rightly argued that the main point of the story is to deny the Mimamsaka position on language, which held that only Sanskrit is suitable for religious and ritual texts.[10] Since Siddhasena was a Brahmin by birth, the story also ties language usage to socio-religious hierarchies. This is not primarily a story about translation (or the impossibility thereof), but certainly indicates one socio-religious context within which concerns about translation might arise.

## Three Modes of Translation

At the centre of this essay is the analysis of "translation" as a text that in its intention is not independently authored, but explicitly brings into the new language a text previously authored in another language. If there is a known author to the first text, the name of that author is attached to the new text. This is what A.K. Ramanujan, borrowing terminology from

---

*Benares to Beijing: Essays on Buddhism and Chinese Religion*, ed. by K. Shinohara and P. Granoff (Oakville, Ont.: Mosaic Press, 1991), pp. 17-33.

9 In both the versions of the story that are available to me, there is no technical term for "to translate". Instead, Siddhasena simply says that he will make the texts into Sanskrit, using a form of the Prakrit verb √*kara* and the Sanskrit verb √*kṛ*, "to do, to make". In the Prakrit *Ākhyānamaṇikośavṛtti* (verse 57.32) of Amradevasuri, composed in 1134 CE, Siddhasena says, "I will make all the scripture into the Sanskrit language" (*siddhantaṃ savvaṃ pi hu karemi bhāsāe sakkayāe ahaṃ*). In the Sanskrit *Prabandhakośa* (p. 18) of Rajashekharasuri, composed in 1349 CE, Siddhasena similarly says, "I will make all the scriptures Sanskrit" (*sakalānapyāgamānahaṃ saṃskṛtān karomi*). I return to the Indic vocabulary for "translation" below.

10 On this point see also Paul Dundas, 'Jain Attitudes towards the Sanskrit Language', in *Ideology and Status of Sanskrit: Contributions to the History of the Sanskrit Language*, ed. by Jan E.M. Houben (Leiden: Brill, 1996), pp. 137-56; and 'Becoming Gautama: Mantra and History in Śvetāmbara Jainism', in *Open Boundaries: Jain Communities and Cultures in Indian History*, ed. by John E. Cort (Albany: State University of New York Press, 1998), pp. 31-52.

Charles Sanders Pierce, has called an iconic translation, in which "Text 1 and Text 2 have a geometrical resemblance to each other, as one triangle to another".[11] Of course, a fully iconic translation is impossible, as theorists of translation in many cultures have argued for millennia. A fully iconic translation would in fact be nothing other than the first text itself. This is the conundrum explored by Jorge Luis Borges in his famous short story "Pierre Menard, Author of Don Quixote"—a text which George Steiner has described as "arguably… the most acute, most concentrated commentary anyone has offered on the business of translation".[12] The goal of Borges's fictional author was not to "translate" Cervantes's famous novel, but "to produce pages which would coincide—word for word and line for line—with those of Miguel de Cervantes".[13] Despite its logical impossibility, however, the "faithful" iconic translation has been the ideal of translators in European languages and Abrahamic religious traditions for 2,000 years.

The other two types of translation in Ramanujan's schema do not aim for iconic faithfulness to the original. The first of these is indexical translation, in which the new text shares the same basic elements of plot, but differs in many specifics. This is what in Western classical music might be called a "variation on a theme". The other is symbolic translation, in which the new text "uses the plot and characters and names… minimally and uses them to say entirely new things".[14] This takes us into literary texts and genres that push the boundaries of any definition of translation, and are more often termed by scholars as "adaptations", "versions", and "renderings", and even, as I discuss later in this essay, "commentaries". If one expands the definition of translation to include these latter two modes, then Indian literary traditions have long been filled with translations. But the practice of faithful iconic translation would appear to have been rare.

11 A.K. Ramanujan, 'Three Hundred *Rāmāyaṇas*: Five Examples and Three Thoughts on Translation', in *Many Rāmāyaṇas: The Diversity of a Narrative Tradition in South Asia*, ed. by Paula Richman (Berkeley: University of California Press, 1991), p. 44.

12 Steiner (1992), p. 73.

13 Jorge Luis Borges, 'Pierre Menard, Author of Don Quixote', trans. Anthony Bonner, in *Ficciones* (New York: Grove Press, 1962), p. 49; cf. trans. by James E. Irby, in *Labyrinths* (New York: New Directions, 1964), p. 39.

14 Ramanujan (1991), p. 45.

# *Anuvad*

The absence of any sustained thinking about translation is indicated in the languages of India themselves. The word used most commonly in contemporary North Indian vernacular languages for "translation" is *anuvad* (*anuvād, anuvāda*).[15] A look at the Sanskrit original indicates that this usage is a modern one—created from the English to "translate", one can say, the word "translation" into Hindi and other vernaculars, to describe a concept that wasn't as fully present in Indian languages as in European ones. In Sanskrit the primary meaning of *anuvāda* is "to say after, to say again, to repeat", as a means of explanation.[16] Monier-Williams cites Yaska's *Nirukta* for this meaning. In the *Brāhmaṇas*, *anuvāda* means "a passage... which explains or illustrates a rule (*vidhi*) previously expounded". Monier-Williams also cites "translation" as a meaning for *anuvāda*, but gives no examples. I suspect this was a modern Sanskrit usage that found its way into his dictionary as a back-formation from vernacular usage. The term was also used in Sanskrit poetics: something that was *anuvāda-ayukta* was an example that did not in fact adequately explain a rule.[17]

The modernity of this meaning for *anuvad* is seen by looking at its usage in several modern vernaculars. R.S. McGregor gives "translation" as the second meaning for the Modern Standard Hindi *anuvad*, with the first meaning being, as in the Sanskrit, the repetition of something already said.[18] He also indicates that "translation" is now the prominent sense of the word; that a formerly secondary meaning is now the primary one indicates a shift—probably relatively recent—in its usage.

Gujarati also indicates the recentness of the use of *anuvad* to mean "translation". Its first meaning in the *Bṛhad gujarātī koś* is "to say again

15 Winand M. Callewaert and Shilanand Hemraj, *Bhagavadgītānuvāda: A Study in Transcultural Translation* (Ranchi: Satya Bharati Publication, 1983) pp. 75-77 and Harish Trivedi, 'In Our Own Time, On Our Own Terms: "Translation" in India', in *Translating Others*, ed. by Theo Hermans (Manchester: St. Jerome Publishing, 2006), Vol. 1, pp. 108-16 for similar investigations of these and other Indic terms for "translation".

16 Monier Monier-Williams, *A Sanskrit–English Dictionary* (Oxford: Oxford University Press 1899), p. 38.

17 D. Varma (1963), Vol. 1, p. 62 cites the Sanskrit literary theorists Mammata's *Kāvyaprakāśa* and Vishvanatha's commentary, and further adds that Mammata's formulation was brought into Hindi poetics by Bhikharidas in his *Kāvyanirṇay*, composed in 1689 CE.

18 R.S. McGregor, *The Oxford Hindi–English Dictionary* (Oxford: Oxford University Press, 1993), p. 38.

what has been said" (*boleluṃ pharī pharī bolavuṃ*), and then the second meaning is "translation" (*bhāṣāntar, tarajumo*).[19] The two Gujarati synonyms for "translation" further indicate the relative recentness of the importation of the concept into Indian languages. *Bhāṣāntar*, literally "other (*antar*) language (*bhāṣā*)", is a *tat-sama* derivation from the Sanskrit that sounds very much like a literal neologism. While it is also found in Monier-Williams, he again gives no example of its usage in classical Sanskrit literature.[20] *Tarjumo* (Hindi *tarjuma*) entered the North Indian vernaculars from Central Asia with the Persianate literary culture of the Mughal and related courts.

Brian Hatcher has recently subjected the Bengali *anuvada* to a preliminary historical investigation by looking at the usage on the title pages of published translations of Sanskrit texts into Bengali in the nineteenth century. He found that early in the century, Bengali authors referred to their publications as *saṃgraha bhāṣāte* ("compiled in the vernacular") or *bhāṣā vivaraṇa* ("vernacular exposition"). While these same authors when writing in English referred to the act of "translation", it was not until the middle of the 1830s that Bengali authors began to use the term *anuvada*, and from then it rose to increasing prominence.[21]

It is clear that the vocabulary for translation as a distinct, nameable practice is recent in South Asia. Does this mean, however, that translation as a practice is something new? Is it yet another feature of modern South Asian life for which we must attribute responsibility, for better or worse, to the British colonialists?[22] As I have argued elsewhere, before we attribute changes in India to colonial influence, we need a clearer understanding of India "on the eve of colonialism", to borrow a phrase from Sheldon Pollock.[23] To attempt even to begin a history of translation in South Asia is beyond the reach of this essay, for the materials for

19 K.K. Shastri, *Bṛhad gujarātī koś*, 2 vols (Ahmedabad: Yunivarsiti Granth Nirman Bord, 1976), Vol. 1, p. 76.

20 Monier-Williams (1899), p. 755.

21 B. Hatcher, 'Writing Sanskrit in the Vernacular: Vidyāsāgar, the Śāstras, and the Reading Public', paper presented at the Annual Meeting of the Association for Asian Studies (Philadelphia, 2010).

22 Trivedi (2006), for one, takes such an ideological postcolonial stance, arguing that importing the modern Indic terms into the emerging field of translation studies is to do injustice to Indic languages and therefore Indic people.

23 John Cort, 'Defining Jainism: Reform in the Jain Tradition', in *Jain Doctrine and Practice: Academic Perspectives*, ed. by Joseph T. O'Connell (Toronto: University of Toronto, Centre for South Asian Studies, 2000), pp. 165-91; '*Sanskrit Knowledge-Systems on the Eve of Colonialism*', ed. by Sheldon Pollock, *Journal of Indian Philosophy* 30 (2002).

such a history have not begun to be collected. I do think, however, that we can see one significant moment in a history of translation in South Asia emerge in Agra in the seventeenth century. Let me now turn to the details of this specifically Jain setting.

## Religious and Literary Performance among Digambar Jains in Seventeenth-Century Agra

The city of Agra was one of the centres of both political and economic power during the Mughal era.[24] Thousands of Jains migrated to the city in response to the opportunities available there. Many of them occupied positions at all levels of the Mughal administration. Others used the city as a base for trading networks. They made Agra into a rich Jain cultural centre as well. In 1594 Pandit Bhagavatidas made a pilgrimage to Agra from his home in Ramnagar, and described the metropolis in his *Argalpur jinvandanā*.[25] He said that there were forty-eight Digambar Jain temples in the city.[26]

Two of those temples were the seats of *bhattaraks*, the landed and domesticated Digambar pontiffs at the apex of the Jain religious community.[27] Bhattarak Shubhkirti resided at the Tihuna Sahu temple, and Bhattarak Jagatbhushan resided at the Sahu Narayani temple.[28] Many of

24 My discussion here overlaps with that in Cort, 'A Tale of Two Cities: On the Origins of Digambar Sectarianism in North India', in *Multiple Histories: Culture and Society in the Study of Rajasthan*, ed. by L.A. Babb, V. Joshi, and M.W. Meister (Jaipur: Rawat Publications, 2002), pp. 40-50.

25 Balbhadra Jain summarises the *Argalpur jinvandanā* on the basis of a single unpublished manuscript in Ajmer; in *Bhārat ke digambar jain tīrth*, ed. by B. Jain (Bombay: Bharatvarhiya Digambar Jain Tirthakshetra Kameti, 1974), Vol. 1, pp. 59-60.

26 By contrast, there were only thirty-six Digambar temples in 1974. Catherine Asher has discussed the way that Jain temples and icons have mirrored the mobility of Jains themselves in urban North India in recent centuries; 'Urban Growth and Decline: Housing the Moving Jina in Jaipur, Delhi and Lucknow', *Jinamañjari* 34.2 (2006), 79-91.

27 There had been no naked Digambar monks (*munis*) in North India for several centuries by the time of Mughal rule. The revival of the naked *muni* tradition began in the early twentieth century; P. Flügel, 'Demographic Trends in Jaina Monasticism', in his (ed.) *Studies in Jaina History and Culture: Disputes and Dialogues* (London: Routledge, 2006), pp. 347-54.

28 The Bhattarak Jagatbhushan mentioned by Bhagavatidas was possibly the same as the monk who was head of the Ater Shakha (branch) of the Balatkar Gana, as attested by several icon, yantra, and temple inscriptions from Agra, as well as one manuscript colophon; V. Johrapurkar, *Bhaṭṭārak sampradāy* (Sholapur: Jain Samskriti Samrakshak Sangh, 1958), pp. 127-28. The inscriptions date from 1629 to 1638, so he must have been a boy or very young man when Bhagavatidas visited Agra.

the temples in the city would have been affiliated with one or the other of the two *bhattarak* seats, and the *bhattaraks* assigned ritual specialists known as *pandits* or *pandes* to the temples under their control. These specialists, who might be celibate (*brahmachari*) or married, oversaw and conducted devotional and tantric rituals in the temples, and organised and supervised the many annual celebrations of the Jain ritual calendar. They also engaged in the production of knowledge: they wrote and copied texts in Sanskrit and vernacular, and delivered public sermons on a regular basis. Almost every Digambar temple in North India has a large courtyard—sometimes covered, sometimes open—for the performance of congregational rituals and for delivering sermons. Many temples also have covered verandas off of the courtyards, where men or women can gather. There they perform rituals involving the worship of icons (either portable metal icons, or stone icons on subsidiary altars placed in the walls of the verandas). They gather to sing devotional songs. They also engage in the study of texts, either by themselves or under the guidance of a more learned person.

Balbhadra Jain has written of Agra during this period, "In the temples there were scriptural sermons both morning and evening, and also philosophical seminars [*tattva-goṣṭhī*]".[29] We can gain a better sense of these cultural performances through the writings of Banarsidas (1587-c.1643). In his autobiography, the *Ardhakathānak*,[30] he wrote of a seminar that was held

29 B. Jain (1974), p. 59.

30 The *Ardhakathānak* [AK] has been translated into English thrice: in prose by Ramesh Chandra Sharma (1970) and Mukund Lath (1981), and in free verse by Rohini Chowdhury (2009). It has been translated into French by Jérôme Petit (2011). While most early Hindi texts were written in verse, and so verse encompassed both the prosaic and the poetic, Rupert Snell has argued that the craft in Banarsidas's text is such that it should be viewed as poetry, not merely verse. All translations of this text in this essay are mine, unless otherwise noted; 'Confessions of a 17th-Century Jain Merchant: The *Ardhakathānak* of Banārsīdās', *South Asia Research* 25 (2005a), 79-104, and 'Preface', in Banarasidas, *Ardhakathanak: A Half Story*, trans. by Rohini Chowdhury (New Delhi: Penguin Books, 2005), pp. vii-xxii. Both Lath and Chowdhury include the Devanagari text as edited by Nathuram Premi (1957). For ease of access, all references are to the two reprints of the Devanagari text. There is extensive secondary literature on Banarsidas and his times. In addition to the works above, see Bansidhar Bhatt, 'On the Epithet: Nāṭaka for the Samayasāra of Kundakunda', in *Jainism and Prakrit in Ancient and Medieval India: Essays for Prof. Jagdish Chandra Jain*, ed. by N.N. Bhattacharyya (New Delhi: Manohar, 1994), pp. 431-62; Ravindra K. Jain, *Kavivar Banārsīdās (jīvan aur kṛtitva)* (Varanasi: Bharatiya Jnanpith Prakashan, 1966), Jérôme Petit (2013), R.C. Sharma, 'Life of a Middle-Class Man in the Seventeenth Century', *Journal of Indian History* 52 (1974), 389-403, and Eugenia Vanina, 'The *Ardhakathanaka* of Banarsi Das: A Socio-cultural Study', *Journal of the Royal Asiatic Society*, Third Series, 5 (1995), 211–24.

in 1635 under the leadership of Pandit (or Pande) Rupchand.[31] Banarsidas wrote, "Pandit Rupchand was well-known, and an expert on the scriptures. He came to Agra. He stayed at the temple built by Tihuna Sahu. All the spiritual seekers held a seminar, in which he lectured on a text, the *Gommaṭasāra*".[32]

This is the same temple mentioned by Bhagavatidas forty years earlier as the seat of a *bhattarak*. Pandit Rupchand, therefore, must have been a disciple of the *bhattarak* who oversaw the temple and its congregation. Banarsidas referred to a circle of spiritual seekers (*adhyatmis*); we will return to them shortly. This group was engaged in religious study. The term Banarsidas used for this was *bichara*; and the modern standard Hindi *vicār-goṣṭhī* is a term for seminar or symposium.[33] The group took advantage of the presence of this intellectual, who was well-known (*guni*) as a scholar of the scriptures (*agama-jana*), and requested that he conduct a course of study (*banchayau*; cf. Hindi *vanchan*, *bachna*) on the *Gommaṭasāra*. This is a tenth-century text, written by Nemichandra, which provides a detailed summary of Digambar doctrine.[34] The seminar was a key event in Banarsidas's spiritual evolution. He described the effect of hearing Rupchand's exposition: "Pande Rupchand was an authoritative teacher; my mind became happy from hearing the text".[35]

Banarsidas gives us one more description of the way these seminars worked. The text for which he is best known among Jains is his 1636 *Samaysār nāṭak*, a Brajbhasha indexical translation of one of the foundational

31 See Cort (2002), p. 73, n. 22 on Rupchand.

32 AK 630b-631; Lath (1981), p. 272; Chowdhury (2009), p. 264:
*... nagara āgare thāna / rūpacanda paṇḍita gunī āyau āgama jāna //*
*tihunā sāhu deharā kiyā / tahāṃ āi tini ḍerā liyā //*
*saba adhyātamī kiyau bicāra / grantha bañcāyau gomaṭasāra //*

33 R.S. McGregor (1993), p. 919.

34 The original of this text is in Sauraseni Prakrit. Banarsidas did not specify whether Rupchand's seminar was based upon the Prakrit original, or upon one or both of the subsequent (and undated) Sanskrit commentaries, by Keshavavarni and Abhayachandra Siddhantachakravarti. As I discuss below, I am suspicious of the abilities of seventeenth-century Digambar intellectuals to read Prakrit without the aid of Sanskrit commentaries, so I assume that the seminar was based on the Sanskrit versions. A century later, the famous Digambar Terapanth intellectual Ṭodarmal used these two Sanskrit commentaries to prepare the *Samyagjñānacandrikā*, his Hindi commentary on the *Gommaṭasāra*; M. Mehta and H.R. Kapadiya, *Jain sāhitya kā bṛhad itihās*, Vol. 4, *Karm-sāhitya va āgamik prakaraṇ* (Varanasi: Parshvanath Vidyashram Shodh Sansthan, 1968), pp. 40-41.

35 AK 634c-d; Lath (1981), p. 272; Chowdhury (2009), p. 266:
*pāṇḍe rūpacanda gura pāsa / sunyau grantha mana bhayau hulāsa //*

texts of Digambar philosophy, the *Samayasāra* of Kundakunda.[36] Banarsidas had first encountered Kundakunda's text three years earlier during a visit to his wife's natal town of Khairabad. This had been another crucial turning point in his spiritual life. There he met a man named Arathmal Dhor, who was an enthusiastic proponent of the two-truths doctrine expounded in Kundakunda's text. In Banarsidas's words, Arathmal "spoke enthusiastically" on the subject.[37] Banarsidas went on to say that Arathmal gave him a manuscript of a vernacular commentary on the *Samayasāra* out of a concern for Banarsidas's spiritual welfare (*hita*). Banarsidas read (*banchai*) and studied (*bhasha aratha bocharai chitta*) the text on his own, but was unable to come to an adequate understanding of it. Only after studying the *Gommaṭasāra* under the guidance of Rupchand was he able to return to the *Samayasāra*. In the *Ardhakathānak* he simply said, "Now I had attained right faith, and knew the true nature of God. In 1639, with zeal and joy, I composed the vernacular *Samaysār nāṭak*".[38]

In the conclusion of the *Samaysār nāṭak*, Banarsidas gives us a longer account of its composition:

> The pleasant *Samayasāra* was read by *pandits* together with its Sanskrit commentary, so they understood it. But the common people could not understand its meaning. The Jain Pande Rajmall loved the *Samayasāra*, and so he wrote a commentary on it known as the *Teacher of Children* [or *Beginner's Textbook*: *Bālbodh*] which was easy to understand. Thus conversation about this wisdom spread. This became the doctrine of those who follow the Spiritual [*adhyatma*] style. The Jina's teachings became known everywhere, and people talked about the *Samayasāra* in every household. It became famous in Agra, and people became knowledgeable about it. Five skillful men began to talk about knowledge day and night. First there was Pandit Rupchand, and the second was Chaturbhuj. The third man was Bhagotidas [Bhagvatidas]. Then there was the virtuous Kaunrpal. Together with Dharamdas they were five men, who met and sat together. They would discuss the supreme truth, and nothing else. Sometimes they discussed the *Samayasāra*, sometimes other texts. Sometimes they would continue to discuss wisdom even after they had

---

36 The dates for Kundakunda, which range from the first through the eighth centuries CE, have been the subject of extensive scholarly debate. See Bhatt (1994) for a discussion of both Kundakunda's Prakrit original and Banarsidas's Brajbhasha translation.

37 AK 592a-b; Lath (1981), p. 269; Chowdhury (2009), p. 246:
*taba tahāṃ mile arathamala ḍhora / karaiṃ adhyātama bātaiṃ jora //*

38 AK 638-639a; Lath (1981), pp. 272-73; Chowdhury (2009), pp. 266-68:
*aba samyak darasana unamāna / pragaṭa rūpa jānai bhagavāna //*
*solaha sai tirānavai varṣa / samaisāra nāṭaka dhari harṣa //*
*bhāṣā kiyau…*

> stood up [to leave]. ... This work continued for many months—how many I can't say. It became known in Agra that a man named Banarsidas had a little knowledge on the subject. The *Samayasāra* is beneficial, and the commentary on it by Rajmall makes it easy to understand. If it were composed in metre, everyone could read this vernacular text. So the thought came to Banarsi to publicise these teachings of the Jina. He received permission from the five men to compose it in metre.[39]

This passage gives us valuable insight into the cultural performance space in which Banarsidas worked. While the professional intellectuals—the *pandits* and *pandes*—were literate in Sanskrit as part of their training and occupation, they were also expected to transmit the contents of the classical scriptures in the vernacular, through both vernacular commentaries and sermons. In the cases of the *Samayasāra* and the *Gommaṭasāra*, the linguistic gulf between the original and the vernacular was even deeper, for both of these texts were composed in Prakrit. It is not clear how fluent even *pandits* and *pandes* were in Prakrit, and I suspect that in many cases they relied extensively, and in some cases exclusively, upon the later Sanskrit commentaries.[40] The vernacular prose *Bālbodh* commentary on the *Samayasāra* by Pande Rajmall (also Raymall), for example, was not based on the original 415-verse Prakrit text, but rather on the *Samayasāra kalaśa*, a 278-verse Sanskrit metrical commentary composed by Amritachandra in about the twelfth century.[41]

Banarsidas then described a circle of five men who gathered to study and discuss these texts. This was a trans-sectarian group of Jains who were interested in the new style of religiosity known as Spirituality (*Adhyatma*).

39 *Samayasār nāṭak*, pp. 416-21. This translation is modified from the one I give at Cort (2002), p. 46.

40 This is certainly the case in some contemporary Digambar settings. While the many college-trained Digambar lay *pandits* demonstrate a high level of Prakrit fluency, as a result of a widespread standardisation and improvement of Digambar pandit training over the past century, many mendicants use Sanskrit almost exclusively (in addition to the vernacular). In this they contrast with the liturgical familiarity with Prakrit exhibited by Shvetambar mendicants. This seems to be a Digambar pattern of some duration, as there are very few compositions in Prakrit from the past half-a-millennium at least. Again, this is in contrast to the Shvetambar situation, in which composition of at least short texts in Prakrit has continued to be an expected occupational skill among mendicant intellectuals.

41 Bhatt (1994), p. 435. Rajmall was a professional pandit, and disciple of Bhattarak Kumarsen of the Pushkar Gana of the Mathura Anvay of the Kashtha Sangh (Nathuram Premi, *Jain sāhitya aur itihās* [Bombay: Hindi Granth Ratnakar, 1956], p. 398). He was a prominent enough figure that he was possibly patronised in the Mughal court of Akbar; Bhatt (1994), p. 450.

One of these, Pandit Rupchand, was another trained intellectual. He was not the same as the Rupchand who had lectured on the *Gommaṭasāra*. The other four were laymen. Banarsidas gave a striking description of the intense nature of their discussions, when he said that even as they got up to leave the seminars they would continue their conversations. Finally, Banarsidas indicated that it was within the setting of this seminar that he composed his own Brajbhasha rendition of the *Samayasāra*, basing his text on Rajmall's version of Amritachandra's Sanskrit commentary. While Banarsidas did not say this explicitly, I think we can read between his lines to see that the final product was the result of his own study and poetic skills combined with the critical comments and assistance of his five companions.

Banarsidas's *Samaysār nāṭak* in turn became a textbook for seminars in Agra. In his colophon to the 1644 *Banārsī vilās*, the posthumous collection of Banarsidas's shorter works, the editor Jagjivan—whose family were *divans* in the Mughal court[42]—mentioned a "circle of scholars" (*jñānīn kī maṇḍalī*) that engaged in the study (*vicāra*) of Banarsidas's text.[43] Jagjivan included in the *Banārsī vilās* the *Jñān bāvanī*, a poem written by the poet Pitambar in 1630 in praise of Banarsidas. In it Pitambar describes an assembly (*sabha*) that sat together at the Digambar temple of Kapurchand Sahu under the leadership of Kaunrpal and studied the writings (*vachan*) of Banarsidas: "They sit happily in the Kapurchand Sahu temple. They sit in the assembly hall (*sabhā*) where they meet for intellectual considerations, and study the writings of Banarsidas".[44]

The Jains in Agra did not just conduct seminars devoted to the details of Digambar Jain philosophy. There were also poetic gatherings. In India at this time the performance of poetry was a musical event. In his autobiography Banarsidas recounted a time earlier in his life, in 1610 or

42 According to Gadadhar Singh, *Hindī sāhitya ke vikās meṃ jain kaviyoṃ kī yogdān* (Muzaffarpur: Prakrit, Jain-Shastra aur Ahimsa Shodh Sansthan, 1994), p. 495, Jagjivan's father Abhayraj was a *divan* of the *umrāṃv* (*umrao*) Jafar Khan, who in turn held the post of a 5,000 from Shah Jahan. Kamtaprasad Jain, in his *Hindī jain sāhitya kā saṅkipt itihās* (Banaras: Bharatiya Jnanpith: 1947, p. 161) adds that Jagjivan succeeded to his father's position, as seen in a verse from the colophon to Jagjivan's vernacular translation of Kundakunda's *Pañcāstikāyasāra*:

*tākau pūtabhayau jaganābhī jagajīvana jinamāraganāmī /*
*jāpharakhāṃ ke kāja sambhāre bhayā divāna ujāgara sāre //*

43 *Banārsī vilās* [BV], Bombay edn, p. 252; Jaipur edn, p. 242.

44 *Jñān bāvanī 50a-c*, in BV, Bombay edn, p. 88; BV, Jaipur edn, pp. 89-90:

*khuśī hvai [hai] ke mandira kapūracanda sāhu baiṭhe /*
*baiṭhe kauṅrapāla sabhā jurī manabhāvanī //*
*bānārasīdāsa jūke vacana kī bāta calī /*

1611, when as a young man his father had sent him from his birthplace of Jaunpur to Agra to earn a living in trade. Banarsidas was not successful as a merchant, but did gain some recognition for his poetic and singing skills. He wrote that ten or twenty men would come to his room to hear him sing Qutban's *Mirigāvatī* and Manjhan's *Madhumālatī*, two narrative mystical poems composed in 1503 and 1545, respectively. These two classics of Hindavi verse were composed by sufi poets on the basis of a heterogeneous range of sources that included popular tales, and gave a mystical framework to express the soul's yearning for God.[45] In this we see a foreshadowing of Banarsidas's later spiritual orientation. At this time, however, he was more interested in love poetry, and this was probably what attracted him to these texts.[46] Mukund Lath has said of the *Mirigāvatī* and *Madhumālatī* that "though allegorical in intent, these poems retained the poignancy of a purely human passion, which accounted for their great popular appeal".[47]

In the *Ardhakathānak* Banarsidas provides us with the details of his poetic education, for in the seventeenth century as today, the performance of poetry was a skill that required training and practice. It was common practice for the sons of merchant families to be given basic education in letters and numbers, as these skills were essential for their trade, so Banarsidas was sent to a local Brahmin in Jaunpur. Banarsidas wrote, "As a child of eight years I went to school to learn how to read. My guru was a Brahmin, from whom I learned letters, reading and writing. I studied for one year. Every day my knowledge increased, and I became proficient in my learning".[48] For most merchants this would have been sufficient, but at the age of fourteen Banarsidas studied with another local Brahmin teacher in Jaunpur, a Pandit Devdatt. He engaged in a concentrated course of higher studies. He studied astrology (*jyotisha*) and a work on mathematics,

45 For an overview of this genre see Aditya Behl, *Love's Subtle Magic* (New York: Oxford University Press, 2012b).

46 Banarsidas described a teenage infatuation in which "I was firmly in love with the aching pangs of a Sufi fakir" (AK 171a-b; Lath 1981, p. 237; Chowdhury 2009, p. 72: *karai āsikhī dhari mana dhīra / daradabanda jyauṃ sekha phakīra / /*). Further, he reported that when he was unable to give up his single-minded focus on love (*āsikhī*) and start to earn a living, his elders sat him down and castigated him as a "dervish in love" (*āsikhbāja darbesa*); AK 199d; Lath (1981), p. 239; Chowdhury (2009), p. 84. It appears that for the young Banarsidas, sufi classics, and the core teachings of sufism itself, were all about love.

47 M. Lath (1981), p. 177.

48 AK 98-99c; Lath (1981), p. 231; Chowdhury (2009), p. 44:
*āṭha barasakau hūā bāla / vidyā paṛhana gayau caṭasāla //*
*gura pāṇḍe sauṃ vidyā sikhaiṃ / akkhara bāñcai lekhā likhaiṃ //*
*barasa eka lauṃ vidyā paṛhī / dina dina adhika adhika mati baṛhī //*
*vidyā paṛhi hūā birapanna /*

the *Khaṇḍasphuṭa*. The rest of his studies prepared him to be a poet. He studied two basic lexicographical texts: the *Nāmamālā* on synonyms, and the *Anekārthakośa* on words with multiple meanings.[49] He studied the techniques of poetic embellishment (*alankara*) and also a text on erotics, the *Laghukoka*.[50] Banarsidas said that he spent an entire year in these studies.

During this period Banarsidas also engaged in studies of a more religious nature, under two Shvetambar monks, Bhanchand and Ramchand.[51] In addition to doctrinal and ritual texts, he studied many Jain hymns. He continued his literary studies at the same time. He learned metrics through the *Śrutabodha* and the *Chandakośa*. Under the two monks he also continued his study of other aspects of Sanskrit grammar. In the conclusion of his autobiography, Banarsidas summarised his literary skills: "I can recite both Sanskrit and Prakrit in a correct manner, I am skilled in various vernacular languages, and I understand the nuances of words and meanings".[52]

---

49 Scholars are of the opinion that the former, and perhaps the latter as well, were probably the well-known texts by the ninth-century Digambar Dhananjaya; Lath (1981), p. 160; see also P. Jain Shastri, 'Prastāvnā', in *Nāmamālā of Banārsīdās*, ed. by J. Mukhtar (Sarsawa: Vir Seva Mandir, 1941), pp. 9-10. These two texts were usually studied together.

50 Lath (1981, pp. 161-62) writes that this may have been a digest of the twelfth-century *Ratirahasya* by Kokkoka.

51 Banarsidas by birth was a Shvetambar, and his family was affiliated with the Khartar Gacch. He did not come to study Digambar texts and doctrines until much later in his life. Only Bhanchand was formally a monk (*muni*); Banarsidas described his disciple Ramchand as "still a youth, who wore householder's clothing" (*rāmacanda bālaka gṛha bheṣa*; AK 174b; Lath 1981, p. 237; Chowdhury 2009, p. 74). Nothing is known of either of these two monks except that in Jaunpur in 1606 (six years after Banarsidas studied with him), Bhanchand (known also as Bhanuchandra) composed a Hindi *Mṛgāṅk lekhā caupaī*; Mahopadhyay Vinaysagar, *Khartar gacch sāhitya koś* (Jaipur: Prakrit Bharati Akadami: 2006, p. 162). The story of Prince Mrigank was a folktale adapted by Jain storytellers to narrate the virtues of donation to mendicants (Gulab Chandra Chaudhri, *Jain sāhitya kā bṛhad itihās*, Vol. 6: *Kāvya sāhitya*, Varanasi: Parshvanath Vidyashram Shodh Sansthan: 1973, pp. 312-13). Banarsidas expressed his debt to Bhanchand as his "excellent guru" (*suguru*) in the introductions and/or conclusions to three of his later compositions: the *Ajitnāthjī ke chand*, the *Nāmamālā* (both composed in 1613), and the undated *Praśnottaramālā*. Banarsidas said that the two monks were disciples of Upadhyay Abhaydharm of the Khartar Gacch. Nothing is known about him, either; an Upadhyay Abhaydharm, together with Vachak Nagkumar, composed a Hindi *Daśadṛṣṭāntakathānak bālā* ('Easy Version of the Stories of the Ten Examples'), but the 1522 date for this text would appear to be too early for him to have been Bhanchand's guru (Vinaysagar 2006, p. 84).

52 AK 648a-c; Lath (1981), p. 273; Chowdhury (2009), p. 270:

*paṛhai saṃskṛta prākṛta suddha / vividha desa bhāṣā pratibuddha //*
*jānai sabada aratha kau bheda /*

I interpret his statement about Sanskrit and Prakrit, as I indicate in my choice of "recite" to translate *paṛhai*, to indicate that he could pronounce Prakrit correctly and therefore recite it, but not that necessarily could "read" Prakrit, i.e., understand it

The result of this extensive study was that Banarsidas became a trained poet. He composed a long Hindi poetic text of 1,000 verses in which he explored all the nine *rasas*, but by his own admission the main focus was only love: "I wrote a new book, in which there were a thousand verses. The theme on which I wrote was the nine sentiments, but mainly it just described love".[53]

Banarsidas was sufficiently skilled that he was able to teach these subjects. Several years later the governor of Jaunpur, Chini Kilic, who was also an able vernacular poet, studied several of these texts under Banarsidas's tutelage.[54]

It was these skills that Banarsidas later brought to religious poetry. None of his earlier secular poems survive, but there are a number of extant religious poems that were collected soon after his death in the *Banārsī vilās*. I think we can assume that these were composed and sung in the learned circles of Agra in a similar congregational, cooperative manner as the composition and study of his *Samaysār nāṭak*. Many of them come with an indication of the *raga* in which they were to be sung.[55]

## The Performance of Translation: Banarsidas

In all of this, there was nothing unique about Banarsidas, although the rich detail he provides in his autobiography is largely unmatched for the period. But there was something else about his literary endeavours that was possibly ground-breaking: in addition to being a prolific

---

without the aid of a Sanskrit or vernacular commentary. I have followed Lath (1981, p. 94) over Chowdhury (2009, p. 271) in my translation of the last section, concerning words and meanings. Lath renders this, "In my use of language I am ever alive to nuances of words and meanings", while Chowdhury translated that he "knows the distinctions between words and their meanings".

53 AK 178cd-179ab; Lath (1981), p. 237; Chowdhury (2009), p. 76:
*pothī eka banāī naī / mita hazāra dohā caupaī //*
*tāmaiṃ navarasa racanā likhī / pai bibisesa baranana āsikhī //*

54 Lath (1981, pp. 184-85) gives the known information about Chini Kilic.

55 Mukund Lath (1981, pp. 197-98) has noted that Banarsidas does not mention any musical training nor even any particular skill in music, and so argues that presumably one of his companions was responsible for setting the poems to music. But the inclusion of the *ragas* in many of the poems in the *Banārsī vilās*, coupled with Banarsidas's description of how popular were his singing performances of the *Mirigāvatī* and the *Madhumālatī*, makes it more likely that he also received musical training, but omitted any mention of it in his autobiography. It would have been unusual at that time to be a trained poet and not have received musical training as well.

author of original works, Banarsidas was a translator who produced iconic Brajbhasha versions of classical Sanskrit texts.

Mukund Lath has written of Banarsidas's autobiography that the author "was evidently working without precedents" when he composed a text in this new genre.[56] We can say something similar about his work in translation. Banarsidas composed five texts that we can describe as translations, two of which do not fit easily into established indigenous genres of translation in South Asia.

In several places in his autobiography, Banarsidas gave lists of poetic texts he composed, often as a result of the religious turns in his later life. The first was as a teenager in Jaunpur, while he was still studying with Bhanchand, when he composed two texts that are now lost: his thousand-verse erotic poem on the nine *rasas*, and a book on Sanskrit grammar titled the *Pañcasandhi*.[57]

The second period was in 1613, during his first residence in Agra, in his mid-twenties. He wrote two texts: the five-verse hymn *Ajitnāth ke chand*, addressed to the second Jina; and a grammatical text on synonyms, the *Nāmamālā*.[58] While the first was an original composition, the latter was the first of Banarsidas's compositions that we can call a translation, in this case an indexical translation.

In the period soon after 1623, and his first exposure to Rajmall's *Bālbodh* on the *Samayasāra*, Banarsidas became more influenced by a spirit of aversion to worldly affairs (*vairag bhav*). During this time, he composed several texts: the *Gyān pacīsī*, twenty-five verses on spiritual knowledge; the *Dhyān batīsī*, thirty-two verses on meditation; several mystical songs (*adhyatam ke git*); several miscellaneous songs in the *kabit* (*kavitt*) metre;[59] and a hymn entitled *Sivmandir*.[60]

---

56 Lath (1981, p. i); see also Snell (2005a) and Vanina (1995) on the *Ardhakathānak* as autobiography.

57 AK 176-79; Lath (1981), p. 237; Chowdhury (2009), p. 76. Lath (1981, pp. 166-67), is of the opinion that Banarsidas's grammatical text was based on a fifteenth-century "grammar-made-simple", the *Sārasvata vyākaraṇa* of Anubhutisvarupacarya.

58 AK 386-87; Lath (1981), p. 252; Chowdhury, p. 160.

59 Lath (1981, p.198) writes: "The kabitta, a metre of four feet, each of 31 syllables, was very popular with contemporary poets because it was excellently suited for exhibiting virtuosity. Many one-verse poems of brilliant texture and compact design have been composed in this form"; see also Bangha (2004), p. 33.

60 AK 596-97; Lath (1981), p. 269; Chowdhury (2009), p. 248. Jérôme Petit has recently published translations of the *Dhyān battīsī* and the *Karma chattīsī*.

Banarsidas's text would lead the reader to think that all of these were his original compositions. The last one, however, is another translation. The *Sivmandir* is Banarsidas's Brajbhasha iconic translation of one of the most popular of all Jain hymns, the medieval Sanskrit *Kalyāṇamandira stotra* of Kumudachandra.[61] While its author was a Digambar monk, the hymn quickly became popular among Shvetambars as well. In forty-four verses, the poet praised Parshvanatha, the twenty-third Jina.

A few pages further on in his autobiography, Banarsidas gave another list of more than a dozen texts that he wrote between 1633 and 1645, when he was a mature writer living again in Agra.[62] This list is also deceptive, as mixed in among a number of original texts are two more translations, one an iconic translation, the other an indexical one.

In 1633, Banarsidas finished the *Sahas aṭhottar nām*, or *Jinasahasranām*. As its name indicates, this hymn is a eulogy involving the 1,000 names of the Jina. Its ritual function as an auspicious benedictory text is indicated by its location at the start of the *Banārsī vilās*. This was another indexical translation. Also in this long list was the *Sūktimuktāvalī*, which Banarsidas and his colleague Kaunrpal (also spelled Kumarpal and Kanvarpal) composed in 1634. This was a Hindi iconic translation of a Sanskrit poem of 100 verses by the medieval Shvetambar monk Somaprabha. He composed the *Sūktimuktāvalī*, also known as the *Sindūraprakara*, in 1177. It covers a range of topics in Jain devotion, practice and belief, in the form of epigrammatic verses modeled on secular moral poems in the *niti* genre.[63]

Finally, between 1635 and 1639, after he had studied the *Gommaṭasāra* with Pande Rupchand, Banarsidas composed a number of works

---

61 Dhanki and Shah (1999, p. 23) estimate that the hymn was composed in the first quarter of the twelfth century.

62 AK 625-29; Lath (1981), pp. 271-72; Chowdhury (2009), p. 262.

63 The Shvetambar editor, Pannyas Pradyumnavijaygani, says of the text, on page 4 of his introduction, "Many monks and nuns memorise these aphorisms, and use them in their preaching". It is therefore quite possible that Banarsidas and Kaunrpal had heard verses from the *Sūktimuktāvali* in their childhood and youth in the contexts of sermons from Shvetambar monks. The title of the text is also sometimes spelled *Sūktamuktāvalī*.

It is not clear when Digambars started to read it, but there are dozens of manuscripts of Somaprabha's text in the Digambar libraries of Rajasthan. Many of them are accompanied with the Sanskrit commentary (*Ṭīkā*) composed in 1598 or 1599 by Harshakirti, a monk in the Shvetambar Nagpuriya Tapa Gacch. Since both Banarsidas and Kaunrpal by birth were Shvetambars, it may be that the practice of reading this text was brought by the two when they started to move into Digambar circles in the middle of their lives.

in the spirit of Digambar mysticism (*adhyatma*).[64] Among these was his magnum opus of 1639, the *Samaysār nāṭak*. This was an indexical translation of the *Samayasāra*, the great masterpiece of Kundakunda, the foundational philosopher for the Digambar tradition. His last work was his autobiography, completed in 1641. While he optimistically entitled it "Half a Tale", since he believed (despite all the evidence of seventeenth-century mortality in North India) that at fifty-five years he was only half-way through his life, he died soon thereafter, perhaps in 1643. Most of his poetic works were collected into the *Banārsī vilās* in 1644 by his friend, fellow poet, and fellow spiritual seeker Jagjivan.

Let me turn to a short analysis of Banarsidas's five translations. My goal here is not to render a judgment on these texts as translations in terms of how faithful they are to their originals, nor on their qualities as original writings. Rather, I want to investigate what they can tell us about the practice of translation in the cosmopolitan literary cultures of North India in the first half of the seventeenth century.[65]

## *Nāmamālā*

Banarsidas's first translation was written in Agra in 1613. In his autobiography he wrote that he spent four months that year composing two texts. One of these was the *Ajitnāth ke Chand*, a five-verse hymn, and the other was the *Nāmamālā*. This was a lexicon of synonyms. He had earlier studied with his Sanskrit teacher in Jaunpur a Sanskrit *Nāmamālā*—probably the famous *Nāmamālā* of the ninth-century Digambar lay scholar Dhananjaya—and his vernacular text was in some manner based upon the Sanskrit predecessor. R.K. Jain and Mukund Lath note that Banarsidas's lexicon was one of the earliest texts of its kind in Hindi, being predated only by two lexicons written by the Vaishnava poet and scholar Nanddas sometime in the latter part of the sixteenth century.[66]

---

64 AK 630-39; Lath (1981), pp. 272-73; Chowdhury (2009), pp. 264-68.

65 In his article on Banarsidas's Brajbhasha translation of the *Kalyāṇmandira stotra*, Luigi Tessitori (2000, p. 310) briefly commented on the difficulties involved in translating the Sanskrit *vasantatilaka* metre into the Hindi *pad*. Verse in the former consists of long sentences made up of long compounds that are held in very clear (if complex) grammatical relation through the inflected structure of the language. The *pad*, on the other hand, is, in the words of John Stratton Hawley (2005: 32), "telegraphic", so that "one almost always has to supply a certain number of connections between words in order to render their meaning intelligible".

66 R.K. Jain (1966), pp. 135-39, and M. Lath (1981), p. 180. On Nanddas see R.S. McGregor,

To characterise Banarsidas's *Nāmamālā* as a translation clearly stretches any definition of this genre near to breaking point. He made no direct reference to a Sanskrit original. He simply said of his text, "I compose the accessible *Nāmāvalī*, for the sake of educating the beginner. I make a river of vocabulary to illuminate the correct meanings. Banarsi makes it in the vernacular, according to his own development and thought. I have assembled various words from the vernacular, Prakrit and Sanskrit".[67] The notion that his text is based upon Dhananjaya's is at best scholarly conjecture.[68] Banarsidas's text is only 175 verses, whereas Dhananjaya's is 203 verses in length. Banarsidas perhaps inadvertently acknowledged his debt to Dhananjaya's text when in his autobiography he mistakenly wrote that his *Nāmamālā* was 200 verses long.[69] His statement that he made vernacular a subject from the Prakrit and the Sanskrit for the sake of educating the beginner (*bāl vibodh*) also locates this text within the field of other "translations" which I discuss below.

The order of words for which synonyms are given is unrelated in the two texts, and even the synonyms vary widely. For example, Banarsidas started his text, appropriately enough for a Jain author, by devoting two verses (4-5) to twenty synonyms for *tirthankara*. Dhananjaya, on the other hand, did not come to *tirthankara* until verse 116, when in a single verse he gave nine synonyms. Only five words are found in both lists.

## *Sahas aṭhottar nām/Jinasahasranām*

In 1633, Banarsidas wrote another text that similarly stretches any definition of translation. This was his *Sahas aṭhottar nām* or *Jinasahasranām*, a hymn in which he gave 1,000 (or, more accurately, 1,008) names of the Jina. In the beginning of the hymn, in wording almost identical to that found in his *Nāmamālā*, Banarsidas wrote that the names in it are in vernacular, Prakrit

---

*Nanddas, The Round Dance of Krishna and Uddhav's Message* (London: Luzac and Company, 1973). Nanddas (verse 3: *gūnthani nānā nāma ko / amarakoṣa ke bhāya //*) explicitly said that his lexicon was based on the Brahminical Sanskrit *Amarakośa*, so the two vernacular lexicons tap into different classical Sanskrit lexicographical traditions.

67 Banarsidas, *Nāmamālā*, verses 1cd-3ab:
*racyauṃ sugama nāmāvalī / bāla vibodha nimitta //*
*sabada sindhu santhān kari / pragaṭa su-artha vicāra //*
*bhāṣā karai banārasī / nija gati mati anusāra //*
*bhāṣā prākṛta saṃskṛta / trividhi su sabada sameta //*

68 Lath (1981), p. 160; R.K. Jain (1966), pp. 131-32; Jain Shastri (1941), pp. 9-10.

69 AK 387; Lath (1981), p. 252; Chowdhury (2009), p. 160: *karī nāmamālā sai doi.*

and Sanskrit.[70] He varied the metres in the ten sections, each of which contains 100 names and so is called a *shatak*. The metrical variety enhanced the performance of the text in a temple setting.

Just as he no doubt consulted Dhananjaya's text (and possibly others) when composing his *Nāmamālā*, it is likely that he based his hymn in part on one or both of two very popular Sanskrit *Jinasahasranāma Stavana*s, and so it serves as an indexical translation, not an iconic one. Banarsidas characterised his text at its conclusion as *bhāṣā-jinasahasranām*, so he viewed it as the vernacularisation of an earlier textual tradition in classical languages. The first Sanskrit text was by the South Indian monk Jinasena (c.770-850), and was contained within his *Ādipurāṇa*, the most popular and influential of all Digambar texts on the Jain universal history. The *Jinasahasranāma* within this encyclopedic text has long circulated as an independent text. The second was by the thirteenth-century lay *pandit* Ashadhara.[71] Each of the three texts consists of ten sections, but the titles of the sections differ, as do the lengths of the texts in total.[72] In other words, the Sanskrit texts served as models for Banarsidas, and sources for many epithets, but he did not set out to make an iconic translation of either Sanskrit text.

## *Samaysār nāṭak*

As I noted above, the text for which Banarsidas is best known among Jains is his *Samaysār nāṭak*. This is a translation of the *Samayasāra* of Kundakunda, one of the central texts of Digambara philosophy and mysticism. With this text we come a bit closer to what we might consider as a translation, even if still very much in the indexical sense. It is unlikely that Banarsidas could read Prakrit sufficiently to have used Kundakunda's root text as his source. Instead, his classical source was the Sanskrit *Samayasāra kalaśa*, written in about the twelfth century by Amritachandra. As Bansidhar Bhatt has explained, Amritachandra originally wrote a Sanskrit commentary on Kundakunda's text, which he entitled the *Ātmakhyāti*. The commentary

70 *Sahas aṭhottar nām*, verse 2: *bhāṣā prākṛta saṃskṛta trividha śabda paramāna*.

71 According to Nathuram Premi, in his "Nivedan" (p. 3) to his edition of all three texts, in the early twentieth-century Ashadhara's text circulated largely in Bundelkhand, while Jinasena's was found throughout the whole country.

72 Jinasena's text is between 120 and 165 verses (the number of verses varies in each published edition; almost no Digambar texts have been subject to adequate collection of manuscripts and subsequent critical editing, and so most of them in their printed editions exhibit a similar variability in length and therefore content), while Ashadhara's text is 143 verses, and Banarsidas's is 103 verses.

consisted of both prose and 278 Sanskrit verses. In time, the verse portion of the commentary was separated from the prose, and became treated as an independent text with the name *Samayasāra kalaśa*. Amritachandra's text was to a significant extent responsible for the widespread Digambar adoption of Kundakunda's two-truth mystical philosophy, according to which from the absolute perspective (*niścaya-naya*) the self (*atman*) is the only existent that is "really real", whereas everything else is only provisionally real from the relative perspective (*vyavahāra-naya*).[73] Amritachandra's text further influenced subsequent Sanskrit commentaries on Kundakunda's text and also generated vernacular commentaries, starting with a fourteenth-century Kannada prose commentary (*vachanika*) by the monk Balachandra.

In this vernacular tradition was also the prose *Bālbodh* of Pande Rajmall, composed in the sixteenth century. As we saw above, this in turn was the inspiration and guide for Banarsidas's *Samaysār nāṭak*. According to Bhatt, Banarsidas's text followed Rajmall's fairly closely, with the main difference being that the former "is more elaborate and poetic", and the latter "philosophic and precise".[74] This is not surprising, given that Banarsidas by training and personality was a poet, while Rajmall by training and personality was a philosopher. Bhatt has also carefully delineated the relationship between Banarsidas's *Samaysār nāṭak* and Amritachandra's *Samayasāra kalaśa*:

> The *Samayasāra-nāṭaka* contains 732 rhymes in Hindi for 278 *kalasha*-verses, that is, more than two rhymes have been allotted to each *kalasha*-verse, on the average. But the rhymes are not so evenly distributed. Strictly speaking, the rhymes are not a translation, nor do they have any explanatory character. They just touch on the *kalasha*-verses and run independently as a lucid poetry.

## *Param jyotī stotra/Kalyāṇamandira stotra*

If Banarsidas's *Nāmamālā*, *Jinasahasranām* and *Samaysār nāṭak* were vernacular texts that bore varying degrees of indexical translation relationship to their Sanskrit forebears, the other two texts were clearly translations in the most iconic sense.

---

73 The best introduction to Kundakunda's two-truth doctrine remains Bansidhar Bhatt, 'Vyavahāra-naya and Niścaya-naya in Kundakunda's Works', in *XVIII. Deutscher Orientalistentag vom 1. bis 5. Oktober 1972 in Lübeck, Vorträge. Zeitschrift der deutschen Morgenländischen Gesellschaft, Supplement II*, ed. by Wolfgang Voigt (Wiesbaden: Franz Steiner Verlag, 1974), pp. 279-91.

74 B. Bhatt (1994), p. 439.

Banarsidas's 1633 translation of the *Kalyāṇamandira stotra* is also known as the *Param joti* (or *Param jyotī*) *stotra*, after the first two words of the first verse.[75] This has long been a common way of "titling" hymns; for example, the Sanskrit original starts *kalyāṇamandira*, "auspicious temple". For reasons of metre, Banarsidas translated this as *śivmandir*, also "auspicious temple". The first verse of Banarsidas's poem, a simple *doha*, is not found in the original, and so serves as an independent invocatory verse.[76] Only with the second verse did Banarsidas begin directly to translate Kumudachandra's text. Banarsidas then in forty-three subsequent verses in a variety of metres reproduced in Braj the forty-four verses (all in the Vasantatilaka metre) of the original Sanskrit.

The final verse is a slightly longer one, of six feet, allowing Banarsidas to provide a signature colophon, in which the translated nature of his composition was made clear:

> The wise Kumudachandra made this *Kalyāṇamandira*.
> Banarsi said it in the vernacular, for the sake of pure right faith.[77]

## *Sūktimuktāvalī*

The joint translation of the *Sūktimuktāvalī* by Banarsidas and Kaunrpal, done the following year, in 1634, gives us a further indication of the ways in which textual practice in seventeenth-century Agra was a shared, perhaps even semi-public performance. By this time in his life Banarsidas was obviously a highly skilled and well-practiced poet. Kaunrpal, on the other hand, was a younger poet. He was the nephew of Dharamdas, one of Banarsidas's business partners and a fellow participant in the

---

75 In this form a partial edition of the hymn was first published by Luigi Tessitori in *Indian Antiquary* in 1913, on the basis of an incomplete manuscript; Luigi P. Tessitori, 'Paramajotistotra: An Old Braja Metrical Version of Siddhasenadivākara's Kalyāṇamandirastotra', *Studi Gianici* (Udine: Società Indologica Luigi Pio Tessitori), pp. 307-15 (originally in *Indian Antiquary* 43 (1913), 42-46). Because the manuscript lacked the concluding signature verse, Tessitori did not know the identity of the translator.

76 *Kalyāṇamandira stotra 1*, in BV, Bombay edn, 126; BV, Jaipur edn, p. 124:
*paramaj[y]otī paramātamā paramajñāna paravīna /*
*bandauṃ paramānandamaya ghaṭa ghaṭa antaralīna //*
The supreme light, the supreme soul, the supreme knowledge, skillful:
I venerate the one made of supreme bliss, the essence of every being.

77 *Kalyāṇamandira stotra* 44, in BV, Bombay edn, p. 130; BV, Jaipur edn, p. 128:
*yaha kalyāṇamandira kiyau kumudacandra kī buddhi /*
*bhāṣā kahata banārasī kārana samakita suddhi //*

spiritual seminar. Kaunrpal outlived Banarsidas, becoming the leader of the Adhyatma circle in Agra after him. It is likely, therefore, that he was younger by one or two decades. Mukund Lath describes him as "an occasional writer of verses on spiritual themes".[78] He is known to have composed only one other text, a short poem on Jain right faith called the *Samakit battīsī*. He composed it in 1630, four years before he and Banarsidas finished their joint translation.[79]

In the signature colophon to their translation, Banarsidas and Kaunrpal gave a hint of how they worked together. They wrote:

> It's called the *Sūktimuktāvalī*, and has twenty-two chapters.
> In total extent the text has one-hundred verses.
> The pair of friends Kunvarpal and Banarsi are like-minded (*ikacitt*).
> They did the text in the vernacular, in verses of various meters.[80]

The key word here is *ikacitt* (pron. *ikachitt*), literally "of one mind", and which I have translated as "like-minded". It indicates that they saw eye to eye, or thought in the same way, and hence that this was a joint project. In Gujarati the word also has a range of spiritual meanings, of a person who is fixed in meditation (*dhyan-stha*), or who is absorbed in a spiritual state (*tallin*),[81] so Kaunrpal and Banarsidas may have used it here to indicate a deeper spiritual harmony that suffused their task of collaborative translation.

Within their translation, however, we also see indications of a different modus operandi, as perhaps the two divided the task. Many of the individual verses contain a signature. In twenty-three verses the signature is of Banarsidas, and in only five do we find the name of Kaunrpal. This may indicate that Banarsidas did the bulk of the work, and that Kaunrpal contributed only a few verses. That the verses with Banarsidas's signature all occur in the first half of the poem, and those with Kaunrpal's signature all in the last half, may indicate still another way in which the labour was divided. But the use of *ikachitt*

78 Lath (1981).

79 Premi (1957), p. 101.

80 *Sūktamuktāvalī*, colophon 1-2, in BV, Bombay edn, p. 68; BV, Jaipur edn, p. 71:
*nāma sūktimuktāvalī dvāviṃśati adhikāra /*
*śataśloka paramāna saba iti grantha vistāra //*
*kuṅvarapāla banārasī mitra jugala ikacitta /*
*tinahiṃ grantha bhāṣā kiyo bahuvidha* [*bahuvidhi*] *chanda kavitta //*

81 Shastri (1976), Vol. 1, p. 345.

would appear to argue against a division of labour and in favour of a collaborative method of translation.[82]

Collaborative composition was a common practice of the time, and probably was part of the cultural practice of a circle meeting in a temple. One of the five companions whom Banarsidas mentions in the *Samaysār nāṭak*, and who also features prominently in the *Ardhakathānak*, was Dharamdas. He was Kaunrpal's uncle, and for many years a business partner of Banarsidas. He and Banarsidas both settled in Agra in their later years, and evidently also shared in the practice of poetry. There is only one poem by Dharamdas that is extant, the seven-verse *Guruśiṣyakathanī*. In Mukund Lath's description, it is "in the form of a discourse by a guru to his disciple, teaching the hollowness of all worldly things and the superior merits of the spiritual life".[83] To quote Lath further, in this poem "the metre and rhyme are interestingly unusual". It maintains a strong rhyme scheme throughout the poem, with the final consonant in every case being a doubled retroflex -*ṭṭ*-. This results in a poem that is baroque in its artificiality. It is most likely not a coincidence that there is a poem by Banarsidas that exhibits a similar form, his *Mokṣapaiḍī*, "The Steps to Liberation". In this poem the rhyme scheme involves the equally baroque use of a doubled -*ll*-. Banarsidas's poem is significantly longer—twenty-two verses in addition to a two-verse colophon—perhaps indicating his greater skill at sustaining this difficult form. Lath comments, "the two friends had evidently decided to try their skill in a new, exciting metre together". One can easily imagine the two friends meeting in the veranda of a temple and spending the afternoon engrossed in the shared composition of poems that displayed their literary skills.[84]

---

82 See also Lath (1981, p. 200), who hypothesises: "The two translators seem to have divided much of their work between them, and many stanzas, therefore, bear their individual signatures. But a sizeable number do not carry any name, and may have been joint efforts".

83 Ibid., p. 179.

84 A verse from each poem will indicate what the two poets were doing.
Dharamdas, *Guruśiṣyakathanī*, verse 1 (Premi 1957, p. 103):
*iṇa saṃsāra samudrakau tākai paiṃ taṭṭā /*
*suguru kahai suṇi prāṇiyā tūṃ dharaje dhrama baṭṭā //*
Banarsidas, *Mokṣapaiḍī*, verse 1 (BV, p. 132):
*ikka samay rucivantano guru akkhai sunamalla /*
*jo tujha andaracetanā vahai tusāṛī alla //*
The artificiality of these poems is seen in that the editors of the Jaipur edition of the *Banārsī vilās* had to provide an extensive gloss to explain the *Mokṣapaiḍī*. R.K. Jain (1966, p. 169) adds that in the *Mokṣapaiḍī*, a composition unique within Banarsidas's oeuvre, the poet employed many Panjabi verbs and inflections.

## The Continued Performance of Translation after Banarsidas

The performance of iconic translation that seems to have begun—or at the very least raised to a new level of visibility—with Banarsidas in the middle of the seventeenth century in Agra did not end with him. One of the leaders of the Adhyatma seminars in Agra after the death of Banarsidas was Hemraj Pande.[85] He was the author of both indexical and iconic translations.

The first extant reference to Hemraj Pande is from 1644, when he was described as participating in a seminar (*gyan mandali*) along with Bhagavatidas (also Bhagotidas), one of the men Banarsidas had mentioned earlier in the context of the Adhyatma seminar.[86] Hemraj was a disciple of Rupchand Pande. Premi argues that this was the same Rupchand who delivered the sermons on the *Gommaṭasāra* in 1635,[87] and so Hemraj was in the tradition of professionally trained intellectuals working under the leadership of the *bhattaraks*.

In 1652 Hemraj composed two texts at the request of Kaunrpal, presumably for use in the seminars.[88] One of these was a summary of eighty-four points of disagreement between the Digambars and Shvetambars, entitled *Caurāsī bol*. The other was a vernacular commentary (*Bālbodh*) on the *Pravacanasāra*, another central text on Digambar spirituality by Kundakunda. In his colophon Hemraj wrote: "Please listen to how I prepared this simple rendering of this great work. There is in Agra a prominent authority and learned man named Kanvarpal. At his request I rendered this extremely difficult text into the vernacular".[89]

---

85 For information on Hemraj, see Padmanabh Jaini, 'Caurāsī Bol of Hemrāj Pāṇḍe', in *Jambū-jyoti (Munivara Jambūvijaya Festschrift)*, ed. by M.A. Dhaky and J.B. Shah (Ahmedabad: Shreshthi Kasturbhai Lalbhai Smarak Nidhi, 2004, pp. 374-98) and (2007), pp. 31-35; Kaslival (1986), pp. 204-54, and Premi (1957), pp. 107-08.

86 Premi (1957), p. 36.

87 Ibid., p. 89.

88 Hemraj gave the year as VS 1709. Jaini (2004) calculated this as 1653, assuming that the difference between VS and CE is 56 years. While this is true for Gujarat, a more accurate calculation for North India requires a difference of 57 years.

89 Translation slightly altered from Jaini (2007, p. 31); original at *Pravacanasāra*, p. 346:
*bālabodha yah kīnī jaise so tuma sunahu kahūṃ maiṃ taisai /*
*nagara āgare maiṃ hitakārī kaṅvarapāla gyātā avikārī //*
*tina vicāra jiya maiṃ iha kīnī jo bhāṣā iha hoi navīnī /*

Hemraj's vernacular version of the *Pravacanasāra* was in the long-standing tradition of vernacular commentaries. He explicitly modelled his version on the earlier vernacular commentary on the *Samayasāra* by Rajmall.[90] Hemraj composed vernacular commentaries on at least five other important Digambar doctrinal texts, and a number of original works in Brajbhasha.[91]

Hemraj also composed an iconic translation of the c. sixth-century Sanskrit *Bhaktāmara stotra* of Manatunga, the most beloved of all Jain hymns. While there have been other Digambar translations of Manatunga's text into Hindi, Hemraj's remains the most popular; there are many manuscript copies of it in the Digambar libraries of North India, and it is included in almost all of the locally produced hymnals found in every Digambar temple in North India. Hemraj followed Manatunga's text faithfully, reproducing in forty-eight Brajbhasha verses the forty-eight Sanskrit verses of the Digambar version of the hymn. In a manner similar to Banarsidas's translation of the *Kalyāṇamandira stotra*, he began with a simple auspicious verse not found in the original, and then proceeded with the translation proper. Manatunga's text concluded with a signature verse. Hemraj retained it, and then added his own signature, indicating clearly that he was translating Manatunga's text:

> Devotion will arise in the mind of any man who memorises this hymn.
> Manatunga is absorbed in his soul, and has attained the wealth of liberation.
> Hemraj rendered the *Bhaktāmar* in the vernacular for the sake of well-being.
> Whoever recites it with the right spirit will attain the land of liberation.[92]

The Digambar practice of iconic translation has continued unabated ever since the work of Banarsidas and Hemraj. Many of the leading Digambar

---

90 *Pravacanasāra*, p. 346:
*yaha vicāra mana maiṃ tina rākhī pāṇḍe hemarāja sauṃ bhākhī /*
*āgaiṃ rājamalla naiṃ kīnī samayasāra bhāṣā rasalīnī //*

91 See Kaslival (1986), pp. 207-24.

92 Hemraj, *Bhaktāmara Stotra Bhāṣā*, verse 48:
*je nara paharaiṃ kaṇṭha bhāvanā mana meṃ bhāvaiṃ /*
*mānatuṅga te nijādhīna śivalakṣmī pāvaiṃ //*
*bhāṣā bhaktāmara kaiyau hemarāja hita heta /*
*je nara paḍhaiṃ subhāvasauṃ te pāvaiṃ śivakheta //*
See John Cort, 'Devotional Culture in Jainism: Mānatuṅga and His Bhaktāmara Stotra', in *Incompatible Visions: South Asian Religions in History and Culture: Essays in Honor of David M. Knipe*, ed. by James Blumenthal (Madison: Center for South Asia, University of Wisconsin, 2005), pp. 93-115.

Hindi poets of North India composed translations. For example, in Agra, Dyanatray (1676-1726) translated the Sanskrit *Svayambhū stotra* of Samantabhadra (c. fifth century) and the Sanskrit *Ekibhāva stotra* of Vadiraja (c. tenth century), and Bhudhardas (fl.1724-1749) also translated Vadiraja's hymn. Poets in other Digambar religious and cultural centres engaged in the constant practice of translation as well. Starting in the late nineteenth and early twentieth centuries we see the introduction of British colonial conceptions of translation, but for several hundred years before this it was an indigenous tradition.[93]

## Iconic Translation in Agra: Something New?

To what extent was the Digambar Jain practice of iconic translation in Agra in the mid-seventeenth century something new? In the absence of explicit theorisation about translation on the part of the translators themselves, or other contemporary literary theorists, this is a difficult question to address.

As I have indicated above, the practice of translation was not new in South Asia. The Jains in particular were accustomed to working in and between multiple languages. Their sacred scriptures and other early authoritative texts were in various dialects of Prakrit, while from early in the Common Era the Jains had been full participants in the intellectual and literary cultures of Sanskrit (and later Apabhramsha). The many

93 For example, in 1905, Nathuram Premi, the well-known Jain scholar, and also one of the leading publishers of modern Hindi literature in the first half of the twentieth-century, said the following in defense of his decision to publish what he called a "new verse translation" (*navīn padyānuvād*) of Manatunga's *Bhaktāmara stotra*, the Brajbhasha translation of which by Hemraj was so widely known and loved: "No doubt Hemraj's translation (*anuvād*) is very beautiful, full of virtues, and excellent. But it is an independent translation (*svatantra anuvād*), in which only the sentiment (*bhāv*) is grasped. The respected translator has not given the full sense of every verse and word... There is one more thing I want to say about Hemraj's translation, which is this, that for the translation of this *stotra* the *chaupāī* metre is inadequate. Due to the restrictions of metre, in many places the translation is difficult to understand and strays from the intention. I don't want to criticise the respected Hemraj, but just show that while his translation is good, it is not without faults". Nathuram Premi, *bhūmikā* to his translation of Manatunga, *Bhaktāmara stotra* (reprint, Mumbai: Hindi Granth Karyalay, 2012), pp. 3-4 ; for Premi, see Manish Modi, 'Pandit Nathuram Premi: Jain Scholar and Publisher', *Jaina Studies: Newsletter of the Centre of Jaina Studies* 2 (2007), 42-44.

Sanskrit commentaries of Prakrit texts often included a literal word-for-word trot or *chāyā*, in which the Prakrit was as directly as possible rendered into Sanskrit. This was also a common practice for the Prakrit passages in Sanskrit dramas.

Then there was the practice of vernacular commentarial translations (the difference between the two genres usually being one of degree, not kind), often known as *bālbodh* or *bālāvabodh*, which Phyllis Granoff has translated as "Instructions for the Unlettered". While this was an especially popular genre among Jains, it was also widely found among Hindu authors. Jnaneshvar's thirteenth-century Marathi version of the *Bhagavadgītā* is one of the best-known examples in this genre, although we have no direct evidence that Banarsidas and the other Jain Brajbhasha poets in seventeenth-century North India knew it. Banarsidas's *Samaysār nāṭak* fits firmly within this practice of translation-as-commentary.

There was also a long and well-known tradition of indexical and symbolic translations in South Asia, especially of narrative texts. The Jains for centuries had been among the most prolific at composing such texts, with their many versions of Jain Puranas and other narrative texts existing in all the languages in which they wrote. Mughal North India saw other examples of the vernacularisation of classical texts, such as Tulsidas's *Rāmcaritmānas*. In his introduction, Tulsidas explicitly said that he was retelling the story of Rāma in the vernacular.[94] Poets in most of the languages of North India composed vernacular versions of the Hindu classics such as the *Rāmāyaṇa*, *Mahābhārata*, and *Bhāgavata-purāṇa*.[95] Some of these were indexical and symbolic

94 *Rāmcaritmānas* 1.7. Jains have posited a connection between Tulsidas and Banarsidas that may represent an attempt to bring the latter more firmly within the circle of the stars of Hindi devotional poetry. Both Mulchand Jain and Ravindra Kumar Jain (1966, pp. 112-13) relate an oral tradition (*kimvadanti, jan-shruti*) that connects the two. Tulsidas heard about Banarsidas, and so travelled to Agra to meet him. Tulsidas gave Banarsidas a copy of his newly composed *Rāmcaritmānas*, and Banarsidas in return composed a poem on the spot. Later the two exchanged poems: Banarsidas gave Tulsidas a Hindi *stotra* to Parshvanath, which Tulsidas adapted as his *Bhakti viradāvalī*, and returned to Banarsidas, Mulchand Jain, *Jain kaviyoṃ kā itihās yā prācīn hindī jain kavi* (Damoh: Subhchintak Press, 1937), pp. 34-36; while Ravindra Kumar Jain does not cite Mulchand Jain, he clearly derived his telling from the earlier text.

95 While Tulsidas was fluent in Sanskrit, it is possible that not all the other translators were. Grahame Niemann has argued that many of the authors of vernacular *Bhāgavata-purāṇas* did not know Sanskrit 'Bhūpati's *Bhāgavat* and the Hindi *Bhāgavat* Genre', in *Bhakti in Current Research, 1979-82*, ed. by Monika Thiel-Horstmann (Berlin: Dietrich Reiner Verlag, 1983), pp. 257-69. Their translations, therefore, were either simply vernacular retellings, or else "translations" from the same language, much in

translations, and hence most scholars in English have characterised them as "versions", "retellings", "reworkings", or "adaptations", not as "translations".[96] Some of these, however, such as Nanddas's Brajbhasha *Bhāṣā dasamskandh*, an unfinished translation of the tenth book of the *Bhāgavata-purāṇa*, more closely approximated iconic translations.[97] How aware Banarsidas, Kaunrpal, Hemraj, and the other Jain authors were of these contemporaneous developments in "Hindu" (both Brahminical and non-Brahminical) circles is difficult to know, although the Jains have always been avid readers, as is evidenced by the number of non-Jain texts found in Jain manuscript libraries. As we saw in the case of Banarsidas, Jains have also been dependent upon Brahmins for "secular" education in both basic literacy skills and the more advanced skills needed for literary production. The intellectual and literary boundaries between these communities were highly porous.

There was also a vibrant culture of literary translation in the Mughal court itself, as well as in other Islamicate courts. Classics of Indic narrative and science were translated into Islamicate languages, and in other ways Persianised and Islamicised, as in the example of the *Mirigāvatī*, *Madhumālatī*, and other Indic folk texts that were recast in sufi and courtly settings. There were also translations of Islamicate texts from Persian into Sanskrit and Indic vernacular languages.

---

the spirit of Robert Bly's popular "translations" of Kabir and Mirabai, in which he worked from existing English translations. This raises, of course, the difficult question of what it means to "know" a language, and the relationship of such knowledge to the distinction between iconic and indexical translations. This issue lies behind the argument of some contemporary theorists that only a "native speaker" can translate from a language, as anyone else lacks the depth of linguistic knowledge to render a faithful translation.

96 For examples, see the articles and books by Bangha and McGregor in the bibliography. An alternate way of thinking about translation in the South Asian context, especially in the period when many Sanskrit classics were being rendered into Brajbhasha, is that of "recycling"; see H. Pauwels, *Kṛṣṇā's Round Dance Reconsidered: Harirām Vyās's Hindi Rās-pañcādhyāyi* (Richmond: Curzon, 1996).

97 We have already encountered Nanddas, who lived a generation or two before Banarsidas, in the context of the *Nāmamālā*s each of them wrote. McGregor (1973, p. 34) estimates that Nanddas died "within a few years of 1585"). In other words, he may be an important precedent and model for Banarsidas in two genres: the lexicon, and the iconic translation of poetry. There is no evidence, however, that Banarsidas knew of Nanddas. But we know precious little of what Banarsidas or any other author of his time read, and it is conceivable that Banarsidas heard about Nanddas, and even read some of his works, through his early teacher in Jaunpur, the Brahmin Pandit Devdatt.

Here again we run into silences in the literary and historical record that limit our ability to speak of how aware Banarsidas and his fellow poets were of these literary developments in Islamicate circles. As Rupert Snell has recently observed, "An often-felt frustration for those concerned to read Hindi literature against its own historical backdrop has been precisely the lack of connectivity between the literary texts on the one hand and historical data on the other".[98] While the work of scholars such as Allison Busch and Audrey Truschke certainly allows us to say much more about literary and social interactions within and without Mughal court circles, we are still somewhat in the dark concerning where the Jains fit into those interactions.[99] This problem of silence is exacerbated in the case of Jain Brajbhasha poets, who are invisible in the writings of their Hindu and Muslim contemporaries.[100]

Banarsidas himself makes no mention of any literary activities in Agra except those of the Jain seminars. The Jains (both Digambar and Shvetambar) played crucial economic and administrative roles in the Mughal court, so we have to accept that his silence may indicate a lack of interaction on literary matters. He was explicit about such interactions in the provincial court of Jaunpur where, as we have seen, he taught and practiced poetry with the governor, Chini Kilich. Social and literary interaction might have been easier in the provinces than in the imperial centre. It was presumably also in Jaunpur that he learned the *Mirigāvatī* and *Madhumālatī*, which he publicly sang during his first residence

98 R. Snell, 'Introduction: The Study of Pre-Modern Hindi Literature', *South Asia Research* 25 (2005), 9. Addressing this lack of connectivity is, of course, a major goal of the current volume. See also *After Timur Left: Culture and Circulation in Fifteenth-century North India*, ed. by F. Orsini and S. Sheikh (New Delhi: Oxford University Press, 2014).

99 Allison Busch, *Poetry of Kings: The Classical Hindi Poetry of Mughal India* (New York: Oxford University Press, 2011); Audrey Truschke, *Culture of Encounters: Sanskrit at the Mughal Court* (New York: Columbia University Press, forthcoming). See also the articles by Busch in the bibliography, and Muzaffar Alam, 'The Pursuit of Persian: Language in Mughal Politics', *Modern Asian Studies* 32, 2 (1998), 317-49. There is a body of scholarship on the Sanskrit epic poems (*mahakavyas*) written by a number of Shvetambar authors that describe the interactions of Shvetambar with the Mughal court, as well as the Mughal observations of these monks; P. Dundas, *History, Scripture and Controversy in a Medieval Jain Sect* (London: Routledge, 2007), pp. 53-72.

100 This erasure continues to the present. Standard histories of Hindi make scant mention of Jain authors, with the exception of Banarsidas, and then the attention is solely on his *Ardhakathānak*. Students in graduate programs in Hindi in India read Jain Apabhramsha literature as a linguistically necessary precursor to Hindi, and the *Ardhakathānak* as the first autobiography in Hindi, but otherwise are taught nothing about the centuries of vibrant Jain writing in all the various forms of Hindi.

in Agra as a young man. His very knowledge of these Hindavi sufi classics bespeaks a literary culture that was not hindered by religious boundaries. In his *Banārsī vilās* we also find an eleven-verse *Śāntināth Jin stuti*, with the notation that it "is in the style of the *Candavā* of Vaki [Baqi?] Mahammad Khan".[101] While this author and text are unknown to me, this is evidence of further knowledge on the part of Banarsidas of Islamicate literature. Banarsidas's curiosity about matters literary and spiritual (and, in his youth, erotic) meant that he was clearly widely read.[102] But we cannot judge whether or not his possibly innovative approach to translation was in any way influenced or shaped by translation practices in the Islamicate courtly circles of Agra.

It is possible that Ramanujan's tripartite classification of translation is less helpful than it seems at first. What makes sense in twentieth-century Chicago from a Piercean semiotic stance may be less applicable in the literary circles of seventeenth-century Agra, as the concerns about different modes of translation were different in the two settings.[103] Nonetheless, Ramanujan's typology does allow us to see much more clearly that questions of accuracy and faithfulness that are central in the long-standing Western practice of iconic translations tend to disappear in communities that put more emphasis on the practice of indexical translation. Ramanujan allows us to see that South Asian concerns about "translation" have for many centuries simply been different from those in the literary cultures that collectively make up the "Western" tradition. Theorists of translation from the times of the Greek translations into Latin, and of Biblical translations into Greek, Latin, and European vernaculars, have been concerned primarily with issues of "faithfulness". Winand Callewaert and Shilanand Hemraj, in their wide-ranging study of translations of the *Bhagavadgītā*, wrote, "It

101 BV, pp. 189-91: *vākī [bāqī?] mahammad khāna ke candavā kī ḍhāla.*

102 To give just one more example, the *Banārsī vilās* also includes a 7-verse *Gorakhnāth ke vacan*, indicating another direction in which Banarsidas's spiritual questing took him.

103 As alternatives, one might apply a widespread tripartite distinction used by modern authors in all the North Indian languages, among translations as *shabdarth* (literal, word-for-word translation), *bhavarth* (translating the underlying, deeper message and intention), and *chhaya* (free adaptation or "transcreation"); Cort (1994), Callewaert and Hemraj (1983), pp. 75-77. Another set of distinctions was employed by Saroj Agraval in her book on the *Prabodhacandrodaya* tradition in Hindi, in which she distinguished among *anuvad* (translation), *rupantar* (adaptation), *svatantra* (texts influenced by or in the style of the original), and *anshatah* (texts partially influenced by the original); *Prabodhacandroday aur uskī hindī paramparā* (Allahabad: Hindi Sahitya Sammelan, 1962).

would appear that in the Indian tradition translators have been more concerned with the communication of the message rather than with the scrupulous preservation of the form".[104] While scholars almost always want to ask why certain issues do not appear to be matters of significant concern in a given culture, nonetheless it may very well be the case that anxiety over the faithfulness of premodern translations was rare in South Asia.

The issue of genre is also significant here. The three iconic translations by Banarsidas, Kaunrpal, and Hemraj which I have discussed are of Sanskrit poems. In translating a narrative text it is easy, and even expected, for the translator to expand, contract, and in other ways modify the source as he brings it across into a new linguistic home. The translation is less of a set "text" as found on paper or in oral memory than of the entirety of the narration itself. The same is true of a philosophical or theological work such as Banarsidas's *Samaysār nāṭak*, in which his goal was to bring across into Brajbhasha the concepts of the original, not necessarily the words and style. Here we see again how "translation" in many ways is simply a mode of "interpretation" in another language, and hence blends into the genre of "commentary". We must also be mindful of the ways that techniques of mechanical reproduction, coupled with the growth of concepts of property rights as extended to literary activity, have profoundly shaped both the practice and theory of translation in the West in recent centuries. What a literary critic or a lawyer might today decry as plagiarised and even actionable was in many other historical and cultural settings simply a matter of standard practice.

I argue that a poem, however, involves a higher degree of unity between form and content than does a narrative or philosophical text.[105] Theorists throughout the world have often advanced poetry as a primary example of untranslatability, as a poem in many ways has no content or meaning outside of the very linguistic form itself. In translating a poem, therefore, whether a religious *stotra* or a more "secular" poem in a *niti* genre, we should expect a stronger degree of "faithfulness" to be displayed by the translator. The exact number of verses of a longer poem

104 Callewaert and Hemraj (1983), p. 75.

105 I leave aside here the related question of how one defines "poetry" in medieval India. While both the classical and vernacular languages distinguished between non-metrical (*gadya*) and metrical (*padya*) language, this does not neatly overlap with the modern distinction between prose and poetry. Much premodern South Asian literature in metre bears a closer resemblance to prose than to poetry.

in Sanskrit is often well-known; to alter the length too significantly would be seen as an act of infidelity.[106]

## Translation and Society

Let me conclude with some comparative observations on the practice and the framework of translation in seventeenth-century Agra and after. The same time that Banarsidas and his colleagues were (perhaps) initiating a new practice of translation in North India also saw the golden epoch of translation in England, as well as the widespread practice of and theorisation about translation elsewhere in Europe. Comparing the contemporaneous situations in North India and England is quite revealing. By looking at this alternative setting we can see the extent to which the local situation in seventeenth-century Agra could have been different. Comparing the two cases shows us ways that translation in India did not have the same implications that it did in England, and thereby gives us further insight into cultural and social practices and structures in seventeenth-century North India. In particular, I briefly discuss two facets of the practice and social location of translation that were dominant in England and largely missing in India.

The first concerns philosophical and theological reflection upon the very practice of translation. As I indicated in the beginning of this essay, translation had been the subject of extensive theoretical reflection since the time of the Roman translation of Greek classics into Latin, and then the Christian translation of scripture into first Greek and then Latin.[107] Sixteenth- and seventeenth-century English authors gave much thought to central issues of translation, such as the relationship between language and meaning, and the tension between faithfulness and creativity in translation. They asked the basic question of whether translation is even possible, or if meaning is so deeply imbedded in any linguistic form that essential elements of meaning are inevitably lost when a text is transported into another linguistic frame.

---

106 In the case of the *Jinasahasranāma* the key element is not the number of verses in the *stotra* but the number of names. As a genre, the *sahasranama* exhibits less unity of form and content than does a *stotra*.

107 Within the voluminous scholarship in European languages that has developed over the past several decades on the subject of translation, see in particular in English Steiner (1992), Venuti (1995), *The Oxford Guide to Literature in English Translation*, ed. by Peter France (Oxford: Oxford University Press, 2000), and, most recently, David Bellos, *Is that a Fish in Your Ear: Translation and the Meaning of Everything* (New York: Faber & Faber, 2011).

One way in which this second-level reflection upon the practice of translation can be seen is through the many metaphors advanced by authors for the translator and his work.[108] The well-known and oft-cited Italian play on words, *traduttore-traditore,* which implies that the translator is merely a traitor to meaning, indicates the depth of anxiety in European thinking on translation. The translator is someone who follows in the footsteps of others. He engages in a contest that he inevitably loses. He is a mere labourer, or even a slave, in the service of a master. He offers glass and imitation jewels in place of diamonds. He shows only the back of a tapestry, not its front. The reader of a translation dons a poor garment, not a rich one. The translation is a pale star that only dimly reflects the sun. It is only a shadow, not a body.

The richness of the metaphorical language in Europe is evidence of widespread thinking about the nature of translation. This stands in stark contrast to the very lack of a word to describe the act in seventeenth-century India. Banarsidas, Kaunrpal, Hemraj, and their successors simply said that they were "making it vernacular", using the noun *bhasha* (*bhāṣā*) and a form of the verb √*kar*. Nor do the Jain poets exhibit any anxiety concerning the relative merits of their vernacular translations *vis-à-vis* the Sanskrit or Prakrit originals. Translators in Europe and North America ritually express the inadequacies of their translations in their prefaces; the Jain poets express no such angst.

This is not to say that vernacular poets did not make value judgments concerning the importance of classical and vernacular languages. The very language of the *balbodh* or *balavabodh,* in which the vernacular text is expressly aimed at an intellectually less-advanced audience, indicates that the truly educated reader or hearer would be able to access the classical original, and would not need the prop of a vernacular version. Banarsidas, as we have seen, said in his *Samaysār nāṭak* that educated people (*pandits*) could read the Prakrit original and Sanskrit commentary, but that common people with little understanding (*alpmati*) required the vernacular versions of Rajmall and Banarsidas himself. A similar value judgment is found in the *Bhāṣā dasamskandh* of Nanddas, who, in the opening verses of his translation, wrote, "This is the *Daśam skandh,* in which I have given some descriptions in the vernacular. The words

108 Theo Hermans, 'Metaphor and Imagery in the Renaissance Discourse on Translation', in *The Manipulation of Literature: Studies in Translation,* ed. by Theo Hermans (New York: St. Martin's Press, 1985), pp. 103-35.

are like the Sanskrit, but that is difficult to understand. I have therefore made it easy by making it vernacular".[109]

Deven Patel has discussed an articulation of the value of Sanskrit over the vernacular by the fifteenth-century Bhalan in his *Nalākhyān*, a Gujarati translation of the Nala episode of the *Mahābhārata*. Bhalan's comments bear striking similarity to the metaphors used by European translators that I mentioned above. He wrote that he was presenting "glass set in cheap metal" in place of "real diamonds, embedded in gold ornaments", that his poem was the "coarse millet" eaten by a poor man instead of the delicacies enjoyed by a rich king, and that his poem was a "leaf hut" of the down-trodden in lieu of a seven-storey high-rise building inhabited by the successful.[110] Here again, I think that the anxiety expressed by Bhalan is not the same as expressed by his contemporaneous European translators. Bhalan was bemoaning having to compose in the lowly vernacular instead of the truly polished and sophisticated Sanskrit in which Vyasa had been able to compose the *Mahābhārata*. Bhalan was making a twofold hierarchical judgment: Sanskrit authors are superior to vernacular authors, and an audience that understands Sanskrit is superior to one that only understands the vernacular. He was not, however, raising a philosophical or theological question concerning the very possibility of translation. Bhalan wrote in the vernacular with the full confidence that by doing so "even a child could understand".[111]

While there does not appear to have been any reflective discourse on the practice and possibility of translation on the part of the Jain authors, the

---

109 Nanddas, *Bhāṣā dasamskandh*, p. 216:

*tina kahī daśama skandha ju āhi / bhāṣā kari kachu barano tāhi //*
*sabada saṃskṛta ke haiṃ jaisaiṃ / bho pai samujhi parata nahiṃ taisaiṃ //*
*tātaiṃ sarala su bhāṣā kījai /*

In other contexts these lines would be read rather as customary self-effacement.

110 Bhālan, *Nalākhyān* 1.3-5:

*sācā hīrā heme jaḍiyā vaibhava no śaṅgāra /*
*durbalane to kāc kathīre bhūkhaṇa hoe apāra //*
*dhanavanta bhū-patine bhojana sarava sañjoge thāe /*
*niradhana tivārāṃ ati ānande juvāra bājarī khāe //*
*siddhivantane sapta-bhomanāṃ mandira ūcā avāsa /*
*parṇa-kuṭi rehe sukha pāme ata durbala pāmī vāsa //*

I thank Deven Patel for generously sharing these verses with me in an e-mail dated 30 March 2010. See also Deven Patel, 'Source, Exegesis, and Translation: Sanskrit Commentary and Regional Language Translation in South Asia', in *Journal of the American Oriental Society* 131 (2011), 245-66.

111 Bhalan, *Nalākhyān* 1.2b: *kālāṃne prīchavā bhālaṇe bhākhāe e kīdhī.*

sort of anxiety that has long underlaid European thought on the subject was not absent.[112] As George Steiner has noted, one source of anxiety about translation is theological: "So far as speech is divine and numinous, so far as it encloses revelation, active transmission either into the vulgate or across the barrier of languages is dubious or frankly evil".[113] This is a religious theory of untranslatability. We find such a theory in India as well. The best-known case is perhaps the Brahminical Vedic literature, which is untranslatable due to the way that the "meaning" of the text inheres to the very sounds themselves at a level beneath the surface sense.

We find a similar mantric rejection of the possibility of translation among the Jains. Due to the Jain theory of mantras, the vernacular translations of hymns such as the *Bhaktāmara stotra* and *Kalyāṇamandira stotra* never supplanted the Sanskrit originals in Jain ritual culture.[114] Jains understand that a Sanskrit (or Prakrit) *stotra* is not simply a communication event. It is also a performance event. A *stotra* is understood to be *mantra-maya*, i.e. "made of mantras". While the expectation is that the person who recites or sings it is full of faith, and that the intention embodied in that faith is important for the efficacy of the performance of the *stotra*, there is a significant extent to which by its very mantric nature the *stotra* is efficacious all on its own. This efficacy does not translate into the vernacular. The vernacular versions of Banarsidas and Hemraj are widely acknowledged to be beautiful, and they are found in most contemporary Digambar hymnals. But they are not *mantra-maya*, and so the number of people who sing or recite them daily pales in comparison with the numbers who perform the Sanskrit originals.

A second key aspect of translation in sixteenth- and seventeenth-century England also appears to have been missing in India. As Michaela Wolf has succinctly put it, "Any translation, as both an enactment and a product, is necessarily embedded within social contexts".[115] As a result, translation needs to be placed within these contexts; there needs to be

112 In part this discussion echoes and builds on Cort (1994).

113 Steiner (1992), p. 251.

114 See also Cort (2005) and 'A Spell against Snakes and other Calamities: The *Uvasaggahara Stotra* Attributed to Bhadrabāhu Svāmī', *Jinamañjari* 34.2 (2006), 34-43. Unlike Brahmins, Jains considered Prakrit as also capable of bearing the same *mantric* power as Sanskrit; Dundas (1998).

115 M. Wolf, 'Introduction: The Emergence of a Sociology of Translation', in *Constructing a Sociology of Translation*, ed. by M. Wolf and A. Fukari (Amsterdam: John Benjamins Publishing Company), p. 1.

what Wolf and others term "a sociology of translation". Translators live in specific social locations, and so the very act of translation has social implications.

This is clearly seen when we look at the English contemporaries of Banarsidas, Kaunrpal, and Hemraj. Translation in England was part of two larger social processes. One was the discovery and appropriation of the classical past. In the words of F.O. Matthiessen, "A study of Elizabethan translations is a study of the means by which the Renaissance came to England".[116] Translation was also part of the broader Protestantising of European Christianity. The process of vernacularising the Bible began before the Reformation, but in the early sixteenth century any attempt to translate the Christian scripture was inevitably done within a charged religious context—and in an era when religion and state were thoroughly intertwined, it was therefore done within a political context as well. This was a lesson William Tyndale learned all too well when he was tortured and executed for heresy in 1536 for daring to translate the Bible into English.

In seventeenth-century England translation as a cultural practice was still deeply implicated in contemporary social and political processes, for it was inseparable from the production of literature more broadly. This was not a period in which freedom of expression was taken for granted. Rather:

> the ideological policy of the English monarchial, ecclesiastical, and patriarchal state during and after the reformation was to maintain political and institutional control over individual and group reading. Reading, here, encompasses interpretations and translations of the texts of Scripture, the law, and classical antiquity [...] *all* directed reading and translation was to redound to the good of the commonwealth.[117]

Especially in the contentious decades of the Civil War and the Restoration, all publications were seen by whichever party was in power as having social and political implications. This was a time of printed pamphlets, so the lag between composition and publication was very short. Printed literature had a social and political immediacy that nowadays we associate with media such as newspapers, radio, television, and now

---

116 F.O. Matthiessen, *Translation: An Elizabethan Art* (1931), quoted by W. Boutcher, 'The Renaissance', in France (2000), p. 45.

117 Boutcher (2000), p. 52.

the blogosphere. All publication, therefore, was done within the social context of government censorship.[118]

In such a setting, many authors turned to translation of the Greek and Roman classics as a way of saying things for which they would be jailed if it were an "original" work.[119] The loyalist John Dryden, for example, found it safer to express many of his pro-monarchy opinions in the words of classical authors than as his own thoughts.

Here again by turning to seventeenth-century England we see features of translation as a social practice that were missing in Agra. The Jain poets were clearly aware of the political conditions within which they lived and worked. Banarsidas's *Ardhakathānak* is full of discussions of the doings of the Mughal rulers and their agents. The colophon to his *Nāmamālā* includes praise of the Mughal Emperor Jahangir: "Every day his glory and majesty is victorious, and there is always bountiful food. The emperor is the source of steady radiance, that Emperor Jahangir".[120] Many colophons of manuscripts include explicit reference to which Mughal emperor was on the throne.[121]

The Jain poets' translations, however, were not politics by other means. They did not turn to translations of classical and medieval Prakrit and Sanskrit works to say things they otherwise could not say in Hindi. A very significant difference was one of technology: Banarsidas, Kaunrpal, and Hemraj operated in an economy of the hand-written manuscript, whereas their English contemporaries operated in an economy of the printed, mass-produced pamphlet. Banarsidas made no mention of how he obtained the paper on which he wrote his texts, but we know for certain that writing for him involved ink and paper, and that texts were physical objects on paper. We saw above that Arathmal Dhor gave him a

118 Annabel Pattareson, *Censorship and Interpretation: The Conditions of Writing and Reading in Early Modern England* (Madison: University of Wisconsin Press, 1984).

119 Paul Davis, *Translation and the Poet's Life: The Ethics of Translating in English Culture, 1646-1726* (Oxford: Oxford University Press, 2008); Jack Lynch, 'Political Ideology in Translations of the Iliad, 1660-1715', *Translation and Literature* 7.1 (1998), 23-41.

120 Banarsidas, *Nāmamālā*, verse 172:
*dina dina tej pratāpa jaya / sadā akhaṇḍita āna //*
*pātasāha thira nūradī / jahāṅgīra sulatāna //*

121 To take just two examples: a manuscript of the Banarsidas-Kaunrpal translation of the *Sūktimuktāvalī* was copied in 1639 (just five years after they wrote it) in Agra during the reign of "Pātisāh Sāhijahāṃ" (K. Kaslival and A. Nyaytirth, *Rājasthān ke jain śāstra bhaṇḍāroṃ kī granth-sūcī*, Vol. 5, Mahavirji: Shri Digambar Jain Atishay Kshetra Shri Mahavirji, 1972, #6657); and a manuscript of Banarsidas's *Samaysār nāṭak* was copied in 1651 in Lahore during the reign of "Bādśāh Śāhjahāṃ" (ibid., #5692.4).

manuscript (*likhi, pothi*) of the *Samayasāra* in 1633. Many years earlier, in 1605, Banarsidas had repented of the infatuation with love represented in his long poem about the nine *rasas*. In a fit of regret at what he perceived as misspent teenage years, he threw the manuscript (*pothi*) into the Gomti River in Jaunpur, where the pages (*patra*) floated away.[122] Banarsidas's seeming ready access to paper may have been a sign of his middle-class merchant economic status, and paper may not have been as readily available in seventeenth-century North India as it was in seventeenth-century England. C.A. Bayly indicates that it was not until the later seventeenth and especially the eighteenth centuries that North India began to see the widespread production of paper manuscripts.[123]

Banarsidas's English contemporaries also lived in a society in which the ruling authorities expressed greater concern to control their subjects, as evidenced by the active presence of official censors. While the Jain translators would have been in trouble had they pronounced anti-Mughal sentiments in the public sphere, the Mughal (and more broadly late-medieval Indian) culture of allowing religiously-defined communities a fair degree of "private space" meant that their translations did not inherently carry political consequences. The Mughals sought to gain the knowledge of their subjects that they needed to rule effectively; but Bayly has estimated, "the detailed descriptions of royal intelligence we encounter may have represented more of an aspiration than a reality".[124] The Mughals did not exert detailed control over the religious lives of their subjects, especially outside of the most visible public sphere, as "the close bureaucratic control of heresy and witchcraft which forged the early modern European state had no equivalent in India". Religious communities such as the Jains were expected to police such matters internally, and only if matters "passed beyond the bounds of propriety", or involved major public shrines, did the officials intervene. Banarsidas gave no evidence of Mughal intrusion into his religious life; only as merchants (and therefore sources of ready revenue for a cash-poor government) were he and his fellow Jains subject to close scrutiny and interference.[125] The Mughal court did not have a high ranking post of

---

122 AK 264-68; Lath (1981), p. 244; Chowdhury (2009), pp. 110-12.

123 C.A. Bayly, *Empire and Information: Intelligence Gathering and Social Communication in India, 1780-1870* (Cambridge: Cambridge University Press, 1996), p. 42.

124 Ibid., p. 13.

125 Ibid., pp. 26-27. See also his observation that the Mughal system of surveillance "was designed to cajole the subject into godly submission, rather than to mount a constant

official censor, and the acts of reading, writing, and translating were not seen as inevitably tied to the ruler and the legitimacy of his rule.

Translation was not innocent of all social implications, however. Nathuram Premi has argued that the hundreds of translations of Prakrit and Sanskrit (and, I should add, Apabhramsa as well) texts into the vernacular undermined the traditional authority of the *bhattaraks*. Premi said that this was an intentional program on the part of Terapanth scholars, who were opposed to the domesticated *bhattaraks* of the Bispanth.[126]

The past three centuries have indeed seen a dramatic social and theological transformation in the North Indian Digambar community due to the rise of the Digambar Terapanth sect.[127] While many of the roots of this transformation go back to the Adhyatma movement of Agra and other urban centres in the sixteenth and seventeenth centuries, its more immediate origins are found in the Jaipur area in the early eighteenth century. The Terapanth is a lay movement that has argued against the worship of deities other than the Jinas, against the use of flowers and other living (or formerly living) substances in rituals, and against the authority of the *bhattaraks*. As a result of this movement, many Digambar congregations and temples in North India (and especially in Bundelkhand) now follow Terapanth ritual practices, and have rejected the *bhattaraks*. The movement has been so successful that even Bispanth congregations and temples, that maintained their adherence to the older Digambar ritual culture, have adopted aspects of Terapanth style. In particular, the Terapanth criticism of the *bhattaraks* as false Jain monks has resulted in the extinction of the *bhattarak* tradition throughout North and central India; it survives only in South India, in Kannada and Tamil speaking areas. Premi argued that the translation of classical texts into the vernacular was part of a Terapanth agenda of shifting literary and intellectual authority away from the *bhattaraks* and their trained assistants, the *pandes*, into the hands of the laity.

I am reluctant to make such a strong claim in the absence of any explicit evidence that this was the intention of the translators. Many

---

policing of society as some nineteenth-century European states [and England as well, I would argue, during the seventeenth-century Civil War and Restoration] attempted to do" (1996, p. 19).

126 Nathuram Premi, 'Digambar sampradāy ke saṅgh', in *Jain Śvetāmbar Kānfarens Herald* 11.9 (1915), 538.

127 See Cort (2002) on the Terapanth-Bispanth division among North Indian Digambars.

translations also came from the hands of Bispanth authors. There is no denying, however, that the traditional authority of the *bhattaraks*, which was based on their control over the Sanskrit literary culture of the Digambars, and was institutionally personified in the *pandes* who were their disciples and whom they deputed to various temples to conduct rituals, give sermons and lead seminars, was lessened as Digambar textual culture moved out of their control and into the broader Digambar public sphere. This process was, to a significant extent, connected to the practice of translation.[128]

## Making it Vernacular: Translation in South Asia

In this essay, I have employed A.K. Ramanujan's tripartite categorisation of translation to bring into focus some of the distinctive aspects of translation as literary practice among Jains in seventeenth-century Agra. Translation was nothing new. Just as multi-linguality is a universal aspect of human culture, so is translation, as people have never allowed the existence of multiple and even mutually unintelligible languages to be an impenetrable barrier to linguistic communication. Translation has a deep history in South Asia, and Jains have always been vital participants in that history. They have translated among Sanskrit, Prakrits, Apabhramshas, and other classical and vernacular languages for two millennia.

The medieval and pre-modern period in North India was also a time and place where the need and practice of translation was highlighted. While Islamicate cultures and languages had been present in South Asia for many centuries, the Mughals and their courtiers brought into

128 Premi's argument does, however, highlight one aspect of the social politics of translation that was missing from the Digambar Jain context. Among Hindus in the medieval and pre-modern period, translation was often implicated in challenges to the authority of the Brahmins, both in terms of their monopolistic claims over Sanskrit, and their related claims that only Sanskrit was suitable for the transmission of true knowledge. Translation, in other words, was a site of contestation over hierarchical caste claims. While caste is also integral to the personhood and social identities of Jains, it operates less in terms of hierarchy and more in terms of difference, and so has not been a divisive factor in Jain society; see John Cort, 'Jains, Caste, and Hierarchy in North Gujarat', in *Caste in Question: Identity or Hierarchy?*, ed. by Dipankar Gupta (New Delhi: Sage Publications, 2004), pp. 73-112. Translation among Jains has not been a marker or tactic of subversion of caste hierarchies.

South Asia a renewed emphasis on Persian, Turkic, and Arabic literary cultures. The Mughal courtly culture was also deeply intertwined with indigenous cultures, to the extent that the distinction of foreign and native, imported and vernacular, was often meaningless on the ground. Sanskrit and related classical Indic languages had a vital place in the cosmopolitan urban culture of North India. While Prakrit was clearly waning, and relegated to restricted social settings, it was not totally absent. Fifteenth-century Gwalior saw the final flowering of Apabhramsha.[129] While Brajbhasha and other vernaculars did not always carry the same prestige as the older literary languages in courtly circles, this period saw their rise to a position of prominence.[130] In other words, urban North India in this period was home to many linguistic literary traditions. Many authors were fluent in multiple languages, in continuity with older court traditions that a true poet, to be one of the jewels of the court, should be able to compose in as many as six languages at once.

In all of this linguistic richness and diversity, translation was an inevitable activity. Translation went in multiple directions. Many of these translations were in the time-honoured South Asian tradition of indexical and symbolic translations, as earlier narratives, theological treatises, and philosophical discourses were brought into new languages with varying degrees of innovation and faithfulness. Some of these bore clear traces of their indebtedness to the texts and languages being translated, and others were translations only in the loosest understandings of the term. There were many vernacular commentaries, aimed at a putatively childlike or unlettered audience that was fully comfortable only in the vernacular. While far too few of these translations have received the attention they are due, as scholars have preferred to study texts deemed "original" instead of translated, translation in various forms was ubiquitous. All of these genres of translation also fit easily into long-established modes of translation in the subcontinent.

But there may have been something new, as well. Banarsidas, Kaunrpal, and Hemraj all produced iconic translations of Sanskrit poems. In these translations, the translators explicitly acknowledged the authorship of

129 See Eva De Clercq, 'Apabhraṃśa as a Literary Medium in Fifteenth Century North India', in *After Timur Left: Culture and Circulation in Fifteenth-century North India*, ed. by F. Orsini and S. Sheikh (New Delhi: Oxford University Press, 2014), pp. 339-64.

130 Busch (2010).

the original text by a Sanskrit poet. They faithfully adhered to the length of the originals in their translations. They did not claim to be composing original texts, but rather simply to be "making it vernacular". Whether or not these translators saw what they were doing as something new and innovative is open to question; there is no evidence that they did. But this is part of a larger silence of theorising about translation in the pre-modern South Asian literary tradition. Just how new this mode of iconic translation was is also open to question. Arguments from silence are always hazardous. This is especially the case when the silence concerns vast archives that have barely been studied, and a subject that has been marginalised by generations of scholars.

This essay is a highly tentative foray into a topic that has hitherto received little scholarly attention. Almost all discussions of translation in India are from a postcolonial framework, and concern the power disparities between English and vernacular writing. Translation, however, even faithful iconic translation, is not something that did not exist in India until the coming of British colonialism. This essay, therefore, serves as an introduction to one particular, local instance of translation as a cultural and social practice. It is also an invitation to other scholars to explore other literatures in pre-colonial India using the framework of translation. Among the Jains of seventeenth-century Agra, at least, the performative aspects of North Indian literary culture involved translation in addition to other genres.

# 3. World Enough and Time: Religious Strategy and Historical Imagination in an Indian Sufi Tale[1]

*Muzaffar Alam*

Stories and anecdotes have been integral to sufi discourses, doctrinal expositions, and rhetorics. A large number of *malfuz* texts are comprised mostly of anecdotes, while even in others where the discussion is predominantly doctrinal, the exposition is interspersed with stories. Nizamuddin Auliya, Mir Hasan Sijzi reports in *Fawā'id al-fu'ād*, related stories from Baghdad, Bukhara, and other cities of the Islamic East in almost every gathering with his disciples and devotees. In some sufi texts, such as Khwaja Nasir Ali Andalib's *Nāla-i 'andalīb*, compiled in eighteenth-century Delhi, the entire *tariqa* code is outlined through/cloaked in tales.[2]

1 "World Enough and Time" is taken from the poem "To his Coy Mistress" by the seventeenth-century poet Andrew Marvell, which begins:

Had we but world enough, and time,
This coyness, Lady, were no crime
We would sit down and think which way
To walk and pass our long love's day.
Thou by the Indian Ganges' side
Shouldst rubies find: I by the tide
Of Humber would complain. I would
Love you ten years before the Flood,
And you should, if you please, refuse
Till the conversion of the Jews [...]

From *The Poetical Works of Andrew Marvell*, ed. by H. Rogers (London: A. Murray, 1870), p. 49. A fuller version of this essay has appeared in *The Indian Economic and Social History Review* 49.2 (2012), 151-96.

2 See Riazul Islam, *Sufism in South Asia: Impact on Fourteenth Century Muslim Society*

 http://dx.doi.org/10.11647/OBP.0062.03

The text that concerns us here, the Persian treatise *Mir'āt al-makhlūqāt*,[3] written in 1041AH/1631-32 by the eminent Mughal sufi 'Abd al-Rahman Chishti (d.1638), weaves together/uses stories drawn from a wide range of Islamic and Puranic materials, in order to construct an original argument about the origin of the world, pre- and post-Adamitic history, the coming of Islam to India, and the complementarity of Islamic and Hindu historical narratives.[4] More specifically, to connect and combine these traditions 'Abd al-Rahman Chishti uses stories with familiar characters but in unfamiliar combinations and doing and saying sometimes unfamiliar things. In line with the conventions of his putative source text of which it claims to be a "translation", the *Bhabikottar* [*Bhaviṣyottara*] *purāṇa*, the narrators are the god Shiva (to Parvati) and the *rishi* Bashist (Vashishta), yet 'Abd al-Rahman Chishti remains firmly in control of the narrative, adding quotations from the Qur'an, *hadis*, and Persian poets, introducing digressions, and stating his own arguments and conlcusions. The ability to tell a good story and the rhetorical skill to draw home an argument and convince through a story are linked to the "embodied knowledge" of the *pir*—and of the storyteller—and

(Karachi: Oxford University Press, 2002), pp. 1-67, for a discussion on stories and parables in sufi texts. See also, for example, Amir Hasan Sijzi Dihlawi, *Fawā'id al-fu'ād* (Lucknow: Nawalkishor, 1302H/1885), trans. by Bruce Lawrence as *Morals of the Heart* (New York: Paulist Press, 1992); and *Fawaid Al-Fuad: Spiritual and Literary Discourses of Shaikh Nizamuddin Awliya* by Ziaul Hasan Faruqi (New Delhi: D.K. Printworld, 1996); Khwaja Muhammad Nasir Andalib, *Nāla-i 'andalīb* (Bhopal: Matba' Shajahani, 1894).

3 The text, still unpublished, is one of five major books by 'Abd al-Rahman Chishti. Several manuscripts are available in India and abroad. I have read and collated three of them: the Aligarh MS (Maulana Azad Library, Aligarh Muslim University, Aligarh, Habibganj Collection, *Fārsiyya taṣawwuf*, 21/343), the Chishti Khanqah, Sarkhej, Ahmadabad MS (microfilm, Noor Microfilms Centre, Iran Cultural House, Embassy of Iran, New Delhi), and the British Library, London MS (India Office Library Or. 1883). All references here are from the British Library MS, which is bound and paginated continuously with several other manuscripts, including 'Abd al-Rahman Chishti's rendering of the *Bhāgavadgītā*, entitled *Mir'āt al-ḥaqā'iq*. Since the texts I refer to are all unpublished and untranslated, I have chosen to provide liberal quotations from them. Svevo d'Onofrio and M. Karimi Zanjani-Asl are preparing a critical edition and translation of the text.

4 For biographical details and some descriptions of his writings, see S.A.A. Rizvi, *A History of Sufism in India* (Delhi: Munshiram Manoharlal, 1983), Vol. 2, pp. 27, 289, 368-69, and 396; Carl W. Ernst and Bruce B. Lawrence, *Sufi Martyrs of Love: Chishti Sufism in South Asia and Beyond* (New York: Palgrave Macmillan, 2002). See also Simon Digby, 'Mas'udi', in *Encyclopedia of Islam*, New Series, 1991, vi, pp. 783-84; Shahid Amin, 'On Retelling the Muslim Conquest of Northern India', in *History and the Present*, ed. by Partha Chatterjee and Anjan Ghosh (Delhi: Permanent Black, 2002), pp. 24-43; idem, 'Un Saint Guerrier: Sur la conquête de l'Inde du Nord par les Turcs au XI siècle', *Annales: Histoire, Sciences Sociales* 60.2 (March-April 2005), 265-93. See also N.R. Faruqui, *Medieval India: Essays on Sufism, Diplomacy and History* (Allahabad: Laburnum Press, 2006), pp. 52, 54, 62, and 126n.

the effects are achieved, as we shall see, through precision, self-assurance, a wealth of details, and by invoking specific sources of authority.

This book argues that, as a genre, stories are particularly amenable to reworking, experiments of combination, substitution, etc. Storytellers can count on the audience's familiarity with certain elements and characters, which they manipulate and combine in new ways. The case of 'Abd al-Rahman Chishti's texts shows how stories (presumably told and listened to as well as written and read) elaborated and transmitted original religious ideas. The *Mir'āt al-makhlūqāt* centres on the figures of Mahadeva and Krishna. It effectively makes use of the concept of *yugas* in order to present a relativist argument that places the Prophets Adam and Muhammad (and his grandson Husain) in a narrative continuum with events from the time of the early Hindu tradition. The text bears some generic resemblance to versions of the *Bhaviṣya-purāṇa* that we know from the nineteenth century—particularly in the device of Mahadev's prophecy about the "future past" that here serves to include Adam and the Prophet Muhammad within a narrative of the destiny of the gods—but it precedes them by two centuries. *Mir'āt al-makhlūqāt* also seems to draw upon several other Puranas that 'Abd al-Rahman Chishti may have read or *kathas* based on the Puranas that he may have listened to; it employs to great effect the Puranic narrative strategy of multiple narrators and multiple time-frames.[5] I shall show how the *Mir'āt* and its author combined rhetorical and political strategies to provide a reconciliation between Hindu and Muslim traditions while manipulating them in such a way as to give the Muslim tradition the upper hand.

## The Age of the World and the Coming of Adam

'Abd al-Rahman Chishti's account of human genesis should be seen as part of the broader interest of Mughal rulers and intellectuals in India's Hindu religious traditions and its "Hindu past". Mughal emperors commissioned translations into Persian of several major Hindu texts, including the *Mahābhārata*.[6] With the appearance of these translations,

5 The argument for oral sources rests on the phonology of the Indic names, common words, and toponyms used, e.g. *bhabhik*, *jug*, *Kishan*, etc.

6 Described by Abu'l-Fazl as "the most honoured, most sacred and most comprehensive book" of the Hindus; *Mahābhārat*, Persian translation by Mir Ghiyas al-Din 'Ali Qazvini, ed. by S.M. Reza and N.S. Shukla (Tehran: Kitabkhan-i Tahuri, 1979/1358

Muslim scholars and religious divines were given access to pasts and legends that stretched their imaginations. For instance, Muslims traced the origins of this world to the birth of Adam, who in their estimate lived around 7,000 years ago, while they now learned that, in the Hindu tradition, the world and its inhabitants had existed for hundreds and thousands of years. Many of them must have dismissed these new discoveries as mere myth, but many others struggled to make sense of them, faced, as they were, with the need to develop effective strategies for affirming their views and authority in a heterogeneous religious environment.[7]

In *Mir'āt al-makhlūqāt*, 'Abd al-Rahman Chishti begins by describing the four eras (*yugas*) according to the Hindu calculation of Time and aligning the age of the world with the *hijri* calendar. This chronology corresponds to a typology of beings that is crucial to his argument: *jinns*, a.k.a. *devatās* and *daityas* (gods and demons), lived in the two earlier ages, while Adam and his descendants lived in the latter two:

> The first of the four ages was Satjug [Satyayuga], comprising over seventeen lakhs twenty-eight thousand years (1,728,000), the second was Traitya [Treta], comprising over twelve lakh ninety-six thousand years (1,296,000), the third is known as Dwapar which comprised over eight lakhs sixty-four thousand years (864,000), and the fourth is Kaljug [Kaliyuga], comprising over four lakhs and thirty-two thousand years (432,000). Today, which is the one thousand forty-one year (1041 AH) since the *hijrat* of our Prophet has passed and four thousand seven hundred and thirty-years (4731) since the Kaljug [...] In two of these four ages the *jinns* reigned supreme in the inhabited portion of the earth (*rub'-i maskūn*). They had a law (*sharī'at*), given by God, and acted according to it. During the third era most of them became too involved in this world (*ghalba-i kasrat-i dunyā*), and began to turn their faces from and revolted against the Divine Commands. [Subsequently] God commanded the angels to chastise them until they were annihilated.[8]

---

*shamsi*), Vol. 1, Abu'l Fazl's Introduction, pp. 18-19. See Audrey Truschke, 'The Mughal *Book of War*: A Persian Translation of the Sanskrit *Mahabharata*', *Comparative Studies of South Asia, Africa and the Middle East* 31.2 (2011), 506-20.

7 See e.g. Abu'l Fazl, *Ā'īn -i Akbarī*, ed. by Saiyid Ahmad Khan (reprint, Aligarh: Aligarh Muslim University, 2005), *Aḥwāl-i Hindustān*, Vol. 3, pp. 360-556; English trans. by H.S. Jarrett (reprint, Delhi: Low Price Publications, 2008), pp. 1-358; Dara Shukoh, *Majma'-ul-baḥrain*, ed. with English translation and notes (Calcutta: Asiatic Society, 1929), p. 182. See also Bikrama Jit Hasrat, *Dara Shikuh: Life and Works* (Calcutta: Viswabharati, 1953), Part Two, pp. 174-292.

8 *Mir'āt al-makhlūqāt*, f. 240a.

Already in earlier Islamic literature, the time before Adam had been divided into four ages, even though the duration of each of the four ages was much shorter than that of a Hindu *yuga*.[9] Further, according to the sufi tradition, as we will see below, the world had existed long before the creation of Adam. 'Abd al-Rahman himself drew upon this tradition when he wrote about this topic in his *tazkira Mir'āt al-Asrār* (1065AH/1655). In his account of the thirteenth-century sufi Shaikh Sa'ad al-Din Hamawi, 'Abd al-Rahman introduces the topic of different accounts of the beginning of time and draws upon the authority of Ibn 'Arabi to propose an even more mathematically precise comparative calculation of the age of the world:

> The Indian, Chinese, and Firangi philosophers put the beginning of creation to several thousand years ago [...]. This belief is supported by Chapter 331 of the *Futūḥāt al-Makkīya* of the Great Shaikh [Ibn 'Arabi], in which he narrates a *ḥadīs̱* of the Prophet: "Verily God created hundred thousand Adams".[10] In the same chapter the Great Shaikh relates a story: "While circumambulating the Ka'ba, I witnessed a vision in the World of Similitudes (*'ālam-i mis̱āl*) that a group of pious people were circumambulating the Ka'ba with me, but I did not recognise them. Upon this, they said that some years ago we too were circumambulating the Ka'ba sanctuary, just as you are doing it now". Then the Great Shaikh relates: "When I heard this, a thought came to my heart that these must be bodies belonging to the World of Similitudes. As soon as this occurred to me, one of them turned to me and said: 'I am one of your forefathers.' I asked: 'How long has it been since you left this world?' He said: '40,000 years passed since I died'. Astonished, I said: 'But it was only 7000 years ago that Adam died'. He asked: 'which Adam are you talking about? This Adam was in the beginning of the first cycle of these 7000 years'".
> The Great Shaikh says: "Upon hearing this, I remembered the *ḥadīs* of the Prophet according to which God Most High created one hundred thousand Adams the way he created the Father of the Mankind (*Abū al-bashar*)". Following this, the Great Shaikh writes that it is possible that after every cycle of 7000 years the descendants of one Adam become extinct and

9 See Mir Khvand (d.1498), *Tārīkh-i rawżat al-ṣafā'* (Tehran: Markazi Khayam Piroz, 1338 *shamsi*/1959), Vol. 1, pp. 20-21. According to Ibn 'Arabi, the *jinns* had lived and been in control of this world for sixty thousand years before the creation of the humankind. There were twelve principal groups of them and they also fought among themselves; see Muhyi al-Din Ibn al-Arabi, *al-Futūḥāt al-Makkīya* (Cairo: Al-Hai'at al-Misriyya al-Amma and Paris: Sorbonne, 1972), Vol. 2, pp. 276-86.

10 *'Innallāha khalaqa mi' atah alfin Ādama'*; in Ibn 'Arabi (1972), Vol. 3, p. 549. See also William C. Chittick, *Imaginal Worlds: Ibn 'Arabi and the Problem of Religious Diversity* (Albany: State University of New York, 1994), pp. 81-95.

descendants of another Adam come into existence, and this chain will go on as long as the world is contingent, until the Resurrection comes (*wa badīn waża' ta qiyām-i qiyāmat muntahī gardad*), because all prophets had brought us news regarding this, and on the day of Resurrection God Most High will bring to life the progeny of all Adams, all at once; this is not anything difficult for the Omnipotent (*Qādir-i muṭlaq*). And God knows the best.[11]

Confronted by apparently conflicting traditions—the Indic historical imaginings of *yugas* populated by gods, *rishis*, and heroic kings, and the sufi and also non-sufic Islamic imaginations—'Abd al-Rahman Chishti had enough support in his own tradition to enable him to blend the two, at least in the imagination of the origins of the world, for in sufi circles too, then, "the world and the people of the world" were much older than the 7,000 years ascribed to them in the Islamic tradition.[12] And it is interesting, for example, that in 'Abd al-Rahman Chishti's narrative the originary being is always named Adam. By comparison, we may note here that Shaikh Ahmad Sirhindi considered the 100,000 Adams, even

---

11 "Because the father of the humankind (Adam) came into existence in the Cycle of Saturn (*Zuḥal*), or, at the end of the third period, his life span and the life span of his descendants that were born in this period, was longer. In this way Adam's life span was thousand years, or, according to a different tradition, 930 years. Likewise, the life spans of his sons too were long. Because the appearance of our Prophet is connected with the Cycle of the Moon, or, the fourth period, in which the life spans are in between 60 and 70 years, with some reaching to 100 years, for this reason the Prophet said the life span of the people of my community is within 70 years (*bain al-sab'īn*). Therefore, the scholars, verifiers of the Truth hold the view that when 7000 years are completed, one week of God's days—one of which is equal to thousand years—is completed. But it should be known that according to them [these scholars], there are two types of the days of God, short (*ṣighār*) and long (*kibār*). The short days are also called temporal days (*ayyām-i zamānī*, 'days of time') and the long ones [are called] God's days. The duration of the short day is a thousand years, as the venerable verse of *Qur'an* has it: 'Verily a Day of your Lord is like a thousand years of your reckoning' (*'wa-in yauman 'inda rabbika ka-alfi sanatin mimmā ta'uddūn, Qur'an*, 22:47), while the long day, which is from God's days, is equal to about 50,000 years. The venerable verse of *Qur'an* 'The angels and the Spirit ascend unto Him in a Day that equals fifty thousand years' (*'ta'ruju-'l-malā'ikatu wa-'r-rūḥu ilaihi fī yaumin kāna miqdāruhu khamsīna alfa sanatin', Qur'an*, 70:4) points to this truth. This is the reason why the author of the *Futūḥāt al-Makkīya* writes that in the Hereafter (*ākhirat*) one day is equal to 50,000 years, while one day in the World of Similitudes is equal to thousand years"; *Mir'āt al-asrār*, ff. 243a-244a.

12 Relevant here are also the *hadis* regarding Moses' queries to God regarding the origins of the world, which are traced to one million years ago; see Alam (2012), 184-85. Such *hadis* were of questionable authenticity from the point of view of orthodox theologians, but they continued to be cited in Islamic literature, and became part of the Muslim imagination.

as they appeared in Ibn 'Arabi's vision, to have lived in the World of Similitudes (*'alam-i misal*) and in that world alone.[13]

To return to *Mir'āt al-makhlūqāt*, it is worth noting that 'Abd al-Rahman Chishti begins with inclusive and universalist language that would have been intelligible to his Hindu audiences. At the same time he exercises intellectual authority and distinction by arguing that it is incorrect to think ("as some people do") that Rama, Krishna, and Arjun were the descendents of "the father of humankind" (Abu al-Bashar), Adam. Hindu gods, he argues, had lived before Adam, and Rama, Krishna, and Arjun had no connection with him:

> Ramchand lived during Traitya [Treta] and Bashist has written that he was a descendent of Brahma, who lived in Satjug. Mahadev also lived in Satjug and both these two person were created by absolute God, without mother and father. Brahma was created out of light (*nūr*) and fire (*nār*) and Mahadev from fire and air (*bād*), while Adam was created towards the end of the Dwapar age. Although Kishan and Arjun were contemporaries of the descendants of Adam, Biyas [Vyasa] has traced their genealogy to Raja Jadu [Yadu]. Raja Jadu also lived in Traitya age and because of this connection Kishan is known as *Jadu bansī*, that is, from the family (*nasl*) of Raja Jadu. In fact, until the time of Kishan and Arjun, Adam's descendents had not come to the country of Hind and the *jinns* and *'unṣūrī*, i.e. non-*nūr*, angels were still in command there.[14] Biyas writes that the coming of Kishan was for the annihilation of Kans and for the killing of the entire community of the *jinns* in the battle of Mahabharat. The purpose was to vacate Hind so that Adam's descendents would take it over. Thus ended the time of the *jinns*.[15]

Note that both Brahma and Shiva-Mahadev in this scheme are *jinns* created by the absolute God. As we shall see, in 'Abd al-Rahman Chishti's narrative Mahadev plays a crucial role in prophesying the coming of Adam and of the Prophet Muhammad and his descendants, while Kishan's (Krishna) conflict against his uncle Kans (Kamsa) merges

---

13 Shaikh Ahmad Sirhindi, *Maktūbāt-i Imām Rabbānī*, ed. by 'Aziz al-Din Dehlavi (Delhi: Matba Murtazavi, 1873), Vol. 2, pp. 42-44.

14 Earlier in his introductory note in the *Mir'at*, Chishti mentions two categories of the angels (*mala'ik*), one *nurani*, i.e. made of light, and the other *'unsuri*, made of elements, and he says that these angels are the same that are identified as *nari*, i.e. made of fire; *Mir'āt al-makhlūqāt*, f. 238b.

15 *Mir'āt al-makhlūqāt*, f. 240b. For Kans (Kamsa), the notorious demon King of Mathura who was killed by Krishna, and Kishan (Krishna) and Ram (Rama), the Hindu gods, see Vettam Mani, *Purāṇic Encyclopaedia* (reprint, Delhi: Motilal Banarsidas, 1998), pp. 382-83, 420-29, and 631-40.

with his role as avenging and exterminating angel in the Mahabharata war, a war that here marks the end of the rule of *jinns* on Indian soil.

'Abd al-Rahman Chishti had already indicated that each era had its own "law (*sharī'at*), given by God, and acted according to it"; at the end of this remarkably synthetic narrative he adds that in the exterminated past the world had been graced with the Divine Truth, too, which was brought from Heaven by the Hindu gods and sages. This is what he projects to be the true religion (*mashrab*) of the sufis, who in any case are instructed to "appropriate the good thing and good word (*sukhan-i nīk*) from each community":

> Mahadev *jinn* was made of fire but in his own community he was matchless, both in physical and spiritual perfection. He would come out with the message of oneness of God/Unitarianism (*tawḥīd*) and would divulge the divine secrets. The *Qur'anic* verse, "I did not create the *jinns* and the humans except to worship Me alone",[16] is a proof of the (divine) gnosis of the *jinns*. It is written in the *Tafsīr-i Zāhidī* that before the coming of our Prophet, the Devs and the *jinns* would rise high to the sky, and listen to the conversation of the angels. After the advent of the Prophet, however, their way to the sky has been closed [...] In believing this there is no harm. The religion of the sufis is that we should appropriate the good thing and good word from each community. This is the message in the *ḥadīs̱* of the Prophet, "take what is good and pure, reject what is dirty and impure".[17]

While inserting Islamic chronology within Hindu time, 'Abd al-Rahman Chishti's historical narrative follows a logic of insubordination and punishment that appears modeled on the story of Iblis. Here it is Mahadev and Hanwant (Hanuman) who get inserted within an Islamic

16 *"ma khalaqtu'l jinna wa'l insa illa liya' budūn"*. Qur'an, 51:56.

17 *Mir'āt al-makhlūqāt*, f.241a. The *hadis "khuẕ mā safā, da' mā kadir"*, is oft-cited in sufi texts, see Izz al-Din Mahmud bin Ali Kashani, *Miṣbāḥ al-hidāya wa miftāḥ al-kifāya*, ed. Iffat Karbasi and Muhammad Riza Barzgar Khaliqi (Tehran: Intisharat-i Zavvar), 1387 *shamsi*/2008, p. 281; Baqir Sadriniya, *Farhang-i māsūrāt-i mutūn-i 'irfānī* (Tehran: Intisharat-i Sukhan, 1387 *shamsi*/2009), p. 230. The *Tafsīr-i Zāhidī* by Abu Nasr al-Raruha, a notable sufi commentary on the Qur'an, is still unpublished; an important manuscript is available in the Khuda Bakhsh Oriental Public Library in Patna, see *Catalogue of Arabic and Persian Manuscripts in Khuda Bakhsh Oriental Public Library, Patna, Vol. XIV*, ed. by Khan Bahadur Abdul Muqtadir (reprint, Patna: Khuda Bakhsh Library, 1970), no. 1112. Unfortunately I have not had access to any of these manuscripts and have therefore been unable so far to verify Chishti's statement. For a summary of Qur'an commentaries see Alan Godlas, "Sufism", in *The Blackwell Companion to the Qur'an*, ed. by Andrew Rippin (London: Blackwell, 2006), pp. 350-61.

sufi scheme. It is also here that Mahadev becomes the narrator of the 'true story' in response to his wife Parvati's queries:[18]

> Since during the time of Satjug (*zamān-i satjug*), that is the first age, the *'unṣurī* angels and the *jinns* led their lives in comfort and luxury, without any problems, they grew haughty. During the entire period of Traitya, the second age, they did things contrary to the divine commands. At that time, Mahadev told them that "if you wish your welfare, you should not give up the path of the divine law (*sharī'at*)". They did not listen to his advice out of their arrogance. They were too attached to the world [of their own]. Mahadev felt ashamed [when his advice was turned down by his own community]. He told these rebels: "Beware that, God willing, during the time of Dwapar God will create a person who will not leave a trace of you in the inhabited part of the earth". Having said this, he set out for Kailash.[19]
>
> Mahadev's wife, Parvati, heard all this in astonishment. She also followed her husband. One day when Mahadev was well settled in his appointed place on the Kailash mountain and was resting, Parvati considered it a good opportunity to ask a question. She asked, "Since the day when you said that in the Dwapar age God will create a person who will annihilate the entire community of the *devatās* (gods) and *daits* (*daityas*, demons), and so on and will take over the inhabited part of the earth, I have not ceased to be amazed. Now do please tell me the nature of that person". Since Mahadev had immense love for his wife, he started telling the true story (*bayān-i wāqi'*).[20]

After a digression on the chain of transmission of the story, to which we will turn later, Mahadev continues the story by prophesying the coming of Adam. Not only is it remarkable that we have Mahadev praising Adam as God's favourite creature in distinctly Islamic tones, but Chishti has Mahadev use Hanuman as an *exemplum* to deliver a small sermon on the evil of haughtiness. The dig at Hanuman—a most popular figure in contemporary North Indian devotion—suggests that 'Abd al-Rahman Chishti's inclusivism had a competitive edge.

---

18 For a useful discussion of the Puranas as a genre constructed around the central principle of "revealing mysteries", see Ludo Rocher, *The Purāṇas* (Wiesbaden: Otto Harrasowitz, 1986); idem, 'Reflections on one hundred and fifty years of *Purāṇa* studies', *Purāṇa* 25.1 (January 1983), 64-76; see also Giorgio Bonazzoli, 'Remarks on the Nature of the *Purāṇas*', ibid., 77-113; idem, 'Composition of the *Purāṇas*', *Purāṇa* 2 (July 1983), 254-80. For the style of the *Kathāsaritsāgara*, see Arshiya Sattar, *Tales from the Kathāsaritsāgara, Somadeva: Translated from the Sanskrit with an Introduction* (New York: Penguin Books, 1994), Introduction and p. 2 in particular.

19 The mount Mahameru with the golden colored peak of Himavan, the seat of Siva according to the Puranas, Mani (1998), pp. 364-65 and 462-63.

20 *Mir'āt al-makhlūqāt*, f. 241.

Adam is pivotal in suturing the history of Hindu gods and demons with the origin and spread of the human race throughout the world, and into the local geography of Hindustan:

> "O Parvati he will have a long life and will be the best of all creatures. His eyes will be bulging like the lotus (*nīlofar*) flowers, his face will be illuminated like thousands of full moons. O Parvati, when Brahma manifests that world-adoring and matchless person in the being of Adam, the people will be helpless all around and will fall prostrate before him. It is about this situation that Shaikh Farid al-Din 'Attar [d. ca 1230] writes:
>
> *Gar nabūda zāt-i haq andar wujūd,*
> *Āb o gil rā kai malak karda sujūd.*
>
> If God Himself were not manifest in his person,
> How would then angels have prostrated before a person made of mud and water?[21]
>
> O Parvati, at that time God will command all the creatures to prostrate before Adam, all *devatās, rishīs, daits, rākshas,* and so on will then fall in prostration. God has said, 'And when we said to the angels "Fall prostrate before Adam", they all fell prostrate except Iblis; he refused, and was arrogant and a disbeliever'.[22] O Parvati, when all the creatures have fallen in prostration, a *devatā* named Hanwant, that is Azazil [i.e. Iblis], will refuse to prostrate out of jealousy; in contempt he will utter a word and say that 'this is the worst creature, created out of dirty earth, while I was created from a delicate fire'. He will then address the other *devatās* and will say, 'O dear ones please do justice, how can I prostrate before him? The Word of God—he [i.e. Iblis] said—"I am better than he; you created me from fire, and he created him from clay",[23] carries the same meaning'. O Parvati, Hanwant[24] *devatā* will turn disobedient because all

---

21 There are several verses by Farid al-Din 'Attar bearing strong affinities to this verse, besides being in the same metre; see *Musībat-nāma* (Tehran: Zawwar, 1959), pp. 58, 242, *Ushtur-nāma* (Tehran: Chap-e Taban, 1961), pp. 30, 302-03, under *Hikāyat-i Ādam*. In the *Asrār-nāma* (Tehran: Chap-e Sharq, 1959, p. 47) 'Attar gives the same verse in a different order: "*dar ādam būd nūrī az wujūd-ash / wagarna kai malak karda sujūd-ash*" (there existed a light in the existence of Adam / otherwise how could the angels have prostrated before him). Interestingly, another poet, Amir Husaini Haravi, cites the same verse with a difference in the second part of the first line of the verse. Instead of 'Attar's "*ẕāt-i ḥaq andar wujūd*", Amir Husaini writes "*partav-i ḥaq dar wujūd*", in *Maṡnavī-hā-yi 'irfānī* (Tehran: Mu'assasah-i Chap va Intisaharat-i Danishgah-i Tihran, 1993), p. 44.

22 "*wa iz qulnā lil malā'ikati usjudū fasajadū illā iblīs aba wa istakbara wa kāna min al-kāfirīn*", Qur'an, 2:34.

23 "*anā khair minhu khalaqtanī min nārin wa khalaqtahu min ṭīn*", Qur'an, 38:76.

24 Since *-want* is the same suffix as *-mān*, so Hanuman and Hanuwant are the same

*devatās* see that God made Adam with his own hands and instilled his own light into him [Adam]. After Brahma observed this and the *devatās* will prostrate before him. Hanwant will humiliate himself because of his arrogance and ignorance. He will live neither in the heaven nor in any other place where Brahma will live, nor in my place, nor in the home of any other *devatās* or *gandharbas* (a category of angels). He will be nowhere near any rishi or rajas, not even in the company of the jogis. No one will give him a place and he will become a vagabond (*sargardān*), roaming between the earth and the sky. O Parvati, arrogance is the worst vice, a real *'ārif* [man of gnosis] is the one who regards God as present and watchful everywhere and remains humble and obedient. Since he looked at Adam with contempt, Hanwant was thrown into Hell. O Parvati, God has given Adam the rule of the seven climes (*bādshāhā-yi haft iqlīm*) and has endowed him with full strength, bravery and all kinds of sciences of the people of ancient times. God says, "and He taught Adam all the names".[25] O Parvati, all beings created of fire will fear Adam, he will dominate over all others and make the entire earth the residence of his descendants, and he will thus bring the world under his control".[26]

In a way, then, Adam acts as the point of suture between the Hindu and Islamic histories of time and creation—a suture strengthened by the analogy between Mahadev and Parvati and Adam and Eve. 'Abd al-Rahman Chishti then shows how the birth of Adam inaugurated the history of the human beings who inhabit the world of the time that he and the others—including both Muslims and Hindus—live in. The names of Adam's sons and daughters that 'Abd al-Rahman Chishti gives are unusual: even though some details remind us of the Biblico-Islamic story of the clash between Habil and Qabil (Gabel/Abel and Cain), the survivor takes the girl with him to Koshal, a country with a clearly Indian name, thus giving the Islamic story an Indic colour.

"O Parvati, the first son that will be born of them will be called Badila, he will be very strong and will perform several miracles. Then there will be a daughter who will be married to him. Then Badila, accompanied by his wife, will leave Adam to settle [in other parts of] the earth. Within a short time there will be so many sons and daughters, steadily taking control of the world. A second son of Adam will be named Hansila, he will be so brave and strong that all the *jinns* and *daits* will fall obedient to him.

---

name; "Hanivant" is the common Avadhi spelling in Malik Muhammad Jayasi's *Padmāvat*, ed. by V.S. Agrawal (Jhansi: Sahitya Sadan, 1998 edn), index p. 781. This could be an earlier "birth" of the very popular Hanuman.

25 *"wa allama adam al asmā'a kullahā"*. Qur'an 2:31.

26 *Mir'āt al-makhlūqāt*, f. 242.

Whosoever will refuse to obey him will be killed (*halāk*). And then there will be another daughter who will be handed over in marriage to Hansila. The third son of Adam will be named Dahanki and will be fearless, he will not accept Brahma and Bishun [Vishnu] and will contemptuously annul all the rituals and prayers of their faith. Wherever their places of worship will be, he will urinate over them. Thus our faith will encounter evils. Dahanki will do everything, religious or worldly, in opposition to our *devatās*. Adam's fourth son will be named Badhal. Five *iqlīms* [climes, countries] will be under his control, some of these he will forcefully wrest from the *deotās* [*devatās*] and *daits*. He will also forcibly collect *kharāj* [tributes, revenues] from them. He will do the thing that should never have taken place, all rulers will be obedient to him, and he will bring in a new *sharī'at*. O Parvati, in the same manner each son of Adam will be married to the daughter who will follow. In all there will be twenty-one sons and twenty-one daughters, and one son will clash with another over one daughter, as a result of which one of the sons will be killed. Taking that girl with him, he will set out for the country of Koshal where he will grow in power and strength and accumulate piles of gold and silver, extracted from the mines as well as the mountains, and he will distribute them to the people. Thus many will go to his country and will get the gold and silver according to their own desire. He will be a great king and will repent for the sin he had committed and will do excessive prayer, all the time dressed in blue. O Parvati, from the sons of Adam countless people will be born. One son there will bear one thousand, from one thousand there will be one lakh, and from the one lakh there will be one crore, and so on. I cannot in fact give you the exact figure of the descendents of Adam".[27]

As an astute narrator, after giving us the pre-history, 'Abd al-Rahman Chishti brings the story up to present times. The next stage is the birth of Muhammad, his mission for the people in the Kali age, the Qur'an, and Islam:

"[After] six thousand years [when "Adam's descendants will have adopted strange ways of living and the earth will be fed up with their sinfulness"], the Almighty (God) will create a wonderful person from among the children of Adam in the country of Mundali, which is located between the seas, a land which will be appropriate for [God] Bishan [Vishnu]". Upon hearing this, Parvati asked Mahadev, "Tell me the truth, whether the person who is going to be created by God in such a blessed place will be born in the house of a *devatā* or a *rishī*". In response Mahadev said, "O Parvati, he will be from the loin of Kant Bunjh, who in wisdom and

27 *Mir'āt al-makhlūqāt*, f. 243.

> gnosis will be like an ocean, so that from him [whatever] emerges [will be] the pearl. And the name of his wife will be Sak Rekha [Sagarika?]. He will have read the three *Beds*, *Siyām Bed*, *Rig Bed*, and *Jajar Bed*, and the fourth *Bed*, *Atharban Bed* he would give up after having read only up to the letters *alif*, *lām*".[28]

The name of Kant Bunjh for Muhammad's father Abdullah is also given in a much later commentary on 'Abd al-Rahman's text by Maulana Sayyid Rahat Husain Gopalpuri.[29] The detail of the "hidden fourth Veda" is tantalising and clearly significant for 'Abd al-Rahman's argument, and we will return later to this issue and to the digression that occurs here. 'Abd al-Rahman then moves to the praise of the Prophet, this time drawing upon familiar/popular Islamic literature. Mahadev tells Parvati that Byas [Vyasa], too, attributes to Muhammad manifold virtues—in fact nearly all the virtues and miraculous qualities that were then popular in Indian sufi Islam. Kant Bunjh will have three sons and the name of the third son, who survives, will be Mahamat, i.e. Muhammad, who will be endowed with excellent etiquette (*awżā'*), will already be circumcised, will have no hair anywhere on his body except for the hair on his head and face, and will not worship the gods venerated by the people of his tribe. Mahadev tells Parvati:

> "Biyas has also written in his book, the *Bhavikh* [*Bhaviṣya*] *Uttarpurān*, that in the future, i.e. in Kaljug, Mahamat will take birth, who the Muslims will call Muhammad. He will always have the shade of a cloud over his head and he will not have his own shadow. No fly will ever sit on his body. And for him the earth will shrink (*ūrā ṭayy-i zamīn kwāhad būd*) and he will have enormous virility, he will struggle only for the *dīn* (faith, religion) and will have no concern for *dunyā* (this world), and whatever he will gain he will spend in the name of God. He will eat little; the king of the time will be his enemy but he will be the friend of the people. The Almighty will send to him a *Purān* of thirty *adhyāy* (divisions), i.e. the *sīpāras* of the Qur'an will be revealed to him, and everyone acting

---

28 A version of this part is also available on the website http://www.ezsoftech.com/akram/prophetprophecies.asp, which shows the nineteenth-century milieu of religious disputations in India. It cites and translates from the introduction to a commentary on the Qur'an titled *Anwār al-Qur'ān* by one Maulana Seyyed Rahat Husain Gopalpuri. Gopalpuri apparently read this part as drawn from a "Baran Uttar khand" (Brahmottarakhand?).

29 Gopalpuri glosses the names "Kant Bunjh" and "Sank Rakhiya" mentioned by Mahadev with those of Muhammad's own father and mother, Abdullah and Amina; ibid.

according to this book will reach God. At that time there will not be any path left to reach God except for this".

Mahamat, Mahadev reports, will not simply set aside

> "all the prayers and *sharī'at*s of previous ages, he will impart the teaching of his own *sharī'at* to the people of his time. He will struggle to make the world like his own self and... in the manner that we write the *sankh*, that is era, in our books, in the same way they will have their *sanat* (era) of Mahamat until the end of the Kaljug age in their books".[30]

Just as Mahamat's *sharī'at* will supersede "all the prayers and *sharī'ats* of previous ages", so, 'Abd al-Rahman Chishti implies, will time be measured according to a new calendar that will supersede previous measurements, and nothing will be left outside of it. Not only does Islamic theology provide the overarching frame for 'Abd al-Rahman's narrative, then, it also provides the conclusion to his story of time.

The martyrdom of Husain, the Prophet's grandson, forms the third important part of the narrative, and here we note not only the familiar trope of dissent and insubordination leading to conflict, but also a significant feature of 'Abd al-Rahman Chishti's ideology, namely the high stature of Ali and his scion.[31] The Prophet Muhammad, 'Abd al-Rahman Chishti writes (reporting of course Mahadev's words, mediated through the words of Vashistha), will have a daughter, better than a thousand sons, very beautiful, peerless, and extremely devoted to the worship of God; she will never lie and will be free from all minor and major sins. Through the intercession of her father, she will be close to God, who will bestow upon her two auspicious sons. The sons will both be men of gnosis, brave, courageous, generous, and matchless in all good works. God will make nobody as perfect as them, either physically or spiritually. These sons of hers will be the Prophet's successors. Here, too, 'Abd al-Rahman Chishti adds his own voice to the narrative by citing a *hadis*, while giving impression that this also comes from the mouth of Mahadev.[32] He then continues by saying that the descendants of the

30 *Mir'āt al-makhlūqāt*, ff. 244a, 244b.

31 I have discussed this feature in my essay 'The Debate Within: A Sufi Critique of Religious Law, *Tasawwuf* and Politics in Mughal India', in *Religious Cultures in Early Modern India: New Perspectives*, ed. by Rosalind O'Hanlon and David Washbrook (London: Routledge, 2011), pp. 8-39.

32 The *hadis* is "*inallāha ja'la ẕuriyata kulli nabfī sulbayhi wa ja'ala ẕuriyatī fī sulbi 'alī ibn abī ṭālib*'" (God placed the descendants of every prophet in his backbones/loins, but He placed my descendants in the loins of 'Ali ibn Abi Talib). The *hadis* is reported in

Prophet's grandsons will be many, and through them Islam will grow day by day. The Prophet will love his grandsons, and all of their deeds will be in keeping with the Divine Will. They will always endeavour to perform God's duty and will attend to the plight of the poor and seek to ameliorate it. After the death of the Prophet, some unlawfully born miscreants (*harāmzādas*) will kill them unjustly, and thus the entire earth will be left without a leader. Their killers will be renegades (*malechh, murtad*), dishonoured and rejected both in faith (*din*) and worldly matters (*dunya*). They will have little devotion to the Prophet in their hearts though they will outwardly claim so. Gradually, many people will join them and will act in opposition to the shining path the Prophet and his descendents had shown.[33] Here 'Abd al-Rahman Chishti is clearly stating his own position regarding the martyrdom of Husain and his killers, i.e. the Umayyid Caliph Yazid, his commander Ibn Ziyad, and their army, a position to some extent in polemical dialogue with his own community. The polemical overtones become louder as he nears the end of the story and asserts—through Mahadev—the triumph of his faith *vis-à-vis* that of Hindus and dissenting Muslims alike:

> "Towards the end of Kaljug the strength of the miscreants will increase, with the entire world facing turbulence (*fasād*). O Parvati, at that time God will send a perfect man (*mard-i kāmil*) to support the faith of Mahamat. He will bring the entire inhabited part of earth under his control and will put the hypocrites (*munāfiq*) to shame. Then all will tread on the right path, the shining path that Mahamat and his descendents will have bequeathed. The [true] faith will again be triumphant from east to west, and there will no one left who opposes it. There will be no Hindu or hypocrite to be seen. Mahamat's faith will everywhere triumph in perfect form in the last phase of Kaljug. All people will act upon the *sharī'at* of Mahamat that the incomparable God (*bīchūn*) had laid down in *Atharban Bed*, that is, the fourth book".[34]

---

several collections, *manaqib*, *tazkira*, and history books. See Shams al-din Muhammad ibn Abd al-Rahman al-Skhawi, *Al-ajwibat al-murdīyya*, ed. by Muhammad Ishaq Muhammad Ibrahim (Riyad: Dar al-Raya fi al-Nashr wal-Tauzi', 1418AH/1997), Vol. 2, pp. 424-25; 'Ala al-din 'Ali al-Muttaqi, *Kanz al-'ummāl fī sunan al-aqwāl wa al-af'āl*, ed. by Shaikh Bakri Hayyani and Shaikh Safwat al-Saqa (Beirut: al-Mua'ssasat al-Risala, 1405AH/1985), Vol. 11, p. 600. Chishti mentions this *hadis* as copied from *Mishkāt* (*kamā fī al-Mishkāt*). I could not locate it in *Miṣhkāt al-masābīḥ* in these very words, but he may have referred to *Mishkāt al-anwār*.

33 *Mir'āt al-makhlūqāt*, f. 245.

34 Ibid., f. 246a.

'Abd al-Rahman suggests here—again through Mahadev—that this future "perfect man" will convert the whole world to Islam. Yet—perhaps in accordance with the general decay of Kaljug?—even this happy outcome will not last for long. Mahadev adds that since the rule is that everything that rises will also decline, the power of that perfect man will also eventually wear off after his death. The world will once again acquire a different hue; chaos and disturbance will prevail all around. People will start living like animals, without discriminating between mothers and sisters. Fearing its total destruction through the excessive sin of the people, the earth will then appeal to God for deliverance. What follows is an impressive combination of the idea of cosmic conflagration (*pralaya*) under the final avatar of Kalki, with the Islamic end of the world (*qiyamat*), and of cosmic regeneration with a renewal of Islamic creation and a second (and final) Day of Judgement, all expressed through Mahadev's prophecy:

> "O Parvati, God will accept the earth's prayer and will subsequently appear in Sambhal in the house of a Brahmin, in the form of the powerful (*qahhār*) Kalki. The sky and the earth will be shaken, a forceful storm will blow, and the Day of Judgment (*qiyāmat*) will descend upon the people of the earth. Everything will be annihilated, darkness will prevail over the world, and the world will remain in the same state of ruination and desolation for some time. At that moment God will recreate Adam along with all his descendents. He will then address Mahamat's daughter and ask her to appeal for justice on behalf of her sons. God will command: 'Go there to Heaven to meet your sons'. God will again command her to request anything she wants. Mahamat's daughter will then raise her hand and say: 'O God, be kind and deliver those who recited the word (*kalima*) of Mahamat'. In kindness God will then say: 'I have forgiven the community of Muslims.' Mahamat's daughter will then lie in prostration together with her sons and will then take the entire community of Muslims with her to Sarg, i.e Bihisht. Their time (*daura*) will thus end. Kaljug will be over". These are the words (*kalimāt*) that Mahadev communicated to Parvati. God knows best what is right.[35]

Here 'Abd al-Rahman Chishti either borrowed literally from a late medieval Vaishnava text, the *Kalki-purāṇa*, a continuation of the *Bhāgavata-purāṇa* that deals with future events and describes the deeds of Vishnu that will take place at the end of the Kaliyuga, or from stories

35 Ibid.

about Kalki that circulated orally.[36] He apparently also conflates other parts of the *Kalki-purāṇa* that mention the creation of Adharma, the degradation of the people and God and the earth approaching Brahma together to get redress, but in 'Abd al-Rahman Chishti's story the coming of Kalki is not in order to free the earth from the influence of the Kali age and establish *varnashrama dharma*, a perfect version of which to him was obviously in the teachings of Muhammad. What is notable is that 'Abd al-Rahman Chishti once again integrates his own Islamic voice into the story—for instance here he states that the human time that began with the birth of Adam is not cyclical but linear and will terminate with *qiyamat*, when all people finally are given the reward and punishment for their deeds. And while 'Abd al-Rahman disputes and refutes the notion of cyclical time, he also takes issue with his own community when he condemns the killing of Husain as the gravest sin committed in Kaljug. Thus, among the first things that God will do on the Day of Judgment is to award justice to Fatima, who is portrayed as the most compassionate intercessor for Muslims. Here 'Abd al-Rahman also introduces a directly polemical note: "in sum the speech (*kalām*) of Mahadev clearly repudiates [the idea of] the transmigration of human soul (*tanāsukh*) which implies continuity of time, whereas time eventually has an end".[37]

As I note in a longer version of this essay, it is on the subject of transmigration that 'Abd al-Rahman Chishti displays most explicitly and impressively his knowledge of Sanskrit texts and Indian philosophy.[38] For the purpose of this book, it is worth noting how he employs the narrative structure of the Puranic tale to further a philosophical-theological argument—namely by using Mahadev as spokesman for his own ideas. Not only does 'Abd al-Rahman Chishti present the debate between Hindu philosophers on transmigration, he intervenes in it while demonstrating his knowledge of Vyasa's *Vedanta*:

---

36 cf. R.C. Hazra, *Studies in the Upapurāṇas, Vol. I, Saura and Vaiṣṇava Upapurāṇas* (Calcutta: Sanskrit College, 1958), pp. 303-08, where Kalki is said to be the son of Visnuyasas and Sumati of Sambhalnagarama. For a brief description of Kalki Avatara, see also Abu'l Fazl, *Ā'īn-i Akbarī*, ed. by Saiyid Ahmad Khan (2005), p. 532, trans. by H.S. Jarrett (2008), pp. 318-19.

37 *Mir'āt al-makhlūqāt*, f.245a.

38 See Alam (2012), 185-89. 'Abd al-Rahman quotes Udayanacharya, Vyasa (as author of the *Vedānta sūtra*) and Shankara—though he considerably over-simplifies their views.

> The third *ashlok* is from Jabal Rishi and Biyas, available in the third chapter (*charn*) in the *Bedānt*, which rejects Jamin and Gautam who advocate transmigration and support *avātar*. They say that one earns the returns of both the good and the bad deed in this world itself. It is because of this assumption (*wahm*) that they had adopted the *mazhab* (belief) of transmigration (*tanāsukh*). Jabal and Biyas say that, "You have misunderstood it; the returns of good and bad are *surg* (*swarg*) and *narg* (*narak*), that is heaven and hell. And, as one gets the result of vice and virtue, then what will be the purpose of the souls coming back again into the different bodies in this world? It is sure that the seeds of vice and virtue blossom into flowers in heaven. As they get this return the seeds get terminated, and without seeds nothing can grow".[39]

'Abd al-Rahman then gives his own assessment of Vyasa and Jabal as supreme theologians and saints, while he calls Gautam and Jaimini mere philosophers "who had gone astray (*ba-jānib-i dīgar rafta and*)". They were nonetheless great—"Plato, too, was Gautam's pupil"—he says.[40] 'Abd al-Rahman thereafter concludes *Mir'āt al-makhlūqāt* with a polemical and interesting message. He writes that "the Hindus are Adam's descendants, but they have forgotten their ancestors, the religion of their ancestors, and their own selves, indeed. They are wrong in tracing their genealogy to the community of *jinns*. They do so unknowingly and out of ignorance".[41] This argument, as we shall see, is central to 'Abd al-Rahman's position in the text.

## Geography and the Age of Humankind

We have already noted 'Abd al-Rahman's strategy of beginning with pre-history and coming to a more recent and familiar time. He employs a similar strategy when dealing with geography: while the earth is divided in to quarters (*rub'*) and domains (*iqlim*), and there exists an

39 *Mir'āt al-makhlūqāt*, f. 246a.

40 This remark, while it shows 'Abd al-Rahman's close reading of Indian philosophy and his contacts with the Brahman scholars of his own time, is not so fictitious. There is a fragment, preserving a memory of the claim that Indian philosophers taught Plato, via Socrates, particularly concerning theology. Cf. Joachim Lacrosse, 'Some Remarks about a Meeting between Socrates and an Indian (Aristoxenus 53)', *Archiv fur Geschichte der Philosophie* 89.3 (2007), 247-63. Islamic philosophers also noticed the similarity of Indian and Greek ideas of transmigration, and in some cases sought to show a diffusion of ideas. For example, Suhrawardi in his Philosophy of Illumination places the doctrine of the Pythagoreans and Plato on reincarnation in the mouth of the Buddha (*bodasaf*). See John Walbridge, *The Wisdom of the Mystic East: Suhrawardi and Platonic Orientalism* (Albany: State University of New York Press, 2001), p. 79.

41 *Mir'āt al-makhlūqāt*, f. 249b.

underlying polarity between the inhabited world and the world of forests and mountains, more familiar names also crop up—one of Adam's son comes to settle in Koshal; a future "perfect man" will be born in Sambhal. When he comes to the part of his narrative devoted to the end of the age of the *jinns*, *devatās*, and *rishis* and the coming of the age of humankind, 'Abd al-Rahman moulds the story of the *Mahābhārata* to his own purposes and introduces toponyms like Nimkhar and Qannauj that were familiar to his audiences, a territorialising gesture similar to those of the Dadupanthi sermons analyzed by Monika Horstmann in this volume. At the same time, the narrative of conflict for supremacy between the recalcitrant *jinns* and the advancing sons of Adam (with their new *sharī'at*) reads also as a narrative of Hindu-Muslim competition, with Krishna as the avenger sent by God to punish the *jinns*. This time Bashisht [Vashishta] is the narrator—and a witness to the event that occurred millions of years ago.

After all the creatures at God's command had prostrated before Adam, Bashisth narrates, God proclaimed that He had given the whole inhabited part of the earth to Adam and that the community of the *jinns* would have to move to the forests, mountains, and islands. On hearing this, some *devatās* left for heaven, while Mahadev, accompanied by Parvati, left for Kailash mountain, "where they are still living luxuriously". Most of the sensible *rishis* left the earth and set out for the mountains. But some rulers of that community and others did not vacate the earth at once. As the number of Adam's descendants increased and pushed ahead, these rulers and the people who were gradually being dislodged from the earth decided to resist the advance, and in the scuffle that ensued they actually gained the upper hand. Some of Adam's descendants who were close to God then complained to Him about it. God accepted their entreaty and ordered Narad to go down to earth to tell the *jinns* that the three Vedas that contained their *sharī'at* had been annulled and that their *shlokas* and prayers were no longer of any use. Whereas in their *sharī'at* the cow was worshipped, in the new world it would be slaughtered and eaten.[42] Narad was particularly instructed to warn them of the dire consequences they would have to face if they refused to act upon God's command. Narad, initially hesitant to descend to earth since the country of the *jinns* had turned into a "breeding

42 Besides moving to the mountains, the *jinns* also had the option of giving up their worldly life and going up to Heaven to live in the world of the spirits, *Mir'āt al-makhlūqāt*, f. 248b.

ground of sins", eventually communicated God's message to the leaders of the *jinns*. He remained on earth for twenty years in the attempt to persuade them. The *devatās* who set out for Kailash met Mahadev there and told him about Narad's visit and God's orders. Mahadev is said to have told them: "I live in one branch (*shākh*) of Kailash, there are still two more branches vacant, you should go and settle there"—in other words, Mahadev advised them to retire to the mountains. Those *jinns* then retired to these branches and began to live there, "where from the power of God they have the elixir of life (*āb-i ḥayāt*) at their disposal". This is where the story in Vashistha's words (*sukhan-i Bashist*) ends, and Byas comes in.[43] Among the disastrous consequences of which Narad warned them, the following is of special interest for us, since it bears upon a significant feature of 'Abd al-Rahman's narrative. Narad said:

> "If you disobey the Divine Command out of your arrogance, you will be ruined. It is to your advantage if you leave this land, otherwise God will create in your own community a person named Kishan who will be endowed with His [God's] attributes. He will annihilate you so completely that no trace of your existence will ever be found".[44]

In Vashistha's story it was Mahadev, Lord Shiva, who had predicted the birth of Adam, the beginning of human time and its triumph. 'Abd al-Rahman Chishti now shows Lord Krishna too as the one who fights the demons in order to facilitate the settlement of Adam's descendants in India. Mahadev, Krishna, Adam, Muhammad, and Husain, in 'Abd al-Rahman's narrative, all fought against evil and struggled to establish truth on earth, though they belonged to different sets of time.

The 'Bharata *katha*' and the stories of Krishna from the *Bhāgavata-purāṇa* circulated widely in oral performance and in Sanskrit and vernacular written versions in North India at the time (see Hawley and Orsini in this volume), as well as in Persian translation.[45] 'Abd al-Rahman weaves together in his narrative the details of the battle of the Mahabharata (the Pandavas, Kauravas, Arjuna, and Krishna) and

43 *Mir'āt al-makhlūqāt*, f. 247.

44 Ibid., f. 248b.

45 See Muzaffar Alam and Sanjay Subrahmanyam, *Writing the Mughal World* (New York: Columbia University Press, 2011), pp. 396-428 for some seventeenth- and eighteenth-century works that include these histories; also Truschke (2011).

the exploits of Kansa and Jarasandha and their annihilation at Krishna's hands in order to fashion his own story of the transition to the current period of human history.

The way in which 'Abd al-Rahman manages to weave together all these stories and characters in order to advance his vision is highly dramatic. Once again, it is Bashist and his disciples Sut and Saunak (on whom more below) who, together with Krishna, act as God's instruments in the story and in God's plan of vacating the earth for the descendants of Adam.

The *jinns* who had not left for the mountains assembled at Sut and Saunak's place in Nimkhar and requested their advice with a pledge to follow it, considering their authority "as respectable members of the community", their knowledge of the Vedas and of Divine Will. Sut and Saunak gave them the same advice as Mahadev and instructed them that, since Kaljug would soon descend, they would all have to give up their "transient lives" anyway.[46] Many of the *jinns* agreed, but once again some of the *daits* (*daityas*, demons), like Kans, Saspal (Sisupala), Jarasandh, and others who were big kings, did not heed their advice out of arrogance and haughtiness. Most of these tyrants lived in India (Hindustan), Byas's narrative continues, and for this reason Adam's descendents, who by then were in control of several countries, could not enter the land. After observing the situation, Narad, accompanied by Bashisht, returned to Heaven and reported it to God. It was at this juncture and for the purpose of punishing the recalcitrant *daits* of Hindustan that God created Krishna. Byas sums up Krishna's "well-known story" as follows:

> "[Krishna] was born from the womb of Devaki, the sister of Kans *Dait*. Basudev, an *'unṣurī devatā*, was Kishan's father. This Kans was a cruel king and lived in Mathura. He had a huge army and power, had subjugated all the rajas of Hind, and was a source of a variety of mischief and turbulence. Tired of his tyranny, the people approached the pious people of their own community. They consoled them and assured that Kishan, born from the womb of Devaki, would kill Kans. Some of the astrologers had also forewarned Kans of this. Kans thus got every child born of Devaki killed, as this story is well-known, and he made great plans to destroy Kishan. God however kept Kishan safe, and after some time he destroyed Kans

46 *Mir'āt al-makhlūqāt*, f.248a.

and brought the country under his control. After that Jarasandh, Kans's father- in-law, mobilised another army together with several other rajas and invaded Mathura. Kishan defeated him, too".[47]

'Abd al-Rahman Chishti thus portrays Krishna as the destroyer of all the evil forces that were in power on the eve of the Kaliyuga. Even after his retreat from Mathura to Dwarka following his triumph over Kans, Jarasandha the king of Magadha, Sisupala the king of Cedi and commander-in-chief of Jaransandha's armies, and Vajranabha, another demon king and the famed warrior Chanur, Kishan returned to kill all the other remaining demons.[48] He never failed, because "the all-knowing God, using His absolute power, manifested Himself in the guise (*kiswat*) of Kishan; no one therefore could overpower him".[49] 'Abd al-Rahman thus neatly combines a nod to Krishna's status as the avatar of God, the end of Dwapar and beginning of Kaliyuga, and Krishna's instrumental role as exterminator of all remaining *jinns*, a job he concludes with the Mahabharata war.

The description of the Mahabharata war concludes the narrative part of *Mir'āt al-makhlūqāt*. Yet, as with many of the earlier stories, the ending is never final: here some of the descendants of the Pandavas who had not left for the Himalayas continue to live in Hindustan. And some of the descendants of Cain, who had come to India after the murder of Abel, married the daughters of the *jinns*, "forgot the book of Adam, embraced the religion of the *jinns* and read the *Beds* [Vedas]". Is this mixed parentage and the forgetting of their true descent a possible explanation of why, centuries after the coming of the sons of Adam to Hindustan, the religion of the *jinns* was still practiced in India? As 'Abd al-Rahman writes (and Byas says):

"Thereafter the battle of Mahabharat took place between the Kauravs and Pandavs. They [Kauravas] were a hundred brothers and there were several lakhs of people in their retinue. Kishan subjugated them all in one fell swoop (*ba-yak qalam*). He then advised the Pandavs to perform *jagsmed* [*yajña Aśvamedha*]. Together with their armies they took a round of the whole earth. And wherever [the old] rajas were left, they killed them. When no haughty person was left on this earth, Kishan wanted to depart and go into hiding. At that time he summoned Arjun, Udhav,

47 Ibid., f. 248a.
48 Ibid. For Jarasandha, Sisupala, Chanura, and Vajranabha, see Mani (1998), pp. 177, 349-50, 719-20, and 821.
49 *Mir'āt al-makhlūqāt*, ff. 249b-250a.

and Ankod and told them that 'since Kaljug has arrived, I am going into hiding. You, too, take all the Pandavs and go to the snow-clad mountains. Give up your transient existence since you have no more time left anymore to live on this earth.' He told Udhav to go to Badri Kedar mountain and engage in the worship of God. Ankod was advised to go to Mansarvar [Mansarovar] and stay there. Kishan then went into hiding. He lived in this world for one hundred and eight years. After him the Pandavs climbed the snow-clad hills and sacrified their lives. About one thousand years later, some of the rajas from their [i.e. Pandavas] lineage who had stayed back on earth gained in strength around the time when several of Adam's descendants had settled there. Their power grew day by day. Some descendants of the son who had killed his brother and had run away had become rulers in India, married the daughters of the *jinns*, and built and settled in [the city of] Qanauj, named after their father, Qabil (Cain). Deprived of the book of Adam, they embraced the religion of the *jinns* and read the *Beds*. After some time, as the time of the advent of Mahamat drew close and the succession of lineages of the *jinns* began to be discontinued, they were constrained to adopt the descendants of Adam as their sons and settled them in their place instead. They themselves disappeared and [then] the entire inhabited quarter of the world came in control of Adam's descendants. Whatever God desired became manifest. This is the meaning of what God said, 'Allah does what He wants, and He commands what He intends'".[50]

As we noted above, 'Abd al-Rahman's pointed conclusion to the text is that this is the history that Hindus have forgotten, a history of which he is reminding his audience.

## Books and Oral Transmission

While *Mir'āt al-makhlūqāt* models itself on the dialogic model of the Puranas and retains much of their oral quality of discourse, the authority of books is invoked many times and in multiple ways in the text: from the putative Sanskrit book of which it purports to be a translation (and from which it quotes), to the scriptural quotes and other Arabic, Persian, and Sanskrit authorities that are invoked, to the question of the "hidden fourth Veda" that Mahamat revealed to the world.

---

50 "*yaf'al-ullāhu mā yashā-u*", and "*wa yahkamu ma yurīd*", Qur'an, 14:27 and 5:1; *Mir'āt al-makhlūqāt*, ff. 249-250a. Udhav (Uddhava) was a Yadava, a friend of Krishna who plays an important role in the "songs of the bee" exchange with the Gopis; see Mani (1998), pp. 803-04.

Though, as we have seen, the *Mir'āt al-makhlūqāt* is a deeply creative narrative, 'Abd al-Rahman Chishti invests considerable energy in showing that it is in fact the faithful and authentic translation of a Sanskrit book. He begins the text with the claim that he had read several well-known Indian history books and scriptures, written in antiquity, in search of an account of Adam, the father of humankind. Initially he had failed in his search, but "after a great effort" he had "discovered a book written by Bashist Muni in which the births of Adam and Muhammad along with their descendents were given in detail".[51] 'Abd al-Rahman Chishti calls it *Malfūż-i Bashist*,[52] invoking the well-known sufi genre of the "table-talk" of a master, even though it is written in the style of a Purana, as we have seen, and purportedly borrows from the "*Uttarākhaṇḍa*" (i.e. the last book) of the text in question. The leaders of the Hindu community had deliberately taken the text out of their "books" and kept it secret (*makhfī midāshtand*) because of their prejudices (*ta'aṣṣub*), he alleges.[53] This statement allows 'Abd al-Rahman Chishti both to justify *why* the version he presents of the "Purana of the future" was not known and in circulation, and to buttress his own superior knowledge. The implication being that the "leaders of the Hindus" hid the text because it contained evidence in support of Islam and the beliefs of Muslims. His tone is therefore polemical here, even as he invokes a set of equivalences (on which more below) and a close relationship between the traditions of the two communities:

> Bashist was an accomplished member of the community of *jinns* and had a position of *muni*. Muni in their terminology is used for prophet. Bashist communicated the knowledge to that community, having received it from Mahadev. Mahadev was Abū al-Jinn (father of the *jinns*) and he was the [principal] prophet (*rasūl-i mursal*) of the *jinns*. Tabari and other historians agree to the fact that there were prophets amongst the *jinns* for their guidance and education.[54] The Qur'an says 'and the *jinns*, we

51 *Mir'at al-makhlūqāt*, f. 238a.

52 Ibid. The Sarkhej Ahamadbad ms (f. 1) has *Malfūż*, only the Aligarh MS (f.1a) calls it *Kitāb-i Bashist*. This is probably the reason why Rizvi (1983, Vol. 1, p. 14) identified the text as a translation of the *Yoga-Vasiṣṭha*; see Alam (2012), 153.

53 *Mir'āt al-makhlūqāt*, f. 239a. It is difficult to say what exactly this treatise was. Chishti generally mentions unknown books as sources for his writings elsewhere too. See his *Mir'āt-i Madārī* (British Museum Manuscript, f. 2b), where he mentions *Īmān-i Maḥmūdī*, a biographical account of Shah Madar by one Qazi Kanturi, as his source. See also Amin for *Mir'āt-i Mas'ūdī*.

54 In his history, Tabari (d.922) mentions *jinns* in the context of his discussion of the angels and of Iblis's position in their midst, and also in his discussion of the creation of Adam. See Abu Ja'far Muhammad bin Jarir al-Tabari, *Tārīkh al-rusul wa al-mulūk*,

> had created before, from the fire of a scorching wind'[55] [...] The author of *Rawżat al-ṣafā'* reports from Ibn Abbas [a companion and cousin of the Prophet] that the name of Abū al-Jinn was Soma with the title of Jann and that in the Book of Adam it is written that Jann's name was Tarnus... In sum the author Tabari and *Rawżat al-ṣafā'*[56] have mentioned the four ages (*zamāna*) as four cycles (*daura*) of the stars (*s̲awābit*).[57]

We noted above 'Abd al-Rahman's attempt to bring together Islamic and Indic accounts of the origins and age of the world. What is worth noting here is his swift and skillful move of buttressing his statement about Bashist with unimpeachable Qur'anic, prophetic, commentarial, and historical authorities. Also skillful is the way in which he makes the authorities he quotes serve his argument, even if this involves a careful selection.[58]

---

ed. by Muhammad Abu'l-Fazl Ibrahim (Cairo: Dar al-Ma'arif, 1960), Vol. 1, pp. 81-90. In his commentary on the Qur'an, however, interpreting the verses "O you assembly of *jinns* and humans! Did you not receive messengers from among you, who told you of My Signs, and warned you about the meeting of this day?" (Qur'an, 6:130), Tabari mentions several *hadis* and views of early Muslim scholars to discuss whether there were prophets from among the *jinns* themselves; idem, *Jāmi' al-bayān 'an ta'wīl āy al-Qur'ān*, ed. 'Abdullah bin 'Abd al-Muhsin al-Turki (Riyad: Dar-i Alam al-Kutub, 2003), Vol. 9, pp. 559-62. See also Vol. 14 for his comments on the verse, "I did not create the *jinns* and the humans except to worship Me alone" (Qur'an, 51:56). It is significant that in some commentaries on the Qur'an written in India in the later Mughal period, Hindu deities are identified with some such *jinn* prophets, e.g. Qazi Sana-Allah (d.1810), *Tafsīr-i maẓharī*, Urdu trans. Abd al-Dayim al-Jalali (Delhi: Dar al-Musannifin), Vol. 4, pp. 217-18. For Qazi Sana-Allah (Qadi Thana'-Allah Panipati), see S.A.A. Rizvi, *Shah 'Abd al-Aziz: Partisanism, Sectarian Polemics and Jihad* (Delhi: Munshram Manoharlal, 1982), pp. 558-73.

55 "*wa'l jānna khalaqnā-hu min qablu min nār is-sumūm*". This verse follows the verse, "We created man from sounding clay, from mud molded into shape"; Qur'an, 15:26 and 27.

56 Here the text has signs of deletion following the word "Tabari" and "*awurda*" (has mentioned) and has to be read with some care. Since 'Abd al-Rahman mentioned Tabari and *Rawżat al-ṣafā'* earlier in the text, when he summed up here the scribe first wrote both and then deleted Tabari. He deleted the verb "*awurda*", too, which is an obvious error, for the verb for this sentence ('*qarār dāda and*') comes later.

57 *Mir'āt al-makhlūqāt*, f. 239b; for cycles of time, Mir Khvand (1959), pp. 36-38. Mahadev in the Hindu tradition is the God Siva, and Bashist (Vasistha) is a noted *rishi* whose sayings form the well-known text, *Yoga-Vasiṣṭha*; see Mani (1998), pp. 723-31 and 834-37.

58 E.g. we know that the discussion of time (*zaman*) in Tabari's history is totally different, see *Tārīkh al-rusul wa al-mulūk*, Vol. 1, pp. 9-80. But Mir Khvand in the *Rawżat al-ṣafā'* does mention cycles (*dauras*) of time as well as cycles of "recompense", a notion echoed in 'Abd al-Rahman's description of the *jinns'* time as a sequence moving from their glory to their dishonour and decline; see Mir Khvand (1959), pp. 20-21; see also *The Rauzat-us-Safa, or, Garden of Purity: Containing the Histories of Prophets, Kings, and Khalifs*, trans. by E. Rehatsek, ed. by F.F. Arbuthnot (reprint Delhi: Idarah-i Adabiyat-i Delli: 1982), Vol. 1, pp. 36-38.

Another striking instance of 'Abd al-Rahman's negotiation between Sanskrit "sources" and Persian text, and between orality and writing, regards the matter of authentic transmission, and here again he creatively combines Puranic and Islamic traditions. At one point 'Abd al-Rahman Chishti breaks his narrative and digresses into a clarification as to how the conversation between Mahadev and Parvati came down to this world through Bashist Muni, and why he, 'Abd al-Rahman, has translated it from Sanskrit, "the language of the gods", into Persian. He writes that when Mahadev started telling the story,

> Bashist Muni, who was busy with prayers at the base of the Kailash mountain, overheard it. Since he had immense devotion for Mahadev he wrote (*dar qalam āwurd*) all the details. From Bashist Sut and Saunak, who were great scholars in Nimkhar, report these details (*dar qaum-i khwud mujtahid-i kāmil būdand, wa 'ābid wa zāhid, ānha az Bashist Mun naql mīkunand*),[59] the *ashloks* of which are translated here. Initially, I had intended to communicate and copy these *ashloks* verbatim, but since not everybody can understand them, I have given here only one of the [original] *ashloks* as evidence. The rest are in translation so that everybody understands them without any difficulty (*bītakalluf*).[60]

Several moves are in evidence in this statement about the chain of transmission: first we have strong oral transmission (supported by devotion) and transcription, then faithful written transmission from Bashist to Sut and Saunak, in other words through an authoritative chain of transmitters, to 'Abd al-Rahman, who *could have copied* the text

---

59 Sut (Suta) was the disciple of Vyasa who learnt from him the Puranas and the *Mahābhārata* and recounted them to Saunaka and the other *rishis* assembled at Naimisharanya (Nimsar in the modern district of Sultanpur, Uttar Pradesh). Saunaka was the one who organised the assembly; Mani (1998), pp. 517 and 774. Abu'l Fazl writes Nimasar as Nimakhar and describes it as a "shrine of great resort", with numerous temples, a tank called *Brahmawaratkund*, and the springhead of a stream about which the Brahmans say that "its sand shapes itself into the form of *Mahadeo* and quickly disappears again, and of whatever is thrown in, as rice and the like, no trace remains"; Abu'l Fazl, *Ā'īn-i Akbarī* (2005), p. 327, trans. (2008), p. 183.

60 *Mir'āt al-makhlūqāt*, f.240b. Chishti cites here a *shloka*: *'ado manya pra'it bodha ait mahesha nilakanthi hast maha kotaha tarkand hadiya'*, which appears to contain Sanskrit words but is totally unintelligible. I have approached several Sanskrit specialists to make sense of this *shloka*, but to no avail. The *shloka* may have been distorted because of the Persian copyists' ignorance of the language; Chishti instead seems to know Sanskrit. We know that he translated the *Bhāgavadgītā* as *Mir'āt al-ḥaqā'iq*; see Roderic Vassie, 'Persian Interpretations of the Bhagvadgita in the Mughal Period, with Special Reference to the Version of Abd al-Rahman Chishti' (PhD dissertation, School of Oriental and African Studies, University of London, 1988). We have already seen his unusual familiarity with Sanskrit philosophical texts.

in Sanskrit but chose to translate it into Persian for the sake of general understanding (among new audiences, is the implication). Yet a Sanskrit *shloka* is copied as proof both of 'Abd al-Rahman's reliable knowledge and of the existence of the original Sanskrit text. A further ring to this chain is added in another digression towards the end of the narrative, when Sut and Saunka question Bashisht on the precision of Mahadev's prophecy about Adam and his world. Bashisht berates their lack of faith in the prophecy, which they could test empirically since the events occurred before their own eyes. But Mahadev's words were not just his but were given to him—Qur'an-like—from above:

> Sut and Saunak asked Bashist, "You knew what Mahadev said about the world of Adam; later his birth and the birth of his descendants also took place in your presence. Was all that happened later the same way as Mahadev had forecast or was there any discrepancy?" Bashist replied, "You and I have lived all through this world, and still you have not gained full knowledge (*'irfān-i kāmil*). They all were born in our presence (*ḥużūr-i mā wa shumā*). What difference (*tafāwut*) did you see that you dared ask this question and doubt the truth of what Mahadev said?"[61]

Bashisht then adds:

> "O my dear ones, what Mahadev said was not from himself; he reported what was written there in the Surg (*Swarg*), i.e. heavens (*aflāk*). Where will the discrepancy then be?"[62]

Finally, 'Abd al-Rahman displays his superior knowledge of hidden mysteries and secret texts in the intriguing detail of the "fourth Bed", the Veda that the Prophet Muhammad's father knew but refused to write down (see above). Once again, the explanation is provided through a digression. Sut and Saunak question Bashist once more about the truth and meaning of his story. 'Abd al-Rahman Chishti writes:

> Sut and Saunak asked Bashist why he [Kant Bunjh], who was going to be like the ocean in gnosis, refused to proceed beyond *alif lām* in the fourth *Bed*. Bashist replied: "Brahma created the four *Beds* [for us in the four different ages], which were all taught to some of the *'unṣurī devatās* who were really able and who were advised to work according to the *Siyām* in Satjug, *Rig* in Traitya, and *Jajar* in Dwapar. The Almighty

61 *Mir'āt al-makhlūqāt*, f. 246.

62 Ibid., f.246b. Surg (*Swarg*), i.e. heavens (*aflāk*) here probably refers to the *lauḥ-i maḥfūẓ*, which according to Muslim beliefs are the tablets preserved in Heaven on which the transactions of mankind were written by God from eternity.

> would then created people from the globe (*kura*) of the earth who would practise according to the *Atharban Bed*. There are four *charans* (sections) in the *Atharban Bed*. Three of these will be read by Adam and his other descendents. The fourth one, which will combine in itself the purpose and substance (*maqṣūd*) of all the *Beds*, will be practiced by none other but Mahamat. If anyone will read the fourth *charan* without the permission of Mahamat he will not get any benefit. Kant Bunjh will not read this fourth *charan* of *Atharban Bed* so that it remains intact as held in trust (*amānat*)". Up to this point was the speech of Bashist.

'Abd al-Rahman Chishti's language of universalism here assumes added density. The prophets before Adam, even though the Divine Truth was revealed to them, were *jinns*, genealogically different from Adam and the other prophets of humankind. But the Books of both the Hindu and Muslim worlds, Bashistha affirms through 'Abd al-Rahman Chishti's words, share the same lineage—they are what the Hindus of his time identified as the Vedas. The first three of them were guides for the eras of the *jinns*, whereas the last one found expression for humankind in the four major Divine Books—the Zabur (Psalms), Torah, Injil (Gospel), and Qur'an—at different stages of their history. In one stroke, 'Abd al-Rahman manages to assimilate the Qur'an into the Indic history of revelation (the Vedas), while at the same time he suggests that it is in fact the appropriate Book for the present age.

## Conclusions

'Abd al-Rahman Chishti lived in a milieu that confronted him with conflicting cosmologies and theological principles. He wanted to carefully craft something that sounded plausible, did not offend anyone, and allowed him to argue and maneuver his position while maintaining his inherited identity and traditions in the complex religious and political space of Mughal India. There is no doubt that the narrative of *Mir'āt al-makhlūqāt* is a remarkable feat that achieves several striking effects. These effects are made possible through a set of equivalences, by slightly twisting familiar narratives and extending familiar tropes, and by having familiar characters like Mahadev and Bashisht saying some unfamiliar/unusual things. Through Mahadev and Bashisht, 'Abd al-Rahman manages to align Hindu and Islamic (including sufi) calculations of the age of the world and of the origin of humankind; through the equivalences of *devatās* and *daityas* with *jinns* he manages to give them (including Shiva, Rama, and Krishna) an honourable place, but in an earlier age. The Islamic trope of rebellion and punishment of unruly angels takes a new guise with the rebellion of Hanuman (Hanwant) and Krishna's punishment of the recalcitrant *devatās*. Brahma creates Adam but is subordinated to *Qadir-i Mutlaq* (Absolute God); God manifests Himself in Krishna, comes down to earth to fight the evil, but Krishna is not God himself. Historical narrative combines with geography in the history of the coming of Adam's children (more specifically Cain's children) to India and their intermarriage with local women, the descendants of the last *jinns*. Having Mahadev prophesy the coming of Adam, of the Prophet Muhammad, and the Qur'an is a masterstroke. It is a strategy both of accommodation (between *yugas* and Islamic time, a *sharī'at* for every age) and of one-upmanship, in which 'Abd al-Rahman repeatedly tells his audiences, Hindus and Muslims alike, that he knows more than the Hindus who have forgotten the history of the defeat of their *jinn* ancestors and of their common origin as children of Adam, and more than the "leaders of the Hindus" who chose to keep secret the inconvenient truth of the fulfillment of the prophecy through Muhammad and the Qur'an.

'Abd al-Rahman used the religious concepts of the others in such a way that the key concept of his beliefs remained unimpaired. Central and startling in *Mir'āt al-makhlūqāt* is the idea that both Hinduism and Islam are many-stranded and internally plural, and thus there can be significant similarities between individual strands of Islam and Hinduism. This breaks down the abstract and comprehensive difference between the two religions that completely obstructs any mutual curiosity or accommodation. We cannot however ignore the polemic in his position, whatever its politics. He endeavours to have his tradition emerge paramount.

'Abd al-Rahman Chishti's reflection on time was esoteric, and included questions about the age of the world, human genesis, and so on. He found that the scales of Hindu time are much vaster than the scales in "orthodox" Islamic thought. He used this discrepancy not simply to say that Hindus believe in fanciful and false things but subsumed one time scale within the other; and what is even more remarkable is that the subsumption is of Islamic time within the larger cycles of Hindu cosmogony. Islam had encompassed several aspects of Judaism and Christianity—admitting, for instance, the prophetic status of Moses and Jesus. Early Islamic scholars had discussed the significance of such integration. But it was much easier to do, as the Qur'an is full of Biblical prophets and Muhammad proclaimed himself to be their successor. To describe the Indic gods and sages as prophets was a far more difficult task. None of them is mentioned anywhere in either the Qur'an, the *hadis* or for that matter in any early Islamic text of the "classical" Islamic period. But in a sense what 'Abd al-Rahman Chishti does here with reference to his discourse on time is the opposite. He subsumes Islamic time into Hindu time, even as he makes the latter the time of the *jinns*. I assume that he does so to explain the discrepancy in Islamic terms and thus to enhance his position's acceptability within his own community. I might add that 'Abd al-Rahman Chishti makes a distinction between the core and the secondary beliefs of his religion. His intellectual move relates to secondary ideas. He does however modify the hard separation and necessary conflict between the doctrines of the two religions and employs a fundamentally dialogic mode. Is there an implicit piece of advice to Muslim theologians, the Naqshbandi shaikhs who were so close to the royal family, and a significant section of the nobility that in order to live and function in this world they should take seriously and interact with the serious central ideas of the other religion, and not live in ignorance of it? The question could be addressed with some amount of certainty only if we were sure about 'Abd al-Rahman Chishti's audience. If we imagine that, as a story, the *Mir'āt al-makhlūqāt* circulated both orally (in Hindavi) and in written form (in Persian), we can envisage at least three, if not four audiences: first, local Muslims (both sufis and non-sufis), to whom he says that accepting these other worlds and truths is not forbidden or *haram*; second, local Hindus, before whom he parades his knowledge of *their* scriptures and stories, in fact his superior knowledge, as we have seen; and third, Mughal authorities, before whom Chishtis like him showed that they had a lot to offer, including embodied authority as well as textual knowledge. To these one could also add Persian-educated Hindus, who read these and other texts that attempted to combine the Indic and Islamic worlds.

# 4. Hearing *Mo'jizat* in South Asian Shi'ism

*Amy Bard*

## Introduction

Contemporary Urdu miracle stories, *mo'jizāt* [pl.], related in intimate settings in Shi'i Muslim households, hold a unique allure among devout families. The stories' templates draw on a North Indian/Pakistani folkloric reservoir of scenes, characters, and social categories, while their oral realisations reflect explicitly Shi'i devotional themes. Miracles and miracle *tellings* are both termed *mo'jizat* and both have multivalent, multi-level significance.

My interest is in the social life of miracles as evidenced in 1) formal *mo'jizat kahanis* (miracle stories), which are ritual or *niyaz* narratives, and 2) informal/casual *mo'jizat*. These represent two locally recognised distinctions, although individuals may apply the term story (*kahani*) in slightly variable ways. Their mostly domestic recountings reveal that genres of miracles do not necessarily derive from normative Islamic distinctions between *mo'jizat*, miracles of the Prophet, and *karamat*, miracles performed by saints.[1] Rather, distinct purposes, modes of mediating authority, and narrative formats inhere in formal vs. informal/casual *mo'jizat*. The two types of narrative have commonalities, such as layers of framing utterances and repeated similar incidents, yet are associated with different performance contexts.

1 John T. Platts, *A Dictionary of Urdū, Classical Hindī, and English* (New Delhi: Munshiram Manoharlal, 1997 [1884]), p. 1048; Joyce Flueckiger, *In Amma's Healing Room: Gender and Vernacular Islam in South India* (Bloomington: Indiana University Press, 2006), p. 168.

 http://dx.doi.org/10.11647/OBP.0062.04

The *mo'jizat* complement, rather than duplicate, the directive lessons of orators in more public mourning assemblies (*majalis* [pl.]) and the emotive language of honour and suffering in Shi'i poetry about the tragedy of Imam Husain at Karbala (680 CE). Miraculous stories (henceforth *kahanis*) echo Karbala motifs, but do not directly reference Husain's martyrdom. The informal ones often feature the mysterious spiritual guides and revelatory dream states that are also standard in more formal *niyaz* narratives, but bring Shi'i sacred geography "home", with localised miracles and evidential discourse from Pakistani or Indian narrators. How do "casual" miracle tales fit into more textually-based expressive traditions in South Asian Shi'ism? Who transmits "ritual" and "casual" *mo'jizat*? How do the audience and the storytelling context affect the testament, revelation, or comfort that the idea of a "miracle" proffers?

The sheer plentitude of miracle stories and testimonies in Shi'i social circles is noteworthy, particularly since the reasonably comprehensive scholarly literature on contemporary South Asian Shi'ism privileges lament genres, hagiography in text and ritual, and mimesis of Karbala through relics such as tomb replicas, cradles, and battle standards.[2] The stories' ubiquitous popularity was underlined for me as I researched Shi'i liturgical poetry between 1996 and 2010: although I never intended to elicit miracle stories, my fieldwork recordings contain dozens of "casual" *mo'jizat*. Friends and consultants were wont to cite miraculous occurrences—always witnessed by a relative or acquaintance, if not by themselves—in any discussion of Shi'i literature or popular devotions.

2 Studies of South Asian Shi'ism to date have helpfully compared the intercession of the *ma'sumin* (the 14 "impeccables", i.e. the Prophet, Fatima, and the twelve *imams*) with the attributes of saints in other religions; Mahmoud Ayoub, *Redemptive Suffering in Islam* (New York: Mouton, 1978); David Pinault, *The Shiites: Ritual and Popular Piety in the Muslim Communit* (New York: St. Martin's Press, 1992). Recent scholarship has also documented Shi'i rites as an arena where local and transnational artistic forms are mediated (Wolf, this volume), and theorised Shi'i hagiography in its imitable and transcendent aspects; see Karen G. Ruffle, *Gender, Sainthood, and Everyday Practice in South Asian Shi'ism* (Chapel Hill: University of North Carolina Press, 2011). This and other literature has emphasised ritual processes, often those whereby today's mourners are transported to the site of Karbala or into a "subjunctive mode" where they put themselves to a test: what would they have done had they been at Karbala? See e.g. Vernon Schubel, *Religious Performance in Contemporary Islam: Shi'i Devotional Rituals in South Asia* (Columbia: University of South Carolina Press, 1993). Akbar Hyder, following the key narrative of Husain beyond the Shi'i community, has illuminated the versatility and explanatory power of the "Karbala trope" in Urdu's twentieth-century progressive literature, sufi *qawwali* texts, and the oeuvre of the great Urdu poet Iqbal; Akbar S. Hyder, *Reliving Karbala: Martyrdom in South Asian Memory* (New York: Oxford University Press, 2006).

In family settings, the tellings frequently became exchanges among household members, who left any queries of mine by the wayside as they quibbled over sequence or details. The story I initially present exemplifies such a milieu. After this taste of an informal miracle anecdote, I briefly situate *mo'jizat vis-à-vis* the Karbala narrative and related expressive traditions, survey formal (*niyaz*) narratives, and then identify some of the most resonant elements in additional "informal" tellings. I conclude with observations about the curiously anonymous power of storytellers, rounding out an overall focus on *listening* to miracles, and show how personal experience of locally-grounded, virtuous suffering lies at the heart of one family's reverence for miracle tales. This approach heavily mines traditions in this one Pakistani family; nonetheless, by comparing performance contexts, formats, and rhetoric, I demonstrate, first, how different miracle genres provide for broad-based, "normative" as well as local Shi'i religious identification, and, second, how miracles can communicate intimacy as well as, or instead of, awe and humility.

## A Casual Recollection of the Miraculous

It is May 1997. In a cramped home in Lahore, Pakistan, Baqir Ahmad Shamsi, Nana-jan (maternal grandfather) to his family, recounts a *mo'jiza* [sing.] at the behest of his grandchildren. It happens to be Muharram, the high ritual season for Shi'ahs, but it is early—day three—in the main ten-day sequence of mourning assemblies and processions. Household life still moves at a relatively relaxed pace, but anticipates the emotional charge that will heighten after the fifth of Muharram. Nana, who lives in turns with his various offspring around Lahore, has a penchant for staying here, in the Shi'i part of Rang Mahal in the old city, during Muharram's mourning observances. The accommodation is not luxurious—he has to negotiate his way through the inner lanes and up a set of narrow stairs—but for him, the two-room flat is warm and welcoming. It also safely houses his widowed daughter and three grandchildren above a courtyard, away from prying eyes.

Muharram or not, whenever Nana visits this decrepit building, the younger generation pump him for his recollections of *mo'jizat*. He is the "go-to" source for stories in general, sometimes for ritual *kahanis*, as well as for informal reports of *mo'jizat*, such as today's.[3] Rahat, Nana's daughter,

3 Although no stigma attaches to *kahani* as the usual label for the printed and oral *niyaz*

despite the many personal misfortunes she has suffered, is a jolly, rotund, middle-aged lady. Her own demure daughters, Sadaf and Najaf, are eighteen and thirteen years old respectively.

**Nana:** I remember a woman in Pindi who had cancer, mouth cancer. These people were certainly Shi'ahs. They were very devout (*Voh mānte the bahut zyāda*). Her desperate family took her to an old *imambargah* [a Shi'i worship hall]. Nursing her in her terminally ill state was beyond them. They bound her to an *'alam* [decorated battle standard] with *rassi* [ropes] and *zanjir* [chains]. "Show us a miracle", they prayed: "Either cure her or let her go. We can't stand to watch this suffering anymore". And they left her.

Night fell. The place had very, very, very high walls. A rider jumped over the wall, the horse's hooves sank deeply in the dirt because it landed with such impact.

**Rahat:** The rider loosed her bonds.

**Sadaf:** (exclaiming) NO! the *rassi*s ripped by themselves.

**Nana:** The rider said, "now you're OK".

**Sadaf:** NO! There was *no* conversation... and the bonds fell apart themselves.

**Nana:** They came and found her in the morning. She had been cured... and the marks of the horse's hooves were there. She explained it to them: that a rider on horseback had come, jumped the wall, the bonds fell away. That spot is still there. They put a plate of glass above the spot,... the hoofprint.

Then, on the strength of that incident (*us kī dekhā-dekhī*) they tied a paralyzed man there.

The same thing happened to him, a miracle. He was also cured. People go there.

---

narratives, the weighty evidential discourse around "casual" *mo'jizat* emphasises the "truth value" of the narratives, and in so doing sometimes displaces the term *kahani*/story. While the history of Hindi/Urdu writing suggests that *kahanis* are not invariably make-believe, recent controversies about memoir-like or biographical/autobiographical narratives that are "wrongly" published or marketed as "*kahanis*" reveal, like the *mo'jizat* tellings, an anxiety about the border between "real-life" events that can be substantiated and fictional *kahanis*; Amy Bard, 'Everyday Life in a Lucknow Locality: Histories, Stories, and Lies', paper delivered at South Asian Religion Symposium in Honor of Jack Hawley, University of California-Santa Barbara, 17 November 2011. In parallel, a number of (mostly less formally-educated) Shi'i informants over the years have insisted that the epic *marsiya* genre detailing Imam Husain's martyrdom was *not* "poetry" (*sha'iri*) but "truth" (*haqiqat*); idem, 'Desolate Victory: Shi'i Women and the Marsiyah Texts of Lucknow' (PhD dissertation, Columbia University, 2002).

**Sadaf:** People SAW it, too! He also explained what happened, exactly: that a rider on horseback had come, jumped the wall, the bonds fell away.

**Rahat:** We don't remember the name of the *imambargah*, but my younger sister Tahsin heard about the incident from someone who had been there. She [Tahsin] said to me, "You also go there, *baji*, you make *ziyarat*, you pray", but then... in the meantime, the girls' Abbu [their father, Rahat's husband] died.

**Sadaf:** The next day!

**Rahat:** Yes, she said to me, "you go there also". But then I couldn't. Because her [Sadaf's] Abbu used to take me everyplace.

The motifs that link this Pakistani account with the Karbala narrative (which we will review shortly) are potent: an *'alam* that represents the fighting ferocity and steadfastness of the Karbala martyrs; a horse and rider recalling Husain and his magnificent horse Zuljinah; a hoofprint like the prints and horseshoes revered as relics in many Shi'i shrines; and finally, the bonds and chains that recall the fate of the widowed women captives of Karbala, and how they rose above that fate.[4]

Shi'ahs associate the *'alam* with Husain's brother 'Abbas, his army's standard-bearer, in particular. They make offerings during Muharram and on occasions of need to household *'alams*, hoping that Abbas, with his dual reputation for fierce power and healing, will intervene on behalf of the ailing. This family's interaction around the *'alam* story generates excitement and an aftermath of resigned regret, a sense that the missed opportunity to make a pilgrimage (*ziyarat*) to the *'alam* and the hoofprint clouds the death of the girls' father.

Here, as with other "casual" *mo'jizat*, the younger generation perform the essential role of "*huñ kār*". That is, they encourage the unfurling story with murmurings of assent and appreciation.[5] They also go further, prompting their feeble grandfather, sometimes filling in gaps, even disputing details, when his voice or his memory fails. Ritual *niyaz kahanis* provide little

4 Reverence for "sacred places where animals carrying early Islamic figures passed or are believed to have left footprints in the ground or rock" span much of the Islamic world. See, for example, Jo-Ann Gross, 'Shrines of the Pamirs', in *Tajikistan and the High Pamirs*, ed. by Robert Middleton and Huw Thomas (Hong Kong: Airphoto International, 2012), p. 635.

5 See Ann Gold, *A Carnival of Parting: The Tales of King Bharthari and King Gopi Chand As Sung and Told by Madhu Natisar Nath of Ghatiyali* (Berkeley: University of California Press, 1992).

room for such negotiating of authenticity. Those recited ritual stories, with their formal trappings—namely food offerings (*niyaz*) in the name of the Prophet's family and published pamphlet texts—have received something of their due in scholarly literature as an important anchor for Shi'i women's religiosity. Their relationship to casual *mo'jizat*, though, including, for example, their standardisation relative to accounts such as Nana-jan's, has received little attention.

The two entrenched forms of *mo'jizat* point up how Shi'i communities in India, Pakistan, and Bangladesh today manifest their devoted remembrance of Karbala and the *ahl-e bait* (family of the Prophet), not only in a wide array of highly choreographed Muharram mourning rites, but in more versatile, personal recollections. In the frequent instances where Sunni Muslims and Hindus join in the more public dimensions of Shi'i Muharram commemorations (reciting laments, for example, or carrying tomb replicas in procession), the manifold layers of symbolism that Shi'as access, their magnified sense of intimacy with *imams* and martyrs, and their attunement to miracles, may mark their special connection to Karbala even as they welcome broader participation. Frank Korom has carefully analyzed such layers of reception as far afield as the Caribbean in his work on the polyphonic Muharram (*Hosay*) commemorations of Trinidad, which have roots in Iran and India.[6]

## At the Heart of all Tales

The kernel narrative of the murder of Imam Husain, grandson of the Prophet, on the plains of Karbala in 680 CE is the touchstone for Shi'ism's defining rites as well as popular miracle tales. A skirmish in the desert between Husain's little band of supporters and the forces of the Muslim Caliph of the day, the Ummayad Yazid, is historically attested, but the lingering, poignant details of each martyr's suffering are accretions that have developed, ramified, and varied over the centuries and with the geographical spread of Shi'i devotion. According to both historical sources and Shi'i religious tradition, Imam Husain's entire family suffered bitterly, besieged without food or water, at the hands of Yazid's henchmen because Husain refused to take an oath of fealty to the corrupt Yazid.

6 Frank Korom, *Hosay Trinidad: Muharram Performances in an Indo-Caribbean Diaspora* (Philadelphia: University of Pennsylvania Press, 2002).

The Husain-Yazid conflict, in the Shi'i view, is far more than a battle over temporal power; it is the culmination of a timeless struggle between *Husainiyat*, "Husain-ness", all that is good and virtuous, and *Yazidiyat*, the world's evil counter-force. Its historical dimensions harken back to the early days of Islam when factions of Muslims supported either the first Caliph, Abu Bakr, or the Prophet's son-in-law and cousin, 'Ali, as leader after the Prophet's demise in 13 AH/632 CE. The actual emergence of Shi'i and Sunni sects was a gradual process, during which followers of various descendants of 'Ali and the Prophet's daughter Fatima also branched off from the main group of partisans of 'Ali (Shi'as). Some of these groups (Isma'ilis, Bohras, etc.) maintain distinct identities today, while others have been re-aggregated into majority "Twelver Shi'ism", so called because of its lineage of twelve *imams*.[7] A rudimentary distinction between Shi'as and Sunnis lies in Sunnis' respect for Abu Bakr, Umar, and Uman as the first three Caliphs (Ali attained power as the fourth Caliph only later), and Shi'i belief that 'Ali, the first *imam*, and his descendants through the Prophet's daughter Fatima, are the legitimate and divinely-guided successors to the Prophet. 'Ali, the Shi'as feel, should have been appointed leader of the Muslims after the Prophet's death; he and his blood are seen as having been denied their rightful role by the three Caliphs and their supporters.

After what many Sunnis term the "golden age" of the three Caliphs, Mu'awiya, an erstwhile governor, assumed the Caliphate. 'Ali and his son Hasan were both deposed and murdered. Yazid, reputedly a drunken reprobate, came to power upon his father Mu'awiya's death in 60 AH/680 CE. The political and spiritual conflict between Hasan's brother Husain and Yazid eventually came to a head at desolate Karbala, where Yazid's enormous army ultimately massacred Husain as he travelled to Kufa to meet with supporters. After Husain's enemies beheaded him as he bowed in prayer, the general Ibn Sa'd paraded the women of the *imam*'s household, unveiled, to Damascus. Shi'as have for centuries related the whole Karbala story in minute detail; their renderings encompass both the majesty and the human frailty of Husain as he fought tirelessly in the face of certain defeat, willingly sacrificed his life, and witnessed the painful persecution of every member of his family.

---

7 See Moojan Momen, *An Introduction to Shi'i Islam* (New Haven: Yale University Press, 1985), pp. 45-60; Yann Richard, *Shi'ite Islam*, trans. by Antonia Nevill (Cambridge, MA: Blackwell, 1995), pp. 35-38; Mohammad Ali Amir-Moezzi, *The Divine Guide in Early Shi'ism: The Sources of Esotericism in Islam*, trans. by David Streight (Albany: State University of New York Press, 1994), p. 61.

The dozens of Karbala sub-plots elaborated in prose and poetry during annual commemorations of Muharram fall into several categories of attested "authenticity". Careful historians would omit from their accounts a number of occurrences otherwise almost universally deemed central to the Karbala tragedy, such as Husain's death at the hands of Shimr. The earliest historical accounts attribute the deathblow to another man, but even the most informed of South Asian preachers usually name Shimr as Husain's murderer.[8] The veracity and details of other episodes, such as that of Husain's son Akbar's death, are disputed by a larger number of commentators, including some Shi'i clerics who accept as strictly true only the skeletal outlines of the Karbala story sketched above.[9] A third class of scenarios is fully embraced in popular piety, although many people realise that certain of the incidents are not historically attested; Husain's nephew Qasim's battlefield wedding perhaps stands as the best example.[10] Miracle tales of the twentieth and twenty-first centuries, then, emerge from a fertile historical ground of frame narrative and emotive embellishment. Poetic juxtapositions such as weddings and deaths; deserts blossoming with roses in the *imam*'s blessed presence; noble, sacred figures in shabby guises—all radiate from the core of Karbala. The transcendent power of devotion to Allah and family manifests itself locally at Lahori shrines, the deathbeds of the Lakhnavi devout, and in household rituals throughout the subcontinent.

## The Reliability of Miracles: "Formal" and "Casual" *Mo'jizat*

Narrative is central to popular Shi'ism in India, Pakistan, and Bangladesh, whether in the form of *mo'jizat kahanis*, or the far better-known, highly participatory *majlis* ("assembly") commemorations detailing the martyrdom and virtues of the Shi'i *imams*, especially Imam Husain. Faithful suffering, devoted remembrance of the *imams* and the martyrs of Karbala, and subsequent miraculous rewards in some sense offer "proof" of the *imam*'s supernatural powers. For impoverished families like Rahat's, though, miracle tales yield as much in the way of sustenance in the course of everyday

8 Ayoub (1978), pp. 108, 111, 127; Momen (1985), p. 30.

9 Ayoub (1978), p. 117; Momen (1985), pp. 28-31; see also Saiyid Athar Abbas Rizvi, *Shah Abd Al-Aziz: Puritanism, Sectarian Polemics, and Jihad* (Canberra: Marifat Publishing House, 1982), pp. 43-47.

10 Ruffle (2011).

travails as in the form of supernatural intervention. Sadaf, Rahat's daughter, asserted that in her family and Sayyid community, encounters with revered personages of the Prophet's family—which she labels *mo'jizat*—happen all around, all the time. "They help us, they help us a lot", she said simply. In her family's case, this help often seems to take the form of an affirmation of elect Shi'i identity and/or Sayyid lineage (descent from the Prophet) and status. While Sadaf imbibes *majlis* sermons and energetically compiles notebooks full of dirges—which she recites in movingly clear, mellifluous tones—these choreographed activities don't soothe her family's particular social stresses as readily as loosely scripted miracle testimonies in a domestic context do.

One way that *mo'jizat* fit into a wider framework of expressive traditions is as sub-components of mourning assembly sermons.[11] Preachers often cite, for example, inscriptions of the name 'Ali in the features of especially reverent individuals or in cosmological form in the skies or the moon. Yet in contrast to rhetorically variegated Shi'i sermons, with their self-conscious drama, hectoring, and emotional extravagance, domestic miracle stories consistently privilege accessibility instead of esotericism, listeners rather than individual narrative "specialists", and affective emphasis on intimacy and encounter with the sacred rather than wonder and distance from it. Casual and formal/ritual miracle tales, furthermore, potentially align with more generally manifested intersubjective categories of interiority and exteriority. Here I am thinking of the private/public dyads of *akam* and *puram* in Tamil poetry, *batin* and *zahir* in sufi and Shi'i discourse, and so on. It would be a stretch to posit very strong parallels between these "classical" conceptual frameworks and *mo'jizat kahanis* in their various settings, but there are some compelling resonances, as we shall see.

Formal miracle narratives, often the centrepieces of rituals of petition, have an impact beyond ritual spaces in part through the tangible blessings—medical cures or financial assistance—that they procure. They also influence other tale-telling, however. Their morphology and that of the less fixed casual miracle *kahanis* or *vaqe'as* (incident, anecdotes) often appear mutually constitutive. For example, in a miracle recounted below by Nana-jan, a person known to Nana emerges from a visionary experience with real blessed food (*tabarruk*) in his hand, much as the woodcutter in the ritual narrative of "'Ali *mushkil-kusha*" (see Table 4.1, below) awakens holding miraculous stones that 'Ali presented to him during a dream-like

11 E.g. Bard (2002); Pinault (2001), pp. 60-61.

encounter. The more casual tales like Nana's can be told at nearly any time, usually garnering their narrative authority with claims of eyewitness testimony (even if at second-, third-, or fourth-hand).

Both the formal *kahanis* and casual miracle accounts reinforce distinctions between the elect and the ignorant, the dutiful and the wanton, every bit as much as they bestow blessings.[12] Humble, impoverished devotees in the *kahanis* who trust in and obey Fatima the Prophet's daughter, for example, usually have inherent moral potential. They may err, but then thoroughly learn their lessons through the consequences of their lapses. Haughty and arrogant characters, whatever their backgrounds, are often beyond redemption or must work harder for it. A supposed Shi'i believer who scoffs at the power of miracles is more likely to reap punishment than a non-believer of another faith background converted by the powers of the *ahl-e bait*, the progeny of the Prophet.

## Formal *Kahanis*: Popularity and Purpose

Formal miracle stories and the rituals around them may in practice be more separable than some scholarship on popular religion might lead us to believe. In the early twenty-first century, *kunda niyaz* offerings of food in the name of Imam Jafar-us-Sadiq (the sixth *imam*) on the date of 22 Rajab have sometimes been executed without even performing the associated *kahani*, "The Woodcutter's Story", even though, as Schubel points out, the story "helps to emphasise the niyaz as an act of Shi'i piety".[13] And conversely, when we scrutinise the dynamics of stories that are told during rituals, a multitude of clues in recited and printed versions of the most popular Shi'i miracles—including their layers of stories within framing stories and narrators constructing the speech of further narrators—stress that it is *listening* to a miracle story, not reading it or even telling it, and *not* its associated trappings, that is meritorious. Failures of piety in the stories repeatedly hinge on failing

12 This emphasis on constituting ethical/moral difference runs somewhat counter to a trend documented by Vernon Schubel (1993, p. 37), as well as in recent work on South Asian miraculous traditions more broadly, wherein accessible miracle narratives and the blessings that conclude their performance, usually in the form of mass distribution of sweets or snacks, can extend the aura of the miraculous to a wider community than the family or sectarian group performing a particular ritual. I do not claim that impulses towards inclusiveness and spiritual hierarchy cannot co-exist, but it is possible that Schubel's analysis in general overprivileges notions of sharing, social leveling, and communitas.

13 Schubel (1993), p. 66.

to "hear", *not* "read", or "tell" the miracles. "*Janāb-e Sayyida*", which acclaims Fatima Zahra, the Prophet's daughter, most emphatically reinforces that one cannot keep one's side of a bargain with the *ahl-e bait* by simply reading the story (to) oneself. Below I provide a basic schematic overview (based on recorded performances, pamphlet versions of the stories, and secondary literature) of the most popular "ritual (formal) *kahanis*". The only story I will actually summarise briefly is that of "*Janāb-e Sayyida*".

Table 4.1: Formal (*Niyaz*) *Kahanis*

| **Name** | **Date or Occasion** | **Dedicated to** | **No. of Stories in Narrative** | **Pamphlets** | **Web** |
|---|---|---|---|---|---|
| *Janāb-e Sayyida's* (or *Bibi Sayyida's*) *Story* | In instances of need or hardship | Bibi Fatima, Daughter of Prophet Muhammad | Frame + 2 | Printed in Bombay; Karachi (Hindi and Urdu) | Urdu in Roman script |
| *The Woodcutter's Story* | 22 Rajab; date aligned variously with the death of Caliph Usman, or death of Muawiya | Sixth Imam Jafar-us-Sadiq, who assigned this date to the *kahani* | Frame + 1 (with the one inner story featuring the sixth Imam recounted several times within the larger narrative) | Printed in Karachi (Urdu, Hindi; also (Gujarati?) | Multiple Websites English; Urdu in Roman script |
| *Das bībiyon̲ kī kahānī (or the Story of the Ten Women* | In instances of need or hardship | Maryam (Mary) Fatima Sara (wife of Ibrahim) Asiya Hagar, and 5 women of Karbala. | Frame + 1 | Printed in Karachi, Bombay (Hindi, Urdu) | No text, but many debates about whether recitation of the *kahani* is permissible in Islam |
| *Story of 'Ali, the Resolver of Difficulties* | Thursday nights; occasions of need or hardship | 'Ali | 1 (with multiple invocations of a vision of 'Ali) | Printed in Karachi (Urdu) | On internet in English |

How do these *mo'jizat* narrations associated with popular rituals compare with the less-documented "casual" miracle stories? While casual *kahanis* are commonly exchanged, discussed, even chuckled over in ritually unmarked settings, the formal *mo'jizat* above are recited in sanctified household ritual settings either on Thursdays, on specified dates such as 22 Rajab, or (especially in the case of "*Das bībiyon̲ kī kahānī*" and "*Janāb-e Sayyida*") on personally determined occasions of pressing need for otherworldly intervention. A current educational Shi'i website, for instance, urges:

> In order to do niaz it is suggested that momin/momannen/nat [*the faithful, believers*] should get up early in the morning of 22 Rajab and should clean the house and purify themselves by taking Ghusal (bath/shower), put on fragrance (etar) and light agarbate [*incense*]/use air freshener in their home and spread a clean 'tahir' sheet in a clean room. One should make sure all the utensils to be used in the preparation of niaz are clean and Pak [*ritually pure*]. [italic glosses mine][14]

The following are the main noteworthy points concerning "formal" *kahanis*, which are readily available in printed form: these traditions appear to be relatively recent, perhaps at most two hundred years old, but many of their components echo folkloric, fantastic elements of older North Indian tales. The petitions and pledges conjoined with these *kahanis* put one in mind of *mannats*, vows to unbind amulets or decorative bands, or to make a charitable offering, when a plea to the divine is fulfilled, and Hindu *vrat kathas*, narratives linked to periodic fasts in honour of one deity or another.[15] Indeed, Schubel observes that, "Generally, it is the case that a favor is asked of the holy person and the intention is made to read a particular story—for instance the story of Bibi Fatima or 'Ali *mushkil-kushā*—along with the distribution of sweets—when the request has been granted. Sometimes it is read beforehand, with the assumption that the vow will be fulfilled".[16]

---

14 https://www.hubeali.com; compare with *Mojizāt wa munajāt* ([n.d.]), cited by Schubel (1993), pp. 39-40: "Light incense, cover your head, sit down courteously and consider that you are at this time in the presence of the sinless Sayyidah [in general a *sayyidah* is a female descendant of the Prophet; here the allusion is to Fatima, Sayyidah *par excellence*]. Refrain from foolish and frivolous conversation. Refrain from laughing. Listen to the miracle which is being related with a trusting and pure heart. And then with respect eat the sweets which you have gathered for distribution".

15 The fasts please the divine by controlling and curbing the supplicant's desires. Most commonly known as *upvas* or *vrat*, the traditions mandate that devotees abstain from food—typically they avoid specially designated kinds of food—or water. Fasts in the name of different gods and goddesses, and associated with their characteristic stories, are observed on specific days; many are held weekly.

16 Schubel (1993), p. 37.

In my experience, upon hearing the most cursory description of Shi'i miracle *kahanis*, even a younger, college-educated generation of practicing Hindus in India and the diaspora draw an analogy between these tales and the traditional Indic *vrat kathas*. Shi'i consultants, on the contrary, professed ignorance of the genre of *vrat kathas*. This was true for both present-day lay preachers in India, and women who migrated to Pakistan from Lucknow, a Shi'i stronghold with eclectic religious rituals, at Partition. Interestingly, anxieties over the Islamic legitimacy of sponsoring *kahani* recitations and their associated rituals (see Table 4.1 above, and also below pp. 152 and 155) permeate web debates among young South Asian Muslims, strongly implying that the practices bear the taint of Hindu influence.

Among the best-known *kahanis* are the *kahani* of *"'Alī mushkil-kushā"* ('Ali, the Remover of Difficulties), *"Janāb-e Sayyida kī kahānī"*, "The Woodcutter's Story" (or *"Mo'jiza* of Imam Jafar-us-Sadiq"), and *"Das bībiyoṉ kī kahānī"*. A typical *kahani* amalgamates two or more brief stories related in a "once upon a time" mode, and devotes as much or more time to frame narratives, wherein a narrator instructs people to hear the story, as to the innermost tale.

In the frame story of *"Janāb-e Sayyida"* (a title for Fatima), the power of Husain's mother (Fatima Zahra/Bibi Fatima/Janab-e Sayyida) revives a child after his fatal fall into a potter's kiln. The miracle is effected when the child's mother, who has fainted from grief, encounters in her unconscious dream state a veiled woman who tells her to recite Janab-e Sayyida's *kahani*.[17] With the little boy miraculously restored, his mother makes all haste to fulfill her promise, but no one else cares to listen to the story. She nonetheless has the good fortune to hear the tale via a second encounter, now in a waking state, with the veiled (*niqabposh*) woman. This mysterious narrator reveals the core miracles of the story set: Fatima intercedes with Allah to resurrect a Jewish bride who has been struck dead (dazzled, apparently, by Fatima's glory) at her own wedding. This, in turn, converts dozens of Jewish onlookers to Islam. These wonders are accomplished by a humble, modest Fatima who displays exemplary obedience to her father and husband, yet exercises an authority of her own. The story's setting, during the lifetime of the Prophet, in Medina, anchors her in a familial and historical role—in contrast to her supernatural appearance as a veiled narrator.[18]

---

17 Schubel (1993); *Janāb-e Sayyida* ([n.d.]).
18 Ibid., p. 4.

The nameless woman appends to this story a folktale-like "clincher" about a princess and her friend, daughter of her father's *vazir*. The two girls are lost in a storm during a royal hunt but rescued, through the intercession of Janab-e Sayyida, by a neighbouring ruler. When these aristocratic characters forget to listen in gratitude, as promised, to Janab-e Sayyida's story (i.e. the wedding story that incorporates the Prophet, 'Ali, the resurrected bride, and the Jews who convert to Islam) their fortunes take another, complicated turn for the worse, and they go from brides to prisoners in the blink of an eye. Once they weep themselves into an unconscious state and make contact with a veiled lady, they realise their grave error, recite the story to one another, and all is restored.

After all of this, we step back abruptly into the frame story: the mother (a goldsmith's wife) of the first-mentioned resurrected child, pledge fulfilled, returns to her house only to see that "the houses of those who had refused to hear the story had all caught fire". Significantly, the intervention of Bibi Fatima/Janab-e Sayyida had explicitly saved her child from burning in a kiln. The pamphlet text then closes with the *darud*. This formalised Arabic salutation to the family of the Prophet is to be intoned by all present, preceded by the supplication, "Pray that the purposes of all faithful believers, men and women, be fulfilled just as the purposes of the goldsmith's wife and the two girls were fulfilled through the devotion of Muhammad and the family of Muhammad".[19]

Schubel has pointed out that certain themes in Shi'ism's better-known martyrological narratives, detached from Muharram's martial surroundings, are recombined in these folksy frames. The separation and death of children; mourning that opens a path to communication with the family of the Prophet; marriage celebrations that turn funereal; and imprisonment scenarios recur. In every standard *kahani* people are saved by the remembrance of Fatima or 'Ali *mushkil-kusha*, but if they forget to hear the (core) story as promised, they fall on bitter times, even starve. Worse is the fate of those who cast aspersions on the power of the *imams*, *ma'sumin* (Shi'ism's fourteen "impeccables": the Prophet, Fatima, and the twelve *imams*), or the *kahani* itself: their children die, the touch of their hands rots food and lays everything to waste. But when the afflicted acknowledge the *ma'sumin*'s miraculous powers and listen to the story, these reversals of fate are themselves reversed. The *kahani* insistently underlines its own efficacy by incorporating examples of the core story's outcomes. Listeners in

19 *Janāb-e Sayyida* ([n.d.]), p. 16.

contemporary times then hope to attain what they seek through their own aural experiences of "*Janāb-e Sayyida*". Just as A.K. Ramanujan discovered with efficacious religious tales in South India, here the story "is a program for mimetic behavior: it invites the listener to... worship... in the belief that whatever happens to a mythic character can happen to a worshipful listener".[20]

## Miraculous Worlds and Their Words: Stories and Standardisation

The characters in the world of standard *mo'jizats*, a world usually unmarked by earthly geopolitical signposts, resemble more those in folktales or short *qissas* than in the tragedy of Karbala: they are goldsmiths, woodcutters, potters, and their families.[21] Curiously, the formal *kahanis* display fewer overt lexical gestures towards Persian genres than some more localised Karbala laments. On this level, these texts almost echo sufi romances such as the *Mirigāvatī* (1505), in which, Aditya Behl notes, the rarity of Persian words renders the few that appear very noticeable.[22] In contrast, the *dah* lament, for example, references the eighteenth-century Urdu version of Kashefi's (Persian) *Rawżat al-shuhadā*, even though its texts are in the Awadhi language from the region around Lucknow and are even occasionally laced with Krishna imagery. Formal *kahanis* illustrate a counter-trend: they feature characters similar to the kings, *vazirs*, and princesses so conventional in the medieval romances of the subcontinent—Urdu *dastans*, Hindavi *kathas*, or sufi *masnavis*—but lack direct generic links with Persian or Arabic antecedents. The formal *kahanis'* stock characters would also be very much at home in secular entertainments such as Insha'allah Khan Insha's fantastical early nineteenth-century Hindi *Ranī Ketakī kī kahānī* (1803). In many of these tales, as in "*Janāb-e Sayyida*", two best friends, daughters of a *badshah* and *vazir*, are heroine and sidekick who face hazardous journeys away from home and family.

20 A.K. Ramanujan, 'Two Realms of Kannada Folklore', in *Another Harmony: New Essays on the Folklore of India*, ed. by A.K. Ramanujan and Stuart H. Blackburn (Berkeley: University of California Press, 1986), p. 54.

21 See e.g. the *qissa* tales in F. Orsini, 'Tales Between Two Scripts', *Print and Pleasure: Popular Literature and Entertaining Fictions in Colonial North India* (New Delhi: Permanent Black, 2009), pp. 109-61.

22 Aditya Behl, *The Magic Doe: Qutban Suhravardī's Mirigāvatī* (New York: Oxford University Press, 2012a), p. 203.

Whether or not these stock folktale features are emphasised, studies of Shi'ism and of vernacular Islam in general tend to strongly associate miracle tales with women's religiosity.[23] Yet, even if women on the whole have more evident investment in *kahani* devotions than do men, in the present day, command of a *kahani* repertoire appears to depend on age as well as gender. Internet forums reveal a high level of curiosity about (and often anxiety about the religious authenticity of) these wholly vernacular traditions and their murky South Asian origins on the part of young women, both Sunni and Shi'i. Some in the diaspora as well as in India, facing the problem of Urdu script illiteracy, have created a market for *kahani* pamphlet and internet texts in Devanagari and Roman script. When these texts in turn pique further interest, even if they come under reformist scrutiny, it is to the oldest living generation that family members often turn to learn more about miracle *kahanis*. My friend Kehkashan from Karachi commented that her India-born *dadi* (paternal grandmother) "used to do the Das bibiyon ki kahani" in the 60s and 70s, but since she passed away the tradition has died, at least in their family. In the instances I cite below, the main teller of casual miracle tales is a maternal grandfather.

When we consider gender in relation to the content of the standardised *kahanis*, it is the case, as Schubel and Pinault have claimed, that female characters and their devotional agency are powerfully showcased. Yet a significant dark side bedevils this agency: one of the most consistently punished characters in the *kahani* is the proud, imperious woman (*maghrur aurat*). In "*Das bībiyoṉ kī kahānī*", it is the proud woman's husband who realises that the couple have forfeited house, sustenance, and children because of her arrogant dismissal of the auspicious *kahani*. It is he who makes *laddu* sweets out of sand to offer in the *imam*'s name as they finally compensate for her horrific lapse by hearing the story.

Ritual *kahanis* also contain linguistic features which studies to date have not analyzed attentively. Among the most notable are the particular uses of the verbs "*sunnā*" and "*paṛhnā*". *Parhna* (to study, or read, or recite aloud) is here the less important word. This is so even though the term readily conveys the *niyaz kahanis*' modes of transmission: the stories are both recited (occasionally without a book) and read in family settings, with *parhna* referring to both acts. In practice, the widespread use of pamphlet literature, available for about five rupees in either Urdu or Devanagari (not

---

23 See Schubel (1993); Pinault (2001); Flueckiger (2008); Ruffle (2011).

to mention internet sources), has tended to produce fairly standardised recitations of the ritual *kahanis*.[24] The pamphlets sometimes contain guidelines for the appropriate preparation of a *niyaz kahani*'s ritual setting or for prefatory prayers, but no instructions regarding the reading of the *kahani*. My observations suggest that recitations range from a droning, monotone reading of the text to a consciously performative style, entertaining, if somewhat subdued. Devotees also render poetry—quatrains, couplets, and longer *marsiya* laments—in chanting, melodic, or declamatory styles, but the printed text would seldom reveal what form any given performance might take. The prominent point in the miracle narratives is that their protagonists are always and repeatedly told to "listen to" or "hear" the story or "have it heard", not to *parhna* it or *parhvana* it [arrange for it to be read]. The *kahani* reciter is invariably either obscured or anonymous.

In surveying four written and four performed versions of "*Janāb-e Sayyida*" (see summary above), one finds few differences in diction or plotline. One of the rare variations is that one pamphlet printed in Bombay presents more of Janab-e Sayyida's/Fatima's words in direct speech, or constructed dialogue, as opposed to summarising or writing *about* what she says, than other versions.[25] A Bombay Devanagari version of "*Das bībiyon̲ kī kahānī*", sold widely in Lucknow, meanwhile, uses virtually the same lexicon as a Pakistani Urdu version, but startlingly glosses in Hindi common Urdu words such as *maghrur* (*ghamandi*, proud), and *muflis* (*gharib*, poor), and even *khwab* (*sapna*, dream) and *shauhar* (*pati*, husband) (*Das bībiyon̲*, [n.d.]). Most of my consultants would likely argue that the audience targeted here is their community's Hindi-knowing, Urdu-illiterate, younger generation.

24 Other older and more regionally inflected devotional genres, including *soz*, *salam*, selections from *marsiya* poetry, and even sermons, are gradually becoming homogenised, partly as a result of the internet's impact on *majlis* performance. "Sha'ista", a widely travelled Shi'a woman raised in Karachi, also noted the international effect over the past few decades of influential cultural and political forces within Shi'ism on rituals and expressive genres: "Some recent Shia practices in Karachi Imambaras—such as the recitation of *dua-e-kumail* on Thursday nights, as well as before some *majalis*—have been introduced by Shia Khojah communities. [Khojas are an affluent sect of Shi'as who prominently observe Muharram rites. Those to whom Sha'ista refers to are Twelver Shi'as whose ancestors split from their Ismaili brethren in the nineteenth century.] I don't know where they get them from; maybe from their travels to Iran? These 'new' practices are also frequently seen in imambaras in Canada and the United States" (personal communication 2009).

25 It would be interesting to pursue whether such a version, presumably enlivened by direct speech, has any verifiable link with the intensity of dramatic performativity in *kahani* recitation, given that women's recitations range from virtuosic to monotone droning in other ritual expressive traditions.

## Everyday Miracles, Everyday Stories

Ideal prerequisites for hearing formal *kahanis* today include a gathering of at least a few people—most often the extended family—personal purification, a clean and perfumed ritual setting, sweets, snacks, or a meal (the *niyaz*) to be distributed at the end of the *kahani*, and final formulaic prayers.[26] More "casual" miracle stories range all the way from relaxed iterations of formal *mo'jizat kahanis* to brief anecdotes that fall under the rubric of "weird things that happened to people I know". These anecdotes can be told by nearly anyone. Whereas non-Shi'as may occasionally participate in *niyazes*, or even recite/read the formal *mo'jizat kahanis*, they would generally have limited access to these largely unwritten, raw anecdotes. Casual *kahanis* may gesture towards local religious shrines or sites such as Karbala—the axes of Shi'i sacred geography—in contradistinction to the folktale neverland of much of the formal *kahani* tradition. They generally share with ritually-framed *mo'jizat kahanis* the tropes of an encounter with the immediate family of the Prophet or the Karbala martyrs in a dream state, of steadfast Shi'i devotion and remembrance, and punishment of those who fail to recognise the powers of the *ahl-e bait*. These narratives, again, are explicitly labelled "*mo'jizat*".

In the course of my ethnographic work, dozens of people in India and Pakistan proffered these accounts, the topics of which ranged from Saddam Hussein's failed attempts during his rule to block geysers of blood that spurted from the ground of Karbala, to the mysterious fevers that befall those who fail to feed starving Sayyids (descendants of the Prophet). The narratives also extended to more general Islamic stories of the miraculous, such as that of a virtuous child who died as a result of his insistence on fasting during Ramzan, but was raised from the dead. Many of the stories have the rough-edged ring of half-remembered family history, while others turn out to have been recast from religious cassettes or the authoritative words of a *maulvi* or *zakir* in a mourning assembly sermon. In comparison to the *majlis* context—as demonstrated in our initial tale of how the holy *'alam* channeled a cancer cure—casual miracle tellings draw out local evidential

26 A few cosmopolitan Shi'as, particularly in urban or diasporic settings, describe modifications they have made to the *kahani* not only by dispensing with the ritual apparatus but by simply reading it to themselves when they face severe personal difficulties. These consultants say they place few restrictions on the time or place when they employ the *kahani*, but they do reiterate that "hearing" the narrative is more important than reciting it, i.e. that reading it silently is not the efficacious ideal.

discourse and opportunities for substantive, even collaborative, interaction between teller and audience, whatever the story source.

The modes of storytelling evoke the flavours of jokes, fables, family reminiscences, or yarns, rather than hard-edged instruction delivered by formally qualified religious experts. Nonetheless, the consensus that the substance of the stories are "true" strongly underlies the use of the term *mo'jizat*, which is more insistent here than in the case of the *niyaz* (formal) *kahanis*. That said, Rahat and Nana's family, along with virtually all of my consultants, incorporate all of the ritual and casual anecdotes we have encountered into the *mo'jizat* category. While they did also employ the word *kahani*, especially for the more standardised *niyaz* narratives, family members such as Sadaf showed an explicit preference for the term "*mo'jiza*" or the clarification "true story", lest the label *kahani* be misconstrued as a fictional incident (personal communication, 1997). Scholarly texts and dictionaries, meanwhile, often underline the distinctions in Islam between *mo'jizat*, "miracles performed by prophets and intended to be public", and *karamat*, "those performed by saints and intended to be secret or private".[27] These categories, Flueckiger asserts, may "analytically help us to understand the dynamics and potential controversy"—including the anxieties expressed over the internet about Shi'i *kahanis*—"of miracles in practice". She also concurs, however, with my findings that "in contemporary vernacular practice", Shi'i "mujizat are performed by the twelve *imams*" as well as the Prophet, and that "the distinction between mujizat and karamat is often not maintained".[28]

In the interests of illustrating something of the range of narratives within a familial repertoire, I have chosen short informal stories told in one Lahore household. The main narrator is the late Sayyid Baqir Ahmed Shamsi ("Nana-jan" to all of us in the storytelling setting) of Lahore, who was a very young man at the time of Partition. Over a year or more, his family shared at least twenty of these stories in Urdu, with some parenthetical Panjabi commentary. By their own description, they were relating *mo'jizat*, though occasionally one of the girls would request a miracle story only to be told that

27 Flueckiger (2006), p. 168; see also Platts (1997 [1884]), p. 1048.

28 Flueckiger (2006), p. 168. In the milieu of Flueckiger's consultant, the sufi healer "Amma", most miracles (not only the ones she performs) seem to be "linguistically conflated as simply *karamat*". In the Shi'i context, the term *mo'jiza* is stressed and includes the intervention of Fatima as well as of the Prophet and *imams*. This is so even when that intervention is implied rather than specified, or even when the label *kahani* is also used.

it was an inappropriately "*sada vaqe'a*" (plain, ordinary incident or anecdote). *Sada vaqe'as* might dramatise mysterious illnesses and divine punishments, but lacked the transformative dream state, or visions of the *imams* or Fatima. All of Nana's miraculous or mysterious incidents, however, referenced an eyewitness, either by name or kinship status. Thus, conversations around the *mo'jizat* mark for the younger generation, as well as for the researcher, what does and does not constitute a miracle: it cannot be utterly mundane, it cannot be fictitious; it should have witnesses and include the appearance of the Prophet's family members or evidence of their intervention.

Here is a story Nana-jan tells about two great classical Urdu elegists (*marsiya-go*) of Lucknow, India, who are still renowned among Urdu speakers today: Mir Babar Ali Anis (1802-1874) and Salamat 'Ali Dabir (1803-1875).

> This was the way of it: Anis and Dabir used to compete. Consequently, two parties were formed, and there was always a fight going on. In order to end the fight, two elders said, "You [each] write a *marsiya*, a 'top' *marsiya*". [Having written them] they sealed those up, and took them off to Hazrat 'Ali's tomb in Najaf. There they submitted this prayer: "Maulah, place your seal (*mohur*) on whichever is the best marsiyah". That night the *imam* came in a dream to those who had gone there [to Najaf], and to the ones in Lucknow, too, and said, "Anis, yours is better, but you're a Sayyid, so I won't stamp [yours with] my seal, or Dabir will say, 'Oh, he's a Sayyid [i.e. a "relative"of the *imams*], so that's why he applied his seal...'" He applied it to Dabir's. Anis's was the better *marsiya*, though; he [the *imam*] came in a dream and said it!

Commenting on this miraculous *vaqe'a* of her father's, Rahat somewhat exasperatedly spelled out to me something that was fundamental to her: that miracles and their tellings function differently, and offer different messages, for different people.

> It should be clear to you why Hazrat 'Ali [cousin and son-in-law of the Prophet] would miraculously appear and affix his seal of approval to a work by the poet Dabir instead of to Anis's better elegy. Anis was a Sayyid, a descendant of the Prophet, like us. *We* must have faith in 'Ali no matter what. Whether our prayers are answered or not, whether we are provided with comforts or not—we believe. The reason they appear and show miracles to others is so that they will believe in the *imams*. We people continue praying, continue our weeping for Imam Husain, continue beating ourselves; if our prayers are accepted, very well, and if not, that's the way it is. Nevertheless, it is our heritage to do so. But in the case of those people who don't believe,

> Sunnis, if they see a miracle and are convinced by it, their prayers are instantly answered. I've witnessed this many times myself.

The story itself turns on a Sayyid/non-Sayyid distinction between the nineteenth-century Shi'i poets, one an elect descendent of the Prophet, the other a "common" individual. Rahat, however, casually extends the category of "others" who are shown miracles to "people who don't believe, Sunnis". This reflected the social situation in much of Pakistan at the time, when tensions between the two sects were high.

Whereas the dubious require "proof", Rahat suggests, pious Sayyids take interaction with revered, transhistorical figures in stride. Here, Hazrat 'Ali, addressing the poet Anis, assumes a familial understanding, an attitude that almost implies "you can see what I'm up against, my boy". Nana's authoritative but friendly, confidential manner as tale-teller somewhat parallels 'Ali's stance. His little story features the dream vision that marks the more formal *kahanis*, but unlike most of those *kahanis*, makes geographical allusions to cultural and religious centres. And, finally, it provides an interesting case of what is at least presented as an oral tradition arbitering the quality of canonical Urdu poems.

A more personalised anecdote also involves these two great poets, and is attributed by Nana-jan to a contemporary of his who was a poet and the grandson of a poet, one Zulfiqar 'Ali. Nana became acquainted with the grandson after he heard his virtuoso performance of a *marsiya*.

> Syed Zulfiqar 'Ali went on *ziyarat* [pilgrimage] to Karbala. On the way, he met a *buzurg* [an elder] who helped him find his way there. After staying there six years, one night he was woken up by a voice in the middle of the night telling him to go to attend a mourning assembly. He was baffled, not sure if he was awake or dreaming, but agreed to go.
>
> Two black-clad men were there. A disembodied voice called out, "Is Anis there?"
>
> One of the men stood up.
>
> "OK", he was instructed, "recite a *marsiya* about Hazrat Abbas [Imam Husain's half-brother, the army standard bearer]". He recited it and sat down.
>
> "OK", came the voice, "I've heard it. Now is Mirza Dabir there?"
>
> Dabir stood up and recited a *marsiya* about Akbar.

> Zulfiqar 'Ali heard the *marsiyas*, wept, and sorrowfully beat himself. Then, still not knowing if he was conscious or asleep, he took the *tabarruk* (the food distributed at the end of a mourning assembly), and departed.
>
> In the morning he woke up to find the *tabarruk* was in his hand.

At this point Nana-jan's granddaughter Sadaf proclaimed, most emphatically and sincerely, "This is a miracle!"

Rather than developing narrative tension between the poets, this anecdote renders them both as stereotypically garbed guides on the path to faith. Like the anonymous elder who helps Zulfiqar 'Ali or the seemingly undistinguished veiled women of the *niyaz kahanis*, these characters are flat, minimally described. Like them, Anis and Dabir turn out to mediate transformative powers, but in their case their role hinges on their local, historic cultural credibility. Nana-jan is invoking Karbala as the ultimate sacred space, yet suggests that the great elegists and mourning practices of the subcontinent have extraordinary leverage even in the Shi'i heartland, even for a man who goes to Iraq in hopes of bettering his religious knowledge. As in the *niyaz kahanis*, it is explicitly stated that Zulfiqar 'Ali (attentively) heard or listened to the poems, not just that the poets recited them. As in the formal *kahani* of 'Ali *mushkil-kusha*, when the main character emerges from his dream-like encounter, the words he has heard have virtually been distilled into tangible blessed objects.

Nana-jan's account is rich in allusions to Karbala figures: Husain is tacitly, automatically evoked by the site itself; two of Karbala's most prominent heroes, Akbar and Abbas, "star" in *marsiya* poems; and Zulfiqar 'Ali's very name conjures 'Ali's sword Zulfiqar, used by Husain in battle. Nonetheless, miracles in Karbala or Najaf serve more to consolidate the *barkat* and cultural richness of South Asian Shi'ism than to confer a hierarchical stamp of authority on them from the heartland.

Zulfiqar 'Ali was also the source of a second, more piquant, story centred on another pious man who paid special reverence to the site of Imam Husain's martyrdom:

> There was a *buzurg* who lived at a place a few miles from Karbala who would go there every Thursday after ablutions. He would perform *namaz* and spend the night there, and come back the next day.
>
> One time, he met a *daku* [bandit] on the way to the *imambargah*:
> "Give me your money".
> "I don't have any money".

"No money! Well then take off your clothes and give them to me".
"Are you out of your mind? I'm going to the *imam*'s *darbar* [shrine, or "court"]. Where am I going to get anything else to wear?!"

In short, he had no choice but to take off his clothes and give them to the brute.

So he went back home, changed, set off again for the *imambargah*. He got up to leave the next morning, but realised he had forgotten to make a complaint to the *imam*. He sat down again and registered his grievance with the *imam*:
"Listen to the kind of treatment I've been subjected to…!"

He bemoaned his state, "What sin could I have committed to merit such treatment?"
The *imam* appeared, but immediately disappeared. The man got even more upset:
"Now you appear, but you came only to disappear in an instant?!"
He moaned and grieved some more.
The *imam* reappeared and said, "What d'you want me to do? Kill the *daku*? I can't. I'm obliged to him. (*Un kā ahsān hai mujh par.*) I can't say anything to him".

The man was stunned, and determined to search for this mysterious *daku*. He finally located him in a godforsaken wilderness, and asked him, "You're a *daku*, why should the *imam* be obliged to you?"
The *daku* replied, "Remember when I made you remove all of your clothes, and you had to go back and change?"
"Yeah".
"And you didn't call on the *imam* until later . . . ?"
"Yes".
"Well, I'm a thief, and one time I looted a huge caravan, and came away with more than my share of goods. I had to run and hide with all my swag, but then couldn't find water anywhere. I searched and searched, and was about to die of thirst, when I remembered Imam Husain and addressed him saying, "Oh, Maula, it's you who could withstand unbearable thirst; ordinary humans can't do so. Please help me".

And the *imam* had to acknowledge and help the *daku*, because in his hour of need he beseeched him so devoutly.

And so the *daku* says, "Yet you, a devotee, did not remember, until much after the fact".

There is no way the *imam* could punish the *daku*, he was obliged to him for his devotion.

"You should have called on the *imam* in your hour of need".

The theme of devotion outweighing criminal sins, of course, pervades ancient Indic texts, medieval devotional poems, and contemporary Hindi folktales.[29] Combined with it here, we have the discernibly Shi'i tropes of agonising thirst, Husain's own suffering, and the critical, continual necessity of remembering the *imams* and their power. The *daku*'s emotional reliance on Imam Husain is total and immediate; he really shares Husain's experiences of liminality and thirst. This combination trumps not only the elder's social stature and regard for appearances, but his conventional piety and adherence to ritual as well. Consigned to the wilderness, the *daku* attains a bond with Husain that eludes the elder who already lives near sacred Karbala, and strives so desperately to get physically closer. This tale, too, tacitly validates the devotion of sincere Shi'as outside of the heartland, who are likely to "experience" Karbala only locally, through mimetic relics, laments, orators' evocations, and seasonal austerities. Dozens more casual *mo'jizat* repeat this theme of re-creating Karbala wherever one is; the replication may serve anyone separated from Husain by time and space, and has special salience for those women who perform their devotions at home rather than even venturing out to a local *imambargah*.

A final story of Nana-jan's is poignantly situated in a time "when there was no Pakistan":

> Before Partition, there was a Hindu devotee of Husain who regularly took Husain's *darshan* [the beholding of an auspicious deity, personage, or object]. The day for *darshan* came, he wanted to offer a *niyaz* for Husain. But the man's daughter was being continually hassled by the boy next door all the time. So they didn't take her from the safety of the house and go for worship (*'ibadat*) during the day, but when it was almost evening they were afraid the day would pass without observing the *niyaz*.
>
> The husband said to his wife, "We have to go for Husain's *niyaz*". The couple cleaned the house, locked the door and went, just the two of them.
>
> The boy came and jumped over the gate and was about to assault the girl. "Who will save you now?!" he taunted.
>
> "Guru Husain", she replied.

29 E.g. Ann Gold, 'Showing Miracles in Rajasthan: Proof and Grace', in *Miracle as Modern Conundrum in South Asian Religious Traditions*, ed. by C.G. Dempsey and Selva J. Raj (Albany: State University of New York Press, 2008).

> Suddenly a horse bearing a fearsome headless rider launched itself over the wall into the courtyard. The rider said, to the girl, "Get out of here! See, the lock's disappeared. I'm Guru Husain and I'm going to kill this wretch. Tell them that it is me, Guru Husain, who killed him".
>
> And he killed him. And he disappeared.

## Universal Loyalties Converge with "Local" Needs and Comforts

It is hard *not* to read Guru Husain and this rather raw depiction of miraculous communal boundary-crossing amidst high walls, locks, vacated homes, and assaults on the honour of women as a tortured kind of reflection on Partition itself. It's even harder to imagine members of a Pakistani generation that hasn't lived through Partition adopting with ease the Hindu-inflected vocabulary of *darshan* and guru that Nana-jan summons so readily. In pointed contrast to "*Janāb-e Sayyida*"'s and his own daughter's emphasis on miracles that testify to or convert non-Shi'as, in this pre-Partition story world, it is the dramatic form the Hindus' reward takes that is miraculous; their unwavering devotion is underlined, but seemingly unremarkable.

The time around the 1947 Partition (referred to at least once in my hearing in Pakistan as "the time before *India* was made") often has a mythic quality in contemporary oral genres. As it happens, there is considerable anecdotal evidence that the formalisation and popularisation of *niyaz kahanis* burgeoned in the decades just after Partition. A woman who migrated with her family from India to Pakistan as a tiny child in 1947, for example, recollects how *mo'jizat kahanis* entered her awareness:

> I am very familiar with *Bibi Syeda ki kahani* and it is a big favourite in our family when there is a difficult situation. But interestingly, I did not grow up knowing it. I did not know about it till I was almost 20 [which would be in the mid 1960s] and no one in our family knew it or read it till then. All of a sudden it was in vogue. Before this, my *bari Phuphi* (older aunt) used to use *beri* fruits for *mannats*, which was also Bibi Syeda *ki niyaz*, but without the *kahani*. I have been completely unfamiliar with *Das bibiyon ki kahani* all my life, but some cousins just told me in detail the whole special *niyaz* procedure involved in ten bibis' *kahani*. (pers. comm. 2009)

The survival narratives implied in both *niyaz kahanis* and casual *mo'jizat* echo the desperate victories of the bereaved women at Karbala who kept alive Husain's memory. More immediately, they reinforce a Shi'i identity across fraught national borders, and the resilience of the faith community to endure, whether as a minority in an Islamic Republic or a minority within a minority in India. Finally, the folksy motifs and feel of these *mo'jizat*, especially those like the "criminal devotee" story, also clearly testify to Shi'ism's thorough immersion in broader South Asian expressive traditions and to the inter-religious appeal of such stories.

Shi'ism's philosophical impulses, broadly speaking, towards relaying and interpreting miraculous messages at differential levels, for the esoterically initiated versus the simple devotee, are well documented.[30] The idea of overt lessons for the general population and hidden messages accessible only to the elect, in fact, pervades Shi'i expressive culture in many forms: conceptions of the "true", hidden Qur'an; of knowledge held by *imams* that would endanger ordinary people, of *zahiri* (apparent) and *batini* (hidden, inner) forms; and of saints' imitable, human qualities versus their transcendent ones.[31] The community's minority status tends to promote this stress on multiple audiences and multivalent messages in the *kahani* context as well. Related assumptions underlie Nana-jan's daughter Rahat's explanation that the *imam*'s seal, the *outward* sign, offers proof of a miraculous occurrence for "ordinary" people, but is more profoundly emblematic, for Sayyids, of their direct, *inner* relationship with the *imam*. In more general and often implicit ways, instances of miracles the world over elicit socially or spiritually particular responses to the same event. Corinne Dempsey, for example, observes that for an "insider" audience of Hindu devotees at a Sri Vidya temple in New York State "[...] seemingly supernatural experiences are not only desirable, but are fully anticipated, and, as such, are not necessarily miraculous. [...] In the end, one person's miracle will be another's explicable, routine experience".[32] In the Shi'i domestic context, even given the potency attributed to "hearing" and "listening", a *mo'jiza* is in some sense some "person's miracle", because it is the teller who determines that this event is indeed a *mo'jiza*.

30 See Bard (2002); Amir-Moezzi (1994); Korom (2002).

31 See Ruffle (2011).

32 Corinne G. Dempsey, 'The Science of the Miraculous at an Upstate New York Hindu Temple', in Dempsey and Raj (2008), p. 121.

## Tellers of Tales

While much of this essay foregrounds the attitudes of miracle *kahani* consumers, the figure of the *kahani* reciter, whether a contemporary narrator or a narrator depicted *in* the *kahani*, enjoys a significant, unusual, and fruitful mutability. In the case of casual miracle anecdotes, the status, age, or personal history of a narrator have some capacity to enhance or situate a story. Nana-jan could almost always attribute his story to a named, local person or a relative. Even if this information—for example, that the "original" narrator was Nana-jan's uncle, or a poet—was not a crucial part of the prefatory material of a *kahani*, it lent the anecdote's formulaic content a local sheen and a sense of direct connection to a particular family audience. Along with this superficial temporal or geographical anchoring, Nana's *kahanis* often hinged on hierarchical relationships (Sayyid versus non-Sayyid; pious man versus bandit) even if they sometimes appeared to subvert them. They also emphasised, through the appearance of the *imams* and the *ma'sumin*, the interpenetration of the miraculous and workaday worlds.

Another family authority, who presides over a large clan in Lucknow, is Sofia Apa. Apa, who has blithely preached to packed *imambargahs* about the miraculous through decades of Muharrams, was visibly moved, almost overwhelmed, as she recounted, in an intimate household setting, Fatima Zahra's visitation to the deathbed of her mother-in-law. Sofia Apa witnessed the dying woman suddenly opening her eyes wide, addressing reverential greetings to the Prophet's daughter by name, and bowing from the waist three times before collapsing into final unconsciousness. Although Sofia did not herself "see" the figure of Fatima Zahra, the holy woman's presence and her interaction with the old lady were palpable. As Sofia gave her unsolicited account of the incident, emotion and quiet conviction suffused her face and voice, a vast departure from the rhetoric and drama she deploys to tell the miracle stories embedded in her Muharram sermons.

Ritual *mo'jizat kahanis*, by comparison, both privilege receptiveness (if not critical "evaluation") through listening, and efface narrators more thoroughly. Listening and the devotion of the listener are front and centre. The prevalence of "*sunna*", restricted use of the terms *parhna* or *parhvana*, and the mysterious veiled narrator widely portrayed in pamphlet texts render the tale-teller in the ritual *kahani* tradition anonymous. And truly, with cheap, simplified texts, almost anyone can read/recite such *kahanis*; in a way, that is the whole idea.

One enduring social lesson this approach to narration imparts is that the teller of a *kahani* may be a generic anywoman, but such an anonymous, undistinguished person can reveal miracles to the receptive. And there is always the probability, in the *niyaz kahanis*, that the faceless narrator reporting the utterances of the holy ones is 'Ali *mushkil-kusha* or the *niqabposh* daughter of the Prophet, Janab-e Sayyida herself. This disguised, "mysterious" performer epitomises motifs of maskings, un-maskings, and reversals of power that run through Shi'i lore. Through miracle narratives, those with limited formal religious or general education can, in daily life, purvey some of the same lessons and values imparted in more learned language by highly compensated, erudite male and female preachers.

## "Whether our prayers are answered or not…": Tales that Testify, Stories that Sustain

Through the reciter's versatile, formulaic voice, the narration of even spectacular, transformative miracles can acquire a certain "everydayness". The devout encounter the generic narrator's hidden powers or cloaked identities in a context of narrative predictability, intimacy, proximity, and shared emotional experiences. In the informality of a household setting, the *mo'jizat* proffer some of the same moral values and narrative interest that similar miracle tales display in sermons, but without the hortatory frame of the ritual *majlis*. Another thing the ritual *kahanis* provide is a forum for petition to the family of the Prophet and hope for intercession that will effect medical cures, respite from hard times, or passing grades in exams.

For devout South Asian Shi'as, then, miracle narratives sometimes inspire awe, but more importantly, they often relay a powerful utility and intimacy. The Urdu narratives referenced in this essay affirm the efficacy of simple, stylised devotional language, and cultivate proximity with Shi'i holy figures, namely the family of the Prophet and the martyrs of Karbala. The basic parameters of miracle narration suggest that some miracles prove, convince, or testify. In such cases, the contact miracles offer with the sacred, whether helpful or harmful, is likely to be at least somewhat surprising and transformative. The miracles within the *niyaz kahanis* often dramatically impress non-Shi'i characters, even as they also carry more subtle resonance for practicing Shi'as. Generally, we may say that testimonial miracles often but not always overlap with "public" miracles. Shi'i processions featuring spectacular tomb replicas and choreographed self-flagellation, for example, can become a context for contemporary miraculous encounters (bleeding rosaries, healings, possession) in spaces that include "outsiders" or non-believers.

Shi'i ritual miracle stories, however, generally "do not face out into the larger community of Islam. They are meant to reinforce certain attitudes and ideas within the community".[33] Flueckiger, analyzing narratives about sufi Muslim *pirs* in Hyderabad, India similarly asserts that "narrativizing the *pir*'s miracles helps both to build the *pir*-disciple relationship and relationships *between* disciples".[34] Yet something else is also transpiring in the charged atmosphere that surrounds Nana-jan in Rang Mahal. Nana's *vaqe'as* do not construct a circle of adepts or initiates, nor do they underline, as many Shi'i sermons do, the link between esoteric knowledge and the mysterious powers of the revered members of the Prophet's family. Nana's family readily accept those powers, and, in doing so, suggest that there are miracles that consistently sustain believers. These tend to be anticipated, comforting, even familiar, rather than amazing or surprising.

These complementary patterns demonstrate not only different locii on a spectrum of "signs and wonders", but that people may individually tailor their modes of revealing, telling, and hearing miracles.[35] This localising, comforting character manifests itself in devotional Islam in many parts of the world. In Tajikistan, Central Asia, for example, women of conviction share, in conversation and through the internet, the miracle (*mu'jiza*) of forty devout Sunni Muslim girls who were turned to stone when non-Muslim men tried to assault them during the recent civil war (1992-1997).[36] This story apparently reconfigures a motif known as the wonder of "*chahel* (or *chīl*) *dukhtarān*", associated with sites in both Afghanistan and Iran, and alluding to forty virgins in ancient times who "were miraculously taken

33 Schubel (1993), p. 39.

34 Flueckiger (2006), p. 182.

35 This functional categorisation scheme counters the trajectory outlined by Kenneth Woodward, for example, wherein miracles themselves have a "story", in the Abrahamic religions, of being performed early on by the Divine, then by Prophets, with their impact moving historically from more public to more private spheres. Eventually, they all but disappear, he asserts, from accounts of the sacred; K. Woodward, *The Book of Miracles: The Meaning of the Miracle Stories in Christianity, Judaism, Buddhism, Hinduism and Islam* (New York: Simon & Schuster, 2001).

36 Mehrangez Gulova (personal communication 2012).

into the earth to escape Zoroastrian armies".[37] No distinctively Shi'i motifs at all figure in this narrative, but the centrality of purity and faith (especially on the part of women) in traumatic local circumstances echo the *mo'jizat* set during Partition or during Saddam Hussein's oppressive regime. The *mu'jiza* reinforces the values of chastity and sacrifice among the women so profoundly moved by this story, while some eerily-shaped stones outside of Dushanbe are supposed to testify to others about the event.

In the South Asian Shi'i milieu, *mo'jizat* rely more heavily than almost any other rituals on Indic popular culture, and have a great deal in common with pleas and petitions to the Almighty across cultures. *Husainiyat* ("Husain-like" virtue, or as Ruffle [2011] thoughtfully glosses the term, *Husaini ethics*) is only part of what the *mo'jizat* exemplify. Untethered from the schematic repertoire of Karbala itself, family-centred miracle narratives urge listeners not so much to replicate (for example) Bibi Fatima's impeccable behaviour, as to trust in and empathise with her. The characters who most exemplify imitable behaviour in the *niyaz kahanis* are the listeners in the frame narratives who excel or lapse in their devotions. *Mo'jizat kahanis*, both formal and informal, teach their lessons through storytelling, unelaborated by exegesis. They offer entertainment that may not be invariably cheerful, but is "good, clean fun" for the everyday, outside the festive celebrations of the *ma'sumin*'s birthdays and the overarching solemnity of the mourning assemblies outsiders most commonly associate with Shi'ism.

*Mo'jizat* which demonstrate that devotion is manifested in the status and prestige that come with that loyalty, especially when one is a Sayyid or a person of extraordinarily pure intention, offer a special comfort to a class of "poor Sayyids", who allow donors to accrue merit (*savab*) through charitable giving to them. Rahat, with her insistence on the eternal calling of the "elect" with the Shi'i community to "believe, no matter what", is one of those poor Sayyids. Her comments reveal that while visible rewards to pious entreaties are always welcome, a superior definition of devotion stipulates honouring the Prophet's family in the very face of long-term disappointment, grief, and poverty. "Others" may need to witness miracles, but the devout exemplify their faith, and enjoy themselves, through the very acts of hearing and transmitting miracle narratives, whether their hardships are alleviated or not.

---

37 *Encyclopaedia of the World Muslims: Tribes, Castes and Communities*, ed. by Nagendra Singh and Masud Khan (Delhi: Global Vision Publishing House, 2004), p. 183.

# II. BOOKS AND PERFORMANCES, BOOKS FOR PERFORMANCE

# 5. Note to Self: What Marathi *Kirtankars*' Notebooks Suggest about Literacy, Performance, and the Travelling Performer in Pre-Colonial Maharashtra

*Christian Lee Novetzke*

In modern scholarship on non-modern, and especially non-Western, subjects, we tend to treat the dialectic between orality and literacy as if all theoretical and historical questions in this regard have been answered. After several decades of reconstruction around the problems posed by postcolonialism and postmodernism, we still have a tenacious hold on the idea that whatever is literate or literary is more highly valued than whatever is ("simply") oral. If a thing is written down, it must be important; and everywhere it is the important and powerful (kings, for example) who first write things down. It is perhaps one of the unfortunate side-effects of the interventions of postmodernism, particularly of Foucauldian thought, that we see power as the essential category of all critique: find the powerful and you will find the essence of a thing or time. However, I have argued elsewhere that we should abandon the distinction between orality and literacy and instead explore the relationship between performance and permanence—and in the process try to avoid the power relations and modern conceits tied up with the idea of literacy.[1] In this essay I make

1 C.L. Novetzke, *Religion and Public Memory: A Cultural History of Saint Namdev in India* (New York: Columbia University Press, 2008), chapter 3. This essay draws substantially from this chapter though the argument it presents is different.

 http://dx.doi.org/10.11647/OBP.0062.05

a different argument. I show how a particular logic of practice within an ostensibly written tradition tends to emphasise orality and especially performance, and how this practice institutes a set of formal conventions that resist the static encroachment of literacy, conventions that invite the creativity of live performance. This is an essay that explores how to read a text that resists its own literacy by emphasising its secondary position in relation to performance.

It is the paradox of using texts to study practices that were essentially oral that traces of writing endure where collective memory fades, and we are often left with the impression that cultures which merely used literacy were dominated by that usage. This is particularly true of the plethora of regional, public, performative religious expressive modes that have come under the rubric of *bhakti* or "devotionalism" more generally. In these contexts we often trace textual remnants to refashion a literary corpus out of what must have been a vaster oral context. This essay shows how the Varkari religious practice of Maharashtra prompts us to develop a critical engagement with literacy and orality mediated through a theory of performance in order to establish a theory of literacy that is subjected to the demands of performance. This prompt is inchoate in the very written texts that form the literary archive of the Marathi Varkari sants that guide us in this direction, in particular the mode of writing used by a specific kind of religious public performer in Maharashtra, a *kirtankar*. Through this mode of writing I'll contend that literacy here is subservient to performance, and that writing is seen as a tool, a carefully contained tool, in the practice of performance.

Public memory in India recalls that in the thirteenth century a precocious teenager, the Marathi sant Jnaneshwar, placed his final touches on his paraphrase and commentary in Marathi on the *Bhāgavadgītā*. Indeed, the main text attributed to him, popularly known as the *Jñāneśvarī*, is so important that it earned its own stamp issued by the Government of India seven years before its author's biographical stamp was issued—the text precedes the author, a testament to the modern power of the written word (see Figure 5.1). In this time, which witnessed a plethora of sants, most of them are remembered to have been literate. In the sixteenth century, we have the sant Eknath who is remembered as not only literate but a textual critic who culled together all available versions of the *Jñāneśvarī* and created its first critical edition. Perhaps Maharashtra's most famous sant, Tukaram, of the seventeenth century, is said to have written his own songs down by hand, a manuscript under glass in the town of Dehu near Pune. He also had a duplicate of his manuscript produced by his tabla player, Jaganade, a meticulous back-up copy. Observing this legacy, one might conclude that literacy, and indeed a proto-philology of a sort, was of primary importance to the Varkari tradition in Maharashtra for well over four hundred years.

Fig. 5.1 (L) Jnaneshwari Stamp, issued in 1990 to commemorate the 700th anniversary of the composition of the *Jñāneśvarī*; (R) "Saint Dnyaneshwar" stamp, issued in 1997 in memory of Jnaneswhar/Jnandev. Public Domain.

In fact, very little of the dissemination of Varkari materials is through writing. The most common way to consume the songs of the sants of Maharashtra is through a live performance, called *kirtan*. Though *kirtan* is a pan-Indian performance art, it as different in its many articulations as the traditions that use it. In Maharashtra, a *kirtan* is essentially a didactic public performance. This can be religious or not—a common *kirtan* subject is family planning and AIDS prevention, for example. But the focus of this paper is in the religious kind of *kirtan* in which the performer chooses a devotional song attributed to a sant and provides a good deal of exposition. This kind of *kirtan* is sort of a religious variety show, usually with a clear moral or political theme. There is often a story from the life of a sant that goes along with the song, and usually other songs or texts are brought in that can range from Sanskritic philosophy to sufi mysticism to the wisdom of political leaders and popular adages and sayings of unknown provenance in any language, including English. Usually a core text, an *abhang* or another type of devotional song, is interlaced with other scripted material, like the songs of other sants, as well as non-scripted, improvised material, and this all alternates between song, didactic narrative, and general storytelling and humour, with musical accompaniment. There is almost always only one lead performer, a *kirtankar*, and sometimes musicians are attached to the *kirtankar* forming a kind of troupe.

Depending on the kind of *kirtan* being performed, the *kirtankar* stands and the audience sits (e.g. *Eknathi-kirtan*, *Rashtriya-kirtan*, *Naradiya-kirtan*), usually segregated by gender. In some cases everyone stands and dances (e.g. *Varkari-kirtan*). Most often, however, *kirtan* is a seated affair for all but the *kirtankar*, and generally this marks what I would call a didactic rather than ecstatic kind of *kirtan* performance. An audience participates in many ways, singing along with the songs, finishing well-known verses along with the *kirtankar*, sometimes interacting with the *kirtankar*, and so on. Indeed, the audience is there to be won, to be engaged, and this is readily apparent when, at the end of a "sit-down" *kirtan*, the audience will present the *kirtankar* with gifts, often of cash (though the *kirtan* performance itself is either done for free or for a fee paid by a patron). Though *kirtankars* can be of any caste,[2] they follow in the footsteps of a *shudra* performer, Namdev, a sant who is said to have flourished in the fourteenth century.

The origins of Marathi *kirtan* are traced to Namdev, who is remembered to have been born in Pandharpur to a low caste tailor or *shimpi* of the shudra *varna*, though his *varna* designation is often disputed, especially in northern India. Though born in Maharashtra and speaking Marathi as a mother tongue, he is remembered as having travelled all over India performing *kirtan*, and thus we find his songs in the Dadupanth, Kabir Panth, Sikhism, and so on. His role as the epicentre of *kirtan* in Marathi contexts is constantly reinforced. An illustration from a nineteenth-century publication of the Marathi hagiographer Mahipati's eighteenth-century text shows Namdev performing a *kirtan* accompanied by Krishna (see Figure 5.2). While Narada, the maverick sage, is considered the first *kirtankar*, his quasi-divine status makes Namdev its first fully mortal practitioner, and of course the first to perform *kirtan* in Marathi. But Namdev's legacy as a *kirtankar* is primarily within Maharashtra, and the kind of *kirtan* he is said to have performed is different from Sikh *kirtan* or the *kirtan* of most other regions and religions in India.[3]

---

2 Though caste is no bar to the performance of *kirtan*, there is still some general regularity. For example, Naradiya and Rashtriya *kirtan* tends to be performed by upper castes (both men and women), whereas Varkari *kirtan* tends to be performed by "middle" or Maratha castes and occasional Dalits. This is a very general observation on the author's part, however.

3 Novetzke (2008).

Fig. 5.2 Namdev Performing a *Kirtan*, folio from a nineteenth-century publication of Mahipati's eighteenth-century biography [1890]. Public Domain.

Namdev's association with *kirtan* must be juxtaposed to his attributed position on literacy. As mentioned above, almost all the other Marathi Varkari sants of his ilk could write, and in typical iconographic depictions they are usually displayed seated before manuscripts. Namdev, by contrast, is never seated before a book. Indeed, he is almost never depicted as seated in Marathi contexts—he's always dancing, singing, and in thrall to the moment of *kirtan*. In other words, he is always performing publicly, never writing privately. Indeed, various songs attributed to him concur that he disdained books and writing, and considered only the public performance of *kirtan* to be an appropriate way to express the sentiments of *bhakti*. Interestingly, most references to Namdev performing *kirtan* occur during the death ceremonies, the *samadhis*, of his friends and family, as if in the face of death Namdev is insisting on the immediacy and survivability of performance.

As far as I know, Namdev's songs never describe him as writing anything, nor do the songs of his companions suggest that he wrote his verses down. When the verb "to write" appears in songs attributed to Namdev it usually refers to the "writing of fate". Even when a contemporary of Namdev is linked to writing, Namdev is neatly set apart, as in this song by Janabai, his so-called "maid", who is attributed the verse, "Nivritti wrote the words that Vitthal placed on his tongue [...] and Namdev expanded the practice of *kirtan*".[4] What is far more common in the songs of Namdev and his contemporaries is speaking and listening to the speech of others. As for books, Namdev suggests that "the tongue makes a good book (*pothi*)", and states in a song's refrain:

> I don't know Veda or Purana.
> I've ignored paper and books.
> Without verses like pearl-white clouds
> I have only the spotless gem of my mind.[5]

As a non-literate performer, Namdev is an apparent anomaly in the context of Varkari sants. But these two aspects of his remembrance—being the Marathi originator of *kirtan* and presenting a disdain for writing as a *bhakti* mode of expression—establish Namdev as the archetypical *kirtan* performer in Maharashtra. Indeed, he comes to embody the ideal conception of what a *kirtankar* does—he provides, in a sense, the *kirtankar*'s theory of practice. This is a theory that not only places orality at the centre of *bhakti* practice, but requires that orality be public, something open to all in the *kirtan*. And this theory casts some suspicion on writing, insisting instead that the antidote to death and decay—to the kinds of loss to which the written archive also addresses its preservative powers—is not appropriate for *bhakti*. In Namdev's theory of practice, *bhakti* is on display, through the body and voice, and never on paper. And as the archetypical *kirtankar*, this theory of practice has been inherited, for many centuries, by those who revere him as the originator of their art. If this contention is correct, that despite the rather impressive rate of literacy among the Marathi sants the logic of the practice of Varkari religious expression has been oral, or rather performative, and not written, is there a way in which we can see it inscribed in the written record, and if so, how?

The oldest written records of Namdev's songs in Marathi date from the early sixteenth century, though most material is from the seventeenth and early eighteenth centuries. These literary remnants appear not in organised compendia of any sort, but in small notebooks, called *badas* or *vahis*, that were compiled and carried by *kirtankars* (see Figure 5.3). Over the years,

4 *Śrī Nāmdev gāthā*, ed. by S. Babar et al. (Bombay: Maharashtra State Government Printing Press, 1970), p. 513 (song 1240, verses 4 and 6).

5 *Śrī Nāmdev gāthā* (1970), song 2218, in the Hindi section, p. 836. See Winand M. Callewaert and Mukund Lath, *The Hindī Songs of Nāmdev* (Leuven: Departement Oriëntalistiek, 1989), p. 323 (song 112), where it is contained in manuscripts from the early seventeenth century.

those who have handled these notebooks have often referred to them as "*kirtan akhyane*" or the "moral stories for performing *kirtan*". In other words, they are remembered as resources for the composition of *kirtan*, objects that serve performance; they were not meant to displace the human voice and body. These notebooks are distinct in terms of orthography, content, etc., from manuscripts as such, which are often called *pothi* in Marathi, signifying a different class of document altogether. *Badas*, by contrast, are truly notebooks, loosely organised and often hastily constructed with lots of margin corrections, lines crossed out, and other emendations. The material used to make these notebooks was not meant to weather the ages, but to hold for a short time the notes and jottings of *kirtankars*. The use and status of *badas* is far different from the carefully copied manuscripts of Sanskrit and Persian literature, or even those manuscripts associated with most of the other Marathi sants. Major archival institutions—such as university libraries, research centres, and other institutes—amid their many collections of *pothis* do not generally collect *badas*. Even the concern with which these notebooks are preserved today differs from the careful attention given to manuscripts—*badas* are alien to the teak-wood glass case, rarely have an index or catalogue citations, and generally rest in haphazard stacks or even piles in the closets of institutions and private collectors.

Fig. 5.3 Four typical *badas* or "notebooks" in the collection of the Bhandarkar Oriental Research Institute. Author's photograph, CC BY.

Most notebooks are a jumble of information far beyond the enumeration of songs attributed to famous sant-singers. Although some *badas*—perhaps one tenth of the ones I examined—contain only songs, the majority are filled with an array of information, and this varying content in the *badas* speaks to the professional lives of their former owners. The *badas* contain all kinds of mundane information: astrological charts; notes on crop prices, geography, weather conditions; surveys of general news. I have found in *badas* love potions and bawdy songs called *lavani*. These materials indicate the diverse applications of the *kirtan* profession, which required a *kirtankar* to be a peripatetic, multi-tasking jack-of-all-trades, carrying information about neighbouring villages or entirely different regions of the subcontinent. *Kirtankars* kept track of births and deaths, changes in commerce, politics, and the lives of famous personalities. A *kirtankar* was part journalist, part foreign correspondent, part actor, part scholar, and part religious commentator, all in the context of the *kirtan* performance. Records of royal patronage to *kirtankars* make clear that monetary rewards reflected the entertainment value of a performance—the *kirtankar* had to sing for his supper. The best records of the economy of this and other kinds of live performance are from the Peshwa period, which obsessively documented the daily life of the Peshwa in Pune and in other areas of the Maratha Confederacy throughout the eighteenth century. Here it is clear that the performers of *kirtan* and the folk variety show, often bawdy in nature, called *tamasha*, were the same people. There was no line between "religious" and "secular" performance—a market economy of public reception governed the strategies of performers. However, for the professional performer appearances at the Pune *darbar* were few. The regular terrain of the *kirtankar* consisted of the many village centres, pilgrimage networks, and holy sites that dotted the Deccan. In these locations they performed the sacred stories, biographies, and songs of those figures that had ascended from ordinary life to hagiographical stardom, and they mixed in political parody, racy love songs, and the buffoonery of the *vidushak*, often portrayed as a bumbling, Sanskrit-mumbling Brahmin.

Clearly, this is a lot to scribble down in a small notebook as you're moving from town to town in the tumult of the late medieval Deccan. So the written record of this heterogeneous performance tradition, the *bada*, is itself a peculiar kind of writing that had, as a matter of necessity, to serve orality and performance. No one wanted to *read* a *kirtan* or an *abhang*, after all—they wanted to see it, hear it, and experience it displayed before them. The *kirtankar*, summoning the collective memory of a sant and his or her verses, could mediate a public experience of *bhakti* for devotees. Still, *kirtankars* kept records, and those records collectively give us the literary archive of the Marathi Varkari sants (and many outside the Varkari fold).

When I first started investigating these old Marathi notebooks to search out Namdev songs, I noticed a peculiar pattern. I would find songs grouped together by theme or purported author, which in itself was not peculiar. But the songs within such a cluster would be intersected by the songs of another sant. For example, notebook number 5 in the collection of the Bhandarkar Oriental Research Institute, dating probably from the late seventeenth century, begins with a few verses by Namdev about the death of Jnaneshwar, part of a series of songs called the *Samādhi*, a eulogy for Jnaneshwar. As mentioned, such moments around death were usually celebrated with a *kirtan*, and here we have an *abhang* by Namdev that is to be understood as being performed by Namdev at this moment diagetically in the Samadhi narrative sequence—so it is a song within a song, so to speak. The *kirtan* song, which in the printed editions of Namdev's verses is ten lines long, stops here after two lines. Two new songs are inserted, one by Janabai, Namdev's "maid" mentioned earlier, and another by Tukaram, both of which are about the glories of listening to *kirtan*. Then the Namdev song is restarted from where it was interrupted, from its third line until the end. Another *bada*, from a private collection in Dhulia and probably finished around the eighteenth century, gives only songs by Namdev and Tukaram, but they are, again, sliced, edited, and intermingled, as if offering only first and second lines as reminders, but positioned together to bear out their thematic interaction. I found this pattern to be quite common in manuscript collections of the late seventeenth and eighteenth centuries, as several more notebooks revealed the same alternating pattern.

Let me highlight another example. *Bada* number 52 in the collection of the Bhandarkar Oriental Research Institute contains a section that tells us it will relate "the beginning of the story of Uddhav's arrival" (*Uddhav āgamana prārambha*), i.e. the arrival of Krishna's messenger to give word to the *gopi*s as to whether Krishna has survived his encounter with the evil king Kamsa in Mathura (see Figure 5.4). The text begins to divide songs in Hindi, called *sakhis*, and Namdev's Marathi *abhangs*. This goes on for ten pages, moving through four Namdev Marathi *abhangs* interspersed with Hindi *sakhis*. While this may seem a strange way to record songs, it is perfectly normal from the point of view of the performance of *kirtan*. Most *kirtankars* interweave songs in exactly this way. They select a single, exemplar *abhang*; then they give one couplet, or sometimes simply a single line, of this *abhang*; and follow with a short portion from another sant's songs, or a brief story, or an aphorism, or a Sanskrit *shloka*, etc. In the context of performance, these interwoven items can come from any source—and indeed Namdev is not the most commonly invoked. But in most texts I've seen it seems that Namdev is the one who allows for the interlinear commentary to be enacted—his songs appear most frequently in such intermingled contexts. The format that can be seen in the notebook is, I believe, a transcription, or perhaps a plan, for a *kirtan*. It is as close as the text can come to replicating the oral performative context.

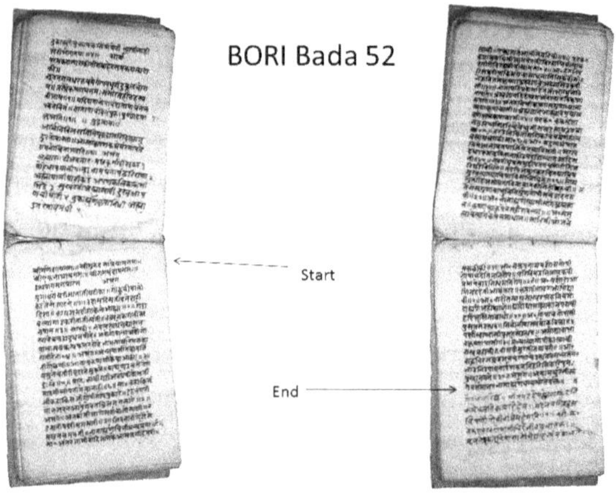


Fig. 5.4 Transcript of a *kirtan* from a Marathi *bada*, c. eighteenth century. Bhandarkar Oriental Research Institute. Author's photograph, CC BY.

Yet this peculiar form is more than just transcription. One sees this format abundantly in the *kirtan* primer handbooks that have been published over the last hundred years or so. The *Kirtan mārgadarśikā* (*Exposition on the Kirtan Tradition*) is a series of *kirtan* primers produced by Krishnadas Lohiya, a famous *kirtankar* of Pandharpur (see Figure 5.5). The layout of his primers follows almost the same pattern as we saw in the *badas* above: a "*kirtanace abhaṅg*" is chosen, which provides the exemplar and theme for the *kirtan*, and it is delivered in lines and couplets interspersed with songs from other sants. Lohiya also gives his own commentary among the interspersed lines, but one presumes that this voice, the voice of the *kirtankar* (as opposed to the voice of the sants whose songs are being used) would change according to the performer and the performance context. If one removes the *kirtankar*'s voice, the format is exactly the same as one finds in *bada* 52.

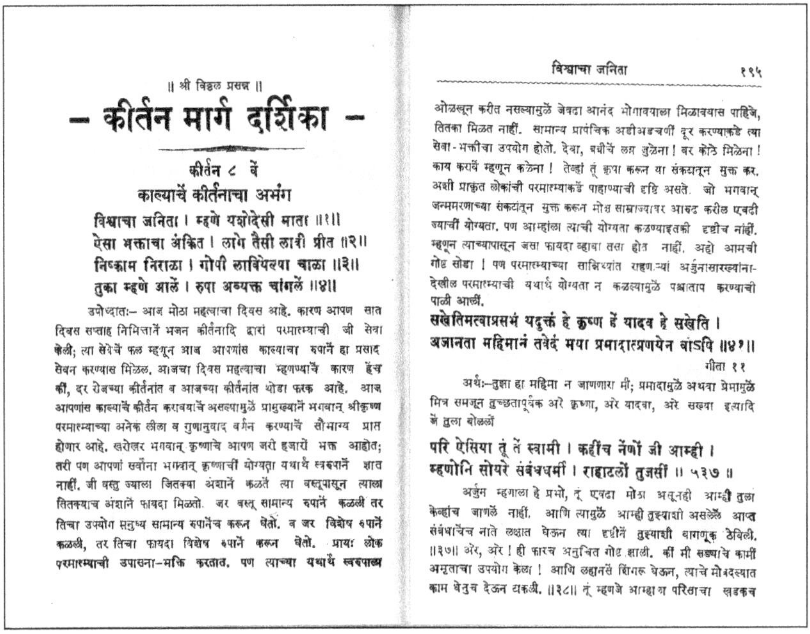

॥ श्री विठ्ठल प्रसन्न ॥

# – कीर्तन मार्ग दर्शिका –

कीर्तन ८ वें

काल्याचें कीर्तनाचा अभंग

विश्वाचा जनिता । म्हणे यशोदेसी माता ॥१॥
ऐसा भक्ताचा अंकित । लागे तैसी लावी प्रीत ॥२॥
निष्काम निराळा । गोपी लाविंयेल्या चाळा ॥३॥
तुका म्हणे आलें । रुपा अव्यक्त चांगलें ॥४॥

उपोध्दातः– आज मोठा महत्वाचा दिवस आहे. कारण आपण सात दिवस सप्ताह निमित्तानें भजन कीर्तनादि द्वारां परमात्म्याची जी सेवा केली; त्या सेवेचें फल म्हणून आज आपणांस काल्याचा रुपानें हा प्रसाद सेवन करण्यास मिळेल. आजचा दिवस महत्वाचा म्हणण्याचें कारण हेंच कीं, दर रोजच्या कीर्तनांत व आजच्या कीर्तनांत थोडा फरक आहे. आज आपणांस काल्याचें कीर्तन करावयाचें असल्यामुळें प्रामुख्यानें भगवान् श्रीकृष्ण परमात्म्याच्या अनेक लीला व गुणानुवाद वर्णन करण्याचें सौभाग्य प्राप्त होणार आहे. खरोखर भगवान् कृष्णाचे आपण जरी हजारों भक्त आहोत; तरी पण आपणां सर्वांना भगवान् कृष्णाची योग्यता यथार्थ स्वरुपानें ज्ञात नाहीं. जी वस्तु ज्याला जितक्या अंशानें कळते त्या वस्तूपासून त्याला तितक्याच अंशानें फायदा मिळतो. जर वस्तू सामान्य रुपानें कळली तर तिचा उपयोग मनुष्य सामान्य रुपानेंच करून घेतो. व जर विशेष रुपानें कळली, तर तिचा फायदा विशेष रुपानें करून घेतो. प्रायः लोक परमात्म्याची उपासना–भक्ति करतात. पण त्याच्या यथार्थ स्वरुपाला

विश्वाचा जनिता १९५

ओळखून करीत नसल्यामुळें जेवढा आनंद भोगावयाला मिळावयास पाहिजे, तितका मिळत नाहीं. सामान्य प्रापंचिक अडीअडचणी दूर करण्याकडे त्या सेवा-भक्तीचा उपयोग होतो. देवा, मुलीचें लग्न जुळेना! वर कोठे मिळेना! काय करावें म्हणून कळेना! तेव्हां तूं कृपा करून या संकटातून मुक्त कर. अशी प्राकृत लोकांची परमात्म्याकडे पाहाण्याची दृष्टि असते. जो भगवान् जन्ममरणाच्या संकटांतून मुक्त करून मोक्ष साम्राज्यावर आरुढ करील एवढी ज्याची योग्यता. पण आम्हांला त्याची योग्यता कळण्याइतकी दृष्टीच नाहीं. म्हणून त्याच्यापासून जसा फायदा व्हावा तसा होत नाहीं. अहो आमची गोष्ट सोडा! पण परमात्म्याच्या सान्निध्यांत राहणाऱ्यां अर्जुनासारख्यांना-देखील परमात्म्याची यथार्थ योग्यता न कळल्यामुळें पश्चाताप करण्याची पाळी आली.

सखेतिमत्वाप्रसभं यदुक्तं हे कृष्ण हें यादव हे सखेति ।
अजानता महिमानं तवेदं मया प्रमादात्प्रणयेन वांऽपि ॥४१॥
गीता ११

अर्थः–तुझा हा महिमा न जाणणारा मी; प्रमादामुळें अथवा प्रेमामुळें मित्र समजून तुच्छतापूर्वक अरे कृष्णा, अरे यादवा, अरे सख्या इत्यादि जें तुला बोललों

परि ऐसिया तूं तें स्वामी । कहींच नेणों जी आम्ही ।
म्हणोनि सोयरे संबंधधर्मी । राहाटलों तुजसीं ॥ ५३७ ॥

अर्जुन म्हणाला हे प्रभो, तूं एवढा मोठा असूनही आम्ही तुला केव्हांच जाणलें नाहीं. आणि त्यामुळें आम्ही तुझ्याशी असलेलें आप्त संबंधाचेंच नाते लक्षात घेऊन त्या दृष्टीनें तुझ्याशी वागणूक ठेविली. ॥३७॥ अरे, अरे! ही फारच अनुचित गोष्ट झाली. कीं मी सड्याचे कामीं अमृताचा उपयोग केला! आणि लहानसें खिंगरू घेऊन, त्याचे मोबदल्यात काम धेनुच देऊन टाकली. ॥३८॥ तूं म्हणजे आम्हास परिसाचा खडकच

Fig. 5.5 A representative page from Lohiya, K. 1997. *Kirtan mārga darśikā* (Pune: Sharada Sahitya), pp. 194-95. 

This is a format that privileges performance. Text here is submitted to the demands of performance. The text is a tool, a means and not an end. Furthermore, its role is not preservation—it may function as an archive, but its composition is not intended to ossify a text and convey it into the future as a fixed form. Instead, the text is dynamic, meant to trigger and prompt a performance, existing as a kind of outline of a *kirtan*, but containing no narrative, typological, or historical logic independent of performance. In other words, it cannot stand alone, as can a *pothi* or a fixed, complete composition. The sort of format seen here is always a "work in progress" because it is a means not an end. Other scholars have noted the echoes of performance in manuscript collections. Winand Callaewart and Mukund Lath, for example, in their wonderful work on Namdev in Hindi contexts have found that Namdev's songs were eventually standardised according to *raga*, much as the songs of the *Ādigranth* and other collections in North India were standardised.[6] Yet I would argue that this process reveals not a secondary status *vis-à-vis* performance. Over time, *raga* associations become fixed to particular compositions in their

6 Callewart and Lath (1989); see also Miner in this volume.

entirety—words and music are joined—and a new kind of text emerges. The categorisation by *raga* suggests an origin in performance, but becomes its own literary organisational strategy. In time, *raga* categorisation became a fixed system, a literary logic to manage a growing corpus of songs. But in the case of *bada* 52, for example, the textual format resists distillation into a new literary type (like the word-music association of *pada* and *raga*) because it remains self-consciously incomplete. Such *badas* record fragments of songs arranged for performative effect—hints and indications to a performer. But taken alone, these are fractured compositions unified only when plugged into the music-narrative-embodiment matrix of a *kirtan* performance.

These examples concur to show that performance, not literacy, dominated the pre-modern public sphere of performative devotion in Maharashtra. Literacy was everywhere, there is no doubt. And it was not just a technology of the elite, but clearly part of the daily work of performers who were not in any real sense elites. Literacy did not have the patina of mystery we often associate with the "literary" classes, high caste priests, scribes, and authors, nor was it central to the conveyance of devotion. *Kirtan*, embodied in the roving *kirtankar*, was the nexus of the public culture of *bhakti*, and of public entertainment in general. In this context, a *kirtankar* might be considered an intermediary between text and orality, though his bread and butter, as it were, was the oral public *kirtan*.

The logic of performance has remained within the written record of the *kirtankar* up to the present, even though most archived *badas* were composed before the twentieth century. *Kirtankars* still carry notebooks and use them in the same way *badas* were used, only now, of course, they also have many more printed aids—the *kirtan* handbooks produced by people like Lohiya and the many editions of the songs and hagiographies of the sants. So perhaps the last example of the kind of logic of writing before the advent of generous printed resources I can point towards can be found in the monumental works of Mahipati, who lived throughout the eighteenth century, dying in 1790. He was a Deshastha Brahmin *kulkarni* or village accountant of Taharabad, but he is more famous now as a *kirtankar* who specialised in the stories of the lives of the sants. Around the middle of the eighteenth century, Mahipati is said to have written his most famous composition, the *Bhaktavijay*. In this work, Mahipati clearly relies upon other materials, especially earlier hagiographies and biographical or autobiographical songs attributed to various sants, the most important of which, for the earliest strata of Varkari lore, is Namdev. If we take, for example, Mahipati's retelling of a purported journey to North India undertaken by Namdev and his companion, Jnandev, we find that Mahipati follows an earlier version of this story, attributed to Namdev, almost word for word (see Figure 5.6). In the illustration given, on one side you see the record of this composition attributed to Namdev from a manuscript dated 1631 CE. On the other side you see Mahipati's retelling dated 1762 CE. The bolded portions are common to both versions, whereas the unbolded text in Mahipati's version represents Mahipati's inventions in, I would argue, the style of a typical *kirtankar*. We can see that Mahipati adds many interlinear comments to Namdev's song in a manner very similar to the format of *bada* 52 and other manuscripts. He combines lines 2 and 3 from Namdev's song to make his line 87, fills in his own presumably improvised materials from the performance of a *kirtan*, and then returns to lines 4 and 6 from Namdev for his line 93. The format is again that of a *kirtan*. Though Mahipati self-consciously refers to his works as *"pothis"* and *"granthas"* (literally, book), throughout his hagiographies he calls upon his audience to "listen" and to "hear" of the lives of the sants and always refers to himself as a *kirtankar*. Indeed, in his lifetime, he was famous for his *kirtans*. Only after his lifetime did the written texts he left behind come to flesh out his fame in religious culture.

# Mahipati's *Bhaktavijay*

From the *Tirthavali* attributed to Namdev 1631 CE

The two walked along the road pleasantly enough, but Nama's thoughts were on Pandurang. || 1 ||

**From time to time, wherever they might be, Nama would turn around and look back, unable to bear separation from Pandhari, || 2 ||**

**Saying, "Tell me, O Mother, Lord of Keshi, why did you allow me to leave? You have not come along with me to watch over me. || 3 ||**

**I've fallen in among strangers and I'm very anxious. I can see no one dear to me. || 4 ||**

My heart is split, stuck in two places, and it's made me feel terribly depressed. || 5 ||

**You're my mother and my father, my brother and my uncle, Lord of Pandhari. || 6 ||**

From the *Bhaktavijay* attributed to Mahipati 1762

**In the meantime Nama looked back very often || 87 ||**

**He cried, 'O, God, you've forsaken me. You've not come to see me off."** Saying this, he fainted. || 88 ||

Just as a child cries when separated from its mother; as a young deer feels when losing sight of its mother, the baby deer searches for its mother everywhere || 89 ||

And just as a man overcome with hunger needs food; and as someone overcome with thirst needs water; and as the *chatak* bird, dying of thirst, scans the clouds for rain || 90 ||

And as a the *chakor* bird, at the new moon, searches for the heavenly orb in vain; and as a fish in a draught longs for water || 91 ||

And as when a young turtle is hungry and does not see its mother anywhere; just so was Nama, separated from Panduranga, overcome with grief || 92 ||

**He said to himself, "I find myself in a forest overcome with anxiety. I see no one who is near and dear to me. Though art my mother and father." || 93||**

Fig. 5.6 (L) section is taken from the *Śrī Nāmdev gāthā* (1970), p. 343; (R) is taken from Abbott and Godbole's translation of the *Bhaktavijay* 1996 [1933], pp. 164-65. Image by the author, CC BY.

At the conclusion of his *Bhaktavijay*, Mahipati makes his ability to connect oral performance and literacy clear. He writes:

> I have written every single letter in this book
> Just as Rukmini's husband has commanded.
> Like the puff of breath blown by a musician,
> I am the wind that sounds the flute.[7]

Mahipati's peculiar metaphor, mixing literacy and the sound of the flute, is clearly meant to invoke a performance, not the preservation of literacy—he is not the ink of the pen, for example. Yet he is explicit that he has "written every single letter" just as each note of an instrument is sounded. Mahipati concludes his *Bhaktavijay* this way:

> To some you have given knowledge of the soul.
> Some have begged to dwell in the union of self and universe.
> My heart's desire is that I will sing [*varṇīn*]
> About the character [*guna*] of Hari.
> Some sit on beds of nails,
> Some sit with Vishnu in heaven.
> For me, in the *kirtan* of your servants
> I have become lost in supreme love.[8]

Mahipati is both producer and consumer of the *kirtan* of the sants. Indeed, as we have seen, he takes their voices and adopts them into his own in a format that I've referred to elsewhere as corporate authorship, following the work of Jack Hawley and others on authorship in *bhakti* contexts.[9] Mahipati does not tell us when he is quoting Namdev and when we are hearing his original voice. But Mahipati is no plagiarist either—he is a performer, whose performance is crystallised, by his own hand, into a text, i.e. a permanent, non-performative form. Mahipati closes what is probably his most famous hagiography by invoking the oral context of performance, set down on the written page. Within fifty years of his death, this text, the *Bhaktavijay*, would enter the world of print as one

7 Mahipati, *Bhaktavijay* (Bombay: Saka, 1890): chapter 57, verses 220-21, pp. 387-88. My translation.

8 Ibid., chapter 57, verse 212, p. 387. My translation.

9 See J.S. Hawley, 'Author and Authority in the *Bhakti* Poetry of North India', *Journal of Asian Studies* 47.2 (1988), 269-90, and C. Novetzke, 'Divining an Author: The Idea of Authorship in an Indian Religious Tradition', *History of Religions* 42.3 (2003), 213-42.

of the first and most popular devotional texts published in the Marathi colonial public sphere.

In this essay I have tried to demonstrate how one can read the written archive of Marathi *bhakti* materials in a way that reveals the logic of *kirtan* and oral performance and emphasises the telling rather than the text. In other words, certain texts themselves suggest that sometimes the telling is the text, fossilised in literacy, imperfectly cemented in time. The written materials I have reviewed here are all the product of a performance economy, in a sense, a literary space that served the performance of *kirtan* before the modern period. Clearly, orality and literacy existed in a symbiotic relationship. In his study of the practices of "everyday life" Michel de Certeau has suggested that the modern idea of writing and authorship occurred because writing had lost its connection to orality when progressive developments in writing and the accumulation, especially through print, of vast bibliographic genealogies began to refer to earlier written sources, rather than to "original" oral ones.[10] At this point writing took on a character all its own, made up its own genealogy resting on replication and consumption, and the symbiotic connection between orality and literacy was lost. In our case we could say that when Mahipati the oral performer became Mahipati the literary and printed author, his fame as a *kirtankar* faded in lieu of his fame as a writer of books about the *bhakti* past. A similar historical-teleological notion is readily apparent in the work of Goody and Watt, for example: although they clearly state that literacy is always afloat in a sea of orality, the dominance of literacy is also the advent of history and of sustainable rational thought, the foundations of modernity.[11] This shift to a self-referential writing system can also be seen to mark a loss of cultural integrity, or a schism that takes on the shape of class differences. Indeed, as I have pointed out, the "oral" texts of the *bada* are of a different class than the "literary" texts of the *pothi* or *grantha*.

Very few concrete examples exist anywhere in the world of a clear transition from an oral society to a literate one—this distinction is one of the key problems of the orality-literacy debate, and has been

---

10 Michel de Certeau, *The Writing of History* (New York: Columbia University Press, 1988).

11 "We must reckon with the fact that in our civilization, writing is clearly an addition, not an alternative, to oral transmission"; Jack Goody and Ian Watt, 'The Consequences of Literacy', *Comparative Studies in Society and History* 5.3 (1963), 345.

rejuvenated in the "cyber" world where text, image, video, and live human interaction can now take place in rapid and simultaneous ways as if technology were constantly trying to replicate the experience of "being there" at a live performance. In the public performance of *kirtan* in the pre-colonial era and later we see a systematic interweaving of orality and literacy that nevertheless privileges orality. I have argued in this essay that the logic of practice at the heart of the public performance of *bhakti* among Varkaris in Maharashtra not only coexisted with forms of literacy but recognised the "threat" of literacy, as well as its necessity. The tradition, through figures like Namdev and centuries of performers, innovated ways to integrate writing and performance, but was always careful to maintain the necessary privilege of performance over writing, to control the power of literacy. I have tried to demonstrate this logic of practice for *kirtankars* by noting how writing functioned in a system of performance that sought to guard against the loss of the immediacy of cultural memory, physical display, and devotional interaction. For the Marathi *kirtankar*, who remains the lifeblood of the devotional tradition of Varkaris, the tongue would always make the best book.

# 6. A Handbook for Storytellers: The *Ṭirāz al-akhbār* and the *Qissa* Genre[1]

*Pasha M. Khan*

The rise of the Urdu novel in the late nineteenth century and the growing celebration of the "natural" at the expense of the marvellous in the twentieth century pushed the Urdu and Indo-Persian romance genre—the *qissa* or *dastan*—into relative obscurity. When it has been studied by modern critics, there has been an unfortunate tendency to treat it as a primitive and imperfect ancestor of the novel. In order to recover a sense of what the *qissa* genre may have been before this recent period, we must examine the concept of genre itself as well as the concept of the *qissa* as a genre. As it turns out, the particular genre of the *qissa* sheds much light on questions of genre in general. One of the keys to understanding the

1 I must acknowledge my debts to four people without whom this contribution would never have existed. First of all, Shamsur Rahman Faruqi, who first mentioned Fakhr al-Zamani to me in New York in September 2008, and who has already written about him at some length. Secondly, my friend and colleague Azfar Moin of the University of Michigan, who regaled me with his tales and ideas about Indian history over tea at the British Library that same Autumn, and who reminded me of Fakhr al-Zamani and gave me access to Mahjub's article—I am especially in his debt. Soon thereafter Francesca Orsini graciously invited me to the SOAS conference on orality despite my misgivings about my lack of access to the MS of the *Ṭirāz al-akhbār*. Finally, in Chicago in March 2009, Paul Losensky introduced me to Shafi'i-Kadkani's description of the same MS, thereby enabling me to make a historical argument regarding the multiplicity of generic strands running through the *qissa*. Thanks are also due to Maria Subtelny for providing helpful comments on the penultimate draft. Research was supported by a Social Sciences and Humanities Research Council of Canada Doctoral Fellowship.

 http://dx.doi.org/10.11647/OBP.0062.06

*qissa* as it may have been understood in its heyday is that it was an oral genre, and indeed a fully performative one, as I will show.

The text I examine in this paper, 'Abd al-Nabi Fakhr al-Zamani's manual for storytellers, is *sui generis* itself, but it gives us a uniquely clear window onto the process of *qissa* performance, shows us one manner in which the *qissa* was defined or "encoded", and, most importantly, lays before us the materials with which the *qissas* that it describes could be built. In doing us this last-mentioned service, it also in a sense undermines the very idea of monolithic genres, in a way that this study will explain. Connected to the fragmentation of the genre is the way in which the *qissa*'s prescribed use or purpose ought to be approached. The understandable aversion in some quarters to instrumentalising texts and spoken words should not blind us to the fact that they were meant to have certain effects, which were sometimes announced by the discourse itself, but more often implied within the discourse's genre as a result of its genre code.[2] A volume on oral performance has the advantage of highlighting the worldliness of the performed discourse—the music that is sung before the emperor or the tale that is told in the bazaar—making it difficult to ignore its relation to the world and its effects on its listeners. The healing properties of music discussed by Katherine Schofield, for instance, are as purposive as the disciplinary, "*adabi*" properties of the *qissa*. How the purposive nature of the *qissa* genre in particular relates to its fragmentation is a problem that will be considered at the end of the paper.

Given that this study will look at a particular conception of the *qissa* genre from the seventeenth century, it is legitimate to ask why this definition of the *qissa* is important and whether it was not a dead end. Indeed, one of the fascinating things about this very specific *qissa* "genre code", which has been discussed by only one Urdu critic so far, is that it appears to have survived well into the nineteenth century before falling into oblivion. To begin with, let us consider the most interesting later expression of this definition.

---

2 I will use the term "discourse" rather than "text" in order to signal my inclusion of non-written language; it is to be understood as approximating *sukhan* or *kalam* (see also d'Hubert in this volume).

# Traces of Continuity and Influence

One of the most successful versions of the story of the Prophet's uncle Amir Hamza was published in 1855 in Calcutta. This is the source of the version that Musharraf Ali Farooqi has recently translated as *The Adventures of Amir Hamza*, and the basis of the translation written by Frances Pritchett in *The Romance Tradition in Urdu*. The 1855 text, entitled *Tarjuma-i dāstān-i Ṣāḥib-qirān* (*Translation of the Story of the Lord of the Auspicious Conjunction*), was written by Mirza Aman 'Ali Khan "Ghalib" Lakhnawi (not to be confused with his more famous Delhite contemporary, the Urdu poet Mirza Asad Allah Khan Ghalib). In his preface, Ghalib Lakhnawi is found making the customary self-effacing remarks about being a blithering know-nothing,[3] and claiming in the next breath that he is married to the granddaughter of no less than Tipu Sultan, the late ruler of Mysore. Beyond these remarks, we know little about Ghalib Lakhnawi aside from what 'Abd al-Ghafur Nassakh tells us in his prosopography (*tazkira*) about ten years after the *Tarjuma*'s publication, which is that Ghalib was a Deputy Tax Collector, the disciple of a poet named Qatil, and a Hindu convert to Islam. He had lived in Patna as well as Lucknow and had at last settled in Calcutta.[4] Whoever he was, he appears to have been coaxed into writing the *dastan* by a friend, a physician of Calcutta named Hakim Imdad 'Ali b. Hakim Shaikh Dilawar 'Ali, who then printed the book using what seems to have been his own personal press.[5] It appears that the Hakim wished to translate the *dastan* himself (from a deliciously withheld Persian

3 That is, "*hec ma-dān-i kaj-maj zabān*", 'Abd al-Ghafur Nassakh, *Sukhan-i shu'arā* (*Speech of Poets*, Lucknow: Uttar Pradesh Urdu Academy, 1982), p. 3. All translations are mine unless otherwise indicated.

4 Nassakh was himself Deputy Collector and Deputy Magistrate for Rajshahi (now in Bangladesh), making it likely that he met Ghalib while on the job; Nassakh (1982), p. 349 cited in Shamsur Rahman Faruqi, *Sāḥirī, shāhī, sāḥib-qirānī: Dāstān-i Amīr Ḥamza kā mutāla'a* (New Delhi: Qaumi Council bara'e furugh-i Urdu zaban, 1999), Vol. 1, p. 209. Here is my translation of Nassakh's entry on Ghalib (1982, p. 149):
Pennamed Ghalib: Mirza Aman 'Ali Khan 'Azimabadi ['Azimabad = Patna]. Author of the Urdu *Qiṣṣa-i Amīr Ḥamza*. Disciple of Qatil. For a time he was Deputy Collector. For a long while he has chosen to reside in Calcutta. He also composes verses in Persian. He was formerly a Hindu, but was then graced with Islam. I met him in Chandannagar, popularly known as Fransidanga. I have seen his *Qiṣṣa-i Amīr Ḥamza*. [A selection of verses by Ghalib follows.]

5 The Matba'-i Hakim or Matba'-i Imdadiyya.

text), but did not do so, on the grounds that his medical practice would suffer. Ghalib's account tells of Hakim Imdad 'Ali's distraction and his reluctant delegation of the task in the Hakim's own words:

> I receive no respite from the clinic, for which reason it is difficult for me to finish [the *dastan*]; and if I abandon the clinic I am helpless to cure the servants of the Absolute Sage (*Ḥakīm*).[6]

Imagine the scandal had Imdad 'Ali sidelined his practice: perhaps he might have been busy scribbling scurrilous accounts of the artistic flair with which the trickster 'Amar 'Ayyar painted polka-dots on the hapless King Nausherwan, while his patients clamoured to consult him about their venereal diseases.[7] (Colonial records of the famous ailments of Lucknow were not kept until the passage of the Contagious Diseases Act nine years later.[8])

In response to Hakim Imdad 'Ali's appeal to Ghalib's "regard for an old friend [*liḥāẓ-i muḥibb-i qadīm*]" caught up in his medical work, Ghalib Lakhnawi took on the task of writing the *dastan*, and the Hakim published it himself. Alas, Ghalib's fame quickly faded thanks to the *dastan*'s superb plagiarism by 'Abd Allah Bilgrami, who stuffed, padded, and ornamented his version, which ultimately eclipsed Ghalib Lakhnawi's work.[9] The *dastan* became very popular in this puffed-up form and was thenceforth famous as Bilgrami's child.[10] The Bilgrami

6 Ghalib Lakhnawi, *Tarjuma-i dāstān-i Ṣāḥib-qirān* (Calcutta: Matba'-i Imdadiyya, 1855), p. 2.

7 My speculations on the nature of the illnesses distracting Hakim Imdad 'Ali are admittedly the products of my fancy. However, 'Amar 'Ayyar does indeed apply a *pointillé* pattern to the royal cheek that I have mentioned, along with other pranks of a gross nature: "*Nausherwān kī dāṛhī mūṅcheṅ peshāb se mūṅḍ ke hama tan barahna kar ke hāth pāṅw to nīl se range aur mūṅh kālā kar ke cūne ke ṭīke diye*"; Ghalib Lakhnawi (1855), p. 358. In Musharraf Ali Farooqi's translation, "He lathered up Nausherwan's beard and whiskers with his urine and shaved them all off. Amar then stripped Naushervan naked, dyed his hands and feet with indigo, and after blackening his face, made spots all over it with lime"; 'Abdullah Husain Bilgrami and Mirza Aman Allah Ghalib Lakhnawi, *The Adventures of Amir Hamza: Lord of the Auspicious Planetary Conjunction*, trans. by Musharraf Ali Farooqi (New York: Modern Library, 2007), p. 663.

8 See Veena Talwar Oldenburg, 'Lifestyle as Resistance: The Case of the Courtesans of Lucknow, India', *Feminist Studies* 16, 2 (1990), 260.

9 See Frances Pritchett, 'Introduction', *The Romance Tradition in Urdu: Adventures from the Dastan of Amir Hamza* (New York: Columbia University Press, 1991), p. 30.

10 In the Summer of 1985 Frances Pritchett and Shamsur Rahman Faruqi unearthed a rare copy of the 1855 edition. Pritchett subsequently made a copy of the Ghalib Lakhnawi text available to the Library of Congress in microfiche form (call number LOC Microfiche 85/61479 (P) So Asia). I am obliged to her for allowing me to peruse her copy of the *dastan*.

editions naturally omitted Ghalib Lakhnawi's telltale preface with its concern for Hakim Imdad 'Ali's patients and its important throwaway remark on the four pillars of the *dastan*—a remark which appears to be a reformulation of a statement about the genre made more than two centuries previously.

It is to this remark that I now turn. "There are four things", Ghalib wrote, "in this *dastan*: battle, courtly assemblies, enchanted worlds and trickery" (*is dāstān men̲ cār cīzen̲ hain̲ razm bazm ṭilism aur 'ayyārī*).[11] Later in the nineteenth century, the Lakhnawi intellectual 'Abd al-Halim Sharar echoed Ghalib's assertion, with one difference: according to him the four elements were "*razm, bazm, ḥusn o 'ishq*" (love and beauty) and "*'ayyārī*".[12] Whence this substitution of Ghalib's third pillar of the *dastan* genre, the *tilism*, for Sharar's *husn o 'ishq*? Shamsur Rahman Faruqi suggests that Sharar may have chosen *husn o 'ishq* rather than *tilism* due to the influence of an Iranian style of storytelling.[13] But Faruqi's hypothesis that the category of *husn o 'ishq* might be from Iran is not based on a notion that Iranians are incurable romantics. Rather, it stems from the striking fact that the same four elements recounted by Sharar—*razm, bazm, husn o 'ishq, 'ayyari*—are enumerated in the early seventeenth century by 'Abd al-Nabi Fakhr al-Zamani, who was a storyteller in Jahangir's India, but who was born in Iran and professed to know a good deal about the Iranian tradition of storytelling.

## Genre Codes and Purposes

Before we broach the subject of Fakhr al-Zamani's work, which evidently inaugurated or at least accorded with a long-lasting definition of the *qissa/dastan* genre, there is a word or two to be said about the idea of genre.[14] Many literary critics have noted that genres (or their *codifications*—a concept to be explained shortly) tend to specify expected

11 Ghalib Lakhnawi (1855), p. 2. For a lengthy discussion of these elements, see S.R. Faruqi (1999), Vol. 1, p. 197ff.

12 'Abd al-Halim Sharar, *Guẕashta Lakhnau*, ed. by Rashid Hasan Khan (Delhi: Maktaba-i Jami'a, 2000), p. 149.

13 S.R. Faruqi (1999), Vol. 1, p. 410.

14 The words *qissa* and *dastan*, which I will use interchangeably, are generally used to denote a narrative account, especially a fictive one. The line between the two is fine almost to the point of non-existence: see Pritchett (1991), p. 5; however, see Faruqi's insistence that narratives such as Mir Amman's *Bāgh o Bahār* and Rajab 'Ali Beg Surur's *Fasāna-e 'ajā'ib* do not qualify as *dastans*; S.R. Faruqi (1999), Vol. 1, pp. 29, 194-95.

uses for the texts through which they flow;[15] it seems probable that codifications of the *qissa* genre do something similar. In fact, as we will see, Fakhr al-Zamani's formulation responds quite appropriately to the question, "what is the purpose of the *qissa* genre?"[16]

I concur with the view that no genre inheres essentially and irrevocably in a written or oral discourse as a fact of its nature. Genres are socially instituted laws, whose institution may be recorded. Tvetzan Todorov's bipartite model of the constitution of genres is useful: any given genre is marked by (1) a trait or a series of traits, but in order for those traits to be recognised as signals of a discourse's participation in a genre, they must be (2) *encoded* as traits of that genre by way of another discourse.[17] Such a *genre code*, if recorded, might take the form of a critical or metadiscursive text which explicitly describes or prescribes a genre. At least this is the most obvious form of the genre code, of which we have examples in the above statements on the *qissa* genre by 'Abd al-Halim Sharar and Ghalib Lakhnawi. These codes, as I have hinted, have a much more extensive antecedent in a text by 'Abd al-Nabi Fakhr al-Zamani, which will be the focus of this study. I will examine the traits of the genre as Fakhr al-Zamani presents them in his own codification.

The information that we possess regarding Fakhr al-Zamani's activities and ideas with regard to the *qissa* genre comes from a singular book of his: the *Ṭirāz al-akhbār* (*The Embroidery of Tales*), a manual for storytellers, to which we now turn.[18] Three manuscripts of the never-printed *Ṭirāz*

---

15 For instance, Fredric Jameson, *The Political Unconscious: Narrative as a Socially Symbolic Act* (Ithaca, NY: Cornell University Press, 1981), p. 106.

16 I am grateful to my friend and colleague Abhishek Kaicker for initially posing this question.

17 Tzvetan Todorov, *Genres in Discourse* (Cambridge: Cambridge University Press, 1990), p. 198. This other discourse might be *within* the discourse whose genre it encodes.

18 The title is polyvalent. *Tiraz* or *taraz* means "embroidery", with secondary meanings including "workshop, factory"—a particularly apt metaphor for the productive function of Fakhr al-Zamani's manual. The additional meaning "form, kind, type" seems the most appropriate one when we consider the division of the book into twelve sections, each called a *tiraz*. Finally, the word may also be read as *tarraz*, meaning an "embroiderer". The most complete MS is in the library of the Majlis-i Sina-yi sabiq, no. 358. Two others exist in Tehran University's Central Library and the Ayat Allah Mar'ashi Library in Qom; see Shafi'i-Kadkani, 'Nigāhī ba Ṭirāz al-akhbār', *Nāma-yi bahāristān* 1.5 (138), 109. This made it difficult, at the time of writing this essay, to access the text itself, though I was subsequently able to obtain and read it. My translation of the opening portions will appear in a forthcoming *Festschrift*. Therefore it is necessary to stress the strictly provisional nature of this study, which does not make use of the manuscripts.

*al-akhbār* are extant, not in South Asia but in Tehran and Qom in Iran; therefore for this chapter I have had to rely on two descriptive articles by the Iranian scholars Muhammad Ja'far Mahjub and Muhammad Riza Shafi'i-Kadkani. The former describes and quotes large swathes of the *Ṭirāz*'s fascinating *muqaddama* or Foreword, while the latter outlines the body of the text. It is possible that this distance from the source text means that my paper is not far from being a collection of bald lies. If this is so, at least it has the interesting quality of surreptitiously reflecting the genre it purports to describe.

## Fakhr al-Zamani and the *Ṭirāz al-akhbār*

Given the unwarranted obscurity of the *Ṭirāz al-akhbār*, it seems proper to say a few words about its author and his life. We may deduce from what he writes of himself in the *Mai-khāna* that familial networks played an important role in his working life, and we may also see the usefulness of storytelling in gaining patronage. 'Abd al-Nabi Fakhr al-Zamani was born in the city of Qazwin in Iran in the late sixteenth century, a time when Iranian emigration to India was not infrequent. He writes that his father Khalaf Beg was a retiring man of a sufistic bent who had the prescience to foretell the hour of his own demise, predicting that he would die on such-and-such a day during the Friday prayer.[19] However, 'Abd al-Nabi recognised the atavism of his own poetic skill, and changed his sobriquet from 'Izzati' to 'Fakhr al-Zamani' in honour of his more learned and famed paternal grandfather Fakhr al-Zaman. He claims that in his youth his memory was so powerful that when "out of youthful desire he sought knowledge of *qissas*, [...] by the absorptive force of his memory he retained the entire *qissa* of Amir Hamza 'Abd al-Mutallib in his mind after hearing it only once".[20] At the age of nineteen he made a pilgrimage to the shrine of Imam Riza in Mashhad, where he was enthralled by merchants' and travellers' accounts of India. As a result, he found himself trekking through Qandahar and on to Lahore, where he made his entrance in 1609.

He stayed in Lahore for four months before moving on to Jahangir's capital at Agra. Fakhr al-Zamani's account makes this move appear

---

19 'Abd al-Nabi Fakhr al-Zamani Qazwini, *Tazkira-i maikhāna*, ed. by Ahmad Gulcin-i Ma'ani, 3rd edn (Tehran: Iqbal, 1983), p. 758.

20 Fakhr al-Zamani (1983), p. 760.

more or less fortuitous, but it is telling that in Agra he met a relative named Mirza Nizami Qazwini, who was at the time a royal *waqi'a-nawis* or chronicler (and later the *divan* of Bihar). In all likelihood Fakhr al-Zamani knew of his kinsman's presence in the Mughal capital and exploited it as a way to gain employment. Given this probability, it is likely that his apparent drifting off to India was quite purposeful and that he had been captivated by accounts not simply of India's beauty, but also of the opportunities it afforded of self-promotion.

It seems that Mirza Nizami was fond of hearing the *qissa* of Amir Hamza, and it was at his urging that Fakhr al-Zamani honed the skills that he had acquired in his youth and properly learned the art of storytelling.[21] When Mirza Nizami moved with the royal court to Ajmer, Fakhr al-Zamani tagged along, and there he met another of his compatriots, named Masih Beg, who was in the employ of the *amir* Zamana Beg Mahabat Khan "Susani". With Masih Beg's help, Fakhr al-Zamani gained an audience with Mahabat Khan's son Mirza Aman Allah "Amani", who appears to have been a fan of *qissas* as well. Fakhr al-Zamani writes of this meeting:

> After I had been at his service for a little while, as per his command I presented a section of the *qissa* before that Issue of Lords. After he had given ear to this speech, that Master of Speech became, to some degree, desirous of this beggar.[22]

After all, the "youthful desire" which had led Fakhr al-Zamani to memorise the *qissa* and to become a storyteller—beginning perhaps at home, outdoors, or in the coffee-house—proved to be the making of a skill that could be used to secure patronage, not imperial, perhaps, but certainly courtly. The possibility of this process highlights the difficulties involved in drawing a bold line between courtly and popular *qissas*, especially before the age of print, when evidence is relatively sparse. If Fakhr al-Zamani's progress is any indication, *qissas* that began at the "popular" level could, given a chance and perhaps with some stylistic alterations, eventually be performed in the courts of nobles and preserved as manuscripts in their libraries. Fakhr al-Zamani was far from oblivious to the success of storytellers like Zain al-'Abidin Takaltu Khan at the court of the Safavid ruler Shah Isma'il, and 'Inayat Allah

21 Ibid., p. 762.
22 Ibid., p. 763.

Darbar Khan at the Mughal Emperor Akbar's court.[23] He also shows that he was aware of his own contemporary, the storyteller Mulla Asad, who was lavished with gifts by Jahangir and given a *mansab* of two hundred.[24] Perhaps Fakhr al-Zamani desired similar emoluments for his storytelling skills. He claims to have become highly intimate with Mirza Aman Allah "Amani" but was later forced to leave his service under ignominious circumstances, and eventually wound up in the employ of Sardar Khan Khwaja "Yadgar" in Bihar.

It was to Yadgar that Fakhr al-Zamani dedicated his most famous work, the *Mai-khāna* (*Wine Tavern*), a prosopography of poets who wrote *saqi-namas* (poems addressed to the *saqi* or cup-bearer). In the *Mai-khāna*, Fakhr al-Zamani mentions a book that he wrote in Kashmir as a guide for storytellers, and particularly for the tellers of the story of Amir Hamza. This book, entitled *Dastūr al-fuṣaḥā'* (*Rules for the Eloquent*), was probably finished around 1616 or 1617 according to Muhammad Shafi'.[25] Whenever it may have been written, it appears to have vanished without a trace, perhaps reduced to cinders when Fakhr al-Zamani's house in Patna caught fire in 1620.[26] Surviving the *Dastūr*, we have a book entitled *Ṭirāz al-akhbār*, a creature halfway between a professional storyteller's handbook and a glorified *bayaz* or commonplace book. If the chronogram ("*zebā Ṭirāz-i akhbār*") is correct, it was finished in 1041 AH (1631/2 CE), and the colophon of the most complete manuscript tells us that the scribe Sayyid Muhammad b. Mas'ud Ahmad Husaini Bihari finished copying it two years later on 27 Safar 1043 AH (1 September 1633), not 7 Safar 1043 AH in Patna ("*dar balda-i Ṭayyiba-i Patna itmām yāft*").[27] The perplexing question is how it came about that manuscripts

23 See Muhammad Ja'far Mahjub, 'Tahawwul-i naqqali wa qissa-khwani', *Irannama* 9 (1991), 191.

24 Fakhr al-Zamani Qazwini (1983), pp. 458ff., for example; for the reward, see Nur al-Din Muhammad Jahangir, *Jahāngīrnāmah (Tūzuk-i Jahāngīrī)*, ed. by Muhammad Hashim (Tehran: Bunyad-i Farhang-i Iran, 1359 AH), p. 215.

25 In fact the *Mai-khāna* provides a chronogram for the *Dastūr al-fuṣaḥā'* ("*dastūr ba-anjām rasīda*") that yields 1046 AH (1636/37 CE); Fakhr al-Zamani Qazwini (1983), p. 770. However Shafi', in trying to square this date with the period of Fakhr al-Zamani's Kashmiri sojourn, concludes that if the *Dastūr al-fuṣaḥā'* was finished in Kashmir as Fakhr al-Zamani claims, it would have to have been completed between the years 1025-1026 AH (about 1616-1117 CE); Shafi' (1983), p. xiv. The *Mai-khāna* itself was not completed until 1028 (1618/19 CE); Fakhr al-Zamani Qazwini (1983), p. 924. The chronogram appears, therefore, to be erroneous.

26 Fakhr al-Zamani Qazwini (1983), p. 886.

27 For the 1633 colophon, see the facsimile in Shafi'i-Kadkani (1381 AH), 122.

of this work are now non-existent in India and Pakistan. The only other extant work by Fakhr al-Zamani is a now-rare collection of tales called *Nawādir al-ḥikāyāt* (*Rare Tales*), supposedly consisting of five volumes, only the first of which remains in the British Library. This volume was composed in 1041 AH (1631/2 CE).[28]

The *Ṭirāz al-akhbār* is divided into a *muqaddama* (foreword) and a main body, which I am comparing to a well-organised *bayaz* (a commonplace book for snatches of poetry). It is in the *muqaddama* that the genre code is most evident, and in the discussion that follows I will focus at first upon Fakhr al-Zamani's descriptions in this section of the book. The *muqaddama* itself is divided into five sections (*fasl*) according to Mahjub: (1) Regarding various accounts of the origin of the Dastan-i Amir Hamza, (2) On the attributes of the *dastan*, (3) On the storyteller's superiority to the poet, (4) On the storyteller's religious leanings and moral conduct, and (5) On the performance of the *dastan*.

## Avicennian Mimesis

Elsewhere I have examined the post-Enlightenment identification of the *qissa* genre with the newly re-encoded English "romance" genre, the identity of which was often thrown into relief in the eighteenth century by setting it against its sister genre, the novel.[29] A particularly strong classificatory force was the text's mode of imitation which, focused through Enlightenment empiricism and rationalism, allowed for the sharp disambiguation of history from fiction, and worked within the genre of prose fiction to separate probable fictions (novels) from improbable ones (romances). Duncan Forbes' preface to *The Adventures of Hatim Tai: A Romance*—his translation of the Indo-Persian *qissa*, the *Haft sair-i Ḥātim*—is one of a number of nineteenth-century writings that take for granted the sameness of the improbable romance genre and the genre that Indians called the *qissa* or *dastan*. Forbes makes an apology for the improbability of the story of Hatim Ta'i, begging the reader to remember that the Eastern

28 Charles Rieu, *Catalogue of the Persian Manuscripts in the British Museum* (London: Gilbert and Rivington, 1883), Vol. 3, p. 1004.

29 Pasha M. Khan, 'Genre Identifications: Hatim-namas as Romance and Qissa', paper presented at the annual meeting of the Association for Asian Studies (Chicago, 28 March 2009).

mind remained in thrall to a credulous belief in things whose existence was, for the English, irrational or unempirical.[30]

Leaving aside the Orientalist valuation that might be perceptible in Forbes' comments, is it possible that there were epistemologies prevalent in India that would have caused *qissa* to be received as statements of truth? After all, magical arts such as geomancy (*raml*) and the creation of *tilisms* (talismans and, in *qissas*, enchanted worlds) were not always perceived as charlatanry, and the existence of creatures such as the *jinn* is attested to by the Qur'an. Fakhr al-Zamani weighs in significantly on this question, but before getting back to his *muqaddama*, it will be useful to better historicise the categories we are dealing with when we refer to literary truth and lies.

Commenting on the Arabic version of Aristotle's *Poetics* (*Kitāb al-shi'r*), the philosopher Abu 'Ali al-Husain Ibn Sina spoke of two somewhat opposed modes of representation: *sidq* or veraciousness, and *muhaka* or mimesis. Its opposition to veracious representation does not mean that mimesis is simply false representation. But at least in part, mimesis is defined by its being mendacious (*kadhib*), a mendacity that, particularly when involved in *takhyil* (incitement of the imagination), has the ability to make the mimetic discourse more effective in certain ways than veracious discourse. Following the Arabic Aristotle, Ibn Sina speaks of poetry as the prime example of mimetic discourse.

It is important to note that for Ibn Sina, as for Al-Farabi before him, poetry *must* be mimetic and therefore mendacious. As an illustration: In the Autumn of 2008 at the Lahore Museum, I came across a manuscript of a versified Urdu tract on medicine (*hikmat*), in *masnavi* form, describing cures for two of the most grievous ailments of the day, *faqr-i sahl* and *ihtilam*—constipation and nocturnal emission. In the Avicennian scheme of things, such scientific treatises (as well as versified grammars and so on), however they may tickle us, are not mimetic but veracious, and therefore are not classifiable as poetry even if they are in verse.

30 Duncan Forbes, *The Adventures of Hatim Taï: A Romance* (London: Oriental Translation Fund, 1830), pp. v-vi. My remark is not meant to deny the usefulness of translating "*qissa*" or "*dastan*" as "romance"; it is only necessary to be attentive to what it meant to perform this translation in eighteenth- and nineteenth-century Britain, and to the kinds of assumptions that came along with such a genre equation. When speaking of the Urdu or Indo-Persian "romance", we must understand the previous history of the genre code of the "romance", we must have a sense of what the *qissa* was without reducing it to this pre-existent notion of the romance, and we must alter our ideas of what we mean by "romance" if we wish for this term to encompass the *qissa*.

However, despite the stress that he places on poetry, Ibn Sina notes that some prose works may also be imagination-inciting (*takhyili*) and mimetic.[31] But if we were to apply the Avicennian distinction to prose discourses, historiographical genres (*tarikh, sira, nasab, safar-nama*, etc.) are not likely to have been considered mimetic, given that mimesis involves mendacity (*kidhb*), whereas historiographical genres cause the reader to expect a veracious (*sadiq*) discourse.

On the other hand, is it possible that the *qissa* was, in Avicennian terms, a veracious genre, similar to a history, rather than a mimetic one? Generalising from the example of *Kalīla wa Dimna*, Ibn Sina insists that such stories ("*amāthil wa qiṣaṣ*"), though they lack metre and do not aim primarily at *takhyil* or imagination incitement, are in fact mimetic, like poetry.[32] A full investigation of this issue would, however, require attention to borderline cases such as Indian versified histories by authors known primarily as mimetic poets, such as Amir Khusrau's *Qirān al-sa'dain* (*Conjuction of the Two Fortunate Planets*), in which Khusrau, as Sunil Sharma reminds us, professes his preference for truthfulness (*rasti*) over falsehood (*durogh*).[33] Other examples include Keshavdas' *Jahāngīrjascandrika* or *Moonlight of the Fame of Jahangir* and the same author's remarkable *Ratnabāvanī* (*Fifty-Two Verses in Honour of Ratnasena*), about which Allison Busch has written; the fact that the latter text has "gods weaving in and out of the story" is only the beginning of its fascinations.[34] Indeed we have yet to come to grips with the alleged prevalence of mimetic elements in the historiography of the post-Mongol Islamicate world, whether in verse or in prose, which often pivot on the under-examined topos of the *kharq al-'ada* ("custom-breaking", extraordinary), exemplified by but not limited to *'aja'ib* (mirabilia) literature.[35] Other problematic texts include

---

31 Abu 'Ali al-Husain b. 'Abd Allah Ibn Sina, 'Fann al-shi'r', in *Fann al-shi'r*, ed. by 'Abd al-Rahman Badawi, 2nd edn (Beirut: Dar al-thaqafa, 1973), pp. 168, 183

32 Ibn Sina (1973), p. 183. In Ibn Sina's view, their aim is not *takhyil*, but the "diffusion of views (*ifādaṭ al-ārā'*)" (ibid.). Ibn Sina also differentiates these two genres from poetry on the basis of their "fantastic" representations, like the English romance critics of the eighteenth century.

33 Sunil Sharma, 'Amir Khusraw and the Genre of Historical Narratives in Verse', *Comparative Studies of South Asia, Africa and the Middle East* 22.1 (2002), 113.

34 Allison Busch, 'The Courtly Vernacular: The Transformation of Brajbhaṣa Literary Culture (1590-1690)' (PhD dissertation, University of Chicago, 2003), p. 212ff. For the *Jahāngīrjascandrika*, see Allison Busch, 'The Anxiety of Innovation: The Practice of Literary Science in the Hindi/Riti Tradition'. *Comparative Studies of South Asia, Africa and the Middle East* 24.2 (2004), 45-59, and her essay in this volume.

35 The ongoing work of Travis Zadeh on the marvellous in Islamicate writings is useful

*qissas* that present themselves as participants in historiographical genres, such as the aforementioned *Haft sair-i Ḥātim*.

## Falsehood and the Sin of Performance

Faced with the bewildering potential of such liminal cases, we may be relieved to find that Fakhr al-Zamani does not compound the sin of lying for a living by pretending in the *Ṭirāz al-akhbār* that he is telling the truth. In the foreword to the *Ṭirāz al-akhbār* we find him confirming expectations: he declares the *qissa* to be a falsehood (*durogh*), "devoid", he says, "of the fine ornament of truthfulness" (*az ḥilya-i ṣidq maḥrūm*).

Moreover, there was a malign aspect to this mendacity; the falsehood of the *qissa* was not value-neutral, but had a negative ethico-religious valence. This comes across most forcefully in the fourth section of the foreword, which concerns the religious conduct of the professional storyteller. In an exhortation worthy of an ethical manual, Fakhr al-Zamani enjoins his storytelling colleagues to practice *muruwwat* (roughly, "humanity")[36] towards their fellow creatures and help them in their time of need: "The best conduct for the speaker [i.e., the storyteller] is [...] to expend in God's path whatsoever he acquires, and to behave with humanity towards everyone".[37] The storyteller's incentive for behaving with *muruwwat* is important to note:

> Perhaps in this way he will win the heart of some afflicted person, and ease a frustrated mind—so that it might be the cause of expiation in this world for his telling of lies, and of an honourable acquittal (*surkh-ru'i*) in the next.[38]

Virtuous conduct is valuable, according to Fakhr al-Zamani, as an antidote to the sins that are necessarily committed by the storyteller, given that the sin of telling lies is an insuperable part of the *qissa* genre. The mimesis inherent in the genre is therefore perceived by Fakhr al-Zamani as blameworthy; elsewhere he says that the *qissa*'s lies may bring disgrace (*ruswa'i*) upon

in this regard. See his PhD dissertation, 'Translation, Geography, and the Divine Word' (Harvard University, 2007), and his recent article 'Wiles of Creation', in *Middle Eastern Studies* 13.1 (2010), 21-48.

36 *Muruwwat* is an originally pre-Islamic Arabian complex of ethical virtues as changeful and difficult to define as it is old; "humanity" is an unsatisfactory translation. See "Murū'a" in the *Encyclopedia of Islam*.

37 In Mahjub (1991), 193.

38 Ibid.

their teller.[39] More than this, they are eschatologically harmful, as evidenced by the need for a life of *muruwwat* to counter the difficulties that mendacity will cause on the Day of Reckoning.

Fakhr al-Zamani's comments regarding the sinfulness of the *qissa* lies already present the *qissa* as a thoroughly oral genre, which does not stand aloof from the context in which it is recited in the way that written texts are sometimes imagined to do. Its production, as we read in the *Ṭirāz al-akhbār*, has material, social, and soteriological effects on the storyteller who speaks it into being. In his landmark study, *Sāḥirī, shāhī, ṣāḥib-qirānī* (*Sorcery, Kingship, Lordship of the Auspicious Conjunction*), Shamsur Rahman Faruqi energetically stresses the orality (*zabani-pan*) of the story of Amir Hamza even when it appears in written form, for instance in the massive Naval Kishore printed cycle, which was itself authored by storytellers. At the outset Faruqi defends oral genres such as the *dastan*, *qissa*, and *masnavi* from Orientalist belittlement and goes on to present an impressive system of poetics based on the *Dāstān-i Amīr Ḥamza*'s orality.[40] When we read together Faruqi's study of Fakhr al-Zamani and the passages from the *Ṭirāz al-akhbār* that Faruqi cites, it becomes clear that "orality" is a central and seminal element of the genre, but also that the *qissa* or *dastan* as Faruqi describes it is not only oral, but, moreover, *performative*.

The *Ṭirāz al-akhbār* makes it clear to us that the term "*qissa-khwan*" does not convey the full range and force of the storyteller's activities. Impressive as it seems that storytellers like Fakhr al-Zamani recited and improvised the interminable *Dāstān-i Amīr Ḥamza* from memory, they did not *simply* read them, but performed them. In his description of the presentation of the *qissa*, Fakhr al-Zamani prescribes not only modulations of the voice, but gestures and postures for the storyteller. The term *naqqali*, designating a sort of professional acting in which a performer conveys a story with words and actions, attempting to *embody* the narrative and its characters, might be a more expressive alternative to *qissa-khwani* in terms of its meaning, although *naqqali* was generally lower on the scale of professions than *qissa-khwani*, and I do not know that Fakhr al-Zamani ever uses the word. In the late nineteenth century Sharar described Lakhnawi storytellers as "imaging"—becoming *taswirs* of—the stories that they performed, allying the art of storytelling to the visual arts.[41]

39 Ibid., 192.
40 S.R. Faruqi (1999), Vol. 1, p. 198.
41 Sharar (2000), p. 149.

Similarly, Fakhr al-Zamani states in the *Ṭirāz al-akhbār* that in the Iranian style of *qissa-khwani* (as opposed to the Indian and Turanian styles, which he also describes), the storyteller must marshal his gestures and postures in such a way that the audience members find themselves beholding the action with the imagination's gaze ("*naẓar-i taṣawwur*"). When a character in the *qissa* escapes from captivity, the storyteller must speak and act in such a way that the audience perceives him to be the one breaking out of his chains. In other words, the storyteller, in bodying forth the *qissa*'s characters, must engage in a mimesis and therefore a kind of mendacity that is not merely oral, but fully performative, for he pretends to be what he is not.[42]

Fakhr al-Zamani's wariness with regard to such imposture may be gauged from his comments on religious performance, which are so remarkable as to merit full translation:[43]

> The possessor of this heart-stealing art and the master of this assembly-adorning craft [i.e., that of storytelling] must be confined by his creed, not by the bonds of religious prejudice, because every one of the sultans of the day and the high-ranking nobles has a different religion and a separate law. Some are Sunni, a few are Shi'a. There is a group that affirms the unity of God, and a lot that disbelieve the resurrection of the dead. The storyteller must deal with each differing faction in each region according to need. First of all, he must not proclaim his own creed inconsistently in order to mix with the great men of each kingdom. For if he makes himself out to be Sunni in one place and makes himself known as a Shi'a in another, he will not be able to maintain this to the end. Because it is possible that, before he shifts locations, the reality of his religion will have been disseminated to every corner of the kingdom where he has long resided.[44]

This is an odd piece of advice—it is difficult to resist the biographical temptation, and to leave off wondering whether Fakhr al-Zamani had tried this trick out himself. What is notable for our purposes is the way in which the negative religious valuation of performative mimesis in the case of the *qissa* performance is paralleled by the analogous mimesis of *taqiyya* or religious dissimulation—the false performance of religion itself.[45] It is as if the

42 Mahjub (1991), 194.

43 Azfar Moin first noted and alerted me to this section of the *Ṭirāz*, for which kindness I am deeply grateful.

44 Mahjub (1991), 192-93.

45 With regard to specifically Shi'i *taqiyya*, we should remember that our storytelling émigré from Shah 'Abbas's Iran lived in a Mughal state whose relationship to Shi'ism was complexly fraught given the presence of other émigrés such as Nur Jahan on the one hand, and, on the other hand, the Shi'a qazi of Lahore, Nur Allah Shushtari,

storyteller's predilection for performance, which should have been restricted to storytelling situations, has burst its bonds, engendering characters that rampage about in the real world. The parallel, while by no means complete, is particularly strong given the chances, in each case, of prior knowledge on the part of the audience that an act is being put on. However, we will soon come to an important difference between the two types of performance.

## What the *Qissa* is Good For

The storyteller, despite the sin implicit in his occupation, can redeem himself through doing good in his life. But how is the *qissa* genre itself redeemed? The *Ṭirāz al-akhbār* does not treat the *qissa* simply as "literature" in the poststructuralist sense summed up by Derek Attridge, as a discourse inhabited by otherness and irreducible to uses, ideologies, and the like.[46] It is easy to see how such a view of literature has participated in a crisis of genre theory, as it dissociates itself from the implicitly prescribed *uses* and *effects* to which genre is so often tied. Jameson writes pithily that "genres are essentially literary institutions, or social contracts between a writer and a specific public, whose function is to specify the proper use of a particular cultural artifact".[47] To take some examples of Arabo-Persian genres, the *marsiya* (lament) is meant to provoke mourning, the *hajw* (satire) to provoke laughter or ridicule, and the *qasida* (praise-poem, in the Persianate sense of this word) to please the one who is praised, to excite admiration, and possibly to earn a reward for the poet. Sunil Sharma's essay in this volume draws attention to the force that words were understood to have in the world, even to the extent of being able to kill. In this spirit, Fakhr al-Zamani deals with the *qissa* as something of the order of *adab* in the classical sense of a culturing, disciplinary discourse. Just as Indian music has curative properties, as Katherine Schofield explains in this volume, the *qissa* ameliorates its audience in particular ways. Fakhr al-Zamani very specifically spells out the genre's beneficial effects for the

executed at Jahangir's order in 1610; Sajid S. Alvi, 'Religion and State During the Reign of Mughal Emperor Jahăngīr (1605-1627): Nonjuristical Perspectives', *Studia Islamica* 69 (1989), 111-112.

46 Derek Attridge, *J.M. Coetzee and the Ethics of Reading: Literature in the Event* (Chicago and London: University of Chicago Press, 2004). This is not to say that this view of literature is incorrect—far from it—nor has genre theory's crisis been unfruitful.

47 Jameson (1981), p. 106.

listener, and, in doing so, offers answers to the question, "What is the purpose of the *qissa*?"

Fakhr al-Zamani lists three benefits of *qissa* recitation for the audience (aside from its benefits for the storyteller himself or herself, which we have glimpsed in the biographical accounts of his ingratiation with Mirza Nizami and Mirza Aman Allah). These may be characterised as linguistic, practical, and moral. First, by exemplifying speech that is eloquent ("*fasih*"), discursively mature ("*baligh*"), and current ("*roz-marra*"), it improves the listener's ability to manipulate language. Second, it serves as a prescription for worldly and state affairs ("'*umūr-i dunyawī wa ashghāl-i mulkī*'") and inculcates prudence ("*tadbir*") in the listener.[48] S.R. Faruqi reminds us that Ghalib Lakhnawi also mentions this purpose, stating that those who hear *qissas* "are able to imagine plans for battle, for subduing forts and conquering states, which is why they [i.e., *qissas*] were always told to emperors".[49] Finally, it deters the listener from vain thoughts, acting as a moral example. This last point is crucial because of its connection with the lie. What the *Ṭirāz al-akhbār* says is that "despite its own falsity, it [the *qissa*] casts the powerful off the rope of false thoughts".[50] The term *batil* and its cognate *butlan* can be synonymous with *durogh* or *kizb*, for instance in the Qur'an we find the admonition "Do not clothe the real in untruth ("*lā talbasū al-ḥaqqa bi al-bāṭil*", 2.42). But *batil* also connotes nullity or void-ness, as in *batil al-sihr* or countermagic: that which renders enchantments null and void. The *qissa* is a kind of lie that has the effect of nullifying false thoughts, a lie which is also a counter-lie, and which therefore has a salutary moral effect despite its essential sinfulness.[51]

We may speculate that the anti-mendacious property of the *qissa* may be enabled by its announcement of its own falsehood, either explicitly or by virtue of its genre—note that this is quite unlike the dissimulation

48 Mahjub (1991), 191.

49 S.R. Faruqi (1999), p. 421; Ghalib Lakhnawi (1855), p. 3. The preface to the 1803 Fort William version of the story of Amir Hamza, written by Khalil 'Ali Khan Ashk, also contains this assertion in words similar to Ghalib Lakhnawi's; Khalil 'Ali Khan Ashk, *Dāstān-i Amīr Ḥamza* (Bombay: Matba'-i Haidari, 1863), Vol. 1, p. 2.

50 "*daulat-mandān rā az sar-rishta-i andesha-i bāṭil bā-wujūd-i buṭlān-i khwesh mī-andāzad*", quoted in Mahjub (1991), 191.

51 Faruqi clearly reads this generic purpose as moral, and even religiously moral, stating, by way of example, that "in the *dastan* sorcerers are always defeated eventually [...] but they are not simply defeated; indeed they die very ordinary and even commonplace deaths, and so it is fully proven that there is no difference between them or any other of God's servants"; S.R. Faruqi (1999), Vol. 1, p. 421.

of the hypothetical religious pretender that Fakhr al-Zamani imagines above. Let us put it simply, and refer to this announced falsehood of the *qissa* as a form of fictionality. When Fakhr al-Zamani announces that the *qissa* is a lie shorn of the finery of truthfulness (*az ḥilya-i ṣidq 'āṭil*), he fixes this fictionality of the genre in the genre code that he is producing. His statement speaks to the Qur'anic phrase *"lā talbasū al-ḥaqqa bi al-bāṭil"*, responding to it by inverting it: the *qissa* is not an untruth clothed in the true; it presents itself as a *naked untruth*. And it is perhaps for this reason that it is able to counter untruth despite its own falsehood.

## The Four Repertoires

We will return to the question of purposes and particularly the multiplicity of purposes enumerated in the *Ṭirāz*. But the *qissa* is not encoded merely as a performative fictional genre with linguistic, practical, and moral uses. We must not forget the four categories with which this essay began: *razm, bazm, husn o 'ishq,* and *'ayyari* (the third of which, the reader will recall, was substituted for *tilism* by Ghalib Lakhnawi). A look at the organisation of the main part of the *Ṭirāz* tells us that Fakhr al-Zamani conceived of these four not simply as elements of the genre but as the discursive and, moreover, *performative* bricks with which the storyteller built the edifice of the *qissa*, the repertoires from which the *qissa* was pastiched together.

We have already analysed the foreword of the *Ṭirāz al-akhbār*; let us now turn to the body. This *bayaz*-like portion consists of prose and verse quotations from a variety of written sources, from the Persian poet Zuhuri's poems to the tales of Sindbad, from odes to the cupbearer to tales of Alexander to animal fables. But rather than being scattered randomly like verses in a standard *bayaz*, they are corralled into the four categories of *razm, bazm, husn o 'ishq,* and *'ayyari*. Each of these four chapters (each one called a report or *khabar*) is subdivided into twelve sections or workshops (*tiraz*), and finally there is an extra chapter, seemingly for leftover odds and ends, subdivided into nineteen sections, for a total of forty-nine sections.

These classified quotations were meant to be memorised and recited or reworked extempore by the storyteller during the performance of the *qissa*. For example, the storyteller might be describing a battle (*razm*) when the story's focus falls upon a war-elephant. His searching memory might then take him to the sixth section of the first chapter of the *Ṭirāz*, which contains descriptions of elephants and wolves, and it might alight on this passage from the *Taj al-ma'āṣir* (*Crown of Great Deeds*):

> *abr-hay'ate bād-ḥarkate barq-sur'ate ażhdahā-kharṭūme dahān-i mauhūme kih dandān-ash go'ī sutūn-i īn bār-gāh-i mu'allaq-i Bīstūn* [or *be-sutūn*] *ast wa kharṭūm-i khamīda-i caugān miṡāl-ash go'ī rubāninda-i īn saqf-i gardūn*...[52]

> Cloud-shaped and moving like the wind, with a serpentine trunk and a fantastical mouth. Its tusks: you would think that they were the pillars of a palace [i.e., the head] attached to Mount Bistun [the body], and you would think its trunk, curved like a polo stick, might be able to steal from the arched vault of the heavens.

The chapter from which this quotation is taken deals with various descriptions of battle (*razm*). Similarly, when describing courtly situations, the storyteller would dip into the chapter on *bazm*, and the same goes for *husn o 'ishq* and *'ayyari*. The four elements of the genre were, as we can see, codified by Fakhr al-Zamani according to the exigencies of the performance. They were not simply there as inert facts, they were toolboxes to be selected properly or improperly.

These four styles were not simply textual; they were fully performative. Fakhr al-Zamani prescribes postures and modulation of the voice for each style. During the narration of a battle, the storyteller must slowly raise his body (sitting on one knee, rising to a standing position) as he reaches the climax. When narrating a courtly scene, he must ease his voice, and in the narration of love scenes, he must perform the expected *naz o niyaz*, the blandishments of the beloved and the pangs of the lover.[53] The *Ṭirāz al-akhbār* seems, in other words, to provide a repertoire of four major performative styles—or perhaps we might say that it provides four repertoires to be used in the correct parts of the *dastan*. But these repertoires are not only memorised collections of classified verse and prose—they are distinct narrative situations that cue the storyteller to summon up prescribed quotations *and* which demand from him a certain set of vocal and physical shifts. It is difficult to imagine that the styles did not intermix at all, but Fakhr al-Zamani frowns upon undue movement between two different styles as evidence that the storyteller lacks *jam'iyyat-i hawass*, which is to say that his senses are scattered and unfocused.[54]

52 Shafi'i-Kadkani (1381 AH), 111.
53 Mahjub (1991), 194.
54 Ibid., 192.

## What Ails the *Qissa*

But, having described the four repertoires which supposedly define the *qissa* genre, I want to return to my initial caveats regarding the category of genre, and to recall that genres, by which I mean codifications of what constitutes various genres, are not inherent or given. They are products of socio-historical forces: ideologies, commercial and practical exigencies, and so on. As such they change over time, and they are objects of contention in any given period.[55] This means that it is possible that another contemporary authority whose testimony we have lost may have defined the *qissa* differently, but just as compellingly, as Fakhr al-Zamani. But Fakhr al-Zamani's codification of the genre, which turns out to be tied to the technicalities of the performative production of *qissas*, is important. This is not only because it presents uses for the genre beyond that of "mere entertainment", but also because it appears to have been re-cited and adapted by Ghalib Lakhnawi and Sharar. It is certainly the case that the nineteenth-century comments are sparse, and it is difficult to understand just how it is that the genre code was perpetuated, given that the quantity and present location of the *Ṭirāz al-akhbār* manuscripts with which we are now familiar do not inspire confidence that they were circulating widely in nineteenth-century Awadh. It is very much possible that the notion of the *qissa* genre that we have discussed travelled orally, and that Fakhr al-Zamani's genre code was neither unique nor directly influential. Nevertheless, it is at the very least the most well-articulated example we have of a genre code that clearly survived, continuously or in stints, over several centuries.

What Jameson and others might call the institutionality of genres—the fact of their being "instituted" under particular socio-historical circumstances—is trouble enough; furthermore, we must consider intertextuality, which obviates the possibility of there being a chaste *qissa*, innocent of the crime of miscegenation. Any law of genre that implicitly prohibits the mixing of genres must overlook or repress this miscegenetic intertextuality.

This is not the place to elaborate a theory of genre mixing, but I will at least rehearse my argument. Without intertextuality, genres cannot

55 My view of genre as synchronically and diachronically divided has largely developed from Ralph Cohen and Hans Robert Jauss; Ralph Cohen, 'History and Genre', *New Literary History* 17. 2 (1986), 203-18, particularly 207-09; Hans Robert Jauss, *Toward an Aesthetic of Reception* (Minneapolis: University of Minnesota Press, 1982).

exist; the family resemblance that allows us to group discourses into genres is intertextual. But even as intertextuality is the condition for such a classification, it shatters the image of the pure genre by virtue of the fact that each intertext is already marked by a genre (or genres, rather) of its own. Therefore we might consider each *qissa* as something of an intertextual tapestry that cannot be taken as a "pure" *qissa* and can only be comprehended as a complex of *multi-generic* intertexts that fall under the order of the master genre code of the *qissa*. Even as we read or hear a discourse overall as a *qissa*, submitting to the social force that encodes it as such, it is instructive to peel back the skin that gathers the discourse together into a single genre, and to view its multigenericity or heterogeneousness as well. Francesca Orsini first alerted me to this possibility with her suggestion of a "dual genealogy" for the Hindi-Urdu *qissa*, descended on the one hand from the *dastan* and on the other hand from the shorter *naql*.[56] To continue in this biological vein, Sunil Sharma has written of Khusrau's verse histories as "hybrid texts".[57] Riding on Orsini's and Sharma's coattails, what I am suggesting is that *all* genres—including the *dastan* and the *naql*, for instance—are already mixed and impure. As much as we try to fix a discourse's genre and decide that there is only one, close observation of its bloodstream will reveal that is infected with myriad others.

Unsurprisingly, an important formulation of the idea of heterogeneity appears in Mikhail Bakhtin's work, and particularly in his essay "Epic and Novel". Here literary history is envisioned as a conflict between a weatherworn host of ossified classical genres led by the epic, and the plastic, heteroglossic "novel" or, rather, *roman*.[58] The importance of Bakhtin's codification of the *roman* lies in the fact that the *roman* is defined precisely by its heteroglossia and therefore its heterogeneity.

56 Francesca Orsini, *Print and Pleasure: Popular Literature and Entertaining Fictions in Colonial North India* (Ranikhet: Permanent Black, 2009), p. 115.

57 Sharma (2002), 114.

58 Mikhail Bakhtin, *The Dialogic Imagination: Four Essays*, trans. by Caryl Emerson and Michael Holquist (Austin: University of Texas Press, 2004). The scare quotes give voice to my uneasiness about the translation of what Bakhtin refers to as "*roman*" into the English "novel". The eighteenth-century sundering of the novel genre from its backward sister, the romance, appears to have been expressed much less vigorously outside of Britain, and Bakhtin often uses the word *roman* to designate what English speakers would think of as medieval romances. Therefore I prefer to leave the word untranslated.

Unlike Aristotle's traditional genres (epic, lyric, tragedy),[59] the *roman* engulfs other genres, playing with them and parodying them—even and especially "extraliterary" genres such as the newspaper report and the letter.[60] In effect *romans* are diseased bodies riddled with heterogenous discourses of various genres, and during periods in (Western) history when the *roman* genre is in the ascendant (as it was in the Greek classical period, classical Rome, and neoclassical Europe), epidemics take place in which *romans* infect other genres on a large scale. It is the effect of this contagion that is referred to by Bakhtinians as *romannost* or *roman*-ness: other genres are *roman*-ised ("novelised")—they become like *romans* by virtue of being contaminated.

Bakhtin's idea is useful and consonant with the vision of the *qissa* genre revealed by Fakhr al-Zamani. At the same time, Bakhtin's argument regarding the essentially sealed-off nature of "high genres" such as the epic is unconvincing, and "*roman*ization" arguably affects all genres; therefore it does not seem justified to single out the *roman* as the originary touchstone for this kind of heterogeneity. Finally, while Bakhtin's account seems to represent *roman*ization as a fate that befalls an originally pure genre, I wish to stress that a discourse in any genre may be regarded as heterogeneous from the start.

Once we look at them through such a lens, it is easy to see that the *qissas* whose performance Fakhr al-Zamani describes are shot through with intertexts of many different genres. Based on the *Ṭirāz al-akhbār*'s list of quotations, we know that in Fakhr al-Zamani's *qissas*, excerpts from the *Shāh-nāma* and Farid al-Din 'Attar's sufi *Manṭiq al-ṭair* (*Speech of the Birds*) might mingle freely with epistolary specimens (*insha'*), *saqi-namas*, and the moral fables of Kalila and Dimna.[61] Most strikingly, the very genre of truth-telling historiography to which we might oppose the lying-mimetic *qissa* ends up infecting it. Mir Khvand's history, the *Rawżat al-ṣafā* (*Garden of Purity*): Hatifi's *Timūr-nama* (*Book of Timūr*); the *Tāj al-ma'a̱sir* (*Crown of Great Deeds*); the *Ḥabīb al-siyār* (*Vademecum of Biographies*); Amir

59 Bakhtin's Manichaean vision of literary history seems wrongheaded insofar as it appears to posit the existence of epics and so on as monoglossic non-*roman* genres, unsullied by *roman*ization, often because they are supposedly older and predate the very appearance of the *roman* on the historical stage. But given the intertextuality of all discourses and, indeed, the intertextual foundations of language itself, the myth of a pure, pre-Babelian genre does not stand up to scrutiny.

60 Bakhtin (2004), p. 33.

61 See Shafi'i-Kadkani (1381 AH), 111, 113, 121, 110 respectively.

Khusrau's *Qirān al-sa'dain*; and the *Tārīkh-i mu'jam* are all quoted in the *Ṭirāz al-akhbār*.[62] This irruption of historiographical genres into the *qissa* does not make the *qissa* simply historiographical, but it suggests that we cannot ignore historiographical elements when we consider the purposes that the *qissa* serves.

It is important to remember that Fakhr al-Zamani mentions *more than one* purpose to the *qissa*: it makes the hearers eloquent, it makes them prudent, and it wards off falsehood. To the question, "What is the purpose of the *qissa*?", we must answer that there is no *single* purpose to the *qissa* because no *qissa* is reducible to a *single genre*, as it will always incorporate intertexts of various genres. At least, this is the view that I have attempted to justify.

62 Shafi'i-Kadkani (1381 AH), 113, 110.

# 7. Did Surdas Perform the *Bhāgavata-purāṇa*?

*John Stratton Hawley*

An old and very rusty saw in the scholarly literature on Surdas is the notion that Sur translated the *Bhāgavata-purāṇa* from Sanskrit into Hindi. It is easy to take potshots at this idea, and I have done so quite a bit myself.[1] Instead of adding to that fusillade here, however, I suggest that we frame the issue somewhat differently and see if that might open the door to a more interesting answer. Is it possible that Sur was not translating the *Bhāgavata*, but performing it?

What does it mean to perform the *Bhāgavata*? Several years ago I travelled to the ancient Shaiva pilgrimage town of Gokarn, on the banks of the Arabian Sea. There I had a chance to talk with an octogenarian Agnihotri Brahman named Samba Dikshita, who told me he had been performing the *Bhāgavata-purāṇa* all his life and that his family had been doing so for seven generations before him.[2] For seven days in the month of *karttik* every year (now his nephew has taken over the job), Samba Dikshita would recite a portion of the section mandated by tradition. As much as he could: he didn't have the command of the text that his father did, he explained. His father knew the text so perfectly, so inside out, that he was able to recite the entire Purana in the course of seven days, as mandated by the text that

1 Most recently, *The Memory of Love: Sūrdās Sings to Krishna* (New York: Oxford University Press, 2009), pp. 15-18.

2 I am deeply grateful to Vidvan Samba Dikshita for granting me interviews on 23 and 25 December 2007, and to his son Gajanan Dikshita for a supplementary conversation on 25 December 2007.

 http://dx.doi.org/10.11647/OBP.0062.07

celebrates this very practice, the *Bhāgavata māhātmya*. But Samba Dikshita did something his father had not always done. After performing the Purana in the morning at the *pathshala* just down the street, he would convene another gathering towards evening, in which he returned to the "portion" for the day, this time selecting from it and developing his own exposition in Kannada. For people who did not care about the Sanskrit text in the same way he did—perhaps because of their linguistic limitations or other commitments—this was a significant occasion. Samba Dikshita mentioned women particularly as belonging to this group. Maybe some children came too. And yes, there were also the men.

Samba Dikshita explained that his family had initiated their practice of performing the *Bhāgavata* those many generations ago because they knew the efficacy of the text. His ancestor had been unable to produce a son and therefore keep the line alive—keep the fire, quite literally, burning. The *Bhāgavata* worked its magic and there was Samba Dikshita to prove it, eight generations later.[3] By my estimate, this crucial event might have transpired sometime around the turn of the eighteenth century, and it was precisely then, so far as we can tell, that manuscripts of the *Bhāgavata māhātmya* first appeared, detailing in its sixth and final chapter the exact conditions under which the *Bhāgavata-purāṇa* ought to be performed and describing its benefits.[4]

I have sometimes wondered just what led to the production of this interesting text, the *Bhāgavata māhātmya*, at just this point in time, and I've considered whether it might have happened because there had come to be too many of Samba Dikshita's afternoons, so to speak, in relation to his mornings—too much else happening in the name of the *Bhāgavata* and too little in the way of its actual, proper performance from a certain conservative Brahmin point of view. Anyone who has recently travelled in North India will know the kind of thing I have in mind. In Brindavan, for example, numerous billboards trumpet this or that world-famous *acharya* performing *shrimad bhagavat saptah*. These aren't just

3 Several years ago I heard a paper from a retired member of the medical faculty at Pune University describing the *Bhāgavata*'s expertise in the field of embryology: Padmakar Vishnu Vartak, 'Embryology and Chromosomes from Śrīmad Bhāgavatam', National Seminar on "Śrīmad Bhāgavatam: Its Philosophical, Religious, and Social Themes", Ananthacharya Indological Research Institute (Mumbai, 28 March 2009).

4 See J.S. Hawley, 'The *Bhāgavata Māhātmya* in Context', in *Patronage and Popularisation, Pilgrimage and Procession: Channels of Transcultural Translation and Transmission in Early Modern South Asia; Papers in Honour of Monika Horstmann*, ed. by Heidi R.M. Pauwels (Wiesbaden: Harrassowitz, 2009), pp. 81-100.

seven-day performances as mandated in the *Bhāgavata māhātmya*, though certainly the authorisation of that number by that text is basic. They are not primarily recitations—Samba Dikshita's "mornings"—but rather expositions, primarily vernacular expositions involving sermon and song. And they are not just *saptahs* or *kathas*, if the signs are to be believed, but *yajnas*—in fact, *mahayajnas*, "great sacrifices".

I wonder whether a similar proliferation of forms and formats claiming the *Bhāgavata* as their end and origin in late seventeenth-century North India might have led to the articulation of the stringent set of performance standards that appears in the *Bhāgavata māhātmya*. These focus on an expositor of great intelligence who is a Brahmin householder capable of teaching the Vedas and is surrounded by other Brahmins; who is purified by an early morning toilet, a bath, and the shaving of his head and chin, etc. The audience, similarly, must be comprised of men who have vowed sexual abstinence for the duration of the performance; who pledge to sleep on the ground, survive on milk and ghi if at all possible, eschew anger and other untoward forms of behaviour; and who will refrain from speaking with a menstruating woman, *mlecchas* and *shudras* (i.e. impure foreigners and low castes), and so forth.[5]

As to the performative environment that might have been sought to be disciplined by this set of prescriptions, one has a great deal to choose from in the records that have come down to us from sixteenth- and seventeenth-century North India. In Braj, a man named Ghamandi—or alternatively, Narayan Bhatt—is said to have created something like the kernel of the *ras lilas* we recognise today—or perhaps they were already there before these South Indian aficionados arrived.[6] Guru Nanak knows about enacted Krishna stories like this, and he does not like them one bit:

*ketīāṃ kanna kahāṇīāṃ kete beda bīcāra*
*kete nacahi maṅgate giḍi muḍi pūrahi tāla*
*bājārī bājāra mahi āi karḍhahi bājāra*

How many Krishna-tales there are, how many opinions on the Vedas!
How many beggars dance and, twisting and falling,
beat time with their hands!

5 I follow the text given in the Gita Press edition: *Śrīmad Bhāgavata Mahāpurāṇa (with Sanskrit Text and English Translation)*, trans. by C.L. Goswami (Gorakhpur: Gita Press, 1995 [orig., 1971]), 6.20-50, pp. 38-42.

6 Norvin Hein, *The Miracle Plays of Mathurā* (New Haven: Yale University Press, 1972), pp. 223-30.

The mercenary fellows go into the market-place and draw out
the market crowd.[7]

Then there are the Ahirs whose performances of the Krishna story fascinated Malik Muhammad Jayasi, as he tells us in his *Kanhāvat* of 1540; he is eager to elevate such performances to a level where they have a chance of capturing the attention of more refined audiences.[8] A decade before Jayasi, Lalachdas "Halvai" had been active in a place he called Hastigram, near Rae Bareilly, creating his own Avadhi shortening of the tenth book of the *Bhāgavata*.[9] Before the end of the century (1595), there appeared a vernacular commentary on the eleventh book by Chaturdas, and let us remember that when Eknath produced his famous Marathi treatment of the eleventh book in the sixteenth century, he was sitting in Banaras.

The *Bhāgavata*'s tenth book, the famous *dashama skandha*, must have risen to almost canonical status at that point—particularly the five "core" chapters describing the *ras lila*—since just about then Hariramvyas, in Brindavan, was shaping his *Rāsapancādhyayī*, to be followed not long afterward (c.1560-1570) by a similar composition written by Nanddas.[10] Nanddas also produced what one might call an actual "translation" of the tenth book of the *Bhāgavata*, his *Bhāṣā dasamskandh*, which he seems to have abandoned after he completed the twenty-eighth chapter. Or perhaps he did not stop but rather changed gears. After all, chapter twenty-nine brought him to the section of the text that had the most obvious dramatic possibilities—the section in which the *ras lila* was portrayed. Hariramvyas

7 *Gurū Granth, āsā dī vār*, p. 464 in the standard edition. The translation is that of Hein (1972), p. 116. See also Norvin Hein, 'Guru Nanak's Comment on the Vaishnava Lila', in *Perspectives on Guru Nanak*, ed. by Harbans Singh (Patiala: Punjabi University, 1969), pp. 493-501. I am grateful to Gurinder Singh Mann for drawing the latter to my attention and for checking the Gurmukhi original.

8 Francesca Orsini, 'Inflected *Kathas*: Sufis and Krishna *Bhaktas* in Awadh', in *Religious Interactions in Mughal India*, ed. by Vasudha Dalmia and Munis Faruqui (New Delhi: Oxford University Press, 2014b), pp. 195-232.

9 *Lālacdās-racit Avadhī-kāvya Haricarit*, ed. by Acharya Nalinavilocana Sharma and Shriramanarayan Shastri (Patna: Bihar-Rashtrabhasha Parishad, 1963), Vol. 1. See also R.S. McGregor, *Hindi Literature from its Beginnings to the Nineteenth Century* (Wiesbaden: Otto Harrassowitz, 1984), p. 96. McGregor's treatment of related works is valuable for the subject as a whole (pp. 96-101, 156ff.). Orsini (2014b) also discusses the *Haricarit* of Lalachdas.

10 Heidi Pauwels, *Kṛṣṇa's Round Dance Reconsidered* (Richmond, Surrey: Curzon, 1996); R.S. McGregor, *Nanddas: The Round Dance of Krishna and Uddhav's Message* (London: Luzac, 1973).

had already celebrated it, as we have seen. It may be that Nanddas simply skipped the rails at this point, moving from the simpler *chaupai-doha* diction of the *Bhāṣā dasamskandh* into the more distinctive *rola* register of his *Rāsapancādhyayī*, which may have seemed more suitable for a fully literary rendition. He never returned to his earlier task.[11]

It seems to have been a whole century, until 1687, before we got a complete and in this sense "faithful" *bhasha* version of the tenth book of the Sanskrit original—this at the hand of Bhupati, who declares at the beginning of this document that he is producing it in Brajbhasha.[12] Bhupati's *Dasamskandh* was widely copied and widely known, yet it was not the only text of its ilk that began circulating at just this moment in time.

Another Brajbhasha *Dasamskandh*, this one richly illustrated in the Malwa or Central Indian style, shows up in two parts in 1686 and 1688. The former gives us episodes from the first half of the tenth *skandha*; the latter, from the second. Intriguingly, however, these two dated manuscripts are not sufficiently compatible to be regarded as parts of a single project, and other undated versions of both parts also exist; copying is involved.[13] Thus the whole cluster makes us vividly aware of a performative domain we have not yet mentioned, one in which the text of the *Bhāgavata*—or its *bhasha* equivalent—would be displayed simultaneously in words and pictures, whether for the pleasure of an individual reader or to provide the basis for a show-and-tell that would require the services of a professional reciter/raconteur. Illustrated *Bhāgavatas* that make use of the Sanskrit text date back to the first half of the sixteenth century in North

11 Nanddas says he is conveying the luminosity of the *Bhāgavata* into *bhasha: Nandadās Granthāvalī*, ed. by Vrajaratnadas (Banaras: Nagari Pracharini Sabha, 1949), 1:14-16, Vol. 2, p. 2. On the shift from the *Bhāṣā dasamskandh* to the *Rāsapancādhyayī*, see also McGregor (1973), p. 35. Note also that the status of the 29th chapter of the *Bhāṣā dasamskandh* is not entirely clear: it is absent from the 1757 VS manuscript that otherwise forms the principal basis for the text that appears in the *Nandadās granthāvalī*, as well as in a similar manuscript that forms a part of the Kankarauli collection, and is therefore described in Vrajaratnadas's edition as an appendix (1949, *pariśiṣṭ*, Vol. 2, p. 272; cf. Vol. 1, pp. 51-52).

12 Grahame Nieman, 'The Bhāgavat Daśam Skandh of Bhūpati', *IAVRI Bulletin* 8, 3-8; Nieman, 'Bhūpati's *Bhāgavat* and the Hindi *Bhāgavat* Genre', in *Bhakti in Current Research, 1979-1982*, ed. by Monika Hostmann (Berlin: Dietrich Weimer Verlag, 1983), pp. 257-67.

13 W.G. Archer, *Central Indian Painting* (London: Faber & Faber, 1958), p. 12. The colophon page is now damaged. On the 1688 Kanoria Bhagavata and its copies, see Neeraja Poddar, 'Krishna in his Myriad Forms: Narration, Translation, and Variation in Illustrated Manuscripts of the Latter Half of the Tenth Book of the Bhāgavata Purāṇa' (PhD dissertation, Columbia University, 2014).

India, and quite a number seem to emerge in the region bordered by Delhi and Agra—greater Braj, one might say.[14] But what is interesting about our Malwa *Dasamskandhs* is that there, for the first time, the seemingly elite practice of manuscript illustration is clearly linked to a Brajbhasha version of the *Bhāgavata* text, not to its Sanskrit parent.

Seen from a wider angle, this may come as no surprise. From the fifteenth century onward, numerous vernacular adaptations of the *Bhāgavata* had begun to appear in various regions of India, not just in Brajbhasha but in Kannada, Gujarati, Malayalam, Bengali, Orissi, and Assamese.[15] Then there were more distant relatives. The Maithili poems of Vidyapati are hardly vernacular transcriptions of the *Bhāgavata*, but it does appear that the poet took the trouble to copy at least a portion of the text for his own use in the second or third decade of the fifteenth century.[16]

Of course, there was also a long history of literary activity around the *Bhāgavata* in Sanskrit itself, as indicated, for example, by the digest of its contents that Vopadeva prepared way back in the thirteenth century—his *Harilīlā*—or the systematic marshalling of its *bhakti*-related passages that he provided in his *Muktāphala*. And by the seventeenth century we have various indications of Brahminical resistance to the production of written vernacular works that could, as Sheldon Pollock has said, threaten "an old economy of literary-cultural power based on Sanskrit and a whole class of bilingual intermediaries".[17] The enthusiastic reception of poets such as Nanddas and Bhupati may have caused certain groups of North

---

14 See Daniel J. Ehnbom, 'An Analysis and Reconstruction of the Dispersed Bhāgavata Purāṇa from the Caurapañcāśikā Group' (PhD dissertation, University of Chicago, 1984), pp. 25-42; and Harsha V. Dehejia, *Celebrating Krishna: Sacred Words and Sensuous Images: The Tenth Book of the Bhagavata Purana* (Ahmedabad: Mapin, 2005), pp. 54-55, 122-23, 164-67, 172-77.

15 Especially helpful for the subject as a whole is Bimanbehari Majumdar, 'The Bhāgavata Purāṇa and its Influence in the Sixteenth Century', *Journal of the Bihar Research Society* 47.1-4 (1961), 381-93. The range Majumdar describes is impressive, and his perspectives are helpful as well. I know from his treatment of Surdas, however, that one would need to evaluate some of his conclusions on the basis of further manuscript work.

16 The date specifically claimed in the Nepal manuscript upon which Subhadra Jha bases this assertion is *lakṣmaṇ samvat* 309, but there are debates about exactly when this occurred. See Jha, *Vidyāpati-Gīt-Saṅgrah or The Songs of Vidyāpati* (Banaras: Motilal Banarsidas, 1954), p. 57.

17 Sheldon Pollock, *The Language of the Gods and the World of Men: Sanskrit, Culture, and Power in Premodern India* (Berkeley: University of California Press, 2006), p. 312. Cf. William L. Smith, 'The Turkish Conquest and the Dark Age of Bengali Literature', in *Ludwik Sternbach Felicitation Volume*, ed. by J.P. Sinha (Lucknow: Akhila Bharatiya Sanskrit Parishad, 1979), Vol. 2, pp. 709-11.

Indian Brahmins to want to reign in this vernacular efflorescence by putting forth just the sort of performance prescriptions that we meet in the *Bhāgavata māhātmya*. There may also have been a caste dimension, not just a linguistic one. Bhupati, after all, was a Kayasth, and it was another Kayasth, a man by the name of Asanand, who took it upon himself to finish the *Haricarit* that Lalach had begun; he had made it to chapter 45 in 1614, when he stopped.[18] Still another Kayasth, a Gujarati named Keshav Kayasth, had composed a *Kṛṣṇakrīḍākāvya* in the late fifteenth century. Against the polyglot, poly-caste backdrop that these texts suggest, did Brahmins want to reassert their own perspective—not just the power of the original text but the power conveyed by their own unique capacity to perform it?

We will be trying to figure out where Surdas stands in this complicated terrain in a moment, but let me mention a few more players on the scene before we do. Consider, for example, the Gaudiya community, so firmly entrenched in Braj by the latter half of the sixteenth century. Not only did their leading theologians—Sanatana, Rupa, and Jiva Gosvami—create an impressive set of new commentaries on the *Bhāgavata*, the community also pioneered a genre in which the ever more elaborately articulated *lila* format that was seen to structure Krishna's life served as the basis for various mappings of the life of his avatar Chaitanya.[19] Think also of the more conservative theologian Vallabhacharya, who was based in Arail just across the *sangam* from Allahabad. Vallabha launched into a massive new commentary on the *Bhāgavata*—his *Subodhinī*—which he was unable to complete, but he did succeed in finishing book ten.[20]

Vallabha's life, in turn, became the seed for the genre known as *varta*—literally, "conversation"—which sometimes made reference to his commentarial effort (as in the *varta* on Surdas), but was not actually structured along the lines of the *Bhāgavata* in the way that happened with the Chaitanyites. Yet that did not mean the *lila* idea could not be enacted elsewhere in the Vallabhite theological imagination. The author of the Vallabhite *Caurāsī vaiṣṇavan kī vārtā* depicts Surdas's life in just those terms. He tells us that at end of his life, Sur disappeared into the *nitya lila*

18 Sharma and Shastri (1966), pp. 7-9.

19 An indispensable treatment of the latter subject can be found in Tony K. Stewart, *The Final Word: The Caitanya Caritāmṛta and the Grammar of Religious Tradition* (New York: Oxford University Press, 2010).

20 The *Subodhinī* is complete for *skandhas* 1-3 and 10, incomplete for *skandhas* 4 and 11, and lacking for the remainder of the *Bhāgavata*.

that brought him into the direct presence of Radha and Krishna. This was possible because the poet had been initiated into a consciousness of that realm when Vallabha whispered to him, in mantraic form, the entirety of his *Subodhinī* commentary at the outset of his life as a religious poet—according to Vallabhite standards, that is. His conversion from being a poet of "simpering", someone who sang laments and petitions, into someone who worked out of a Krishnaite framework was accomplished by means of his initiation, when Vallabha vouchsafed to him the true and entire meaning of the *Bhāgavata*.[21]

This great Sanskrit text is strikingly ubiquitous in the recollections of sixteenth-century Braj that have come down to us. (We cannot be sure Sur lived there, but he clearly worked in its linguistic medium.) It seems Rupa Gosvami had turned his attentions to producing a Sanskrit *Uddhavasandeśa* even before he met Chaitanya.[22] His guru-brother Raghunath Bhatt is remembered as having recited a portion of the *Bhāgavata-purāṇa* itself on a daily basis "at the assembly of Rupa Gosvami", as the *Caitanya caritāmṛta* puts it, probably at the temple of Govindadev.[23] The Chaitanyite leader Gadadhar Bhatt made a similar commitment, not only to Govindadev but to Radharaman, Gopinath, and Madanmohan.[24] Elsewhere in the *sampradayik* spectrum, the Vallabhite writer known as Gadadhar Bhatt Dvivedi remarks that Keshav Kashmiri, the leader of the Nimbarka community in sixteenth-century Brindavan, was known for his seven-day *Bhāgavata* performances. Hariramvyas, who also lived in Brindavan in the latter half of the sixteenth century, appreciated the importance of

---

21 Just because it is hard to accept the historicity of this account, that is no reason to underestimate the importance of the sentiment it expresses—not in regard to Surdas but in relation to the period (mid-seventeenth century?) and *sampradaya* context associated with the writing of the text where the story appears. I discuss historical difficulties associated with this and related *varta* passages in *Sūr Dās: Poet, Singer, Saint* (Seattle: University of Washington Press and Delhi; Oxford University Press, 1984), pp. 14-22. On the *varta*'s view of the *Bhāgavata* as a template for the poetry of Surdas, see also my *Three Bhakti Voices: Mirabai, Kabir, and Surdas in Their Time and Ours* (Delhi: Oxford University Press, 2005), pp. 185-88.

22 Sushil Kumar De, *Early History of the Vaiṣṇava Faith and Movement in Bengal* (Calcutta: Firma K.L. Mukhopadhyaya, 1961), p. 646; see also McGregor (1973), p. 48.

23 *Caitanya Caritāmṛta of Kṛṣṇadāsa Kavirāja: A Translation and Commentary*, ed. by Edward C. Dimock, Jr. and Tony K. Stewart (Cambridge: Harvard Oriental Series, 1999), 3.125, p. 924.

24 Thanks to Shrivatsa Goswami for clarifying this matter to me. Gadadhar Bhatt's vow has been carried out by his descendents until the present day. See also Swapna Sharma, *Gadādhar Bhaṭṭ: paramparā aur sāhitya* (Vrindaban: Vrajagaurav Prakashan, [n.d.]), p. 31.

"*Bhakti* and the *Bhāgavata*", but he hated that *pandits* recited it for money.[25] The presence of the *Bhāgavata* is frequently felt in various vignettes that appear in the *Caurāsī vaiṣṇavan kī vartā*, a seventeenth-century text, but we must wait until the eighteenth century before we meet the idea that Vallabhacharya, like Keshav Bhatt Kashmiri, was known for reciting the great text over the course of a seven-day period, as is prescribed in the *Bhāgavata māhātmya*. This we learn in the *Caurāsī baiṭhak caritra*, a treatise that celebrates Vallabha's travels and worldwide fame.[26]

So I repeat our initial question: Should we also be making a place for Surdas on this already crowded stage?

First of all, we must disabuse ourselves of any notion that Surdas ever made an attempt to answer this question himself. There is plenty in the Surdas tradition that tries to do it for him, but that is all after the fact. The Surdas about whom I wish to speak in this essay is the Surdas who lived in the sixteenth century—the *real* Surdas, if I may put it that boldly. While it is certainly true that there is no way in principle to separate him from the poets who contributed literally thousands of poems to the Surdas corpus after his death, I am convinced that beneath this pile of other Surdases also stood a single renowned poet who lived in the sixteenth century itself. Poems that we can trace to that century, thanks to manuscript evidence and the exacting critical edition prepared by Kenneth Bryant, are notably tighter, more difficult, and more elegant than the more recent ones.[27] Using the name Surdas (admittedly, somewhat loosely) to designate this sixteenth-century corpus of poems, we can see clearly that nowhere does Surdas come out and say that he is either translating or performing the *Bhāgavata*. No poem that we can be sure circulated in the sixteenth century even mentions the *Bhāgavata*, as a certain number of later ones do. No

25 Heidi R.M. Pauwels, *In Praise of Holy Men: Hagiographic Poems by and about Harirām Vyās* (Groningen: Egbert Forsten, 2002), pp. 98-99.

26 *Chaurasi Baithak: Eightyfour Seats of Shri Vallabhacharya*, trans. by Sham Das (Baroda, Shri Vallabha Publications, 1985), 84, p. 83. The seventeenth-century figure Gokulnath is traditionally claimed to be the compiler of the *Caurāsī baiṭhak caritra*, but this seems impossible. See Alan W. Entwistle, *Braj, Centre of Krishna Pilgrimage* (Groningen: Egbert Forsten, 1987), pp. 263-64. In an email communication of 9 April 2008, Shandip Saha points out that the *Caurāsī vaiṣṇavan kī vārtā*, which is almost certainly earlier than the *Caurāsī baiṭhak caritra*, makes no mention of Vallabha performing *bhagavat saptah*.

27 Surdas, *Sur's Ocean: Poems from the Early Tradition*, ed. by Kenneth E. Bryant, trans. by John Stratton Hawley (Harvard, MA: Harvard University Press, 2015). The materials, principles, and technology underlying this edition, which seeks to reconstruct the extant corpus of Surdas poems that can be shown to have circulated in the sixteenth century, are substantially different from any earlier edition of the *Sūrsāgar*.

one has yet come along and organised Surdas *padas* so that they appear to replicate the *skandha*-by-*skandha* organisation of the *Bhāgavata*—that would not happen until almost the turn of the nineteenth century[28]—and certainly no one has composed a poem anything like the following (NPS 225):[29]

*śrīmukha cāri sloka dae brahmā kauṃ samujhāi*
*brahmā nārada saun kahe nārada byāsa sunāi*
*byāsa kahe sukadeva sauṃ dvādasa skandha banāi*
*suradāsa soī kahe pada bhāṣā kari gāi*

Vishnu, from his sacred mouth, explained four *ślokas* to Brahma;
Brahma told them to Narad, and Narad to Vyas in turn;
Vyas told them to Shukdev, setting them out in twelve books,
And these Surdas told as songs sung in the common tongue.

All of this is late, late, late. Nonetheless, it is important. It reveals the desire of eighteenth- and nineteenth-century editors to make plain a perceived link between the great Sanskrit Purana and this prestigious vernacular text. The *Sursāgar* was indeed perceived—at least by some—as a *text* by that point in time, and someone felt it was essential that it be construed in relation to the *Bhāgavata-purāṇa*, which was in its turn regarded by many as the definitive commentary on and sum of all Vedic knowledge. That claim was already being made in the sixteenth century.[30]

But the absence of this external scaffolding doesn't mean that the poet himself was either ignorant of or indifferent to the *Bhāgavata*. This, I think, was not so. But how, precisely, was Sur sensitive to the *Bhāgavata*? And how did he perform it?

It would certainly be wrong to suggest that every poem circulating in Surdas's name in the sixteenth century can be regarded as in some sense

28 Hawley (1984), p. 39. The oldest manuscripts I have seen that adopt this organisational scheme are Nagaripracharini Sabha no. 496, dated 1847 VS =1790 CE, and NPS no. 4469 (269/26), dated 1850 VS = 1793 CE.

29 The abbreviation NPS designates the Nagaripracharini Sabha edition of the *Sūrsāgar*, a critical edition that has served as the standard text of reference for the poetry of Surdas since its partial publication in 1936 and complete publication in 1948. The version currently available is *Sūrsāgar*, ed. by Jagannathdas "Ratnakar", Nandadulare Vajpeyi et al., 2 vols (Varanasi: Kashi Nagaripracharini Sabha, 1972 and 1976). The critical apparatus appears only in the portion published in 1936.

30 E.g., Jiva Goswami, *Tattvasandarbha* 19, 22a, and 24, as given in Stuart Elkman, *Jīva Gosvāmin's Tattvasandarbha: A Study on the Philosophical and Sectarian Development of the Gauḍīya Vaiṣṇava Movement* (Delhi: Motilal Banarsidass, 1986), pp. 91, 100-01, 111-12; see also De (1961), pp. 261-65.

a performance of the *Bhāgavata-purāṇa*, though the themes and narrative episodes in the poetry do often match those in the great Sanskrit text. Occasionally, however, we find ourselves faced with a much more direct connection between the *Bhāgavata* and the words of Surdas. Let us consider two such poems—poems that also relate to one another, in that they share a common phrase. Here is the first:

1 *mādhau kopi cakra kara līnau* (Bryant §356, NPS 273)[31]
2 *chāḍi beda bānī apanau panu jana kauṅ bhāyau kīnau*
3 *ratha te uteri avani ātura hvai leta carana ati dhāi*
4 *sahi na sakati bhū bhāra bhīta hvai capala bhaī akulāī*
5 *kachuka aṅga kachu adhara upara paṭu unati bāhu bisāla*
6 *sveda sroṇi sobhā ati tana mai ghana baraṣyau mani lāla*
7 *sura subhaṭṭa sameta sudarasana deṣi birañci bhramyau*
8 *mānahu āna sṛṣṭi karibe koṅ ambuja nābhi jamyau*

1 Madhav, in anger, took the wheel in his hand.
2 Abandoning the word of the Veda, his own promise,
he did what would please his devotee.
3 He stepped from his chariot to earth, all astir,
and the moment his foot touched the ground he ran.
4 The earth could not endure the weight
and shuddered fearfully, as if deranged.
5 His upper garment slipped down his limbs
and as he lifted his vast, strong arm
6 It revealed a torso radiant with sweat and blood—
a thundercloud raining pearls and rubies.
7 Sur says, when Brahma saw that fine warrior
and the discus he held, called Fine Vision,
8 He fell into confusion, as if this were a new creation
and he a baby lotus-born upon an umbilical stem.

The first task that faces the audience of most Surdas *padas* is to identify the narrative moment to which the poem refers. This poem is a good example of the audience's quandary, but the poet makes their task easier than he sometimes does: he announces the episode in his title line rather than challenging his listeners to deduce it on their own. On the basis of

31 The symbol § marks the position of this poem in the Bryant edition. I am grateful to Ken Bryant for permission to quote his reconstructions of §§ 356-357 in this essay. As previously stated, NPS refers to the standard Nagaripracharini Sabha edition of the *Sūrsāgar*. In the text that follows the abbreviation Mbh will refer to the *Mahābhārata* in the critical Pune edition, for which V.S. Sukthankar served as general editor. BhP denotes the *Bhāgavata-purāṇa* in the Gita Press edition.

what he says, knowledgeable members of his audience will recognise immediately that Sur is referring to events that transpired on the third day of the great Bharata war (Mbh 6.55.83ff.). But more is involved. The way Sur approaches his subject shows that he assumes at least on his own part, if not also on the part of his audience as a whole, a knowledge of the manner in which that story is reported in the *Bhāgavata-purāṇa* (especially BhP 1.9.37-39). Bhishma, the aged but ever-agile commander of the Kaurav army, was the staunchest devotee (*jana*, v. 2) of Krishna, who had joined the forces of the opposite side as Arjun's charioteer but had vowed never to take an active role in the fighting. It was Bhishma's fondest wish to see Krishna arrayed against him in battle, however, and he attempted to provoke Krishna to fight him by raining countless arrows upon Krishna and Arjun, both of whom sustained multiple wounds. When Krishna sensed in Arjun a residual unwillingness to retaliate against Bhishma, who was his own elder and preceptor, he feared for Arjun's safety and sprang into the fray himself, thus fulfilling Bhishma's wish. In doing so, he broke his earlier oath, "the word of the Veda" (*beda bānī*, v. 2), but all in the cause of making a countervailing vow come true—the vow of his devotee. Bhishma had vowed that he would cause Krishna to take up a weapon in the Bharata war, and when Krishna reached for the wheel, that vow was complete.

The *Mahābhārata* is content to present this about-face in its own terms, but the *Bhāgavata* is more guarded. Rather than have Krishna simply attack with his own weapon, the *sudarśan* discus (cf. Mbh 6.55.83-86), it depicts him as having been unarmed. Krishna therefore has to reach for the wheel of the chariot he was driving (*dhr̥tarathacaraṇo*, BhP 1.9.37) and use that as if it were his accustomed discus. Surdas does not definitively commit himself to the latter position, in that he designates the weapon with the word *chakra* (v. 1), which can mean either "wheel" or "discus", but the fact that Krishna "takes it in his hand" (*kara līnau*, v. 1) does seem to lean in the direction of the *Bhāgavata*. The "fine vision" (*sudarśan* > *sudarasana*, v. 7) that Bhishma then saw was at once the gorgeously bloody sight of Krishna that Surdas conjures up in verses 5-6 and the disc of that name, whether in function (if it was the chariot wheel) or in essence (if the discus itself).

The pun on *sudarshan* guides the poem to its completion and introduces another startling juxtaposition. It is this. Clearly the person who sees this vision is Bhishma, who bows before Krishna and, according to the

*Bhāgavata*, delivers an extended hymn of praise describing what he sees (BhP 1.9.32-36). Bhishma is the devotee, servant, or subject (*jana*, v. 2) to whom reference is made near the beginning of the poem. Yet when the vision has been described and the poet uses his signature to indicate that he is about to conclude, he suddenly changes perspective by naming the beholder of the vision not as Bhishma but as Brahma (*birañci*, v. 7). The gods are often thought of as witnessing momentous events in the life of Krishna, so Brahma's presence makes sense to that degree, but there is a more particular stimulus for the confused manner in which Brahma reacts to seeing Krishna. He is disoriented by the affinity between the sight of Krishna raising the wheel or discus on his arm and the image of a lotus emerging from the dark waters of a lake on its stem. He finds himself in a powerful time-warp, since he himself was emitted from the navel of Vishnu on an umbilical lotus at the beginning of time. Considering the vast power of Krishna's discus for destruction, this vision of a return to creation is a stark event, perhaps foreshadowing the new age that will emerge from the global carnage of the great Bharata war as a whole.

In the *Mahābhārata* (6.55.89-90), the simile of the primeval lotus is used to describe the appearance of Krishna's arm and weapon at this moment, but it is apparently Sur's own invention to bring Brahma himself on the scene. Once again I think it is likely that his impetus for doing so came from the *Bhāgavata-purāṇa*. Although the *Bhāgavata* makes no mention of Brahma, the personal deity, it does feature his antetype, the impersonal Brahman, at just this point in the story. The *Mahābhārata* goes on to describe a series of further confrontations before Bhishma actually expires, and makes it clear that Arjun was the one who killed him. But it is the *Bhāgavata* that focuses its account of Bhishma's death on the encounter with Krishna himself. It says this caused Bhishma to arrest his own breathing and merge into Brahman (*brahmaṇi niṣkale*, BhP 1.9.44).

Where is Surdas between these two master narratives? Somewhere in the middle. He seems to personify Brahman and thereby arrive at a new perspective on the *Mahābhārata*'s navel-lotus simile, while at the same time suggesting a close identification between the aged warrior-sage Bhishma and the aged god Brahma. These two are made to share a common vision, though with very different reactions. Bhishma's calm is Brahma's disquietude, and Bhishma's death is Brahma's birth.

It is a remarkable ending, I think, a remarkable way of re-envisioning a moment absolutely pivotal to the way in which the great Bharata battle will unfold. This recasting is very much in the spirit with which the *Bhāgavata* tells the story, yet with a spicing—or rather, to follow the metaphor of soup, a stock—that takes us back to the Epic. Sur seems to invite his hearers to recall that there are distinctive disparities between the ways in which these two great authorities treat this tale, but his mode of displaying this is not to point it out in the fashion of a commentator. Rather, he performs his way through to a new solution. In doing so, is he performing the *Bhāgavata* more than the *Mahābhārata*? No, in the case of this poem I don't think we want to be forced into making that decision. In fact, it would be precisely false to do so.

Now let us take a look at a second performance of this same episode—an encore, so to speak, though most likely it was originally performed independently of the composition we have just studied. Intriguingly, though, one verbal sequence that it contains—the first half of verse 3—actually repeats what we have already heard in "Madhav, in anger, took the wheel in his hand". Here is our second poem:

1 *vā paṭa pīta kī phaharāni* (Bryant edition §357, NPS 279)
2 *kara dhari cakra carana kī dhāvani nahi bisarati vaha bāni*
3 *ratha te uteri avani ātura hvai kaca raja kī lapaṭāni*
4 *mānahu siṅgha saila te nikase mahā matta gaja jāni*
5 *jihi gupāla merau panu rāṣyau meṭi beda kī kāni*
6 *soi ba sura sahāi hamārai nikaṭa bhae prabhu āni*

1 The way his yellow garments fluttered,
2 The wheel in his hand, how swiftly he ran—
I'll never forget how he appeared
3 When he stepped from his chariot to earth, all astir.
With bits of dust smeared through his hair he seemed
4 Like a lion emerging from a mountain lair
on sensing some great, mad elephant.
5 The same Gopal who fulfilled my vow,
who brushed aside the Vedic sense of right—
6 This is the one who's coming to my aid:
such a Lord, says Sur, and yet so near.

This time we quickly recognise the moment. But now we see events directly through Bhishma's eyes; it is he who speaks. In consequence, the principal metaphor he offers for what he sees—that Krishna's wild hair looks like the dusty mane of a lion moving in for the kill (v. 4)—is more in keeping with his own dramatic situation. It is martial rather than cosmological.

The individual elements of this image are put forward when the *Bhāgavata-purāṇa* (BhP 1.9.32-42) recounts the battle of Krishna and Bhishma, and there too Bhishma is the narrator. In the *Bhāgavata*, however, the description of Krishna's hair being suffused with dust that horses had kicked up (BhP 1.9.34) is at several verses' remove from the brief reference to his acting as ferocious as a lion faced with an elephant (BhP 1.9.37), which also occurs in the *Mahābhārata*. Sur displays his originality by drawing these two into direct proximity with one another.

The vow mentioned in verse 5 refers to Bhishma's pledge to see Krishna standing before him as a warrior before he dies. To fulfill this wish, Krishna must abrogate his own pledge, his Vedic oath (*beda kī kāni*, "the Vedic sense of right", v. 5) not to step upon the field of battle and take sides in the Bharat war (BhP 1.9.37). Like the author of the *Bhāgavata*, Sur depicts Krishna as a person who places the honour and desire of those devoted to him above any other morality, even when the latter is thought of as being sanctioned by the Veda as in the case of a promise that ought to be kept. In both texts—the *Bhāgavata* and the *Sursāgar*—the lesson is that with Krishna the religion of *bhakti* is victorious over its predecessor, the religion of royal and martial *dharma*.

The poet's use of the title Gopal (*gupāla*, v. 5) seems intended to contribute to this shift of emphasis. As the darling of the cowherds and protector of cattle, Gopal is not strictly speaking a figure who belongs in the epic milieu where this poem is set. But once again there is a precedent in the *Bhāgavata*, which allows Bhishma, in the course of a long encomium to Krishna, to mix in a reference to the lad who had such a profound effect on the cowherd women of Braj (*gopavadhvaḥ*, BhP 1.9.40). As in the case of the lion metaphor, however, Sur achieves a sharper juxtaposition, and one can say the same for the note on which he concludes. When Krishna comes to Bhishma's aid, drawing near to fulfill his vow, everyone in the audience knows what form this help will take: death!

Here we do seem to have left the *Mahābhārata* behind in favour of the *Bhāgavata*'s telling of the tale. But does that alter the balance sufficiently that we can now be convinced we ought to think of Sur as specifically "performing the *Bhāgavata*", given the evidence that these two poems provide us? Obviously not in the sense that might be expected on the basis of the roster of *Bhāgavata* performers with which we began. Sur is far too independent a poet to allow for such a characterisation. He not only presents what he has received; he kneads it, he contests it. One might even say he twists it.

This is hardly the only occasion on which we can see such a process at work. The most famous is undoubtedly presented by Sur's *bhramargit* poems, where the gopis of Braj are visited by Uddhav, the messenger Krishna has sent to console them after he has departed for Mathura. As the *Bhāgavata* reports this moment, the gopis receive Uddhav's *advaita* sermon about how Krishna is always with them despite his seeming absence with a measure of equanimity, even satisfaction. When Surdas approaches this theme, by contrast, the gopis reject Uddhav's message altogether. In the *Bhāgavata* both they and Uddhav get a chance to say their piece; in the *Sursāgar* Uddhav is practically reduced to silence.

One might think that this disparity merely reflects two storytelling traditions that have moved apart from one another as independent performative genres, and there must surely be an element of that. But every so often we can see that the *Bhāgavata* is specifically on Sur's mind—or at least that certain of its distinctive phrases echo in his consciousness. Consider, for example, the *bhramargit* poem in which Sur's gopis say they are suspicious of the message Uddhav brings because the very form of its delivery—by a messenger they perceive as a "bee"—shows Krishna has been consorting with a species famous for "cheating hearts" (*kaitava cita*).[32] In putting things this way, Sur does not repeat or "translate" the *Bhāgavata*, but, rather, turns it on its head. At the appropriate point in the *Bhāgavata*'s narration it is Uddhav, not Krishna, who is excoriated for being "the friend of a cheat" (*kitavabandho*, BhP 10.47.12), while in the words of Surdas that allegation, made with exactly the same term (Skt. *kitava* > Brj. *kaitava*), is leveled against Krishna instead. Knowledgeable members of Sur's audience would surely have appreciated the reference and understood its ironic relation to the poem they were hearing.

Given all this, it is perhaps fitting that we do not really know—contrary to what we are told by the *Caurāsī vaiṣṇavan kī vārtā*—just what Sur's performative circumstances might have been. This Vallabhite text wants him to be a straightforward temple musician, serving Krishna in *kirtan* at the great shrine atop Mount Govardhan or serenading him in the *mandir* of Navanitapriyaji in Gokul. Yet there is actually no reason to believe that these temples—or any temples—were his exclusive métier. Certainly there is no reason to believe he was a Vallabhite. Sur may indeed have performed in temples, but it is also possible to envision him singing his

32 Bryant §268.3. The Nagaripracharini Sabha edition, which follows a more recent manuscript tradition, loses this meaning (*kaisaiṅ cita*, NPS 4211.3).

poetry in homes, in *satsangs*, in what Anantadas calls *mahotsavs*, in salons, or in courts. And which court, if so? It seems to me unlikely that the Surdas Abu'l Fazl mentions was the same as "our" Surdas,[33] so I like the fact that Muhammad Kabir, the author of the *Afsānah-i shāhān*, written early in the seventeenth century, wants to argue instead for the court of Islam Shah, his Afghan forebear.[34] But there too we encounter a record that can hardly be taken at historical face value.

We also do not know what Sur's musical situation was, except that to characterise it as *dhrupad*, as is often done, skirts a number of difficulties attending that characterisation. The most striking of these is that poems attributed to Surdas in the sixteenth century show no preference for the four-verse pattern that seems to have been considered to be one of the great hallmarks of classical *dhrupad* practice.[35] In fact, such poems are rare. Eight-verse *padas*, which could also be performed on a four-part scheme, are much more numerous, but no more so than poems that contain six verses instead; other lengths are also possible. In all this one sees that the contrast between Surdas and Tansen or Haridas, true exemplars of the *dhrupad* style, is marked.[36] For Sur, the term *vishnupad/bishnupad*, invoked for example in 'Abd al-Hamid Lahori's *Pādshāhnāma* (1627-1647), may be more accurate, but we do not know exactly what it connoted—if indeed the connotation was exact.[37]

---

33 I have argued this point in several places, most recently Hawley (2005), p. 190, and (2009), pp. 21-23.

34 I reproduce the text from the edition of Parameshvari Lal Gupta along with Aditya Behl's translation in Hawley (2005), pp. 191-92; see also Hawley (2009), p. 19. See also Gupta, *Kutuban kṛt Mṛgāvatī* (Varanasi: Vishvavidyalay Prakashan, 1967), p. 39; and *Mīr Sayyid Mañjhan Shattārī Rājgīrī: Madhumālatī, An Indian Sufi Romance*, trans. by Aditya Behl and Simon Weightman, with Shyam Manohar Pandey (Oxford: Oxford University Press, 2000), pp. xii-xiii.

35 *Sahasarasa: Nāyak Bakhśu ke dhrupadoṅ kā saṅgrah*, ed. by Prem Lata Sharma (New Delhi: Sangeet Natak Akademi, 1972); cf. Richard Widdess, 'The Emergence of Dhrupad', in *Hindustani Music: Thirteenth to Twentieth Centuries*, ed. by Joep Bor, Françoise "Nalini" Delvoye, Emmie te Nijenhuis, and Jane Harvey (New Delhi: Manohar, 2010), pp. 117-40.

36 See Hawley, Introduction, part 2, section 5, "Performance, Past and Present", in *Into Sūr's Ocean: Poetry, Context, and Commentary* (Cambridge, MA: Harvard Oriental Series, 2016).

37 Françoise "Nalini" Delvoye, "The Verbal Content of Dhrupad Songs from the Earliest Collections", *Dhrupad Annual* 5 (1990), p. 98. The association between Sur and *vishupad* apparently remained strong enough in musical memory that N. Augustus Willard worked it into the taxonomy of vocal compositions he provided when writing his *Treatise on the Music of Hindoostan* at the court of Banda in 1834. See William Jones and N. August Willard, *Music of India* (Calcutta: Susil Gupta, 1962), p. 70.

There are also problems with *raga*. Early manuscripts of the *Sursāgar* often associate quite different *ragas* with a given *pada*. Luckily the distance between *shabd* and *svar* or alternatively *matu* and *dhatu*—between verbal text and musical rendition—is sufficiently great in the genre of the *pada* that we can discern something of the poet's performative sensibility even without knowing how it might have been expressed musically on any particular occasion (cf. d'Hubert and Miner in this volume). As can be judged from the Bhishma poems we have considered, the verbal logic of these early Surdas *padas* is often sufficiently rigorous and tight that their force can be appreciated without actually hearing them sung.[38] Similarly, we do not have to know where Sur himself performed or where other early singers sang "his" *padas* to sense at least something of the impact that might have been felt when sixteenth-century audiences encountered them.

The multiple *ragas* that could be assigned to a given Surdas poem in early manuscripts suggest a considerable malleability, as does the range of performative circumstances that were imagined for them early on, ranging from temple to court. And yet, the world in which we may envision this poet flourishing is not infinitely diverse. If we miss the fact that sometimes he is positioning himself in relationship to the *Bhāgavata*—not just the way in which it tells the story of Krishna, but even its actual words—we miss something quite important about the world out of which Surdas comes and to which he sees himself as contributing. He may not require each of his listeners to command a close knowledge of the Sanskrit text of either the *Mahābhārata* or the *Bhāgavata-purāṇa*, but I would argue that if they do, they are "ideal listeners" at least for poems of the type on which we have been focusing. Not every *pada* that circulated in Surdas's name in the sixteenth century was as closely calibrated to precedent as our two Bhishma poems seem to have been, but by contrast to the general

38 Here the classic analysis has been provided by Kenneth E. Bryant, *Poems to the Child-God: Structures and Strategies in the Poetry of Sūrdās* (Berkeley: University of California Press, 1978), even though he does not restrict himself to *padas* that can be traced to the sixteenth or seventeenth century. Bryant demonstrates how these poems developed in "real" time, as against being the more or less static statements that might be anticipated on the model of *rasa* theory (especially pp. 40-42). Richard Widdess has observed, in a intriguingly parallel way, that early musical treatises on *prabandha* relevant to a consideration of the historical meaning of the term *dhrupad* make a strong distinction between verbal content (*bani*, *matu*) and performance realisation (*dhatu*), being far more interested in the former than the latter. See Widdess (2010).

run of *padas* that appear in standard editions of the *Sursāgar* today, the proportion of such poems is surprisingly high. In poems like these, the singer expected his hearers not just to experience a familiar telling of a familiar tale but to reframe what they thought they knew, to see it all again. Clearly, it was the function of the best performances to make that possible, and in this regard Sur was often a master performer.[39]

We learn from the *Bhāgavata māhātmya* that when its adored parent text is properly performed, the hearers come to life. In the frame story, Bhakti, who has been restored to radiant youth in Brindavan, is burdened by her two bedraggled sons Jnana and Vairagya: knowledge, that is, and the sort of religious discipline that implies detachment from the workaday world. The *Bhāgavata māhātmya* achieves its climax when, in its last chapter, Jnana and Vairagya join their mother in hearing a seven-day performance of the *Bhāgavata-purāṇa* at Haridwar. The result: they spring back to life. Sur's performance of the *Bhāgavata-purāṇa* is obviously very different. It does not rigorously repeat—it rigorously unsettles and recovers—and in that way it seems to do just the opposite of what the *Bhāgavata māhātmya* prescribes. But note the similarity as well. Unlike what has so often been said about the excellence of these poems, they appeal not just to *bhakti* but to knowledge and discipline—a knowledge of the tradition out of which they come, and the discipline that makes it possible, with discrimination, to enter it all over again.

Was Surdas performing the *Bhāgavata-purāṇa*? Certainly not as the *Bhāgavata māhātmya* leads us either to expect or to desire. Nor after the manner of poets like Lalachdas or, in certain of their works, Hariramvyas or Nanddas. Sur's relation to the *Bhāgavata-purāṇa* is far more independent. It may sometimes be his subject, but it is never his master. Does this make Surdas less a performer of the *Bhāgavata* than these quite explicit *Bhāgavata* poets? In a certain sense, obviously, yes. But if we can be more expansive in our view, if we can let Sur engage the *Bhāgavata* in his own way—inventive, ironic, sometimes even contrary—then it makes sense to say that Sur often performs the *Bhāgavata* even better than they do. In imagining such a possibility, it may be helpful to think of Sur enunciating the *Bhāgavata* not just in relation to a "parent text", something learned in the course of a decent Vaishnava education and held in memory thereafter,

---

39 See Bryant (1978), especially pp. 26-39, 134-41.

but in relation to the several genres of live *Bhāgavata* performance with which he was probably surrounded.[40] If so, he would evidently have been reacting to—and contributing to—this range of performative possibility from roughly the opposite point of view than comes forward from the author of the *Bhāgavata māhātmya* a century or so later. Sur was crafting, nuancing, expanding the boundaries of the text; the *Māhātmya* was trying to standardise and clamp down.

A lovely window onto the sort of tensions that may have emerged as various performers of the *Bhāgavata* reacted to each other in early modern, Brajbhasha-speaking North India comes to us from an unexpected source. It is once again the *varta* literature of the Vallabha *sampraday*, but this time not the original collection of eighty-four such *varta*s attributed to Gokulnāth, the *Caurāsī vaiṣṇavan kī vārtā*, but the subsequent 252 *varta*s that emerged from the hand of his nephew Hariray, *Do sau bāvan vaiṣṇavan kī vārtā*. In one of these *varta*s we hear that the Chaube Brahmins of Mathura didn't like the idea that Nanddas, the major Pushtimargi poet to whom we have already referred, had set about to render the entirety of the *Bhāgavata*'s tenth book into *bhasha*. They were sure it was going to cut into their own storytellers' (*kathavachak*) business, and they appealed to Nanddas's guru, Vitthalnath, to make his pupil stop. We are told that Vitthalnath obliged.[41]

How is this story to be received? Does the author expect us to smile at the self-serving anxieties of Mathura's famously irascible old guard, or should we be recalling that actually Vitthalnath had good reason to try to keep the peace with these Chaubes? After all, by the time this account was being written his *sampraday* was making substantial inroads into Mathura society. Whichever the more likely scenario, it is doubtful we should take the *Do sau bāvan vaiṣṇavan kī vārtā*'s story at face value, any more than we

40 To a lesser extent the same must have been true for the *Mahābhārata*, as well. Sheldon Pollock has drawn attention to "the continuing importance of the auditory experience" as hinted in the opening *dohas* of Vishnudās's vernacular *Mahābhārata*, written at Gwalior in about 1435 (2006, p. 306 n43). And we know that the *Mahābhārata* was translated into Persian (as *Razm-nāmā*) at the court of Akbar during the early 1580s and, interestingly, that the *Harivaṃśa*, traditionally considered to be its appendix (*khila*), was included in the project. Both were handsomely illustrated; see Robert Skelton, 'Mughal Paintings from the Harivaṃśa Manuscript', *Victoria and Albert Museum Yearbook* 2 (1970), 41-54.

41 Dinadayalu Gupta, *Aṣṭachāp aur Vallabh-sampradāy*, 2nd edn (Allahabad: Hindi Sahitya Sammelan, 1970), Vol. 1, p. 146 (pp. 140-41). Sheldon Pollock has taken note of the significance of this passage (2006), p. 312.

should accept its claim, offered in the preceding *prasang*, that Nanddas was the younger brother of Tulsidas.[42] As suggested earlier, I find it far easier to believe that Nanddas abandoned his *Bhāṣā dasamskandh* for his own reasons. After he had ratcheted up his performative gears to meet the demands of the *Bhāgavata*'s celebrated chapters on the *ras*, as he did in his *Rāsapancādhyāyī*, he may have found it unappealing to return to the straightforward task of translation that he had earlier begun. This seems natural enough if we think of the career of the poet himself, but the idea of such a lapsed project on the part of one of the *sampraday*'s most famous figures might well have seemed embarrassing to Hariray later on, given his systematic temperament and devotedly sectarian point of view. So he blamed the work-stoppage on others—the famously recalcitrant Chaubes—while at the same time preserving the *sampraday*'s own claim to agency by invoking the compassionate largess of Vitthalnath.

To Vallabhite eyes, at least in the mid- to late seventeenth century, Nanddas and Surdas were guru-brothers. These two were very likely the most luminous among the "eight seals" (*ashtachhap*) that the Pushtimargi community claimed as its own, even if in point of historical fact Surdas was not bound to Vallabha in the same way that Nanddas revered Vitthalnath. Never mind. The Pushtimarg leaders felt they had to claim Sur, and their efforts have borne impressive historical fruit: contrary to fact though it is, few people today doubt that Sur's inspiration came from Vallabha. As the Vallabhites asserted their own *Bhāgavata* credentials, adding to Vallabha's foundational commentary a performance milieu that pivoted on the *ashtachhap*, they crossed the boundary from Sanskrit to the vernacular. They played an important part in baptising Brajbhasha as a language of refinement, a "Sanskrit" of its own.

It is amusing to see the Chaubes deployed against Nanddas. If indeed these local Brahmins stood for older modes of Braj religiosity and textual accreditation—a *Bhāgavat kathā* tradition in which only the original Sanskrit text had the right to be inscribed on the page—they ought to have felt less anxiety in relation to Nanddas than in relation to his fictive *ashtachhap* brother, Sur. Nanddas and his Vallabhite community were a threat to the older Chaube networks, for sure, but an even greater threat to any text-reciting expertise on the part of the Chaubes would have

42 Stuart McGregor comments on the manifest improbability of such a relationship, observing among other things that if these two poets had been brothers, that fact could hardly have gone unnoticed in the *Bhaktamāl* of Nabhadas (1973), pp. 33-34.

come from Brajbhasha poets and *kathavachaks* who were uninterested in being anchored to this or that sectarian lineage. No other poet stands more powerfully for the independence of Brajbhasha than Surdas. In this respect he even more than Nanddas stands as a fitting symbol for the liberal thrust of *Bhāgavata* performance that the *Bhāgavata māhātmya* seems so eager to discipline and cap.

Given all this, it was only a matter of time until some editor cast a glance at the *Sursāgar*, saw a text that had burgeoned with the compositions of performers who took Sur's seal as their own, and determined that it should be aligned with the *Bhāgavata-purāṇa* rather than developing in some protean fashion of its own. This moment occurred in the late eighteenth century, a century or so after the *Bhāgavata māhātmya* seems to have been composed. The editor in question grouped the Sur *padas* before him in such a way that they seemed to correspond to the twelve-*skandha* template by means of which the *Bhāgavata* itself is organised. Some *skandha*s could claim very few Surdas poems, which may have meant he had to commission several new *padas* to make his efforts seem plausible. Is this enterprise to be interpreted as a stern exercise in Sanskritic discipline or as an exuberant celebration of what vernacular performance could achieve—a *Bhāgavata* of its own, one truly based on the rhythms and practices of Brajbhasha? To me, both estimations seem possible. Personally, I like the second.

# 8. Text, Orality, and Performance in Newar Devotional Music[1]

*Richard Widdess*

We are accustomed to thinking of texts as existing either in written form, read, silently or aloud, and transmitted by copying and re-copying; or else in memorised form, rendered and in some sense re-created through performance, and transmitted orally.[2] In both cases we tend to assume that the meaning of a text resides primarily in the words themselves, and is understood by the reader or listener through the act of reading or listening. But there are traditions of performance in South Asia where these assumptions do not hold: traditions where written documents, oral transmission, and performance co-exist; and traditions where the meaning of the words plays only a small part in the overall meaning of their performance. Both conditions apply in the genre of Newar devotional singing called *dapha*.

1 This article draws on ongoing research and on materials in two other places: in my 2011 article '*Dāphā*: Dancing Gods, Virtual Pilgrimage, and Sacred Singing in the Kathmandu Valley", *Musiké* 5.6 (2011), 55-79; and in my book *Dāphā: Sacred Singing in a South Asian City: Music, Performance and Meaning in Bhaktapur, Nepal*. SOAS Musicology Series (Aldershot: Ashgate, 2013). Full acknowledgements will be found there; for the present article I am particularly indebted to Shamsher Nhuchen Pradhan for help with ethnographic research in Bhaktapur, and to Nutandhar Sharma for his advice on *dapha* song texts.

2 The distinction between orality and literacy has often been questioned, for example by Ruth Finnegan, *Literacy and Orality: Studies in the Technology of Communication* (Oxford: Blackwell, 1989); and that between text and performance has recently been challenged by Karin Barber, *The Anthropology of Texts, Persons and Publics* (Cambridge: Cambridge University Press, 2007).

 http://dx.doi.org/10.11647/OBP.0062.08

The study of *dapha* takes us to the Kathmandu Valley, a region that has been in close communication with other parts of the Indian subcontinent for at least two millennia. From the twelfth century until 1768-1769 it was divided into three small kingdoms, centred on the three cities of the Valley, Kathmandu, Lalitpur, and Bhaktapur. The rulers of these kingdoms called themselves the Mallas, and the inhabitants were principally of the ethnic group now known as the Newars, who speak the Tibeto-Burman language Newari. Following the defeat of the Mallas in 1768-1769 by the king of Gorkha, Prithvi Narayan Shah, who set up the capital of his empire in Kathmandu, positions of power have been mainly occupied by members of a different ethnic group, the Parbatiya, who now constitute about half the population of the Valley, and speak the Indo-Aryan language Nepali, the national language of modern Nepal.

A rich tradition of *dapha* performance is to be found in Bhaktapur, in the eastern part of the Valley.[3] Once the most powerful of the Malla kingdoms, Bhaktapur remains a predominantly Newar town. About half its population belong to farmers' castes, who live in the town and go out to their fields during the day. The farmers (*maharjan*, *jyapu*) occupy the middle band of the complex local caste system and they take great pride in preserving many performance traditions of music and dance that date back, they claim, to the time of the Malla kingdoms.[4] One of these traditions is *dapha*, performed by groups of men in temple courtyards or other outdoor locations, when they are not working in the fields: in the early morning or evening, or during the day on festival days. About sixty *dapha* groups exist, performing with varying degrees of regularity, from once a year to every day.

Figure 8.1 shows a typical *dapha* group. Its members have assembled in Suryamarhi Square, at the eastern end of the town, to celebrate the Buddhist festival of Panchadan or Five Offerings; they sit on the brick paving of the square, surrounded by standing devotees, while behind them, on a raised platform, five Buddha statues are being installed and worshipped by the crowds (Hindus interpreting them as the five

3 For a discussion of this genre as it is practised in Kirtipur, at the western end of the Kathmandu Valley, see Ingemar Grandin, *Music and Media in Local Life: Music Practice in a Newar Neighbourhood in Nepal* (Lingköping: Lingköping University, 1989), pp. 8-10 and 71-85.

4 See David N. Gellner, 'Introduction', in *Contested Hierarchies: A Collaborative Ethnography of Caste among the Newars of the Kathmandu Valley, Nepal*, ed. by David N. Gellner and Declan Quigley (Oxford: Oxford University Press, 1995), pp. 10-19; R.I. Levy, *Mesocosm: Hinduism and the Organization of a Traditional Newar City in Nepal* (Berkeley: University of California Press, 1990), pp. 625-29.

Pandava brothers from the *Mahabharata*). The photograph shows one half or side of the *dapha* group, who face the camera; the other half sit facing them, close to the camera but with their backs towards us. The two sides sing alternately, never together. Between the two sides, on the left, are two drummers, playing the barrel drum *lalakhin*, an indispensable accompanying instrument; some of the singers play cymbals, *tah*, but these are hard to see in the photograph. Clearly visible, in the centre of the photograph, is the oblong shape of a folding manuscript songbook (*dapha saphu*); the singers nearer the camera have an identical book (not visible in the photograph). In the open space between the two sides, oil lamps and plates of offerings indicate the ritual context of the performance, while hookahs acknowledge the singers' need for periodic refreshment. The boy sitting on the lap of one of the singers, clapping his hands in time to the rhythm of the cymbals, reflects the importance of *dapha* as a means of enculturation into Newar male society.

Fig. 8.1 *Dapha* group performing in Suryamarhi Square, Bhaktapur. September 2007. Author's photograph, CC BY.

## Historical Origins

*Dapha* singers themselves say that *dapha* singing originated with the higher castes in a palace context, in Malla times, and was taken over by farmers for their own use. There is considerable evidence to support this idea.

The manuscript songbooks contain the texts of poems dating back many centuries. Some of these are ascribed to well-known poets of northern India: Jayadeva, Namdev, Vidyapati, Kabir, Surdas, and other familiar names appear (cf. Novetzke and Hawley in this volume), and the most popular of these is Jayadeva, whose *Gītagovinda* is contained complete in some *dapha* songbooks. I assume that the works of these poets circulated at the Malla courts, having been brought there by *pandits* and *bhaktas* from India: the *Gītagovinda* certainly did, because manuscripts survive from as early as the fifteenth century. But a much larger proportion of *dapha* songs are ascribed (in the last verse) to local authors, namely the Malla kings of the seventeenth and eighteenth centuries. The earliest of these poets to appear in Bhaktapur songbooks is the king of Bhaktapur Jagajjyoti Malla (r.1614-1637), who was a prolific and versatile patron and exponent of the arts. The last is Ranjit Malla (r.1722-1769), the last Newar king, who was driven into exile by the conqueror, Prithvi Narayan Shah. Ranjit is the most popular author in the Bhaktapur songbooks, and dozens of songs bear his name, including one that records his melancholy thoughts on leaving Nepal for the last time.

The songs in the *dapha* songbooks are written in Maithili, Newari, or Sanskrit, with some songs combining vocabulary from more than one language. Similar texts survive in manuscripts of seventeenth-century or later date, preserved in the National Archive, Kathmandu.[5] These include anthologies of poetry by Jagajjyoti and other Malla authors, as well as songbooks for general use. Of particular interest is a collection of Jagajjyoti's poetry entitled *Gītapañcāśika*, dated 1628, and therefore contemporary with the author.[6] It includes three songs that still appear, still ascribed to Jagajjyoti, in Bhaktapur *dapha* songbooks today. A tenuous textual continuity can thus be demonstrated between the early seventeenth-century palace context and twenty-first-century farmers' music.

Records of the Malla courts in the seventeenth and eighteenth centuries also demonstrate that the theory and aesthetics of music were well known in that milieu. For information about music theory (*sangitashastra*), Newar scholars looked to Indian sources in Sanskrit (cf. Miner, d'Hubert, and Schofield in this volume). Some of the earliest palmleaf manuscripts of the *Nāṭyaśāstra* survive in Kathmandu, and later texts such as the *Saṅgītaratnākara* were also known. But again, imported texts are outnumbered by local

5 I have consulted microfilm copies kindly provided by the German Nepal Research Project, through the good offices of Nutandhar Sharma.

6 *Gītapañcāśika*, National Archives of Nepal, MS no. 1-399, dated Śāke 1550/1628 CE. Microfilm no. B288/12. Various languages. (Catalogue of N. Sharma.)

productions: Jagajjyoti alone wrote or commissioned at least five treatises on music, and his successors produced more in their turn. These are digests of material from Indian sources, in Sanskrit or occasionally Newari. A related subject of interest was the pictorial imagery of *raga*, as expressed in poems and paintings (cf. Miner in this volume). Two fine *ragamala* albums survive that are believed to have been painted for Jagajjyoti himself, on the basis of a treatise he wrote (the *Saṅgīta-cintāmaṇi*), which itself was based on the eastern Indian treatise *Saṅgīta-dāmodara* of Shubhankara (sixteenth century).[7] Figure 8.2 shows a typical page from one of the *ragamalas*. It demonstrates the lively way in which familiar images from the Indian *ragamala* tradition were re-interpreted in a Newar style of painting that shows the influence of Rajput exemplars.[8] These various productions demonstrate that the Mallas were familiar with the traditional South Asian theory and aesthetics of *raga* and *tala*. In practice, we may assume that they transformed Indian models in music, as they did in painting.

Fig. 8.2 Raga Lalit. Bhaktapur, early seventeenth century. Photograph by Gert-Matthias Wegner, CC BY.

7 See Gert-Matthias Wegner and Richard Widdess, 'Musical Miniatures from Nepal: Two Newar Ragamalas', in *Nepal: Old Images, New Insights*, ed. by P. Pal (Mumbai: Marg Publications, 2004), pp. 81-91. See d'Hubert and Miner for the circulation of this text in northern and eastern India.

8 The half arch in Figure 8.2 is a convention in Newar art signifying "on the threshold". Here it is used to convey the conventional interpretation of *raga* Lalit as a lover leaving the house of his mistress at dawn.

Another art-form assiduously cultivated at the Malla courts was Newar dance-drama, to which the Malla kings themselves contributed many texts, especially in the seventeenth and eighteenth centuries. According to a European witness who visited the Bhaktapur court in the eighteenth century, the performance of these dramas contained little dialogue: there were two choruses who "sing the whole", while the actor "dances constantly", fitting "the movements of his face, feet and hands to the meaning of the words they are singing".[9] This description reveals that the songs were sung, not by the actors themselves or by other solo singers, but by a group of singers; furthermore, the group was divided into two "choruses". The parallel with the antiphonal sides of a *dapha* group is striking. A connection is further strengthened by close similarity between the *raga* and *tala* names assigned to songs in dramas of the time and in contemporary *dapha*; and by the fact that the term *nandi-gita*, used to denote the opening song in Newar drama, is still used, in some Bhaktapur groups, to denote the opening song of a *dapha* singing session.[10]

Evidence that a form of religious group singing akin to *dapha* was being performed at the Malla courts in the seventeenth century is provided by a painting published by Anne Vergati.[11] It shows a ceremony performed in Kathmandu, in the year 1664, by King Pratap Malla at the temple of Taleju, the tutelary goddess of the Malla kings. On the steps of the temple, just below the king and his courtiers, a small vocal group is depicted (see Figure 8.3), comprising eight singers divided into two sides of four each, sitting to either side of a central drummer. The latter is playing what appears to be a *lalakhin*, and the singers all play cymbals. The court robes, seated posture, and closeness of the singers to the court distinguish them from groups of standing ritual and processional musicians visible lower in the painting, strongly indicating that this is a courtly form of music-making. This may well be the earliest depiction of a *dapha* group.

---

9 Cassien in 1740, cited in H. Brinkhaus, *The Pradyumna-Prabhāvatī Legend in Nepal* (Stuttgart: Franz Steiner Verlag, 1987), p. 115.

10 One performance tradition featuring dance accompanied by *dapha*-style singing (*Kha Pyakhan*) is said to have survived in Bhaktapur until about a decade ago. Information from the Khairguli Dapha group, March 2009.

11 Anne Vergati, 'Gods and Monuments in Late Malla Period Paintings', in *Nepal: Old Images, New Insights* (Mumbai: Marg Publications), pp. 92-106.

Fig. 8.3 *Dapha* group performing at the Taleju temple, Kathmandu, in 1664. Detail of a painting now in the Collège de France, Paris. Author's sketch, CC BY.

## Texts and Meaning

There is thus good reason to trace the origins of *dapha* to the Malla courts of the seventeenth and eighteenth centuries, whence it was adopted by the farming community in Bhaktapur. The process of adoption would no doubt have been facilitated by the fact that the farmers not only rented and farmed fields owned by the upper castes, but were also employed by the upper castes in a number of capacities, including assistants in temples, cremation specialists, midwives, and messengers, and therefore had direct access to the aristocratic milieu.[12] Following the Gorkhali conquest, in the nineteenth and twentieth centuries upper castes tended to move away from Bhaktapur to Kathmandu, the centre of political and economic power, and thus withdrew from patronage and performance of the arts in Bhaktapur, leaving the farmers and other lower castes as principal bearers of Newar music and dance traditions. Nevertheless, one *dapha* group with exclusively upper-caste membership survived until the 1980s: significantly, it was attached to the temple of Taleju, the tutelary goddess of the Malla kings, whose temple is within the palace compound,

12 D. Gellner and Rajendra Pradhan, 'Urban Peasants: The Maharjans (Jyāpu) of Kathmandu and Lalitpur', in *Contested Hierarchies: A Collaborative Ethnography of Caste among the Newars of the Kathmandu Valley, Nepal*, ed. by D. Gellner and D. Quigley (Oxford: Oxford University Press, 1995), pp. 168, 172-73.

in Bhaktapur as in Kathmandu. This important group must have served to some extent as a model for other, lower-caste groups.[13]

In this process of transmission from higher to lower castes, song texts were imperfectly preserved and incompletely understood. This was inevitable given that Maithili and Sanskrit are not generally known among the farmers (Maithili was the court language, because the Mallas were partly descended from Mithila royalty); even the Newari of *dapha* includes unfamiliar archaisms and formalities. Literacy was until recently relatively low among middle and lower castes, and indeed training in *dapha* was often the only formal education available. Unlike the *kirtankars'* notebooks analysed by Christan Novetzke in his essay in this volume, *dapha* manuscript songbooks preserve only a very approximate rendering of the original texts, as we can see from a comparison of the incipits of three songs that appear in the *Gītapañcāśika* manuscript of 1628 with the versions found in present-day songbooks (see Table 8.1). Some of the errors indicate oral transmission (/r/ and /l/ or /ṭ/ and /t/ interchange, for example), while others are evidently writing errors (e.g. confusion of /n/ and /t/, or /y/ and /p/).

Table 8.1: Incipits of three *dapha* songs in early and modern manuscripts

| *Gītapañcāśika* MS (dated 1628) | *Dapha* songbooks |
|---|---|
| fol. 5:<br>*Bhavabhayabhañjani asura vināśini* | Yachen, no. 107, p. 111:<br>*Bhavabhayaṃjani asura vināsinī* |
| fol. 5:<br>*Gharanahi samvara yahiriva* | Yachen, no. 101, p. 107:<br>*Ghalanahi saṃvatsa pahilivā* |
| fol. 7:<br>*Kṛmikiṭa jaga dekhi sakṣa sarūpa* | Yachen, no. 114, p. 118:<br>*Kimikṛta janadeki sa asaluye*<br>Barahi, no. 50, p. 25:<br>*Kimikīna janadeṣi sava akṣarūpe*<br>Tekhadola, no. 80, p. 19:<br>*Kimikita jatadeṣi sava aha salupe*<br>Dattatreya, no. 32, p. 10:<br>*Krimikita janadoṣi sava asa rūpa* |

13 This information is derived from a survey of *dapha* groups conducted by Gert-Matthias Wegner in 1984, and is confirmed by present-day singers. Compare the dissemination of court-based oral text genres in Rwanda described by Barber (2008), pp. 58-66.

Not only the texts, but also their meanings become obscured, or transformed. Figure 8.4 is a *dapha* song that is very frequently performed in Bhaktapur, *Ganamani*, in mixed Newari and Sanskrit.[14] A tentative translation follows, worked out with considerable difficulty on account of the uncertain state of the text by a Newar historian, Nutandhar Sharma. It is clear that the poem was written by, or at least attributed to, Ranjit Malla, the last king of Bhaktapur. According to *dapha* singers from whom I learned this song, it is in praise of Ganesha. Sharma's translation, however, reveals a song in praise of an unnamed goddess; and according to Sharma, this can only be the Tantric goddess Taleju, since she is described as dominating gods and demons, even Shiva himself.

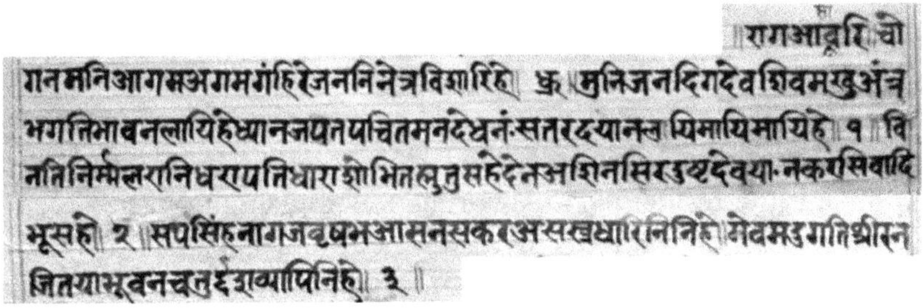

Fig. 8.4 *Ganamani*. Dattatreya Navadapha songbook, song no. 63 (fol. 20r-20v). Public Domain.

Rāg Āsāvari | | [tāl] Co[kh]

O Mother with big eyes, [you are] the jewel of [the] retinues, esoteric, impossible [and] deep [to understand]. Sages, the gods of [different] directions [and] Śiva do not devote to others [but only to you].

Meditate on [her], repeat [her] name, do penance, keep attention [and] feeling [on her], [offer] wealth [and] sacrifice oblation; [to] the compassionate mother, O Mother. | | 1 | |

[I] bow down [to you,] the pure[,] queen [and] mistress of the lord of the world, with graceful face, O [mother] goddess; Sitting on the head of the evil god[s] [and] all ghosts (*bhūta*) including Śiva. | | 2 | |

14 A recording of the song *Ganamani*, performed by the Dattatreya Navadapha group, can be found on the CD accompanying the book *Dāphā: Sacred Singing in a South Asian City* (see fn. 1).

> [You, decorated with] braided hair, a lion [as a vehicle], snakes, sitting on a bull [and] holding all kinds of arms, O [goddess]. No other place to get salvation for Śrī Ranajita, O [mother, you, who is] pervasive over [all] fourteen [directions]. | | 3 | |

For *dapha* singers, it seems, the first word, *Ganamani*, is enough to suggest that the song is about *Gaṇapati*, Ganesha. Consequently the song is often sung at Ganesha temples, and is often the first or second song taught to beginners—in the latter case, the first will be a song to Nrityanatha (*Nāsaḥdyaḥ*), who for Newars is the patron deity of music and dance. Thus a single word of the text acts as a pointer to its entire meaning and hence to a network of associations and usage. The original meaning of the text seems not to have been transmitted to, or has been forgotten by, the farmer community. Taleju was of central importance to the Malla court (literally, since her temple is in the palace itself), as the ultimate wielder of *shakti* and hence source of the Mallas' power; but she is perhaps less significant to the farmer community than the deities who inhabit the residential areas of the town, including Ganesha. The fact that Newari does not distinguish gender morphologically makes it easier to understand the switch from female to male deity.

This example is of course an extreme case, since for most songs the meaning is more explicit in the text. Singers discuss the meaning of particular words and phrases in the breaks between songs,[15] and can usually tell the investigator at least the gist of a song, which may be reflected in the time or place of its performance. But another case where little is understood is the *Gītagovinda*. Singers know that this text includes the divine names of Vishnu, and that it concerns the erotic relationship of Krishna and Radha; this is sufficient for them, and some say it is better not to know the precise meaning in view of its erotic content. When I asked one group why they go to the trouble of singing the entire *Gītagovinda*, in one all-night performance, when they do not understand the words, they explained that the *objective* is to sing all night. Therefore they *choose* to sing the *Gītagovinda*, because it takes that length of time. Here we see very clearly how the process of performance itself, elaborated and prolonged to the maximum extent, is what is important; the text becomes a means to that end, losing most of its intrinsic meaning in the process.

---

15 Information from Simonne Bailey.

## Performance and Meaning

What then is the meaning of performance, as distinct from the meaning of what is performed? To begin to answer this question we have to recognise that *dapha* performance has not one but many meanings. It has meanings for the individuals who participate as singers, instrumentalists, or helpers, and for the larger community who do not participate directly. It has meanings at 6.00 am on a cold winter's morning on the verandah of a small neighbourhood temple, and other meanings on a warm afternoon at the start of the Biskah festival in Tahmarhi Square, the central square of the town.

The performance of *dapha* can be seen as a form of religious exertion akin to the pilgrimages, rituals, fasts, and festivals that punctuate Newar life with remarkable frequency. Michael Allen observes that various forms of "highly organised human physical activity", designed to bring the human and the divine into "productive contact", constitute "the primary mode of worship" in Newar religion.[16] *Dapha* is certainly one of these forms. A *dapha* singing session is in itself a complex ritual. It begins with three rings on the *tah* cymbals, followed by a lengthy instrumental invocation (*dyahlhaygu*). An odd number of songs must be sung, at least three, but usually more; the first will be a short song in praise of Shiva, and the last will be accompanied by *arati*, in which a multi-branched candelabra will be lit and worshipped, followed by another instrumental invocation and worship of the *tah* cymbals. Between the first and last songs, others will be sung in praise of various deities, selected partly according to inclination and partly to reflect the season of the year or the day of the week (each day being presided over by a different deity).

Not only the whole singing session, but the performance of each individual song is an elaborate ritual. Each song is preceded by the appropriate *raga*: an unmetered, wordless melody, sung by one or two individual singers without instrumental accompaniment. The name of the *raga* is specified in the songbook for each song, as is the musical metre or *tala*; some songs require two or more different *talas*. The song itself comprises a variable number of lines or couplets, of which the first is usually repeated as a refrain (*dhuva*) after each of the others. Each couplet is sung many times, at slow and fast tempi, the two sides

16 Michael Allen, 'Procession and Pilgrimage in Newar Religion', in *Change and Continuity*, ed. by S. Lienhard (Turin: Edizioni dell'Orso, 1996), p. 209.

of the group alternating according to a standard formula. The *lalakhin* player, sometimes aided by a player of the natural trumpet *pvana*, guides the singers by punctuating each stage of the expansion process with cadential formulae, and varying his patterns to initiate and maintain changes of tempo. In each line, increasingly fast tempo, loud volume, and high pitch generate the musically-induced state of heightened emotional involvement that Edward Henry terms "intensity".[17]

The ritual complexity of *dapha* performance is paralleled by the complexity of the social mechanisms required to transmit and maintain it. Each *dapha* group constitutes a society, or *guthi* (< Skt *goṣṭhī*). *Guthis* for a variety of social, religious, and musical purposes are a pervasive feature of Newar society, "a network undergirding the whole of Newar social and religious life".[18] (*Guthi* membership may be voluntary or hereditary, and is often based on residence in the neighbourhood and/or membership of a particular caste.[19]) A *dapha guthi* appoints officers in rotation to organise its activities, holds regular feasts to consolidate social bonds, and in some cases owns land, the produce of which pays for the repair of instruments and songbooks, and for the feasts. Membership of such a *guthi* is one way for Newar males to secure a respected position in a caste-based neighbourhood community: as Gellner and Pradhan observe, "participation [in music groups] is equivalent to belonging to the neighbourhood".[20]

Participation in a musical *guthi* requires a process of initiation. Once every ten to twelve years, a *dapha guthi* will recruit local boys (with the active support of their parents) and teach them, over a period of several months, to sing and play the essential repertoire. In this process the teacher uses the manuscript songbook to ensure faithful transmission of its text, *but the boys are not taught to read it*,[21] and must memorise the

17 Edward O. Henry, 'The Rationalization of Intensity in Indian Music', *Ethnomusicology* 46.1 (2002), 33-55.

18 Anne Vergati, *Gods, Men and Territory: Society and Culture in Kathmandu Valley* (New Delhi: Manohar, 1995), p. 124.

19 Further details are given in Widdess (2014). For *guthi* as a pervasive feature of Newar society, see, for example, G. Toffin, *Newar Society: City, Village and Periphery* (Kathmandu: Social Science Baha, 2007), and Vergati (1995).

20 Gellner and Pradhan (1995), p. 179.

21 Particularly able boys may be taught to read the songbook at an advanced stage of their training.

songs through imitation and repetition. The process culminates in an all-day *puja* to the patron deity of music, Nasahdyah (= Nrityanath), at which the new trainees perform in public for the first time, followed by a feast. The following day, there is yet another performance and a picnic feast at the temple of Ganesha called Surya Binayak, on a wooded slope to the south of the town. The trainees are then entitled to participate in the regular singing sessions of the *dapha* group; although few keep up their participation on a regular basis, some may well return to singing in later life.

Performance of *dapha* thus has meaning for the neighbourhood community, which invests significant resources of time and money in its periodic renewal. It also has significance for the wider community of the whole town, since major festivals are regularly enhanced by the singing of *dapha* along with other music genres. Thus several local *dapha* groups participate in the Panchadan festival, including that seen in Figure 8.1. One of these groups represents the local community of oil-pressers (Manandhar), who are low-caste Buddhists; others represent the Hindu potter caste, also resident in the neighbourhood. Their participation represents the local community at a major civic event that happens in their neighbourhood.

Similarly at the start of the festival of Biskah, the Newar New Year festival dedicated to Bhairav, the *dapha* group attached to the Bhairav temple in Tahmarhi Square comes out of the temple to sing in the square itself, between the temple and the wooden chariot on which an image of Bhairav will be paraded through the whole town (see Figure 8.5). Surrounded by crowds from all over the town, they sing the song *He Śiva Bhairava*, the subject of which is immediately apparent from its opening words, and whose last line contains the signature of Ranjit Malla. In Malla times the king himself would have attended this ceremony. Today he is represented by a sword, carried by one of the royal priests who maintain the cult of Taleju in the former royal palace. Here we find a situation akin to that depicted in the 1664 painting discussed earlier, with the chariot of Bhairav taking the place of the Taleju temple, and the priests of Taleju representing the king and his court.

Fig. 8.5 One side of the Bhairav Navadapha group performing on the first day of Biskah, Tahmarhi Square, Bhaktapur. The chariot of Bhairav is visible behind the singers. April 2003. Author's photograph, CC BY.

# Conclusions

The meanings of *dapha*, therefore, are generated as much by its performance as by its texts, if not more so. In the transition from high-caste palace culture to the middle-caste farmers' community (*jyapu*), much of the original meaning of the texts, along with their original form, may have been lost. Now the texts provide *clues to meaning*: a word, name, or phrase evokes a network of meanings and associations, which may in turn determine when and where the song is sung. What is important, however, is the performance, which has its own meanings and values independently of the text: as religious exertion, as an expression of social identity, and as a component in urban ritual. In consequence, musical elaboration of the song, by both singers and instrumentalists, is paralleled by the elaboration of social processes by which the tradition is maintained and renewed.

Musical elaboration of songs, going far beyond a straightforward rendition of the text, is of course not unique to *dapha*, but is typical of many traditions in South Asia. Devotional singing in Vrindaban and other parts of Braj indulges, like *dapha*, in multiple repetitions of lines or parts of lines, with periodically increasing "intensity". In classical Hindustani *khayal*, the musical elaboration of *raga* and *tala* through solo, virtuoso improvisation, with intensity gradually increasing throughout, occupies far more time than the rendering of the song, whose text is often at least partly obscure to audience and singer alike: a word here or a phrase there may be sufficient to evoke a familiar topos or suggest a mood. The ultimate case, perhaps, is the *marai kirtan* of West Bengal, where the text of every song is replaced by the ubiquitous mantra *Hari bol* in performances that are maximally intense from the start.[22] Such cases suggest that some South Asian musical forms escape such conventional categories as *orality* and *text*, but are better understood as *performance*: a process in which text may be present, in written and/or oral form, but is subsumed by musical elaboration and the enactment of religious and social meanings.[23]

22 I am indebted to Jyotsna Latrobe for information about this genre.

23 For a discussion of the meanings of performance in a different genre of Newar music, see Widdess, 'Musical Structure, Performance and Meaning: The Case of a Stick-Dance from Nepal', *Ethnomusicology Forum* 15.2 (2006), 179-213.

# III. WRITTEN CLUES ABOUT PERFORMED TEXTS

# 9. Listening for the Context: Tuning in to the Reception of *Riti* Poetry[1]

*Allison Busch*

Beginning in the sixteenth century, Indian poets began to cultivate new styles of vernacular literature that became spectacularly successful at the courts of the Mughal period (1526-1857). Instead of adopting the Sanskrit language preferred by their forebears, the members of this (generally) Brahman community chose to express themselves in Brajbhasha, a literary dialect of Hindi. And thus was born a style of poetry today known as "*riti*", so called because of the tradition's signature genre, the *ritigranth* or poetry manual that drew significant inspiration from classical *alankarashastra* (rhetoric).

At first glance, the performative dimensions of these often highly scholastic texts are less obvious than those of their *bhakti* ("devotional") counterparts (see Hawley and Novetzke in this volume). *Bhakti* literature was often set to *ragas* and collectively sung, whereas it is the exception rather than the rule for music to figure overtly in the transmission of courtly Hindi literature. Virtually no paratextual evidence points towards musical accompaniment. Nor do *riti* authors generally discuss the connections between poetry and music, despite their prolix discourses on nearly every

1 Research for this contribution was supported by grants from the American Institute of Indian Studies in conjunction with the National Endowment for the Humanities, the American Council of Learned Societies, and the Columbia University Summer Grant Program in the Humanities. Special thanks go to Shefalika Awasthi, Pankaj Sharma, Chandramani Singh, and Giles Tillotson for their assistance at the Jaipur Pothikhana. I am grateful to Francesca Orsini for her detailed feedback and also to my research assistants Justin Ben-Hain, Ronnie Dreyer, and Christine Marrewa Karwoski.

 http://dx.doi.org/10.11647/OBP.0062.09

other topic, from figures of speech (*alankara*) to characters (*nayikas* and *nayakas*) to metrics (*chhand*) to literary mood (*rasa*).[2]

And yet for those with eyes to see—or, more aptly—ears to listen, it is possible to reconstruct some of the aural landscape of early modern Hindi court culture. Some genres, like genealogy and panegryic, have embedded performative features and appear insipid or even unintelligible if confined to the written page. Occasionally one also finds suggestive textual evidence about the performance cultures of early modern India. I begin with a few general examples culled from the extensive oeuvre of Keshavdas—widely hailed as the progenitor of Hindi's *riti* style. Keshavdas was employed by the rulers of Orchha, a small regional kingdom that, like many others, was incorporated into the Mughal Empire during the reign of Akbar (r.1556-1605). Select poems by other *riti* poets like Amrit Rai, Narottamdas, and Padmakar, some marked by dazzling aural acrobatics, will confirm some of the evidence about courtly performance that we see in Keshavdas. Another approach is to consider how court poetry, like music, functioned as a repertoire that could be tailored to suit different contexts, as with the poetic competitions known as *samasyapurti*. A range of disparate sources, including Sanskrit poems and treatises on rhetoric, Brajbhasha song texts and commentaries, as well as memories from the Persian tradition, uncover further intriguing signs of the reception contexts for *riti* literature. We encounter recitations and other types of "tellings": debates from within a *mahfil*, snatches from long-ago conversations between an author and his patron, as well as hints about what teachers told their students and their styles of imparting knowledge (see also Pellò in this volume).

## Tellings in the Texts of Keshavdas

Keshavdas's *Kavipriyā* (*Handbook for Poets*, 1601), a foundational Brajbhasha work in the *riti* style, is a good place to begin this investigation. Sanskrit *kavya* (poetry) and the formal vernacular poetry traditions that partially derive from it are unthinkable without a written textual culture,[3] but certain

---

2 A rare exception is the *Kāvyaras* attributed to Jai Singh (probably not one of the famous Kachhwaha kings by that name), which concludes with a short section on *raga* and *svara* (musical notes); *Kāvyaras*, vv. 501-21, ed. by Devendra (Jodhpur: Rajasthan Oriental Research Institute, 2002), pp. 149-51.

3 When it comes to early modern Hindi, Keshavdas's profoundly transformative contributions to a phenomenon that Sheldon Pollock has called "literarization" cannot be overestimated. Pollock distinguishes literization—simply writing the vernacular—

elements of Keshavdas's poetry also bear strong performative markers. Take the *Kavipriyā*'s opening chapter on royal genealogy (*rajavamsha*), which can be seen as stemming both from documentary compulsion and a ritualistic urge to orally proclaim the glory and longevity of his patrons:

*brahmādika kī binaya teṃ, harana sakala bhuvabhāra*
*sūraja-baṃsa karyo pragaṭa, rāmacandra avatāra*

***tinakeṃ*** *kula kalikālaripu, kahi 'kesava' ranadhīra*
*gaharavāra ihi khyāti juta, pragaṭa bhayo nr̥pa bīra*

*karana nr̥pati* ***tinakeṃ*** *bhae, dharanī-dharma-prakāsa*
*jīti sabai jagatī, karyo bārānasī nivāsa*

*pragaṭa karana tīratha bhayo, jaga meṃ jinake nāma*
***tinakeṃ*** *arjunapāla nr̥pa, bhae mahonī grāma*

*gaṛhakuṃḍāra* ***tinakeṃ*** *bhae, rājā sāhana pāla*
*sahaja indra* ***tinakeṃ*** *bhae, kahi 'kesava' ripukāla*

At the request of Brahma and the other gods
and to lighten the suffering of the world,
[Lord Vishnu] incarnated himself as Rama,
[the first king of] the solar dynasty.

Keshavdas says, that dynasty gave rise to King Bir of Gahadavala fame,
Fearless in battle, an enemy of wayward times.

He had a son named Karan—the very embodiment of virtue on earth.
He conquered the entire world and made his home in Varanasi.

Karan sponsored a pilgrimage place, known in the world after his name.
He had a son named Arjunpal, who settled
the village of Mahoni [in Bundelkhand].

He had a son named Sahanpal, [founder] of Garhkundar.
Keshavdas says, his son was like Indra himself, a destroyer of enemies.[4]

Keshavdas continues in this vein for thirty or so verses before reaching his own contemporaries. The continuous string of *dohas* (couplets) and the

from literarization, the forging of literary discourse. See Sheldon Pollock, *Language of the Gods in the World of Men* (Berkeley and Los Angeles: University of California Press), p. 298.

4 Keshavdas, *Kavipriyā*, vv. 1.6-10, ed. by Vishvanathprasad Mishra (Allahabad: Hindustani Academy, 1954), pp. 94-95. In the last line *sahaja indra* can also be taken as a proper name (and some manuscripts read *sahaja karana* instead). All translations from the Hindi are my own, unless otherwise specified.

trochaic cadences of the end rhyme stress the continuity of the lineage over countless generations and produce an almost ritualistic effect, as do tag phrases such as *tinakeṃ*, a recurring honorific genitive (highlighted in bold type) that links one generation to the next.[5]

One strategy, then, for determining the likely mode of reception of a text is to try to identify potential performative features. Another is to be alert to references *within texts* that bring into view the importance of performance in the daily life of Indian courts. For instance, in the same chapter of the *Kavipriyā*, Keshavdas concludes his description of Orchha dynastic history with a detour into the musical culture sponsored by his patron. Raja Indrajit, the poet proclaims, "had a full command of music and gathered together an assembly (*akhāro*) [of talented people]". This is the first attribute he mentions, as if he saw it as his royal patron's special distinguishing feature.[6] Equally if not more interesting, Keshavdas also composes an extensive paean to a group of six female courtesans (*patura*), celebrated variously as musicians, dancers, and poet-composers, whose talents animated the cultural life of that court:[7]

> The fingers of Rangray are the epitome of expertise.
> As soon as she touches the drum, the room comes to life with sound.
> Rangmurti's lovely feet dance to the beat of Rangray's drum.
> They are perfectly synchronised,
>     having mastered the study of music in tandem.
> The experts have expounded every theoretical aspect of music—
> Rangmurti reigns over them all, embodying perfection in her dance poses.
> These courtesans are skilled in dancing, singing, and playing the vina.
> They are all studious [or: they all recite] and the incomparable
>     Pravinray composes poetry.[8]

---

5 As in "*tinakeṃ... bhae* [of X was born]", that is, X had a son.

6 Keshavdas, *Kavipriyā*, v. 1.41 (1954), p. 97.

7 Ibid., vv. 1.42-61, pp. 97-99. On the figure of the *patura* (also *patara*), see Premlata Sharma, 'Sampādakīya bhūmikā', in *Sahasras*, ed. by Premlata Sharma (New Delhi: Sangit Natak Akademi, 1972), pp. 125-29. Skilled female performers (some of them acquired through the slave trade or conquest) were highly prized status symbols in this period, according to Ramya Sreenivasan, 'Drudges, Dancing Girls, Concubines: Female Slaves in Rajput Polity, 1500-1850', in *Slavery and South Asian History*, ed. by Indrani Chatterjee and Richard M. Eaton (Bloomington and Indianapolis: Indiana University Press, 2006), pp. 140-46.

8 Keshavdas, *Kavipriyā*, vv. 1.53-56 (1954), p. 98. Additional verses from this passage are translated in Allison Busch, *Poetry of Kings* (New York: Oxford University Press, 2011), p. 39.

The last line is ambiguous. Often the Brajbhasha term *kavitt* simply means "poetry", but this was precisely the period when one of the premier *riti* metres, a quatrain known as the *kavitt*, was gaining a wide following.[9] *Kavitts* (along with *savaiyas*, another popular verse that became all the rage in courtly literature) have a distinctly musical rhythm. They are assumed to have been sung or chanted,[10] and to this day they comprise part of the *kathak* dance repertoire.

Another major work by Keshavdas, the *Vīrsiṃhdevcarit* (1607), an idealised biography of Indrajit's brother Raja Bir Singh Deo Bundela (r.1605-1627), contains countless references to performed poetry. Traversing the narrative in various places is an almost bewildering array of bard-like figures with names like "*magadh-sut*", "*bandani ke put*", "*bandijan*", and "*dasaundhi*". The division of labour among these various court professionals is not always easy to fathom over the gulf of centuries, but a few details can be made out. Keshavdas informs us that the *magadh-sut* and *bandani ke put* called out benedictions (*baranata jaya/jaya bolata*) to the king at the commencement of a polo match.[11] Later in the same scene, a musician beats his drum in celebration and a *baital* (i.e. Baitalik, a panegyrist) commends Bir Singh's prowess at polo with a recitation (*paṛhyau gīta*).[12] The tasks of the *bandijan* included waking up the royal household and praising the king as he entered the *darbar*.[13] During the coronation scene that caps the work, a *dasaundhi* named Sahibray is honoured with a gift of cloth.[14] Dr Kishorilal, who wrote a painstaking modern commentary on this complex work,

9 Tulsidas, for instance, composed an entire collection of quatrains, his *Kavitāvalī*, within just a decade or so of the *Kavipriyā*. See Imre Bangha, 'Writing Devotion: The Dynamics of Textual Transmission in the *Kavitāvalī* of *Tulsīdās*', in *Forms of Knowledge in Early Modern Asia: Explorations in the Intellectual History of India and Tibet, 1500-1800*, ed. by Sheldon Pollock (Durham: Duke University Press, 2011), pp. 144-46.

10 On the *kavitt*, see R.S. McGregor, *Hindi Literature from its Beginnings to the Nineteenth Century* (Wiesbaden: Harrassowitz, 1984), p. 118; Rameshchandra Sharma, *Hindī kavitt-sāhitya kā vikās* (Jaipur: Aruna Prakashan, 2007), pp. 23-24, 25-31, 51-60.

11 Keshavdas, *Vīrsiṃhdevcarit*, ed. by Kishorilal (Allahabad: Hindi Sahitya Sammelan, 1997), v. 19.3; here and elsewhere I refer to this edition, unless otherwise noted.

12 Keshavdas, *Vīrsiṃhdevcarit*, vv. 19.17-18 (1997), p. 379.

13 Ibid., vv. 21.16-17, 26.48, pp. 402, 484. Other *riti* works suggest that *bandijan* had additional roles, for this same term is used to describe the performers of a *virudavali* in a military environment, discussed below in Padmakar's *Pratāpsiṃhvirudāvalī*, in *Padmākargranthāvalī*, ed. by Vishvanathprasad Mishra (Varanasi: Nagari Pracharini Sabha, 1959).

14 Keshavdas, *Vīrsiṃhdevcarit*, v. 33.23 (1997), p. 596.

glosses the *dasaundhi* as a *charan*,[15] who along with *bhats* were charged with keeping written genealogical records and reciting poetry at Rajput courts.[16]

The presence of these various figures seems to indicate that performed poetry was a staple of daily life at Orchha,[17] but it is not clear whether Keshavdas always records the actual practices of his court, for in some cases he may simply have been emulating the normative descriptions of Sanskrit *kavya*, in which it is expected that perfect kings have stately assemblies, and their courts should naturally bustle with devoted retinues.[18] Although he never cites his classical sources directly, he had carefully studied authorities such as Kalidasa, Bana, and Dandin. And for Keshavdas the encounter with Sanskrit classics was through texts, not tellings: he knew them because he read them. The assiduous copying of manuscripts and commentaries throughout the early modern period illustrates how *readership* was absolutely central to literary culture.

In an elaborate description of the court of Bir Singh Deo Bundela, Keshavdas even mentions Orchha's flourishing book culture: "*baiṭhe lekhaka likhata apāra dasa sata sahasa lakṣa lipikāra*" [There sat countless writers writing, hundreds and thousands of them].[19] Words such as

---

15 Ibid.. This meaning is confirmed by R.S. McGregor, *The Oxford Hindi-English Dictionary* (Delhi: Oxford University Press, 1993), p. 485, and *Hindīśabdsāgar*, ed. by Shyamsundardas, Balakrishan Bhatt, Amir Singh, and Ramchandra Shukla (Varanasi: Nagari Pracharini Sabha, 1965), p. 2236. The term is evidently attested in both Jayasi and Sur.

16 The functions of Bhats and Charans are briefly described in Norman Ziegler, 'The Seventeenth-century Chronicles of Mārvāṛa: A Study in the Evolution and Use of Oral Traditions in Western India', *History in Africa* 3, 1976, pp. 129-31, 137-38; Janet Kamphorst, *In Praise of Death* (PhD dissertation, Leiden University, 2008), pp. 31-36, 221-30, 256-60.

17 In a few scenes Keshavdas also employs a considerable amount of technical terminology from music and dance. See, for instance, Keshavdas, *Vīrsiṃhdevcarit*, vv. 20.32-38 (1997), pp. 394-97.

18 Compare the references to Magadha-sutas and Bandi in Valmiki's *Rāmāyaṇa: Ayodhyā (Book Two)*, trans. by Sheldon Pollock (New York: New York University Press and JJC Foundation, 2005), pp. 64-65; 114-15. Imre Bangha (drawing on Gopalnarayan Bahura's edition of the *Pratāpprakāś*) notes the importance of poetic performance in some strikingly similar daily routines of King Pratap Singh of Jaipur recorded at the turn of the nineteenth century. See 'Courtly and Religious Communities as Centres of Literary Activity in Eighteenth-century India: Ānandghan's Contacts with the Princely Court of Kishangarh-Rupnagar and with the Maṭh of the Nimbārka Sampradāy in Salemabad', in *Indian Languages and Texts Through the Ages: Essays of Hungarian Indologists in Honour of Prof. Csaba Tottossy*, ed. by Csaba Dezso (Delhi: Manohar, 2007), pp. 313-14. The parallels are suggestive but do not allow us to decide definitively whether poets relied largely on literary formula or recorded the lived experiences of their courts.

19 Keshavdas, *Vīrsiṃhdevcarit* v. 27.5 (1997), p. 487, preferring the "likhata" of the

"*lekhaka*" (writer), "*likhata*" (writing), and "*lipikara*" (scribe) leave no room for doubt that Orchha—and this became typical of Rajput courts of the Mughal period—was actively transmitting literature, scholarship, and historical records through manuscripts.[20] Indeed, within a half century of Keshavdas's completing the *Kavipriyā*, its genealogy served as a written archive for the Jodhpur historian Mumhata Nainsi, who based his account of the Bundela dynasty on it.[21] Raja Indrajit, the patron of the *Kavipriyā*, was himself a scholar who painstakingly wrote a Brajbhasha commentary on the Sanskrit works of Bhartrhari.[22] Nonetheless, written texts, while important, are not the only medium that had currency at this court.

A "description of the city" (*nagaravarnana*), also from the *Vīrsiṃhdevcarit*, highlights the importance of recitations of religious texts at Orchha in the early seventeenth century:

> The city resounded with the sweetness of song,
> enchanting like Madhava's Mathura.
> Bells, cymbals, horns, pipes, and sitars played.
> The city was bustling with *kirtan* in the towering temples.
> Some were listening to *harilila*,
> others were singing songs of Rama and Krishna. …
> People were honouring their ancestors with rites and worshipping,
> paying homage to Hari.
> One would recite the Puranas, another would listen,
> yet another intoned the prescriptions of grammar.
> Still others were practicing mantras and teaching yoga.[23]

As always, the relationship between a poetic genre like the *nagaravarnana* and the lived experience of the citizens of Orchha in the seventeenth

---

Vishvanathprasad Mishra edition for "likhana". It is possible that Keshavdas or Raja Bir Singh Deo intended a comparison with the Mughal *kitabkhana*. On the arts of writing at Akbar's court, cf. *Ā'īn-i Akbarī*, Abu'l Fazl, ed. by D.C. Phillot, trans. by H. Blochmann (Delhi: Low Price Publications, 2008), I, pp. 102-13.

20 The disproportionately high number of Hindi manuscripts surviving from the seventeenth century has been noticed by many scholars. According to Imre Bangha (2011, p. 141), hundreds of thousands of Hindi manuscripts are extant from the seventeenth to nineteenth centuries and relatively few from before. On the increasing tendency to document historical events by the seventeenth century, see Ziegler (1976), pp. 131-35.

21 See *Naiṇsī rī khyāt*, ed. by Badariprasad Sakariya (Jodhpur: Rajasthan Oriental Research Institute, 1960), I, pp. 128-31. I thank Dalpat Rajpurohit for the reference.

22 R.S. McGregor, *The Language of Indrajit of Orcha* (Cambridge: Cambridge University Press, 1968).

23 Keshavdas, *Vīrsiṃhdevcarit*, vv. 18. 1-2, 7-8 (1997), pp. 368-70.

century is difficult to assess.[24] It is arresting, though, that a poet famed for his written contributions to the formal traditions of *riti* poetry and rhetoric *should* highlight the auditory nature of certain forms of textual experience: the communal performance of religious songs and the oral transmission of knowledge systems such as grammar and yoga.

Perhaps the most intriguing case of a "telling" in Keshavdas's oeuvre is a description of *his own performance* at the court of the Mughal Emperor Jahangir. This occurs in his last work, the *Jahāngīrjascandrikā* (*Moonlight of the Fame of Jahangir*, 1612), which is set in Agra. The opening frame story likens the text to a sermon (quite literally a telling!) delivered by the poet Keshavdas on the relative importance of Fate (*bhagya*) and Human Effort (*uday*). His listener (and the probable patron of the work) is Iraj Shahnavaz Khan, the son of the famous Mughal general and acclaimed Hindi poet 'Abd al-Rahim Khan-i Khanan. Another intended listener, as evident from the title as well as numerous panegyric poems, was Emperor Jahangir (r.1605-1627). In the final scene Keshavdas mentions that the emperor enjoyed his work, purportedly addressing the poet with the following Braj *doha* (couplet):

> Ask for your heart's wish, Keshavray [i.e. Keshavdas],
> I am pleased (*rījhe*) with your poetry in every respect (*mana krama bacana*).[25]

Keshavdas uses the suggestive verb *rījhna*, to be pleased, which specifically connotes a connoisseur's delight upon hearing a poem or song performed, one possible implication being that the *Jahāngīrjascandrikā* was read out loud to the emperor. Among the features that make performance the most likely mode of delivery for this text is the following panegyric verse, part of a larger poetic sequence on Jahangir's ostensible vassals. Keshavdas engages in intense verbal acrobatics, concatenating carefully-chosen place names that begin with specific Nagari characters (in the case of this verse "ga", "a", "sa", and "kha").

> *gaura gujarāta gayā goṛavāne gopācala,*
> *gandhāra gakhkhara gūṛha gāyaka ganesa ke*
> *araba airāka ābū āsera avadha aṅga*

24 A helpful introduction to the genre of the "description of the city" is A.K. Ramanujan, 'Toward an Anthology of Indian City Images', in *Urban India: Society, Space, and Image*, ed. by Richard G. Fox (Durham: Duke University, 1970).

25 Keshavdas, *Jahāngīrjascandrikā*, v. 198, ed. by Kishorilal (Allahabad: Sahitya Bhavan, 1994), p. 148. Unless otherwise indicated, subsequent references are to this edition.

*āsāpurī ādi gāṃva argala subesa ke*
*sambhala singhala sindhu soraṭha saubīra sūra,*
*khandhāra khuresa khurāsāna khāna khesa ke*
*sāhina ke sāhi jahāṃgīra sāhijū kī sabhā*
*"kesaurāya" rājata haiṃ rājā desa desa ke*

The kings of Gaur, Gujarat, Gaya, Gondwana, Gwalior,
Gandhara, and Gakkar, special admirers of Ganesh;
The well-appointed kings of Arabia, Iraq, Mt. Abu, Aser, Avadh,
Ang and Ashapuri, have established residence.
The nobles and dependents of Sambhal, Sinhala, Sindh, Saurashtra,
Saubir, Sur, Kandahar, Khuresh, and Khorasan—
Keshavdas says, the kings of many countries adorn the court of
the shah of shahs, Emperor Jahangir.[26]

Although I have attempted a rough translation here, the "meaning" of this verse can only be realised in performance. Note the long list-like quality of the passage, almost hypnotising with its heavy alliteration. One of the text's modern editors stresses that the verse displays Keshavdas's geographical knowledge,[27] and to be sure some of the places—Kandahar, Khorasan, Sindh, etc.—were areas of pronounced Mughal political concern. Others, such as Arabia and Iraq, were part of a wider Muslim geographical imaginary. A palimpsest of an older Sanskritic worldview, fully consonant with the poet's training, is also visible. Place names like Anga (Eastern Bihar) and Sinhala (modern Sri Lanka) were not relevant Mughal administrative terms but instead hearken back to an ancient tradition of geopolitical description in *kavya* that gave expression to universalist political aims through representations of sovereigns claiming authority over all the Indian regions. Employing virtuoso alliteration, Keshavdas cleverly assimilates both older and newer political paradigms to present Jahangir as supreme among kingly vassals in the style of a universal emperor (*maharajadhiraja*) from classical India.[28] While virtually incomprehensible on the printed page, in

26 Keshavdas, *Jahāngīrjascandrikā*, v. 99 (1994), p. 94. Three more verses follow in the same vein. My translation draws on Kishorilal's modern Hindi rendition.

27 *"Is se keśav ke bhaugolik jñān kā bhī patā caltā hai"*, ibid., p. 95. Some of the place names are obscure but glosses of the less obvious ones include: Gaur, either a region near Kandahar (in the reading of Kishorilal) or Bengal; Gondwana, near the Narmada river in modern Madhya Pradesh; Gakkar, a region in the Northwest of Punjab; Aser (also Asir), an important medieval fort town in central India; Sambhal, possibly Sambhalpur; Saubir, a region near the Indus river; Sur, a city in Afghanistan.

28 These verses are reminiscent of the famous *digvijaya* (conquering of the quarters) passage from canto four of Kalidasa's *Raghuvaṃśa*, in which Rama's ancestor King Raghu proclaims his universal sovereignty by traversing all four quarters of the subcontinent. See *Raghuvaṃśa*, ed. by Rewa Prasad Dwivedi (New Delhi: Sahitya

performance this and related verses would have had the effect of suggesting the immense power and reach of the Mughal Empire with Jahangir at the helm.[29]

## Performative Features of Poetry

Certain types of verses, like the panegyric just cited, allow us to infer their performative settings through style. Linking together a chain of epithets (*virudavali*) was another aural technique that Brajbhasha (and Sanskrit) poets used to express the power of their royal patrons. Amrit Rai, an approximate contemporary of Keshavdas from a regional kingdom further west, begins his *Māncarit*, a biography of the Kachhwaha ruler Man Singh (r.1589-1614), with a long series of epithets that combine literary flourishes with specific references to his patron's accomplishments:

*govindamandirasthitishāpanācārya*
*rāṇapratāpasindhukumbhodbhavadeva…*
*mayūmaidānamānamardanapravīṇa*
*udayācala-āvairimārttaṇḍa*
*uttarakhaṇḍapracaṇḍagaḍhagūḍhavajrābhighāta*
*khurasānavīrakhetajaitikhambha*
*khurasānamīranīrapravāhasahasrārjuna…*
*ḍhillīśvarasāhiakabarapratāparūpa…*
*mahārājādhirājakūrmmeśvara māna ciraṃ jīva*

He presided over the establishment of the Govindadev temple.
A second Agastya, he drank up the ocean of Rana Pratapa…
A consummate crusher of enemy pride on the battlefield at Mau,
A sun rising over the morning mountain of Amber,
A lighting bolt striking the formidable,
    impenetrable forts of the Northern lands,
Victory pillar on the battlefields of Khorasan,
Thousand(-armed) Arjuna to the lifeblood of the Mirs of Khorasan…
The embodiment of the strength of Shah Akbar, lord of Delhi…
Long live lord of the Kurma dynasty, emperor among kings, Man Singh.[30]

---

Akademi, 1993). On this classical model of representing political sovereignty in the Sanskrit cosmopolis, see Pollock (2006), pp. 239-58.

29 Similar "geographical" set pieces are attested in other more or less contemporary works (such as Amrit Rai's *Māncarit*, written for Man Singh Kachhwaha, and the *Kavīndrakalpalatā* of Kavindracharya, who was connected to Shah Jahan and Dara Shukoh. Both works (although not these specific passages) are discussed further below.

30 Amrit Rai, *Māncarit*, in *Māncaritāvalī: amber ke suprasiddh rājā mānsiṃh ke carit se*

The mostly Sanskrit discourse achieves a significant portion of its meaning from the rhythmic, incantatory effects of its stately compounds. To be present in a royal assembly where such a list of epithets was intoned would have been to partake of the body politic in a symbolic but also profoundly experiential manner. Scholars have remarked on the ritual dimensions of courtly panegyric, an effective tool for political incorporation.[31] This chain of epithets is also noteworthy for the peculiar eruptions of distinctly non-Sanskrit language into its otherwise heavily Sanskritised register, including expressions such as the "mirs of Khorasan" or a Persian word for battlefield ("*maidān*"). This text comes down to us, then, as a performance of Man Singh's authority powerfully expressed in classical Indic tropes that simultaneously encode the contemporary Rajput reality of service in a Persianate imperial order.

Amrit Rai's *Māncarit* is filled with performative elements. At one strategic moment in his "description of the city" he uses a four-verse sequence in the *jiya* metre for a sustained description of the gardens that ennoble his patron's realms in the Kachhwaha capital of Amber (near modern Jaipur). Note how the expressive punch is handled entirely by performative features, from the brilliant alliteration to the sense of sheer plenty conjured up by the long, cantering list:

*dekhe vicitra su bāga bahu bidhi phūla phala taruvara ghaṇe*
*campā caṃpelī mālatī vara veṣa maurasirī vaṇe*
*ketakī kuñja kumoda kūjāṃ kevarā pāḍala mahā*
*piya pārijātaka marua maṇi jāhī juhī johī jahā*

Many varieties of gardens could be seen,
    dense with flowers, fruits, and fine trees.
There were champa and jasmine flowers of magnificent form,
    groves of pines,
Clusters of ketaki blooms, water lilies, screwpines, grand trumpet flowers,
Lovely coral trees, basil, and jewel-bright jasmine.

---

*sambandhit pāṃc rājasthānī racnāoṃ kā saṅkalan*, ed. by Gopalnarayan Bahura (Jaipur: Maharaja Savai Man Singh II Sangrahalay, 1990), p. 2. The word "Kurma" refers to the Kachhwaha lineage.

31 Cf. Julie Scott Meisami, *Medieval Persian Court Poetry* (Princeton: Princeton University Press, 1987), pp. 43-44. Stewart Gordon has drawn attention to the practice of *khil'at* (symbolic gifts of cloth) and, in South Asia, the exchange of *pan* (betel nut) as rituals of political incorporation. Publicly performed panegyric can perhaps be considered in a similar light. See *Robes of Honour: Khil'at in Pre-colonial and Colonial India*, ed. by Stewart Gordon (New Delhi: Oxford University Press, 2003).

*āṃle amba anāra aṃvilī nimba nimbū nāragī*
*sundara sadāphala sada supārī seba sapatālu ṣagī*
*jāmūṇa jaṃbhīra vijaura aṃjira jarada jaradālū ghaṇe*
*kaṭahala karauṃdā nāliyara baḍhi veli vaṇa vaḍhahala vaṇe*

Dense orchards of myrobalan, mangoes, pomegranates,
tamarind, neem, lemons, and oranges.
Delectable citrus fruits, excellent betel nut, apples, and plums flourished.
Jamuns, limes, figs, and copious orange apricots,
Jackfruits, corindas, coconuts, large bels, and barhal trees.

*pīpala palāsa palaraka pīlū mahu makoī phārase*
*bara bāsa beri babūra bāriva tūta taiṃdū tāri se*
*khīraṇi khajūrī khaira khūhaṇi jāhi kivaṃ agaṇita gaṇe*
*baranau banāi binoda bāhira bāga ati bahu bidhi baṇe.*[32]

Pipal, palash, palarak (sheesham) and pilu trees,
mahuas and gooseberries and phalasas
Consummately fragrant jujubes, acacias, barivs,
mulberries and musk melons sweet as palm fruit.
Khiranis, date palms, mimosas, milkhedge—
countless in number are the varieties!
I joyfully describe all the types of gardens and groves
on the outskirts of the city.

While I have attempted a literal translation here, it hardly does justice to the impact of a verse like this at its moment of delivery. That English is an impoverished idiom when it comes to distinguishing subspecies of jasmine, limes, and other Indian flora is a trivial problem in comparison to how a silent written medium is unable to recapture the mood of an original that positively exploded with sounds. Note how the lines crescendo in their enumeration of the various plants (*jāhī juhī johī jahā, āṃle amba anāra āvilī, nimba nimbū nāragī*) and nearly succeed in recreating the lushness of three-dimensional space.

The western Indian provenance of Amrit Rai's text partly explains his affinity for bardic techniques, such as the flair for alliteration and comprehensive description. Another is his social location, for, according to Gopalnarayan Bahura, Amrit Rai was probably from the Bhat community whose literary compositions had a special relationship to performance.[33] He uses similar language effects in a lively sequence of verses (also from the description of the city) on the subject of performance itself:

---

32 Amrit Rai, *Māncarit*, vv. 97-99, in Bahura (1990), p. 16. The printed Hindi spellings have been lightly emended for clarity.

33 Ibid., p. 89.

Here (*kahūṃta*) brahmans recite the Vedas in their distinct manner,
Consecrating King Man Singh with their mantras.
Elsewhere (*kahūṃta*) *pandits* recite (or read)
with all their intellectual might,
Debating every domain of scholarship under the sun.

In one part (*kahūṃ*) of the realm authoritative sermons
on ancient lore take place all day long.
Elsewhere (*kahūṃ*) the *Rāmāyaṇa* and *Mahābhārata* are recited.
Somewhere (*kahūṃta*) well-trained performers
play the *vina* with concentration,
Accompanied by dedicated percussionists.[34]

Amrit Rai uses enriched, sonorous language to convey the sumptuousness and sophistication of the royal capital. The insistent repetition of the indefinite "somewhere" (*kahūṃ, kahūṃta*) at the beginning of most lines strengthens the feeling that Man Singh's kingdom is simply brimming with knowledge and artistic expertise. Clever *pandits*, talented storytellers, and expert musicians bring lustre to the realm. As the poet remarks hyperbolically, "When the king listens (*suṇai*) to music and is swayed by the lilt of poetry, Sheshanaga himself is entranced by the singular sounds (*amolita bola*)".[35]

Another biography of Man Singh from the same court, written about a decade later by one Narottamdas, also contains a description of the city that celebrates the king's musical soirées. "Nobody hosts better musical performances than King Man Singh", remarks the poet.[36] He composed this verse to cleverly mimic the *bols* or structured syllables called out during a dance recital:

*tāgṛidi tāgṛidi tāgṛidi theiyam,*
*jāṃkhina jāṃkhina jāṃkhina leiyam*
*gāṃmana gāṃmana gāṃmana geiyam,*
*pāṃgura pāṃgura pāṃṃgura seiyam.*[37]

34 Ibid., vv. 130-31, p. 21. Compare the passage from the *Vīrsiṃhdevcarit* cited above in note 23.

35 Ibid., v. 142, p. 22.

36 Narottamdas, *Māncarit*, v. 100, in Bahura (1990), p.156. The Kachhwahas are also associated with the patronage of music treatises during Akbar's period. See R. Sathyanarayana, 'Introduction', in *Nartananirṇaya of Paṇḍarīka Viṭṭhala*, ed. by R. Sathyanarayana (Delhi: Indira Gandhi National Centre for the Arts and Motilal Banarsidass Publishers, 1994), I, pp. 15-21.

37 Narottamdas, *Māncarit*, v. 101, in Bahura (1990), p. 156.

Inert on the page, these lines do not make much sense. Read aloud, they bring to life the courtly salons of Mughal India, conjuring up the rhythms and whirls of a Kathak performance.

Rich, aurally-infused verses of this type are entertaining but they are also a suitable testament to both the righteousness and the good taste of the king, whose duty it was to enrich the agricultural bounty of the land and promote the arts. While traditional in style, the writers of this court may also have felt a special compulsion to celebrate Amber's gardens and musical culture because of the contemporary Mughal concern with them.[38] And the praise of Amber also makes a crucial argument about local sovereignty in an age when Hindu rulers had been subsumed ineluctably into the Mughal imperial system: Rajput kingdoms are stately and controlled by just, luminous rulers who provide amply for their subjects. The auditory experience of such luscious verses would have served to dramatically underscore this political point.

## The Performance of Martial Poetry

The many performative set pieces in Indian court literature of this period reflect different moods, since poets deliberately suffused their sense with layers of sound to suit particular contexts. One important domain was martial poetry, where onomatopoeia and the manipulation of specific combinations of phonemes was thought to impart *ojas* or "martial spirit" and was thus considered especially effective for conveying military prowess in works characterised by *vira rasa* (the heroic sentiment).[39] Whereas Amrit Rai prefaced a larger narrative poem with a "chain of epithets", two centuries later Padmakar, who spent part of his career at the same court, devoted two entire works to this motif, both in a heroic vein. His *Pratāpsiṃhvirudāvalī* is an extended paean to the exploits of his Kachhwaha patron Raja Pratap Singh (r.1778-1803) and includes several lively scenes that stress the bustle and cacophony of battle:

---

38 Babur famously complained that India lacked proper gardens (which for him meant those with running water), as though it were a major civilisational deficiency. See *Bāburnāma*, trans. by Wheeler Thackston (New York: The Modern Library, 2002), pp. 350, 359-60.

39 A representative statement from classical poetics is in V. Raghavan, *Bhoja's Śṛṅgāra prakāśa* (Madras: Punarvasu, 1963), p. 348.

*udagga khagga jaggamagga tyoṃ umagga soṃ gahaiṃ*
*samagga agga agga hvai su bairi bagga koṃ dahaiṃ*
*umaggi jaggi jāmagīṃ samagga magga meṃ lasai*
*alagga ugga uggahūṃ su dugga dugga meṃ trasai.*

Riled up with passion, the soldiers grabbed their fiercely gleaming swords.
The entire battalion surged ahead to decimate the enemy forces.
Fuses ignited, the canonnonballs exploded forth,
    lighting up the whole battlefield.
The [enemies] who were unscathed were filled with wrath;
    they sheltered in the forts, taking fright.

*su opa kopa opacī su cāu copa soṃ saje*
*karāla kāla jāla se utāla phāla soṃ gaṃje*
*humaṃki haṃka haṃka kai bamaṃki baṃka jhaṃkahīṃ*
*tamaṃki teja tāu meṃ tanaṃkahūṃ na saṃkahīṃ…*

Fiery-tempered, the armour-clad warriors deployed energetically.
Fearsome as the noose of death, they rushed forward in a wave.
They leapt, roaring their battle cries, swelling with anger,
Sparked with a passionate inner light, unwavering.

*tahaṃ jakkājakkī ṭhakkāṭhakkī ṭhakkāṭhakkī ḍhālana kī*
*tupakana kī taṛataṛa bānana saṛasaṛa macata su khaṛakhaṛa bhālana kī*
*gajaghaṇṭana ghanananana golī gananana kānana sanananana māci rahī*
*topana kī ararara bhūpara bhararara gharaghara ghararara ati umahī.*

Crazed with intensity they jostled, shields clanging.
Guns blazed, arrows whirred by, and lances crashed together.
Elephant bells jingled, bullets shot forth,
    and the nearby jungles echoed with sound.
Cannons boomed, the earth trembled,
    as people everywhere were agitated.[40]

These are quintessential examples of poetry that incites *vira rasa*. Thanks to an abundance of guttural and geminate consonants, we hear the din and clamour of warfare, the metal-on-metal sound of swords and shields clashing; we see the terrifying cannonballs flashing through the sky; we feel the intensity of battle as soldiers dash into the fray, ready to fight to the death. These verses remind us that battlefields were soundscapes as well

40 *Pratāpsiṃhvirudāvalī*, vv. 71-73; 88-89, in *Padmākargranthāvalī*, ed. by Vishvanathprasad Mishra (Varanasi: Nagari Pracharini Sabha, 1959), pp. 283, 286.

as landscapes and, in fact, martial styles of music and recitation were part of the very ambience of war.

In his *Himmatbahādurvirudāvalī*, Padmakar concludes a dramatic opening verse sequence on the mustering of the armies with a description of the conch shells, drums, and horns that spurred the warriors to fight:

> When warriors blow the conches,
> The Elephants who guard the cardinal points scatter in all directions.
> The incessant rumble of the kettledrum resounds, riling up the soldiers.
> Martial odes blare forth, accompanied by music,
> proclaiming their might everywhere.
> The sound of the drums pervades the earth,
> fomenting anxiety in enemy kings.
> The rising percussive tempo booms like thunderclouds.
> Fine poets recite a *virudāvalī*—upon hearing it,
> the warriors rush forward, galvanised.
> Wherever bards intone martial verse,
> they become excited and are eager to fight.[41]

There is no reason to think that Padmakar is indulging in mere poetic licence, for his mention of instruments and the like is supported by other evidence on the importance of the soundscape of battle for his milieu.[42] Aside from its aesthetic and panegyric properties, *vira rasa*-infused poetry would have served the practical purpose of spurring on the warriors.

## Poetic Repertoires and Tailoring Production to Diverse Patrons

Alongside performances *in* poems and poems *as* performances we can also investigate the ways in which poets were performers (see also d'Hubert and Sharma in this volume). Sometimes poets literally did double duty as singers. The Sanskrit term *vaggeyakar*, "poet-composer", nicely

41 *Himmatbahādurvirudāvalī*, vv. 39-42, in ibid., p. 8. Later in the work the performers known as *bandijan* are said to declaim the *virudavali* (vv. 57, 182-83), and Muslim performer castes such as *nakib* and *dhadhi* are also mentioned (v. 81), pp. 9, 26, 12.

42 None Arjun Singh, the captain of one of the warring parties featured in this poem, apparently invented his own style of tambourine, known as a *laggī*, for leading his warriors into battle; Lala Bhagvandin, 'None arjun siṃh kā saṅkṣipt hāl', in *Padmākarkṛt himmatbahādurvirudāvalī*, ed. by Lala Bhagvandin (Varanasi: Nagari Pracharini Sabha, [n.d.]), pp. 31-32.

encompasses this dual role. For instance, Akbar's famous court musician Tansen performed his own compositions, and seventeenth-century writers like Kavindracharya Sarasvati and Jagannatha Panditaraja are remembered as singers in Mughal sources.[43]

Whether or not poets were also active as singers, they shared with their musical brethren the need for technical mastery and developing a repertoire. Rigorous immersion in poetics can indeed be considered comparable to musical training—musicians knew their *ragas* (melodic modes), *talas* (beat cycles), and would have memorised snatches of lyrics, while *riti* poets were highly trained practitioners of a sophisticated craft who sharpened their skill by mastering literary theory, which in India was considered a *shastra* or formal science. Knowledge of the correct use of *alankarashastra*, the "science of ornaments", was essential since poets were sometimes expected to compose extemporaneous verses on diverse topics in *samasyapurti* competitions, on which more below.[44]

Many *riti* poets were also itinerant, and factoring in shifting performance environments goes a long way towards explaining the striking repetitions of compositions that we find across an individual author's oeuvre. Expected to participate in poetry competitions and to present occasional verses, poets would have been prompted to recycle lines or to retool them for changing contexts. Thus they, like musicians, developed repertoires. The technology of modern publishing makes repetitions easy to spot, but in premodern times patrons probably just assumed that a given panegyric was composed for him alone. The following *kavitt* by Keshavdas occurs with only very minor changes in two separate places in his collected works. The first appearance in the *Kavipriyā* reflects a pedagogical setting—the point

43 On Tansen, see Françoise "Nalini" Delvoye, 'Les chants *dhrupad* en langue braj des poètes-musiciens de l'Inde Moghole', in *Littératures médiévales de l'Inde du Nord*, ed. by Françoise Mallison (Paris: École Française d'Extrême-Orient, 1991), pp. 141-43; idem, 'The Image of Akbar as a Patron of Music in Indo-Persian and Vernacular Sources', in *Akbar and His India*, ed. by Irfan Habib (New Delhi: Oxford University Press, 2000a), p. 200. On Kavindracharya, see Allison Busch, 'Hidden in Plain View: Brajbhasha Poets at the Mughal Court', *Modern Asian Studies* 44.2 (2010), 289-92. The case of Jagannatha is discussed in Audrey Truschke, 'Cosmopolitan Encounters: Sanskrit and Persian at the Mughal Court' (PhD dissertation, Columbia University, 2012), pp. 54-55.

44 As Keshava Mishra puts it in his *Alaṅkāraśekhara*, a Sanskrit poetry manual composed in a township near Delhi in the sixteenth century: "*kurvanti kavayaḥ śaktāḥ samasyāpūraṇādikam*" (skilled poets engage in the completing of verses and other similar activities). *Alaṅkāraśekhara*, v. 18.2, ed. by Pandit Shivadatta and Kashinath Pandurang Parab, 2nd edn (Bombay: Nirnaya Sagar Press, 1926), p. 63. Keshava Mishra provides some examples of the technique in the subsequent canto.

is to illustrate how to use numbers as the basis for poetic ornamentation. Keshavdas outlines objects and concepts associated with the numbers one through ten before consolidating the lesson through two examples (a companion poem treats the numbers from six to ten).[45] Doubling as a eulogistic poem, in the *Kavipriyā* the *kavitt* is dedicated to his then-patron, Raja Indrajit of Orchha. In writing the *Jahāngīrjascandrikā* more than a decade later, Keshavdas updated the poem.[46] Here I excerpt the version from the *Kavipriyā*, marking with square brackets the small portions that were later changed in the *Jahāngīrjascandrikā*:

*eka thala thita pai basata prati jana* [*jiya*][47]
*dvikara pai desa-desa kara ko dharanu hai*
*triguna kalita bahu balita lalita guna,*
*gunina ke gunataru phalita karanu hai*
*cāri hī padāratha ko lobha* [*cita nita-nita*][48]
*dībe kauṃ padāratha-samūha ko paranu hai*
[*kesodāsa indrajīta bhūtala abhūta*][49] *pañca-*
*bhūta kī prabhūti bhavabhūti ko saranu hai*

He lives in one place, but inhabits the hearts of one and all.
He has only two hands, but collects taxes[50] from all the lands.
He is comprised of three elements, endowed with many beautiful qualities.
He brings the talent-trees of the talented to fruition.[51]
He himself craves only the four aims of life,[52]
While vowing always to give generously.
Keshavdas says, Indrajit is unprecedented on this earth:

45 Keshavdas, *Kavipriyā*, vv. 11.1-23 (1954), pp. 160-63.

46 Compare *Kavipriyā*, v. 11.22 (1954), p. 163, with *Jahāngīrjascandrikā*, v. 33 (1994), p. 50.

47 Spelled *jīya* in both the Kishorilal and Vishvanathprasad Mishra editions of *Jahāngīrjascandrikā*, a variant that does not alter the meaning.

48 In *Jahāngīrjascandrikā* the text indicated in square brackets is replaced with the poet's signature and a correlative marker: *kesaudāsa jihi*.

49 In this line Keshavdas makes a major change, switching out the name of the patron to whom he addresses the verse: *sāhina kau sāhi jahāṃgīra sāhi āhi*.

50 Here there is a pun on the word *kara*, which means both "hand" and "taxes".

51 The poet cleverly plays on different meanings of the Brajbhasha word *guna* (Sanskrit/Modern Standard Hindi *guṇa*). The three elements are the three *gunas* from *Sāṃkhyā* philosophy: *tamas*, *rajas*, and *sattva* (lethargy, energy, and quiescence); *gunas* are also "qualities" in the sense of virtues; in Indian literary theory *guna* is, additionally, a technical term referring to the phonological properties of words; and *guṇī* or *gunī* (singular of the Brajbhasha *gunina*) means a talented person, often a musician, poet, or scholar.

52 In the classical Hindu conception the four aims of life are *dharma*, *artha*, *kama*, and *moksha* (virtue, gain, pleasure, and release).

He is made up of the five elements,
yet he protects the material prosperity of the entire earth.

Much of the wording is verbatim. The only significant emendation is in the service of invoking the new patron: the half-line "Keshavdas says, Indrajit is unprecedented on this earth" is replaced with the metrically equivalent "the emperor of emperors, Jahangir, is…". Perhaps one quarter of the *Jahāngīrjascandrikā* draws in similar fashion on earlier material, especially *Kavipriyā* and *Vīrsiṃhdevcarit*.[53] It is natural that poets would have wished to refine their compositions over time, but they also clearly recycled favourite poems to please new patrons.[54] The substitution of patron names has been noted for the performance of *dhrupad*, as well.[55]

The preference for free-standing verses (*muktaka*) over longer narratives (*prabandha*) among writers of this period also points towards the need to see compositions as units of entertainment from the poet's repertoire that were presented in performance venues on different occasions, rather than constituting a coherent written text. As Lakshmidhar Malviya observes, poets did not just set out to write a work of *muktaka*: they gathered together material into a collection crafted—and performed—over time.[56]

---

53 Also compare Keshavdas, *Jahāngīrjascandrikā*, vv. 34-35, 43-45 (1994), pp. 51-52, 61-62, with (respectively) idem, *Kavipriyā* 11.23, 8.5, 8.28, 8.26, 6.7 (1954), pp. 163, 139, 143-44, 118. Close parallels can also be drawn between the performance of poetry in the courtly assembly in *Jahāngīrjascandrikā*, vv. 185-92 and Bir Singh Deo's coronation scene in *Vīrsiṃhdevcarit*, vv. 33.32-47 (1997), pp. 600-10.

54 Examples abound. Jagannatha Panditaraja probably wrote his *Jagadābharaṇa* (Ornament to the world) originally as an encomium to the Mewar ruler Rana Jagat Singh (r.1628-1652), but the work is nearly identical to *Prāṇābharaṇa*, a panegyric presented to Maharaja Prananarayana of Koch Bihar (r.c.1632-1659; 1661-1665) and one manuscript also suggests the use of its praise addresses for Mughal royalty. See P.S. Ramachandrudu, 'Introduction to the Second Edition', in *Panditaraja Kavya Samgraha*, ed. by K. Kamala (Hyderabad: Sanskrit Academy, Osmania University, 2002), pp. xlv-vi; and Jatindrabimal Chaudhuri, *Muslim Patronage to Sanskritic Learning* (Delhi: Idarah-i Adabiyat-i Delli, 2009), pp. 62-63. For another example of such repurposing, see Audrey Truschke (2012), pp. 79-80.

55 In the *Sahasras* commissioned by Shah Jahan, the lyrics of the famous composer Nayak Bakshu were collected, but the names of the original patrons (Man Singh Tomar, Muzaffar Shah of Gujarat) were replaced with the name "Shah Jahan". See Françoise "Nalini" Delvoye, 'Indo-Persian Accounts on Music Patronage in the Sultanate of Gujarat', in *The Making of Indo-Persian Culture*, ed. by Muzaffar Alam, Françoise "Nalini" Delvoye, and Marc Gaborieau (Delhi: Manohar and Centre de Sciences Humaines, 2000b), p. 270.

56 Thus, the *Satsaī* of Matiram, a lengthy compilation of 700 or so stanzas, contains 176 couplets recycled from *Lalitlalām* and his other works. See Lakshmidhar Malviya, *Bihārīdās kī satsaī* (New Delhi: Aditya Prakashan: 2008), I, p. 3.

## Performance, Improvisation, and the Transmission of Literary Knowledge

As much as we can surmise about premodern literary performances, a fuller understanding is all too frequently thwarted by the dearth of detailed accounts.[57] Still, the evidence, while sparse, is not entirely lacking. A suggestive passage in chapter seven of the Sanskrit rhetorician Rajashekhara's *Kāvyamīmāṃsā* (*Investigation of Poetry*, early tenth century) discusses recitation practices, which he intriguingly classifies according to regional styles. Thus, the southern (*draviḍa*) *kavi* is said to be heavily inclined towards sung poetry, Kashmiris (*kāśmīraḥ*) prone to nasalisation, and those from the plains (*pāñcāla-maṇḍala*) praised for their mastery of versatile poetic forms and proper pronunciation.[58] *Riti* writers were as a rule silent on this subject, but modern scholars have speculated about different recitation styles for the *kavitt*, proposing a distinction between the more archaic and dramatic *ludhakant* mode, often associated with martial poetry, and the gentler rhythms of the so-called *padmakari shaili*, said to be suited to erotic compositions.[59] There is also some evidence, as we shall see, that poets would explain their verses at the time of performance.[60]

As far as the setting for such recitation, it is reasonable to envision a scenario, much like the *baithak* or *mahfil* associated with other related performance cultures, in which a poet recited his work (or another's) in front of a specialised audience of connoisseurs, whether at court or in a private salon. The *sabhā* or *mahfil* was a place for entertainment, but also a space in which participants might display or hone their cultural knowledge in oral discussions. The anonymous author of the *Ghunyat al-munya*, a fourteenth-century treatise on Indian music and dance, notes how his

57 We know much more about modern *kavi-sammelans* and poetry competitions. See Dayashankar Shukla, *Hindī kā samasyāpūrti kāvya* (Lucknow: Ganga Pustakmala Karyalay, 1967), pp. 32-33, 87-212; Francesca Orsini, *The Hindi Public Sphere 1920-1940* (New Delhi: Oxford University Press, 2002), pp. 80-89. How closely modern performance practices reflect those of earlier times is difficult to assess.

58 Rajashekhara, *Kāvyamīmāṃsā*, ed. by C.D. Dalal, R.A. Sastry, and (revised and enlarged by) K.S. Ramaswami Sastri Siromani, 3rd edn (Baroda: Oriental Institute, 1934), pp. 33-34.

59 Rameshchandra Sharma (2007), pp. 55-57. Sharma draws on the work of Nagendra, a leading post-independence Hindi scholar. "Padmakari" is in all likelihood a reference to the late *riti* poet Padmakar (1753-1833), who of course did write plenty of martial poetry as well.

60 Pollock (2006), p. 87.

patron, Abu Raja, occasionally arranged a concert of Persian and Indian music in order to foster "sweet relaxation". Various discussions evidently ensued in the intervals between songs:

> Those present in the assembly often requested the intricacies of verses (*shi'r*)... to be explained to them. And my patron... out of his vast ocean of eloquence, brought to [the] surface the pearls of meaning. ... Sometimes they enquired about the mysteries of sound; he by the vibrations of the moods of that master of exposition rendered threadbare the screen concealing music, thereby revealing her to all.[61]

While this passage references a musical soirée, the emphasis on how the patron would discuss the meaning of the lyrics is directly relevant to the reception of poetry.[62] In this scene, the *mahfil* was a place where the patron showed his mettle. More frequently, performances involved the rigorous assaying of the skills of those employed by the patron, whether musicians, poets, or scholars.

Poets who may have spent some of their time in a quiet study composing their verses at leisure also had to compose publicly, under pressure, and to offer, using the apt phrase of Rao and Shulman, "a poem at the right moment".[63] There is much general anecdotal evidence about how the patron or convener of a literary assembly would set exacting topics (*samasya*) and poets oblige them by fulfilling (*purti*) the demand. *Samasyapurti* anecdotes typically feature in literary lore as evidence of a poet's brilliance.[64] Tales of one-upmanship abound, as with Padmakar and Thakur, whose rivalry is said to have manifested in poetic duels at the court of Anupgiri Gosain.[65] Some legends stress the defiance of political authority. Often a courtesan

---

61 *Ghunyatu'l Munya: The Earliest Persian Work on Indian Classical Music*, trans. by Shahab Sarmadee (New Delhi: Indian Council of Historical Research in association with Northern Book Centre, 2003), p. 4.

62 An illuminating discussion of this text is in Aditya Behl, *Love's Subtle Magic* (New York: Oxford University Press, 2012b), pp. 292-94.

63 Velcheru Narayana Rao and David Shulman, *A Poem at the Right Moment* (Delhi: Oxford University Press, 1999).

64 We see many examples of poetic bravura in the *Bhojaprabandha*, a sixteenth-century account of purported proceedings from the court of the celebrated King Bhoja of Dhara, but the text is not exactly amenable to historical inquiry of a positivist sort since competitions for line-filling occur among wildly asynchronous poets such as Kalidasa, Bhavabhuti, and Dandin; Narayana Rao and Shulman (1999), pp. 159-68. Various *samasyapurti* competitions are detailed in Shukla (1967), pp. 24-27, 72-86.

65 Imre Bangha, *Scorpion in the Hand* (Delhi: Manohar, 2014), p. 18.

or devout *bhakta* scores a point against the Mughal emperor with a timely poem.[66]

Extemporaneous compositions might be required in various contexts. Motilal Menariya relates a somewhat fanciful tale about how the *riti* poet Vrind supposedly secured employment at the Mughal court (Aurangzeb's grandson Azim us-Shan became his patron). Aurangzeb presented him with the following *samasya*: "*payonidhi pairyo cāhai misarī kī putarī*" [a figurine made of sugar seeks to swim the ocean]. The first *purti* was unsuccessful:

> Placing all their faith in the supreme godhood,
> sages and holy men bear witness.
> God sustains the existence of life forms both movable and movable,
> whom He holds dear.
> Vrind says, He is supremely powerful in everything
> and from his grace the miraculous unfolds:
> The lame can scale a mountain, the mute can recite scripture,
> so why shouldn't a figurine made of sugar seek to swim the ocean?

Having failed to impress the emperor with these bland pieties, the poet tried a less pedestrian approach and was rewarded with an appointment at the court:

> Seeing the terrifying, cruel glance of Agastya, it did not budge.
> The jostling of the waves ceased,
> curbed were the whirling eddies and sea spray.
> Says Vrind, all of this was unprecedented, unheard of.
> The waters stilled, placid like a mirror, and remained miraculously calm.
> When the ocean faced so fearlessly the wrath of Agastya,
> why shouldn't a figurine made of sugar seek to swim the ocean?[67]

Poetry composition could be a grueling test. In this imagined encounter between Aurangzeb and Vrind it becomes the skill to be measured in an interview-like situation. And sometimes *samasyapurti* was *actually a test*. Records from an eighteenth-century Braj academy in Bhuj, Gujarat, for instance, indicate that filling in verse lines was a component of the annual

---

66 Select examples of encounters with Mughal emperors are discussed in Busch (2011), pp. 132-33.

67 Motilal Menariya, *Rājasthānī bhāṣā aur sāhitya* (reprint, Jodhpur: Rajasthani Granthagar, 1999), pp. 134-35; cited in Sudhir Kumar Sharma, *Kavivar Vṛnd, vyaktitva aur kṛtitva* (Delhi: Swaraj Prakashan, 1998), p.12.

examination of aspiring court poets.[68] In a courtly rather than educational context, the clever handling of a *samasya* was an entertainment for onlookers. Both Vatsyayana (author of the *Kāmasūtra*, a famous treatise on erotics) and Rajashekhara included *samasyapurti* in their enumerations of characteristic courtly pastimes.[69]

One rare account of what by all indications was a real *samasyapurti* in a Deccan court context comes from Jayarama Pindye's *Rādhāmādhava-vilāsacampū* (*Love Play of Radha and Krishna*, c.1650), a collection of mixed Sanskrit and vernacular poetry performed for the Maratha king Shahaji Bhonsle (father of Shivaji). Both Shahaji and his son were well-known seventeenth-century patrons of *riti* poetry in Brajbhasha, but they also hosted *pandits*, poets, and connoisseurs conversant in numerous *deshabhasha* or regional vernaculars. Jayarama Pindye, unusually, claims to be proficient in twelve languages, and his *Rādhāmādhavavilāsacampū* features poetry in all of them.[70]

The text also brims with evidence about performance. In a passage near the beginning of the sixth canto, the recitation of what has until this point been exclusively a Sanskrit text is briefly interrupted as Jayarama is formally introduced at court. Here the language of tellings becomes particularly explicit. Jayarama's poem, we are informed, is being intently read out loud (*asmin prabandhe pāpaṭhyamāne*) before a community of connoisseurs (*rasikajanasamāja*), who after hearing it are overcome with wonder (*tacchravaṇena paraṃ kautuhalam avāpya*) and address the professional cantor (*prabandhapāṭhakam*) to learn more about the provenance of the work and

68 Françoise Mallison, 'The Teaching of Braj, Gujarati and Bardic Poetry at the Court of Kutch: The Bhuj Braj-bhāṣā Pāṭhśālā (1749-1948)', in *Forms of Knowledge in Early Modern Asia*, ed. by Sheldon Pollock (Durham: Duke University Press, 2011), p. 175. This "testing" may go back much further to a tradition of *kavi-parikshas* (testing of poets) in the medieval period; Dayashankar Shukla (1967), pp. 23, 32, speculates that the original inspiration for *samasyāpūrti* may have been the testing of poets, and mentions the modern continuation of this practice for the degree of *acharya* at Kashi Sanskrit Vishvavidyalay.

69 For the canonical 64 courtly arts listed in the *Kāmasūtra*, see the chart excerpted in Daud Ali, *Courtly Culture and Political Life in Early Medieval India* (Cambridge: Cambridge University Press, 2004), pp. 76-77. Several others are focused on the literary arts, including "pratimālā", an apparent ancestor to modern parlor games like Antakshari (also a popular game show) and Bait Bazi, where the challenge is to sing/recite a verse that begins with the last letter used by another contestant; cf. *Kāvyamīmāṃsā* (chapter 10, p. 53), cited in Shukla (1967), pp. 23-24.

70 Knowledge of India's regional vernaculars, "*deśabhāṣāvijñāna*", is one of the 64 courtly arts mentioned in the *Kāmasūtra*. See note 69.

its author.[71] Throughout, Jayarama frequently invokes the language of listening with words like *śrotavya* ("to be heard"), *śrotum* ("to hear"), and *ākarṇya* ("having heard").[72]

The sixth canto is also the occasion for a *samasyapurti* competition in the court. One by one, various individuals (often named, underscoring the likely historicity of Jayarama's account) enter the arena to present their verse(s). The Sanskrit authors are, predictably, Brahmans, some of whom have professions and talents with close connections to performance. Thus, Nilakantha Bhatta and one Tukadeva are praised for their skill in reciting the Puranas, and Vireshvara Bhatta is lauded as a "bee on the lotus in the lake of musical nectar".[73] The *samasyas* often consist of an intriguing first or last line, or sometimes just a partial line. "What shall I do, lord who reigns over Varanasi [Shiva]?" engenders a lament about the futility of learning and pious behaviour when all who die in this holy place—even the lowborn—are automatically granted release.[74] Nilakantha Bhatta has to complete a verse that ends with the phrase "why a dispute about the goad when the elephant has already been sold?"[75] Prahlada Sarasvati, justly extolled as "a gladdener of the hearts of poets", is successful in completing the *samasya* "*gatāgatair eva gatā triyāmā*" [the night passed in equivocation] using a clever *yamaka* (homonym, a subspecies of the pun) that plays on the word *Rāmāyaṇa*:

> Should I drink in the *Rāmāyaṇa*, or gaze upon a beautiful woman in bed?
> Thus for the aging gentleman the night passed in equivocation.[76]

In the eleventh canto, various Bhasha (vernacular) poets are also shown to perform. One Raghunath Vyas uses the tag "the wives of your enemies roam the forests" as an opportunity to expatiate on Shahaji's military prowess, the premise being that he routs his enemies and reduces their women to the status of helpless, impoverished widows.[77] Some poems relate to specific

71 Jayarama Pindye, *Rādhāmādhavavilāsacampū*, ed. by V.K. Rajvade (Pune: Varda books, 1989), p. 226.

72 See, for instance, ibid., p. 228. Also note the references to singers (*gayaka*) and singing style (*gayana-riti*) on p. 246.

73 Ibid., pp. 230-31.

74 This results in ibid., p. 229, v. 204.

75 Ibid., p. 230, v. 211.

76 The *yamaka* in the first line reads, "*Rāmāyaṇam vā śravaṇena peyam rāmāyane vā nayanam vidheyam*" *Pindye* (1989), p. 230, v. 212.

77 Ibid., p. 246. For a brief discussion of this verse and other noteworthy passages

military campaigns, as when one Alli Khan, extolled as a "*gunijana*" or man of talent, commemorates a recent campaign at Allanggarh by singing a *karka* or martial poem.[78] In one case a request to illustrate a particular figure of speech is entertained, resulting in a virtuosic quatrain that employs the literary ornament of *yamaka* in all four lines:

*sāheba toṃ sama kona aheṃ* ***sūraju sūraja*** *upara tāpa tapo haiṃ*
*kaunu kahuṃ aba tere mu****kābala kābala*** *te kārabhāra layo hai*
*bāndhi jamaddhara sāheṃ teṃ* ***majāku*** *sāhe ta****mājaku*** *bhaiju bhayo hai*
*sāhiju hi kara leta phiranga,* ***phiraṅgina*** *koṃ* ***phira raṅga*** *gayo hai.*

Oh lordly one, what warrior is greater than you?
Your fierceness blazes brighter than the sun.
Can anyone anywhere compare to you?
Your influence extends as far as Kabul.
You bind your sword as though it were child's play
But its slicing instills fear (?)
Shahaji collects taxes abroad and the foreigners turn pale.[79]

Arguably, a Bhasha poet has a special advantage when it comes to homonyms because unlike his more grammatically precise Sanskrit colleagues he can fudge words and add Perso-Arabic vocabulary to augment his lexical stock. Note the last line, which takes the Persian word *firang*, "Frankish" or foreign (probably a reference to the Portuguese), and redistributes the lexemes to create the satirical meaning "*phira raṅga gayo hai*" [then they lost their colour] (i.e., paled due to fright).

The *yamaka* verse just quoted showcases creativity and a poet's ability to think on his feet, but the whole enterprise of courtly literature was made possible because Indian authors and audiences knew their literary theory.[80] The patron Shahaji Bhonsle himself references the vernacularisation of motifs from classical rhetoric:

---

from this text, see Sumit Guha 'Transitions and Translations: Regional Power and Vernacular Identity in the Dakhan, 1500-1800', *Comparative Studies of South Asia, Africa and the Middle East* 24.2 (2004), 28-29.

78 "*Karakā... allīkhānā gunijana vaha gāyo sāheba pāsa*", Pindye (1989), pp. 259-60.

79 Ibid. p. 247. The meaning of line 3 of the Bhasha quatrain remains somewhat cryptic. Perhaps "*majāku*" is from *mazāq*, "joke, jest", and "*tamājaku*" may be related to the Arabic *mazak*—"to cut". I am grateful to Vivek Gupta for the latter suggestion.

80 In fact, the *Rasamañjarī* of Bhanudatta, a recognised authority in Sanskrit poetics, comes in for special mention in this *champu* when in the Sanskrit section poets are asked to elucidate some of his formulations of *nayikabheda*, the cataloguing of female characters according to literary conventions. Pindye (1989), p. 233.

On one occasion the crest jewel among kings spoke as follows
in the assembly (*majlis māhi*):
Nobody has yet described in Bhasha
the setting or rising of the sun and moon.
Just as the rays of the sun bring a cluster of flowers to bloom
So vernacular poets transform [motifs] and clarify them.
And so a single female character may have many vernacular clothes.
Accordingly, I will elaborate further on the envisioned topic.[81]

The passage shows how technical literary knowledge was a basis for performance—and through performance, debate—among connoisseurs. The poet had to demonstrate his knowledge of sometimes subtle distinctions between types of female characters or figures of speech.

That courtly performances had educational potential in which poet-performers set themselves up as instructors to their patrons is a point underlined by other contributors to this volume (d'Hubert, Schofield). A suggestive example from the Braj world is the *Kavīndrakalpalatā* (*Kavindra's Wish-fulfilling Vine*, c.1650) of Kavindracharya, the esteemed pandit, vernacular poet, and *dhrupad* singer who had close contact with the Mughal court in North India during this period. The *Kavīndrakalpalatā* is a remarkable collection of diverse Braj compositions associated with the patronage of Shah Jahan (r.1628-1658). It contains (in this order) 108 *kavitt*s in a panegyric vein, all praising Shah Jahan; 55 *dhrupads* or song texts[82] containing the emperor's name; 10 *bishnupad*s or "Vishnu songs"; 60 verses in typical *riti* metres (especially *kavitt*, *savaiya*, and *doha*) that are labeled "*tattvajñān*", which collectively constitute a poetic sermon on Indian philosophy; and a separate set of poems and *dhrupads* dedicated largely to Prince Dara Shukoh. The work thus has the air of being assembled over time through a series of performances and lectures rather than being the product of sustained effort directed at a single coherent written composition.

The *dhrupad* section of the work especially commands our attention. Many of the verses portray light, erotic moments, and are typical of the courtly repertoire of occasional poems: the exultations of the Holi festival as well as scenes where a woman longs for her lover, rejoices in his company, or gives him the cold shoulder with a display of pique.[83] Occasionally

81 Ibid., p. 250.

82 Although this section of the work is labeled as "*sāhijahāṃ viṣayaka dhruvapadāni*" in the colophon, it contains a few instances of other styles like *kavitt*, *doha*, and *jhulana*.

83 E.g. Kavindracharya Sarasvati, *Kavīndrakalpalatā*, ed. by Rani Lakshmikumari

Kavindracharya draws attention to more technical subjects, however, as when he announces to his patron:

> *dakṣina nāyaka ke lachani je kahiyata,*
> *te saba tumaheṃ aru granthani meṃ je gāī nikāī*
>
> I have explained to you the characteristics of the *dakshina nayaka*
> And they have also been well explained [lit., sung] in books...[84]

The *dakshina nayaka* is a well-known term from the Indian *alankarashastra* referring to a man who can manage his love affairs with more than one woman.[85] This construct of an "adept lover" has natural salience for a king with multiple wives, but this alone cannot account for the insistent focus on such terminology in Kavindra's songs. A lengthy *dhrupad* on the theme of Holi begins:

> *kanaka mahala madhi ritu vasanta maiṃ, khelata śāhi ihi vidhi kī horī*
> *vasana amola ābhūṣana pahiraiṃ, prauḍhā mugdhā madhyā gaurī*
> *uttima gāvati, uttama nācati, uttima vāda bajāvati*
> *rāga rasa rūpa parasapara nirakhi sukha pāvati.*[86]
>
> It's the spring season and this is how Shah Jahan
> plays Holi in the golden palace.
> His fair women—innocent about love, somewhat knowledgeable, and
> mature alike—are wearing their priceless jewels and garments.
> Finely do they sing, finely do they dance,
> finely do they play their instruments.
> Swayed by love and beauty, they behold each other and are delighted.

---

Chundavat (Jaipur: Rajasthan Oriental Research Institute, 1958), *dhrupad* section, vv. 18-20, 29-30, 35, 40-44, 52-54, pp. 24-33. A few verses (e.g. v. 49, p. 32) have more political overtones, emphasising Shah Jahan's might. References are to this printed edition of the text except where otherwise indicated.

84 Ibid., *dhrupad* section, v. 14, p. 24. The expression *gāī nikāī* probably here means "well explained" (*"vistār ke sāth kahnā"* is one definition from the *Hindīśabdsāgar*, p. 1271), but the Hindi verb "gā-" also of course means to sing.

85 Sundar Kaviray, a *riti* poet (and diplomat) at Shah Jahan's court, distinguishes between an *anukūla* ("agreeable") and *dakṣina nāyaka* as follows: "An agreeable lover is unacquainted with other women even in his dreams; an adept lover looks upon all his women equally and remains constant so that all are happy"; *Sundarśṛṅgār*, in *Sundar kavirāy granthāvalī*, ed. by Ramanand Sharma (Delhi: Lok Vani Samsthan, 2004), v. 224.

86 Kavindracharya Sarasvati, *dhrupad* section, v. 20 (1958), p. 25. I emended from *nūpa* to *rūpa* (here and elsewhere I have also made a few other minor modifications in spelling, such as replacing *suṣa* with the more standard form *sukha*).

Here, as elsewhere, Kavindra uses the highly marked terms typical of *riti* poetry manuals for *mugdha* ("innocent" in the ways of love), *madhya* ("somewhat knowledgeable") and *praudha* ("mature") female characters.[87] Like many *dhrupads* composed for royal patrons, the composition is partly intended to be flattering—praise for the sexual charisma of kings surrounded by exquisitely beautiful women has a long history in India. But the insistence on *nayikabheda* terminology in Kavindra's *dhrupads* goes hand in hand with the polymathic brilliance on display in other songs. Thus a number of verses touch upon the science of gems.[88] Elsewhere it is Shah Jahan's musical expertise that is praised: he is *sura-jñān*, a connoisseur of melodies/notes.[89] It is not unheard of for *dhrupad* song collections to be quite broad in their range of topics, and some patrons were very well-versed in Indian music knowledge.[90] As Nalini Delvoye has noted:

> The various historical and cultural contexts in which those [*dhrupad*] songs were composed account for the variety of the themes dealt with in the *dhrupads* compiled in the main collections or recensions known to date. Besides religious and eulogistic subjects, *dhrupad* songs deal with a wide range of other topics such as *nayak-nayika bhed* (dealing with particular kinds of love and types of lovers in different circumstances), the description of nature and seasons, and philosophical or more personal views of life and

87 Ibid., vv. 31, 35-36, 38, pp. 28-30.

88 One verse refers to the traditional stipulation that *ratnas* or jewels total fourteen in number (v. 4); another extols Shah Jahan's throne (*takht*) with its costly gems (v.24); the next enumerates several types of jewels to praise Shah Jahan as exemplary in the Indic royal practice of *dana* or charity (v. 25). One of the manuscripts of the text from the Jaipur royal palace collection (Pothikhana) includes a short lesson on the science of gems that begins shortly after v. 25: this was omitted from the only published edition of the text (Chundavat, 1958). Some of the discussion is in Sanskrit, but the manuscript uses the abbreviations "bhā" and "pā" for Bhasha (i.e. Brajbhasha) and Parsi (i.e. Farsi or Persian), respectively, in order to signal equivalences across languages. Thus we are informed that the Persian word for *mānik*, ruby, is *yākūt*, etc. *Kavīndrakalpalatā*, Pothikhana, manuscript no. 1174, Maharaja Sawai Man Singh II Museum, Jaipur, ff. 18-21. Emma Flatt has pointed to a similar process of linguistic but also cultural translation in an astrology treatise from the Bijapur court authored by Sultan 'Ali Adil Shah (r.1557-1579). See 'The Authorship and Significance of the Nujūm al-'ulūm: A Sixteenth-century Astrological Encyclopedia from Bijapur', *Journal of the American Oriental Society* 131.2 (2011), 240-41.

89 Kavindracharya Sarasvati, *dhrupad* section, vv. 21, 34 (1958), pp. 25-26, 29.

90 Françoise "Nalini" Delvoye, 'Dhrupad Songs Attributed to Tānsen, Foremost Court-Musician of the Mughal Emperor Akbar', in *Studies in South Asian Devotional Literature*, ed. by Alan W. Entwistle and Françoise Mallison (New Delhi: Manohar, 1994), p. 413. On the Mughal nobility's mastery of Indian music as a *shastra*, see Katherine Schofield, 'Reviving the Golden Age Again: "Classicization", Hindustani Music, and the Mughals', *Ethnomusicology* 54.3 (2010), 484-517.

similar topics, which are roughly the same as those treated by Brajbhasha court poets for the same period.[91]

Kavindracharya was evidently keen to purvey information about Indian knowledge systems through the medium of *dhrupad*. Two songs in the *Kavīndrakalpalatā*, extensively laden with recondite terminology from the Nyaya and Vaisheshika schools of Indian philosophy, include such mouthfuls as *sapta padārtha* ("seven elements"), *ṣaṭ-bhāva* ("six states"), *catura abhāva* ("four absences"), *vyadhikarana* ("concomitance without co-existence"), and *upādhi binu vyāpati* ("invariable concomitance"). Imagine somebody in the Western tradition trying to sing Hegel! Both of the "philosophy" *dhrupads* praise Shah Jahan as "*mahājāna*" (supremely wise, suitably assonant with the emperor's name), and one of them concludes with the line, "the learned Shah Jahan knows all of the fine points (*bheda*, also "secrets") of these matters, the subtleties of the world".[92] A Sanskrit panegyric by one Purnananda Brahmacharin points to how Kavindracharya would regularly address the emperor on points of *shastra*.[93] The *tattvajñān* verse sequence that occurs later in the text, devoted to philosophical concerns, does suggest that the pandit gave some kind of Braj lectures on philosophy. A probable teacher-student relationship goes a long way towards explaining the two *dhrupads* focused on Indian philosophy and speaks to a concern with imparting knowledge of traditional Indian disciplines to the members of this Persianate court (see also Schofield in this volume).

The memorisation and oral transmission of knowledge have of course a very long history in India, and many Indian *shastras* bear mnemonic features.[94] At least some evidence suggests that elements of oral transmission even pertain to the written Brajbhasha poetry manuals characteristic of *riti* literary culture. The very structure of the *ritigranth* genre, which operates

91 Delvoye (1994), p. 412.

92 Kavindracharya Sarasvati, *dhrupad* section, vv. 33, 44 (1958), pp. 28-29, 31.

93 "*Dillīśvarasya nigamāgamaśāstrabudhyā sambodhayan pratidinam trijagatkavīndra*" (Kavindra, famous in the three worlds, would address the emperor every day on the wisdom of the *shastras*, Vedas, and ancillary texts). Cited in V. Raghavan, 'Kavīndrācārya Sarasvatī', in *D.R. Bhandarkar Volume*, ed. by Bimala Churn Law (Calcutta: Indian Research Institute, 1940), p. 161.

94 The *Nāṭyaśāstra*, for instance, contains some verses labeled *anuvaṃśya* or "passed down"; Bharata, *Nāṭyaśāstra*, ed. by K. Krishnamoorthy, 4th (revised) edn (Baroda: Oriental Institute, 1992), I, p. 308. Mark McClish and Patrick Olivelle have suggested that the *Arthaśāstra* owes its survival to its use in an educational setting. A redactor introduced "memorable" verses to make topics more teachable. Mark McClish and Patrick Olivelle, *The Arthaśāstra* (Indianapolis and Cambridge: Hackett Publishing Company, 2012), pp. xvi, xlii.

by first proposing a definition of a literary concept and then presenting a relevant example verse (the panegyric to Jahangir cited above was an illustration of the *ganana alankara* or trope of poetic enumeration), may owe something to the instructional practices of premodern Indian teachers. One important "performance" of a text like Keshavdas's *Kavipriyā* was probably for the poet's own students.[95] A favourite student singled out early in the work is Pravinray, one of the six *paturas* or courtesans who graced Raja Indrajit's assembly discussed above. The text is peppered with imperatives such as *sunahu* (listen!) and vocatives, including *prabina*, which may mean either "clever one" or, more likely, address Pravinray herself.[96] Keshavdas also enjoined his students to memorise his *Kavipriyā*.[97] Probably this was not mere hubris on the part of a poet since the sentiment is common enough.[98] As we have seen, a good command of the literary apparatus was a basic requirement of courtly connoisseurship and extemporaneous performance.

Although only the written traces survive, the practice of scholarship in early modern India would have been profoundly oral, interactive, and communicative. The *Jorāvarprakāś*, a commentary on Keshavdas's *Rasikpriyā* by the influential eighteenth-century Braj writer Surati Mishra, is set in the *praśnottarī* or "question and answer" format, itself suggestive of an oral environment in which the questions of a patron or student prompted the scholar to address particular issues.[99] Surati Mishra was also one of the leading scholars at a conference convened in Agra in 1737 that attracted literati from all over. The "proceedings" of the conference have come down to us in textual form in an unpublished work called *Sarasasāra*. In describing the "rationale for the book" (*granthakārana*), the compiler Ray Shivdas points to discussions among poets and singers:

---

95 Keshavdas explicitly mentions the reasons for composing his *ritigranth* in *Kavipriyā*, v. 3.1 (1954), p. 101: "So that boys and girls would understand the fathomless ways [of poetry composition]".

96 See, for instance, Keshavdas, *Kavipriyā*, vv. 3.14-15, 3.45, 6.14, ibid., pp. 103, 106, 119. Vocatives are a common occurrence in *ritigranths*.

97 'Wear my *Kavipriya* like a necklace (*kaṇṭhamālā*), by committing it to memory', ibid., v. 3.3, p. 101. There is a double entendre: the noun *kaṇṭha* means "neck", whereas *kaṇṭha kar-* is a verbal phrase meaning "to memorise".

98 See also Bhikharidas, an authority on Indian *alankarashasta* from the eighteenth century, *Kāvyanirṇay*, in *Bhikhārīdāsgranthāvalī*, ed. by Vishvanathprasad Mishra (Varanasi: Nagari Pracharini Sabha, 1957), Vol. 2, v. 1.9, p. 4.

99 Surati Mishra, *Jorāvarprakāś*, ed. by Yogendrapratap Singh (Allahabad: Sahitya Sammelan, 1992).

I will now tell (*kahata*) the rationale for the book,
listen carefully (*suniyauṃ cita lāi*)
to the way that we have stated new categories, applying our intellects.
Clever poets had heard (*sunai*) many individual poems and *dhrupads*
that engaged new categories of *nayakas* and *nayikas*.
They looked to the discussions of them in available books
and became aware of new categories that had never before been treated.[100]

Poets and singers had begun to notice literary schemes that were not covered by the existing books and thus resolved to draft a new *ritigranth* to update the categories. In other words, performance practice had the potential to affect theory.

That poetic theory was a source of public debate in literary salons is also confirmed by Azad Bilgrami in his *Ma'āsir-al kirām*, a rare Persian *tazkira* (see Pellò in this volume for the genre) that commemorates the achievements of both Persian and Hindi writers. In his entry on Diwan Sayyid Rahmatullah, the governor of Jajmau (near modern Kanpur), Azad recounts an incident that sheds further light on how concepts from *alankarashastra* were assumed knowledge in many early modern *mahfils* and not just for Hindu literati but also for Muslim poetry aficionados. One day, a student of the famous *riti* poet Chintamani Tripathi recited (or read[101]) a poem that was intended to illustrate the *ananvaya alankara*, a trope in which the object under consideration (*upameya*) is so spectacular as to brook no standard of comparison (*upamana*). The student's example verse was found wanting by the convener of the *mahfil*, Sayyid Rahmatullah, who ruled it an incorrect usage of this figure of speech.[102]

On the strength of this and other examples given here, knowledge of *alankarashastra* was available to the audiences of *mahfils* who listened to poetic performance. The main subjects of *ritigranths*, such as taxonomies

100 Note the emphasis on listening in lines one and three. *Sarasasāra*, Hindi Sahitya Sammelan, MS 2715/1492, folio 28, vv. 119-20 (my emendation, since two verses are mistakenly marked "119"). A related passage from this colophon is discussed in Busch (2011), pp. 197-98.

101 Ghulam Ali Azad Bilgrami, *Ma'āsir al-kirām* (Hyderabad: [n.p.], 1913), p. 364. Azad uses the verb *khwāndan*, which means both to read and to recite, an ambiguity that speaks eloquently about the tellings and texts problematic. The Sanskrit root *pāṭh-* (modern Hindi *paṛh-*) is similarly bivalent. Cf. Pollock (2006), p. 85 on the Sanskrit word *vācayati*, which "literally means to make [a text] speak".

102 The poem is about the beauty of the *nayika*'s eyes, which in keeping with the trope should have been compared with her own eyes. The inexperienced poet mistakenly uses the epithet "*mṛgākṣī*", "doe-eyed". A more extensive discussion of the passage is Busch (2011), pp. 154-56.

of figures of speech and different types of female characters, were not just the bookish learning of *pandits* (*pāṇḍitya-pradarśan*, as Hindi scholarship sometimes likes to put it), but the basis for energetic debates that were part of a rich performance culture.

## Conclusion

A close reading of diverse *riti* works uncovers numerous hints about performance in one of the least expected domains of Hindi literary culture that has today become synonymous with dry scholasticism and pedantry. In certain key respects, the stunning achievements of classical Hindi authors like Keshavdas or Surati Mishra are incomprehensible without understanding the degree to which the *riti* corpus was underwritten first and foremost by a *textual* engagement with the Sanskrit past. Moreover, the explosion in written documents during the early modern period means that much of Hindi literature—even the vaunted song texts of *bhakti* religiosity—was closely tied to manuscript culture. And yet understanding the dynamics of performance is critical even for formal written traditions like the *riti* styles cultivated by the higher echelons of literate society.

Performance leaves few written traces, posing a considerable challenge for literary historians. There are, thankfully, some exceptions, as when Keshavdas celebrates the brilliant *paturas* patronised by Indrajit, or Jayarama Pindye records the spectacle of Shahaji Bhonsle's court as each poet handles a challenging *samasya*.[103] One way around the paucity of specific records is to track the features of poems that especially mark them for oral delivery. We can learn to listen for the context. For instance, the virtuoso use of alliteration or a predilection for bardic styles in some texts is a good indication that they were probably appreciated in dramatic public presentations. Specific genres like the "chain of epithets" and praise poems

---

103 Doubtless there are still many untapped sources. A short manuscript from the royal palace library in Jaipur provides written evidence of *samasyapurti* poems by one Prananath Shrotriya, active during the late seventeenth century. It is just one of more than two dozen works attributed to him, quite a few evidently on *prastavik* ("occasional") themes that were inspired by specific requests. See Prannath Shrotriya, 'Basant kī khabari hai', Pothikhana, MS 3398 (4), Maharaja Sawai Man Singh II Museum, Jaipur; Gopalnarayan Bahura, *Literary Heritage of the Rulers of Amber and Jaipur with an Index to the Register of Manuscripts in the Pothikhana of Jaipur (I. Khasmohor collection)* (Jaipur: Maharaja Sawai Man Singh II Museum, 1976), pp. 314-15. Further written evidence of premodern *samasyapurti* competitions must still be available in manuscript collections, awaiting further research.

in the *muktaka* style are unthinkable without a listener on the receiving end. As with *dhrupad* songs, the patron, or, to use explicitly auditory language, addressee, is even signaled by his name.

Analogies between music and poetry, both staples of courtly assemblies, often prove instructive, which means we do well to study how poems behave like songs, or poets like musicians. Singers and poets alike drew on established repertoires. They shared a penchant for improvisation. They also transmitted knowledge to their patrons through performance. We discover that not just poetry but elements of *shastra* or formal works of Indian theory were read out loud and debated in *mahfil*s.

If we grant that patrons were not always silently reading a text (sometimes of course they were), then of necessity a *social* dimension enters into the experience. There is the social complexity of the patron-performer relationship, but also the collective participatory moment of the *mahfil* in which a work is vetted, where multiple listeners interact with a text at the same time. This was a world of listeners *and* readers. Sometimes listeners and readers were one and the same. For instance, a king might enjoy a lively performance in his court and also engage in private perusal of a work (many early modern kings had libraries). But sometimes listeners may not have been readers, particularly in a multilingual environment with various language capacities in play. This raises the possibility that what was a written literary document for some communities was experienced as an auditory culture by others.

A surprising number of Brajbhasha and even some Sanskrit works can be linked to Mughal settings, and yet it is not clear that the patrons always read them.[104] Possibly some works were experienced as tellings, since the dissemination of the *riti* literary ethos did not depend on an exclusively written engagement. Hundreds of poetry manuals were produced in early modern India, and the manuscript tradition is robust, as I have stressed. But evidence does suggest that they may have been experienced in, or in some cases sparked by, oral contexts.

Did the Persianate Mughal emperors access Brajbhasha poetry by listening or by *reading*, by a telling or a text? The *Jahāngīrjascandrikā* is

104 Audrey Truschke (2012), pp. 70-81 discusses the complexities of the Mughal reception of texts in Sanskrit, a language the emperors did not know. Since they did know Hindi, perhaps they partially understood some Sanskrit; possibly a Hindi translator helped to mediate the text; in some cases Mughal elites (such as 'Abd al-Rahim Khan-i Khanan) were linguistically proficient and would have been able to understand; other texts might have served more as symbolic objects.

framed as a sermon by Keshavdas to Rahim's son Iraj Shahnavaz Khan, and the poet claims that he presented the work to the emperor, though nobody claims that Jahangir read it. Emperor Muhammad Shah (r.1719-1748) once gave Surati Mishra an audience at his court and the poet presented several verses to him.[105] Were they also available to him as texts? It was certainly common for Persianate emperors and the Mughal nobility to have considerable cultural competency in local knowledge systems—literature among them—but one can readily access a literary tradition without reading.[106]

When we measure texts and readership in terms of a manuscript census, looking for both quantity and indications of script communities, we may vastly underestimate the number of users of a text. A collection of praise poems may exist in a single manuscript at a single court. Some poetry manuals survive in relatively few numbers. As evident from the case of the Braj couplet that was presented in the assembly of Diwan Rahmatullah, reading was in some cases a public performance and thus may not necessarily leave written traces. Clearly much work remains to reconstruct the experiences of Indian literary life in the pre-print era. We come closer the more we learn to factor in both "tellings" and "texts".

---

105 A few details are Yogendrapratap Singh, 'Bhūmikā', in *Jorāvarprakāś* (Allahabad: Hindi Sahitya Sammelan, 1992), pp. 8-9.

106 See Sudipta Kaviraj, 'The Two Histories of Literary Culture in Bengal', in *Literary Cultures in History*, ed. by Sheldon Pollock (Berkeley and Los Angeles: University of California Press, 2003), p. 511 (here drawing on Bhudev Mukhopadhyay's distinction between spoken language and intelligible language).

# 10. Reading the Acts and Lives of Performers in Mughal Persian Texts

*Sunil Sharma*

In classical Persian literary culture, despite the primacy of the written word, the recitation of texts was as important, if not more so, than reading books. Extemporaneous or rehearsed performances of verses in a *musha'ira* (poetry contest), declamation of formal *qasidas* in a courtly setting, and listening to tales in prose or in mixed forms were part and parcel of the lives of rulers, princes, and courtiers. And although participation in literary activities, including the recitation of poetry, was part of the accomplishments of every educated person, there were various classes of professionals associated with poetry. On the highest level were the professional court poets who composed verses, and then, with some overlap, there was a special professional class of people whose oral skills were prized for various reasons, whether for their mellifluous voice, physical beauty, place of origin, or connection to powerful people. At the most formal level, court poets continued the age-old tradition of composing and declaiming long panegyrics (*qasidas*) in praise of the sultan or another highly placed patron, often on festive occasions such as 'Id al-fitr and Nawroz or to mark a military victory. Poets who were gifted declaimed their own laudatory poems, while some would have their poems read by a professional declaimer (*ravi*). To mark other special events such as births, deaths, completion of buildings, etc., poets composed poems containing chronograms (*tarikhs*), or just the chronogram itself, that may have been part of an oral culture as well.

In studying the topic of orality in early Mughal Persian culture, the influence of the earlier Timurid forms of literary production is discernable

 http://dx.doi.org/10.11647/OBP.0062.10

in the way texts were produced and performed at court. Local performative practices, especially in the fields of music, dance, and Hindi, Urdu, and Persian poetry, gradually became an essential part of this repertoire.[1] While textual sources, and to some extent the visual archive in the form of paintings from manuscripts,[2] provide us with details about the setting and performers of texts, it is also possible to piece together information about both the normative and experiential aspects of oral culture through the lives of the people who were involved in these activities, whether they were patrons and listeners, or poets and performers. My focus here will be to read the fragmentary information about these lives within the larger context of the Mughal Persian literary culture of the sixteenth and seventeenth centuries in an effort to improve our understanding of the place and the range of oral performance and oral performers of Persian literature at court, and at times beyond it.

Already Amir 'Unsur al-Ma'ali Kay Kavus (d.1098), in his eleventh-century *Mirror for Princes*, *Qābūsnāma*, discusses the subject of the oral culture of texts in some detail. Although dating from an early period in Northern Iran, this influential work offers insight into the normative rules on oral culture that also apply to courtly Persianate societies of later times. In chapters 35-38, the duties of a poet, musician, courtier, and boon companion are described, since all poets were ideally expected to be able to supply material for conversation and quotation. To the poet the author

1 My study is limited to the courtly culture of the sixteenth and seventeenth centuries for the reason that there was a major shift in practice of oral texts in the late seventeenth century. I refer at the end to the eighteenth-century *Muraqqa'-yi Dihlī*, a unique work that contains biographies of singers and performers of mid-eighteenth century Mughal Delhi, seen from the point of view of the author, Dargah Quli Khan, a visitor from the Deccan. The change from earlier sources is that the descriptions of performances are now largely non-courtly and the settings much more socially diverse, suggesting that a new audience of townsmen and bourgeois gentlemen had emerged by the eighteenth century. In her study on this period, Katherine Schofield's remarks on the musical *mahfil* have some bearing for the transformation in the culture of poetic performances in general, as when she draws attention to "the changed relationship between patron and musician in one of the most exclusive of Mughal male social spaces, the princely mehfil"; Katherine Butler Brown (now Schofield), 'If Music be the Food of Love: Masculinity and Eroticism in the Mughal *Mehfil*', in *Love in South Asia: A Cultural History*, ed. by F. Orsini (Cambridge: Cambridge University Press, 2006), p. 65.

2 Many such visual representations of performances and performers from the Mughal period can be found in Bonnie Wade, *Imaging Sound: An Ethnomusicological Study of Music, Art and Culture in Mughal India* (Chicago: University of Chicago Press, 1998). Women are mostly absent in these sources except as dancers, but their participation as poets and performers emerges in the eighteenth-century sources.

advises, "Learn anecdotes, rare quips and amusing tales in abundance, and repeat them to your patron".[3] To the musician he says, "[E]xert yourself to become a *raconteur*; by telling a number of stories, witticisms and jests you can rest yourself and diminish the strain of minstrelsy"; he adds that "minstrels are rhapsodists for poets in general and not mere reciters of their own verse".[4] In connection with the duties of a boon companion, the author cautions, "[Y]ou should be a *raconteur*, retaining in your memory a large number of anecdotes, jests and clever witticisms; a boon companion without stories and quips is imperfectly equipped".[5] These statements illustrate the pervasiveness of the spoken word in daily courtly life, and in multilingual Persianate societies the complexities of interaction would have increased significantly due to individuals from different social groups with differing artistic preferences and knowledge of Persian.

Closer in time to the Mughals, in a normative work from the late Timurid period by Husain Va'iz Kashifi (d.1504), the *Futuwat-nāma-yi Sulṭānī*, the author prescribes both reading and listening to stories as beneficial activities for people in general.[6] In a section of the chapter on the class of eloquent men (*maddāḥān* and *ghurra-khwānān*), Kashifi prescribes rules to professional performers for the recitation of both prose and poetic works.[7] Kashifi avers that the purpose of reading and listening to stories about the past is didactic. In terms of delivery, the author recommends a modulated approach to reciting works so that they are pleasing, comprehensible, and captivating. The short prescriptive guidelines, although written in a sufi milieu, would also have ramifications for Mughal courtly culture and can help us better understand the state of oral literary culture in sixteenth- and seventeenth-century Agra, Delhi, and Lahore.

3 Kay Kavus, *A Mirror for Princes, The Qābūs nāma*, trans. by Reuben Levy (New York: E.P. Dutton, 1951), p. 185.

4 Ibid., p. 187.

5 Ibid., p. 198.

6 Husayn Va'iz Kashifi, *The Royal Book of Spiritual Chivalry (Futūwat nāmah-yi sulṭānī)*, trans. by Jay R. Crook (Chicago: Great Books of the Islamic World, 2000). For a practitioner's manual on storytelling, see Khan's essay in this volume on 'Abd al-Nabi Fakhr al-Zamani's *Ṭīrāz al-akhbār*, dating from Emperor Jahangir's time (r.1605-1628).

7 Kashifi (2000), pp. 296-98. In a more courtly milieu and in earlier times, the role of the storyteller "was significantly different from that of the poet and the minstrel.... He was not allowed to perform on formal occasions, in which the poet and minstrel played important parts. The storyteller neither recited poetry nor sang songs, which was done by the minstrel. Instead, his principal duties consisted of telling, by implication, prose stories in the evening and delivering messages", Kumiko Yamamoto, *The Oral Background of Persian Epics: Storytelling and Poetry* (Leiden: Brill, 2003), p. 56.

The brief biographical notices of professionals in various artistic fields in the Mughal period suggest that in fact Persian court poets often did double or triple duty as musicians, storytellers, and calligraphers (see also Pellò in this volume). Biographical dictionaries (*tazkiras*) from the Timurid, Safavid, and Mughal periods attest to the widespread practice of composing poetry across social and communal groups in the Persianate realm.[8] Paul Losensky has noted the wider social spread of Persian poetry in the fifteenth century and the importance of multi-talented poets:

> The sociological growth of poetry begun in the Timurid-Turkmen period continued unabated in the following two and a half centuries of Safavid and Mughal rule [...] Private homes, *khanqahs* and mosques, small shops in the bazaar and, in Safavid times, coffeeshops all served as forums for this new class of poets. [...] This new popularity of poetry among craftsmen and shopkeepers was matched by a widespread and burgeoning enthusiasm for writing verse at all levels of court society. Some knowledge of literature and an ability to improvise a few verses had long been a desirable talent among the king's boon companions (*nudamā*), but in Timurid-Turkmen times fluency in the poetic tradition became one of the expected accomplishments of any member of the court. We thus find numerous artists and artisans attached to the court—engravers, calligraphers, and musicians—who also achieved recognition as poets. Professional poets conversely were often noted for their competence in other art forms.[9]

But if it was true that every person educated in Persian was also a part-time poet, it would have been a smaller number who would have been active as professional poets, and what was true for Safavid Iran, where Persian was not only an elite language, may not have been true of Mughal India, where Persian always remained a learnt language.

What is also apparent is that performers who may not have been part of the elite Persophone element at court, i.e. Indians rather than Central Asians or Iranians, were only cursorily mentioned by Mughal Persian writers, perhaps because their accomplishments were not sufficiently of interest for an audience in the larger Persianate world, in an elitist cultural milieu where place of origin and the register of language used were prized attributes. In the *Ā'īn-i Akbarī*, the historian and biographer of the Emperor Akbar (r.1556-1605), Abu'l Fazl, writes that there were Indians, Iranians,

8 Paul Losensky discusses some of these in detail in his book, *Welcoming Fighani: Imitation, Influence, and Literary Change in the Persian Ghazal, 1480-1680* (Costa Mesa, CA: Mazda, 1993).

9 Ibid., pp. 138-39.

Turanian, and Kashmiris, both men and women, among the musicians at court. He provides a list of thirty-six male musicians (*khunyāgarān*), twenty of whom sing (*gūyanda*) or chant (*khwānanda*), or do both.[10] Twenty-three among the singers in Abu'l Fazl's list were of Indian origin (from Gwalior, Dhar, Agra, Multan, and Malwa), six from Khorasan (Herat, Mashhad), and one was a Qipchaq. No biographical account of them is provided here, although people like Miyan Tansen and Baz Bahadur were well-known figures of the time.

The place of origin of these individuals was important because, as the Safavid historian Iskandar Munshi in *'Ālamārā-yi 'Abbāsī* writes, "the best singers came from Iraq and the best chanters from Khorasan".[11] It is likely that to a certain extent the same value was attached to these places in Mughal India, especially since native speakers were considered the arbiters of Persian usage. The poet Liva'i Pirzada-yi Sabzavari is an example of someone who both sang and chanted. He is also mentioned by 'Abd al-Qadir Bada'uni in the *Muntakhab al-tavārikh* as being "peerless in the valley of song and chanting" [*dar vādī-i naghma u surūd bī-'adīl būd*].[12] As the name of this singer indicates, Sabzavari was of Iranian stock, and being from the Persian heartland probably helped raise his position among the ranks of singers.

## Storytelling and Storytellers

Mughal sources inform us that the Emperor Akbar was fond of listening to all kinds of stories, whether of Islamic-Persian or Indian origins, and he was also somewhat of a storyteller himself. In discussing his library, Abu'l Fazl notes that books in Hindavi, Persian, Greek, Kashmiri, and Arabic, in both prose and poetry formed part of the royal library:

> From day to day experts present books to the emperor who hears every book from beginning to end. Every day he marks the spot where they have reached with his pearl-strewing pen. He rewards the readers with gold and silver according to the number of pages read. There are few well-known books that are not read in the royal assembly. Which are the ancient stories

10 Abu'l Fazl, *Ā'īn-i Akbarī*, ed. by Sir Sayyid Ahmad Khan (reprint, Aligarh: Aligarh Muslim University, 2005), p. 251.

11 Iskandar Munshi, *History of Shah 'Abbas the Great, Tārīk-e Ālamārā-ye 'Abbāsī*, trans. by Roger M. Savory (Boulder: Westview Press, 1978), Vol. 1, p. 281.

12 'Abd al-Qadir Bada'uni, *Muntakhab al-tavārīkh*, ed. by Maulvi Ahmad 'Ali Sahib and Taufiq Subhani (Tehran: Anjuman-i Asar va Mafakhir-i Farhangi, 2000-2001), p. 219.

> (*dāstānhā-yi bāstānī*), curiosities of science (*gharā'ib-i 'ulūm*), or fine points of philosophy (*navādir-i ḥikam*), which the leader of wise men does not appreciate? He does not tire of hearing a book again and again, but listens with great interest. The *Akhlāq-i Nāṣirī* [by Tusi], the *Kīmiyā-yi sa'ādat* [by Ghazzali], the *Qābūsnāma*, the letters of Sharaf Maneri, the *Gulistān* [by Sa'di], the *Ḥadīqa* by Hakim Sana'i, the *Maṣnavī-i ma'navī* [by Rumi], the *Jām-i jam* [by Auhadi], the *Būstān* [by Sa'di], the *Shāhnāma* [by Firdausi], the *khamsa* of Shaikh Nizami, the *kullīyāt*s of [Amir] Khusrau and Maulana Jami, the *dīvān*s of Khaqani, Anvari, and other history books are read out to him.[13]

This canonical list of classical Persian prose and poetic works, however, reads remarkably like a curriculum of a Persian literature programme of study, and it is through listening to these texts that Akbar sought to educate himself and the court. If it was true that Akbar was illiterate, it would explain why he was fond of *listening* to this broad range of classical Persian texts. In the *Akbarnāma*, Abu'l Fazl states that, "Among books of poetry, he recites Rumi's *Maṣnavī* and Hafiz's *divan* fluently and finds pleasure in their meaningful and enjoyable aspects".[14]

Not all the books on this list would have been conducive to reading aloud, nor were they usually used in that way. Works like the *Shāhnāma* and the *Gulistān* were meant to be read aloud in sections, though their orality was accompanied by an equal value placed on these works as books, and it was usually through the copying and use of manuscripts of these texts that they were transmitted with the seals of the members of the royal family and nobility. As we shall see below, in the Mughal context storytelling, poetic recitation, and discussion also functioned as forms of re-enacting and validating the canon in the face of new literary developments and challenges, especially when it came to poetry.

One of Akbar's favourite stories was the popular romance (*dastan*) of Amir Hamza, the uncle of the prophet Muhammad, which also enjoyed immense popularity in Urdu literary culture in later centuries. Such tales provided entertainment not only when the court was in residence in the capital city, but also while it was on the move. Abu'l Fazl writes that after a hunting expedition in Malwa in 1564, "for the sake of delight and pleasure he [Akbar] listened for some time to Darbar Khan's recital of the story of

13 *Ā'īn-i Akbarī* (2005), p. 96. All translations in this paper are mine unless otherwise indicated in the bibliographic reference.

14 Abu'l Fazl, *Akbarnāma*, ed. by Agha Ahmad Ali and Maulawi Abd-ur-Rahim (Calcutta: Asiatic Society of Bengal, 1873), Vol. 1, p. 271.

Amir Hamza".[15] Akbar is said to have been so fond of this text that "inside the palace he even recited it in the style of the storytellers".[16] It was the extreme enjoyment of the emperor in listening to and performing this narrative work that led to the production of a lavishly illustrated manuscript of the *Hamzanāma*.[17] The extremely large paintings from this manuscript attest to their use in performances of the text, in which the pictures functioned as visual aids. In a study on oral aspects of Persian *dastans*, Julia Rubanovich concludes that such stories "were composed in writing by authors who were part and parcel of the world of medieval literacy".[18] Thus, in all aspects of the production and performance of stories, certain literary standards had to be met.

Akbar's pleasure in listening to the recitation of the adventurous tales from the *Hamzanāma* would have been enhanced by the performance of the reciter, Mulla 'Inayat Darbar Khan, whose biography was later recorded in the eighteenth-century biographical dictionary of Mughal nobles, *Ma'āṣir al-'umarā* by Shahnavaz Khan. Shahnavaz Khan writes that the emperor "favoured literary gatherings" [*tavajjuh bi-majālis būd*], but apparently those where storytelling was the chief entertainment rather than *musha'iras*. His biographical account of Darbar Khan stressed the lineage and status of the storyteller-cum-courtier, and the remarkable closeness he enjoyed with the emperor:

> Darbar Khan: Inayat-fam, son of the story-teller (*qiṣṣa-khwān*) Taklu Khan, who was specialised in story-telling in the service of the Safavid Shah Tahmasp [r.1525-1576] and was the object of a variety of royal favours. When his son entered India he distinguished himself in the same hereditary manner by the fortune of intercourse in the service of the felicitous 'Arsh Ashiyani [Akbar]. He was rewarded with a *mansab* of 700 and the title of Darbar Khan. In the fourteenth year after the victory of Ranthambor, when the emperor

15 Abu'l Fazl, *Akbarnāma*, ed. by Agha Ahmad Ali and Maulawi Abd-ur-Rahim (Calcutta: Asiatic Society of Bengal, *Akbarnāma*, 1881), Vol. 2, p. 223.

16 *"hattā kih khvud andarūn-i maḥal bi-ṭaur-i qiṣṣa-khvānān mīguft"*, Shahnavaz Khan, *Ma'āṯhir al-umarā*, ed. by Maulvi 'Abd al-Rahim (Calcutta: Asiatic Society of Bengal, 1888), Vol. 2, p. 2.

17 For the Mughal manuscript of this work, see John Seyller, *The Adventures of Hamza: Painting and Storytelling in Mughal India* (Washington, DC: Smithsonian Institution, 2002). Shahnavaz Khan (1888, p. 3) goes on to describe the production of this sumptuous volume.

18 Julia Rubanovich, 'Tracking the *Shahnama* Tradition in Medieval Persian Folk Prose', in *Shahnama Studies II: The Reception of Firdausi's* Shahnama, ed. by Charles Melville and Gabrielle van den Berg (Leiden: Brill, 2012), p. 660.

> left for pilgrimage of the shrine at the Dar al-Khair Ajmer, due to a severe illness Darbar Khan left for the Dar al-Khilafa Agra. Upon reaching there he quit the mortal world. Since 'Arsh Ashiyani was very attentive towards him he was greatly saddened.[19]

The account goes on to narrate that in his will Darbar Khan asked to be buried near the tomb of Akbar's faithful dog, who had predeceased him, thus indicating the high degree of intimacy between him and the emperor that would not have been possible for all literati at court. Darbar Khan's authentic credentials as a native speaker of Persian, as an Iranian, and as the son of someone who had served the Safavid ruler as reciter would certainly have elevated him above others and helped him obtain his position at Akbar's court, and it was thus that he came to be included in a biographical dictionary of nobles.

From the early Mughal period we encounter the names of at least two other such storytellers, Iskandar of Iraq and Mir Muhammad Hashim of Badakhshan, whose lives are recorded in the biographical section of 'Abd al-Baqi Nihavandi's *Ma'āṣir-i Raḥīmī*, a work completed in 1616 for his patron, the Mughal general 'Abd al-Rahim Khan-i Khanan. Nihavandi describes the Khan-i Khanan's interest in storytelling in several languages: "He also knows the stories and traditions of the Turks better than those people such that he likes to listen to tales and stories to induce sleep; sometimes they are recited in his presence in Turki, sometimes in Hindi, sometimes in Persian".[20] A portion of this work recorded the lives of notables in Mughal service, including religious men and poets.[21] The reason that notices of the lives of the two storytellers, *qissa-khwan* and *afsana-gu* respectively, made it into this work is because they were also professional poets. Nihavandi writes thus about Hashim:

> Mir Muhammad Hashim, the storyteller (*qiṣṣa-khwān*): His lineage is from the exalted *sayyids* of Badakhshan. He was adorned with perfect talent and

19 Shahnavaz Khan (1888), Vol. 2, pp. 1-2.

20 'Abd al-Baqi Nihavandi, *Ma'āṣir-i Raḥīmī*, ed. by M. Hidayat Husain (Calcutta: Asiatic Society of Bengal, 1925), Vol. 2, pp. 590-91.

21 The biographical part of the work was published in a new edition recently. John Seyller's point about artists' biographies in this work also extends to those of performers, "'Abd al-Bāqī often indicates an area of expertise within a particular field—especially in calligraphy—but never cites distinctive qualities of the individual's work, let alone specific examples. Indeed, the second-hand nature of most of his information is highlighted by his eagerness to corroborate his statements with his own personal testimony whenever possible"; Seyller (2002), p. 53. This is characteristic of many kinds of *tazkiras* from this period.

> used the pen-name "Muhtaram". He is a peerless storyteller of and also has complete mastery in poetry. In the time when this general of kingly qualities was occupied with the conquest of Gujarat and lived in that province, he [Hashim] was appointed in his retinue of slaves and servants. For a long time Mulla Mulhami Shirazi, one of the special attendants of the general, used to say that the Mir was in the service of the lofty and victorious cavalry for ten years, and according to some reports another eight years in this person's service. He was a panegyrist, storyteller, master of the stables (*'alūfa*) and *jāgīrdār*. Now in the year 1024 (1615) he is in Golconda.[22]

This account shows a remarkable degree of social mobility for someone who was a poet and entertainer in the first place, but his social background played clearly to his advantage in furthering his career. This is also seen in the case of the biographical sketch of the second performer, Iskandar, who was in the service of Emperor Jahangir:

> Iskandar the storyteller is from Iraq and is said to be among the eloquent and sweet-tongued. He recites (*mīkhwānad*) and performs (*adā mīnumāyad*) old stories and fictional tales (*bāstānī qiṣṣa-hā va afsāna-hā-yi ghair-i vāqi'ī*) written by men of good temperament and taste in such a way puts on airs that he is praised by experts and literati. Out of the delicacy of his nature and personal poise, he also displays finesse in his poetic style. Every time that he engages in wonderful innovations he does not refrain from his own sayings and embellishes with other styles as well. Presently he has the high-ranking position of candle and lamp of the Emperor Nur al-Din Muhammad Jahangir. He considers himself one of the panegyrists and well-wishers of the general and is said to have composed lustrous verses in praise of him.[23]

In all three cases the storytellers hailed from the central Iranian heartland, with their credentials as native Persian speakers in their favour.[24] One can infer that it was facility with the language that was a selling point rather than simply pronunciation, but a native speaker's authority was certainly something that native Persian speakers would have exploited. This is a compelling argument in light of the fact that, as far as the textual evidence shows, no other individual, especially of Indian origin, was accorded

---

22 'Abd al-Baqi (1931), Vol. 3, pp. 1004-05.

23 Ibid., p. 1242.

24 On the subject of native speakers of Persian at the Mughal court, see Muzaffar Alam, 'The Pursuit of Persian: Language in Mughal Politics', *Modern Asian Studies* 32.2 (1998), 341. Jean Calmard mentions the "unidirectional flow" of such professionals at this time, 'Safavid-Persia in Indo-Persian Sources and in Timurid-Mughal Perception', in *The Making of Indo-Persian Culture: Indian and French Studies*, ed. by Muzaffar Alam, Françoise "Nalini" Delvoye, and Marc Gaborieau (New Delhi: Manohar, 2000), p. 355.

such honours. In both the cases he mentions, the biographer Nihavandi recorded their original compositions in Persian and highlighted their role primarily as panegyric poets (*maddahan*) in the service of the emperor and of his own patron, the Khan-i Khanan. As with Darbar Khan, in the *tazkiras* these two storytellers appear as professional poets first, though their skill at storytelling was clearly much prized by the Mughal court.

## Recitation and Narrative Texts

When it came to poetic texts, it seems that portions of long narrative poems were frequently recited aloud, but actually we know less about the use of narrative *masnavis* in an oral context, apart from those mentioned by Abu al-Fazl as Akbar's favourite works. The fact that many Mughal poets, especially during Shah Jahan's period (r.1628-1656), wrote short topical poems in this form suggests that they were meant to be recited, and that these poems gradually replaced the ceremonial *qasida* as the traditional poetic form to mark formal occasions.

As for the *Shāhnāma*, whereas in Safavid Iran *shahnama-khwans* were a popular sub-group of storytellers,[25] in North India reading parts of the epic rather than reciting it seemed to be the prevalent practice. In Iran, professional reciters of the epic summarised the most dramatic parts, such as the feats of the hero Rustam, in their own words with occasional and appropriate quotations from Firdausi's original text. In the Iranian lands

25 "The real flourishing of storytelling as an art of entertainment came in the Safavid period... here we see a more obvious mingling of the courtly and common threads of storytelling", Mary E. Page, '*Naqqāli and Ferdowsi: Creativity in the Iranian National Tradition*' (PhD dissertation, University of Pennsylvania, 1977), p. 128, quoted in Karin Rührdanz, 'About a Group of Truncated *Shāhnāmas*: A Case Study in the Commercial Production of Illustrated Manuscripts in the Second Part of the Sixteenth Century', *Muqarnas* 14 (1997), 119, who discusses the influence of oral narratives on textual production and illustration of manuscripts. Also see Yamamoto (2003), pp. 20-28, for the practice of storytelling and coffeehouses; she writes, "Little research has been done on the social background of the storytellers. In general, they came from the middle to lower classes" (p. 23). Rubanovich's study of the use of the epic in folk literature is enlightening; she cautions, "in contrast to the court literature, the fortunes of the *Shahnama* in medieval Persian folk literature remain elusive and neglected. Generalised assertions as to the epic's broad popularity in oral tradition are based mainly on scant and mostly oblique references to *shahnama-khvans* and *shahnama-khvani* in medieval sources and do not take into account the diachronic development of the reception of the *Shahnama*"; (2012), p. 11.

Firdausi's epic carried connotations of national identity, while in Mughal India the *Shāhnāma* probably never had the same cultural associations for Indian audiences as the *Rāmāyaṇa* and *Mahābhārata* did. Tales from the *Shāhnāma* may have been read as a standard classical text, and perhaps occasionally performed as a form of entertainment, but not as a national epic. Several condensed versions of the *Shāhnāma* appeared in Mughal India in a mixed prose and verse (prosimetrum) form that included the heroic stories popular in India but excluded the more obscure historical parts.[26]

But the *Shāhnāma* also acted as a template, and imitations of Firdausi's epic were produced by court poets in India who replaced the epic heroes with contemporary figures.[27] A poet named Manzari Samarqandi composed one the many pseudo-*Shāhnāmas*, i.e. a continuation or imitation of Firdausi's poem, on the battle between Sikandar Sur and the Mughals. Bada'uni tells us that the general Bairam Khan suggested some corrections be made to the text, which is not extant, and in one night the poet revised the poem of 300-400 couplets and in the morning recited it in an assembly.[28] The Emperor Shah Jahan was particularly interested in literary works that included contemporary history, and his court poets produced at least two *Shāhnāma*-like epics to honour him, parts of which may have been read aloud at court.

Due to its mystical contents and its appeal to a more universally Muslim audience, Jalaluddin Rumi's *Maṡnavī-yi ma'navī* was known in Mughal India across multiple social levels. According to Annemarie Schimmel, Indo-Persian works "contain much information about famous *mathnavi-khwāns* who excelled in the recitation of Rumi's verses. Among them we may mention a certain Sayyid Sa'dollah Purabi (d.1726) who wrote a *resāla-ye chehel beyt-e Mathnavi*".[29] The Emperor Aurangzeb's

---

26 See Brittany Payeur, 'The Lilly Shamshir Khani in a Franco-Sikh Context: A Non-Islamic "Islamic" Manuscript', in *The Islamic Manuscript Tradition: Ten Centuries of Book Arts in Indiana University Collections*, ed. by Christiane Gruber (Bloomington: Indiana University Press, 2009), pp. 221-48; and Pasha M. Khan, 'Marvelous Histories: Reading the *Shāhnāmah* in India', *Indian Economic and Social History Review* 49.4 (2012), 527-56.

27 See Sunil Sharma, 'Amir Khusraw and the Genre of Versified History', *Comparative Studies of South Asia, Africa and the Middle East* 22.1 (2003), 112-18.

28 Bada'uni (2000-2001), Vol. 3, p. 233.

29 Annemarie Schimmel, *The Triumphal Sun: A Study of the Works of Jalaloddin Rumi* (Albany: State University of New York Press, 1993), p. 377.

(r.1658-1707) fondness for Rumi's *Masnavī* is mentioned in an anecdote involving the Qadiri sufi Mulla Shah Badakhshi (d.1661), who fell out of favour with the emperor for having been closely associated with his rival Dara Shikoh.[30] Although such anecdotal evidence suggests that Rumi's work was occasionally recited in both courtly and non-courtly settings, among the larger populace it was, like other *masnavis*, probably more part of a reading culture than an oral one.[31] In the end, there is not sufficient evidence to explore this issue in depth.

Much more is known about the performance of the *ghazal*, the privileged poetic form of the sixteenth and seventeenth centuries, whose recitation and practice were not limited to elite gatherings and included alternative settings such as gatherings of sufis, women, and general townspeople. As mentioned above, the fifteenth and sixteenth centuries witnessed a large-scale broadening of the literary communities, with poets emerging from all classes of society. This is specifically linked to the rise of the *ghazal* genre, as Losensky explains:

> The social spread of poetry, for example, is generally accounted to be a major factor in the rapidly growing popularity of the ghazal. The lyric was *the* genre of choice of the new class of amateur poets, among both the urban classes and courtiers, and makes up the bulk of poetic citations found in the tazkirahs. The panegyric qasidah was too closely associated with courtly politics and ritual to have much appeal outside of this context, while the narrative masnavi was usually too lengthy for the literary assemblies in which most poetry was now presented and received. For the most part, the ghazal does not demand the time or leisure required by the other major genres.[32]

Mughal sources mention a few examples of this social spread of poetry (see Pellò in this volume), but these are fewer than in Iran and Central Asia.

30 "Kabil Khan [Shaikh Abu al-Fath, *munshī al-mamālik*], one of his [Mulla Shah's] friends, said to him one day, 'Formerly our sovereign Aurangzeb loved to listen to discourses on the subject of mysticism, and I have often had the honour of reading before him passages from the Masnavi of Jalaluddin Rumi. The Emperor was often so touched by them that he shed tears; certainly when he comes to Lahore he will wish to see you'. 'No', replied Mullah Shah; 'we shall never see him…'"; Claud Field, *Mystics and Saints of Islam* (London: F. Griffiths, 1910), p. 64.

31 For the larger subject of the reception of Rumi's works in India, see Franklin Lewis, *Rumi, Past and Present, East and West: The Life, Teaching and Poetry of Jalāl al-Din Rumi* (Oxford: Oneworld, 2000), p. 470.

32 Losensky (1993), p. 142.

One poet with a direct link to the old culture of Timurid Herat, Qasim Kahi (d.1580), the last disciple of the great poet-mystic Jami (d.1492), was brought to Delhi by the Emperor Humayun (r.1530-1540, 1555-1556). Bada'uni did not approve of the poet's antinomian ways and association with dervishes, courtesans, and especially dogs, and accused him of plagiarising ideas from other poets. But he records that Kahi wrote on music and sang in a good voice, so that some lines of his *ghazals* became the rage and were recited in assemblies.[33]

Despite the popularity of the *ghazal* form, the social origins of the *ghazal* poet were as important as his poetic talent, especially if he planned to gain access to royal courts and generous patrons. In Pritchett's words, "the whole interlocked literary culture of ustad, shagird, and mushairah documented in the tazkirahs was primarily devoted to the cultivation of the *ghazal* as an elite oral performance genre".[34] Thus, Bada'uni notes that the poet Qasim 'Ali "Ghubari", who was very handsome and used to sing at social gatherings and had pretensions to be a Quraishi, used to be embarrassed that his father was a grocer.[35] Social mobility and the importance of lineage are both in evidence here, in mutual tension.

Thus poetic assemblies or *musha'iras* were the occasions for complex forms of social interaction. As Pritchett puts it, they "were not only complex competitive arenas and technical workshops but hothouses of gossip and general social rivalry as well".[36] In addition, "[i]mpromptu composition was highly valued, and many opportunities were available for the poet to show his skill".[37] A single line from a *ghazal* would suffice as the text for an entire performance and give pleasure to its listeners, some of whom would remember and record it in their notebooks. At least from the eleventh century onwards Persian *ghazals* were performed in sufi

33 Bada'uni (2000-2001), pp. 120-23. Of another poet, Bahram 'Saqqa', a disciple of Shaikh Muhammad Khabhushani, Bada'uni writes that he would wander the streets of Agra with his disciples, giving water to the thirsty as he recited verses. He compiled several of his *divans* but when he was overcome by religious ecstasy (*jazba*) he would wash the pages of his notebooks one by one (p. 168).

34 Frances Pritchett, 'A Long History of Urdu Literary Culture, Part 2', in *Literary Cultures in History: Reconstructions from South Asia*, ed. by Sheldon Pollock (Berkeley: University of California Press, 1993), p. 905.

35 Bada'uni (2000-2001), p. 198.

36 Pritchett (1993), p. 894.

37 Ibid., p. 899; see also Busch in this volume.

*khanqahs*, and in the case of Amir Khusrau (d.1325) the same poem could be courtly or mystical depending on the context of its performance.[38]

## Singing Verses, Discussing Poetry

Whereas his father had been fond of listening to stories, Jahangir seemed to have been particularly fond of *ghazal* performances.[39] Anecdotes relating to them show that even as the *majlis* served as the social backdrop for the recitation of poems, mainly of classical poets, it was here that a negotiation over the value of individual poets took place. In his *Majālis-i Jahāngīrī*, a detailed and intimate record of sessions with the emperor dating from 2 November 1608 to 24 November 1611, 'Abd al-Sattar Qasim Lahori writes that during the 105th *majlis* on 10 August 1611, at bedtime all kinds of singers and musicians (*qavvālān va kalāvantān va dīgar gūyandagān*) gathered before the ruler.[40] Among them were two brothers, Maku and Hamza, popular court *qawwals*, who sang a certain quatrain (*dubaitī*). The emperor asked who had composed it (*bar zabān-i mubārak raft ki īn shi'r az kīst?*). Maku informed him that it was by the poet Mushfiqi. The emperor asked where he was from (*Mushfiqī kujā'ī būd?*). The answer was that he was from Bukhara. Having satisfied the emperor's curiosity, they sang this one verse for an hour. The emperor discussed the meaning of the verse and then recited a verse of Baba Fighani (d.1519), a poet who brought in the vogue for what would be later called the *taza-gu'i* or *sabk-i Hindi* poetry.[41] During the 104th *majlis* on 11 August 1611, the emperor asked everyone present who was the greater poet: Sa'di or Hafiz, not in terms of mastery over the *ghazal* because he knew it was the former, but in terms of mysticism (*darvīshī*) and piety (*khudāparastī*).[42]

Anecdotes such as these suggest that oral recitation of poetry also played a role in the process of the canonisation of certain classical figures in the

---

38 See e.g. Sunil Sharma, *Amir Khusraw: The Poet of Sufis and Sultans* (Oxford: Oneworld, 2005), pp. 41-42.

39 He also appreciated storytelling. In his memoirs, Jahangir mentions the *qissa-khwan* Mulla Asad who had previously been in the service of Mirza Ghazi the governor of Sindh in Thatta; Jahangir, *Jahāngīrnāmah, Tūzuk-i Jahāngīrī*, ed. by Muhammad Hashim (Tehran: Bunyad-i Farhang-i Iran, 1980), p. 215.

40 'Abd al-Sattar Lahori, *Majālis-i Jahāngīrī*, ed. by Arif Naushahi and Muin Nizami (Tehran: Miras-i Maktub, 2006), pp. 258-60.

41 See Losensky (1993) for a study of the vogue of this poetry in the sixteenth and seventeenth centuries in the Persianate world.

42 Lahori (2006), p. 256.

same way that *tazkiras* did in writing. Additionally, it was not just the poets but also patrons who wanted to hone their aesthetic tastes and keep up with the latest trends and popular verses in the larger Persianate culture (see also Schofield and Busch in this volume).

Another author from the late Jahangir period has left a similar text to the one by Lahori. Mutribi Samarqandi in his *khatima* (conclusion) to a larger biographical dictionary of poets called *Nuskha-yi zībā-yi Jahāngīrī* (1625) kept a record of meetings with Jahangir. In this work Mutribi attests to the emperor's continuing interest in discussions about poetry centred around performances. During their fifteenth session, the Emperor Jahangir asked the seventy-year-old Mutribi to sing, which the latter did reluctantly, and then a theoretical discussion on music ensued. In their seventeenth meeting the Emperor Jahangir told Mutribi, "The sweet-voiced nightingale [Fasih Khan] has been reading your book to us for hours. We enjoy it very much".[43] At the twenty-third meeting, the emperor informed Mutribi that Fasih Khan had finished reading his anthology and ordered the book to be placed in the royal library. He also suggested to Mutribi that his own anthology, compiled when he was a prince, could be incorporated into the larger work, to which the author acquiesced.[44] Written texts, thus, resulted in these types of oral discussions and recitations that in turn sometimes led to amplifications of the original texts.

## Performance and Memory

Instances of memorable musical and poetic performances are frequently described in sufi sources, testifying to the portentous effect music and poetry could have on one with a sensitive nature. Interestingly, Mughal courtly sources also carry resonances of this perception. In his memoirs Jahangir narrates a strange occurrence (*amr-i 'ajīb va qaẓīya-yi gharīb*) during a performance by *qawwals* on 12 Muharram of the fifth regnal year (8 April 1610). As part of the performance, the singer Sayyid Shah enacted a simulated *sama'* (*bi-ravish-i taqlīd samā' mīnamūd*). Jahangir records that he was curious about the context of the line of Amir Khusrau that was being sung that evening and asked if anyone present could explain it:

---

43 Mutribi Samarqandi, *Khāṭirāt-i Muṭribī*, ed. by 'Abd al-Ghani Mirzayif (Karachi: Mu'assasah-i Tahqiqat-i Asiya-yi Miyanah va Gharbi, Danishgah, 1977), p. 70.

44 Ibid., p. 88.

*har qaum rā-st rāhī dīnī u qibla-gāhī*
*mā qibla rāst kardīm bar simt-i kaj-kulāhī*

Every community has its right way, creed and prayer;
I turn to pray towards him with his cap awry.[45]

From the audience, Mulla 'Ali the seal engraver came forward and explained that during his father's time he had heard the story that provided the background to the composition of these lines. Apparently, one day Nizamuddin Auliya (d.1325), Khusrau's spiritual master, was watching some Hindus perform their religious rituals and uttered the first line. Just then Amir Khusrau joined him and replied with the second hemistich as a compliment to his spiritual master. Jahangir writes that as soon as Mulla 'Ali recited the second hemistich, he became so affected that he fell down before the throne. Concerned, the emperor himself got up from the throne and the royal physicians rushed to Mulla 'Ali's side thinking he was having an epileptic fit, but there was nothing to be done because he was dead. He was taken away to be buried. This remarkable occurrence encapsulates several layers of parallel performative contexts taking place around this one line of poetry that is actually found in a *ghazal* by Khusrau's contemporary Hasan Sijzi (d.1338)—the original interaction between poet and *pir* to explain the meaning of the verse, and the later Mughal reception of it. There is perhaps also a hint of a suggestion that a price had to be paid for enacting a mock *sama'* session, although it was the innocent and pure-hearted Mulla 'Ali who became a martyr for love in the retelling of the story.

The aforementioned author of the *Majālis-i Jahāngīrī*, Lahori, provides another, and more detailed, eyewitness report of the same event in the seventy-sixth *majlis* that took place on 15 Muharram 1020 (11 April 1610). He writes that there was a *sama'* session at court and the *qawwals* of Delhi sang this line of Amir Khusrau. The poet Maulana 'Ali Ahmad "Khalifa" narrated the context of these lines to the emperor as he had heard it from his father—the same narrative given by Jahangir. Lahori also pinpoints the exact moment of the event, one hour after nightfall, and gives a brief biographical sketch of the respected Maulana, whose father was an accomplished dervish and who was himself appointed as tutor to the princes. In contrast to this esteemed figure, he mocks the fake dervish

45 Jahangir (1980), p. 97.

who was imitating the *sama'* (*yakī az darvīsh-ṣūratān ki khvud rā sayyid guft... bi-taqlīd samā' mīkard*). In the end, in order to emphasise the uniqueness of this event he only has recourse to the written word by declaring that nothing like this can be read in books of history (*kutub-i tārīkh*). But this was not the end of the life of this memorable performance. Twenty years later the Mughal court retained a memory of this event. During his extended visit to the Mughal court, the aforementioned Mutribi, in one of his sessions with the emperor, was describing a certain Central Asian dervish youth who heard a schoolboy sing the poems of the antinomian poet Qasim Anvar (d.1433) and died on the spot. Upon hearing this, the courtier Maktub Khan told Mutribi about the unfortunate Ahmad 'Ali who had died after reciting Amir Khusrau's verse two decades earlier, and Mutribi affirmed that he had read this story in the *Jahāngīrnāma*. Mutribi added that he also saw a painting of this event, presumably in a manuscript of the text. This story has even more re-tellings,[46] but the intriguing question is why it lingered for so long in the memory of the Mughals. On one level, the three versions of this event in different Mughal works reiterate the point that the performance of Persian mystical poetry had the power to move people's hearts to an extreme degree, but the story itself was strange enough to be included in various texts as entertaining material. The strange context of the story, the biography of the reciter, and the use of Amir Khusrau's verses in *qawwalis* are defining aspects of Mughal oral culture that link the Timurid past to the present, the sacred to the profane, and the spoken word to the written.

The Mughal fascination with this story may be connected to a hagiographical tale in the history of the sufis of Delhi concerning Qutbuddin Bakhtiyar Kaki (d.1235),[47] a story that also had a life in Mughal texts. The following account is taken from the *Mūnis al-arvāḥ*, a collection of biographies of Chishti sufis written in 1640 by princess Jahanara, daughter of the Emperor Shah Jahan, who along with her brother Dara Shikoh was mystically minded. She writes:

> It is narrated that one day the *qawwals* were singing this line:
>
> Those who are slain by the dagger of submission
> Have another life at all times from the unseen.

46 Yet another version is found in *Ma'āṣir-i Jahāngīrī* by Khvaja Kamgar Husaini, ed. by Azra Alavi (New York: Asia Publishing House, 1978), p. 128.

47 I am grateful for Katherine Schofield for bringing this to my attention.

> An ecstatic state overcame the Khvaja [Qutbuddin] and for three days the singers repeated these same lines. He was unconscious and at the time of prayers he regained consciousness, asked the singers to sing the same line and lost consciousness. This went on for four days. On the fourth night his condition changed and his auspicious head was next to Qazi Hamiduddin Nagori and feet next to Shaikh Badruddin Ghaznavi. When Qazi Hamiduddin saw this state of his he asked him [the Khvaja], "Who among the *khalifas* should sit on the prayer mat?" He said, "Give the robe, staff, bowl and sandals that I received from the guiding master [Mu'inuddin Chishti] to Shaikh Fariduddin Mas'ud Ajodhani". And then the bird of his soul flew to the highest heaven.[48]

In another work of this period, *Siyar al-aqṭāb* (1646), the sufi Shaikh Allah Diya recounts the same story, providing additional information in the names of the singers, Salahuddin and his sons Karimuddin and Nasiruddin. The parallel occurrence of the two anecdotes in Mughal texts of the same period shows that, as far as the performance of the *ghazal* is concerned, by the sixteenth century sufi and courtly practices overlapped to some degree. It is somewhat unclear whether the same singers performed *qawwali* at sufi shrines and at the Mughal court, although it would seem likely if the emperor or governor summoned the performers for a private performance. The increasing use of Hindavi/Hindi lyrics at court may have been an influence in the blending of boundaries between sacred and profane, courtly and non-courtly.

## Multilinguality at the Mughal Court

We have seen that the place of origin of performers was an important identity marker for practitioners of the arts, much more so in the early Mughal period, when the notion of purity of language was hegemonic and the recitation of stories or chanting of poems were the exclusive domain of native speakers of Persian. Courtly Mughal Persian sources from the sixteenth and seventeenth centuries are uncannily silent about performances or recitations in languages other than Persian. This, of course, does not demonstrate that only Persian performances took place at court, as Allison Busch has convincingly shown with reference to Brajbhasha Hindi poetry, but rather that the authors who documented the lives and practices

48 *Mūnis al-arvāḥ*, in *Princess Jahān Ārā Begam, Her Life and Works*, ed. by Qamar Jahan Begam (Karachi: S.M. Hamid 'Ali, 1991), pp. 84-86.

were writing for a specific kind of audience which only prized Persian.[49] As we have seen, the prestige of Persian at this time facilitated the inclusion of the accounts of poets and storytellers in biographical dictionaries alongside more powerful individuals, but excluded others who were part of a multilingual oral culture, even if this overlapped or existed alongside with Persian. This same tendency can be found in the case of poetic *tazkiras* which only commemorate the achievements of poets writing in Persian, or occasionally Turkish or Arabic, but not in local languages.

In this context, the mention Emperor Jahangir makes in his autobiography in the year 1608 of being "taken with the verses for him by a Hindi poet (*charan*) in the entourage of the Rajput prince Raja Suraj Singh" and exclaiming, "I have rarely heard Hindi verses on such a delicate theme" is rather unusual.[50] In fact what is preserved in the text is a Persian version of these verses, not the original Hindi. Another exceptional instance from a few decades later concerns the brothers Mir Muhammad Salih and Mir Muhammad Mu'min, both courtiers of Iranian descent whose father had been a master calligrapher under Akbar and received the title *mishkīn-qalam*. The elder brother was the *darogha* or overseer of Shah Jahan's library and used the pen-name "Kashfi'" in Persian and "Sujan" in Hindi. One of the brothers is said to have written a treatise on music, a fact that is not recorded by other sources who mention the brothers, such as Muhammad Bakhtavar Khan's history of Aurangzeb, *Mirāt al-'Ālam*, demonstrating that a single biographical account only provides an incomplete picture of the complexities of the cultural scene at the Mughal court. The historian of Shah Jahan's time, Muhammad Salih Kanbo, writes about them in his work *'Amal-i Ṣāliḥ*: "Since both are adept at Hindi songs (*naghma-yi hindī*), the singers (*naghma-sarāyān*) of India listen to their performances", suggesting that they listen both for enjoyment and instruction.[51] It is thus possible that rules about including Hindavi/vernacular song-music *within Persian texts* were beginning to loosen up by the mid-seventeenth century,[52] although

49 Allison Busch, 'Hidden in Plain View: Brajbhasha Poets at the Mughal Court', *Modern Asian Studies* 44.2 (2010), 267-309, and her essay in this volume.

50 The first sentence is from Christopher Shackle, 'Settings of Panegyric: The Secular Qasida in Mughal and British India', in *Qasida Poetry in Islamic Asia and Africa*, ed. by Stefan Sperl and Christopher Shackle (Leiden: Brill, 1996), p. 213; the second is from Jahangir (1980), p. 80.

51 Muhammad Salih Kanbo, *'Amal-i Ṣāliḥ*, ed. by Ghulam Yazdani and Vahid Quraishi (Lahore: Majlis-i Taraqqi-yi Adab, 1967-1972), pp. 344-45.

52 Kanbo's reference to the Hindi poet Kavindra is further evidence of this: 'Either the Mughal court's sponsorship of Braj texts was on the rise in Shah Jahan's period or

as early as Akbar's time, the poet Gada'i, son of the renowned sufi Shaikh Jamali and holding the post of *sadr al-sudur*, was mentioned as having a talent for composing and singing in Hindi.[53]

The fascination with, and even anxiety about, the nature of the classical Persian canon, and with forging connections with the Central Asian and Iranian lands, thus underwent a transformation in the later Mughal period, most notably in the representation of what was never a monolingual culture in the first place but a multilingual one, even as the social, ethnic, and linguistic backgrounds of the writers of biographical dictionaries and histories became more diverse. The importance of oral culture embedded in practices such as recitation and discussion about the merits of one poet over another should also be considered when studying the process of canon formation in Persian or Indo-Persian literature. What did remain unchanged was that in the courtly milieu, the oral setting, for poetry at least, was never completely eclipsed by book culture.

In the early textual sources, we have seen, the lives of performers were recorded only when they held other positions of honour. Otherwise they might just have found a passing mention in these works. Professional poets, in addition to their traditional duties as panegyrists and writers, also fulfilled the roles both of storytellers and reciters. The eighteenth-century panoramic text on Delhi, *Muraqqa'-yi Dihlī*, by contrast, paints a lively picture of the world at the fringes of and outside the royal court. It records the names of many singers, dancers, reciters, and *qawwals*, and the genres they performed, but provides us with almost no information about the social or geographic origins of the performers—nor does it provide textual examples of the lyrics being recited, sung, or performed.[54] The focus of this work appears to be rather on the physical qualities of the performers and a hyperbolic and highly metaphoric description of their contribution to the now socially diverse culture of entertainment. Although the *Muraqqa'-yi Dihlī* was written in Persian, it thus symbolically marks the decreased importance of Persian and a transformation of earlier Mughal literary practices. The popularisation of poetry and its recitation was no longer limited to an elite audience and had become the hallmark of cosmopolitan comportment for a larger part of the urban population.

---

something had shifted in the historiography that made it more acceptable for Persian writers to mention Hindi poets'; Busch (2010), 151.

53 Bada'uni (2000-2001), Vol. 3, p. 52.

54 The Persian text was edited and translated into Urdu by Nur al-Hasan Ansari (Delhi: Department of Urdu, University of Delhi, 1982).

# 11. Persian Poets on the Streets: The Lore of Indo-Persian Poetic Circles in Late Mughal India

*Stefano Pellò*

## Memorialising the Present

The early modern Persian *tazkira* can be thought of as an attempt to catalogue and archive, in a narrative-fictional way, specific individual personalities and the internal dynamics of the Persian-writing poetic community, and thus to describe (in terms that are also prescriptive) its protocols with regards to poetic education, poetic production, reception, and criticism. In other words, the genre of literary *tazkiras* can be understood as a kind of autobiography or, even better, auto-hagiography of Persian literature by its own protagonists.[1] "Hagiography" can then

1 In Persian the genre of poetic *tazkiras* is closely related to that of sufi *tazkiras*, and they benefit from much the same conceptual and methodological tools, from protocols to expressive codes; see M.K. Hermansen, 'Religious Literature and the Inscription of Identity: The Sufi Tazkira Tradition in Muslim South Asia', *The Muslim World* 87. 3/4 (Jul–Oct 1997): 315-20. But Persianate poetic *tazkiras* do not just inscribe a "Muslim identity" (Hermansen: 317), they tend to canonise multiple and co-existing identities first of all by recalling, through a shared code of expression, a shared code of social and linguistic practices. The comparison pays off also in the case of saints' and artists' hagiographies in Europe such as *Legenda Aurea*, the famous thirteenth-century Latin collection of lives of saints by Jacobus de Voragine, and the even more celebrated sixteenth-century collection of lives of Italian Renaissance artists, Giorgio Vasari's *Le vite de' più eccellenti pittori, scultori, ed architettori*, ed. by G. Milanesi (Florence: Sansoni, 1880).

 http://dx.doi.org/10.11647/OBP.0062.11

be read here as the institutionalisation of reference figures, a powerful device for modelling lives within an established and prescriptive palimpsest of poetic/suficate language.[2]

Among other things, Persian poetic *tazkiras* reflect the ideas that literati had of the occasions and spaces of poetic experience and exchange, and of boundaries governing them—itself one of the pivotal forms of knowledge of the Persianate world. Using the expressive code of poetry itself, the *tazkira* genre explores, catalogues, and gives rhetorical form to the pre-textual and the con-textual dimensions of poetry both as a meaningful social craft and a powerful way of controlling and exploiting the *langue* of the Persianate cosmopolis. What do I mean by this? As a whole, Persian *tazkiras* are very much concerned with an ideology of harmonic continuity and the textual recreation of a dia-chronic and dia-topic, or even u-chronic and u-topic, *majlis* ("assembly") of poets, who often belonged to different chronological and geographical backgrounds, as the titles themselves indicate.[3] After all, as a verbal-noun deriving from the Arabic root Z̲KR, "to remember, to recall", the word *tazkira* itself declares the primary concern of this wide, multi-purpose, or rather "container-genre" to be the memory of a past, in our particular case the memory of the literary past.[4] More

---

2 For an example of the (self-) inscription of the Vaishnava disciples of Bedil's poetic circles that used this poetic/suficate language, see Stefano Pellò, 'Persian as a Passe-Partout: The Case of Mirza 'Abd al-Qadir Bedil and his Hindu Disciples', in *Culture and Circulation: Literature in Motion in Early Modern India*, ed. by Thomas de Brujin and Allison Busch (Leiden: Brill, 2014), pp. 21-46.

3 Titles signify the shared imaginary textual space-time in which poetic/sufi individual personalities are located and re-located through reference not only to places (including the all-embracing *Haft iqlīm*, "Seven climes") but to other generic collective spaces, such as the *majlis* "assembly", the *rawza* "garden", the *safina* "ship", etc: in Ahmad Gulchin-i Ma'ani's survey on Persian *tazkiras* we meet, for instance, six *majlises* (or the plural form *majalis*), fourteen *rawzas* (or the plural form *riyaz*), nine *safinas*, as well as several other loci of the lyrical *langue* related to the poetic space of the "garden", such as *hadiqas, gulzars, gulistans, gulshans, baharistans, baghs; maykhanas, maykadas, kharabats* (the canonical taverns), *atashkhanas* (the antinomistic fire-temple), *nigaristans* (the pictorial gallery of beauties), etc., all before the beginning of the fourteenth century of the Hijra; Ahmad Gulchin-i Ma'ani, *Tārīkh-i taẕkirahā-yi Fārsī*, 2 vols (Tehran: Intisharat-i Danishgah-i Tihran, 1348-1350/1969-1971).

4 As Marcia K. Hermansen and Bruce B. Lawrence state, "*tazkiras*, as their name suggests, both memorialise individuals and communicate their legacy to a new generation [...] If there is a word for understanding poetic and sufi *tazkiras*, it is *memory*"; M.K. Hermansen and B.B. Lawrence, "Indo-Persian *Tazkiras* as Memorative Communications", in *Beyond Turk and Hindu: Rethinking Religious Identities in Islamicate South Asia*, ed. by D. Gilmartin and B.B. Lawrence (Gainesville, FL: University Press of Florida, 2000), pp. 149-75, p. 152.

specifically, literary *tazkiras* operate as interrelated fragments of a genre both in compilative and (re-)creative continuity, working at the same time as commentaries (*sharh*) and lexicons (*farhang*) of the Persianate literary community. They preserve and adapt a code while codifying and adapting the memory of individual personalities.[5] Yet, predictably enough, the way in which writers framed this concern changed over time and space. The great Timurid and post-Timurid *tazkiras* (from the *Tazkirat al-shu'arā* by Dawlatshah Samarqandi onwards), for instance, appear to be primarily interested in shaping a durable canon, comparing the great masters of the past to the main poets of the present, and connecting the texts produced by the latter to the models of the former.[6] But from the end of the seventeenth century onward in North India, we witness instead a growing interest in shaping the idea of the *present*. In other words, the focus shifts from the relationship between modern poets (the *muta'akhkhirān*) and the classics (*mutaqaddimān*), to the relationship of modern poets with one another: from a memory of the distant past to a memory of the closer and more familiar past, or of the present. Thus, beside providing biographical information and verse selections, these texts communicate the varied and shifting behaviour, tastes, sensibilities, hermeneutic tools, and approaches that the inter-related and ever-expanding Persian-writing literary communities of the wider Persianate world used.

This centrality of the present as a theme to be studied in and for itself, and a related feeling of the newness of doing so, can be found in the introduction of a *tazkira* completed in Delhi in 1682, the *Kalimāt al-shu'arā* by Muhammad Afzal Sarkhush. The author specifies that:

> before this, the venerable people who decided to devote themselves to writing and composing poetic *tazkiras* used to start from the life and the

---

5 Just as Hafiz in the opening *ghazal* of his *diwan* retraces, according to Julie Scott Meisami, "a life in, and of, poetry—his own poetry, and that of the traditions that inform it"; J.S. Meisami, 'A Life in Poetry: Hafiz's First Ghazal', in *The Necklace of the Pleiades: 24 Essays on Persian Literature, Culture and Religion*, ed. by F.D. Lewis and S. Sharma (Leiden: Leiden University Press, 2010), pp. 163-81, p. 172.

6 See Paul E. Losensky, *Welcoming Fighāni: Imitation and Poetic Individuality in the Safavid-Mughal Ghazal* (Costa Mesa: Mazda, 1998), ch. 4. On the fecund centrality of the relationship with the past in the Timurid poetic milieu see also Riccardo Zipoli, *The Technique of the Ǧawāb: Replies by Nawā'ī to Ḥāfiẓ and Ǧāmī* (Venice: Cafoscarina, 1993), and Marta Simidchieva, 'Imitation and Innovation in Timurid Poetics: Kāshifī's *Badāyi' al-afkār* and its Predecessors, *al-Mu'jam* and *Ḥadā'iq al-siḥr*', *Iranian Studies* 36.4 (2003), 509-30.

> poetry of Hakim Rudaki and to arrive to the authors of their own age. As for the people who lived up to and including the age of Emperor Akbar, their memory can be found in every historical writing and in every *tazkira*. The present writer now feels that there is little merit in going on copying from the works of each other and repeating things. [...] Since the present age is full of writers who know how to deal with many-coloured images and fresh new concepts, it will not be inopportune to devote oneself to describe their lives and to speak about the peculiarities of their poetical discourse.[7]

The reference to "many-coloured images and fresh new concepts" evokes the coeval spread of the concepts of newness in writing poetry, variously called *ṭarz-e naw*, *tāzagūyi*, and so on. For our purposes here, it is tempting to connect this explicit historical consciousness and programmatic declaration to the emergence of urban poetic circles (called *maktabs*, lit. "schools"), sometimes based in the houses of the most eminent masters, as sites of poetic production in late-seventeenth-century, and especially eighteenth-century, Delhi and North India in general. These new semi-public spaces and dynamics, such as the "bourgeois" *musha'ira* or the institutionalisation of the master-disciple (*ustad-shagird*) relationship, needed a form to be textualised in while Persian increased its social and ideological reach as the language of choice for a widening class of secretaries and scribes who "took their work home" and needed to find a place for themselves in the sociotextual sphere of Persian literary culture.[8] (It is not by chance that we find several Kayasths and Khatris among the *tazkira*-writers of the period.) "In the *mushā'irah*", Jamal Malik reminds us,

> it was not only "a middle class who was interested in Persian and Urdu poetry and among whom one could count representatives of military, administration, as well as notables and traders" that participated. These public spaces also provided a gregarious forum for communications and the perennial co-option of new members from the lower classes, including barbers, soldiers, perfume vendors, masons, weavers, tailors and

---

7 Muhammad Afzal Sarkhwush, *Kalīmāt al-shu'arā*, ed. by M. H. Mahvi Lakhnawi (Madras: [s.n.], 1951), pp. 2-3.

8 I borrow the term from Sheldon Pollock, who defines the "sociotextual community" as "the community for which literature is produced, in which it circulates, and which derives a portion of its self-understanding as a community from the very act of hearing, reading, performing, reproducing, and circulating literary texts"; S. Pollock, 'Introduction', *Literary Cultures in History: Reconstructions from South Asia*, ed. by S. Pollock (Berkeley: University of California Press, 2003), p. 27.

> carpenters, presupposed permanent social openness [...] And precisely because of the heterogeneous status and the intellectual heterogeneity of the participants, these fora of exchange and expression, which also contributed to the processes of consensus forming and group building, gave rise to a new trend in taste and the formation of a moral institution alternative to the court.[9]

Thus both the space of the urban poetic circle, the non-courtly *musha'ira*, and the master-disciple relationship came actively into play in the creation of new literary identities in the Persian (and increasingly Urdu) context.[10] A model for the new type of Indo-Persian poetic circle was the *maktab* or circle of Mirza Bedil in Delhi, about whom Lachhmi Narayan Shafiq writes, in the introduction of his *tazkira Gul-i ra'nā*, that:

> in the days of Shah 'Alam, Muhammad Farrukhsiyar and Muhammad Shah, thanks to the graceful company of Mirza Bedil—mercy be upon him—many individuals from the people of the Hindus acquired the talent of weighing poetic expressions. And so the Indian parrots tasted a new sugar, as will become clear from the reading of the subsequent pages.[11]

For the purpose of this volume, the questions that we need to ask are: what oral practices flowed into these "new" Persian circles? And conversely, what role did these circles play in producing a particular kind of oral culture, glimpses of which we glean from reading *tazkira* literature? *Tazkiras* were for a long time decried as devoid of "any consistent principle of selectivity, critical evaluation of facts, or analytical framework" and "resistant to critical theory because they are drenched in the minutiae of local detail".[12] Yet precisely these supposed limits of *tazkiras* are providential when we want to explore the closeness of these texts to the domain of their pre-textual orality, a shared set of

---

9 J. Malik, 'Muslim Culture and Reform in 18th Century South Asia', *Journal of the Royal Asiatic Society* 13.2 (2003), 227-43, p. 240, quoting Ali Jawad Zaidi, *Tārīkh-i mushā'ira* (Delhi: [n.p.], 1989), p. 109.

10 See Pellò, 'Persian as a Passe-Partout', passim. The usefulness of focusing on poetic apprenticeship in eighteenth-century North India, and especially Delhi, was noticed by C.M. Naim ('Poet-Audience Interaction at Urdu Musha'iras', in *Urdu and Muslim South Asia: Studies in Honour of Ralph Russell*, ed. by C. Shackle (Delhi: Oxford University Press, 1991), pp. 167-73, p. 173; a more sustained study of master-disciple relationships in the burgeoning Urdu poetic culture is Frances Pritchett, 'A Long History of Urdu Literary Culture, Part 2', in *Literary Cultures in History: Reconstructions from South Asia*, ed. by S. Pollock, pp. 864-911.

11 Lacchmi Narayan Shafiq, *Tazkira-yi gul-i ra'nā* (Hyderabad: 'Ahd Afarin Barqi Press, [n.d.]), p. 2.

12 Ibid.

stories with several variants. *Tazkiras* textualise, so to speak, the open *canovaccios* of the fragmented narratives of Persian literature. The "minutiae of local detail" in particular guide us to the question of how the "local" was made cosmopolitan, and how the ideals of canonical persistence were localised in a context—that of late-seventeenth- and eighteenth-century Indo-Persian literary culture—where we witness an ever-growing interest for the non-Persian and for the *previously* extra-canonical South Asian spaces, subjects, narratives, and texts.[13] In short, if properly analysed *tazkiras* can provide modern readers with insights into the con-textual and pre-textual dimensions of late-Mughal Persian poetry.

How to recover and configure the oral dimension ("tellings") in and around *tazkira* texts is the particular analytical path this chapter seeks to chart. To do so, it concentrates on the web of gossip within Indo-Persian *maktabs* or poetic circles and on their strategies of localisation (the "minutiae of local details"). Besides the already mentioned *Kalimāt al-shu'arā* by the Delhi-based sufi Mirza Afzal Sarkhush (completed in Delhi in 1682, it contains the biographies of 169 poets), my analysis will largely be based on the third volume of the *Safīna-yi Khwushgū* by the *Bais* Rajput Bindraban Das Khwushgu (completed in Delhi in the mid-eighteenth century, it contains 245 biographical notices), and the *Safīna-yi Hindī* by the Kayasth Bhagvan Das Hindi (completed in Lucknow at the very beginning of the nineteenth century, it deals with 335 authors of Persian verse). These last two *tazkiras* are particularly useful given their explicit interest in charting the contemporary world of Persian poetic production and its "new" subjects adumbrated above, their interest in prominent Indo-Persian *maktabs* such as that of Mirza Bedil, and their coverage of almost the whole late Mughal period, from the latter part of Aurangzeb's reign to the emergence of Lucknow as a literary centre.

---

13 I think, for instance, of relatively well-known eighteenth-century works relating to South Asian forms of knowledge such as the *Ghizlān al-Hind* by Ali Azad Bilgrami (see Sunil Sharma, 'Translating Gender: Āzād Bilgrāmī on the Poetics of the Love Lyric and Cultural Synthesis', *The Translator* 15.1 (2009), 87-103), but also of the substantial amount of Persian *masnavi* renderings of Sanskritic literature produced for local patrons in the "new" urban settings, described above well after Dara Shukoh's times and just before the colonial period, still to be explored. The *Jilwa-yi ẕāt* by Bedil's disciple Amanat Ray Lalpuri, a long free rendering of the tenth Book of the *Bhāgavata-purāṇa* in the shape of a Persian *masnavi*, completed in 1733 for Nawab Amjad Khan (Muhammad Shah's foster brother), is only one among many possible examples; see Pellò, 'Persian as a Passe-Partout'.

# Institutionalising Gossip: Stories from the Street

In the introduction of his *Kalimat al-shu'arā*, Mirza Afzal Sarkhush clearly points out that "hagiographic" scope of poetic *tazkiras* I referred to earlier. Indeed, he goes so far as to place poets immediately after the prophets and to intimate that reading about the lives of the poets will be of spiritual use for the audience:

> The relation between the munificent poets and the prophets—peace be upon them—is one of extreme closeness. As a matter of fact, both these groups of people are in constant touch with the primary source of graces (*mabda'-i fayyāż*) and the hidden world (*'ālam-i ghayb*). Mulla Nizami has written:
>
> *Among great people, a group came in the first row, and the other in the second: the first row is that of prophets, and the second is that of the poets.*
>
> There should be no doubt, then, that remembering the lives and listening to the utterings of such elevated natures will not be devoid of general gains and of sure benefits.[14]

Not all the individuals described in Indo-Persian *tazkiras* of the late Mughal period, however, fit comfortably into this elite group of "elevated natures". Nor does the way their lives are presented always point in the direction of spiritual *exempla*. As a matter of fact, some notices come, so to speak, directly from the streets—the second axis of this chapter—and hint at the interaction within poetic *maktabs* of individuals apparently well beyond the pale of hagiographic canons, and sometimes also of the social spaces traditionally connected to Persian literature in South Asia, as in earlier periods. It is the case, for instance, of an individual mentioned in the *Safīna-yi Hindī* who is simply called "Pinki", the Hindi term for an opium addict, a term that subsumes his poetic persona:

> He belongs to the common people of Delhi (*az ahālī-yi Dihlī ast*). Since he was addicted to opium, he chose this Hindi word as his own poetic

14 Lacchmi Narayan Shafiq, *Tazkira-yi gul-i ra'nā*, p. 2. The long pre-codification of the sufi and generally *'irfānī* "gnostic" concepts in the language of Persian poetry (well scrutinised by J.T.P. de Bruijn, *Persian Sufi Poetry: An Introduction to the Mystical Use of Classical Poems* (London: Curzon, 1997)) allowed a non-contrastive overlap of the poets with saints.

name. He wrote a *masnavi* describing opium and was still alive in the age of Muhammad Shah.

*The one who gave opium to Pinki*
*left the tress of Layla in the hand of Majnun.*

*He is a drunkard, a libertine, a shameless man*
*He's not even Pinki, he's opium, nothing else.*[15]

Bhagvan Das's *tazkira* mentions other authors of Persian poetry who were addicted to drugs.[16] One was an Iranian named Muhammad Hasrat, whose social background was very different from that of Pinki:

> He was a *Sayyid* from holy Mashhad. He was warm-hearted and had a good nature and had inherited the title of guardian of the sacred mausoleum of Imam Riza. He was strongly addicted to opium, and because of this he died at the beginning of the reign of Muhammad Shah.[17]

The poetic activity of Pinki and Hasrat appears to be little more than a pretext for textualising the pre-textual. What emerges here is in fact the will to show the strength of the gossip network immediately available to the *tazkira* writer, and to which he himself contributes. While remembering Pinki, about whom we know nothing else, Bhagvan Das conveys to the reader both a glimpse of non-courtly life in Delhi

15 Bhagvan Das Hindi, *Safīna-yi Hindī*, ed. by S. Shah Md. Ataur Rahman (Patna: Institute of Post Graduate Studies and Research in Arabic and Persian, 1958), pp. 37-38.

16 The poets' taste for intoxicants is a common *topos* in *tazkira* tellings, touching even the most prominent "model" authors of the Safavid-Mughal age such as Sa'ib-i Tabrizi and Bedil; for Sa'ib's well known inclination towards wine and opium see, for instance, A.H. Zarrinkub, *Zā'ir-i Hind*, in M.R. Daryagasht, *Sā'ib va sabk-i hindī* (Tehran: Nashr-i Qatra, 1992), pp. 75-83, p. 80; as far as Bedil is concerned, see Bindraban Das Khwushgu, *Safīna-yi Khwushgū*, ed. by S. Shah Md. Ataur Rahman (Patna: Institute of Post Graduate Studies and Research in Arabic and Persian, 1959), p. 109. The motif of debauchery among poets, while narrativising social and economic trends (see, for instance, Rudi Matthee, *The Pursuit of Pleasure: Drugs and Stimulants in Iranian History* (Princeton: Princeton University Press, 2009), pp. 46, 105-08), is perfectly inscribed within the ultra-classical *malamati* mode of Persian suficate poetry (i.e. the quest for the blame of the prudes); not surprisingly, immoral and addicted poets are often the protagonists of late conversions (in Khwushgu's description, Bedil himself is said to have completely quit intoxicants at a certain point in his life), following a bio-literary scheme that can be traced back to the figure of the early Ghaznavid master Hakim Sana'i reconstructed in Timurid works such as Dawlatshah Samarqandi's *Tazkirat al-shu'arā* and Jami's *Nafaḥāt al-uns*; see J.T.P. de Bruijn, *Of Piety and Poetry: The Interaction of Religion and Literature in the Life and Works of Ḥakīm Sanā'ī of Ghazna* (Leiden: Brill, 1983); and R. Zipoli, "The Obscene Sanâ'î", *Persica* 17 (2001), 173-94.

17 Bhagvan Das Hindi (1958), p. 60.

and a literary identity based on an ordinary/everyday practice of urban decadence but expressed through the choice of the poetic name (*takhallus*) and the comparison between opium and the tress of Layla. As far as Hasrat is concerned, we do not even know from Bhagvan Das what kind of relations the poet had with North India, if any: the apparent contrast between the religious affiliation of the poet with the shrine of Imam Riza in Mashhad and his ill-fated taste for intoxicants is enough to justify his presence in the *tazkira*. Both biographical notes lead us to question if and to what extent such observations mirror the subjects of everyday chats within poetic *maktabs*. The *Safīna-yi khwushgū* offers further examples, such as the curious details about the death of Ma'niyab Khan, in which an immediate taste for savoury gossip seems to go well beyond the poetic sphere:

> Ma'niyab Khan passed away while he was having sexual intercourse, most probably because he used to eat very little food. God be praised, what an enjoyable way of dying! This is, in any case, quite an uncanny circumstance, which took place in the year 1157 [1744-1745].

Compare it with the note in the *Safīna-yi Hindī* on Muhammad Ja'far, whom Bhagvan Das calls an "occasional poet" from Tehran who never went to India. More than in his poetry, however, the *tazkira* writer is interested in providing readers with the curious details of his death:

> One night a Sayyid, one of the guardians of the sacred precints of Imam Riza, dreamt that the Imam said to him, "We keep Mir Ja'far very close to ourselves". That person told this fact to everyone the next morning, and three days later the aforesaid Mir passed away.[18]

More significant to us than the binding grace conceded to Mir Ja'far by the *imam* is the introductory caption "*naql*" that immediately precedes the passage. A common Arabic loanword, the verbal noun *naql* (alone or in related constructions with the copula such as *naql-ast* or the derived *manqūl-ast*) carries the idea of transporting something from one place to another and in Persian textual culture it is technically employed to indicate the act of relating (as well writing down) other people's words, as well as to street performance practices. Steingass's Persian dictionary suggests "telling" among the English terms for *naql*, and this seems quite an appropriate rendering here: the caption declaredly introduces

18 Ibid., p. 49.

a telling, a "story" related to the *tazkira* writer by an unnamed source and hinting explictly at the coeval lore of Persian poetic *maktabs*. Similar observations apply to another spectacular death, that of Jugal Kishor Sarvat, which returns us from the Shi'a shrines of Khorasan to the courtly social space of eighteenth-century North India:

> He [Sarvat] was famous for his familiarity with subtleties, his witty speech, and his taste for good living and good company. He lived close to the court of Muhammad Shah, as a member of the deputation of the governor of Bengal, and the emperor got so affectionate to him that he became the object of the envy among the notables of Shahjahanabad. He spent an enormous sum of money for his son's wedding, thus attracting gossip. After the sack of Delhi he moved to Lucknow, and got in close contact with Nawab Shuja' al-Dawla Bahadur, who honoured him highly; eventually he moved to Farrukhabad. It is related that he was killed by his own elephant while he was mounting it.[19]

Again, the details about the pitiful death (preceded by the description of an equally "spectacular" career) of the gossiped-about socialite are introduced by a formula, "*guyand*" (literally "they say"), which is technically analogous to *naql(-ast)* and points to the oral diffusion of this story within the circles of Persianate intellectuals. The source is once again unnamed, but this is not always the rule and gossip is not the only basis for social storytelling in *tazkiras*. The identity of the informants is in fact often specified. While almost purely fictional personas (as far as their role in *tazkira* literature is concerned) like Pinki, Muhammad Hasrat, Mir Ja'far, and Jugal Kishor are more or less identifiable with the tellings about them, stories about more influential authors often come with authorising transmitters, as in the following brief passage by Bindraban Das Khwushgu about the great Delhi master Nasir 'Ali Sirhindi (1638-1696):

> He generally had rough manners with people, in fact he even used to insult them. *The honourable Shah Gulshan reports* that once an old acquaintance of his went to visit him, accompanied by a boy. [Nasir 'Ali] looked at the handsome youth and said: "Is there a way for me to bite your lips?". His guest got offended and left. The day after [Nasir 'Ali] apologised sending him a line by Mirza Sa'ib.[20]

19 Ibid., p. 47.
20 Khwushgu (1959), p. 2, emphasis added.

Shah Gulshan (d.1727), a prominent sufi and Persian poet based in Delhi, was a good friend of both Nasir 'Ali Sirhindi and of Khwushgu, the author of the *tazkira*. Predictably enough, poets talk about fellow poets, and the sources for the textualisation of oral gossip in *tazkira* literature are mostly about the poets themselves. In this specific case, the less-than-saintly account is used to cast aspersions on the main rival of Bindraban's idol Mirza Bedil.

Again predictably, the apparently "extra-poetic" accounts above notwithstanding, a great number of reported stories and repartees deal with the production, reception, and criticism of poetry, including the occasions for composing "poetic responses" (*jawabs*) and for public readings, with authoritative masters offering critical evaluations and corrections (*islah*). Thus the telling also becomes a strategy that configures orality as a site for experimentation—a performative "place to try"—and where tensions between writers can be located, as in this rather comic episode regarding the Mughal poet Shayda and narrated by Mirza Afzal Sarkhush:

> It is related that one day [Hakim Haziq] recited this *matla'*[21] in the presence of Mulla Shayda:
>
> *The nightingale abandons the rose garden if he sees me in the meadow.*
> *Nobody will be left to worship the idols, if the Brahmin looks at me.*
>
> Shayda said: "It is clear that you composed this line feeling like an effeminate young boy!". Hakim [Haziq] got enraged and ended up throwing Shayda in the courtyard pond.[22]

Such anecdotes, of course, are not specific to the literary environment of late Mughal Persian literary circles, be they courtly or non-courtly. In fact, contrasts between poets are a common *topos* in *tazkira* literature, and we can read the frequent recourse to such anecdotes by late Mughal biographers more cautiously as the diligent application of a generic protocol, rather than as the revolutionary desire to talk about real and local events. This is true also in the not uncommon cases where obscene vernacularity is employed, as in the following episode retold by Khwushgu:

---

21 The first line of a *ghazal* that gives the rhyming pattern to the whole poem.
22 Sarkhwush (1951), p. 51.

It is related that one day Miyan Muhammad Sadiq Ilqa, who had a fierce rivalry with him [Sarkhwush] in *musha'iras*, went to visit him. Sarkhwush had a very long white beard, and pointing at it Ilqa said: "You are a poet, such a big beard does not suit you at all!". Sarkhwush replied: "People who have seen me have an image of me with this beard, and if I change they won't recognise me. But it is clear that you are very annoyed by beards, and, indeed, even that light down looks stranger to your face: you should keep it shorter than the fuzz on the testicles of wanton men!"[23]

Satire and obscene discourse (*ḥajw u hazl*) are among the oldest modes of Persian literature, and *tazkiras*, just like dictionaries, are where they are traditionally recorded.[24] To stay with this particular story, we can also note that the beard (with its hygenic and sexual connotations) is among the preferred targets of the genre, and we can even find verse specimens built on the same ungenerous comparison Sarkhwush made to put down his rival's criticism.[25] Generic protocols can of course be profitably employed to talk about the real and the local, and late Mughal *tazkira* writers *do* speak about the present reality of poetic circles through relevant tellings, keeping respectfully within canonical requirements. Consider the following story about Mirza Bedil and Ja'far Zatalli, narrated in the *Safīna-yi Khwushgū*:

He [Bedil] had a very dignified nature. One night Ja'far Zatalli, who was one of the authors of satirical and obscene verse of the age (*ki yakī az hajwiyān u fuḥshgūyān-i 'aṣr būd*), brought to him a *masnavi* which he had written in his praise. As soon as he recited the first hemistich, "I don't give a shit about 'Urfi and Fayzi compared to you! (*chi 'Urfi chi Fayzi ba pish-i tu phish*)", Bedil said: "You were very kind to come, but we, the poor Bedil, are not pleased listening to such stories regarding the great masters". He took two *ashrafi*s from his purse and gave them to him, as a payment for the praise, thus silencing him. No matter how much those present—and especially the poor Khwushgu—insisted on letting Zatalli

23 Khwushgu (1959), p. 74.

24 See Riccardo Zipoli, 'Oscenità poetiche neopersiane: due *tarjī'-band* sulla masturbazione', *Annali di Ca' Foscari* 33 (Serie orientale 25, 1994), 258-59; and 'Elementi osceni nella lessicografia neopersiana', *Annali di Ca' Foscari* 35 (1996), 249-89.

25 Consider for instance the following line attributed to Munjik-i Tirmizi (tenth century) and recorded as an explanatory verse for the word *ramgān* in Asadi Tusi's *Lughat-i Furs* (eleventh century): "*rūy-at ba zīr-i rīshak andar nāpaydā/chūn kīr-i mard-i ghancha ba ramgān bar*" (Your face disappears under a small beard/like the cock of a catamite under his pubic hair); Asadi Tusi, *Lughat-i Furs*, ed. by M. Dabbirsiyaqi (Tehran: Tahuri, 1336/1957), p. 146. The line is quoted in Zipoli (1006), 269.

complete the couplet and thus listen to which word he had chosen to rhyme with *phish*, Bedil refused to do so.[26]

The reconstruction of a verbal exchange, part of a series of stories Khwushgu collected in order to show Bedil's character in poetic interactions, works well not only to communicate the contrast between poets of different status but also to convey a certain view (that of the *tazkira*-writer and of his circle) of the etiquette that ought to govern this specific socio-poetic space: the first-hand account of Bedil's declared respect for the masters of the Mughal past functions as a source of authority for Khwushgu, who can employ his well-informed gossip to build an immediately credible and influential lore. After all, the main audience of the *tazkiras* was made up of literati themselves, and access to the pre-textual orality of poetic circles, be it direct or mediated through the *naql*, provided the *tazkira* writer with an advantageous position to substantiate a more or less open prescriptive approach. In other words, the "minutiae of local detail" in the telling-oriented structure of the *tazkira*, be they Pinki's taste for opium or Bedil's dislike of satirical poems, became a powerful tool in the hands of the gossiper-biographer, who used them to express moral, social, and aesthetic judgements regarding the present time of poetic circles.

## Localisation: Pre-texts, Projections, and Protocols

We are also left, like Bindraban Das Khwushgu and the other participants in the *majlis* held in Bedil's house, with the desire to know which word Zatalli chose to rhyme with *phish*. *Phish* is a colloquial Hindi expression of disdain, and its presence in Zatalli's only utterance in the exchange between him and Bedil directs our attention towards the role of the narrativisation of everyday life and orality in charting a selected view of the specific spaces and cultures surrounding the production of the text.

Outside Bedil's familiar house, but not too far from it, the market is, among the urban spaces of North India, a favourite setting in which to place Persian poets, as in the following story narrated by Khwushgu, with regard once again to Nasir 'Ali Sirhindi:

26 Khwushgu (1959), p. 113.

> Bhagwant Rai, known by the pen-name Qalandar, the son-in-law of Rai Chandar Bhan Barahman, the famous *munshi*, was a friend of his [i.e. Nasir 'Ali's]. He [Bhagwant Rai] told me this story about him: "One day we were sitting together, with a third person, on a *rath*, which is a means of transport, and we were passing through the Delhi bazaar. We saw a vegetable-seller who was having an argument with his beautiful wife, yelling every possible insult at her. Suddenly Miyan Nasir 'Ali got off the *rath* and we thought that he wanted to act as a judge to the fighting couple. After flattering the vegetable-seller with every sort of adulation and false words, he said: "To treat this gracious and fairy-like creature as if she were a horse or a donkey is indeed an inhuman and ignoble behaviour! I am a good person and I have done you no harm: If you are tired of her, please give her to me!" The vegetable-seller and all the other passers-by were struck by the brilliance of his words and the quarrel ended in the twinkling of an eye.[27]

It would be naive to simply take such a narrative at face value. The people of the market are in fact the main protagonists of the classic poetic genre known as *shahr-ashub*, in which the "beauties" of the city are described through their daily activities.[28] The beautiful wife of the fruit-seller is thus not only an aspect of local colour but a literary character in no trivial sense, as the readers of the *tazkira* would have recognised. Thanks to the semantic power of a telling related by an eye-witness, Nasir 'Ali thereby becomes a literary persona himself, somehow acting, and codified, in the textual world he and the readers were familiar with. Analogous remarks can be made about other narrative *topoi* lying behind the tellings within the textualised world of Persian poetic circles shown in the *tazkiras*, such as the "madness" of poets:

> [Maulvi Muhammad Hikmat] was an erudite and skilful man from Jaunpur. When he was thirty he went completely mad. One day he was running through the market in his delirium and some children started throwing rocks at him. He was saved by an acquaintance who took him away and managed to calm him down. He immediately composed this verse:
>
> *My head has become a field of poppies thanks to the childrens' stones:*
> *madness is blossoming, the season of spring has finally come!*[29]

27 Ibid., p. 3.

28 See Sunil Sharma, 'The City of Beauties in the Indo-Persian Poetic Landscape', *Comparative Studies of South Asia, Africa and the Middle East* 24.2 (2004), 73-81.

29 Hindi (1958), p. 63.

In this anecdote, found in the *Safīna-yi Hindī*, the subject of the story and the performance of the public composition and recitation of a verse explicitly coincide with the recognition, by the pretended "mad" poet, of the transformation of his own "real" condition of mental insanity into a textual paradigm, which even an occasional amateur of Persianate literary cultures would have identified with the lover Majnun. The madness of the poet in the Jaunpur bazaar, just like Nasir 'Ali Sirhindi's scene with the vegetable sellers in the market of Delhi, while retelling realistic glimpses of local daily life through oral gossip, transfers them onto the plane of literary codes. Such strategies, while calling upon the imaginary dimension of the characters and *topoi* of the poetic hyperspace, stretch them by adding to them the immediate socio-historical "reality". Thus the world of poetic imagination—the *shahr-ashub*, Majnun—is euhemerised, i.e. tranferred into the immediate historical, specific present. In Khwushgu's *tazkira*, for instance, we see Shah Yaqin actually *composing* his poems while sitting in the Delhi bazaar, as if on the literary stage of the *shahr-ashub*:

> Most of the times he used to sit in the coffee-shop of Chandni Chawk in Shahjahanabad with his good friends, where he was always prone to read and recite poetry and to exercise his ability in composing it.[30]

The locus where the poet produces his craft is the same space in which Nasir 'Ali talks to the vegetable-seller and his beautiful wife, or where another madman, Shah-i Kabuli, dances and recites initiatic lines following Mirza Bedil's horse, according to the latter's autobiography.[31]

The everyday urban setting is also the place where poets/characters meet, in the biographic tellings, other characters/artists (who are, again, often the object of *shahr-ashub* poetry), such as painters and singers: a relatively well-known case is that of the story of the painter Anup Chhatr and the portrait he made of Mirza Bedil.[32] Some of these characters even become the subjects of independent notices in *tazkiras*, as in the case of the female dancer Babri Rindi:

30 Khwushgu (1959), p. 259.

31 Mirza 'Abd al-Qadir Bedil, *Kulliyāt*, ed. by K. Khalili (Kabul: da Pahane wizarat, da Dar al-ta'lif riyasat, 1344/1965-66), Vol. 4, p. 169.

32 Ibid., pp. 281-85. The episode has been described in Abdul Ghani, *Life and Works of Abdul Qadir Bedil* (Lahore: Publishers United, 1960), pp. 67-68 and briefly discussed in Pellò, 'Il ritratto e il suo doppio nel *maṣnawī* indo-persiano di Nāṣir 'Alī Sirhindī', in *La mandorla e il mirabolano: esotismi, contaminazioni, pittura e Oriente*, ed. by R. Favaro (Venice: Cafoscarina, 2007), pp. 111-13.

> The people of the street used to call her *bhori* [innocent, silly], she was one of the dancers of Shahjahanabad. She left her shameful living and her nature was very agreeable. She had no equals in singing (*naghmasarā'ī*) and dancing (*raqṣ*). She used to meet Mirza Bedil frequently, and she composed poetry.[33]

As with Pinki above, the interplay between the real and the imaginary allows the *tazkira* writer to textualise a "marginal" character within the same space as the great masters:[34] Babri Rindi, just like the others, is a real character who embodies a literary character, who then becomes in Bhagvan Das's *tazkira* a fictive character who talks about reality, calling upon the authoritative weight of Bedil's poetic circle and projecting the whole process (and its reverse) onto it. In fact, Bindraban Das Khwushgu, closely related to Bedil's circle, calls upon the same cast of characters and places himself on the *shahr-ashub* stage while telling an autobiographical story about his own ill-fated love for a female dancer:

> When I fell in love with a female dancer, and was extremely distressed because of it, one day I happened to be in his [Shah Gulshan's] presence [at Zinat al-Nisa' mosque]. I couldn't help bursting into tears, and he asked me what was going on. I told him everything and said, "Can you tell me if will finally succeed in having her?". He replied: "I will divine it in my dreams". When he woke up, he said: "You won't have her, in fact I have even seen the person who is entitled to have her. He has the looks of a Kunwar and seems to be a chieftain". I felt desperate. After a few months she was bought for one thousand five hundred rupees by the representative of the *zamindar* of Bikaner, who took that beauty to his province.[35]

Just as important as the poets' house and the street of the bazaar, the temple milieu (*masjid*, *dargah*, *takiya*, etc.) is another main locus for constructing (and remembering) the lore of Indo-Persian poetic circles in *tazkira* tellings, a kind of screen on which we can watch textualised orality at play. The narrative objects of the *tazkiras*, i.e. the poets, are themselves in several cases represented as sufis, renunciates, *faqirs*, and generic holy men, and it is surely redundant to recall that these personas form a substantial part of the Persian literary cast as whole.

---

33 Hindi (1958), p. 90.

34 The presence of the well-known conversion *topos* is a further hint in this direction, see footnote 17 above.

35 Khwushgu (1959), p. 167.

Along the same lines of the examples above, the recovery of the pre-textual and localised orality that is textualised in *tazkira* tellings charts a productive interplay between real(istic), fictional, and imaginary planes. An exemplary story is narrated by Khwushgu about the Naqshbandi shaykh and musician Shah Gulshan, who has already appeared, and whom the *Safīna* describe as the "Amir Khusrau of the times", according to the definition of "most of the accomplished singers", and as living in poverty ("he lived on the *khichhri* of the offerings"), at the mosque of Zinat al-Nisa on the banks of the Yamuna in Delhi. Khwushgu, who boasts about having been in close contact with him, tells us that:

> One day he was travelling back from Lahore and was crossing a perilous desert with very rough terrain, with sharp thorns that were tormenting the travellers' feet. In the middle of the stage (*manzil*), he felt the urge to compose poetry. He saw the shade of a tree and left the caravan. In that unusual place he started thinking of a *ghazal*. A *faqir*, completely naked, appeared out of nowhere and, being extremely surprised, asked him, "O *darvish*, how can you stop here, in this path where even lion-hearted men feel anguish? Get up and continue your walk, otherwise you will die!" He replied "Thanks to the grace of my weakness, I got so estranged from myself that the idea of going back is a danger itself. This ink-holder, this pen, this paper and this torn cloak, is all that remains of me: if the end of my life comes now it would be a blessing". [...] He did not leave that place until he had finished his *ghazal*.[36]

The travellers' misery, the bush thorns on a desert road, the asperity of the stages of the journey, and so on, are all canonical metaphors for the harshness of the spiritual path in Persian and Persianate literatures. Thus the *tazkira* notice sets up a double mirror between experience, fictional narrative, and poetic text: it does not include Shah Gulshan's *ghazal* but the terms it uses to describe the occasion in which the *ghazal* was composed are common in the *ghazal* code, thus raising the question of whether this particular *ghazal* by Shah Gulshan used those terms too. This telling places the sufi poet on the stage of his own craft, adds tridimensionality to this specific theme of suficate poetry, and locates a timeless and placeless literary image in a precise time and place. This manner of bringing the theme to life is comparable to the visual comment of a miniature painting illustrating a *ghazal*. But unlike miniature painting, such a telling also relocates the poetic event to a

36 Ibid., p. 166.

specific historical present, one shared by the characters of the *tazkira* and its immediate readers—it gives the event visible movement and an audible voice.

Similar observations can be made for the following story, this time located in a Hindu temple, regarding the sufi poet and *tazkira* writer Muhammad Afzal Sarkhwush:

> While he was coming back from Ajmer he stopped at Manoharpur and ended up entering the shrine where a Hindu ascetic (*hindū faqīr*) lived. He enjoyed the conversation that ensued so much that he remained there for twenty-five days, no matter how much his travel companions insisted on departing. A brilliant point in that conversation occurred when that monotheist ascetic (*faqīr-i muwaḥḥid*) said during the discussions: "Idolatry and Islam are one and the same thing!". Sarkhwush replied: "If things are like this, then why don't you become a Muslim?". The *faqir* replied: "Things are exactly like this! So why don't you become a Hindu (*chirā hindū namīshavī*)? One side is equivalent to the other, and my point is that sometimes it is necessary to go beyond both". The *faqir* then recited this lines from [Rumi's] *Maṣnavī*:
>
> *When the absence of colour*[37] *becomes the prisoner of colour,*
> *then a Moses starts a war against another Moses.*
>
> *When you reach the colourlessness which used to be yours,*
> *then Moses and the Pharaoh will make a durable peace.*
>
> *And if you still have questions about this subject*
> *then you should know that colour always matches with vain debates.*[38]

In this particular episode, the memorialisation of orality in the telling can also be read as a strategy. Thus the classical theme in Persian suficate poetry of the supreme unity of idolatry and Islam and the recognizable poetic character of the non-Muslim Holy Man make visible and audible space for "new" emerging subjects in the socio-textual realm of Indo-Persian literary culture. The Vaishnava *tazkira* writer is speaking about

37 The text has the form نیرنگی instead of the expected بیرنگی "colourlessness", which is found in Nicholson's edition of Rumi's *Maṣnavī*; see *The Mathnawí of Jalálu'ddín Rúmí, Edited from the Oldest Manuscripts Available, with Critical Notes, Translation and Commentary*, ed. by R.A. Nicholson (London: Luzac & Co., 1925), Vol. 1, p. 152 (vv. 2467-69). I consider نیرنگی, which can also be read as *nayrangī* "magic", a misprint and follow the text established by Nicholson in my translation.

38 Khwushgu (1959), p. 73.

himself (and the social groups he represents) and the canon of Persian poetical culture as well as about the "historicity" of Sarkhwush and his meeting with the "Hindu *faqir*", along the lines I have repeatedly dealt with elsewhere.[39] The ascetic is even made to substantiate his brilliant reply with an impromtu recitation of three famous Persian lines from the first *daftar* of Jalal al-Din Rumi's *Maṡnavī-yi ma'navī*, containing the much-codified imagery of Moses and the Pharaoh, thus locating the ascetic well within the protocol frame of Persian poetic *tazkira*. Moreover, to remain within the intertextual world of Khwushgu's circle, the whole episode can be read in parallel with the telling about the dialogue between his master Bedil and his Brahmin fellow-traveller, a scene retold in the *Chahār 'Unṣur*, where, conversely, Bedil wins an argument regarding the nature of time (and converts the Brahmin to Islam) by technically referring to the whole duration of the life of Brahma as "the twinkling of the eye of Vishnu the black".[40]

Finally, tellings from the "temple" environment like those from other settings, especially the bazaar, can also function as containers to hint at vernacular practices and identities. This is the case in the first-hand account of a meeting between Khwushgu and the Kashmiri sufi 'Abd al-'Ali Tahsin, "who used to stay with Saint Gulshan at the Begam's [Zinat al-Nisa'] mosque":

> One day he was sitting on the banks of a stream, in the shrine of a *darvish*, with two or three friends. With a cup full of *bhang* in his hand, he was talking about it: "Some friends describe *bhang* with the word *rainī*, and Indians call the night "*rain*". Is it because the color of *bhang* resembles that of the night, or is *rain* used to allude to earth, since whoever takes *bhang* is brought down to the earth?" I arrived during this conversation and listened to it. He saw me, and after the greetings I said: "O master, the word *rainī* is a term used by Indian dyers and indicates the vats where they keep colours, especially the colour red, and in which they immerse clothes to dye them. This is the clear similitude between *rain* and *bhang*: if you immerse yourself in it, it makes you colourful!". Tahsin offered the cup to me and said: "Since you are a Hindu, this is your job!"[41]

---

39 See Pellò (2014a), and 'Between Gayā and Karbalā: The Textual Identification of Persian Hindu Poets from Lucknow in Bhagwān Dās Hindī's Tazkira', in *Religious Interactions in Mughal India*, ed. by V. Dalmia and M. Faruqi (New Delhi: Oxford University Press, 2014b).

40 Bedil (1965-66), pp. 41-45.

41 Khwushgu (1959), pp. 266-67.

The telling gives Khwushgu the opportunity to promote himself as an authority as far as Hindi and "Indian" vernacular cultures are concerned, somehow expanding the well-experimented strategy of using *tazkiras* as instruments for including details about the specific cultic space of non-Muslim Persian writers in North India in late Mughal times. Along the same lines, the explicit recognition of Khwushgu's religious identity through Tahsin's persona (and the implicit reference to the ritual use of hemp by *sadhus* and the like) hints at the emergence of the socio-semiotic identity of Vaishnava authors within Indo-Persian poetic circles that I have discussed elsewhere.[42] Equally relevant to our investigation is the philological discussion at the centre of the story. Along with dictionaries and commentaries, *tazkiras* are where the correct meanings and uses of words are discussed, especially those relating to the poetic world, predictably enough. A large part of the discussions taking place during *musha'iras*, *majlises*, and sessions of poem-correction represented in the *tazkiras* deal, in fact, with the etymology, meanings, and metaphorical value of a specific word, and the correct opportunity to use it. Khwushgu places this communicative dynamic in public places such as the streets and mosques of Delhi and matches the subject of the discussion with the place of the story. The use of *bhang* by fellow poets and the vernacular world adumbrated behind it are thus included in the *tazkira* narrative through the frame of a philological discussion, which follows the scheme even to its conclusion, with a well-earned prize given to the author of the most brilliant definition.

## Conclusion: The *Langue* and the *Parole* of the *Maktab*

The relatively large colloquial Hindi vocabulary found in *tazkira* stories about the everyday life of Indo-Persian poets should not go unnoticed. *Pinki* ("intoxication"), *rath* ("cart"), *bhori* ("naive woman"), *phish* ("pshaw!"), *khichhri* (the well known rice dish), *bhang* ("hemp drink"), and *rain/raini* ("night/nocturnal"), the words mentioned in the short excerpts analysed here, are just a few examples from a much larger catalogue of vernacular, everyday words that are very frequently accompanied by their Persian or Arabic-Persian equivalents—as if the

42 Pellò (2014a).

readers would not know.[43] However, Hindi is *not* spoken within the tellings:

> Once he [Mirza Bedil] went out with a stout hand-stick (*chūb-i dastī*), which in Hindi is called "*laṭh*", and met a great shaykh who had had the grace of being a close acquaintance and companion of his for thirty years. [The shaykh] said something about the stick (*'aṣā*), and the honourable Bedil immediately replied with five elegant and rhymed definitions: "*sunnat al-anbiyā*" (the tradition of the prophets), "*zīnat al-ṣulaḥā*" (the ornament of the pious ones), "*mu'nīs al-a'mā*" (the companion of the blind), "*mumidd al-żu'afā*" (the assistant of the weak ones), "*dāfi' al-a'dā*" (defense of the enemies).[44]

Bedil ventures into the unsafe streets of Delhi with a "*laṭh*", but talks to his friend the *shaykh* about an *'aṣā*, improvising five Arabic metaphors for it: Hindi is alluded to, but the official spoken language of the telling is Perso-Arabic. As a matter of fact, notwithstanding the insistence on mentioning and explaining Hindi terms within the Persian texture of the narrations, not much room is left for Hindi in these stories, not even when the poet-actors deal with the small-talk of the *maktab* gossip, the street environment of the bazaar, or the vernacular world of *sadhus* and *faqirs*. The absolute star of Khwushgu's *tazkira*, Mirza Bedil, is quite clear on this matter in his own autobiography. When retelling his meetings with one of his masters, the wandering ascetic Shah Muluk, who was living in Banaras, "stretched out under a tree like a shadow, like grass woven in a clot of earth",[45] Bedil writes:

> In those days he composed almost forty lines, and they became the precious substance of the awakening of the ignorant author of these pages [...] Since most of them were composed according to the expressions of India and followed the rules of Rekhta, *it would have been inappropriate to include them in the present book, which is obedient to the rank of Persian.*
>
> *How many concepts that, due to the strangeness of language,*
> *with all their petulance remained on the pages of secrecy!*[46]

43 I have discussed the implications of this strategy of vernacular inclusion with Persian glosses "as if readers did not know" in my 'Local Lexis? Provincializing Persian in Fifteenth-century North India', in *After Timur Left: Culture and Circulation in Fifteenth-Century North India*, ed. by F. Orsini and S. Sheikh (New Delhi: Oxford University Press, 2014).

44 Khwushgu (1959), p. 120.

45 Bedil (1965-66), p. 20.

46 Ibid., p. 34, emphasis added.

The vernacular utterings of Shah Muluk are not allowed into the Persian frame of Bedil's *Chahār 'unṣūr*, just as the Hindi street conversation about the *laṭh* between Bedil and the shaykh does not fit the generic protocols of Khwushgu's *Safīna* and must be filtered through the Perso-Arabic linguistic and poetic code (i.e. the five rhymed definitions) to properly work within the palimpsest of the *tazkira*. Thus, direct speech is not only represented in Persian (think, for instance, of Nasir 'Ali's exchange with the vegetable seller in the Delhi market) but can just as often be substituted by Persian verse, as in the above case of the "Hindu *faqir*" talking to Muhammad Afzal Sarkhwush in the shrine at Manoharpur.

It would be trivialising to read this as a straightforward strategy of exclusion. The *parole* of Indo-Persian poetic circles cannot be represented as such within the textual space of the *tazkira* but can—and must—be invoked through its projection onto the *langue* of Persian poetic culture. Vernacularity is not absent but hidden and works like a sub-text, continuously evoked by "subtitled" Hindi vocabulary and the oral realm of the localised tellings and gossip, once again "dubbed" in Persian. In more general terms we should keep in mind that *tazkiras*, these "hagiographies of (poetic) language",[47] are written in the attempt to capture not the elusive, unattainable "real" life of the literati but rather their textual existence. Nevertheless, the marked historicity of the biographical tellings is summoned through the use of expressive rules that are expandable, if not changeable. Giorgio Vasari, in his *Vite de' più eccellenti pittori*, projected the everyday life stories of Italian artists (who incidentally are all made to speak literary Tuscan and not their Venetian or Lombard dialects) onto the aesthetic screen of Renaissance figurative art, yet at the same time textualised the vernacular spaces of sixteenth-century Italy surrounding it, as in the tragicomic story of the beautiful young porter whom the Marquise of Mantova manhandled so as to make him a better model for Saint Sebastian's martyrdom.[48] In a

47 Consider, for instance, the opening lines (immediately after the canonical eulogies) of the introduction of the *Kalimāt al-shu'arā*: "Word (*sukhan*) has no beginning and is eternal, because speech (*kalām*) is one of the seven attributes (*ṣifāt-i sab'a*) of God. Since the essence has no beginning and is eternal, its attributes must consequently be eternal and with no beginning as well. Until the spring of the ability of speaking (*nuṭq*) will be flourishing, every tongue will be a flower seller of colourful expressions; and among the totality of mouths and tongues, the dignity of metered words and poetry will forever be superior to non-metered words and prose"; Sarkhwush (1951), p. 1.

48 The episode is found in the life of the Veronese painter Francesco Bonsignori (c.1460-1519); see Vasari (1880), 5, pp. 299-307.

similar fashion, what I have called the lore of later Mughal Indo-Persian poetic circles, their web of tellings, was textualised and translated onto a regulated representational plane, yet at the same time the result of this process can be read as a telling itself, one that surveyed the pre-textual and the con-textual spaces of these poetic circles in order to shape a live, localised, and influential narrative of the specific world of Persian poetical production and reception in late Mughal North India.

# 12. Texts and Tellings: *Kathas* in the Fifteenth and Sixteenth Centuries

*Francesca Orsini*

Wrestlers, mimics, actors perform, *pandits* recite the scriptures.
Songs, sounds, stories full of *rasa*, it's a good pastime,
The fort people are happy and give handsome rewards.[1]

In the ecology of performance genres in early modern India, *kathas* or stories are pretty much ubiquitous. We find them recited at courts and in village assemblies, at the foot of citadels and in courtyards, in temples and sufi assemblies, even occasionally from the pulpits of mosques—and they are also one of the standard markers in the description of cities, as in the quotation above (see also Busch in this volume). In the fifteenth and sixteenth centuries in particular, *kathas* account for a significant percentage of literary production. The *kathas* we have from that period are written texts, typically in verse form, but they are texts that clearly bear the traces of their oral-literate nature—they were meant to be read or recited aloud and mostly refer to themselves with verbs that have to do with telling and listening, as other contributors to this volume also point out.[2] Copied artfully or scrappily in different scripts, with

1 Malik Muhammad Jayasi, *Kanhāvat*, ed. by Shivsahay Pathak (Allahabad: Sahitya Bhawan, 1981), p. 21.

2 The most comprehensive and holistic study of a Hindavi *katha* text *in* performance and of text *and* performance is Philip Lutgendorf's *The Life of a Text: Performing the* Rāmcaritmānas *of Tulsidas* (Berkeley: University of California Press, 1991). About the *Rāmcaritmānas'* (*Mānas* for short) own relationship to written and oral textualities, Lutgendorf notes that although Tulsidas uses the verb "to read" (*bā̃cnā*) when written

 http://dx.doi.org/10.11647/OBP.0062.12

or without illustrations, and translated into different languages, they clearly circulated across, and wove together, the layered and multilingual literary culture of North India, much like songs. In fact, two of the three tales from the fifteenth and sixteenth centuries I discuss in this essay—Isardas's *Satyavatī kathā* (1501) and Alam's *Mādhavānal Kāmakandalā* (991 AH/1582)[3]—were held together in manuscript copies in Kaithi script from the eighteenth century by the same individual in Ekadla village of Fatehpur district (UP), alongside copies of Jayasi's *Padmāvat*, Qutban's *Mirigāvatī*, and Manjhan's *Madhumālatī*—tangible evidence that these tales were once part of a common repertoire.[4]

Whatever their specific topic, Hindavi *kathas* written in this period share two noticeable features. They either anchor the story in or refer to epic and Puranic characters and/or narratives, even when they subvert them or quickly leave them behind. And they combine and blend instruction and entertainment, so that even sections that are specifically marked as dealing with spiritual-philosophical or technical knowledge (*gyana*) often contain a significant amount of humour.

This essay explores these two features across a number of *kathas*, but with particular focus on the rewriting of epic-Puranic women's characters and their agency in Bhima Kabi's *Ḍaṅgvai kathā* and on the display and discussion of musical knowledge in Alam's *Mādhavānal Kāmakandalā*.

---

communications such as letters are "read", nowhere is the verb used in reference to reading the *Mānas* itself—the verbs commonly used are "to recite" (*kathnā*), "to tell" (*kahnā*), "to sing or chant" (*gānā*), and "to listen" (*sunnā*), the same terms used in our *katha* texts (pp. 37-38). The word *katha* occurs as many as 180 times in the *Mānas*, often in reference to Tulsi's own narrative (the term "book" or *granth* is sometimes used but never with reference to his own text), and he speaks of composing the text after having listened to the story of Ram "again and again" from his guru, slowly and gradually grasping and deepening his understanding of it (p. 23).

3 The third is Bhima Kabi's *Ḍaṅgvai kathā* (1493), ed. by Shivgopal Misra (Allahabad: Hindi Sahitya Sammelan, 1966).

4 Shivgopal Misra, *Satyavatī kathā tathā anya kṛtiyāṃ* (Gwalior: Vidyamandir Prakashan, 1958), p. 24. Apart from the epics (*Rāmāyaṇa* and *Mahābhārata*), other tales that were rewritten and retold (rather than translated) across North Indian vernaculars and Persian in this period include *Mirigāvatī* (in Persian *Rāj Kunvar*), *Madhumālatī* (as *Gulshan-i Ma'ānī*), *Padmāvat*, and the *Mādhavānal Kāmakandhalā* discussed here. See R.S. McGregor, *Hindi Literature from its Beginnings to the Nineteenth Century* (Wiesbaden: Harrassowitz, 1984); for the full history of the Padmavati/Padmini story before and after Jayasi, see Ramya Sreenivasan, *The Many Lives of a Rajput Queen: Heroic Pasts in India, c.1500-1900* (New Delhi: Permanent Black, 2007).

How were the *katha* texts from this period performed? Barring Tulsidas's *Rāmcaritmānas* (1574), whose performance "life" continues to the present day and has been studied in an exemplary fashion by Philip Lutgendorf, we don't really know. Yet—and this is one of the assumptions behind this volume—current performance practices help us ask the right questions regarding past performances, even though the actual form of the performance may have substantially changed.[5] For example, Lutgendorf argues that even at the time of the composition of the *Mānas* we should not presume that this written *katha* "was intended to stand by itself without further mediation or that its early 'telling' consisted only of reciting its text".[6] Besides, the "slow, systematic, storytelling recitation, interspersed with prose explanations, elaborations, and homely illustrations of spiritual points" that is typical of *Mānas katha* performances now reflects, Lutgendorf argues, Tulsidas's own point about the Ram *katha* as being "mysterious, profound, enigmatic" and *requiring* exposition, because only a listener who is a "treasury of wisdom" can grasp its inner meaning.[7] Aditya Behl has highlighted the

---

5 Other studies of contemporary *kathas* in performance include Annd Grodzins Gold, *A Carnival of Parting: The Tales of King Bharthari and King Gopi Chand As Sung and Told by Madhu Natisar Nath of Ghatiyali* (Berkeley: University of California Press, 1992); Susan S. Wadley, *Raja Nal and the Goddess: The North Indian Epic* Dhola *in Performance* (Bloomington: Indiana University Press, 2004); J.D. Smith, *The Epic of Pabuji: A Study, Transcription and Translation* (Cambridge: Cambridge University Press, 1991); and Shyam Manohar Pandey's transcriptions of the different versions of the Lorik-Chanda oral epic: *The Hindi Oral Epic Canainī (The Tale of Lorik and Candā)* (Allahabad: Sahitya Bhawan Ltd., 1982) and *The Hindi Oral Epic Tradition: Bhojpurī Lorikī* (Allahabad: Sahitya Bhawan, 1996-2005).

6 Lutgendorf (1991), pp. 119-20. Even completely oral performances, such as the contemporary telling of the stories of King Bharthari and King Gopinath in rural Rajasthan, exhibit a complementarity between (oral) text and oral exposition. Madhu Nath's "performance alternates regularly between segments of sung lines, accompanied by music which he plays himself on the *sārangī*—a simple stringed instrument played with a bow—and a prose 'explanation' (*arthāv*). In this explanation he retells everything he has just sung, using more colourful, prosaic, and often vulgar language than he does in the singing. The spoken parts are performances or communicative events as clearly marked as the musical portions are. Whereas Madhu's ordinary style of speaking is normally low-key and can seem almost muted, his *arthāv* is always enunciated distinctly and projected vigorously. The *arthāv*, moreover, often incorporates the same stock phrases and poetic conceits that occur in the singing"; Gold (1992), p. 9. Interestingly, Gold chose to translate the *arthav* rather than the sung text as more representative of Madhu's artful performance.

7 Lutgendorf (1991), p. 118, quoting *Mānas* 1.30b, and p. 115. Tulsidas seems to occasionally throw in obscure verses, brief allusions, and references to religio-philosophical doctrines that cry out to be explained and developed; for examples of "mysterious verses" and the ways in which *katha* expounders explain them, see

importance of the enigmatic form in Hindavi sufi *kathas*: "Sufi romances are composed enigmatically because of a fundamental problem or enigma with which the spiritual users had to grapple".[8] Obscurities in the text—Lutgendorf and Behl both suggest—can thus be read as clues to points in the narrative text that would attract oral exposition.

Lutgendorf's study importantly shows the *multiplicity* of formal and informal performance practices that have grown around a particular *katha* text, the complementarity between text and exposition, the expert knowledge that both performers and listeners possess and that is orally transmitted, the mixture of knowledge (*gyana*), devotion, emotion, and entertainment that the *katha* text and its performances activate, the formulaic elements and yet the artfulness of it all. But while Lutgendorf understandably considers many of these characteristics peculiar to the *Mānas* as a devotional text, we will see that many of the same elements come into play across a whole spectrum of *kathas*.

## Epic-Puranic Frames

So many are the references to the epics and the Puranas even in *kathas* that have ostensibly little to do with them that we may speak of an epic-Puranic continuum that includes also romances and ritual tales (*prem-kathas* and *vrat-kathas*). Why are such epic-Puranic references and/or framing so ubiquitous?[9] One possible explanation is that authors and storytellers may have wanted to tag their original stories onto the familiar epic-Puranic repertoire to strengthen their value and/or acceptability, and because telling was customarily presented as a "re-telling"—as scholarship on the "many Ramayanas" has amply shown.[10] But while

---

ibid., pp. 221-23. Lutgendorf's book explores a whole range of readings, tellings, and performances of the text, from private reading to public recitation to singing to ritual enactment. Even reading practices (*pāṭh*) range from private individuals to professional reciters, at home or in a temple, including the full recitiation (*pārāyaṇ pāṭh*) in nine days, one month, and the "unbroken recitation" (*akhaṇḍ pāṭh*) within twenty-four hours—usually a sponsored ritual event; ibid., pp. 54, 60, 79.

8 A. Behl, 'Introduction' to *The Magic Doe: Qutban Suhrawardi's Mirigāvatī*, trans. by A. Behl and ed. by Wendy Doniger (New York: Oxford University Press, 2012a), p. 29.

9 Except, for example, Bajid's tales, which do not refer to them; see Bangha in this volume.

10 A.K. Ramanujan's essay 'Three Hundred Ramayanas: Five Examples and Three Thoughts on Translation' first appeared in Paula Richman's collection *Many Rāmāyaṇas: The Diversity of a Narrative Tradition in South Asia* (Berkeley: University of California Press, 1991); see also Richman's further collection *Questioning Ramayanas: A*

A.K. Ramanujan's pioneering work highlighted the subversiveness of oral ("folklore") tellings, we will see that written tales could also offer bold twists on familiar epic characters and stories. Bhima Kabi's *Ḍaṅgvai kathā*, for example, rewrote the character of Subhadra and of other female characters from the *Mahābhārata* in a way that emphasised the importance and agency of the local Rajput women for whom he composed the tale.

Bhima, who also authored a version of the Chakravyuha story from the *Mahābhārata*, tells us that the wife and daughter of his Baghela chieftain or small king patron loved the Puranas and the *Mahābhārata*. Significantly, both women are named: his wife Manikdei is "a [*pati*]*vratī* who knows *vratadharma*"; like Durga and Bhavani personified, she is devoted to *dharma* and always listens to the Vedas and Puranas, while her daughter, Ghatmadei, enjoys listening to the "*Bhāratha kathā*".[11] Such evidence shows that the authors and tellers of these tales also recited the Puranas and the epics—the *Mahābhārata* and *Rāmāyaṇa*—to their patrons.[12]

Puranas proclaim "frequently and often at considerable length" in so-called *phalashruti* verses (lit. "fruit of listening") the efficacy and the benefits that accrue from listening to, reciting, or copying them or making others do so.[13] But *phalashruti* verses and instructions to listen to the tale "with undivided concentration" (*mana lāi*) invariably tag *kathas* from this period, whatever the topic. In Isardas's *Satyavatī kathā* the *phalashruti* stanza at the end declares the merit of listening to (as well as telling) this *katha* to be equal if not surpass that of many other rituals like pilgrimage or gift-giving to Brahmins. Knowledge is again mentioned as one benefit accrued:

---

*South Asian Tradition* (New Delhi: Oxford University Press, 2000). For the *Mahābhārata*, see A. Hiltebeitel, *Draupadī Among Rajputs, Muslims and Dalits: Rethinking India's Oral and Classical Epics* (New Delhi: Oxford University Press, 2001).

11 S. Misra (1966), p. 84, stanza 4.

12 Another indirect piece of evidence is the Brahmin *kathavachak* from Kannauj chided by Vallabhacharya for earning money from expounding the *Bhāgavata-purāṇa* along with other texts; he then turned to reciting the *Mahābhārata* to a "local king"; Shyam Das, *Eighty-four Vaishnavas* (Delhi: Butala Publications, 1985), pp. 31-37.

13 Indeed, listening to a *katha* or a *puran-katha* is presented as one of the most efficacious ways of cultivating a love for God, if not *the* most appropriate way in the Kali age; Lutgendorf (1991), pp. 57, 115; he also quotes the six-chapter *māhātmya* contained in the *Bhāgavata-purāṇa* that details the merits that accrue from reciting or listening to the text or presenting a copy to a devotee (p. 58); see also Hawley in this volume.

Whoever listens intently (*mana lāī*) to the tale of Satyavati loses their great sins (*mahāpāpa*).
Knowledge springs in the mind of the listeners as if they'd heard the Vedas and Puranas,
As if they'd given gifts and money (*dravya dāna*) to the Brahmins
and dispatched them honourably;
As if they'd performed ritual obligations ["*nema, dharma, acārā*"]
and gained *darshan* of Deva Gopala;
As if they'd bathed in all the *tirthas*, visited them, and given gifts.
The fruit of telling the story equals listening to the thousand names of God;
Isar *kabi* sang and it was as if he'd travelled to scores of *tirthas*.[14]

Listening to tales, the evidence shows, was thus presented and perceived as a meritorious and beneficial activity (see Khan, Sharma, and Bard in this volume). But we also see here a generic feature at work, one that we may link to performance context and audience expectations. Each tale modulates and combines registers of instruction and entertainment—through humorous/subversive situations, vivid dialogues, emotional scenes, displays of technical knowledge, and so on—so that drawing a line between "entertaining" and "enlightening/instructive" tales seems quite artificial.[15] Rather, all these seem to have been ingredients that a good author and teller even then needed to be able to combine (and elaborate on depending on the audience's mood). For example, good and bad rule is one of the topics upon which the *Mahābhārata* and *Rāmāyaṇa* instruct. So *katha* authors and tellers included, normally in the introductory section, a discourse on Kaliyuga and the instability and confusion prevailing in the world, and on good and bad rule—often extremely brief but nonetheless there. Even if there is little in Isardas's *Satyavatī kathā* to suggest a courtly milieu—with its focus on a wife's trials, penance, and reward for the sake of her husband's health, the

14 S. Misra (1958), p. 94, stanza 58. See also the *phalashruti* in the *Ḍaṅgvai kathā*, which implicitly equates the tale to a Purana: "If you hear the Purana you have *dharma*, if you listen to the Purana knowledge [*gyāna*] arises. Who has dharma gets wealth and sons, people without it are like beasts. For this reason Bhima proclaims [*gohrāvā*], forget everything and set your heart on Vishnu". A few stanzas later, some lines that may be additions, since they do not appear in all the manuscripts, draw a direct link to this *katha* and the Puranas: 8.1-3, S. Mishra (1966), p. 87.

15 E.g. of the storytelling performances of Bharthari and Gopichand, Ann Gold says, "Like most of Rajasthan's popular folk tradition these meshed with the audience's twin passion for entertainment and enlightenment"; Gold (1992), p. 14.

story reads largely like a ritual *vrat-katha*—its introductory section still contains one stanza about unjust rule:

> In a country where the king is evil (*mada*), no good man dwells.
> The mind of a stupid ruler is like the moon of the fourth night, blank.
> First he makes promises to the Brahmins,
> then he takes all the wealth himself.
> He considers gold equal to glass (*kañcana kāṃca barābara dekhai*), and sin equal to virtue.[16]

This forces us to ask the question of what terms like *gyana* (knowledge), *bhava* (emotion), and expressions like listening to tales "*mana lāi*" (with concentration, bringing the mind-heart to bear upon) meant for audiences in this period.

Intertextual references to other characters and other stories must have been even then one of the pleasures of *katha* performances, and one of the skills that storytellers displayed, in performance possibly through the digressions that are endemic in many storytelling performances and traditions.[17] Such intertextual play was of course based on the assumption that the audience would be familiar with the characters, stories, and situations hinted at and could savour the correspondence while listening to the performance and admire the storyteller's ability to weave those references into the story.[18] Thomas de Bruijn has spoken of the *katha* as a "dialogic genre", so fundamental is this intertextual play to

16 S. Misra (1958), stanza 4, pp. 66-67.

17 Intertextual references often work as terms of comparison in evaluative descriptions: e.g. Indra, Krishna, Rama, *kinnara*, Kama, and Kubera are all invoked to praise in extravagant terms Madhavanal's impressive appearance, his supernatural beauty, his wealth, and his attractiveness. Or else they help making a general point: Madhavanal cannot escape the line of his fate (*karama rekha*) any more than the Pandavas could their exile, or Raghava when he bore the consequences of Narada's curse upon his father; it was because of fate that King Harishchandra found himself a humble water-carrier, and that Bali the king of the monkeys lost everything; *Ālamkṛt Mādhavānal Kāmakandalā*, ed. by Rajkumari Misra (Allahabad: Ratnakumari Svadhyay Sansthan, 1982), pp. 39-40. For intertextual references in Persian *qissas*, see Khan in this volume.

18 For a brilliant analysis of Surdas's use of this device in his song-poems and the effect it has on listeners, see K. Bryant, *Poems to the Child-God: Structures and Strategies in the Poetry of Sūrdās* (Berkeley: University of California Press, 1978), and Hawley in this volume. That the ability to refer to or to link a verse, a name or a situation to other characters and stories is still highly valued in oral exposition is supported by evidence in Lutgendorf (1991) and Gold (1992).

its narrative and performance logic, for example, in Malik Muhammad Jayasi's use of the Rama story in his *Padmāvat* (1540).[19]

In his observation of contemporary *Mānas katha* performances, Philip Lutgendorf notes that the invocation and the communal singing (*kirtan*) at the beginning of a performance, besides setting up the ritual-devotional time-space, "give the speaker a measure of the audience's mood, which will be crucial to the success of his performance". What about the framing that is *written* into *kathas* from this period, what clues does it give us about the way authors, tellers, and audiences perceived tales?

In the case of the *Rāmcaritmānas*, Lutgendorf has drawn attention to the importance of how the four sets of tellers and listeners of the *Mānas* match the four descending ghats to the "Lake of the Deeds of Ram". This Puranic framing turns Tulsidas's Ram *katha* into a kind of Purana while also underscoring the devotional message of the telling. The tellers and listeners include Shiva and Parvati (just as in 'Abd al-Rahman Chishti's *Mir'āt al-makhlūqāt* in Muzaffar Alam's chapter in this volume), the crow Bhushundi and Garuda, the sages Yajnavalkya and Bharadvaj, and finally Tulsidas and his audience.[20] In both the *Mānas* and the *Mir'āt al-makhlūqāt* this framing therefore inserts the story into the Puranic logic of divine intervention—with previous curses and boons explaining the birth and actions of various characters (for Tulsidas particularly in the first book). In the *Mir'āt* the framing also acts as an authenticating and familiarising device. Yet while in the *Mir'āt* the frame helps combine the different Indic and Islamic temporalities of creation, in the *Mānas* the multiple levels of narrators give a tangible sense of the eternal temporality of the story—it has always existed and it is eternally retold, even as or before it happens.[21] The multiple narrators also underscore the special theme of the *Mānas*, i.e. the saving power of devotion and of Ram's name in

---

19 Thomas de Bruijn, 'Dialogism in a Medieval Genre: The Case of the Avadhi Epics', in *Before the Divide: Hindi and Urdu Literary Culture*, ed. by F. Orsini (New Delhi: Orient Blackswan, 2010), pp. 121-42. For a systematic survey of epic-Puranic references in Hindavi sufi romances, see Umapati Rai Chandel, *Hindī sūfī kāvya meṃ paurāṇik ākhyān* (Delhi: Abhinav Prakashan, 1976).

20 Lutgendorf (1991), p. 25.

21 Famously, the first tellers of the story are Ram's own children. Lutgendorf (1991, pp. 24-25) observes that in the *Mānas* Tulsi draws attention to the multiple narrators so often that "one must assume it to be an important element in the poet's strategy; evidently Tulsi expected his audience to remain continuously aware of all four narrative frames".

the Kali age—Bhushundi, Shiva, and Tulsidas are all eloquent on this point.[22]

A simpler epic-Puranic framing device appears almost ubiquitously in the Hindavi tales of the fifteenth and sixteenth centuries—whether they actually reworked epic-Puranic material or not, and not necessarily to produce the same effects. In Isardas's *Satyāvatī kathā*, for example, written at Joginipur-Delhi, this framing device provides simply a stepping-stone for the narrative, though it arguably also lends weight to the tale and underscores the benefits accruing to listening to it.[23] After invoking Ganesha, the power of the Goddess Jalpa (*Jālapā māyā*), and Rama's compassion and listing the requisites of a good king, Isardas has Janmejaya ask Vyasa *rikhi* (*rishi*) where the five Pandavas went while in exile. After naming the places they visited in the first seven years, Vyasa comes to the eighth year, when the Pandavas reached Jharkhanda and had *darshan* of the sage Markandeya. In the ensuing dialogue between the Pandavas and Markandeya, the brothers ask the sage for a "book full of *rasa*" (*grantha rasārā*), so that:

> *listening* to it our dharma may increase,
> we may attain the path of salvation and our sins may be removed.
> The mind wanders if the body/one (*jīu*) is renunciant (*bairāgī*).
> Today we have found a great treasure, o Guru, a great fortune.
> *Tell* us something, Gosain, that will awaken our *gyāna*.[24]

Satyavati's *katha* is, implicitly, that book, and though these two sets of Puranic narrators play no further part in the narrative, the link has been established.

After an invocation to Ganesha, to Sharda (Sarasvati), and to Shiva, Bhima Kabi begins his *Ḍaṅgvai kathā* (in "*pasu bhāṣā*") with a summary description of his story—as one would do in performance—and links it directly to the *Mahābhārata* and its heroes:

---

22 Lutgendorf (1991), pp. 28-29.

23 The *Satyavatī kathā* is only one of a number of tales circulating in this period that have *sat* in the title (the most famous of them is probably *Mainā-sat*) and that deal with women's duty and religion. The story develops very much along the pattern of the *vrat-kathas* that Lutgendorf mentioned above. See also Amy Bard in this collection for Shi'i homoforms.

24 S. Misra (1958), pp. 68-69. A similar stanza is found in the eighth stanza of the *Ḍaṅgvai kathā*, see S. Misra (1966), p. 87.

*sārada au ganesa baru dīnhā, taba maiṃ kathā arambhai kīnhā;*
*tehi pāche saṃvareuṃ gananāha, karahu bhīma daṃgau pargāha.*
*krisna sana kasa maḍī hurārī, kaise pāṇḍau līnha ubārī;*
*so kabi bhīma kahau samujhāī, paṛhe gune te pātakhu jāī.*
*au kahau srāpu urbasī dīnhā, kaise urbasī ghorī kīnhā,*
*jāke kahe anega kali, duritana jāīṃ parāī,*
*kr̥ṣṇa caritra kachu gāvau, bhāratha kathā bicārī* ¦ 2 ¦

Sharda and Ganesha gave a boon, then I could begin my story.
After that I praise Shiva [Gananath], make Bhima look after Dangai [Dangau].
How the fight with Krishna began, and how the Pandavas saved him.
Explain and recount it, Bhima the Poet, so that by reading
and considering it sins may go.
Sing of how Urvashi was cursed and turned into a mare.
So that by telling it the many sins of Kaliyuga may be forsaken,
Consider the *Bharatha kathā* and sing some of Krishna's story.[25]

Then, over two stanzas, Bhima Kabi considers the characteristics of the present age, Kaliyuga: everyone has forgotten ascetic practices, prayers (*japa tapa*), and vigour; hypocrites control everything; Brahmins and cows are no longer revered; temples and pilgrimage places are empty; crooks serve lowly masters and masters praise crooked deeds; nobody thinks about the future or the transience of everything and everyone—which he suggests is the topic of his story.[26] There follows a praise of Kashi (Banaras) and a brief "discussion on knowledge", to which we return below.

But the most striking thing about this tale is the way it uses the familiar characters from the *Mahābhārata* to fashion a story that drastically subverted the epic story in order to speak directly to the concerns of his patron's milieu. Remarkable in this is the important, indeed decisive, role that women characters play. Not so much Urvashi-turned-mare, the narrative ploy, but even more significantly Krishna's sister and Arjun's wife Subhadra, and to a lesser extent Duryodhana's wife. They are the ones who direct the action and who articulate the primacy of kinship ties over those of subordinate rule. Taken together with the explicit mention of the Baghela chieftain's wife and daughter as possible patrons of the tale, already mentioned above, this telling suggests a particular historical moment and location in which women of the local elite could

25 S. Misra (1966), p. 82. Explain (*samujhāī*), consider (*bicāri, gune*—also singing), recount (*kahau*), sing (*gāvau*)—all these verbs are employed to describe the text and its telling.
26 Ibid., pp. 85-87, stanzas 6-7.

and did find a narrative voice through their counterparts in the tale. It is worth spending some time on this aspect of the *katha*.

## Strong Women: The *Kathā* of Dangvai or the Epic Overturned

The *Ḍaṅgvai kathā* is an original take on the *Mahābhārata* that uses epic-Puranic characters—at times deploying their familiar characteristics (Bhima's bravery and strength, Narada's trouble-making, Shakuni's wiliness), but mostly freely twisting them and their relationships to suit the story—to weave a tale that responds closely to the concerns of its own milieu.[27] The *Ḍaṅgvai kathā* comes from a Baghela milieu, though it is difficult to pinpoint exactly where geographically. Simon Digby reminds us that the Baghelas, like the Ujjainiyas and the Bachgotis, were major suppliers of military manpower to the Jaunpur Sultans and later allies of Sher Shah. They were therefore among the "spurious Rajput" groups whose kings (*bhuārā* <*bhūpāla*) were more like chieftains and whose courts would have been rather small affairs, though later in the sixteenth century Virabhanu and his grandson Virabhadra became close to Humayun and Akbar and established themselves at Rewa. The values that the story embraces are those of subordinate chiefs of limited means, who have to negotiate between the call of honour and the reality of subordination.[28] The call of honour demands, for example, that one protects anyone who seeks shelter or supports one's kin. But the reality is one of subordination, forced compliance, exile, and punishment at the hands of one's overlord. In particular, the tale revolves around three issues and choices: whether to surrender a treasured object (or woman) or keep it and flee; whether to give shelter or refuse it; and whether loyalty to one's kin comes before loyalty to one's overlord. Women play a vocal and forceful role in all these choices.

---

27 There a few other works by this name: a *Ḍaṅgvai Parva* by one Balvir (1608Vi, *NPS Khoj Report* 1917, Nr 13), a *Jikrī Daṅg Rājā kī* by one Totaram ([n.d.], *NPS Khoj Report* 1932, no. 220), and an anonymous *Ḍaṅgvai Purāṇa* (*NPS Khoj Report* 1935, Nr 152); S. Misra (1966), p. 51.

28 See Simon Digby, 'Two Captains of the Jawnpur Sultanate', in *Circumambulations in South Asian History: Essays in Honour of Dirk H.A. Kolff*, ed. by J. Gommans and O. Prakash (Leiden: Brill, 2003), p. 165; and Hirananda Shastri, 'The Baghela Dynasty of Rewah', *Memoirs of the Archaeological Survey of India*, no. 21 (Calcutta: Govt. of India, 1925).

In Puranic fashion, the story begins in the god Indra's heaven, where the sage Durvasa (later also called Gorakh and clearly a Nath yogi in appearance) has come as a welcome and honoured guest (*"baṛa pāhuna"*). A dance performance by the *apsaras* Urvashi is organised for him, but the beautiful courtesan (*"pātura"*) is dismayed: his ascetic appearance, described in detail, contrasts horribly with her own beautiful and adorned form.[29] Urvashi decides to dance ungracefully and out of rhythm,[30] and the irate sage curses her to descend to the earth and become a mare (*ghorī*) by day and a woman by night. Only when the magical "three-and-a-half" *vajra* weapons strike will she be freed from the curse.[31] We can see here a further transformation of the character of the heavenly nymph Urvashi and of her story with Pururavas. Unlike the Urvashi of the *Ṛgveda*, the *Mahābhārata*, and Kalidasa's *Vikramorvaśīya*, Urvashi here is a courtesan, there is no love story with Pururavas, and the curse turns her into a mare, not a vine.[32]

After some wandering on earth in a geographical setting that is markedly epic-Puranic, the mare Urvashi ends up in a forest full of local trees and flowers.[33] Informed by his gardener, King Dangvai of Dangi

29 S. Misra (1966), p. 91.

30 *"ulaṭi pulaṭi kai nācai, milai na tārau tāra"*; ibid., p. 9115, *doha*.

31 I was finally able to find out what the "three-and-a-half weapon" was thanks to a Persian translation of another *katha*, *Mirigāvatī*: "the three-and-a-half weapon is an expression relating to four people – one is the Bhim's weapon, one is Parasuram's, one is Hanuman's and the half is Duryodhan's" and it is it is made of copper, iron, and bronze; *Mrigāvatī*, Chester Beatty, ms In 37, fol. 94r.

32 For a brilliant archaeological exploration of the story of Urvashi and Pururavas in Sanskrit sources, see D.D. Kosambi, 'Urvasi and Pururavas', in *Myth and Reality: Studies in the Formation of Indian Culture* (Bombay: Popular Prakashan, 1962), pp. 42-81.

33 The mare initially descends onto the world of men in *"Jambudvīpa desa"* and roams the forests of Dandakal and Kedali, the mountains of Binjha (Vindhya) and Vindhyadhar, Kanauj *des*, the country of the Kurus, Kamani, Banga and the mountains of Tilangi, Kashmir, Jalandhar, Chaupar [?], and Naipar (Nepal) [21], before stopping at a "forest near Kashi" full of local trees and flowers—*"kela, nariyara, dākha khajūrī, candana, arga sīpari pūrī. kaṭahara, baṛahara bera khīranī, aura sadāphara nīmbū jāmunī"*, 22.4-5; S. Misra (1966), p. 93. Ann Gold notes that "Distinctive to Madhu's telling is a general concern for mundane detail: many descriptions of actions and relationships, well understood or easily imagined in village thought, that do not advance the story line but rather situate it in familiar experience... Such familiar scenes or situations may, moreover, be suddenly spiced with magical occurrences or divine intervention: donkeys talk to village elders, a guru's play spoils the carefully crafted pots; messengers come from heaven to straighten out the king and save his subjects. It would seem that Madhu and his teachers, in adapting a traditional tale for village patrons, elaborate both the familiar and the magical to strike a captivating blend"; Gold (1992), p. 63.

*desa* comes to see the beautiful mare and is smitten at once.[34] But after coming face to face with him, the mare escapes. Despite their precious horses (*tokhara* and *tajana*), all his horsemen fall behind in the chase and only King Dangvai is left to follow her at nightfall. He then sees her transforming into a beautiful woman (*triya rupa*) and is frightened at first—is she a female demon or ghost or one of the eighty-four yoginis, was she sent by the gods to ensnare him? Yet he still grabs her reins and mounts her—a metaphor for intercourse since she has already turned into a woman? The figure of the seductive woman-mare who attracts and is pursued by the male protagonist is familiar from other tales from this period (in Qutban's *Mirigāvatī* she is a doe), but notably here Urvashi does not lure away Dangvai but surrenders to him.[35] Urvashi the mare here seems to be a figure of territorial conquest, and a trophy that incites pride and envy.

Urvashi tells him her story and begs him to keep her, though in hiding. Dangvai is overjoyed: "I'll have a nine-fold treasure (*naunidhi*) sitting at home!" he exclaims a few times.[36] Back at the palace, Dangvai's queens ceremonially welcome the mare, decked in all her finery. Dangvai keeps her hidden in his picture gallery (*citrasārī*) and spends all his time with her. Eventually one of his queens, Padmavati, finds out the truth.

Meanwhile Narada—the Puranic messenger and trouble-maker—informs Krishna. He praises the mare's beauty to the skies and advises Krishna to take her from Dangvai by force (*ajorī*). Krishna, who now will have no rest until he has acquired the mare, sends an envoy, ostensibly just to enquire about the truth of this report. Dangvai protests that he knows nothing about it, though he is in no doubt as to what the "enquiry" entails: "I am your slave, he repeated several times. Whichever horse or elephant you want from the treasury, I'll give it to you". Krishna's request then becomes more explicit, and is accompanied by a threat: "If

---

34 The terms used are *lāgi samādhi* (S. Mishra, 1966, p. 94, 23.5.), suggesting a moment of mystical encounter similar to the one in Qutban's tale; see Behl (2012a), pp. 111-16.

35 Wendy Doniger has written extensively on the seductive (and threatening) mare vs. the pacific and nurturing cow, but Urvashi's sexuality here does not appear to be threatening; see Wendy Doniger O'Flaherty, 'Sacred Cows and Profane Mares in Indian Mythology', *History of Religions* 19.1 (1979): 1-26, and *Women, Androgynes, and Other Mythical Beasts* (Chicago: University of Chicago Press, 1980).

36 S. Misra (1966), pp. 97-98, 27.6, 28.10.

Dangvai wants to keep his *ghara* (house), he must give up his *ghori* (mare), so Krishna said".[37] The second envoy adds his own word of advice:

> Who in the three worlds will save you? Krishna will strike wherever you go.
> If you want to save your life and enjoy your kingdom,
> Take the mare with you and flee today to the quick.[38]

Dangvai swears that he will never give up the mare as long as he lives and indirectly accuses Krishna of being a bad king—which lord (*ṭhakura*) has ever been seen taking someone else's wife by force (*barabasa*)?

> Wherever a lord behaves poorly, how can his subjects live?
> If a lord (*ṭhākura*) does not observe dharma, fate/Brahma makes him dwell in hell.[39]

What sin (*gunahbāta*) has Dangvai committed against Krishna? He will rather leave his country (*desa*) for the sake of the mare.

Envoys travel to and fro, each advising Dangvai either to surrender the mare or flee Krishna's wrath. His wives, whom Dangvai consults in the women's palace (*antahpura*), advise him to submit to Krishna, surrender the mare, and beg for forgiveness: thirty-three thousand gods look up to Krishna, who has killed many demons, they remind him; "never be an enemy of one like him, give him the mare and fall at his feet".[40] But Dangvai is determined to leave. A cadence of "*chāṃḍe*", "*chāṃḍesi*" ("he left") marks Dangvai's pathetic exile.

Dangvai's flight takes him to several epic-Puranic characters: the Ocean, Sheshnaga, Vibhishana, Kubera, Duryodhana, and Yudhishthira. Each of them, though, refuses his call for shelter and protection.[41] In the netherworld Sheshnaga, the Lord of the Snakes, feels it is beyond his power to give shelter to Dangvai, since he is indebted to Krishna for his domain ("*Hari ke rākhe rahauṃ patārā*").[42] Ravana's half-brother

---

37 Ibid., p. 100, 32.3.

38 Ibid.

39 Ibid., p. 100, 33 *doha*.

40 Ibid., p. 102, 36.4.

41 The Ocean argues that he has already had to suffer at Murari's hands when, in the Tretayuga, Ramchandra had "tied up" the Ocean in order to cross over to Lanka; in fact, the Ocean retells Rama's story in one stanza. Ibid., p. 104, 38.

42 Ibid., p. 104, 40.2.

Vibhishana, to whom Dangvai turns next, is similarly indebted to Krishna,[43] and moreover Krishna is a "*baṛa ṭhākura*", a great lord.[44]

Dangvai then approaches the *Mahābhārata* heroes one by one. First he goes to Duryodhana, the head of the Kauravas. But Duryodhana trembles when he hears his plea: "Who will give you shelter, *bīra*[45] [...] Who will embrace (*aṅgvai*) enmity with Krishna? Go elsewhere, for I do not dare show pride (*garava na karata*) toward Hari". Besides, Duryodhana adds, Krishna is close kin (*niyari sagāī*).[46] Yudhishthira first asks why Dangvai has come without "Lakshmi or wealth" to offer and without attendants (*parigraha*).[47] He is just as adamant as Duryodhana in refusing to take Dangvai's side against Krishna, their affine.[48] If they give shelter to Dangvai now, they will regret it later, for their fate is threaded with Krishna's ("Whatever the fate of the five Pandavas, it is the fate of the sixth, Narayana"). But Yudhishthira is ready to arrange a reconciliation (*meru*) if Dangvai hands him the mare. To do otherwise would be madness, for who opposes the ruler of the three worlds? And "who will die for someone else's death?"[49]

By this stage the desperate Dangvai is ready to kill himself. Amidst loud cries he prepares a pyre on the banks of the Ganga with the intention of immolating himself alongside the mare/Urvashi. But his luck turns, for it so happens that Subhadra—Arjuna's wife and Krishna's half-sister—has gone to bathe in the river. Deeply struck by the sight of such distress, she enquires after his fate and then resolves to help him, whatever the consequences.[50] And when Dangvai doubts her ability to act upon her offer ("on whose strength do you want to protect me?"), she replies proudly that she is powerfully connected. It is an impressively assertive self-introduction, very far from the elision of women's names

43 Because—as his avatara as Rama—he gave him the kingdom of Lanka.

44 Ibid., p. 106, 42.4.

45 "Brother" as well as "hero".

46 Ibid., p. 108, 45 *doha*.

47 Ibid., p. 108, 46.4.

48 "Hari keeps *gotiyāī* with us, for us the source of much joy". Ibid., p. 109, 47.3.

49 Ibid., 47 *doha*, p. 109.

50 She wonders: "Have you raised your hand against your sister or have you killed a Brahmin? Did you come abroad to trade and have lost all your wealth gambling? Have you been the cause of your family's ruin, or has the king taken all you had? Have highway men robbed you by force, or have you stolen someone else's mare?"; ibid., p. 110, 49.2-6.

and the prohibition to utter their husbands' that we are accustomed to recognise as a feature of patriarchy:

*hauṃ patibratā pārtha kai nārī, au ahibarana kera mahatārī;*
*jeṭh dudisṭila bharahī bhīṃvā, devaru nakule au sahadevā.*
*pāṇḍu sasura au kontā sāsū, indraprastha hama bhūjaiṃ rājū.*
*bāsudeva kai bahinī, nāuṃ subhadrā mohiṃ.*
*aba jani cintā manai, karihauṃ nirabhai tohiṃ.*[51]

I am Partha's *pativratā* wife and Abhimanyu's mother.
Yudhishtira and Bhima the mace-bearer are my *jeṭhas* (older brother-in-laws), Nakula and Sahdeva my *devars*.
Pandu and Kunti are my in-laws, and we enjoy the rule of Indraprastha.
I am Basudeva's sister, Subhadra is my name.
Now stop worrying, I'll relieve you of your fear.

This assertive and active Subhadra is also a far cry from the tearful figure of Subhadra in the *Mahābhārata*.[52] When she suggests that Dangvai go to Bhima, and he again expresses his doubts, since he has tried the Pandavas before, she assures him that Bhima will keep his word to her, as she has had occasion to appreciate in the past:

*taba asa bacana subhadrā kahaī, mohiṃ bharosa bhīma kara ahaī.*
*bācābandha bāṃha mohi dharī, bahuta bharosa kara karī.*

Then Subahdra said: "I trust Bhima.
He keeps his word and will support me, I have relied on him a lot".[53]

Subhadra knows how to work on Bhima. First she has him acquiesce to any request from her, which he happily does, then she praises him at length for his strength and valour (*paurukha*) by reminding him of

51 Ibid., p. 111, 50.7-9, *doha* 1.

52 In the epic Subhadra figures first as the woman Arjuna falls in love with and carries off at her own brother's suggestion. She then has to assuage Draupadi's jealousy by submitting to her. After she gives birth to Abhimanyu she is taken to Dwarka, while the five Pandavas go into exile accompanied by Draupadi. She next appears as Abhimanyu's grieving mother, and once again as a figure of grief who pleads with Krishna to revive Abhimanyu's posthumously (still)born son, Parikshita, who is the only Pandava male left. And when the Pandavas ultimately leave on their "great journey", she is left behind as guardian to the Yadava heir, Vajra Yadava; see textual references in Vanamala Bhawalkar, *Eminent Women in the Mahābhārata* (Delhi: Sharada Publishing House, 2002), Vol. 2, pp. 337-51.

53 S. Misra (1966), p. 112, 51.9-10.

all the heroes he has slain. Finally she mentions Dangvai, saying she has already promised to protect him with Bhima's support. If Bhima now refuses Subhadra will burn herself alive together with Abhimanyu, a final touch of emotional blackmail. But Bhima is unconcerned about consequences. The fact that she could count upon him "is a blessing for me", he says.[54]

So while with Bhima we have the most uncompromising statement of the ideology of valour and protection—he gladly takes on the burden of Dangvai's gratitude and will not surrender him to anyone, for it is now a question of his own honour and shame—the strategist is Subhadra. Such is the strength of Bhima's purpose that Yudhishthira's brothers and Kunti, each sent to make Bhima see sense (otherwise whatever trust they have with Krishna will be destroyed), are won over by Bhima's forceful argument: "If I surrender a man who sought refuge with me, there will be no greatness (*baṛāī*) left among us five brothers":[55]

> Nobody breaks an alliance (*prīti-uccheda*) the day one's lord is in trouble.
> If you die in the service of a Brahmin you reign over thousands of rebirths.
> If you go to a pilgrimage place when death approaches, you either revive
> or you go straight to heaven.
> But if you surrender a man who sought shelter,
> you are reborn twenty-one times in hell.
> One who lusts after the wife of a friend, relative, or guru,
> Earns as much sin as the one who withdraws shelter.[56]

Even with Pradyumna—Krishna's son who has been sent as an envoy and who recounts the ten avataras in order to remind the Pandavas who they are going to war against—Bhima stands firm: glory (*jasa, sobhā*) does not depend on victory or defeat, but on doing the right thing. And Krishna himself will earn no glory in the world by attacking the Pandavas for the sake of Dangvai's mare. Pradyumna can only report back to Krishna that the Pandavas, his close allies in the *Mahābhārata*, are not afraid of him: "They do not talk sense (*sidhai bātā*), they speak of oath (*sapata*) and glory (*jasa*)".[57]

---

54 Ibid., p. 114.
55 Ibid., p. 108, 45 *doha* a.
56 Ibid., 63, p. 120.
57 Ibid., 72.4, p. 126.

So while risking the wrath of Krishna (called *"baṛa sultānu"*) over a petty chief and his trophy woman/mare is presented as foolish and suicidal, it is also what Rajput honour demands. In a still more extraordinary twist, even the Kauravas, after Nakula goes to enlist their support, come to fight Krishna alongside the Pandavas! The logic of the *Mahābhārata* is completely overturned in order to make the point that a Rajput must support his kin and retinue in trouble. True, Duryodhana wavers at first, but again it is his wife Bhanamati who speaks up in support for one's kin over selfish interest—"Glory spreads from winning *and* losing", she says, "Listen *swami*, wealth and the earth belong to no one".[58] If you make the wrong choice you can always blame it on sins and *karma* in previous births (*purbil*), she adds. (Wily Shakuni instead had suggested abstaining and taking over the kingdom after Krishna has killed all the Pandavas.[59]) While the wives of the subordinate chieftain Dangvai advised prudence and compliance, the wives of lineage Rajputs advise supporting kin and the choice of enduring glory over short-term interest—transience is one of the truths at the heart of this *katha*.

As the mighty clash between the two armies approaches—gods and semi-gods enlist with Krishna, while human allies join the Pandavas and Kauravas—Duryodhana has second thoughts. He curses Bhima, saying: "To hell with your manliness (*manusāī*)! The whole army is disappearing in the fight, who will be left to do valorous deeds afterwards? ... Our honour (*pati*) will disappear alongside our army".[60] Like other *kathas* of this period, there is no alternative to going to war, and the preparations, the clash, and the battlefield strewn with corpses and limbs attacked by jackals, crows, and female ghosts provide opportunity for a lively description which one feels storytellers could expound upon at leisure.[61] But who can win? And should Bhima be killed by Krishna, of all people? The story finds another solution. While Bhima and Krishna are locked in combat, their disc and mace get so entangled that Hanuman has to go to disentangle their weapons (*bajra*). In so doing, the magical "three-and-a-half" weapons come together, Urvashi is released from her curse

58 S. Misra (1958), stanza 83.5 and *doha* a, p. 131, emphasis added.

59 Ibid., 84 *doha*, p. 132.

60 Ibid., p. 142, 100.4-5 *doha*.

61 In the *Ḍaṅgvai kathā* the war is narrated with longer stanzas detailing the many participants, the mountain-like elephants, the horsemen and foot soldiers, the earth trembling under their weight, the warriors' individual exploits, and the battlefield (ibid., pp. 134-45); the description is very similar in Jayasi's *Padmāvat*.

and whisked off to heaven, and Bhima can take Dangvai to submit honourably to Krishna:

> "*Deva*, the reason for this great battle, that beautiful woman, has gone to heaven.
> The mare for whom this fracass (*caucadu*) broke out has climbed on an air craft and gone to heaven".
> Dangvai felt regret in his heart: "Fate led my heart astray.
> I disobeyed Basudeva (Krishna), I brought grief to the Kauravas and Pandavas".
> Dangvai thought to himself: "I have been deficient in my action.
> How can I wash the sin (*kalaṅka*) of the mare, Gosain!?"[62]

At first Krishna reproaches the Kauravas and Pandavas: "Those I gave kingdoms to enjoy today rose up in arms against me".[63] But when Duryodhana grasps one of his feet, Karna grasps the other, and Arjun pleads with him, Krishna lifts them all up in an embrace. Proper farewells seal the peace and everyone returns to their domains.

The *katha* captures dramatically the fear (*khabhāru*) and desperate quest for shelter that warriors out of favour must have felt, crying for shelter outside the gates of other chiefs, pleading that they were being persecuted through no fault of their own, and appealing to their helpers' principles (like valour, *purukhārathu*), or else flattering them into taking their side. In the tale, the other chiefs first welcome the wandering chief with respect, but are quick to send him off when they realise what enemy they would make if they gave him shelter.

With regard to the conflict of duty that arises between loyalty to one's lord (and sometimes kin) and assistance to one's brothers, the *katha* articulates several positions: some see it as an opportunity to advance their interests, others (like Yudhishthira) blame the shelterer for jeopardising their position for the sake of a nobody and for abstract principles. Significantly, the wives Bhanmati and Subhadra argue that, when the currency is *sata* (truth and virtue), fame and a good name are more important than victory or defeat, or indeed death. At the same time the *katha* suggests that a good overlord should *not* demand everything and anything from his subordinates and should be quick to accept their apologies if they submit after taking up arms against him. While drawing upon the familiar set of *Mahābhārata* characters, then,

62 S. Misra (1958), p. 146, 105.3-7 and *doha*.
63 Ibid., 106.4, p. 147.

Bhima Kavi fashioned both a gripping tale that turned the epic tale upside down and powerful and articulate women characters in whom his elite women patrons may have wanted to find themselves reflected.

## Varieties of Knowledge

To a greater or lesser extent knowledge (*gyana*) is advertised and included as a theme in many tales from this period. That debates around spiritual knowledge were popular in this period is proved by the genre of imaginary *goshthi* or *samvad* between well-known spiritual figures or between characters embodying opposite views, often with sharply satirical or simply humorous edges. We find *gyan goshtis* mentioned or briefly sketched in several *kathas* from this period.[64]

Take the miniature *gyan goshti* between the sage Durvasa and his body in the *Ḍaṅgvai kathā*. Durvasa, we are told, has caused much suffering to his body by practising ascetic penance in Kashi for a thousand years. The five senses (*pañcabhūta*) decide to leave his body, complaining that "he has given us much trouble (*kaṣṭa*)". When the sage, shaken out of his trance, asks them to explain themselves, they declare over two stanzas that he has been a terrible master, without any desire that they may fulfil and unconcerned with worldly shame. "In this world everything appears as *rasa*, and without Vishnu nothing tastes sweet":

> You find happiness through your body,
> no good comes without the body, they say.
> We are the ones who allow life on earth, who is dearer than us?
> We are the ones who maintain or sway *satta* [*sata*],[65]
> we can destroy or reduce to begging.
> We make people laugh or cry, we are the ones who show disaster;
> If one knows yoga (*joga juguti*), then we are his slaves".[66]

---

64 For *goshthi*, or discussion over points of spiritual knowledge or religious practice, as an early modern devotional genre in Hindavi, often with Gorakhnath as one of the debaters, see David Lorenzen, 'Sain's *The Kabir-Raidas Debate*', in *Praises to a Formless God: Nirguṇī Texts from North India* (Albany: State University of New York Press, 1996), pp. 169-204; see also Eleanor Zelliot, 'A Medieval Encounter Between Hindu and Muslim: Eknath's Drama-Poem Hindu-Turk. Samvad', in *India's Islamic Traditions*, ed. by Richard Eaton (New Delhi: Oxford University Press, 2003), pp. 64-82.

65 A polysemic word whose meanings include "essence", "vigour, energy", as well as "virtue"; see R.S. McGregor, *The Oxford Hindi-English Dictionary* (New Delhi: Oxford University Press, 1992, 32nd impression 2003), p. 977.

66 S. Misra (1966), 11.3-5, *doha*, pp. 88-89.

After "having a *gyan goshti* and assuaging the five senses", Durvasa leaves for Mount Kailasa.[67] The debate is hardly developed here, but since there is much textual variation among the manuscripts at this point, with several verses added to the speech by the five senses, we may take it as an indication that storytellers and scribes found this a good place to expand.[68] Jayasi inserts a fully-fledged *gyan goshthi*, humorous and yet profound, at the end of his retelling of the Krishna *katha*.[69] The debate is between Krishna and Gorakhnath over the relative merits of *bhakti*'s *bhoga* (enjoyment) of *rasa* and of renunciant yoga, and while nobody is the winner, the debate articulates Krishna's "mystery" of *bhoga* more convincingly.

And while *gyana* often refers to spiritual knowledge, there is one particular form of knowledge that tales and their tellers particularly claim to impart, which is knowledge related to music and performance art (see d'Hubert, Miner, and Busch in this volume). The poet-performer (whether singer or storyteller) bestowed authority and value upon himself through his display of technical musical knowledge, usually through performance scenes *within* the tales (e.g. d'Hubert and Miner). The narrative pace slows down, details increase the "density" of the telling,[70] and with a mirroring effect the characters' connoisseurship reflects back the connoisseurship of the poet-performer and of his patrons. The romance between the talented Brahmin musician Madhavanal and the beautiful courtesan Kamkandhala predates this period, yet the numerous retellings in North Indian vernaculars (and one in Persian) from this period suggest a recurrent interest in the characters and the story.[71]

---

67 Ibid., p. 90, 12.1.

68 See ibid., p. 89.

69 See Parameshvarilal Gupta, *Malik Muhammad Jāyasī kṛt Kanhāvat* (Banaras: Vishvavidyalay Prakashan, 1981), pp. 314-18; for a fuller discussion see my 'Inflected *Kathas*: Sufis and Krishna Bhaktas in Awadh', in *Religious Interactions in Mughal India*, ed. by V. Dalmia and M. Faruqui (New Delhi: Oxford University Press, 2014); for a different interpretation, see Heidi Pauwels, 'Whose Satire? Gorakhnāth Confronts Krishna in *Kanhāvat*', in *Indian Satire in the Period of First Modernity*, ed. by Monika Horstmann and Heidi Pauwels (Wiesbaden: Harrassowitz, 2012), pp. 35-64.

70 For density see Lutgendorf (1991), p. 191. In Alam's tale, there are many variants and interpolations in the manuscripts for this episode, suggest that these episodes were particularly important for storytellers.

71 R.S. McGregor lists a Sanskrit play by Anandadhara (c.1300), a narrative poem (*prabandha*) by Ganapati in Gujarati (1528), two Rajasthani versions, a *chaupai* by the extraordinarily prolific Kushallabha (1559); *Hindi Literature from the Beginnings to the Nineteenth Century* (Wiesbaden: Harrassowitz, 1984), p. 62. The editor of Alam's

Musical connoisseurship (*guna*) is a central theme of the story between the Brahmin musician and the courtesan dancer-singer. It is also key to the characterisation of the king and patron. *Guna* is a polysemeic word at this time (see also Busch in this volume)—it refers generically to "talent" (King Gobind Chand of Puhupati is first called "multi-talented", "*bahu gunā*") or specifically to aesthetic, and particularly musical, talent and connoisseurship. The term *catura* (clever) is used as a synonym, while its antonym *mūrkha/mūṛha* (stupid, also *abibekī*) means clueless, devoid of musical understanding. *Gunī* (talented, knowledgeable) can mean talented and knowledgeable, or simply a "musician". Kamkandala is first introduced as "*pātara gunī*"—a talented courtesan—even before the head-to-toe description showcases her beauty and, as Behl suggested, arouses passion (*shauq*) in the listeners as well as in the characters of the tale.[72] But Madhavanal's beauty and talent also arouse dangerous desire in the women of the city of Puhupavati, so much so that their irate husbands force the king to order him to leave![73]

> Listen, King, to what we say, Madhonal has entraced all the women.
> He plays [lit. "does"] *ragas* and bewitches them, they all go after him with doe-like gait.[74]

King Bhopati, reluctant to send away such a talented musician, tests Madhavanal's power by asking him to play at court. Bewitched, all the king's maids forget what they are doing and come running. The king has

---

text, Rajkumari Mishra, also lists a *vilasa* by Madhava (1600), a Gujarati version by Damodar Kavi, a Brajbhasha one by Rajkavi Kesa (1717), a Rajasthani one by Jagannatha Kavi (1744), and several more; *Mādhavānal Kāmakandhalā*, ed. by Rajkumari Mishra (Allahabad: Rajkumari Svadhyay Sansthan, 1982), p. 15. To these should be added Haqiri Kashani, the author of a Persian *masnavi* version called *Maḥż-i 'Ijāz* [*The True Miracle?*, 1091H/1680]; *Haqīriya's Masnavī* The True Miracle (*Mādhavānal Kāmakandalā*), ed. by Yoga Dhyan Ahuja (Delhi: University of Delhi, 1965); see Prashant Keshavmurti, 'Ḥaqīrī Kāšānī, *Maṯnawī-i mādhavānal-kāmakandalā mausūm ba maḥẓ-i i'jāz'*, *Perso-Indica*, http://perso-indica.net/work.faces?idsec=16&idw=122; I am grateful to Imre Bangha for the reference.

72 R. Mishra (1982), 18.1, p. 15, also 26.2, p. 21; Behl (2012a), p. 33.

73 "One woman fell down, entranced; another brought her hands to her lips. One whose eyes locked with his left the pond and came near him. One forgot to keep her clothes in order, another let her hair loose, besotted. One lay aside her ornaments, another took off her waistband. One woman got up and moved towards him, like a spotted doe on hearing a tune. *Doha*: Madana [like Kama, the god of love], took the bow with the five flower-arrows and the woman was struck on the spot. With their graceful gait, they were all entranced, like gazelles by a hunter"; ibid., 10, p. 9.

74 Ibid., 13.4-5, p. 11.

no choice but to exile him. Unlike other sufi tales of quest, Madhavanal's journey as a *bairagi* is very short. In a mere two lines he reaches the city of Kamavati, where the beautiful Kamkamandala resides. By contrast, the two musical performances in Kamavati take up twenty stanzas and include a complete list of *ragas* and *raginis* (cf. Miner and Appendix).[75]

When Madhavanal arrives, a musical performance is about to begin at the court of King Kamaseni. Madhavanal, a stranger, is stopped from entering by the doorkeeper and has to listen from outside:

> Madhav sat at the gate door, there was a tournament (*akhārā*)
> in the abode of the king.
> When the string-instrumentalists (*tantakāra*) sang,
> twelve played the Mridanga,
> The fourth among them was incompetent,
> he had only four fingers in his right hand.
> The rhythm and the melody were broken but the stupid people
> did not understand anything.
> Who would be such a connoisseur of melody (*suragyāni*)
> —everyone was stupid in the king's assembly.
> Who would notice the broken rhythm in the tune of the *mridanga*
> among twelve players?[76]

But Madhavanal, sitting outside the door, beats his head in despair at the fault "since he knew rhythm and bad rhythm (*kutāla*), the seven notes, and could recite (*bakhānai*) all the characteristics (*pramāṇa*) of music".[77] He has recognised that the fourth among the twelve players has a wax finger and is pretending to play. King Kamaseni is duly impressed and rewards him most handsomely, and the whole assembly is equally impressed by Madhavanal's handsome appearance. Alam is spurred to sing the praise of talent/music (*guna*) over two stanzas:

> Seeing this *gunī* (musician/talented one),
> connoisseurs (*guni jana*) were delighted
> —who would be if an ignorant (*niguni*) was there?[78]
> If anyone has *guna* within, from king to pauper everyone respects him.
> No one questions high or lowly status, one who has *guna* sits high.

75 R. Mishra (1982).
76 Ibid., 27.2-5, *doha*, p. 22.
77 Ibid., 28.2, p. 22.
78 *"Nigunī jani koi hoī"* can have several meanings, depending on the meaning of *jani* (people or "don't"): "Let no one be untalented" or "who is untalented?"

The talented man who goes abroad sells his wares at greater price.
Just as a mother rears her son, *guna* always bestows happiness.
Without *guna* one's ancestors fall from heaven,
without *guna* one's mouth utters lowly words.
Without *guna* one is like a man blind, without *guna* one is a bird without wings.
When you fall into bad times and lose your wealth,
if you're talented your talent stays with you.
If you have *guna* in your body then wealth will come and you will get it again.[79]

Kamakandala recognises a fellow *guni* and prepares to sing and dance particularly well for his sake.[80] As in the *Mirigāvatī* passage described by Allyn Miner in her essay, the musical performance is carefully detailed, if not realistically described: the different types of musical instruments played, the different *ragas* and *raginis* (see Appendix),[81] the stage (*rangabhumi*) adorned with lamps and torches, and the various rhythms (*talas*). The list of *ragas* and *raginis* (*ragaputras* are mentioned rather than listed) appears to work more as a display of knowledge and possibly as a mnemonic device than as a narrative/diegetic element.[82] Intriguingly,

79 Ibid., 32 *doha* and 33, p. 25; one of the manuscripts (ms "B", undated, from Bundi) also has the following *soratha*: "*Guna* is your king, *guna* is the garland, *guna* is the friend, *guna* is the mother. God gave fortune to the one with a forehead full of *gunas*"; ibid.

80 "A very clever insightful man has come. There is always an *ausara* [i.e. a *naubat*, a musical session] in the royal court, but no ignorant knows whether it is good or not. This one who has come is bright like a phase of the sun, full of understanding of rhythm, scale, and sound. He has cast off defects far and wide now that he makes *guna* move by knowing the difference between the seven (notes?)"; ibid., 34.1-4, p. 26; the meaning of "*Sāt bheda jau guna sañcārai*" (34.4) is unclear.

81 All "intoned together" (42.1, p. 32). This is where the complete *Ragamala* comes in, stanzas 36-40. The various *talas* are also sung in unison (?! "*sakala tāla milau*", 42.3, p. 32).

82 Alam's *ragamala* is almost identical to that appended at the end of the *Ādi Granth* (which, as Allyn Miner shows in her essay, does not represent the *ragas* actually used in the *Granth*). This has prompted much debate as to its origin and the direction of is circulation, since Alam's *Mādhavānal* (1582) predates the oldest available manuscript of the *Granth* (1604). The *ragamala* fits metrically with the rest of Alam's text, but even here it is more of a set piece than part of the narrative. His list of *raginis* corresponds most closely to Ksemakarna's *Rāgamālā*, composed in Rewa in 1570 (see Table 14.1 in Miner's essay), which could have provided a common source for both Alam and the early Sikh circles. I am grateful to Imre Bangha for telling me about the debate, and to the group who read the *Mādhavānal* together in 2011-2012: Imre Bangha, Richard Williams, Yuthika Sharma, Robert Skelton (for the *ragamala* section), Preeti Khosla, and Professor Shyam Manohar Pande.

the *ragamala* is one of the sections of the *katha* that contains the highest number of variants. Copyists or storytellers found this episode a good place to add comments or to break the long list of *ragas* and *raginis* by coming back to the performance or the characters, or by inserting rhythmic lines like those in real performances. This is how one scribe or storyteller broke the compact list of *ragas*:

> Madhav thought in his mind—"This is how she has done Dipak:
> She has pictured his wives with his sons through her gait,
> that accomplished *apsara*!"
> Dipak gave much joy, Madhav is an expert Brahmin.
> After arranging the women, she harnessed the notes of Sri raga.
> They sang Sri raga all together, combining it with his five women.
>
> Oh Madhav—gem among Brahmins, jewel of the courtiers and skilled—here,
> Forsaking all laziness of his body, and knowing Kandala,
> he displayed all his qualities,
> He expounded Lakshmi (Sri) raga,
> and they drank the immaculate water to the full.
> Their hearts' desire fulfilled their minds' desire,
> the courtly lady took up the Megh raga.[83]

Kamakandala then shows her skill with rhythms (*talas*):

> They all sang together in unison when the courtesan set foot on stage,
> They pronounced the scale (*sargama*) in the Jhakut rhythm,
> they considered the sound of the steady refrain.[84] (?)
> Brahma *tala* and Chutput *tala*,
> all the *talas* were coordinated into one rhythm. ...
>
> Turning over[85] the *dhruva dhrupad*, she sang *bisnupada* verses,
> Clever and accomplished Madhavanala understood all the *bhāvas*.[86]

And here *all* the manuscripts apart from the one used by the editor insert rhythmic lines like those sung in actual performances:

---

83 Ms "B", ibid., p. 30.

84 "*thira riu* (?) *jo sabada bicarai*" is unclear.

85 "*Mura mura*" could also mean, "Turning back to look at him".

86 Ibid., 42 *doha*, p. 33.

*theī theī theī theī saba karahīṃ, tathaka tathaka kai mukha uccarahīṃ*
*dhapaka dhapaka sauṃ dhapaka dhalaṅga, damaka damaka driga drimridaṅga*[87]

Kamkandala is thus said to have sung all the *ragas* with their *raginis* and *ragaputras* in one session. This not only impresses her extraordinary skills upon the listener but provides the author (and storytellers) with the chance to spell out the full system of *ragas*. In a similar fashion, the fact that she and her fellow singer-dancers are said to have "intoned all [the *ragas*] together" and sung all the *talas* in unison is clearly impossible but points to their complete knowledge and extraordinary virtuosity. The density of the text is unmistakeable here.

The narrative rhythm picks up once we turn from this ideal performance to a diegetic incident. Kamakandala is demonstrating another talent by dancing with a bowl full of water balanced on top of her head and explaining her dance movements with syllables when a bee, attracted by the scent of sandalwood paste on her breasts, comes and starts biting her. But—and here lies her virtuosity—Kamakandala does not miss a step. She draws in air from her mouth and nose and pushes it out through her nipple, driving the bee away! Once again, only Madhavanal has noticed her trick, and delighted by her art he promptly gives her all the precious gifts the king had just bestowed upon him—"Clever one met clever one".[88] But his gesture angers the king to no end, and Madhav is thrown out of this city too, though not before berating the king and his assembly for their lack of musical insight:

You, king, are undiscerning (*abibekī*), you cannot discriminate
talent from the talentless.
Am I so stupid and a philistine? I delighted in the art,
and could not keep hold of my life![89]

Though the king has ordered him out of the city immediately, Madhavanal cannot resist spending two nights with Kamkandala. The remaining two-thirds of the tale deal with their pain of separation (*biyoga/biraha*).[90] While Kamkandala is wasting away in Kamavati (and

---

87 Ibid., p. 33.
88 Ibid., 45.1, p. 35.
89 Ibid., 49.1-2, p. 37.
90 At the beginning of the tale Alam had told his listeners that his was a tale of "love and separation" (*siṅgāra viyoga*), ibid., p. 5.

will not sing or dance again), Madhavanal seeks refuge with King Vikramaditya at Ujjain. The king is sympathetic, checks that his story is correct by sending envoys to Kamavati, and then successfully lays siege to the city. Once an emaciated and wasted Kamkandala is brought before him he decides to test her love by announcing that Madhavanal is dead. Kamkandala dies on the spot and, once he hears the news, Madhavanal dies too. But the tale is not over. Horrified by the sin he has incurred—a double murder, including that of a Brahmin—Vikramaditya decides to immolate himself on a pyre. The news of his decision spreads across the three worlds, and his old friend the Betala (Vampire)—of the *Twenty-Five Stories of the Vampire* fame—comes to his rescue by bringing *amrit* (ambrosia) from the netherworld. Adding further intertextual references, Alam compares the king to Hanuman, who brought the magic root that revived Laskshman at a crucial point of the war in Lanka.[91] The king now turns physician and, once revived, Madhavanal and Kamkandala can finally come together, after Vikramaditya defeats King Kamasena in battle.[92] Music and dance, though richly elaborated in the first part of this *katha*, do not appear again.

## Conclusions

Alam has made a katha in *chaupais*, he first heard it with his ears.
Here and there he placed some *dohas*, and elsewhere *sorathas*.
The ears that listen to this beautiful tale,
    full of *rasa* and pleasing to the mind of the learned,
If lovers (*prītivant*) hear it, their love will increase
    and they will be happy.
If sensuous *rasika* men hear it (*kāmī rasika purukh*)
    they will reflect on this tale night and day.
        *Pandits*, clever people (*budhivantā*) and *gunis*, parsing poets,
        praise its qualities (*guna*) *nāma namita* (?) and tell many tales
        again and again. ||172||

91 Ibid., 138 *doha*, p. 99. For a full list of intertextual references in this text, see ibid., 'Introduction', p. 28.

92 Some mss have a longer version that includes the protagonists' former lives; see ibid., p. 19.

At the end of his telling of *Mādhavānal Kāmakandalā* Alam refers both to the metrical structure and to its *phalashruti*—an intensification of love and desire. At the onset he had declared that his *katha* of "love and separation" was "partly mine, partly stolen from others" (*kachu āpana kachu parakrita cūri*) and that "since few listen to this tale in Sanskrit, I have bound it together in *chaupais* in *bhakha*".[93] Taken together, these two statements articulate much of the poetics of Hindavi *kathas* of the time. *Kathas* were tellings, often retellings, and sought to impart spiritual and practical (here musical) knowledge in an entertaining and arresting fashion.

That *kathas* in this period are always re-tellings of earlier—usually epic-Puranic—material is a truism, but we have seen that epic-Puranic framing and intertextual referencing also helped introduce original tales. Some of these drew upon oral traditions—as in the case of Da'ud's *Candāyan* (1389), which inaugurated the rich genre of sufi *prem-kathas* in Awadhi/Hindavi to which Alam's sixteenth-century *Mādhavānal* belongs. Others—like the *Ḍaṅgvai kathā*—took epic-Puranic characters as a point of departure to develop a deeply original and local tale. Textual clues like *phalashruti* verses and abbreviated discussions on Kaliyuga, good and bad rulers, or *gyan goshtis*—present even when they are not relevant to the story—thus help us make a historical argument about how *kathas* in Hindi emerge as an independent textual genre, by tagging along epic-Puranic narrative and performative traditions. And the fact that even a relatively little-known and little-copied tale like that of Dangvai is mentioned several times in *kathas* written hundreds of miles away points towards the intense circulation of tales in this period, and to the capacious repertoire of storytellers.

Like other essays in this volume, this one has drawn attention to the textual clues that evoke some possible performative practices of these tales—references to speaking and listening, to audiences out there, to "dense" moments in the texts that were likely to attract oral exposition, to manuscript interpolations that suggest the insertion of additions and digressions by performers. The striking presence of a complete *ragamala* in Alam's *Mādhavānal* as part of the main performance episode shows that tales like this aimed to display and impart technical knowledge—or at least to provide a model for its memorisation. And though we do not

93 Ibid., 6.3, 5, p. 5.

have a living tradition of exposition or *arthav* for these texts as we have for Tulsidas's *Rāmcaritmānas* or the *Bhāgavata-purāṇa*, or for the oral texts of Bharthari and Gopichand, it is traces such as these that suggest what a storyteller could and would have done with them.

Contemporary studies of storytelling practices remind us of what we do not have and what we need in order to imaginatively transform the text into a telling. Typical of all *katha* performances, Lutgendorf tells us, is a cyclical pattern, "a gradual progression from slowly paced delivery, through a growing involvement by the speaker in his topic reflected in louder and more rapid speech, to an emotional climax"—a pattern similar to that of musical performances.[94] He also notices shifts in what he calls "performance density" and the conscious use of particular language registers, pronunciation, rhythm, timbre/pitch, or chanting—to underline shifts in emotional register, such as the archaic pronouncing of the final inherent "*a*" sound to impart a "metrified" effect or echo the near-monotone chanting style of Vedic recitation (191). It is impossible to recover these effects from texts of the past, but these descriptions help us imagine the artful use of voice that storytellers may have brought to bear upon their performances.

While this essay has focused on quite different tales, the same metrical structure (*chaupai-doha*), forms of address, intertextual referencing, alternation between swift diegesis and slow description, between deep *bhava* and lighter fun, and blending of knowledge, instruction, and entertainment can be found in all of them. As Lutgendorf puts it, "The medium of *kathā* is artful language, but its essence is emotional communication".[95] In some cases the writing is richer in metaphors—Alam's *katha* is particularly original in this respect—in others ornamentation is notable by its absence. But the common coordinates show that both authors and listeners knew how to listen and what to listen for.

94 Lutgendorf (1991), pp. 185, 186.
95 Lutgendorf (1991), p. 242.

# Appendix:
# The *Ragamala* in *Mādhavānal Kāmakandalā*

With each raga are five *raginis*, and she sings (*alāpai*) their eight sons,
First she "did" the Bhairav raga, her mouth composed his five women:
First Bharavi and Bilavali, then she sings Puniki [?][96] and Bangali,
then it was the turn of Asaloh—these are Bhairav's five wives.
Then she did Deskar and Madhav, after them Lalit and Bilavala,
Then Malkosh, together with his five wives,[97]
And their eight able sons—
Kamakandala speaks them with her mouth. ||36||

After that she intoned Godagari, thereafter Dev Gandhari,
Then she did Suhuti and Andhyari properly.
She sang Dhanasiri after that and pointed to the five with Malkosh,
After that she progressed to Maru and Misthanga,
Marvar [Mevada], Parbalchand, Kosar,
Khohkhat and Bhora, Ananda came next, she sang Malkosh with his eight sons.
Then came Hindol, bringing his five *raginis*,
The play of rhythm began, she sang beating the rhythm. ||37||

Telangi and Devgiri came, and the beautiful Basanti and Sindhuri,
She brought the delightful Ahiri to the king, the five wives came along.
Surmanand, Bhaskar came, Chandra-Bimbu, Mangalan were beautiful,
Fifth came Sarasban, and Binoda—she sang Basant and Kamoda full of rasa.
She considered and proposed the eight sons, then came Dipak's turn.
She intoned Kachhali, Patmanjari, Todi,
And after that Kamodi and Gujri with Dipak. ||38||

Kalingi, Kuntala and Rama, Kanvala, Kusuma: the names of the five,
Gaura and Kanhara and Kalyana—here go the eight sons of Dipak.
As fifth she sang Siri [Shri] raga, bringing his five *raginis* along,
She sang Vairati, Gandhari, Gauri and Asavari,
Then she intoned Sindhavi, and established the five with Sri Rag.
Malawa, Sarang, Sagara, and that Gaud, and Gambhir
The eight sons of Sri Raga, Gaud, Gambhir, Hamir. ||39||

Sixth she performed Megha raga, she pronounced with her mouth his five wives:
The tunes of Sorathi and fair Malari, then she sang Asa and Kunkuni.
In high tones she did Suho (Suhavi), she showed the five with Megha raga.

---

96 The text reads "puni Kinnara".

97 Variant manuscript (a): "She does the Bangala and the excellent Harika, making a play, the Madhukar resounded".

Bairati, Gandhar, Kedara, Jaldhar, Nata, and Jaldhara,
Then she sang Sankara and Syama—the names of the sons of Megha raga.
She sang the six *ragas* and the thirty *raginis*,
And all the sons with them: eighteen, ten, and twenty. | |40| |[98]

98 R. Misra (1982), pp. 27-31.

# 13. A Curious King, a Psychic Leper, and the Workings of *Karma*: Bajid's Entertaining Narratives[1]

*Imre Bangha*

The Hindi literary scene in the second half of the sixteenth century underwent a deep change and, thanks to the stability and patronage of the Mughal empire, Brajbhasha started to supersede the earlier layers of Awadhi and sant poetry. Up until that time it was Puranic, epic, and historical narratives and sufi romances—composed normally in the *doha-chaupai* metre, conveying important religious or political messages, and usually of a performative nature—that had been deemed worthy of being committed to writing in the vernacular. Towards the end of the sixteeenth century, however, books began to appear in Brajbhasha that were composed in order to be read and studied and not primarily to be performed (see Busch in this volume). This is also the time when we can

1 I am grateful for Dr Daksha Mistry for copying or photographing many of the manuscripts of Bajid's works. Discussions with her greatly contributed to my understanding of Bajid. I also express my gratitude to Dr Kishori Lal and Prof Ramdev Shukla, who generously shared their deep knowledge of early Hindi by reading through the texts of several works, to Monika Horstmann for sending me a copy of the *Pañcāmṛt* and providing me with useful information about the Dadupanth, as well as to Francesca Orsini for her excellent editorial remarks. The Max Mueller Memorial Fund and the Sub-Faculty of South and Inner Asian Studies at the University of Oxford provided funding for several study tours in India between 2006 and 2009, where among other matters I discussed the poems of Bajid with local experts and copied and consulted his manuscripts.

 http://dx.doi.org/10.11647/OBP.0062.13

spot the beginning of an ever-increasing commitment to writing down Hindi songs that had so far been transmitted by oral performance.

It was also around this time that "lighter" works began to appear on the vernacular literary scene in which the slender message becomes subsidiary to the delight in storytelling.[2] One of the first known proponents of the genre of entertaining narratives committed to writing was the poet Bajid. Bajid is interesting not simply as one of the first storytellers *per se*, but rather because he was widely copied in the world of handwritten books, and as the author of short poems that are still current in the oral lore of Rajasthan he is one of the most dramatic examples of how literary tastes changed with the advent of print culture. The study of Bajid's oeuvre contributes to a better understanding of the popular literary world of the sixteenth and seventeenth centuries and the circulation of popular works in oral *and* written form.

Bajid was a prolific author. About a hundred and twenty unpublished works of his exist in manuscript form. While he was most renowned for the short stanza form *arilla*, most of his works are predominantly narrative compositions (in *doha-chaupai* metre) of fifteen to one hundred couplets each. There are also two anthologies of *dohas*, which prefigure the massive Dadupanthi "storebooks", the *Gañjanāmās* and *Sarvāṅgīs*. Along with the *arillas* and the narrative poems in *doha-chaupai*, Bajid also composed in new poetic forms such as *kundaliya*, *jhulna*, and *nisani*—all forms that seem to emerge in Hindi literature around this time. Bajid also experimented with various voices, linguistic styles, and registers. His *rekhta* composition in mixed language is the first longer composition in Khari Boli in North India, predating the *Bikaṭ kahānī* by several decades.[3]

Bajid is remembered in hagiography as a Pathan disciple of Dadu Dayal (see Horstmann in this volume). And while Dadu is remembered as a great saint and composer of songs, his first-generation disciples—including those with Muslim backgrounds such as Bajid and Rajjab—have

---

2 The distinction between didactic purposes and purposes of providing pleasure was theorised by the Chicago School of Criticism, see *Critics and Criticism: Ancient and Modern*, ed. by R.S. Crane (Chicago: University of Chicago Press, 1952); for criticism of this approach see W.C. Booth, *The Rhetoric of Fiction* (Chicago: University of Chicago Press, 1961).

3 See Imre Bangha, 'Rekhta, Poetry in Mixed Language: The Emergence of Khari Boli Literature in North India', in *Before the Divide: Hindi and Urdu Literary Culture*, ed. by Francesca Orsini (New Delhi: Orient BlackSwan, 2010), pp. 56-58, 62-63; the central theme of Bajid's rekhta, just as of the *Bikaṭ kahānī*, is *viraha* or the pain of separation in both its worldly and transcendental aspects.

left behind a massive written legacy.[4] Bajid's works are testimony to the transition from the performed world to the written and they bear signs of both. A clear sign of the written world can be found in the names of his books, most of which are called are *nāmau*, a Brajified version of the Persian term *nāma*, "book". By doing this Bajid was imitating Mughal Persian literature to an audience that did not necessarily know Persian but surely respected its status. Although the majority of Bajid's works are in non-Persianised Bhasha, he systematically uses words such as *divan* to refer to God acting as a worldly lord, and *dargah* for his court. Bajid's works abound in references to writing. For example, fate is expressed in his *Kaṭhiyārā-nāmau* with the words *likhe/likhyau* or *kalām*, both meaning "what has been written". He also frequently refers to letters, and one of his compositions, entitled *Ciṭhī* ("Letter"), imitates the style of early Hindi letters.[5] The fact that his works were copied so extensively shows that, already in Bajid's lifetime, oral transmission was not felt to be enough to preserve them.

Nonetheless Bajid's works also show clear performative signs. Modern *kathavachaks*—performers and expounders of Sanskrit or Hindi stories—still use Bajid's *arillas* to highlight their points. Bajid himself used *arillas* in a similar fashion at the end of his longer works to underscore their moral message. Normally Bajid's works are instantly comprehensible, lacking as they do any Sanskritic ornamentation. What renders his independent poems and his didactic or narrative compositions lively is the use of proverbs and idioms instead. In this respect Bajid's poetry can be perceived as an alternative to his contemporary Keshavdas, who infused Sanskrit *kavya* tradition into Hindi literary culture (see Busch in this volume).

## Saint and Poet: Bajid Remembered

Notwithstanding the neglect of modern historiography, Bajid is remembered in hagiography as a Pathan disciple of Dadu Dayal, while in the wider literate and oral world he has been popular for his

4 As we shall see, unlike Dadu, Bajid wrote relatively few *padas* and often experimented with new poetic forms.

5 This work can be found on ff. 25r-26v of ms 6588 at Rajasthan Oriental Research Institute (RORI), Bikaner. The title of Bajid's compositions is often preceded with *Gun* or *Guṇ* (virtuous), rather than the more generally used *Śrī* (glorious).

independent quatrains in the *arilla* metre, of which he was considered to be the best exponent.

The earliest manuscript material attests that Bajid was a contemporary of Dadu Dayal (1544-1603) and was active already before 1600.[6] Although his association with Dadu is somewhat unclear, he is very much present in early Dadupanthi literature, both in anthologies and in hagiography. The earliest hagiographic work mentioning Bajid is Raghavdas's Dadupanthi *Bhaktamāl* (1660/1713/1720[7]), where he is counted among the hundred and fifty-two disciples of Dadu, though not the smaller circle of his fifty-two disciples (in verses 361-62). Yet Bajid was important enough to make it into the group of the twelve disciples of Dadu to whom Raghavdas devotes one or more entire *chhappay* stanzas. Bajid's popularity as a poet may well be the reason why Raghavdas provided an independent description for him.

It is Bajid's Muslim background and his conversion that Raghavdas found most interesting. Reference to his literary activity with the polyvalent word *bhajana* ("worship", "devotional singing") merges it with general praise of his pious life. Bajid was a Pathan, and this is probably why Raghavdas uses the Perso-Arabic words *malika* and *khalika* (*khāliq*) in his *chhappay*, where his Muslim birth is not wished away but retained in the vocabulary chosen to describe him:

> He gave up his Pathan lineage and recited the name of Rama;
> through the power of his worship/singing (*bhajana*) Bajid won the game (*bājī*).
> His heart was terrified when he killed a gazelle and out of this terror
> inner strength arose and his evil attitude dispersed.
> He broke his bow and his arrows, cheated his body
> and emerged under the guru Dadu, the compassionate.
> Raghavdas says, his body and his heart delighted
> in the Lord (*mālika*) day and night

6 His earliest manuscript, containing eight works, is dated from 1600 (RORI Bikaner 6588), and we have a manuscript of his *Guṇ Gañjanāmau* from 1613 (RORI Jodhpur 13498(4)), and of his *padas* and *Guṇ Ajāib-nāmau* from 1636 (RORI Jodhpur 11583 (11)).

7 The date *saṁvat satrahai sai satrahotarā* has been interpreted as VS 1777 or VS 1770, but since the work presents no *bhaktas* later than the second generation after Dadu, a third interpretation VS 1717 (1660 CE) is most likely; see Agarchand Nahta, *Rāghavdāskṛt bhaktamāl* (Jodhpur: Rajasthan Oriental Research Institute, 1965), p. da; in *The Hindī Biography of Dādū Dayāl* (Delhi: Motilal Banarsidass, 1988, p. 14), Winand Callewaert considers Raghavdas a fifth-generation disciple and is inclined to accept 1777 VS as the date of composition, relying on Swami Narayandas Pushkar, the modern editor of this work; but in *The Life and Works of Raidās* (New Delhi: Manohar, 1992 p. 20), Callewaert gives the date as 1770 VS.

and he played with the Creator (*khālika*) as if released from
the games of this world.

(Raghavdas, *Bhaktamāl* 428)[8]

This is a familiar topos in hagiographies, suggesting conversion from a previous lifestyle that entailed habitual killing. Valmiki's precedent is the most well-known, but the same topos of conversion arising from killing a gazelle can also be found in a sufi hagiography, the *Chishtiya bihishtiya* (1655), where it is recounted in relation to Bajid's contemporary Baha' al-Din Barnavi (d.1630), the first known composer of *khayal*.[9]

The following *arilla* shows that Bajid himself thought of the conversion as a means to destroy his earlier *kafirpan* "disbelief" or "baseness':

I was a base/unbelieving (*kāphira*) soul not thinking of the Beloved;
I did not talk of compassion or morality;
my filthiness was destroyed by removing disbelief (*kāphirapanā*);
and indeed, my master showed me a blessed slavery.

(*Gurudev kau aṅga* 5)[10]

Later hagiographies follow Raghavdas and agree that Bajid did not make disciples and did not participate in the leadership of the sect but rather dedicated his life to literary activities, which he perceived as devotion.[11] Bajid himself emphasised proper conduct more than literary achievements, as did Dadu in many of his couplets:

8 Nahta (1965), pp. 201-02; Brajendrakumar Simhal (*Sant Bājīd granthāvalī* (Delhi: Dharika Publications, 2007), Vol. 1, p. 14) gives the variant *avigata agama su* ("the unfathomable existent") instead of *dādūjī dayāla guru*. It is in all probability based on *Rāghavdāskṛt bhaktamāl*, ed. by Swami Narayandas (Jaipur: Shri Dadudayal Mahasabha, 1969), which I was not able to consult. This may well be the original reading without the didactic insertion of the name of the guru. All translations in this paper are mine.

9 *Tarjuma-i-Mānakutūhala & Risāla-i-Rāgadarpaṇa*, ed. and trans. by Shahab Sarmadee (New Delhi: Indira Gandhi National Centre for the Arts and Motilal Banarsidass Publishers, 1996), pp. 187-89. I am grateful to Katherine Schofield for pointing out this parallel to me.

10 Bajid's *arillas* are quoted from Sukhadayal Dadu, *Maharṣi Vāzidjī Mahārāj ke aril* (Delhi: Shri Dadudayal Trust, 1976).

11 Bajid is mentioned in Atmavihari's *Dādūjanmalīlā* and Daulatram's *Bhagavat-līlā advait-siddhānt*, and in Swami Champaram's *Dṛṣṭānt-sākhī saṅgrah*; all these works are referred to in Dadu (1976), pp. ka-dha.

*bājida phūlā bhāvarā, sākhī pada ko joṛa;*
*ṭharāvana meṃ ṭhīka paṛai, bāta kahāṁ ke kroṛa.*

(Jagannath: *Guṇgañjanāmā*, 156, *karaṇī binā kathanī kau aṅga*, 2)

Bajid says, the dull swelling with pride composes couplets and songs. One should be proper in one's behaviour. What are millions of words good for?

The fact that the largest accessible collection of Bajid manuscripts—some sixty works—is to be found not in a sectarian institution but in the Khasmohar Collection at the City Palace in Jaipur, which served as the library for the rulers of Amber and Jaipur, suggests that Bajid was once appreciated in the royal court as much in Dadupanthi circles.[12] His popularity—the proliferation of the Bajid manuscripts in Rajasthan tells us that he was one of the most widely read poets in the seventeenth and eighteenth centuries—is in sharp contrast with his absence from many modern histories of Hindi literature, including the canonical one by Ramchand Shukla. (This is paralleled by the neglect of other important Dadupanthi authors with Muslim backgrounds, namely Rajjab and Bakhna.)

## Bajid's *Arillas*

Notwithstanding his religious background, Bajid's popularity in the early modern period was due to his *arillas*, as this *kabitt* by one Gopal testifies:[13]

*canda jū kau chanda, chapai nāmā baitāla jū kau,*
*keso ko kavitta, doha bihārī ke su gāṃsa kau;*

12 By comparison, the Dadu Mahavidyalay in Naraina today has only six manuscripts of his but seemed to have fourteen in 1948, since Swami Mangaldas (in *Pañcāmṛt*, Jaipur: Shri Swami Laksmiram Trust, 1948) mentions only fourteen works of Bajid. Sukhdayal Dadu, the head of the Dadudayal Trust in Narnaul, devoted some twenty-five years to collecting Bajid's works. By 1976 he had collected some 65 works; he wrote that in another Dadupanthi centre he had seen a thick book of Bajid but as soon as he started to consult it a "*sadhu* of that centre snatched away the book from my hands and in spite of repeated requests he did not let me see it"; Dadu (1976), p. na.

13 There are several poets by the name Gopal and the most likely candidate for the authorship of this quatrain is the court poet of Rajsingh of Ratanpur (Vilaspur) (r.1756-1776); see Madanmohan Gautam, 'Piṅgalnirūpak ācārya', in *Hindī sāhitya kā bṛhat itihās: Rītikāl*, ed. by Dr Nagendra (Banaras: Kashi Nagaripracharini Sabha, 1958), p. 483.

*vallabbha rasika māñjha, giridhara kavi kuṇḍaliyā,*
*bājida arilla jo hai atisai prakāsa kau;*
*rasarāsa rekhatā, au bāta bīrabala jū kī,*
*tulasī caupāī au saloka vedavyāsa kau;*
*bhanata gupāla e jahāna bīca jāhira haiṃ,*
*sūra ko pada aura dhurapada haridāsa kau.*[14]

Chand (bardai)'s *chhanda*, Namdev's *chappaya* on Vitthal,
Keshav's *kavitta*, Bihari's *dohas*, which are like arrow-heads.[15]
Vallabh Rasik's *manjh*, the poet Giridhar's *kundaliya*,
Bajid's *arilla*, which is abundant with brilliance,
Rasrashi's *rekhta* and Birbal's sayings,
Tulsi's *chaupai* and Vedavyasa's *shloka*—
Gupal says—all these are well-known in the world,
together with Sur's *pad* and Haridas's *dhrupad*.

For this reason, it is worth dwelling briefly on this genre. The arilla, a poetic form called sometimes *chandrayan*, is a quatrain rhyming in couplets with 11+10 (or sometimes 9+12) morae in a line. In contrast with the trochaic ending of the *doha* suitable for closing a statement, the final sequence of the *arilla* with its cretic (long-short-long) cadence was especially suitable for final exclamations and questions encouraging the involvement of the listener or the reader. As a genre, the *arilla* was already present in Apabhramsha literature, yet in Hindi it emerged as a literary genre around the end of the sixteenth century and became especially popular in the Dadupanth.[16] Its popularity may be linked to Bajid's extraordinarily successful use of it, a practice that included questions, exclamations, proverbs, and idioms expressed in down-to-earth language.[17]

Bajid's *arillas* express general Nirgun sant teachings. Books of his *arillas* were published five times between 1932 and 2007.[18] They even

14 Chaturvedi, Javaharlal, 'Saṅgīt samrāt svāmī Haridās', *Āj* (20 March 1960) quoted in Kishorilal Gupta, *Iśk dariyāv* (Jhansi: Abhinav Prakashan, 2007), pp. 13-14.

15 The text seems to be corrupt here. The word *gāṃs* ("arrowhead") is a reference to the popular *doha* that likens Bihari's couplets to the boatman's arrow.

16 The *chandrayan* is attested in Hemacandra's *Prākṛtapaiṅgalam* and in Abdurrahman's *Sandeśarāsaka*; see Gaurishankar Mishra 'Dvijendra', *Hindī sāhitya kā chandovivecan* (Patna: Bihar Rashtrabhasha Parishad, 1975), p. 79.

17 Kabir and Surdas are also credited with *arillas*; see 'Dvijendra' (1975), pp. 180, 243. Since these *arillas* are not found in critical editions but in sources such as the *Kabīr vacanāvalī* by "Hariaudh", they are probably later additions to these corpora.

18 Their earliest publication, *Vājīnd kī arelāṃ*, ed. by Ayodhyasimh Visharad (1932), is referred to in Dadu (1976), p. *dha*; I have not been able to consult this book. Mangaldas (1948); Simhal (2007); and in Govind Rajnish, *Pañcāmṛt aur Pañcraṃg: Madhyakālīn*

inspired the modern guru Osho to deliver discourses on them.[19] His stray *arillas*, along with some of his other works, have been included in the two Dadupanthi *Sarvāṅgīs* of Rajjab (c.1600)[20] and Gopaldas (1627), and in the *Gañjanāmā* of Jagannathdas,[21] another disciple of Dadu Dayal.[22] They are still current as popular sayings in Rajasthan and storytellers often quote them to prove their words.[23] Like the *dohas*, *arillas* are good vehicles for short religious or general moral teachings, though their greater length allows somewhat greater scope for poetic imagery or verbal play. In these two examples, a warning about inescapable death is vividly matched by the quotidian image of the millstone and the agricultural images of the dike and of grass growing along the road:

*gāphila rahibo bīra kahau kyūṃ banata hai;*
*yā mānasa ke sāṁsa ju jauṃrā ginata hai;*
*jāga lāga hari-nāṁva kahāṃ lauṃ soihai;*
*pari hāṃ cākī ke mukha paryau su maidā hoihai.*
(2 *Sumiran kau aṅga*, 4)

How long can you remain negligent, my friend,
when King Death counts the breaths of this life?
Awake! Be attached to God's name! How long will you sleep?
And indeed, whatever falls into the millstone will become flour.

---

*sant-kaviyoṃ kā prāmāṇik pāṭh-sampādan* (Jaipur: Maya Prakashan Mandir, 2004). Visharad published 131 *arillas*, Mangaldas and Rajnish had 138, Dadu and, relying on him, Simhal had 185.

19 Osho, *Kahe Vājīd pukār* (Poona: Rebel Publishing House, 1995).

20 This date is established by Dalpat Rajpurohit in 'The Dadupanth and Sarvangi literature', in *Bhakti in Current Research 2003-9: Early Modern Religious Literatures in North India*, ed. by I. Bangha (New Delhi: Manohar, forthcoming), since Chote Sundardas (b.1594), a close associate of Rajjab, is not mentioned in it.

21 Jagannathdas of Amber is claimed to be a disciple of Dadu Dayal in the extended title of Nārāyandās Puṣkar 1985, thus suggesting that his anthology dates around the beginning of the seventeenth century.

22 According to Simhal (2007, pp. 53-54), Rajjab's *Sarvāṅgī* quotes 18 *padas*, 39 *sakhis* and *arillas*, and one full composition (*granth*); the *Sarvāṅgī* of Gopaldas quotes 337 *chandas* and *padas* (including four full compositions); and Jagannathdas's *Gun Gañjanāmā* quotes 61 *sakhis* and *arillas*. Considering that Simhal did not notice a fifth full composition in Gopaldas, the *Śrīmukhnāmau*, the total in that compilation goes up to 370. Callewaert (1993, p. 5) credits Bajid only with 433 lines in this work, but even that makes him the third most quoted Dadupanthi author in this anthology, surpassed only by Dadu Dayal (6061 lines) and Rajjab (467 lines). It should be mentioned that not all *Sarvāṅgī* manuscripts give the same texts and these numbers only refer to the versions that Dharm Pal Simhal (*Sarvāṅgī: guṇ gañj-nāmā sahit*. Jalandhar: Dipak Publishers, 1990) and Callewaert used.

23 See Hiralal Maheshvari, *History of Rajasthani Literature* (New Delhi: Sahitya Academy, 1980), p. 126, and Simhal (2007), p. 51.

*kāla phirata hai nāla raini dini loya re;*
*hanai raṅka aru rāva gīnai nahiṃ koya re;*
*yaha dunīyā bājīda bāṭa kī dūba hai;*
*pari hāṁ pānī pahale pāla baṃdhai to khūba hai.*
(5 *Kāl kau aṅga*, 9)

O man! Death walks along with you day and night.
It kills both the lowly and the king, does not consider anyone.
Bajid, this world is grass on the roadside.
And indeed, it is good to prepare a dike before the water comes.

That Bajid's *arillas* were perceived as religious poetry by the scribes and probably by the poet himself is signalled by the fact that in most manuscripts they are organised into "*angas*", just like the *dohas* of the other Dadupanthi poets.[24] But many *arillas* must also have been memorised and transmitted orally, just as in modern times, and eventually included independently into the massive *Sarvāṅgīs*. Bajid's persona remained important in this process of transmission, since even verses without poetic signature are correctly attributed to him in the anthologies by the inclusion of a hypermetrical signature *vājīda* into the text of each poem.

Although one of the modern editors of Vaijid's *arillas* was astonished by the fact that "he used a very pure form of Hindi" (i.e. Brajbhasha) in them, the language of Bajid's works as preserved in the manuscripts is hardly homogenous.[25] There are compositions in Brajbhasha, in Sadhukkari—the language of the sants mixing grammar and vocabulary from various North Indian languages and dialects—in the Dhundhari dialect of the Jaipur area, while his Rekhta used the new literary medium of Khari Boli. Although it is clear that Bajid consciously used various dialects, we should be aware of the fact that the original language of a particular work may have undergone changes during written transmission. A major dividing line is between Brajbhasha and Dhundhari: sometimes manuscripts of the same work prefer one or another, thus dragging the work more towards

24 The some two dozen *arillas* in his earliest available masnucript (Bikaner RORI 6588) dating from 1600 (1657 VS), that is from the poet's lifetime, are not yet organised in *aṅga*s, but most later manuscripts and the modern editions present them distributed into *aṅga*s. This structuring is so widely accepted that it may have been done under the poet's eyes.

25 Mangaldas (1948), p. *ka*.

a higher cosmopolitan court culture (Brajbhasha) or towards a more local Rajasthani environment (Dhundhari).

## Bajid's Other Works

Most of Bajid's works deal with issues important to the sant tradition without being sectarian or expressing explicit allegiance to Dadu Dayal and the Dadupanth. His preferred themes include the pain and longing of the devotee for union with the ineffable being (*Virah-nāmau*, *Virah-vilās*, etc.) and the contrast between false or true devotion. He attacks human shortcomings in the "Book of the Obtuse" (*Mūrikh-nāmau*), the "Book of the Disgraced One" (*Nakaṭā-nāmau*), the "Book of the Negligent" (*Gāfil-nāmau*), and the "Book of the Quarrelsome Woman" (*Karkas-nāmau*). His *Pādsāh-nāmau* is a celebration of Jahangir's remittance of the pilgrimage tax. Some of the titles—e.g. the "Book of the Sufi" (*Sūphī-nāmau*), the "Book of the King" (*Śāh-nāmau*), the "Book of Union" (*Vāsil-nāmau*), and the "Book of Love" (*Muhabbat-nāmau*)—distinctly reference the wider Persianate culture of North India at the time, albeit in a more popular form.

Along with Bajid's earthly language, there are also traces of what we can call realism in his imagery. His *Utpattināmau* uses realistic imagery to describe the worthlessness and suffering of worldly life from the time before birth until death:

*nakha-sikha roma-roma rasa bhīno; sarbasu lye juvatī koṃ dīno.*
*bhayo nisaṅka na māṃnai saṅka; meṭi calyo bidhinā ke aṅka.* (31)
*batalāyeṃ te neka na bolai; galiyārana meṃ eṭhyau ḍolai.*
*ṭeḍhī pāga ukāsai bāṁha; calateṃ phiri phiri dekhai chāṁha.* (32)
*gārai apanaiṃ ganai na koi; hama baḍa hama baḍa hama baḍa, loi.*
*suta dārā mero dhana dhāṁma; chūṭi na sakai kiyo basa kāṃma.* (33)
*aratha-daraba kī lāgo sevā; pūji na sakyo nirañjana devā.*
*mūrikha mana māyā meṃ dīnau; hari nāgara sūṃ heta na kīnau.* (34)[26]

Your every pore from head to toe was drenched in emotion and you
    gave all your wealth to young women;
You were fearless without notions of fear,
    you effaced what was written for you by God.
When you were asked you did not speak,
    you swaggered down the streets;

26 All quotations from the narratives are from the edition-in-progress by Bangha and Mistry.

With turban awry and showing your muscles,
    you gazed at your shadow as you walked.
No one is aware of his own pride; "I am great, I am great,
    I am great, o people!
I have son, wife, wealth and a house!"—you couldn't get free:
    desire subdued you.
You served money and wealth and could not worship the untainted god.
Your obtuse mind was set on illusion; you did not love Hari,
    the one from the town.

Apart from frequent copying there is also a very unusual indicator of the popularity of Bajid's compositions. According to the modern editor of his collected works, Brajendra Simhal, five of Bajid's longer works are included in their entirety in the *Sarvāṅgī* of Gopaldas.[27] This is a clear sign that when compiling his anthology Gopaldas did not work simply from memory but had manuscripts in front of him.

What is the reason of the modern Hindi historians' amnesia about Bajid? There is probably more than one factor at work. Bajid's poetry is not ornate and lacks *alankaras* and even *rasa* in the Indian aesthetic sense. *Arillas* were never considered a major poetic form in Hindi and were hardly used for learned poetry. But their simple style, down-to-earth idiomatic language, and performative practice—as Thibaut d'Hubert points out in this volume, performance provided the ornamentation for unornate poetry—kept Bajid's *arillas* alive even when Hindi high literature in the nineteenth and twentieth centuries neglected it.

## Two Entertaining Tales: *Andhā kubrā kau sagun* and *Rājkirat*

As mentioned above, Bajid is remembered in hagiography as a disciple of Dadu Dayal with a Muslim background and in the wider literate and oral world as the author of celebrated stray *arillas*. Bajid the storyteller, however, is unduly forgotten today. Yet among the most oft-copied manuscripts of

27 His *Utpatti-nāmau* (*Sarvāṅgī* 106, 1-54), *Goru-nāmau* (113/2, 1-88), *Tūtī-nāmau* (119/2, 1-30), *Śrīmukh-nāmau* (16, 78-110), and his *Nirañjan-nāmau*. Its inclusion is claimed by Simhal (2007, p. 15) but I was not able to locate this work there. He also claims that, apart from this, Bajid's 19 *jhulna* verses are included in the *Upades kau aṅga* of the *Sarvāṅgī* (115, 1-19), as well as Bajid's *Kāl kau aṅga* (119, 1-26) and the 31 poems of his *Māyā triṣnā kau aṅga*—but I was not able to locate this work there.

Bajid's narrative works in *doha-chaupai* are several entertaining narratives that display features of oral performance.

While most of Bajid's works are concerned with Nirgun religion and morality and fall into the category of *upades* or "religious teaching", his interest in storytelling is testified to by the title of several of his works about "famous deeds" or *kirat/kīrat*,[28] such as *Māyā kirat, Govind kirat, Dās kirat, Viśvās kirat, Kāyā kirat, Gopāl kirat,* and *Prahlād kirat*.[29] In addition, Bajid's longest independent compositions are two books called *Hitopades*. Some of these narratives recreate *Panchatantra* fables in Bhasha while others seem to be rooted in oral tales. In these narratives religion often receives less attention and Bajid seems keener to investigate psychology. I already remarked on his interest in human shortcomings, and he was similarly attracted to people humble either by birth or by accident, such as low-caste wood-sellers, hunchbacks, blind people, or lepers. If devotional vocabulary and ideas appear in these tales, they are generally voiced in a subversive fashion by his wayward characters. And while these characters often meet with failure, listeners no doubt were expected to laugh at their pious words.

Five of the works by Bajid that I am editing with Daksha Mistry, a colleague from Vadodara, are tales. The story called *Rājkirat*, "The Deeds of a King", is the most popular, with eight documented manuscripts. The *Kaṭhiyārā* or "Book of the Wood-Seller" has five, while three short fables drawing on the *Panchatantra* tradition are preserved in a single manuscript in the royal collection of Jaipur. Although their circulation varied, all narratives belong to the same genre and one can even perceive a development in them. The *Panchatantra* stories do not have much of a religious veneer, the *Kaṭhiyārā* is heavily loaded with philosophical discourse, while the *Rājkirat* is mostly narrative with a touch of the discursive.

Other authors of *chaupai-doha* narratives tend to use the *doha* in order to underline the preceding *chaupais*. Bajid inverts the sequence: the *doha* comes first and introduces the new theme that will unfold in the following *chaupais*. While in the former case, the *doha* provides some rest in the narrative flow, in the latter it creates suspense and expectation. As in Bajid's other compositions, several *dohas* may come together at the

28 This word can be perceived as the vernacularised form of *kṛt* "deeds" and also of *kīrti* "fame"—not without a tinge of irony.

29 A list of one hundred works by Bajid is given in Simhal (2007), pp. 56-64.

end with a concluding *arilla* that enunciates the moral, which in the case of these narratives does not necessarily refer to any sant teaching.

The tales consist of monologues and dialogues full of idioms and proverbs that evoke spoken language rather than narrative discourse, thus using mimesis instead of diegesis.[30] Conversations are lively and tension is created by sudden "cuts" and changes of scene, while the use of conventional elements that stimulate the arising of a certain mood (*uddipanas*) creates a correspondence between event, setting, and mood, as with the terrible storm at night when the king approaches the merchant, or the joyful rain at the meeting of the blind man with the hunchback. The didactic element in Bajid's popular narratives varies in emphasis. In some stories, the use of wit and entertainment is clearly part of religious instruction, as in the *kirtankar* performances discussed by Christian Novetzke in his essay in this volume. In the *Kaṭhiyārā-nāmau* ("Book of the Wood-Seller"), for example, an interesting story raises interesting questions about the relationship between fate and divine power:

> *kalama piyā kai hātha hai kidhauṃ kalama kai pīva;*
> *darigahi lau gudarāiyau araja kahī yaha jīva.*
> (*Kaṭhiyārā-nāmau* 28)
>
> Is fate in the hands of the Beloved or is the Beloved in the hands of fate?
> Take my case to His court. This is the request of the soul.

In this tale a destitute and lowly wood-seller achieves one wish for each member of his family as a boon from the Lord (*divan*) through the mediation of a holy man (*sadha*) who attends his court (*dargah*) and who in the paratext is identified with Narada ("*nāradovāca*"). Once turned into a woman young and beautiful like a queen, the wood-cutter's wife disregards her husband who, thereupon, turns her into a parrot. Eventually their son restores the original situation to everyone's satisfaction. The composition is heavily loaded with verses about fate (*kalam*) and divine power that come from the mouth of the Lord.

30 The emphasis on dialogue and repartee are in line with nineteenth-century stories like the *Qiṣṣa qāżī-e Jaunpur*. See F. Orsini, *Print and Pleasure: Popular Literature and Entertaining Fictions in Colonial North India* (Ranikhet: Permanent Black, 2009), ch. 4, pp. 128ff.

Let us now turn to the story entitled "The Good Omen of the Blind Man and the Hunchback" (*Andhā-kubrā kau sagun*), a satire in 63 *doha-chaupai* stanzas about a blind man and a hunchback who try their hands at burglary. Several values get reversed when related to these two inauspicious figures. The title is already ironical, for "*sagun*" (*shakun*)—good omen—is one of the key words in the story. Whereas the meeting of blind people and cripples in India is considered to be a bad omen (*apashakun*), in the tale the two characters perceive their meeting as a good omen for their successful venture. This inverted language appears already in the introductory *doha*, when the two refer to their miseries with the word for victory ("*jaya*"), although instead of joy they cry out in pain:

> *āndhau ara kubarau mile kathā kahai kai phera;*
> *āpa āpane jaya kau lāge kahana dukha ṭera.* (1)
>
> A blind man and a hunchback met and spoke, taking turns;
> both of them started to tell their own "victories" shouting out in pain.

The first half of the story describes the meeting of the two men in the form of a repartee. In one *chaupai* the hunchback describes his misery as a cripple derided by others, but he quickly goes on to point out the real cause of his gloom:

> *jaga mahi jīye kaunahi kāma; jau pai gaṃṭhi soṃ bhayī na dāma.* (4)[…]
> *niradhana dekhi dhāma kau dhāvahi; mati hama pahi kahu māgana āvahi.* (6)
>
> What is the use of living in this world if
> there is no money in one's wallet?
> When people see a poor man they run into their houses
> lest he come beg from them.

The blind man then reveals to the hunchback that although he is blind he can see everything and is a master thief:

> Hunchback, you do not know my secret, I swear I can outdo any thief.
> Ten others trust in me; I am the head of five thieves. (13)[…]
> Thanks to the gift of the omen I can find hidden treasures,
> it takes me no time to find one. (15)

He adds a few words about the heroism of the thief reminiscent not only of the ideal of the *jivan-mukta*, "those who are detached from their lives", but also of the morals of Ravana's *vairya-bhakti*, according to which even inimical deeds bear the fruit of salvation because in them attention is directed to God, or in this case to the "true ones" (*sāṁce*, an apparently polisemic word referring both to the sants and to those who are not crooked),

> When a thief waits in hiding (for a chance) he does not lust after his life:
> It is the person dying at the feet of the true ones
> who achieves splendour. (17)

This couplet is a parody of another *doha* of Bajid's, in which the message of spiritual heroism has to be taken seriously. The verse is included in the *Sarvāṅgī* of Gopaldas:

> Bajid [says], If he dies, he will earn the fruit of liberation;
> if he stays alive, he will shine in the world;
> When a hero enters the battle, he does not lust after his life.
>
> (Gopaldas 1993: *Sarvāṅgī* 59, p. 29)

All this talk of heroism enthuses the hunchback, who asks the blind man to be his guru and save him, again using *bhakti* vocabulary in a subversive way:

> One cannot take weight on one's bare [i.e. unprotected] shoulder[31];
> who can cross (a river) without a boatman?
> I am being washed away, catch my hands! You are a great tree,
> let me sit in your shade. (22)...
> Then the blind man thought over these words
> and investigated all possibilities:
> is there a shore below or earth above? (27)

Eventually the blind man accepts the golden opportunity, "the golden/ omen bird" (a word-play on *sauna*). While they celebrate, it begins to rain, as if nature is also celebrating with them, and a golden bird comes and sits between them.

31 The meaning of this line is elusive. The above translation takes *dhorī* as "white, simple" (cf. Sanskrit *dhavala*). An alternative interpretation with the meaning "cattle" and the reading *kandhana* would give "It is (the shoulder of) cattle that one loads", i.e. "You are an appropriate person for this load".

They then set off and arrive in front of a closed compound, where the first problem arises: the gate is closed. Somehow they manage to get in through the drain, but once inside the hunchback loses heart. The blind man comforts him by reminding him of the good omen that helped them to get thus far. Fortunately everyone is asleep and the blind man can enter the building. Thanks to his extraordinary sense he finds the hidden wealth, and they make their way out the same way they came. Once again the hunchback loses heart, and this time the household wakes up and the cook and a few men start chasing the two thieves on horseback. The hunchback loses heart even further and foresees their future in prison and their eventual death. The blind man consoles him, once more drawing upon devotional vocabulary towards the end of his speech:

*pota parāi sira dharihauṃ samajhyo hau taba;*
*ika andha ara kubarau doū maribe aba.* (48)
[*tau*] *kubare kahi tau mana kari dhīrau; ko aihai hama tuma doū nīro.*
*hiyau na hāri, hāthi hai sauna; hamakau lagai na tātau pauna.* (49)
...
*musakila saba karihai āsāna; miṭyau tama jaba ugyo bhāna.*
*kubarai bāta sunahi kini aisī; saguna bhayau tau saṃkā kaisī.* (51)
*saguna hamāraiṃ sadā sahāī; saguna pitā saguna hī māī.*
*roṭī daī saguna kī khāhiṃ; saguna binā su āsarau nāhiṃ.* (52)

"Earlier I thought that I would grasp the wealth of others,
but now first the blind man and then the hunchback will die".
Then the blind man said, "Hunchback, take courage, who can come near us?
don't lose heart, the omen is in our hand—not even the wind can harm to us".
...
Every difficulty will straighten out.
Once the sun rises all darkness disappears.
Why don't you listen to me, hunchback? If we have the omen,
why doubt?
The omen always helps us, the omen is our father and mother.
We eat what the omen gives us; without the omen we have no refuge".

Indeed the omen does protect them, and the arrows of their pursuers turn back upon them. Now that they have escaped, the hunchback tries to get hold of the booty by poisoning the blind man's water. However, instead of killing the blind man, the poison cures his blindness. He immediately discovers the hunchback's intention and begins kicking him. And through this kicking the hunchback himself is healed. Now the two become fast friends, and the narrator concludes:

> *naisaka citai kṛpā kī kora; jana bājīda bacāyau cora.* (62)
>
> Just a glance at God's grace, the devotee Bajid says, saved the thief.

The morals are only loosely connected to the story—through his use of devotional vocabulary Bajid seems to suggest in a twisted way that faith in the omen was indeed salvific.

Bajid's skillful characterisation in this story is remarkable. The blind man's assertiveness contrasts sharply with the wailing, pusillanimous, and eventually treacherous hunchback. The miraculous healing of the heroes at the end of the *Andhā-kubrā ko saguṇ* seems based on the story of the three-breasted princess found in some versions of the *Panchatantra*. In that tale a blind man is persuaded by his hunchback friend to marry the inauspicious three-breasted daughter of a king in order to get her dowry. After some time the infatuated hunchback tries to kill the blind man by feeding him a dead cobra. Yet the poison has the opposite effect and cures his blindness. Through the kicks and blows in the ensuing fight both the hunchback and the three-breasted woman are cured of their deformations.[32] In Bajid's version the character of the three-breasted princess is eliminated and a more polisemic bird/omen (the *sauna*) replaces the inauspicious woman and her gold, which in Braj also translates as *sauna*.

Although the story of the hypocrite lion that takes up the first half of Bajid's *Parpañc-nāmau* is absent from the classical versions of the *Panchatantra*, it still echoes the hypocritical animals encountered in some recensions. The second half of the *Parpañc-nāmau* features the story of an ass without ears and heart, which does have a *Panchatantra* lineage.[33]

---

32 It is found in J. Hertel, *The Panchatantra: A Collection of Ancient Hindu Tales in the Recension Called Panchakhyanaka, and Dated 1199 A.D., of the Jaina Monk Purnabhadra* (Cambridge, MA.: Harvard University Press, 1908), book V, tale 10; Viṣṇu Śarma: *The Pañcatantra*, trans. by C. Rajan (London: Penguin, 1993), p. 430; and A.W. Ryder, *The Pañcatantra* (Chicago: University of Chicago Press, 1956), p. 465, though not in Edgerton's influential reconstruction: Franklin Edgerton, *The Panchatantra Reconstructed: An Attempt to Establish the lost Original Sanskrit Text* (New Haven: American Oriental Society, 1924).

33 Hertel (1908), book IV, tale 2; Edgerton (1924), book IV, tale 1. Just like in the story of the blind man and the hunchback, Bajid again downplays the gender issue by doing away with figures of the three she-donkeys waiting to get married to the prey

Bajid thus took current stories—whether he knew they came from the *Panchatantra* or independently—and turned them into self-standing tales. Bajid's example shows that stories could be taken from a wide pool, closely connected to popular culture. Curiously, the only existing manuscript describes these three narratives as the work of "Miyan Bajid"—while the colophons of other works refer to him more often as "Bajidji"—thus suggesting that these works of his were perceived as somewhat more "Muslim" than his other compositions.

The *Rājkirat* or "The Deeds of the King"—in which a king discovers the truth of his previous birth from a leper—is Bajid's most popular tale. The tale follows the common pattern of a seeker being sent further and further to discover the truth for himself in a humble, and humbling, fashion. The story is also a familiar one and usually features King Bhoja as its hero,[34] and the parallel with the almost contemporary story of Garuda and the crow Bhushundi in the Uttarakanda of Tulsidas's *Rāmcaritmānas* (7.58-125) is hard to miss. In this version Garuda wonders why Rama, the lord of the universe, was subject to the snake trap in the war with Ravana. Garuda first asks Narada who directs him to Brahma, who sends him further to Shiva, who perceiving pride in him sends him to the crow Bhushundi who at last answers him. Bhushundi also explains his present lowly state as the consequence of acts of pride in his previous births.

*Rājkirat* tells the story of a king who becomes obsessed with his past life, more precisely with knowing which virtuous act he committed in order to gain the bliss of his present life. In an act reminiscent of *Turandot*-type stories, he imprisons all the Brahmins who are not able to give him an answer. Then he sets out himself in search of anyone who can tell the past and future. Soon the scene changes and we are at the house of a merchant (*mahājana*) who can sense the death of his own son in a distant country. The idiolect of the characters is made more marked by an abundance of proverbs and idioms:

---

donkey. In Bajid's version the jackal herself offers to marry the donkey and lures him to become a prey of a lion.

34 This is how Ray Saheb Munshiram, the secretary to the Radhasoami guru Baba Sawan Singh (1858-1948), presented it in his diary to illustrate the workings of karma; see R.S. Munshiram, *Ruhānī ḍāyrī*, ed. by Sewa Singh (Beas: Radha Soami Satsang, [n.d.]), pp. 143-204.

*jau kahiye tau mānai kauna; beṭai diyo jare pari launa.*
*pūta piyārau jhūjhyau ājū; mūla gaṃvāyau lāhā kājū.* (8)

*sevaga bāta gaï nahī kīnī; gharī mahūrati dina likhi līnī.*
*tela dekhi tela kī dhārā; bina māraiṃ ko karai pukārā.* (9)

*cānda kuṃ ḍārani kahu kyauṃ chāyau; jyauṃ hai tyauṃ ba saṃdesau āyau.*
*sevaga kāni saṃdesau sunyau; masare hātha sīsa pari dhunyau.* (10)

*rājā bipra satāvai bādī; ūṃṭahi chāḍi ajā kina lādī.*
*sāha hamāro būjhau, loī; āsaṃkyā jiya rahai na koī.* (11)

"If I say so, who will believe me? My son poured salt onto my wound;
My beloved son died today, when I sought to gain
I lost my capital in the bargain".

A servant did not let these words go by and wrote down their exact time,
(saying) "I saw the oil and the oil's flow (I have seen it in all its aspects),
why would one who is not hit cry out?"

Can the moon be hidden by branches? The news came out exactly
as it was said.
A servant heard it with his ears, rubbed his hands
and beat his head [in sorrow].

"The king is torturing his priests in vain;
why is he loading a goat instead of a camel?
Ask my master! No doubt will remain in your heart". (11)

The king is directed to this merchant and arrives at his house in the dramatic setting of a dark and stormy night. The merchant sends the king to a carpenter, who has better knowledge than he does. The king first sends out one of his footsoldiers, who finds the carpenter preparing a junk for fractured bones (*khāpa*) because the village headman's son is about to fall from the horse and break his arm. Now convinced that the carpenter knows the future the king comes to him:

*khātī uṭhi ṭhāḍhau bhayau mahārāji kauṃ dekha;*
*cherī kai mukhi tūbarā kyauṃ ba samāvai, sekha.* (29)

*khāya tihārau launa, svāmī, jana yetau bhayau;*
*yā garība kai bhauna kyauṃ paga dhāre, nātha jū.* (30)

Seeing the king the carpenter got up:
"How can a gourd fit into the mouth of a nanny-goat? (29)

I eat your salt, my lord, how did your servant become so important?
Why did you come, my lord, to this poor man's house?" (30)

The carpenter reveals that there is a leper outside the town who will be able to answer the king's query. At this point the narrator inserts a moral comment:

> The merchant knew the events, the carpenter did not reveal them;
> It was in order to get the king rid of his pride (*rājas*)
> that he was sent to the leper. (39)

This is the same argument that Shiva uses with Garuda in the above-mentioned story in the *Rāmcaritmānas*:

> The reason, Uma, why I did not myself instruct him was that by the grace of Raghunatha I knew the secret (of Garuda's infatuation). He must on some occasion have given vent to his pride, and the gracious Lord Rama evidently wished to cure him of it.
>
> (7.61.4, trans. R.C. Prasad)[35]

In Bajid's *Rājkirat*, the king then approaches the leper, who tells the king that in their previous lives all four of them were brothers who lived in poverty. Just as in the story of the blind man and the hunchback and in the *Kaṭhiyārā-nāmau*, there is some description of their poverty as wood-sellers with hardly anything to eat—and even in this tale the four brothers resolve to go thieving! However, a wandering ascetic overhears and scolds them. The future leper's reaction is to throw a stone at the ascetic and break his head. The future king washes the ascetic's wound and covers him with his clothes. The carpenter gives him some dry food, the merchant offers him food cooked in oil, and the king gives him all his food. The narrator then reasserts the common Indian knowledge about *karma*:

> *bhalī karai tākauṃ bhala hoī; burī burā, sandeha na koī.* (50)
>
> If one does good, he will receive good, and if bad, then bad, there is no doubt.

The leper explains that neither the merchant nor the carpenter were proud of their good deeds, whereas the king had the quality of passion

---

35 Ram Chandra Prasad, *Tulasidasa's Shriramacharitamanasa: The Holy Lake of the Acts of Rama* (Delhi: Motilal Banarsidass, 1990; reprint 1999), p. 611.

(*rajas*), which is egotism, pride, and darkness, and was already thinking about attaining royal splendour. Therefore, while the trace of the two brothers' deeds—their *samskara*—disappeared, the king could not see his past good deed. At the end of the story the king himself expresses the moral of the tale:

> *... sukrata binā nara-kāyā kaisī.*
> *jaba laga yā jaga māṃhī rahiye; kari upagāra aura sana kahiye.* (54)
>
> ... How can one attain human birth without good deeds?
> As long as you live, tell everyone to do good to others.

As previously mentioned, the relatively high number of manuscripts attests to the fact that this was a popular work. Its popularity cannot be explained without reference to the work's literary merit, its lively style, and well-designed structure, with well-placed repetitions and rising tension. The three meetings are similar and echo each other, and one cannot miss that with each meeting the king gets closer and closer to the other speaker. While the Brahmins are unable to answer the king's query, it is through rumour that he hears about the merchant's ability. He first sends a man to see the carpenter but later sets off himself, and immediately, to visit the leper. The Brahmins know nothing, the merchant knows what happens far away in the present, the carpenter knows the future, but it is the leper who reveals the past. The lower one lies on the social scale, the more one knows. Instead of the parodic subversion of the story of the blind and the hunchback, we have a different kind of reversal here, in this case connected with pride and the need for humility. The inner development of the king is made explicit by the change in his approach towards the men he meets. As he goes lower and lower, his kingly pride appears less and less. One can almost perceive the story as an early Indian *Bildungsroman*. The simple message about *karma*, pride, and passion is elaborated in an entertaining manner.

The characters in Bajid's tales are not Brahmins but rather people from the lower classes. In fact, Brahmins are useless in *Rājkirat*, just as asceticism is hypocritical in one of his animal fables. Figures outside society, such as the leper or the blind man, appear as liminal characters with extraordinary powers. All this suggests that their audience (and readership) might have been closer to the world of the merchant and of the carpenter. However, the moral of the *Rājkirat* also tells the listener a message about the deeper brotherhood between the various castes, since they all were brothers in a previous life.

## Oral Traces in Written Texts

These tales are told in simple Brajbhasha, using the standard narrative structure of *chaupai-dohas*. Although the reader of the manuscripts encounters these tales as written texts, several traces evoke oral performance. Foremost among them is the frequent address to an imagined audience—"*ho bhiya*" ("hey brothers") or "*loi*" ("people")—normally embedded in the metre. After a *doha*, each new set of *chaupais* normally begins with an unmetrical *tau* ("then") to give the composition a more colloquial tint. Other colloquialisms include the frequent use of emphatics, such as "completely" ("*mūri*"), at the end of the half lines. The second half of the *Rājkirat* introduces pseudo-Sanskrit paratextual indicators to the dialogues—"*rājā uvāca, koṛhī uvāca*" ("the king said", "the leper said")—possibly inserted by the author or by a scribe in imitation of the Sanskrit epics.

While the use of such formulaic expressions is considered typical of oral compositions, John Brockington has observed in connection with the Sanskrit *Rāmāyaṇa* that they may also be used to evoke oral performance: "The tendency to greater frequency of formulaic *pāda*s in the later parts of both epics does seem not to be an index of orality but rather a sign of the decay of genuine oral tradition".[36] In Bajid's case, too, we have literary works that evoke oral embeddedness. Were these works composed for performance or for private reading? Before Bajid's time the answer to this question would have been simple. But the fascination of the early Dadupanth with writing indicates a deeper involvement with textuality.[37] Thus, in spite of the features that suggest oral performance,

---

36 John Brockington, 'Formulaic Expression in the Rāmāyaṇa: Evidence for Oral Composition?', in *The Epic: Oral and Written*, ed. by L. Honko, J. Handoo, and J.M. Foley (Mysore: Central Institute of Indian Languages, 1998), p. 137.

37 A similar broadening of the performance towards the textual can be found also in the case of the seventeenth-century Bengali poet Alaol. As d'Hubert points out in his essay, "The literary self-awareness displayed by Alaol is also accompanied by the broadening of the theoretical paradigm of performance towards more textuality, a central place given to 'speech' (*vachana*) an the metadiscourse it may include", pp. 425-26.

the variant readings in the manuscripts are minimal and do not indicate that the work underwent a phase of oral transmission. The only significant variation is the hesitation between Braj and Dhundhari forms in the *Rājkirat*. In contrast with the metrically correct Braj version, the Dhundhari variants suggest the scribes' uncertainty with the less standardised Rajasthani idiom.

## Conclusion

As the author of verses that circulate as sayings and the writer of tales that evoke oral narration, Bajid stands at the crossroads between performed and written literature. His rich manuscript tradition cannot hide the fact that his narratives still show their embeddedness in oral culture. Bajid used a language that was close to popular speech and genres that were linked to performance.

The approach to religious vocabulary and teaching in his narratives ranges from the didactic to the parodic. His effective characterisation and his clear structuring contributed to the popularity of his tales. Although not all his tales circulated widely in written form, he was clearly a very popular figure in the early modern literary field, whose works spanned the courtly, devotional, and popular domains. A revision of standard Hindi literary history that places greater emphasis on popular works and on performance cannot but pay serious consideration to a figure like him.

# IV. MUSICAL KNOWLEDGE AND AESTHETICS

# 14. *Raga* in the Early Sixteenth Century

*Allyn Miner*

In 2007 Aditya Behl drew my attention to a passage in the *Mirigāvatī*, composed in 1503, describing a magical courtly concert. He was organising a series of mini conferences on the sixteenth century at the time and invited me to prepare a presentation on music. The passage caught my attention at once because it was so detailed. Also, the author Qutban's patron was Shah Husain Sharqi of Jaunpur, who is credited with the origin of *khayal*, the classical North Indian music genre. Soon I was searching for the sources from which Qutban must have drawn, and I was swept into the world of *ragas* and *raginis*, *ragadhyana* visualisations and *ragamala* paintings. These articulations of formal musical melodies in different media were just beginning to circulate across North India in the early sixteenth century, and their complicated paths stretch before and after the period in Sanskrit, Persian, and vernacular texts. As I began to see different ways in which texts presented the idea of *raga*, the project became a search for the idea itself: that is, how did *raga* resonate in this period and at what levels did it work?

This paper is the fourth reworking of the presentation I gave at Penn in 2007.[1] Each has involved rethinking a complicated set of issues, sources, and contexts. In this version, I begin by sorting out the concepts *raga*, *ragamala*, and *ragadhyana*, then trace the treatment of *raga* in several texts directed to different audiences for different purposes. The paper deals not with music but with the evocation of it, and explores how the

1 I presented an expanded version at UCLA in 2008, a summary at the Society for Ethnomusicology Meeting in 2008, and a fourth working in London in 2009.

 http://dx.doi.org/10.11647/OBP.0062.14

idea of melody functioned to carry a layered set of meanings. I think with love of Aditya Behl. Grateful for his warm encouragement, I begin with excerpts of his translation from *The Magic Doe*:

> The prince gave out *pān* and dismissed the assembly,
> but chose a few companions to be by his side…
>
> The instruments sounded, all in rhythm.
> and played the six complete *rāgas*.
> Their thirty wives, the *rāgiṇīs* [*bhārjā*],
> were sung, five by five, after each *rāga*.
> First they sounded a single note,
> then began to play Rāga Bhairava.
> They sang Madhumādhavī and Sindhurā,
> then beat time to Baṅgālī and Bairāṭī.
> After that they sang Guṇakalī complete.
> These are the wives of Bhairava…
>
> In the sixth place they set Raga Śrī
> and sang the high notes pure and clear.
> Then they sang Hemakalī and Malārī, followed by Gujarī and Bhimpalāsī.
> These are the wives of Rāga Śrī. I have told them well, recognizing the *rāga*…
>
> Then the dancers came in, dressed in short saris.
> They put on many airs and graces…
> The whole assembly saw them and was entranced.
> Passionate desire seized their minds and bodies.
> The dancers salaamed the prince, sought his permission.
> The prince ordered them to begin the performance.
> The singers sang intensely, and they were accompanied by spirited dances.
> The *māṇṭha*, the *dhruvā*, the ring-dance, and the *paribandha*—
> these were the songs, those the melodies.
> They danced to all the different rhythms, usages, songs,
> and melodies that existed.
> King Indra came to watch the occasion in amazement,
> accompanied by all the gods.[2]

2 Aditya Behl, *The Magic Doe: Quṯban's Mirigāvatī*, ed. by Wendy Doniger (New York: Oxford University Press, 2012a), pp. 131-33. The text is based on the Avadhi critical edition by D.F. Plukker, *The Miragāvatī of Kutubana: Avadhi Text with Critical Notes* (Amsterdam: published thesis, 1981), http://gretil.sub.uni-goettingen.de/gretil/3_nia/hindi/kutmir_u.htm

# *Raga*, *Ragamala*, and *Ragadhyana*

Qutban's *raga-ragini* list (or as he calls raginis, wives [*bhārjā*]) appears early in the history of the *ragamala* phenomenon in North India. *Ragas* as performed melodies, *raga-raginis* as lists, *ragadhyana* visualisations, and *ragamala* paintings all appear in overlapping contexts in the sixteenth century. Using Qutban's list as a focus, in this chapter I will briefly sort out these practices and propose that *ragas* functioned in three distinct but interlocking spheres: as objects of general aesthetic appreciation; as objects of music-technical specialisation; and as tools of devotional or magical practice.

*Ragas* are defined in texts and in practice by two types of attributes: musical principles of notes and scale; and associations of emotion, season, and the like. A description of *Raga Madhyamādi* in the *Saṅgītaratnākara*:

> It arises from the scale types *gāndhāri, madhyama* and *pañcami,* uses the note *kākali;* has *madhyama* as its final note, low *ṣaḍja* as its fundamental and initial note, and *sauvīrī* as its *mūrchhanā. Madhyamagrāma* intervals are employed in evoking mirth and conjugal love; it is sung in the first quarter of the day in summer for the propitiation of Lord Siva.[3]

The idea of *ragas* as gendered entities is thought to have an early source in the feminine subcategory *bhasha* (*bhāṣā*, Sanskrit. "local language"), but it was in the fourteenth century that music theory texts first portrayed *ragas* as visualised and gendered. The *Saṅgītopaniṣatsāroddhāra*, a text from Gujarat written about 1350 by the Jain author Sudhakalasa is the earliest in which we find visualisations for male and female *ragas*. It contains a scheme of six male *ragas* and thirty-six females called *bhashas*, all described in the style of deities visualised for worship:

> *Śrīrāga* has a fair complexion. He has eight hands and four faces. He carries a snare, a lotus, a book, a goad, and the fruit of a citron tree. In two of his hands is a *vīṇā*, and one hand grants beneficence. He is known for having a swan as his vehicle. He is like a form of Brahma.

3 Based on *Saṅgītaratnākara of Śārṅgadeva: Text and English Translation*, ed. by R.K. Shringy and Prem Lata Sharma (New Delhi: Munshiram Manoharlal, 1989), vol 2, pp. 61-62.

> *Gauḍi bhāṣā* wears yellow clothing. She has fair limbs and has an elephant as her vehicle. *Kolāhalā* wears a red garment, is fair, and has a parrot as her vehicle.[4]

While technical details relating to other topics, especially drumming, are significant in this text and may record contemporaneous practices, the text lacks music-technical definitions of *ragas*. Was the writer more interested in the imaginative idea or perhaps the spiritual efficacy of *raga* over its music-technical details? This idea will be expanded below.

Sudhakalasa's type of *raga* visualisation must have attracted the attention of a wide cross-section of patrons, since poetic and painted portrayals of music and *ragas* spread quickly across North India over the next century. Maharana Kumbha of Chitrakut, Mewar, includes a similar set in his massive compendium, the *Saṅgītarāja*, written in 1456. The two lists of visualisations are not identical but seem to have shared an earlier source.[5] The *Saṅgītarāja*, unlike Sudhakalasa's text, details each *raga*'s musical characteristics as well as a visualisation. The section is more than 200 pages long and includes for each *raga* details of scale, tones, structure, and notation:

> *Śrī rāga* is from the *ṣaḍja grāma* and the *ṣāḍjika jāti*. *Sā* is its *nyāsa*, *aṃśa*, and *graha* [and it is performed] in the high and middle registers. *Pa* is less used in the lower register. According to some, it uses only five tones. It is sung in *vīra rasa* in the rainy season.
>
> Some describe him as fair colored, with eight arms and four faces,
> holding a lotus, a noose, a hook, a citron fruit and a book;
> playing with the sixth hand and holding the *vīṇā* securely in two;
> Like Brahma himself, smiling.
> Sā Sā Sā rī Rī Ga Rī sā Nī Sā Nī Dhā Pā Mā Gā Mā Rī Sā Nī Ni Sā Rī |
> Pā Pā Mā Rī Sā Ni Nī Sā Ga Rī Sā Sā Sā Sālāpa ukto nṛpeṇa | |[6]

Maharana Kumbha would have been interested in creating a thoroughly impressive text as a part of his project of building the reputation of the Mewar state, but he is credited with two other works on music, and his elaboration of material in the *Saṅgītarāja* indicates that he was

4 Sudhakalasa, *Saṅgītopaniṣatsāroddhāra: A Fourteenth-century Text on Music from Western India*, ed. and trans. by Allyn Miner (New Delhi: Indira Gandhi National Centre for the Arts and Motilal Banarsidass, 1998), p. 91.

5 Maharana Kumbha, *Saṅgītarāja*, ed. by Prem Lata Sharma (Varanasi: Banaras Hindu University Press. 1963), Vol. 1, p. 651.

6 Kumbha (1963), p. 407.

indeed a specialist. His interests were in the technicalities as well as the generalised aesthetic appeal of *ragas*.

Within a few decades *raga-ragini* lists with *dhyana* visualisations of a literary-heroic character appeared in several Sanskrit and vernacular texts. The *Saṅgītadāmodara* of Shubhankara is thought to have been written in Bengal in the late sixteenth century,[7] but more clearly dateable texts are the *Rāgamālā* by Pundarika Vitthala, a South Indian who moved north and wrote in the last quarter of the sixteenth century, and the *Rāgamālā* by Ksemakarna of Rewa, some one hundred and fifty miles south of Jaunpur, dated to 1570.[8] The seventeeth-century *Saṅgītadarpaṅa* of Damodara Mishra contains *ragamala* sets of three "opinions" (*mata*) and its *Hanuman mata* scheme is widely found in later paintings and texts.

The pleasure that these verses illustrating *ragas* (*ragadhyana*) provided is thus attested by their quick spread across North India. The *Saṅgītadāmodara* exemplifies the Sanskrit *ragadhyana* tradition and its verses circulated widely:

> He is shining brightly, his lotus-like face having been kissed by a wide-hipped beauty. Wearing bracelets and a garland, feeling in a mood of desire he enters the music room in the evening, he is Mālava, the king of *rāgas*.[9]

Verses from the *Saṅgītadarpaṇa* also travelled across North India:

> Eighteen years old with a body as beautiful as the god of love,
> wearing sparkling earrings.
> Śrīrāga is in the service of the seven notes, wearing red clothes,
> the image of a king.[10]

7 Shubhankara, *Saṅgīta Dāmodaraḥ*, ed. by Gaurinath Sastri and Govindagopal Mukhopadhyaya (Calcutta: Sanskrit College, 1960), p. 15.

8 Emmie te Nijenhuis, *Musicological Literature* (Wiesbaden: Harrassowitz, 1977), p. 23; see also Ksemakarna, *Rāgamālā*, ed. and trans. into Hindi by Vinod Shastri and Rama Gupta (Jaipur: Rajasthan Sanskrit Academy, 2003).

9 Narada, *Pañcamasārasaṃhita Nārada kṛta tathā Saṅgītadāmodara Dāmodarasena kṛta*, ed. by Bimala Rai and trans. into Hindi by Lakshman Tivari (Calcutta: Manipuri Nartanalaya, 1984), p. 36.

10 *Saṅgītadarpaṇa. Damodara Paṇḍita viracita*, ed. by Sridhar Ranganath Kulkarni (Mumbai: Maharashtra Rajya Sahitya Sanskrti Mandal, 1985), p. 195. The text dates anywhere from the second half of the fifteenth century to the early seventeenth century; Klaus Ebeling, *Ragamala Painting* (Basel, Paris, New Delhi: Ravi Kumar, 1973), pp. 112, 114.

> Red-complexioned, a manly figure, holding a shining white staff,
> he is returning from battle against other great warriors.
> He wears a garland of the heads of his enemies around his neck.
> Much honoured, this is Mālavakośika.[11]

> Rāginī Khambāvatī is a giver of pleasure. She knows the theory of aesthetic joy (*rasa*). Her delicate limbs adorned with jewelry, she is enamoured of musical sound (*nāda*). She has a voice like the kokila bird and is the beloved wife of rāga Kauśika.[12]

And if *raga* verses found broad appeal, paintings were to be even more successful. Easily reproducible and showcasing as they did local styles, they proliferated across North India. Tracing the circulation of *ragamalas* in these various scholarly, poetic, and visual forms is quite complex. Texts in Sanskrit and vernaculars list *ragas* and *raginis* in family sets (*mata*), some with *ragadhyana* verses. Most paintings (*ragamala*) that include *ragadhyana* verses in Sanskrit or vernacular follow one or another scheme recorded in the texts, but at least one scheme is found only in paintings. Three schemes are most relevant to the question of where Qutban got his *ragas* and *bharjas* (*raginis*):

a) Damodara's *Saṅgītadarpaṇa*: a widely-circulated text, it lists the *Hanumana mata* as one of the three schemes, one that was relatively widespread in both texts and paintings;

b) The scheme that Ebeling found exclusively in paintings and not in any text and that he calls the Painters System;[13]

c) The scheme found in the Ksemakarna's *Rāgamālā*, composed in Rewa some 130 miles southwest of Jaunpur and notable for its addition of a new category, *putra* (sons).

Table 14.1 shows the *Mirigāvatī raga-ragini* list alongside those of these three nearest relatives. The male *ragas* in the *Mirigāvatī* match those of the others in name and order. Its *raginis* do not match exactly either of the others, but it has many *raginis* in common. The number of similarities and differences across the schemes is comparable, suggesting that Qutban's was in fact one of the *ragamala* sets circulating in the region at the time.

---

11 *Saṅgītadarpaṇa* (1985), p. 91.
12 Ibid., p. 93.
13 Ebeling (1973), p. 18.

Table 14.1: Four early Rāga-Rāginī systems

| *Mirigāvatī* (Qutban, 1503) | *Hanuman mata* (Damodara, 17th C) | Painters system (Ebeling) | *Rāgamālā* (Ksemakarna, 1570) |
|---|---|---|---|
| | | | |
| **Bhairauṅ** | **Bhairava** | **Bhairava** | **Bhairava** |
| Madhumādhau | Madhyamādi | Bhairavī | Vaṅgālī |
| Simdhurā | Bhairavī | Nat | Bhairavī |
| Baṅgālā | Bangālā | Malasri | Velāvalī |
| Bairāṭikā | Varāṭikā | Patmanjari | Punyakī |
| Gunakarī | Saindhavī | Lalit | Snehakī |
| | | | |
| **Mālakausīka** | **Kauṣikā** | **Malkos** | **Malakousika** |
| Gaurī | Toḍī | Gauri | Gundagrī |
| Deukalī | Khambāvatī | Khambavati | Gandharinī |
| Toḍī | Gauṇḍī | Malavi | Srihathī |
| Konkanī | Guṇakarī | Ramakali | Andhreyakī |
| Khambhāvat | Kakubhà | Gunakali | Dhanāśrī |
| | | | |
| **Hiṇḍola** | **Hiṇḍola** | **Hindol** | **Hiṇḍola** |
| Bairārī | Velāvalī | Bilaval | Tilaṅgī |
| Desākha | Rāmakalī | Todi | Devagirī |
| Nāṭika | Deśākhya | Desakh | Vasantī |
| Sānjugutā | Paṭamanjarī | Devgandhar | Sindhurā |
| Desī | Lalitā | Madhumadhavi | Ābhīrī |
| | | | |
| **Dīpaka** | **Dīpaka** | **Dipak** | **Dīpaka** |
| Birasacimda | Kedārī | Dhanasri | Kamodanī |
| Kāmodaka | Kānaṛā | Vasant | Paṭmañjarī |
| Desī | Deśī | Kanada | Toḍī |
| Paṭhamanjarī | Kammodā | Bairadi | Gujjarī |
| Kahesī | Nāṭikā | Desvarati or Purvi | Kahelī |
| | | | |
| **Megha** | **Śrī** | **Megha** | **Śrī** |
| Mālasirī | Vāsantī | Gujari | Vairāṭī |
| Sāraṅgī | Mālavī | Gormalar | Karṇāṭaka |
| Barārī, | Mālaśrī | Kakubha | Sāverī |
| Dhanāsirī | Dhanāśrī | Vibhasa | Gauḍī |
| Gāndhārī | Āsāvarī | Bangal | Rāmagirī |
| | | | |
| **Sirī** | **Megha** | **Sri** | **Megha** |
| Hemakalī | Mallārī | Pancam | Mallārī |
| Mallārī | Deśakārī | Kamod / ini | Soraṭhī |
| Gūjarī | Bhūpālī | Setmallar | Suhāvī |
| Bhīumpalāsī | Gurjarī | Asavari | Āsāvarī |
| | Ṭankā | Kedar | Kokaṇī |

If *dhyana* visualisations of *ragas* and *raginis* as well as their lists were widespread in the later sixteenth century, it is likely that they were known in Sultan Husain Sharqi's court. Paintings may have been circulating as well. The earliest set of paintings depicting a *raga-ragini* set in the literary style is dated tentatively by Khandalavala and Moti Chandra to between 1525 and 1570, from "probably Uttar Pradesh or Delhi".[14] An earlier set illustrating the descriptions in the *Saṅgītopaniṣatsāroddhāra* is found on the border of a Jain *Kalpasūtra* manuscript dating to about 1450.[15]

While the appeal of the *ragamala* is easy to understand, the idea remains a puzzle in terms of music. Musicologists explain family sets as an organising method that replaced earlier categories. Terms in the *Saṅgītaratnākara* such as *bhasha* and *aṅga* ("limb") imply that later categories were seen as derivations of earlier ones. It might be assumed that they shared aspects of scale. That question is open, but scale-based relationships do not seem to have existed between *ragas* and their *raginis* or among *raginis*.[16] Harold Powers, who grappled with the musical meanings of painted *ragamalas*, proposed that since motifs were shared across regions and re-imagined in local painting styles, they reflected the way *ragas* were shared pan-regionally and performed locally.[17] The musical organisation of *raga-ragini* sets is problematic, but a painted *ragamala* was not intended to prescribe musical scales. It conveyed an aggregation of courtly high arts.

With his evocation of a *ragamala*, Qutban conveys the charms of *ragas* as imagined in the aesthetic world of the courtly milieu. This register would have worked across the entire spectrum of listeners to which the *Mirigāvatī* was directed: *ragas* as marvelous sonic entities encompassing all the senses and the arts. But there were other registers on which it also worked. Specialists personified by patrons such as Maharana Kumbha were producing texts that were more directly oriented to the technical requirements of *raga* performance.

---

14 Ebeling (1973), p. 152.

15 See Sarabhai Nawab, *Masterpieces of the Kalpasutra Paintings* (Ahmedabad: Sarabhai Manilal Nawab, 1956).

16 This statement is based on *raga* usage in the modern repertoire. It is well known that *raga* scales can change significantly over a few generations, but to my knowledge no musicologist has found indications that scale was the basis for *raga-ragini* relationships.

17 Harold Powers, 'Illustrated Inventories of Indian Rāgamālā Painting', *Journal of the American Oriental Society* 100.4 (1980), 473-93.

# *Raga* in Specialist Circles

At the same time that the Hindavi of the Gwalior region became a premier language for poetry in the early sixteenth century, Raja Man Singh Tomar (r.1486-1517) was providing an intensely focused environment for music in his court in Gwalior. The *dhrupad* genre would later become the highest ranked song genre of the Mughal court, and in Man Singh's court it was the most celebrated medium for *raga* performance.

The *Mānakutūhala* is a work on *raga* attributed to Man Singh. One copy of the Gwaliyari original has been preserved in the Central Library, Baroda,[18] and a Persian translation of it is included in the *Rāg darpan*, written in 1666 by Saif Khan "Faqirullah", one of Aurangzeb's noblemen.[19] The *Tarjuma-i Mānakutūhala* section of Faqirullah's text is entirely devoted to *raga*. It becomes clear from this text that the musical interests of performers and music patrons lay beyond *ragamalas* and *ragadhyanas*. Faqirullah writes in his introduction that the *Mānakutūhala* was written in consultation with performers and composers:

> It was in the year 1663 CE that an old book, written during the days its author lived, came to my notice. It was called the *Mānakutūhala*, and was attributed to Rājā Mānsingh, the ruler of the state of Gwalior. Contemporaries with whom the Rājā constantly discussed the intricacies of the art and its aesthetic excellences, have been such poet-musicians (*go'indas*) as Nāyaka Bhinnu, Nāyaka Bakhshū, Nāyaka Pāṇḍavī—the last having come from Tilaṅga, en-route to Kurkhet for a holy bath. Besides them were Maḥmūd, Lohank and Karan. When these musicians assembled (at Gwalior), the Raja had an idea: an opportunity like this comes... only once in ages. Why not avail of it, learn and write down everything about every *raga*, complete with illustrations and practical hints.[20]

The *Mānakutūhala* section begins with a *raga-ragini* scheme that includes eight sons (*putra*) for each *raga*. The scheme is the same as that in the 1570 *Rāgamālā* of Ksemakarna mentioned above. The same scheme is also appended at the end of some recensions of the *Ādigranth*, a point

18 Oriental Institute, acc. no. 2125. The editors are grateful to Nalini Delvoye for drawing our attention to this manuscript.

19 The *Mānakutūhala* and the *Rāg darpan* became available in Shahab Sarmadee's English translation; Faqirullah, *Tarjuma-i-Mānakutūhala & Risāla-i-Rāgadarpaṇa* (New Delhi: Indira Gandhi National Centre for the Arts and Delhi and Motilal Banarsidass, 1996).

20 Faqirullah (1996), pp. 11-13, modified from Sarmadee's translation.

to which I return below. There is a difference between the *Rāgamālā* of Ksemakarna, however, and the *Tarjuma-i Mānakutūhala*, which is significant for our interest here. Ksemakarna's text includes *ragadhyana* verses as well as associations of time, season, residence, attire, and ornaments for each *raga*. The *Mānakutūhala* includes times, seasons, *rasas*, and regional associations but no *ragadhyana* verses. Is the lack of *dhyanas* a sign that Man Singh and his circle had limited interest in this type of *raga* characterisation? Following the *ragamala* list in the *Mānakutūhala* is a separate and longer section in which *ragas* are described in quite different terms. Here, more than ninety *ragas* are described in terms of how they are formed from combinations of three, four, five, or six others:

> We name the *rāgs* which combine to produce one particular *rāg*. There are five kinds of *Kānharah*: *Sudah Kānharah*; *Kānharah* sung with *Dhanāsirī* added to it, called *Bāgesarī*; *Kānharah* mixed with *Mallār*, named *Aḍāna*; *Farodast* suffixed to *Kānharah*, known as *Shāhānā*; and *Kānharah* compounded with *Dhavalsirī* and *Mangalashtak*, designated *Pūriyā*.[21]

Sarmadee notes that Faqirullah's choice of terms conveys the sense that *ragas* were to be combined in specific ways. The Arabic and Persian verbs used by him mean "to join", "to mix", "to bring together", and "to adulterate".

> … the *ragas* have not just been mixed, according to him, but mixed in an order of precedence and in a specific measure. As an innovator himself, he knew what has been done and how. That is why he has taken scrupulous care to narrate the exact and whole fact in minimum possible words.[22]

This kind of discussion would sound familiar to a performing musician. While talk of *raginis* may evoke ideas of delicacy or beauty, it is detailed debate about scale- and phrase-based affinities that are of real interest to serious patrons and connoisseurs. Some later texts as well reflect a limited interest in *ragamalas*. Two of the most important late-sixteenth and seventeenth-century Persian texts outlining music theory, the *Ā'īn-i Akbarī* (1593) and the *Shams al-aṣwāt* (1698), both refer to *raga-ragini* sets but neither includes *ragadhyanas*.[23] This is not just a matter of language.

---

21 Ibid., pp. 35-37, modified from Sarmadee's translation.

22 Faqirullah (1996), p. 267.

23 For the *Ā'īn- i Akbarī*, see: http://persian.packhum.org/persian/main?url=pf%3Fauth%3D7%26work%3D002; Ras Baras Khan, *Shams al-aṣvāt*, ed. and trans. by Mehrdad Fallahzadeh (Uppsala: Acta Universitatis Upsaliensis, 2012 [1698]).

*Ragamalas* are found in Persian as well as Hindavi and Sanskrit.[24] Rather, it seems to be a textual manifestation of interest in the music-specific aspects of *raga* performance.

The *Mānakutūhala* section provides other hints that the text was directed to performers and patrons of performance. Many of the *raga* names appear to have come from the oral repertoire. Some Persian names appear here (*Farodast, Shahānā*). Several names are known in modern performance but are not found in *ragamalas* (*Bageshrī, Aḍānā, Puriyā, Tilak Kāmod*).[25] There are speculations about sources: "*Mālasiri* and [other] such *ragas* are to be mixed because *Mālasiri* is the name of a folk-tune". And "*Bairārī*... originated in Tirhut and developed there".[26]

Some *ragas* are associated with iconic figures:

> *Mālasiri* affixed to *Mallāra* produces *Khambhāvatī*. Bharat was the first to melodise it...
>
> *Desakalī, Kalyāna, Gūjarī* and *Shyām* [...] together produce *Abheri*. It ought to be sung in the evening. Kanha was the first to introduce it.[27]

Some are associated with more recent figures:

> *Gūjarī* and *Āsāvarī*... together get the name *Gauṇḍakalī*. Gorakhnath was the first singer of it...
>
> *Pūrbī, Gaurī* and *Shyām*, mingled correspond with *Farodast*. Earliest compositions in it go back to Amir Khusrau.[28]

Qutban's patron, Husain Shah Sharqi, was certainly a specialist. Qutban admires his level of expertise in literature and language:

> He reads the scriptures, difficult of access,
> and speaks the meanings aloud and explains them.
> A single word can have ten meanings:
> *pandits* are struck dumb with amazement.[29]

24 British Library Johnson Album 35 is a *ragamala* set with *dhyanas* written on the back of each painting in Sanskrit and Hindi with a Persian translation.
25 Faqirullah (1996), pp. 35-37.
26 Ibid., pp. 39, 47, modified from Sarmadee's translation.
27 Ibid., pp. 47-49.
28 Ibid., pp. 40-41, 45.
29 Behl (2012a), p. 20.

According to Faqirullah he created and named nineteen *ragas*:

> the twelve *Shyāms*: *Gaurā Shyām, Shyām-mallār, Bhopāl-shyām, Kānharā-shyām, Sāhā-syhām, Pūrbī-shyām sampūran, Shyām-rām, Megha-shyām, Basant-shyām, Bairārī-sampūran shyām, Shyām-koḍāyī, Gauṇḍa-shyām.*
>
> five other mixes: "*Koḍāyī, Śaktivallabha* from mixing *Sughrāyi, Gauṇḍa, Pūriyā* with *Sankarābharana* and *Kānharā*";
>
> and also "*Jaunpurī Āsāvari* [made] from *Āsāvari, Jaunpurī* and *Toḍī*, and *Jaunpurī Basant* from *Basant*, mixed with *Jaunpurī Toḍī*".[30]

Can anything be inferred about the music environment in the Sharqi court from the names of Husain Shah's *ragas*? Only one Persian name, *Muwāfiq*, occurs. In the *Mirigāvatī*, too, Qutban evokes a high court environment and uses vernacular with a Sanskritic lean. The evoked sensibility is one of history and refinement. Notable among the *raga* names is *Jaunpuri*. *Ragas* known to come from a specific time and place are relatively rare. This *raga* has remained in the repertoire to the present day, marking the status of Husain Sharqi in the world of formal music performance.

Qutban must have been writing about the music practiced in his patron's court. He chose to describe it in a language accessible to the widest range of listener. His listeners would have experienced the tale in accord with their varying backgrounds. But his choice to feature a sublime musical experience at a climactic point in the story must have been made for the benefit of spiritual aspirants as well.

## *Ragas* in *Bhakti* Texts

*Ragas* were an organising principle for collections of *bhakti* poetry from an early period without reference to gender or family grouping.[31] *Bhakti* scholars have grappled with questions of the *ragas'* functions. It seems to be fairly well established that *raga* usage corresponds with their associated time of day in Vaishnava and Sikh liturgical practices, but that other associations are not

30 Faqirullah (1996), pp. 63-65.

31 A separate *raga-ragini* list is appended to some recensions of the *Ādigranth*, and it matches the lists in the *Mānakutūhala* and the *Rāgamālā* of Ksemakarna, which would seem to confirm that it dates to an early period; a verbally almost identical *ragamala* passage occurs in Alam's *Mādhavānal Kāmakandalā*, see Orsini in this volume.

consistent.[32] Callewaert and Lath have argued that tune is a natural way of remembering and organising sung material; even more so than the songs' thematic content or other text-based methods.[33] I do not attempt to add to the discussion of liturgical function here. Rather, in the following paragraphs I compare *raga* sets used in three early *bhakti* compilations, and offer the suggestions that: 1) *raga* sets became canonised for *bhakti* use where they took on a life independent of courtly performance contexts; 2) later *bhakti* performances were based on this performance canon rather than on the *ragas* current in court performance; and 2) the *bhakti* composers or compilers who originally specified *ragas* as organising principles were likely linked to courtly music-specialist circles.

If we look at the *raga-ragini* sets of Table 14.1 alongside the *ragas* mentioned in three early *pada* compilations, we can begin to sort out the connections among them over time. Twelve *ragas* organise the earliest collections of *padas* of the *sampradaya* of Swami Haridas (b.1493);[34] fifteen *ragas* organise the *Caurāsī pada* of Hita Harivansha (b.1473 or 1502);[35] and thirty-one *ragas* organise the songs in the *Kartarpur pothi* version of the *Ādigranth* compiled by Guru Arjan Dev in 1604.[36]

Table 14.2 shows the *ragas* of the three *pada* compilations and their occurrences in the *raga-ragini* systems shown in Table 14.1. Their relationships to other systems are too complex to be dealt with here, but several points emerge from this chart. There is clear continuity among the sets. The earlier sets are most closely related to the *raga-ragini* systems. A number of *ragas* have been added to the *Ādigranth* collection. Many of the names are familiar from later practice but they never became a part of *raga-ragini* family groups.

32 *Raga* times with regards to music in Sikh practice are charted in http://www.sikhiwiki.org/index.php/Timings_For_Gurbani_Raag. Snell charts times in Vallabha worship practice. He also makes the valuable speculation that the time of day associations have remained connected over time with the name of the *raga* rather than with *raga* scales as they changed; R. Snell, *The Eighty-four Hymns of Hita Harivaṃśa: An Edition of the Caurāsī Pada* (Delhi: Motilal Banarsidass, 1991), p. 320.

33 See Winand M. Callewaert and Mukund Lath, *The Hindi Songs of Namdev* (Leuven: Departement Oriëntalistiek, 1989), but also Horstmann in this volume.

34 Richard D. Haynes, 'Svāmī Haridās and the Haridāsī Sampradāy' (PhD dissertation, University of Pennsylvania, 1974), p. 67.

35 Snell (1991), p. 30.

36 See Winand M. Callewaert, *Sri Guru Granth Sahib with complete index* (Delhi: Motilal Banarsidass, 1996), Part II.

Table 14.2: *Rāgas* named in three *bhakti pada* compilations and their occurrences in the *rāga-rāginī* sets of Table 14.1

| *Haridāsa* (b.1493) | *Caurasi pada* (Hita b. 1473-1502) | *Ādigranth* (comp.1604) | Table 14.1 |
|---|---|---|---|
| | Dhanāsirī | Dhanāsarī | A.B.C.D. |
| Avārau | Āsāvarī | | B.C.D. |
| Malār | Malāra | Malār | A.B.C.D. |
| Vilāval | Vilāvala | Bilāvalu | B.C.D. |
| Kānharau | Kānharau | Kanara | B.C. |
| | | Gonda | B.D. |
| Kedārau | Kedāra | Kedāra | B.C. |
| | | Sirī | A.B.C.D. |
| | Devagandhāra | Devagandhārī | A.C.D. |
| Gaurī | Gaurī | Gaurī | A.B.C.D. |
| Basant | Vasanta | Basantu | B.C.D. |
| | Toḍī | Toḍī | A.B.C.D. |
| | Lalita | | B.C. |
| | Gūjarī | Gujjarī | A.B.C.D. |
| Vibhāṣ | Vibhāṣa | | |
| Naṭ | | Naṭ Nārāiṇ | |
| | | Rāmakalī | |
| Kalyān | Kalyāna | Kalian | |
| Sārang | Sāraṅga | | A. |
| Gauṛmalār | | | |
| | | Majh | |
| | | Asa | |
| | | Bihāgara | |
| | | Vadahansu | |
| | | Soraṭhī | D. |
| | | Jaitasirī | |
| | | Bairārī | A.C. |
| | | Tilanga | D. |
| | | Suhī | |
| | | Mālī Gaurā | |
| | | Māru | |
| | | Tukharī | |
| | | Bhairav | A.B.C.D. |
| | | Sarag | |
| | | Parabhati | |
| | | Jaijavanī | |

Given that performance practice changes fairly quickly, if the *bhakti* composers chose *ragas* that were prominent in their contemporary repertoires we would expect the core set to show more change over the time represented here. Even the *Ādigranth*'s addition of *ragas* to the earlier set seems to indicate, rather than a wholesale substitution, that the *raga* names represent at least the loose canonisation of a particular core set of *ragas* specific to *bhakti* uses.

The use of *ragas* in *pada* collections is significant for hints about composers and performers. A *raga* is a template for melody. A composer must create a *raga* melody that conforms to scale, phrases, and tonal ornamentations as well as to the metric requirements of a text. Any performer or group may memorise a *raga* melody, but the creator of the melody must be a specialist. Outside classical music, the genres in which *ragas* are used today are those performed by hereditary specialists tied to court, temple, or shrine. *Qawwali*, *haveli sangit*, Sikh *kirtan*, and the music of the Langas and Manganiars of Rajasthan are examples of North Indian genres that use *raga*. Their repertoires are handed down in specialised lineages. Thus it seems reasonable to propose that the assignment of *raga* in *bhakti* texts suggests that the original compiler or composers moved in or were connected with court or specialist circles.

Vernacular *bhakti* poetry famously worked across a spectrum of elite and non-elite populations. I have proposed that *raga* similarly resonated in various ways: as an aesthetic entity across a broad spectrum of listeners; as canon carrying the song repertoires of devotional lineages; and as a specialised object at music-technical levels. But how were *ragas* actually heard and carried? *Raga* melodies are carried in song genres, and the names of genres listed by Qutban and other writers give us further information for tracing how *ragas* moved across time and contexts. In the sections below I consider the song genres mentioned in the *Mirigāvatī*. Qutban has listed an eclectic assortment, some with connections to older practices and some newly emergent, with connections to formal, local, and devotional applications. The purpose of the survey is to explore more precisely the dynamic and various ways in which *ragas* were heard in Qutban's circles and, in the last section, to consider the place of non-*raga*-based genres.

## *Raga*-Based Genres in Qutban's Time

All the instruments sounded; six *sampūran rāgas* were performed in *ālāp*.

(Qutban, *Mirigāvatī*)[37]

The text-free beginning of a *raga* performance, *alapa*, "speech, conversation", is described in *saṅgītaśāstra* texts from the thirteenth-century like the *Saṅgītaratnākara*, but it is not a term that occurs frequently. On the other hand it is a featured part of a *dhrupad* performance. Since *dhrupad* was newly developing in Gwalior around Qutban's time and the term appears so frequently in this passage from the *Mirigāvatī*, one is tempted to see its use as recent and local.

Then beautiful singers sang *māṇṭhā, dhuruvā, jhūmara,*
*paribandha, gīta* and *rāga*…

Then they danced *dhurapada sancārā* and sang *gīta*
with lovely ringing sounds.[38]

All the terms from Sanskritic sources that Qutban uses here—*mantha, dhuruva, jhumara, paribandh,* and *dhurpada*—persisted in textual and oral sources in later periods. The list seems to be a record of songs current in the Sharqi court. *Prabandha*, a "connected narrative", was formal court song described in Sanskrit texts from about the ninth century.[39] *Prabandhas* were sequences of songs, each of which had melodic sections (*dhatu*) and various kinds of text (*anga*). More than seventy types of *prabandhas* are defined in the *Saṅgītaratnākara*. We know from *prabandha* treatment in texts beginning with Sudhakalasa's, mentioned earlier, that the practice had diminished by the fourteenth century. Faqirullah puts it in the category *tasnīfāt-i mārgī*, "arcane compositions":

*Parbanda* is of only two lines, sung to praise the gods or eulogise a ruling chief. Besides this, the call or cry of an animal is also sometimes [...] rendered, the underlying idea being to imitate it.[40]

37 Plukker (1981), stanza 247.1, p. 52, translation mine.
38 Ibid., 251 *doha* and 252.3, translation mine.
39 (Rowell 1992).
40 Faqirullah (1996), p. 95, modified from Sarmadee's translation. Faqirullah defines *jhumara* under the same category: "*Jhūmarā* is composed in four lines, the theme being the praise of gods. Rhythmically, it restricts itself to *tālas* exclusively meant for it"; ibid.

In modern practice the term is used for a 14-beat *tala* cycle and a dance-and-song type associated with Punjab. *Mantha* and *dhruva* are *prabandhas* belonging to the *salagasuda* category described in texts beginning with the *Saṅgītaratnākara*. *Dhruva* seems to have gained prominence in the fourteenth century. Sudhakalasa states that "music without *dhruva* is like a pond without water".[41] Faqirullah mentions it under the category *desī tasānīf*, "current" or "local" genres, and associates it with Dravidian languages. Both terms survived as obscure song types in some twentieth-century performance repertoires.[42]

Of particular interest in the *Mirigāvatī* passage is Qutban's reference to *dhurpad* (i.e. *dhrupad*). This contemporaneous use of the term outside of Gwalior, and in association with dance, may hint at a history for *dhurpad* elsewhere as well as in Gwalior. Man Singh's *dhurpad* was by Faqirullah's account a winning combination of formal and local structures. Faqirullah puts it at the top of his list of "current/local genres":

> *Dhurpad* is an invention of Rājā Mān Gwaliari. It comprises four song parts, and is equally suited to all nine *rasas*. Rājā Mān formulated this favourite of the common people and the elite alike with the cooperation of Nāyakas Bakhshū and Bhinnū, together with Maḥmūd, Karana and Lohaṅka. They gave it finish and an appeal which surpassed that of all the other the prevailing song-forms. I think this was because of two reasons:
> First, once *dhurpad* came out, the *ragas* and the song-forms of the archaic *mārga* style lagged behind. Second *dhurpad* is self-sufficient. It took from both *mārg* and *desī* and grew into the marvel of the age.[43]

Faqirullah also refers in admiring terms to the Gwaliyari language, which had become a model of refinement.[44]

By Faqirullah's account, Husain Shah Sharqi also created a song form of his own, known as *chautukla* or *chutkula*, which he includes in his list of "local/current genres".[45] Faqirullah's description appears to be an

41 Sudhakalasa (1998), p. 13.

42 V. Roy Chaudhury, *Bhāratīya saṅgītakośa* (New Delhi: Vani, 1998), p. 92.

43 Faqirullah (1996), pp. 97-99, modified from Sarmadee's translation.

44 "*Sudesa* is the part of the country with Gwalior at the centre, *Mathura* in the north, *Itawah* in the east, *Unch* in the south and *Bhusawar* to the west. The language spoken in these areas is the most elegant and the most correct, just like the Persian spoken in Shiraz"; Faqirullah (1996), pp. 98-99, modified from Sarmadee's translation.

45 *Chautukla* means "four parts"; *chutkula* means "anecdote or joke". Sarmadee reads it in Faqirullah as the former. Brown [Schofield] accepts *chutkula* and notes its appearance in the *Ā'īn-i Akbarī* of 1593 and the *Pādishāhnāma* of 1637 as well as in the seventeenth-century *Saṅgītanārāyaṇa*. K. Butler Brown, 'The Origins and Early

expansion of previous mentions of the genre in Persian sources, but he takes the opportunity to insert a poke at the Jaunpur ruler:

> Sung in Jaunpur with two non-rhyming verses (*misra*). The rhythmic phrase *paran* climaxes on returning to the first verse. Sentiments of love and lover (*ishq, ashiqi*) the grief of separation and eulogy and praise form its regular themes.
> The author and originator of this song-style was Sultan Husain Sharqi, the ruler of Jaunpur. Absurdly enough he fought with Bahlol Lodi, the Sultan of Delhi, and suffered a defeat. The past records speak of all this.[46]

Faqirullah's mention of the term *paran* is notable. *Parans* are known today as compositions for the *pakhavaj* drum, the predecessor of the tabla. The description seems to hint at a cadence in the sense of a modern *mukhra*, the phrase with which a song line begins and which leads to the first beat of the *tala* cycle. No other technicalities about *chutkula* are known. Following its use in textual sources, Katherine Schofield finds that it later became subsumed under the term *khayal*. She proposes a complex process of exchange between the Jaunpur and Delhi regions that resulted in the development of the *khayal* genre.[47]

## *Ragas* and Sufis

There are two more aspects that we need to briefly consider in order to complete this survey. First, the fact that not all song types, even in courtly contexts, were set to *ragas*. Second, we need to consider the overlap and exchange of musical knowledge, musical forms, and musicians between the Sharqi court and sufi circles.

Qutban uses the term *gita*, the generic term for song, and he may be using it in contrast to *raga*:

> Beautiful singers sang *māṇṭhā, dhuruvā, jhūmara, paribandha*, here a *gīta* and here a *rāga*…
>
> Then they danced *dhurpad sancārā* and sang *gīta*, and the music rang out.[48]

---

Development of Khayal', in *Hindustani Music: Thirteenth to Twentieth Centuries*, ed. by Joep Bor, Françoise "Nalini" Delvoye, Jane Harvey, and Emmie te Nijenhuis (New Delhi: Manohar, 2010), pp. 165, 166.

46 Faqirullah (1996), p. 101, modified from Sarmadee's translation; see also Brown (2010), pp. 166-67.

47 Brown (2010).

48 Plukker (1981), 251 *doha* and 252.3, translation mine.

Faqirullah also describes a genre called *bar* that is sung by lineage performers (*dhadhi*) and may be a genre not set to *raga*. *Var* is one of the poetic categories used in the *Ādigranth*, and directions specified the use of folk tunes (*dhuni*) in its performance:[49]

> *Bār* is sung by the *ḍhāḍhīs*, and no one else. The body of the song has no limit as to the number of lines, but the *tāla* alters itself twice. In it the heroic exploits of a warrior are sung. In the past, no exaggeration or undue eulogizing was allowed to form part of the narration. Less than two persons do not suffice for this song form. The *ustād* leads and begins with the first two lines, followed by the *shāgird* coming out with the third line. In sequence after this, the *ustād* proceeds with the couplets and the *shāgird* keeps on repeating the opening line.[50]

Faqirullah's passage nicely describes the call-and-response format standard to devotional and sufi songs.

On the second point, Husain Shah Sharqi's connections with and patronage of Chishti and Suhrawardi shaikhs are supported not just by the evidence of Qutban's *Mirigāvatī* but also by a *tazkira* of Chishti sufis, according to which Husain Shah built a monastery for his *pir*, Pir Buddhan:

> Shaikh Pir Buddhan became the pir of Sultan Husain Sharqi (862/1458-883/1479) of Jaunpur. Shaikh Pir Buddhan was a wrestler, an archer and above all else, a great patron of musicians. The qaul and taranah melodies invented by Amir Khusrau were his favourites. Hindu musicians from as far as the Deccan would call on him, finding in him a great connoisseur and admirer of Indian classical music. The Shaikh's fame soon turned [his home at] Rapri into an important centre for both Persian and Indian music. The Shaikh was successful in persuading a group of musicians (known as chokh) from the Deccan to settle in Rapri, some of whom later even embraced Islam.[51]

Qutban also names his *pir* as Shaikh Buddhan ("the elderly"), and he may or may have not been the same Buddhan associated with

---

49 See description of Asa di var at http://www.sikhiwiki.org/index.php/Asa_di_Var.

50 Faqirullah (1996), p. 119.

51 S.A.A. Rizvi, *A History of Sufism* (New Delhi: Munshiram Manoharlal, 1983), Vol. 2, p. 276, taking the seventeenth-century *tazkira Chishtiya-i bihishtiya* by Shaikh Barnawi's son as his source. A full account in Urdu of this *tazkira* can be found in the three-part article by Mahmud H. Sherani, *'Makhdūm Shaikh Bahā'ud-dīn Barnāwī'*, *Oriental College Magazine* (Lahore), part 1 (August 1927), 41-58; part 2 (November 1927), 9-26; part 3 (August 1929), 72-99.

Husain Sharqi.[52] What seems clear, though, is that some *shaikhs* of the Suhrawardhi and Chishti orders in the Jaunpur region cultivated court genres and participated in courtly music circles. Faqirullah mentions later *shaikhs* who were professional singers and instrumentalists (*go'indas* and *sazindas*) and singles out Shaikh Baha ud-din Barnawi (d.1628), a descendant of Husain Shah Sharqi's *pir*, as the most accomplished musician of his age. The Shaikh played the *rabab*, *bin*, and *amirti*, and was a vocalist and composer. Faqirullah links him directly to Jaunpur and says that he considered Hussain Sharqi's *chautukla* to be the most difficult of all song forms.[53]

The movement of sufis in and out of courts and courtly patronage for individual sufi leaders became a path for musical exchange and innovation. Katherine Schofield has begun to draw out of textual sources a nuanced story about sufi involvement in the development of the *khayal* genre.[54]

## Conclusion

While the grand concert described by Qutban in his *Mirigāvatī* appears at first to be a beautiful set piece, a close look reveals it to be a window onto the history of *raga* and formal music in the sixteenth century. The thirty-six *ragas* Qutban mentions amount to a full *raga-ragini* set, one of several circulating in the region at the time. The song genres that he mentions were likely in practice in Husain Shah Sharqi's court. The *Mirigāvatī* passage however, is complimented by other contemporaneous sources that represent *ragas* in different ways. Looked at side by side, these sources portray a broader picture in which *ragas* were understood differently among various audiences and practitioners. Considered in this way, the concepts of *raga*, *raga-ragini*, *ragadhyana*, and *ragamala*, so confounding to musicologists and art historians, fall into clearer perspective.

52 Though Behl notes that there were several contemporaneous Shaikhs named Buddhan, and it is not possible to know which was Qutban's pir, the most likely candidate is Shaikh Shams ul-Haqq of the Suhrawadiyya sufi lineage who was close to Husain Sharqi; Behl (2012a), p. 22.

53 Faqirullah (1996), p. 190.

54 Brown (2010).

Qutban's *ragamala* list would have had various resonances among the diverse audiences of the *Mirigāvatī*. Most listeners must have known *ragas* to be the melodies of high court art music. Those with access to courtly literature would have been aware of *ragadhyanas*, visualisations that brought the *ragas* and *raginis* to imaginative life. Some might have seen *raga* paintings that were just beginning to circulate, in which the poetic-musical imaginings were vividly portrayed. These audiences would have relished the idea of *raga* as representing high culture and sublime aesthetics.

A smaller number, consisting of elite connoisseurs and professional singers, would have known the *raga* families and their visual-literary aesthetics, but would have been even more actively interested in the music-technical details of *raga* melodic phrasings, that is, in *ragas* in practice. The *Mānakutūhala* compiled by the ruler of Gwalior in a period roughly contemporaneous to Qutban, expresses those interests, treating *ragas* in terms of their sources and component parts.

In the *Mirigāvatī* passage, Qutban mentions a number of genres in which *ragas* were performed in the divine concert, evoking for all audiences the sophisticated history of musical forms. But the names—*māṇṭhā*, *dhuruva*, *jhumara*, *paribandh*—are also a record of contemporary performance genres, and the information must have resonated for specialist audiences in this way. *Dhurpad*, the pre-eminent song of the later Mughal courts, is associated with Gwalior, but it finds a mention in Qutban's passage, hinting at a wider use of the term, a fact of singular interest to music historians.

Contemporaneous to Qutban and certainly heard by all kinds of audiences were the songs of *bhakti* devotionalism. Whether singers typically used *raga* melodies cannot be known, but *raga* designations in later *bhakti* collections signal an engagement with *raga* among specialist *bhakti* singers. And this use of *raga* is distinct from both that of the general listener and that of the court musician. *Ragas* in *bhakti* collections are used to group poems without references to *raga-ragini* sets, connections among *ragas*, or genre names. We do not fully understand the work of *ragas* in the compilations, but *ragas* have always been coded with associations of time, season, and emotional content. Surely they must have been chosen by specialists to signal the emotions and other associations that the expert singers considered appropriate to the poem. Also, *raga* seems to have always signaled a relationship to courtly environments.

Not all song genres were set to *ragas*. Faqirullah describes a genre called *vār* and mentions practices of Chishti *shaikhs* that were likely not *raga*-based. In Qutban's time, however, some prominent sufis who cultivated connections with the courts are mentioned in connection with *raga*-based music. Indeed, music practices encouraged by sufi elites are now being traced in connection with the emergence of important later concert genres such as *khayal*.

Qutban's passage about the grand concert is a celebration of music as a central feature of intellectual and spiritual life. The passage would have affected listeners in various ways. It would have evoked the rarified atmosphere of a divine court. It would have served as an account of contemporaneous specialist music practices. It would have hinted at sublime codes of musical meaning. But perhaps most importantly, Aditya Behl felt it would have served as a message for Qutban's most select audience, that of sufi aspirants, and for us as well, that in the highest stages of sufi practice "[...] the novices of this order went through a program of musical purification and sublimation in the City of Gold".[55]

---

55 Behl (2012a), p.17.

# 15. Learning to Taste the Emotions: The Mughal *Rasika*[1]

*Katherine Butler Schofield*

In 1691, the North Indian vernacular poet Vrind eulogised his aristocratic patron in the following verses:

> He is handsome, steadfast, valiant, and skilled with a bow.
> Generous, knowledgeable, an enjoyer, extremely generous in spirit,
> Mirza Qadiri is the jewel of his family,
> Clever with emotion, experiencing delight.
> A connoisseur (*rasika*), he understands matters of sentiment (*rasa*),
> And pursues love wholeheartedly.
> He longs night and day for music and pleasure.[2]

This poem sets out in fairly stereotypical fashion the two essential ingredients of elite manhood in seventeenth-century North India: skill in the arts of war, and connoisseurship of the arts of pleasure, here specifically love and music. What may be more unexpected about this poem to modern readers, inured as we are to "Hindu-Muslim" tensions

1 Formerly known as Katherine Butler Brown. In addition to the participants at the "Tellings and Texts" conference, I wish to thank Sunil Kumar and the history students at Delhi University whose thought-provoking response to this paper initiated much-needed revisions; the European Research Council for funding the research that made its way into later drafts; and Steve Dolph for sending me a rare copy of Aditya Behl's last article, '"The Path of True Feeling": On Translating Qutban's *Mirigāvatī*', *Calque* 5 (2009), 68-113. I dedicate this paper with love to Aditya, himself a *rasika*, whose conversations on this and other subjects I miss very much.

2 Vrind, *Śr̥ṅgārśikṣā*, cited in Allison Busch, 'Hidden in Plain View: Brajbhasha Poets at the Mughal Court', *Modern Asian Studies* 44.2 (2010), 299.

 http://dx.doi.org/10.11647/OBP.0062.15

and the Hindi-Urdu divide,[3] is the object of Vrind's praise. Vrind was a Hindu, working within the heavily Sanskritised courtly milieu of Brajbhasha *riti* poetry. But his patron, Mirza Qadiri, was a Muslim, a sufi, and a Mughal office-holder deeply invested in a Persianate cultural universe.[4] Vrind extolls Mirza Qadiri as a *rasika*, translated here as "connoisseur", but literally "one who, in experiencing the arts, can taste or savour the *rasas*", the nine highly distilled sentiments of Sanskritic aesthetic theory.[5] Unless this were mere flattery or convention, for Vrind to describe his Mughal patron as a *rasika* reflected something remarkable.

In this chapter I will address the question of what was required in Mughal India for a patron coming initially from outside the Indic aesthetic tradition to truly become a *rasika* of North Indian (or Hindustani) music:[6] to learn to taste the *rasas* not merely intellectually, as might be possible with poetry, but also experientially, as is central to musical understanding. In other words, I wish to tackle for an historical period Timothy Rice's ethnomusicological conundrum: whether it is ever possible to translate non-verbal experience from one cultural domain into another—in this case from Indic to Persianate—in order to re-experience it on a deeper level in the new domain.[7] My suggestion is that it is possible, and that key to this translation is the notion of *affinity*: of the existence of experiential common ground between Persianate and Indic ontologies of music—that is to say, what music *is* and what it *does*—and particularly music's central role in both traditions in mediating the various moods of love: *'ishq* in Persian, *shringara rasa* in Sanskritic terms.

Connoisseurship practices are widespread cross-culturally, and the domain of connoisseurship practices—male, socially elite, and

---

3 On the latter, see especially Christopher King, *One Language, Two Scripts: The Hindi Movement in Nineteenth-century North India* (New Delhi: Oxford University Press, 1994); also *Before the Divide: Hindi and Urdu Literary Culture*, ed. by F. Orsini (New Delhi: Orient Blackswan, 2010).

4 Busch (2010), 298-300.

5 For a comprehensive treatment of the Indic concepts of *bhava*, *rasa*, and *rasika* in the period of their initial formulation, see Daud Ali, *Courtly Culture and Political Life in Early Medieval India* (Cambridge: Cambridge University Press, 2004), pp. 185-206.

6 Please note that I am not suggesting in any sense that the Mughals were "foreigners" to India, certainly not by the seventeenth century from which I draw much of my material; I am merely reflecting on the remarkable fact that many new Persianate migrants to India in the Mughal era so rapidly became bicultural.

7 Timothy Rice, *May it Fill Your Soul: Experiencing Bulgarian Music* (Chicago: Chicago University Press, 1994), pp. 3-8.

discursively exclusive—tends to remain constant across cultures.[8] What differs are the specific codes of practice and aesthetic content that form the exclusive body of "knowledge" belonging to each culture of connoisseurship. The body of knowledge relevant to Mughal connoisseurs of North Indian music was set down in Persian-language treatises on Hindustani music theory, largely from the mid-seventeenth century onward, all of which were in dialogue with the authoritative Sanskritic theoretical tradition, and which connoisseurs themselves composed, commissioned, collected, and circulated.[9] The knowledge of Hindustani music created and embodied in these treatises reflects the attempt of a Persianate male elite with predominantly sufi inclinations to appropriate into their own systems of logic and modes of connoisseurship a Sanskrit-based Indic musical system that, despite or perhaps because of its otherness, powerfully resonated with their emotional and spiritual sensibilities. The question I want to address here is this: were Mughal patrons able to use this body of knowledge in order to experience Hindustani music in its own Indic terms: as *rasikas*?

In relation to North Indian cultural fields, I define connoisseurship as the cultivation of the emotions and senses through specific aesthetic practices that also engage the intellect, and in which the aim is experiential transcendence. In the person of the *rasika*, connoisseurship is overtly privileged in Indic aesthetic theory. The nine *rasas*, affective essences that are available to be "savoured" by the *rasika* in the visual and performing arts, are the erotic (*shringara*), comic (*hasya*), pathetic (*karuna*), furious (*raudra*), heroic (*vira*), terrible (*bhayanaka*), disgusting (*bibhatsa*), marvellous (*adbhuta*), and irenic (*shanta*).[10] In Sanskrit and Brajbhasha literature of the sixteenth and seventeeth centuries, *rasika* was the generic term most often used to denote connoisseurs of

8 Music connoisseurship practices have been very undertheorised to date. For connoisseurship generally, see Pierre Bourdieu, *Distinction: A Social Critique of the Judgment of Taste* (London: Routledge, 1999); for art and manuscript collecting in Mughal and early colonial India, see John Seyller, 'A Mughal Code of Connoisseurship', *Muqarnas* 17 (2000), 177-202; Natasha Eaton, 'Between Mimesis and Alterity: Art, Gift, and Diplomacy in Colonial India, 1770-1800', *Comparative Studies in Society and History* 46.4 (2004), 816-44; and Maya Jasanoff, *Edge of Empire: Conquest and Collecting in the East, 1750-1850* (London: Harper Perennial, 2006).

9 For a more detailed discussion, see Katherine Butler Schofield, 'Reviving the Golden Age Again: "Classicization", Hindustani Music, and the Mughals', *Ethnomusicology* 54.3 (2010), 484-517.

10 Ali (2004), p. 188. In the *Nāṭyaśāstra*, there were only eight *rasas*; the ninth, *shanta*, was a later addition.

poetry and music. Both arts, due to their high level of cultivation and abstraction, were considered exemplary in their capacity to concentrate and refract the many facets of the nine *rasas* and thereby to provoke the connoisseurs' tasting. In the figure of the *rasika*, Indic aesthetic theory thus emphasises "the role of the perceiving subject" and privileges "*experience* and affect". Artists and their works thereby succeed or fail not on their own terms, but "by [their] ability to evoke aesthetic response in the listener".[11] Critical to the Mughals' extensively attested capacity to appreciate Indic forms of poetry and music was the fact that Persianate aesthetic theory also shared this emphasis on the audience. In particular, the Islamicate discourse on *sama'* or "audition", the devotional use of music and poetry by sufi initiates from which much Persianate music aesthetics derive, focuses so heavily on the knowledgeability and emotional and spiritual preparedness of the audience, that comments on music itself or on musicians may be sidelined.[12]

The theory of the *rasas*, and of how vernacular poetry and song lyrics brought them into being, was certainly known at the Mughal court by the late sixteenth century. Particularly important were the versified catalogues in Sanskrit and Brajbhasha called *nayika-bheda*, which categorised different kinds of heroines (*nayika*) and heroes (*nayak*) using traditional metaphors, and which constituted the lyrical repertory of much courtly song and poetry. Such lyrics were not merely to be read straightforwardly; rather, they exemplified the *rasas*, and the purpose of *nayika-bheda* textbooks was to make "the path of *rasa* [...] understood by everybody".[13] Important Mughal patrons not only knew and commissioned *nayika-bhedas* in Indic languages, but they translated them into Persian, incorporated Persian-language *nayika-bheda*s into treatises on Indian arts, and even used them to guide their own writing of vernacular poetry. Three canonical writers on music—Abu'l Fazl (1551-1602), Mirza Khan (fl.1675), and Saif Khan Faqirullah

11 Martin Clayton, 'Introduction: Towards a Theory of Musical Meaning (in India and Elsewhere)', *Ethnomusicology Forum* 17.2 (2001), 13.

12 Qazi Hasan, *Miftāḥ al-sarūd* [mistransliterated *Miṣbāḥ al-sorūr*], Asiatic Society of Bengal, MS 1629, ff. 2a-4a; also Carl W. Ernst and Bruce B. Lawrence, *Sufi Martyrs of Love: The Chishti Order in South Asia and Beyond* (New York: Palgrave Macmillan, 2002), pp. 34-46. For extensive discussion of sufi appropriation of *rasa* theory in the domain of literature, see Aditya Behl, *Love's Subtle Magic: An Indian Islamic Literary Tradition, 1379-1545* (New York: Oxford University Press, 2012b), especially pp. 59-108, 286-384.

13 Sundar, *Sundarśṛṅgār*, cited in Busch (2010), 287. More widely on Mughal-era *nayika-bheda* and *rasa* theory, see ibid., 281-7.

(d.1684)—incorporated Persian-language *nayika-bheda*s into their works.[14] And a great Mughal office-holder like Abdurrahim Khan-i Khanan "Rahim" (1556-1626) was able to compose a set of *nayika-bheda* verses in Brajbhasha sufficiently accomplished to be praised by his contemporary critics.[15] He at least must have qualified as a *rasika* in the literary sense.

It is particularly important to note that in this poetic tradition, one *rasa* above all others was celebrated and explored: *shringara rasa*, the erotic sentiment, known as the king of *rasas*. Written from the feminine perspective of the *nayika*, Brajbhasha poetry characteristically explores the travails of a heroine waiting for the return of an absent, neglectful, or teasing beloved; this can also be read ambiguously as referring to a human or a divine beloved.[16] The Indic tradition therefore had significant affinities with the Persian poetry central to Mughal cultural traditions. This likewise took as its principal theme *'ishq*, or love, and *firaq*, longing for the absent beloved, and could similarly be read in either a courtly or devotional manner. In sufi readings of such poetry, the soul—the interlocutor—was frequently construed as feminine,[17] even though the interlocutor of Persian poetry is usually construed as masculine.

The peculiar affection of Indian sufis for the female voice of Indian vernacular poetry and song lyrics, particularly in the guise of the *virahini* seeking reunion with her male beloved, is well known.[18] Through

---

14 Abu'l Fazl "'Allami", *Ā'īn-i Akbarī*, trans. by H. Blochmann and Col. H.S. Jarrett (Calcutta: Asiatic Society of Bengal and Baptist Mission Press, 1873-1907; reprint 2008), Vol. 3, pp. 239-44; Mirza Khan ibn Fakhruddin Muhammad, *Tuḥfat al-Hind*, ed. by N.H. Ansari (Tehran: Bunyad-i Farhang-i Iran, 1968), Vol. 1, pp. 297-321; Saif Khan "Faqirullah", *Tarjuma-i-Mānakutūhala & Risāla-i-Rāg Darpan*, ed. and trans. by Shahab Sarmadee (New Delhi: IGNCA and Motilal Banarsidass, 1996), pp. 132-49.

15 Busch (2010), 282-84. A matter for further contemplation concerns Persian translations of Sanskrit and Brajbhasha *nayika-bheda* and *ragamala* verses (*dhyanas*), whose subject matter and evocative purpose are related. While both Brajbhasha and Sanskrit versions explicitly seek through poetical means to evoke the *rasa* associated with *nayika* or *raga* iconography, there is no attempt to do this in Persian translations of the same material. Rather, the latter tend not merely to be in prose, but in prosaic prose, almost as if they are simply guides to the original materials.

16 It is worth noting that in the *Tuḥfat al-Hind*, Mirza Khan inserted his *nayika-bheda* section into the chapter on *shringara rasa*; Khan (1968), pp. 297-31.

17 On the *nafs* or "lower" soul as woman in Persian sufi poetry, particularly that of Jalaluddin Rumi, see Annemarie Schimmel, *My Soul is a Woman: The Feminine in Islam* (New York: Continuum, 2003 [1997]), pp. 69-80.

18 Ibid., esp. 118-38; see also e.g. Shantanu Phukan, ''Through Throats Where Many Rivers Meet': The Ecology of Hindi in the World of Persian', *Indian Economic and Social History Review* 38.1 (2001), 33-58; Katherine Butler Brown [Schofield], 'The Origins and Early Development of Khayal', in *Hindustani Music: Thirteenth to Twentieth Centuries*, ed. by Joep Bor et al. (New Delhi: Manohar, 2010), pp. 159-94; Francesca Orsini,

*nayika-bheda* descriptions of different kinds of romantic heroines in verse and song, a vast proliferation of emotions and scenarios, all of them revealing different aspects of *shringara rasa*, were made available to the Mughal connoisseur for exploration in the person of the Indian *nayika*. Shantanu Phukan makes clear that in seventeenth-century Mughal readings of vernacular poetry, *shringara rasa* as enacted through the romances of heroes and heroines resonated profoundly with *'ishq*.[19] Mughal aficionados of songs may therefore have seized on the *nayika*, the principal embodiment of *shringara rasa*, as a means to enhance and enlarge the emotional experiences of their own exploration of *'ishq* through the shared Indic and Persianate metaphor of the lover yearning for the beloved.[20]

It is the affinity between *shringara rasa* and *'ishq* that most obviously connects the Mughal connoisseur of music to the Indic *rasika*. This affinity goes back at least to the pre-Mughal sufi romances, magical narratives in which sufi vernacular authors used poetical imagery from the Indic tradition as complex allegories, and which when revisited by Mughal noblemen became a renewed source of pleasure and moral and spiritual instruction.[21] Aditya Behl pointed out that the principal object of the hero's quest in the sufi romance, which is a metaphor for the journey of the human soul towards the Divine, is *shringara rasa*. However, along the way, all nine of the *rasas* are explored, savoured, tasted, and transformed for the purposes of teaching the sufi how to control and sublimate his baser emotions[22]—a notion that has clear links with Islamicate understandings of cultivating the emotions through

'"Krishna is the Truth of Man": Mir 'Abdul Wahid Bilgrami's *Haqā'iq-i Hindī* (Indian Truths) and the Circulation of Dhrupad and Bishnupad', in *Culture and Circulation*, ed. by Allison Busch and Thomas de Bruijn (Leiden: Brill, 2014), pp. 222-46.

19 Phukan (2001), 34-36. Phukan's article, with its reflections on the confluence of the "varying emotional resonance[s]" of Hindi and Persian in Mughal literature, has many things to say to my work in this chapter.

20 See e.g. the lyrics of the *dhrupad* and other song compositions in the *Sahasras* compiled for Shah Jahan, and Khushhal Khan's *Rāg-rāginī roz o shab*, compiled for Nizam Asaf Jah III of Hyderabad; *Sahasras: Nāyak Bakhśū ke dhrupadoṃ kā saṅgrah*, ed. by Premlata Sharma (New Delhi: Sangit Natak Academy, 1972); Khushhal Khan "Anup", *Rāg-rāginī-yi roz o shab*, Salar Jung Museum Library, MS Urdu Mus 2.

21 Ibid., 36; Phukan, '"None Mad as a Hindu Woman": Contesting Communal Readings of *Padmavat*', *Comparative Studies of South Asia, Africa and the Middle East* 16.1 (1996), 41-54.

22 Aditya Behl, 'Presence and Absence in Bhakti: An Afterword', *International Journal of Hindu Studies* 11.3 (2007), 321-2; Behl (2009), 73-76.

artistic means in order to balance mental and physical health.[23] There thus appears to be a long tradition within Indian sufism of the sufi as true *rasika*, an idea that is at least obliquely manifested in the treatises on music written at the seventeenth-century Mughal court.

Several Mughal holders of high office and patrons of music were undoubtedly *rasikas*, going by the depth of their musical writings. The most interesting was Mirza Raushan Zamir (d.1669).[24] The author of the 1666 *Tarjuma-yi Pārijātak*,[25] a Persian commentary on Ahobala's contemporary Sanskrit music treatise, the *Saṅgītapārijāta*, he was by far the most sophisticated and knowledgable scholar of Hindustani music and Sanskrit music theory of the Indo-Persian corpus. He is better known to Indian literary history, however, as the Brajbhasha poet "Nehi", and Allison Busch argues that his poems, including several on the *nayika*, "attest to [his] remarkable command of Braj literary style".[26] Zamir demonstrably possessed fluent command of Sanskrit and Brajbhasha, and an expert's understanding of traditional Indic aesthetics and Hindustani music. The author of the late eighteenth-century *Ḥayy al-arwāḥ* memorialised him as possessing "genius (*mahārat*) in both the knowledge and practice (*'ilm o 'amal*) of music", and of composing (*guftan*) "many *dohra*s and *kavitt*s in the *bhākhā* language, which is the idiom for [exploring] *shringāra rasa*, *shringāra rasa* being the beauty and love (*ḥusn o 'ishq*) of women and men".[27] Zamir was by anyone's estimation a *rasika*.

Saif Khan Faqirullah, a very high-ranking Mughal officer, was likewise famed long after his death for having been a *rasika* of Hindustani music.[28]

---

23 Katherine Butler Schofield, 'Sense and Sensibility: The Domain of Pleasure and the Place of Music in Mughal Society', forthcoming; see also Behl (2012b), especially pp. 286-324.

24 For a potted biography see Charles Rieu, *Catalogue of the Persian Manuscripts in the British Museum* (London: British Museum, 1883), Vol. 3, p. 1088; and more extensively Ziauddin, *Ḥayy al-arwāḥ*, John Rylands Library University of Manchester, MS Persian 346, ff. 57b-8a.

25 We derive the title *Tarjuma-yi Pārijātak(a)* from colonial-era catalogues like Hermann Ethé's *Catalogue of Persian Manuscripts in the Library of the India Office* (Oxford: India Office, 1903), Vol. 1, pp. 1117, but this treatise should probably be entitled *Tarjuma-yi kitāb-i Pārijātak*, "Translation of the book Pārijātak", as it is in the colophon, or simply *Pārijātak*; e.g. British Library, MS Egerton 793, f. 211a. In the preface, only the Sanskrit original is referred to, in the phrase *muṣannīf-i kitāb-i Pārijātak ki Ahōbal nām dārad*, "the author of the book Pārijātak, whose name is Ahobal"; ibid., f. 2a.

26 Busch (2010), 296-97.

27 Ziauddin, ff. 57b-58a.

28 Nawwab Samsam-ud-daula Shah Nawaz Khan and 'Abdul Hayy, *The Ma'āthir-ul-*

And he aspired through his writings to induce similar levels of mastery in his fellow Mughal patrons.[29] His technical knowledge of Hindustani *raga* theory was less virtuosic than Zamir's, but it is evident throughout his 1666 *Rāg darpan* that, far more importantly, Faqirullah *tasted* the *rasas* of Hindustani music performance. For Faqirullah, music was about the momentary transcendent experience, the experience primarily of *'ishq*.[30] This is important: I would suggest that even a deep understanding of how the *rasas* were embodied in poetry, and a command of Indic music-technical knowledge, did not necessarily make a Mughal patron a *musical rasika*. This was because Hindustani music itself embodied the *rasas*, and could do so entirely independently of language. Musical sound was a primary vehicle of *rasa* in traditional Indic aesthetics, as exemplified in the *ragamala* tradition of painting the character of each musical mode of the Indian melodic system as a *nayak* or *nayika*. Even down to the present day, each *raga* of the Indian modal system is said to embody one of the nine *rasas*.[31] Music had power in its own right to move the emotions independently of any visual or verbal aid; musical sound was considered to be efficacious (*pur aṣar / bā tā'ṣir*).[32] Combined with textual evocations of *shringara rasa* it was twice as powerful as either on their own. To be a true *rasika* of music, one thus needed to experience the *rasa* in the sound of the *raga* alone.

This presents us with problems in ascertaining the extent to which the Mughal connoisseur of music qualified as a true taster of the *rasas*, as opposed to someone whose head was merely stuffed with textual theory. The most basic is Charles Seeger's "linguocentric predicament"—that it

---

*Umarā*, trans. by H. Beveridge (Calcutta: Oriental Press, 1952), Vol. 2, pp. 683-87.

29 Schofield (2010), 495-98.

30 Faqirullah (1996), e.g. pp. 78-81, 94-95, 110-21.

31 Though for key discussions of the artificiality of correlations between the *rasas* and individual *swaras*, *ragas*, and iconographical forms in both Sanskrit musical treatises and *ragamala* paintings, see Richard Widdess, *The Rāgas of Early Indian Music: Modes, Melodies and Musical Notations from the Gupta Period to c.1250* (Oxford: Clarendon, 1995), pp. 39-48; and Tushara Bindu Gude, 'Between Music and History: Rāgamāla Paintings and European Collectors in Late Eighteenth-century Northern India' (PhD dissertation, University of California, Los Angeles, 2009), pp. 52-55. Harold Powers argues that a single *rasa*, in its many facets, is predominant in *ragamala* paintings: *shringara rasa*; 'Illustrated Inventories of Indian Rāgamāla Painting', *Journal of the American Oriental Society* 100.4 (1980), 482.

32 Qazi Hasan, ff. 8a-b; Zamir, f. 1b; Faqirullah (1996), pp. 78-81; and Muhammad Karam Imam Khan, *Ma'dan al-mūsīqī*, ed. by Sayyid Wajid 'Ali (Lucknow: Hindustani Press, 1925 [1869]), pp. 109-16.

is exceptionally difficult to describe the experience of music in words.[33] As Sher Khan Lodi put it in 1691, "it is simply not possible to capture the essence of music in pen and ink on the surface of a page".[34] The Mughals, like the rest of us, were hamstrung by their difficulty in expressing through the "sibilant scratches of a broken pen" the full emotional, physiological, and often spiritual efficacy of the sound of the *raga* for the listener.[35] More problematically, the musical treatises gloss over the *rasas* rather briefly. Abu'l Fazl and Mirza Khan listed and described the *rasas*, but in relation to literature. Faqirullah named the *rasas* of several *ragas* and provided a definition, but did not otherwise explain them. Zamir briefly identified the *rasas* associated with each of the notes of the scale.[36] Perhaps most inexplicably, Ras Baras Khan, the Emperor Aurangzeb 'Alamgir's chief musician and our most authoritative source, whose own name is indicative of the centrality of *rasa* to the hereditary tradition, did not discuss *rasa* theory in his 1698 *Shams al-aṣwāt*.[37]

Nonetheless, I am going to suggest that the Mughal treatise writers' obvious grasp of the *rasas* within the literary domain, the ways in which they attempted to describe musical experience, and their major stated reason for writing—their concern to explain the unique efficacy of each *raga* for the listener—demonstrate that they did possess an accurate sense of the *rasas* in Hindustani music, and especially *shringara rasa*.

The key lies in the *affinities* between what music is and does in Persianate and Sanskritic ontologies. In the Sanskritic framework, different *ragas* evoke and provoke the nine *rasas*, with a special emphasis

33 Charles Seeger, 'Speech, Music, and Speech About Music', in *Studies in Musicology, 1935-1975* (Berkeley: University of California Press, 1977), p. 23.

34 Sher 'Ali Khan Lodi, *Taẕkira-yi mir'āt al-khayāl*, ed. by Hamid Hasani and Bihruz Safarzadah (Tehran: Rawzanah, 1998), p. 141.

35 Ibid. I translate the word *tā'ṣir* as "efficacy" here (less often as "effect") in order to highlight the link made in the sources between music and medicine, and the *raga* as a quasi-medicinal preparation that possesses medicinal efficacy; see especially Karam Imam (1925), pp. 109-16.

36 Abu'l Fazl (1873-1907), Vol. 3, p. 239; Mirza Khan (1968), p. 71 and elsewhere; Faqirullah (1996), pp. 14-19, 32-33, 94-97; Zamir, ff. 11b-12a. The author of the fourteenth-century *Ghunyat al-munya*, the first known Persian treatise on Hindustani music, translated *rasa* as *kaifīya-i laṭīfa* ("subtle emotional state"), listed all the *rasas* and considered them to saturate Indian poetry, music, and dance (for a discussion see Behl (2012b), pp. 293-94)—but there is no evidence the Mughal theorists knew their masterful Tughluqid predecessor.

37 Ras Baras Khan, *Shams al-aṣvāt*, ed. and trans. by Mehrdad Fallahzadeh (Uppsala: Acta Universitatis Upsaliensis, 2012 [1698]).

on the facets of *shringara rasa*.[38] What music is and does on the most basic level in the Persianate framework comes from sufi discourse. According to al-Ghazzali, music is the manifestation of *'ishq*, love, as it pertains to the sense of hearing:

> We come now to treat of love in its essential nature. Love may be defined as an inclination to that which is pleasant. This is apparent in the case of the five senses, each of which may be said to love that which gives it delight; thus the eye loves beautiful forms, the ear music, etc… But there is a sixth sense, or faculty of perception, implanted in the heart… through which we become aware of spiritual beauty and excellence. Thus, a man who is only acquainted with sensuous delights cannot understand what the Prophet meant when he said he loved prayer more than perfume or women, though the last two were also pleasant to him.[39]

Music is therefore a synecdoche—albeit a lesser one—for the sublimities of love, with direct and immediate access to the soul of the listener, and the power to transform the listener's emotional state. In the words of Abu'l Fazl:

> I cannot sufficiently describe the wonderful power [*nairangī*, magic] of this talisman [*ṭilism*] of knowledge [music]. It sometimes causes the beautiful creatures of the harem of the heart to shine forth on the tongue… The melodies then enter through the window of the ear and return to their former seat, the heart, bringing with them thousands of presents. The hearers, according to their insight, are moved to sorrow or to joy. Music is thus of use to those who have renounced the world and to such as still cling to it.[40]

In other words, what music is, its essence, is the direct aural manifestation of sentiment and especially love, and what music does, its purpose, is to move the listener's emotions. As Faqirullah put it, "*ranjakatāyī*—to arouse tender sympathy [*riqqat*] in the heart [of the listener]—is music's entire essence [*lazzat*] and its result [*mā-ḥaṣal*]".[41]

---

38 Powers (1980), p. 482.

39 Abu Hamid al-Ghazzali, *The Alchemy of Happiness* [*Kimīyā-yi sa'ādāt*], trans. by Claud Field (London: John Murray, 1910 [c.1100]), pp. 100-01.

40 Abu'l Fazl (1873-1907), Vol. 1, p. 611; and Abu'l Fazl "'Allami", *Ā'īn-i Akbarī*, ed. by H. Blochmann (Calcutta: Baptist Mission Press, 1868-1877), Vol. 2, pp. 262-63.

41 Faqirullah (1996), pp. 152-3. For one of the earliest detailed elaborations of the efficacious purposes of music *vis- à-vis* the human emotions, see *Epistles of the Brethren of Purity: On Music*, ed. and trans. by Owen Wright (Oxford: Oxford University Press and The Institute of Ismaili Studies, 2010), pp. 76-81, 124-26, 162-75.

Music's tangible emotional and physiological results are a prominent subject of reflection in the treatises. Several authors foreground the efficacy of music, its *asar* or *ta'sir*,[42] and a large number of words for pleasureable effect are used in conjunction with Hindustani music in this corpus, particularly *zauq* and *lazzat*. Notably, these two words also mean taste, flavour, savour, or "feel", and *zauq* also has a specifically sufi usage, meaning a "[cultivated] taste for things spiritual".[43] That words like *zauq* and *lazzat*, which mean both pleasurable effect *and* taste or flavour, were used so frequently in Indo-Persian treatises to describe the *ragas'* effects is, I would argue, because they had the semantic depth to evoke the Sanskritic concept of *rasa*, centrally embodied in the performance and listening experience of *raga*. Indeed, Mirza Khan translated the word *rasa* as *zauq*.[44] Faqirullah's definition of *rasa*—"which means inflaming the passion and pleasing the heart [through] listening"—maps very closely onto his understanding (above) of the *lazzat*, essence, of music.[45] Elsewhere, a strong link is made, through the use of this language of affect and effect, between music and a deeper aesthetic listening experience verging on sublimity that is capable of being translated, discursively and experientially, from Indic into Persianate terms, even where *rasa* is not invoked explicitly.

That the Mughal treatise writers did understand specific affective essences to be key to understanding Hindustani music is made explicit in the stated concern of several authors with explaining its agreed effects on the listener, largely through highly technical discussions of *raga* and the seven notes (*swara*) of the scale. Zamir's first purpose in writing was musicological, but in order to fulfil a second central purpose: "to describe to a certain degree [the *ragas'*] effect on the listener; how it is that the gentle singing of the beautiful voice causes dusk to fall, that vengeful snakes are tamed by melancholy harmonies, and that deer pass away from listening to heart-stealing music".[46] The purpose of Kamilkhani's 1668 treatise on *raga* was to explain the theory behind why each *raga* must be played at a specific time of day or season of the year in

42 e.g. Qazi Hasan, ff. 8a-b; Zamir, f. 1b; Faqirullah (1996), pp. 78-81; Karam Imam (1925), pp. 109-16.
43 Behl (2012b), p. 22.
44 "*ẕauq o maza* [taste]"; Mirza Khan (1968), Vol. 1, p. 71.
45 Faqirullah (1996), pp. 94-95, 152-53.
46 Zamir, f. 1b.

order to produce a specific, designated effect that "pleases and ravishes the heart".[47]

The Indo-Persian writers knew well which *rasas* were traditionally associated with each *raga* in the Sanskritic tradition. The three authors who particularly took up the topic of attempting to explain the *ragas'* effects on the listener insisted, however, that they inhered not in the overall mode, but in the movements and relationships of its constituent notes, and in particular its strongest and second strongest notes (*vadi* and *samvadi*). Designated effects were caused by the fact that each note was dominated by one of the four elements from Persianate medicinal discourse—fire, earth, air, and water. In this way, each note had specific power over one of the four humours of the body, thus explaining the *raga*'s efficaciousness for the connoisseur in Unani medicinal terms. Shaikh 'Abdul Karim explained that:

> The *ragas* are of four types: one [type of] *raga* is of airy essence, one fiery, one watery, and one earthy [...] From listening to those *ragas* that possess the airy essence one's heart will be buffeted by the grief of separation (*firaq*). From listening to those *ragas* that possess the fiery essence, the stations of the heart will be inflamed with passionate love (*'ishq*). From listening to those *ragas* that possess the watery essence the stations of the heart will be annihilated through proximate union (*wisal*) with Divine Truth within the essence of the Glorious and Great Existence. From listening to those *ragas* that possess the earthy essence the stations of the heart will attain an excess of mystical knowledge (*'irfan*) of their true selves.[48]

According to Ras Baras Khan, the first and fifth notes corresponded with water, the second and fourth with fire, the third and sixth with earth, and the seventh with wind.[49] Zamir/Ahobala's allocation of effect to note was identical to Ras Baras Khan's, but, strikingly, expressed in terms of *rasa*: the seventh note invoked *karuna rasa*, which was indeed the mood of longing caused by separation, and the same two notes that inflamed the fire of *'ishq* were likewise those that provoked *shringara*

---

47 'Ivaz Muhammad Kamilkhani, *Risāla dar 'amal-i bīn o thātha-yi rāg-hā-yi Hindī*, Bodleian Library, MS Ouseley 158, 1668, ff. 123a-125a.

48 Shaikh 'Abdul Karim bin Shaikh Farid Ansari al-Qadiri, *Jawāhir al-mūsīqāt-i Muḥammadī*, British Library, MS Or. 12,857, c.1640, f. 67b; Katherine Butler Schofield, 'Indian Music in the Persian Collections: The Javahir al-Musiqat-i Muhammadi', parts 1 and 2, *British Library Asian and African Studies Blog* (October 2014), http://britishlibrary.typepad.co.uk/asian-and-african/

49 Ras Baras Khan (2012).

*rasa*.[50] Thus the Mughal writers made sense of the *rasas* by reference to Persianate explanations of music's efficacies as medicinal preparations. In this way, Mughal connoisseurs synthesised the *rasas*, through the *ragas*, into their bodily practice and experience of the healing powers of music. Through physiological understanding, they became *rasikas*.

The most important sentiments music provoked in Persianate ontologies were love, *'ishq*; and the pain or grief of separation, *hazin*, *dard*, and *firaq*. Perhaps unsurprisingly, the Hindustani art music genres that were most popular amongst Mughal patrons similarly took the many facets of *shringara rasa* as their subject matter. The most important of these, *dhrupad*, composed in Brajbhasha and performed by the top musicians of the day, was according to Faqirullah capable of evoking all nine *rasas*. Primarily, though, *dhrupad* dealt with "the fascinations of love and its wondrous effects upon the heart".[51] Faqirullah inserted a Persian *nayika-bheda* into his musical treatise, in between sections on musical instruments and different vocal types.[52] The obvious reason why Faqirullah thought a catalogue of heroines was necessary to understanding Hindustani music was to guide connoisseurs who might be less familiar with Brajbhasha with regard to the usual emotional range of *dhrupad*. According to Nalini Delvoye, the 1,004 *dhrupad* texts preserved in the *Sahasras*, a 1637-1646 compilation for the Emperor Shah Jahan, demonstrate that their primary subject matter was indeed love. And with few exceptions Mughal-period *dhrupad* texts drew on two kinds of female lover from the *nayika-bheda* tradition: the *khandita nayika*, the heroine whose lover is unfaithful and absent in the arms of another; and the *patur*, the courtesan, whose life is full of dance, music, and romantic intrigue. The romantic hero, the *nayak*, is described as the ideal *rasika*.[53]

But what is most interesting about all the traditional *nayika-bheda* imagery in extant Mughal *dhrupad* texts is that it maps closely onto the

50 Zamir, ff. 11b-12a; this is a literal translation of and commentary on the Sanskrit original; cf. Ahobala Pandit, *Saṅgītapārijāta* (Hathras: Sangit Karyalaya, 1971), pp. 31-32.

51 Faqirullah (1996), pp. 94-99; Abu'l Fazl (1873-1907), Vol. 3, pp. 251-52. Faqirullah's description is a palimpsest of Abu'l Fazl's, by which I mean verbatim citation with insertions of original commentary.

52 Ibid., pp. 133-49.

53 For detailed discussion see Françoise "Nalini" Delvoye, 'The Verbal Content of Dhrupad Songs from the Earliest Collections, I: The *Hazar Dhurpad* or *Sahasras*', *Dhrupad Annual* (1990), 93-109.

*dhrupad* imagery that 'Abdul Wahid Bilgrami interpreted allegorically as sufi concepts in his 1566 *Ḥaqā'iq-i Hindī*. His purpose was to reveal the deeper meanings sufis read into Brajbhasha terminology, most importantly the *patur*, who is really the seeker after Truth (Schimmel's woman soul); and the *nayak*, the perfect *rasika*, who is really the *pir* or spiritual guide, "the guide to true reality (*murshid-i ḥaqīqat*) or anyone who has been a full recipient of the bounty of God's presence".[54] In other words, it seems that from at least the mid-sixteenth century onwards, Mughal-era adherents to sufism, like their Delhi Sultanate predecessors,[55] had appropriated the language, imagery, and themes of Indian aesthetics, and particularly those that embodied *shringara rasa*, into their hearing of *dhrupad* in devotional settings. How much more likely is it that this absorption would have extended to Mughal appreciation of the emotional resonances of *dhrupad* texts—their evocation of *rasa*—within the aesthetic realm of courtly connnoisseurship?

Of particular resonance to Mughal aficionados of *dhrupad* would have been the figure of the *bahurupi*, who symbolises in Bilgrami's analysis "the real beauty of God [... since] by virtue of being a beloved [he] possesses a special beauty (*ḥusn o jamāl*), and by the quality of being the lover has a special desire and yearning... Since his face had a hundred thousand faces [...] every speck revealed anew a different countenance".[56] As with so many Indic and Persianate song lyrics, the *bahurupi* can be interpreted in many ways. The *bahurupiya* were one of several communities of male street performers who employed beautiful young men who danced, sang, and dressed in thousands of different costumes to trick and tease their spectators. Such beautiful youths were often objects of erotic attention and could be taken by Mughal men as beloveds; but they could also be metaphorically transformed into *shahid*s, witnesses of God's beauty, who could be present in the sufi assembly entirely unproblematically as a visible reminder of the beauty of God.[57] The famous Persian *masnavi* of Muhammad Akram Ghanimat of 1685, the *Nairang-i 'ishq*, concerns the story of just such a love, which is really

54 Orsini (2014a), p. 234.
55 Behl (2012b).
56 Orsini (2014a), p. 234.
57 Abu'l Fazl (1873-1907), Vol. 3, p. 257-58; Katherine Butler Brown [Schofield], 'If Music be the Food of Love: Masculinity and Eroticism in the Mughal *Mehfil*', in *Love in South Asia: A Cultural History*, ed. by Francesca Orsini (Cambridge: Cambridge University Press, 2006), pp. 61-83.

quite homoerotic in places, but which is overtly to be read as an allegory for the soul's quest for the divine.[58] Of course, the human lovers of the *nayak-nayika* tradition were also frequently interpreted in devotional terms, and superimposed particularly on the love of Radha and Krishna.

When *dhrupad* songs travelled from the court to the sufi assembly and back into the courtly setting and out again, they *had* to be capable of being interpreted in a multiplicity of ways—whether sufi, Hindu *bhakti*, aesthetic, devotional, or any combination of these—depending on the listener's history of emotional and cultural experiences.[59] But by the seventeenth century the Mughal patron had long appropriated and reappropriated, through repeated listenings in different contexts and on different occasions, the imagery and the sounds associated originally with *shringara rasa* into his own deeply felt aesthetic experience of Hindustani music, through the powerful affinity he felt between *shringara rasa* and *'ishq*, cultivated in the particular suficate environment of Mughal Hindustan.[60] In this way, some Mughal connoisseurs of Hindustani music became, recognisably, *rasikas*.

58 Muhammd Akram Ghanimat, *Nairang-i 'ishq*, ed. by Ghulam Rabbani 'Aziz (Lahore: Panjabi Adabi Akademi, 1962 [c.1690]); Christopher Shackle, 'Persian Poetry and Qadiri Sufism in Late Mughal India: Ghanimat Kunjahi and his Mathnawi Nayrang-i 'Ishq', in *The Heritage of Sufism: III. Late Classical Persianate Sufism (1501-1750)*, ed. by Leonard Lewisohn (Oxford: Oneworld, 1999), pp. 435-63.

59 Rice (1994), pp. 6-8.

60 On the term suficate, see Shackle (1999), pp. 436-37.

# 16. Patterns of Composition in the Seventeenth-Century Bengali Literature of Arakan

*Thibaut d'Hubert*

*vādya kavilāsa ādi yantra sulalita* ǀ
*keha keha susvare gāhe gīta* ǀǀ[1]

Alaol, *Sikāndarnāmā* (1671)

*ānchi ū naw ast u ham kuhan ast*
*sukhan ast u darīn sukhan sukhan ast*[2]

Nizami Ganjavi, *Haft paikār* (1197)

The divorce between music and poetry is a fairly recent phenomenon and naturally not recognised by all, but it is usually widely accepted that poems are first and foremost texts that demand to be understood with the tools of textual analysis. In the case of premodern Bengali literature, however, neglecting the fact that texts were performed leads to a misunderstanding, not only of the way poems were composed, but also of the dynamics at work in the formation of the literary tradition as a whole. The texts I am dealing with in this article are *panchalis*, a

1 "Some gracefully [played] the *kavilāsa* and other instruments, while others were singing songs with their beautiful voices". The *kavilasa*, also called *kapinasa*, is a stringed, probably plucked, intrument (Sk. *tata-*) which does not seem to be clearly identified by specialists. It is mentioned very often in Bengali and Assamese premodern literature as well as Sanskrit treatises (e.g. Shubhankara, *Saṅgītadāmodaraḥ*, ed. by Gaurinath Sastri and Govindagopal Mukhopadhyay, Calcutta: Sanskrit College, 1960, p. 51). Sukumar Sen gives the following definition for this term: "a kind of lute. Ts. Lit. poetic performance. Ts. (**kavilāsa*) or sts. (**kavilāsya*); cf. *kavilāsikā*. Pada"; *An Etymological Dictionary of Bengali, c.1000-1800 A.D* (Calcutta: Eastern Publishers, 1971), p. 115.

2 "What is both ancient and new is speech, and in this speech dwells another speech".


http://dx.doi.org/10.11647/OBP.0062.16

type of Bengali narrative poem. Though the exact origin of the term remains unknown, *panchali* refers more to a kind of public performance than to a literary form or a genre.[3] In this paper I propose to study the various levels of performance that shaped the compositional pattern of the Bengali *panchali* author Alaol.

Alaol lived in the kingdom of Arakan, in modern Myanmar, in the seventeenth century. His œuvre is constituted of translations from Awadhi (an eastern form of Hindavi) and Persian narrative poems and treatises. Short poems called *padas* have also been collected from several anthologies compiled in Chittagong in the eighteenth and nineteenth centuries.[4] Even though Alaol had a deep knowledge of Hindavi, Sanskrit, and Persian literary cultures, his poems follow the rules of traditional Bengali literature, and all of his translations are *panchalis*. Born in what is modern central Bangladesh, he was brought by Portuguese corsairs to Mrauk-U, the capital of the kingdom of Arakan. He became a royal slave, enrolled in the cavalry, and was finally noticed by Muslim dignitaries for his intellectual skills. He then became a central figure of the artistic milieu of Mrauk-U and worked under the patronage of various dignitaries between 1651 and 1671.[5]

Major changes in the context of the composition and the performance of Bengali poetry occurred in the gatherings (Ben. *sabhā*) attended by Alaol in Mrauk-U. These took place in the houses of the Muslim dignitaries of the capital and, as the poet describes them in his prologues, were informal gatherings in which the etiquette of the court was partly reproduced. The hierarchy was less pyramidal than in royal courts and beside the patron who hosted the assembly, other individuals of similar

3 See *infra* for a discussion of the origin and meaning of the term *panchali*.

4 See Alaol, *Alaol racanāvalī*, ed. by Muhammad Abdul Qayyum and Razia Sultana (Dhaka: Bangla Academy), pp. 607-10. Some *padas* (e.g. *pada* n. 6, 9, 10) found in the anthologies of Chittagong are also present in Alaol's narrative poems (*Padmāvatī* and *Saptapaykara*). These *padas* were first edited by Ahmed Sharif, 'Rāgatālanāmā o padāvalī', *Sāhitya Patrikā* 7.1 (1370 BA), 1-48; see also Yatindramohan Bhattacharya, *Bāṅgālāra vaiṣṇavabhāvāpanna musalmāna kavira padamañjuṣā* (Calcutta: Kalikata Vishvavidyalay, 1984), pp. 38-42. For a study of Alaol's short poems inserted inside the narrative texts, see d'Hubert, *Histoire culturelle et poétique de la traduction. Alaol et la tradition littéraire bengali au XVIIe siècle à Mrauk-U, capitale du royaume d'Arakan* (Paris: École Pratique des Hautes Études, 2010), pp. 284-351.

5 For a presention of Alaol's life in English, see Satyendranath Ghoshal, *Beginning of Secular Romance in Bengali Literature* (Santiniketan: Visva-Bharati, 1959), pp. 63-65. For a reappraisal of the data available on his life and historical context, see d'Hubert (2010), pp. 99-149.

ranks were present, such as other Muslim dignitaries or religious men. After Bengali, the regional culture language, Persian seems to have been the second language of communication.

Alaol's texts contain several references to the audience that is strikingly present as compared to previous and contemporary *panchalis*. In the traditional *panchali*, the audience does not play an active part in the performance, whereas in Alaol's poems it is clearly considered as a component of its complete realisation. The central feature of this common endeavor is speech (*vachana*) and the unfolding of its meaning. Thus the *panchali* provides more than a narrative: it conveys a speech that calls for "another speech". Resettled in the context of the Indo-Persian assembly or *majlis*, the Bengali poetical speech (Pers. *sukhan*) became a subject of speculation and discussion (*suhbat*).

The topic of this article can be summarised in a comment pronounced by Alaol, before performing a scholarly digression on *sangita* (lyrical arts)[6] found in his translation of *Padmāvat* (1540), the Avadhi poem of Malik Muhammad Jayasi. Worried about his reputation, Alaol declared:

> *alapa nā kahõ yabe / baliba paṇḍita sabe / ei kavi saṅgīta nā jāne* | |
>
> If I don't give a short explanation [of this passage], scholars will say: "This poet doesn't know anything about lyrical arts!"

In this verse, the poet uses some key terms—*kavi* (poet), *pandita* (scholar), and *sangita* (*saṅgīta*, lyrical arts)—that will set the tone for our reflection on poetry and public performance in Alaol's texts. We shall see that, through the explicit use of the Sanskrit theoretical knowledge expounded in the *sangitashastras* (*saṅgītaśāstras*, treatises of lyrical arts), he provided his readers/auditors with analytical tools that allowed them to think of the compositional pattern of the existing regional literary tradition that lacked proper theoretical literature.[7] The literary self-awareness

6 My translation of *sangita* as "lyrical arts" rather than "song" or "music" (e.g. the entry 'Saṅgīta' in the *Samsad Bengali-English Dictionary*) is based on the definition of this term given by the theoretical literature studied by Alaol. See below.

7 The first treatise on poetics that was written in Bengali was probably the *Rasakalpavallī* (1673) by Ramagopal Das. Though a treatise on poetics and aesthetics mainly based upon the works of Rupa Goswamin (*Ujjvalalīlamaṇi* and *Bhaktirasāmṛtasindhu*), the author also quotes from Shubhankara's *Saṅgītadāmodara* (see below) regarding topics as central as *bhava* (sentiment) or *nayika-bheda* (the types of heroine). For an overview of the history of technical literature on poetics in premodern Bengal, see Ramagopal and Pitambar Das, *Rāmagopāla Dāsa-viracita Rasakalpavallī o anyānya nibandha, Pītāmbara Dāsa-viracita*

displayed by Alaol is also accompanied by the broadening of the traditional paradigm of performance towards more textuality, a central place given to "speech" (*vacana*), and the metadiscourse it may induce.

## Performance and Authorship in Premodern Bengali Literature

Premodern Bengali literature was meant to be publicly performed, and performance shaped the very idea of literary composition and authorship. The *Caryāgītis* (c. eleventh century), allegedly the oldest texts of Bengali literature, were poems meant to be meditated and commented upon. The potential for speculation in the *charyas* is attested by the very sophisticated Sanskrit commentaries that were written on them. But they were also sung, and legends about their authors often provide a setting in which the poems have been originally composed.[8] The manuscripts of the *Caryāgītis* contain indications about the *ragas* or musical modes and *talas* or rhythms used for musical performance. Similarly, the *Śrīkṛṣṇakīrtana* (c. fourteenth century CE) which, after the *Caryāgītis*, is considered the oldest Bengali text, was recited with specific *ragas* and *talas* and contains lots of theatrical features.[9] We could go on like this up to the nineteenth century and even further, because modern *palagan* singers and *patuyas* are perpetuating this

---

*Aṣṭarasavyākhyā o Rasamañjarī*, ed. by Harekrishna Mukhopadhyay, Sukumar Sen and Praphullacandra Pala (Calcutta: Kalikatha Vishvavidyalay, 1963), pp. 8-10.

8 See Abhayadatta, *La vie merveilleuse de 84 grands sages de l'Inde ancienne*, trans. from Tibetan by Djamyang Khandro Ahni (Paris: Éditions du Seuil, 2005), and compare with the *mise en scène* of the poetical compositions of the *ashtachhap* in Hariraya, *Caurāsī vaiṣṇavan kī vārtā*, ed. by D. Parikha and G. Shukla (Mathura: Shri Govardhana Granthamala Karyalaya, 1970).

9 See Wakil Ahmed, *Bāṃlā kāvyera rūpa o bhāṣā* (Dhaka: Khan Brothers & Co., 1994); Kshudiram Das, *Bāṃlā kāvyera rūpa o rīti* (Calcutta: Desh Publishing, 1994); Selim Al Deen, *Madhyayugera bāṃlā nāṭya* (Dhaka: Bangla Academy 1995); Chaya Chatterjee, *Śāstrīya Saṅgīta and Music Culture of Bengal Through the Ages* (New Delhi: Sharada Publishing House, 1996), pp. 32-40; and Saymon Zakaria, *Bāṃlādeśera lokanāṭaka: viṣaya o āṅgika-vaicitrya* (Dhaka: Bangla Academy, 2008), pp. 5-15. For the text and a translation of the *Śrīkṛṣṇakīrtana*, see Baru Chandidasa, *Śrīkṛṣṇakīrtana*, ed. by Vasantaranjan Ray Vidvadvallabh (Calcutta: Vangiy Sahitya Parishat, 1361 BA), and *Singing the Glory of Lord Krishna: The Śrīkṛṣṇakīrtana*, trans. by M.H. Klaiman (Chicago: Scholars Press, 1984).

tradition and provide living examples of how premodern literature could have been performed.[10]

The Bengali literature that was produced after the fourteenth century may be formally divided into short and long versified texts.[11] On the one hand, we find the *padas*—short poems composed on a variety of metres—that include the two foundational corpora just mentioned, and on the other hand there is the voluminous amount of versified narrative texts called *panchalis*.[12] The lyrical and even dramatic dimensions of short poems or *padas* are systematically referred to by specialists of this literature, but the long narrative poems we are concerned with here are usually not thought about in their performance context by scholars. Yet it is vital to think about narrative texts in performance if we want to comprehend the way they have been composed and transmitted.

10 See France Bhattacharya, 'A propos d'une représentation du Caṇḍi Maṅgal au Bengale Occidental', *Adyatan "d'aujourd'hui"* 3 (1984), 7-26; Philippe Benoît, 'Quatre chansons de paṭuyā du Bengale sur le Rāmāyaṇa', *Bulletin d'Études Indiennes* 10 (1992), 53-87 ; and Zakaria (2008), pp. 37-40.

11 We find this dichotomy in Sen's general definition of "ancient Bengali literature" (*purāno bāṅgālā sāhitya*). Though he first makes the distinction between three formal types, he finally reduces it to only two: *pratham gītikavitā, dvitīya paurāṇik geya athavā pāṭhya ākhyāyikā, tṛtīya a-paurāṇik geya kavitā-ākhyāyikā. śeṣ dui dhārār racanār rūp vā pharm prāy ek-i rakam evaṃ se pharmer nām-o 'pāñcālī'*. "First, there is lyrical poetry, second, come the stories drawn out from the *Puranas* that must be sung or read aloud, third, are the narrative poems meant to be sung. The last two trends of composition or *forms* are almost the same, and the name of this *form* is '*panchali*'" (Sen (2000), Vol. 1, p. 103).

12 The *panchali* type of representation assumed various forms through history. As regards prosody, the main features of a *panchali* are the alternation of narrative parts in *payar* verse and descriptive and more lyrical parts in *tripadi*. A *panchali* may also contain other shorter poetical forms such as *git* ("songs" composed on a variety of metres), *baromasis* (songs of the twelve months), or *cautishas* (acrostic poems based on the letters of the Bengali alphabet). The word *panchali* is found in several narrative poems to designate the text itself or its form. The actual features of *panchali* performances and the way they changed over time are not well known. The original *panchali* would have included puppet dance and would have afterward developed towards modern *yatra* representation (Shambaru Chandra Mohanta, Chandra, 'Panchali', in *Banglapedia* (Dhaka: Asiatic Society of Bangladesh, 2006), CD ROM). But the clear demonstration of this evolution is still lacking. See Sukumar Sen, *Bāṅgālā sāhityera itihāsa* (Kolkata: Ananda Publishers, 2001), Vol. 1, pp. 103-04, Vol. 2, pp. 2: 6-8; see also Ahmed (1994) and Al Deen (1995), pp. 77-82; for contemporary *panchali* representations, see F. Bhattacharya (1984) and Zakaria (2008). About *panchali* as a model for *jarigan* performances, see also Mary F. Dunham, *Jarigan: Muslim Epic Songs of Bangladesh* (Dhaka: The University Press Limited, 1997), pp. 45-46 and 330.

Narrative texts were, and still are in some places in West Bengal and Bangladesh, recited by professionals called *kathak*, *pathak*, or *gayen*. Each term stresses one aspect of their style of recitation: the two first terms refer to a musically tuned reading-cum-commentary, and the second more specifically to singing.

In many cases the poet is presented as a kind of original performer rather than an "author".[13] For instance, a common motif in *mangalkavyas* regarding the creation of the book is that of the "inspired poet".[14] One day the poet, usually a Brahmin, while attending to his everyday affairs, or in a dream, sees the Goddess appear before him. She then gives the order to compose a poem whose text she will fully provide, or for which she will bestow the boon of eloquence on the poet who presents himself as ignorant and unfit to fulfill such a task.[15] This primeval inspiration originating from the Goddess herself is afterward reinitiated through the performance by the ritual gesture of the *gayen* before he starts the recitation of the text. Before the performance begins the *gayen* grasps a *chamar* (flywhisk), and it is from this moment only that he remembers what he will have to recite during the next several hours.[16] In this creative process absolutely no place is left for the poet's role as a composer. He is first and foremost presented as a devotee, and it is through an act of devotion, represented by the holding of the *chamar*, that the poem will

13 On the subject of authorship in premodern South Asian vernacular literature, see J.S. Hawley, 'Author and Authority in the Bhakti Poetry of North India', *The Journal of Asian Studies* 47.2 (1988), 269-90, and Ali Asani, *Ecstasy and Enlightment: The Ismaili Devotional Literature of South Asia* (London: Institute of Ismaili Studies, 2002), pp. 82-99. For a discussion about the author and the performer of oral poetry, see Paul Zumthor, *Introduction à la poésie orale* (Paris: Éditions du Seuil, 1983), pp. 209-27.

14 *Mangalkavyas* are narrative poems about the spread of the worship of a goddess among human beings. Regarding the inspired poet and performer see Y. Bhattacharya (2007), p. xi and F. Bhattacharya (1984), p. 8. For instances of "divine inspiration" see Krittibas, *Kṛttivāsī Rāmāyaṇa*, ed. by Harekrishna Mukhopadhyay (Kolkata: Sahitya Samsad, 2002), pp. 4-5; Ketakadas, *Manasāmaṅgala*, ed. by Akshaykumar Kayal and Chitra Dev (Kolkata: Lekhapad, 1384 BA), pp. 5-7; and Heyat Mahmud, *Kavi Heyāt Māmud*, ed. by Mazharul Islam (Dhaka: Agami Prakashan, 2009), p. 299.

15 The commissioned poet shows a similar humility in order to obtain the "compassion" (*kripa*) not from the divinity, but from his mundane patron. See also David Shulman, 'Poets and Patrons in Tamil Literary Legend', in *The Wisdom of Poets: Studies in Tamil, Telugu, and Sanskrit* (New Delhi: Oxford University Press, 2001), pp. 63-102, and T. d'Hubert, 'Reading Persian Poetry in Seventeenth Century Arakan: The Sāqī as a Guru and the Figure of the Patron in Alaol's Bengali Translation of Niẓāmī's Sharafnāma', in *Patronage in Indo-Persian Culture* (New Delhi: Manohar, forthcoming).

16 See Bhattacharya (1984), pp. 10-11.

come into existence. In terms of representation of the literary activity, it is not only that performance is the main way to share the content of a written text; rather it means that no text is ever able to come into existence without a setting of ritual performance.

The Bengali poetic tradition does not openly stress the poet's skills as a composer. But the performer who recites the poem is expected to be able to provide commentary and improvise new elements, either in verse or prose, in order to highlight a special point regarding the characters' behaviour, to add humorous elements in due time, or to beautify a specific episode.[17] Unfortunately, this part of the performance, which is known from the observation of modern *palagan* representations, was not written down. As a consequence the only reminders we have of this metatextual practice appear here and there through the numerous variant readings found in the manuscripts of very popular texts. The best example in this regard may be Krittibas's *Rāmāyaṇa* (c. fifteenth century) that has proved to be an unsolvable philological puzzle due to its countless variant readings and fragmented transmission.[18]

Bengali literary texts were part of a larger performing tradition that included music, dance, and dramatic improvisation. The production and transmission patterns of literary texts were thus totally dependent on the way they would be performed. This close connection between performance and literary composition appears clearly in the first adaptation into Bengali of the Sanskrit *Mahābhārata* by "Kavindra" Parameshwar Dasa. Kavindra's patron, Paragal Khan, Sultan Husain Shah's (1493-1519) officer in charge of the Chittagong area, made the following request regarding the composition of the text:

> *ehi saba kathā kaha saṃkṣepa kariyā* | *dineka śunite pāri pāñcāli baliyā* | |
>
> Summarise this story and tell it, so that I can listen to this *panchali* in a few days.[19]

17 Zakaria (2008).

18 Regarding the manuscripts of the *Kṛttivāsī Rāmāyaṇa* see Amiya Shankar Chaudhuri, 'Kṛttivāser puthi saṃvād', in *Kavi Kṛttivāsa saṃkalana grantha* (Phuliya: Kavi Krittivasa Smaraka Grantha Prakashak Samiti, 1989), pp. 183-201. For an attempted critical edition by Nalinikantha Bhattashali, see *Mahākavi Kṛttivāsa viracita Rāmāyaṇa, Ādikāṇḍa*, ed. by Nalinikantha Bhattashali (Dhaka: Shrinath Press, 1936).

19 Kavindra Parameshwar Das, *Kavīndra-Mahābhārata*, ed. by Kalpana Bhowmik (Dhaka: Bangla Academy, 1999), p. 332.

The point here was not only to shift from the Sanskrit to the Bengali literary tradition but rather to provide Paragal and his courtiers with a more performable version of the story, which in its original form and in this court milieu, was hardly fit to be publicly performed.[20] What should also be kept in mind is that, unlike Sanskrit texts, Bengali *panchalis* were not at first linguistically sophisticated. Unlike Sanskrit *kavyas*, they were not "ornate" (*alamkrita*), and no commentary was needed to unfold the meaning of the verses and release the *rasa*. The aesthetic pleasure derived rather from the performance as a whole. *Panchalis* were heavily narrative, and it was the theatrical setting that provided the ornamentation.[21] That is why, textually speaking—and, as I suggested before, through the relative absence of the figure of the author as a craftsman of speech—the story was central, not the word. We will see that things seem to be different in the case of Alaol.

## Performance in Alaol's Texts

What material do we have to study performance in Alaol's poetry? To answer this question we need to make a distinction between three kinds of sources that the Bengali poet's texts provide: the description of the *sabha* (assembly), paratextual indications, and the *mise en abyme*, inside the story narrated in the poem, in which performance is present. *Mise en abyme* indicates a formal technique in which an image contains a smaller copy of itself. Often applied to paintings that contain a smaller image of

---

20 One of Kavindra's techniques was to drop the secondary stories found in the Sanskrit recensions, thus reistablishing the linearity of the narrative, which was one of the important features of the composition of Bengali *panchalis*. See the comparative tables given in the introduction of K. Bhowmik's edition; Kavindra Parameshwara Das (1999), Vol. 1, pp. 129-308.

21 This approach is aligned with what P. Zumthor wrote about oral literature and the fragmentary nature of the text (1983, p. 56). The complete aspect of poetry is what he defines as the "œuvre": "L'œuvre, c'est ce qui est communiqué poétiquement, ici et maintenant: texte, sonorités, rythmes, éléments visuels ; le terme embrasse la totalité des facteurs de la performance"; (1983), p. 164. In his article on Bengali and Maithili plays composed in Nepal, Brinkhaus makes the same comment regarding the poor literary value of those courtly dramas; Horst Brinkhaus, 'On the Transition from Bengali to Maithili in Nepalese Dramas of the 16th and 17th Centuries', in *Maithili Studies: Papers Presented at the Stockholm Conference on Maithili Language and Literature* (Stockholm: Department of Indology, University of Stockholm), pp. 67-77.

themselves, I use it to denote the description of performance inside the text (see also Miner, Orsini, and Busch in this volume).

# Descriptions of the *Sabha*

Alaol included many contextual features in his poems, such as descriptions of the assemblies he attended, or his patrons' interventions during the reading of his poem. The first we notice is that poetry is presented as one pleasurable activity among others in the society parties organised by the Muslim notables of Mrauk-U. According to Alaol's account, *sabhas* were held at night and included a dinner, games, dances, music, and discussions on various topics related to some books that had been previously read aloud to the audience.[22] The poet seems to have performed his own poem, and there is no mention of professional storytellers in his prologue. He does mention dancers and musicians, though not in relation with the poem he is about to declaim. Alaol does not give any details regarding the precise setting of the *sabha*, such as the way people were seated, the presence or not of a stage,[23] etc.

# Paratextual Elements

The paratextual elements found in the manuscripts concerning the musical modes (*ragas*) do not leave any doubt regarding the musical aspects of the

22 This matches the usual organisation of *majālis-i shabāna* as described in Mughal sources, where poetry and music often came late at night; see 'Abd al-Sattar ibn Qasim Lahori, *Majālis-i Jahāngīrī*, ed. by Riza Allah Shah 'Arif Nawshahi and Mu'in Nizami (Tehran: Markaz-i Pizhuhishi-i Mirath-i Maktub, 1385S). Theatrical performance in the neighbouring kingdom of Bhulua also took place at night after dinner (Raghunath 'Kavitarkik', *Kautukaratnākara*, ed. and trans. by Dulal K. Bhowmik (Dhaka: Dhaka University, 1997), pp. 25-6. In Alaol's case, the succession of the dinner and the recitation of poetry is the occasion to pun on the various meanings of the word *rasa*—"juice, savour" and "aesthetic emotion"; Alaol (2007), p. 457; see also Pellò and Schofield in this volume.

23 According to Zakaria (2008, pp. 38-39), performances took place directly on the ground and it is with the advent of the *yatra* in eighteenth century that stages were built. Gautier Schouten, who visited Mrauk-U in 1660, seems to suggest that stages were built to perform dramas: "Ensuite, le soir étant venu, les spectateurs finirent la journeé en faisant des danses sur des théâtres; on y joua des comédies: on y fit entendre de la musique; et une partie de la nuit se passa dans ces festivités". Unfortunately, this short account does not allow us to ascertain whether these were Bengali *panchalis*; see G. Schouten, *Voiage de Gautier Schouten aux Indes orientales. Commencé l'an 1658 et fini l'an 1665* (Amsterdam: Pierre Mortier, 1708), p. 194.

recitation. Another clue furnished by the *panchali* tradition itself is the *bhanita*, that is the poet's signature line marking the end of a narrative section or a song. These can contain a short praise of the patron and the name of the poet, and sometimes they are used to introduce questions and comments made by the poet or even the patron about the episode that was just narrated or on some point of vocabulary.[24] The *bhanitas* hint at the performed dimension of Alaol's texts because they address the audience directly and help structure the narrative sequences of the poem.[25] They provide a lively tune to the recitation, and it is not rare to find copyists who, carried away by the flow of the poem, added their own *bhanitas* where they deemed it appropriate.[26]

Performance also surfaces in Alaol's texts in the *mise en abyme* that mirrors the actual recitation of his own poems in the *sabha*. As compared to his models, Alaol lays special emphasis on the episodes that involve some kind of performance. This is often an opportunity for Alaol to provide his knowledgeable audience—the *gunigana*—with very precise technical information (see also Miner in this volume).[27]

Among the topics Alaol discusses, *sangita* and its subsidiary sciences are particularly important to define the poet's view of artistic composition. Moreover, fragments of what seems to have been a treatise on music composed by Alaol are found in later works called *Rāgamālās* and *Tālanāmās*.[28] The fragments of Alaol's *Rāgatālanāmā* partly deal with the myth of the creation of *ragas*, *talas*, and musical instruments.[29] The work appears to be framed around the story found in the *Nāṭyaśāstra* about the origin of Drama, combined with elements of Puranic stories such as the birth of the Ganga (the river Ganges), but it does not match exactly with

24 See for instance Alaol's comments in *Padmāvatī* on the terms *kākanucha* (phoenix) and *gamanā* (new bride) (2007), pp. 43-44, 127-29.

25 The subject of the preceding or following section is often mentioned by the author in his *bhanitas* and helps the audience to follow what is going on in the poem.

26 See for instance the suggestions made by Kshudiram Das concerning the interjections that may have been added by later performers in the *Śrīkṛṣṇakīrtana*; quoted in Ahmed (1994), p. 8.

27 On music and courtly aesthetics in the Indo-Persian courtly culture, see Schofield in the present volume.

28 These fragments have been edited by Ahmed Sharif, 'Rāgatālanāmā o padāvalī', *Sāhitya Patrikā* 7.1 (1967), 16-17, 81-82, 92-93; and have been reprinted in Alaol (2007), pp. 595-606.

29 These treatises are to be understood in connection with the development of *ragamala* paintings in Indo-Persian courts treated by Miner in the present volume.

any version known to me.[30] Alaol also provides lists of the *kalas*, *ragas*, *raginis*, *talas*, and *talinis*, the way they may be combined as well as the directions, colours, and, for the four *kalas*, the elements—fire, earth, wind, and water—they are associated with.[31]

In the *bhanitas* of this technical text the Bengali poet often addresses the assembly in different ways from his narrative poems and he never refers to the name of any of his patrons.[32] This suggests that the fragments were parts of the teaching he delivered to the children of the local elite.[33] Alaol clearly states that he is using the *shastras* in order to explain the science of *sangita* when he states:

*avagata pāiyā* śāstra-pustaketa ǀ
bhāṅgiyā kahiba *saba bujhaha paṇḍita* ǀ ǀ

I learned *in the books of the treatises*
And I will *explain everything*, so that you, knowledgeable audience,
may understand.

30 About the origin of theatre in the *Nāṭyaśāstra*, see Lyne Bansat-Boudon, *Poétique du théâtre indien* (Paris: École Française d'Extrême Orient, 1991), pp. 53-59. The author of the *Saṅgītadāmodara* summarises the myth in this way: "In this regard, we hear that in ancient times, Brahma made the fifth Veda from the [other four] Vedas on Indra's request; that is to say that it was a secondary Veda, because the Vedas are said to be four by the Tradition. Then, Shiva [declared] to Brahma that this secondary Veda is called 'Gandharva'. After that, he taught it to Bharata who spread it in the mortal world. That is why its instigators are Shiva, Brahma and Bharata". The first two chapters of the *Pañcamasārasaṃhitā* of Narada deal with the spread of *sangita* from heaven to western Bengal (Radha) by the descendants of Bharata; Damodar Sen Narada, *Pañcamasārasaṃhitā and Saṅgītadāmodara*, ed. by Guru Bipin Singh and trans. into Hindi by Lalmani Tiwari (Calcutta: Manipuri Nartanalaya, 1984), pp. 1-4.

31 Alaol's use of the term *kalā* differs from the *Saṅgītaratnākara* and seems to refer rather to the non-lexical syllables (commonly called *nom tom*) used as an aid to articulation in *dhrupad alap*, which are often embued with esoteric meanings and power; see R. Sanyal and R. Widdess, *Dhrupad: Tradition and Performance in Indian Music* (Aldershot: Ashgate, 2004), pp. 152-57. The fragment of *sangita* treatise bearing Alaol's signature elaborates on the inner significance of *kalas*, their location, their *dhyanas* (cf. Miner in this volume), and their cosmological associations; the cosmological associations show a clear link with Shaiva tantric teachings, and templates for such cosmological associations can be found in early modern Bengali Qalandari Yoga treatises; *Ālāol Racanāvalī*, ed. by Muhammad Abdul Qayyum and Razia Sultana (Dhaka: Bangla Academy, 2007), pp. 598-99; I am grateful to Allyn Miner for pointing me in the direction of *dhrupad*.

32 The expressions he uses are *sabhā madhye, sabhā praṇāmiyā, sabhā sambodhiyā, sabhāra ālae*; Alaol (2007), pp. 597-98, 600-06.

33 See below for reference to his teaching activity in *Sikāndarnāmā*.

*raciluma ei kathā ādye* lekhā pāi |
I composed this discourse *after obtaining [the knowledge] from the scriptures.*

āgama vicāri *kahe hīna Alaola* | |
The humble Alaol speaks *after reflecting upon the treatises.*[34]

Alaol, like other Bengali poet-translators, used the verb *bhāṅgiyā kah-*, which literally means "saying after breaking", to talk about the process of translation. Without going into the details of Alaol's approach regarding translation, let us just notice the didacticism of the poet, who presents himself as an intermediary between his source and the audience. We shall see that he was not only an interpreter of texts, but also of the performance in its various artistic dimensions. In this case it seems that his source-texts were Sanskrit *sangitashastras*.[35] The didactic dimension of these fragments further appears in Alaol's answer to the audience:

*hīna Alaole kahe śuna guṇigaṇa* |
*uttarera padduttara śunaha ekhana* | |[36]

The humble Alaol says: "Listen connoisseurs!
Listen to the answer I now give to [your] question".

## *Shastras* and the *Panchali* Tradition

We saw that performance is present in Alaol's texts through conventions connected to the *panchali* tradition. Yet by writing a treatise he also expressed a more specific interest in *sangita* (lyrical arts). What did the term *sangita* mean for the poet and his milieu? We will see that this technical term borrowed from Sanskrit treatises provides the relevant epistemological tools to define Alaol's paradigm of performance.

34 Alaol (2007), pp. 593, 603, and 606.

35 In his narrative poems, Alaol explicitly names three of them: Shubhankara's *Saṅgītadāmodara* (c. fifteenth century), Damodara Mishra's *Saṅgītadarpaṇa* (c. 1625) and Narada's *Pañcamasārasaṃhitā* (c. sixteenth century); see Alaol (2007), pp. 109 and 252. The editors of the texts mistakenly read *saṅgita pañcama svara nārade kahila* for *saṃhitā pañcamasāra nārade kahila* (compare with the text of the manuscript given in Alaol, 2002, p. 302) and *Saṃkṣipta-darpaṇa* for *Saṅgīta-darpaṇa*.

36 Alaol (2007), p. 606.

Shubhankara, the author of the *Saṅgītadāmodara*, one of the explicit sources of Alaol on lyrical arts, gives the following definition:

> *tālavādyānugaṃ gītaṃ naṭībhir yat tu gīyate* |
> *nṛtyasyānugataṃ raṅge tat saṅgītakam ucyate* | |[37]
>
> The song performed by female artists accompanied
> by rhythmical instruments[38]
> and dance is called *sangita*.

The term *sangita* provides the widest artistic paradigm—it contains the arts of instrumental music (*tala-vadya*), dance (*nritya*), and *gita*. *Gita* is further divided into two elements, *dhatu* and *matu* (music and text), providing another useful theoretical tool.[39] *Dhatu* and *matu* also appear in another important definition, that of the *vaggeyakara* (the author and composer).[40] It is worth pointing out that by using shastric technical terms to talk about performance, Alaol did not demarcate a "high" tradition separate from that of the regional *panchali* but rather applied the science taught in Sanskrit *shastras* to the regional artistic domain.[41]

---

37 Shubhankara (1960), p. 16. On Shubhankara, his place in the history of *sangitashastras*, and the reception of his work, see Nijenhuis (1977), pp. 19-20.

38 The compound *tālavādya* can either be translated "rhythmical instrument" or "rhythm (*tāla*) and [melodic] instruments (*vādya*)".

39 See the definition given in the *Saṅgītadāmodara*: *dhātumātusamāyuktaṃ gītam ity ucyate bhudhaiḥ* | *tatra nādātmako dhātur mātur akṣarasaṃcayaḥ* | | (What contains *dhatu* and *matu* is called *gita* by wise men. In this concern, *dhatu* is made of sounds and *matu* is [the result of] a combination of syllables); Shubhankara (1960), p. 16.

40 For a Persian definition of the *bayikār* (< Sk. *vāggeyakāra*), see *Ghunyat-ul-Munya: The Earliest Known Persian Work on Indian Music*, trans. by Shahab Sarmadee (Bombay: Asian Publishing House, 1978), pp. 129-30, and for the Persian text *Ghunyat'ul Munya: The Earliest Persian Work on Indian Music*, ed. by Shahab Sarmadee (New Delhi: Indian Council of Historical Research, 2003), p. 109. The *Lahjāt-i Sikandarshāhi*, another Persian text composed in an Afghan Lodi milieu in the second half of the fifteenth century, gives a complete definition of the *vaggeyakar* that closely follows the *Saṅgītaratnākara;* 'Umar Sama' Yahya al-Kabuli, *Lahjāt-i Sikandarshāhī wa laṭā'if-i nā-matnāhī*, ed. by Syeda Bilqis Fatema Husaini (Mumbai: Alhyat Research Center, 2001), Vol. 1, pp. 146-47. On the figure of the *vaggeyakar* in Braj literature during the Mughal period, see Françoise "Nalini" Delvoye, *Tânsen et la tradition des chants dhrupad en langue braj, du XVIe siècle à nos jours* (Paris: Université de la Sorbonne Nouvelle Paris III, 1990), pp. 127ff.

41 This contrasts with South Indian Dravidian literary traditions in which the epistemological frameworks of Sanskrit had been adopted and adapted very early; Sheldon Pollock, 'The Cosmopolitan Vernacular', *The Journal of Asian Studies* 57.1 (1998), 6-37, and *The Language of Gods in the World of Men: Sanskrit Culture and Power in*

We therefore witness the rapprochement of the regional Bengali medium with the Sanskrit epistemological framework in the context of performance. This move becomes clear when Alaol states it himself in the digressions that follow some of the performance scenes depicted in his poems. Damodara in his *Saṅgītadarpaṇa* (Bnf Sanscrit 771, f. 32a) provides the following definition of the author and composer:

> *vāgvarṇasamudayas tu mātur ity u[cya]te budhaiḥ* |
> *geyaṃ dhātur dvayoḥ kartā prokto vāggeyakārakaḥ* | |[42]
>
> The combination of the letters of words is called *matu* by wise men,
> what ought to be sung is *dhatu*, the one who composes both is called
> "author and composer".

According to this definition, Alaol was a *panchali vaggeyakar*, a *panchali* author and composer. Even if he used the regional medium for his compositions, he declared himself a specialist of lyrical arts as taught in contemporary Sanskrit treatises, and he analyzed his own activity of Bengali poet with the tools provided by the Sanskrit tradition. Hence it is legitimate in his case to study his poems using the terminology of the Sanskrit treatises he was familiar with.

I will now try to demonstrate that the above-mentioned performance paradigm obtained from the definition of *sangita* and *gita* can help us define the three kinds of poetical performance present in Alaol's texts. The first kind of performance combines instrumental music, dance, and singing, the second one is the musically tuned declamation of a narrative part, and the third kind of performance is the commentary on a text that has been previously read to the audience in the *sabha*.[43] These three categories are refered to by Alaol himself when he declares that he taught *patha* (reading), *gita*, and *sangita* to the children of the nobles

---

*Premodern India* (Berkeley: University of California Press, 2006). Even sixteenth- and seventeenth-century Brajbhasha literature openly integrated Sanskrit scholarship when reflecting on its own tradition; Allison Busch, 'The Anxiety of Innovation: The Practice of Literary Science in the Hindi/Riti Tradition', *Comparative Studies of South Asia, Africa and Middle East* 24.2 (2004), 45-59. But this was not the case at all in premodern Bengali, which was largely autonomous in its aesthetic and prosody from the prescriptions of Sanskrit *shastras*.

42 Damodara, *Saṅgītadarpaṇa* (MS Bnf Sanscrit 771), f. 32a.

43 This should be compared with the definitions given by Zumthor (1983, p. 164) of *texte*, *poème*, and *œuvre*.

of Mrauk-U.[44] According to this paradigm, the musical aspect (*dhatu*) dominates in the text or in the various episodes contained in a *panchali* when, for example, a *gita* is inserted inside a narrative section, while the textual element (*matu*) will be dominant in highly ornate sections, such as the *nakha-sikha*, and even more in scholarly digressions. The bulk of the narrative parts constitute the middle of this paradigm in which the text is central but requires a musical tune when performed. Here is a pattern using this framework and the technical terms used by Alaol himself to designate the lyrical, narrative, and speculative dimensions of his literary compositions:

Table 16.1: The performance paradigm of Alaol's poems

<table>
<tr><td rowspan="2">[dhatu, music]<br>lacari song<br>katha/vrittanta/vivarana/prasanga tale, narrative, description, episode</td><td>sangita<br>text/music/dance</td><td rowspan="2">Traditional panchali</td><td rowspan="3">Alaol's panchali</td></tr>
<tr><td>gita<br>text/music</td></tr>
<tr><td>bakhana commentary<br>[kavyarasavakya/tattvakatha/<br>nitishastrakatha on kavya, knowledge, ethics]<br>[matu]</td><td>patha reading<br>text</td><td></td></tr>
</table>

The terms used in this Table are found in Alaol's technical vocabulary. Similarly to any other *panchali*, it includes both the *sangita*, involving text, music, and dance, and the narrative part characterised by a musically tuned declamation. Alaol adds the scholarly digressions and other sophisticated parts in which he stresses eloquence and technical aspects of "speech". *Bakhana* means "commentary", and the three compounds indicated underneath are the three main themes of the refined discourse as conceived by Alaol—on the savour of poetry, the essential principals, and mundane ethic.

44 Alaol (2007), p. 313.

## *Mise en Abyme* of *Sangita*: Alaol as a *Gandharp*

In Alaol's texts we find illustrations of the three kinds of performance of *panchali*: complete theatrical performance, narrative performance, and technical speech or didactic discourse. By analyzing one description of a *sangita* performance from Alaol's *Padmāvatī*, we will see how the poet blurs the limit between the performance that is depicted in the story and the *panchali* that is actually taking place in the *sabha* of his patron. In this *mise en abyme*, Alaol also plays the role of an artistic mediator between the show and the audience. In the following passage in *lachari*, that is to say a song composed in the *tripadi* metre which is accompanied by dance steps performed by the *gayen*, Jayasi's text is the model for Alaol's poem and gives the Bengali poet the opportunity to describe a *sangita* performance:

> । । *rāga dīrgha chanda lācārī* । ।
> *tabe rājā ratnasena / vicāri bujhiyā mane / vaśya maraṇa āche tattve* ।
> *yedina ānande yāya / jīvana suphala pāya / sukhabhoga bhālamanda śarte* । ।
> *bhavitavye thāke yei / avaśya haiba sei / vidhi-bale nāhika eḍāna* ।
> *ajñāne bhāvaya dukha / [jñānete bāriba sukha]*[45] */ sadānanda [sārete] pramāṇa*[46] । ।
> *eteka bhāviyā citte / ratnasene ānandite / rājadvāre raci nṛtyaśālā* ।
> *haraṣita sarvajana / nācaya nartakīgaṇa / pañcaśabde kari eka melā* । ।
> *chaya rāga hāṅkāriyā / chatriśa rāgiṇī laiyā / madhusvare kaila ālāpana* ।
> *dakṣiṇā[ty]a aṅga bālā / nānā kāce nāce bhālā / sādhanā hastaka sulakṣaṇa* । ।
> *kahite nṛt[y]era kathā / bahula bāḍaya pothā / nā kahile śānta nahe mane* ।
> *alapa nā kahõ yabe / baliba paṇḍita sabe / ei kavi saṅgīta nā jāne* । ।
> *maneta kariyā kalpa / kahimu kiñcita alpa / bujhaha rasika dhīra jane* ।
> *rasasindhu guṇīśvara / śrīyuta māgana vara / ājñā pāi Alaola bhaṇe* । ।[47]

> Then Raja Ratnasena intensely reflected
> upon the undeniable power of death.
> When time passes in joy and bliss, one plucks the good fruits of life;
> the experience of pleasure depends on the good and bad things [that we do].
> What is part of our destiny will surely happen;
> there is no way to escape the power of Fate.

45 The editor Debnath Bandyopadhyay reads: *janmite bariba sukha*.

46 Bandyopadhyay reads: *sāhase*. The reference here is to the *Vedāntasāra* of Sadananda (c. fourteenth century), a handbook that exposes the basics of Vedanta philosophy. This short text was widely read and has been commented upon by several authors; see Theodore Aufrecht, *Catalogus Catalogorum: An Alphabetical Register of Sanskrit Works and Authors* (Leipzig: F.A. Brockhaus, 1891), Vol. 1, p. 607.

47 Alaol (2002), p. 300.

One worries in ignorance, whereas knowledge increases happiness;
testimony lies in Sadananda's [*Vedānta*]*sāra*.
Thinking thus in his mind, Ratnasena in order to enjoy his self
built a dance hall at the door of the royal palace.
Everyone was cheerful and the dancers danced
accompanied by the festive harmony of all kinds of instruments.
Striking up the six musical modes with their thirty-six *raginis*,
they started singing the prelude with sweet voices.
Beautiful young women from the South skillfully danced in various fashions,
displaying their mastery of hand movements.
If I talk about dance, the book will expand too much,
If I don't, I won't find peace in my mind.
If I don't give a short explanation, scholars will say,
"This poet doesn't know lyrical arts!"
Hence I decide to explain all this briefly;
O wise connoisseurs! Listen carefully!
Alaol speaks on the order of this Ocean of sensibility, the master of all qualities,
the noble and excellent Magana!

In these lines, Alaol exposes various aspects of an artistic performance—from the motivations of the patron to set up a *nrityashala* to the critical preoccupations of the court poet who must show his erudition in order to remain credible in front of the assembly.[48] Again, Alaol slips from text to context. The courtly performance described in the poem mirrors what is actually taking place in the *sabha* of Mrauk-U. The shift from the narrative to the lyrical form, or from *prasanga* to *sangita*, concretely takes place through the metrical change from *payar* to *lachari tripadi*; thus when a

48 Actually the whole argumentation regarding Ratnasena's attitude is Alaol's comments. The Avadhi text only has: *tabahũ rājā hiẽ na hārā / rāja pāvari par racā akhārā*; Jayasi, *Padmāvat*, ed. by Mata Prasad Gupta, 2nd edn (Allahabad: Bharati Bhandar, 1963), p. 437. Alaol translated the first and last words of the *caupai* (*tabe rājā ratnasena / [...] rājadvāre raci nṛtyaśālā* / l. 1-5), and glossed the Avadhi expression *hiẽ na hārā* (lit. "did not lose in his heart"). The additional "philosophical" explanation that Alaol gives may be understood as advice to encourage the patron to play his role of supporter of the arts even in difficult times. Compare with *Satī-Maynā Lora Candrāṇī*, when Alaol describes Lora's pleasures in the Mohara kingdom: *raciyā udyāna ghana / puṣkariṇī upavana / tathā* [*sajjā*] *kari* [*nṛtya*]*śālā* । *gīta nāṭa raṅge ḍhaṅge / candrāṇī loraka saṅge / paricaryā kare kulabālā* ।। ("He made a complete pleasure garden, pools and groves where he adorned a dance hall. In the amusements of chants and dramatic performances, Chandrani with Lorak were served by well born young girls"); Alaol, *Satī-Maynā Lora Candrāṇī*, ed. by Muhammad Abdul Qayyum (Dhaka: Bangla Academy, 1992), p. 90. I have slightly amended Abdul Qayyum's text *śayyā* to *sajjā* and *nitya* to *nṛtya*. These were obvious mistakes in the rendering into modern Bengali of the spelling found in the manuscripts.

*sangita* performance is described in the poem, it is also actually performed in Alaol's *sabha*.

The evocation of dance in the original poem impels Alaol to intervene and provide the assembly with his comments. This attitude is a specific feature of the *gandharva* (Sk.) (>*gandharp*/*gandharb* in Pers.), a key figure of artistic performance dealt with somewhat differently in Sanskrit and Persian treatises.[49] For instance, in the *Saṅgītaratnākara*, composed by Sharngadeva in the thirteenth century, one of the most influential treatises on *sangita* frequently referred to by the *Saṅgītadāmodara* and the *Saṅgītadarpaṇa*, the *gandharva* is briefly mentioned as one type of *vaggeyakar* (author-composer) who masters both *deshi*, i.e. regional, mundane technique, and *marga*, i.e. eternal, divine technique. No further precision is given regarding his role in the *sabha* during the performance. The definition of the *gandharva* as a knowledgeable intermediary between the performers and the audience is furnished by the *Ghunyat al-munya*, a Persian treatise on Indian music and dance composed in fourteenth-century Gujarat.[50] Though Alaol never refers either to the function of *gandharva/gandharp* or to this treatise, typologically speaking this definition seems to match perfectly Alaol's function in the *sabha* as it transpires in his poems:

> mu'arrif-i surūd *ki ānrā* gandharp *gūyand ; waẓīfa-yi ū ān ast ki har rāg u surūd u raqṣ ki maṭlūb-i ṣāḥib-i majlis bāshad, istifsār kunad, wa bar*[51] *ṭawā'if-i mazkūr bagūyad, wa dar athnā-yi surūd u raqṣ chūn bāngī yā shaklī nīk ṣādir shawad taḥsīn kunad, wa nām-i ān bāng u shakl bagūyad ki īn rā īn chunīn gūyand—ū bāyad ki bar majmū'-i anwā'-i surūd wa ashkāl-i raqṣ muṭṭala' bāshad.*[52]

---

49 See Sharngadeva, *The Saṅgītaratnākara of Śārṅgadeva with the Kalānidhi of Kallinātha and the Saṅgītasudhākara of Siṃhabhūpāla*, ed. by S. Subrahmanyam Shastri and V. Krishnamacharya (Madras: The Adyar Library and Research Centre, 1959), p. 153, and the *Saṅgītaśiromaṇi*, ed. and trans. by Emmie te Nijenhuis (Leiden: Brill, 1992), pp. 484-85. The *Lahjāt-i Sikandarshāhī* does not elaborate on the topic: "*dar bayān-i* gāndharb *wa ānchunān ast ki har ki* mārg *u* desī *rā bā badānad, ān rā* gāndharb *nām khwānand… sabab-i īn ma'nī niwishta nashud tā kitāb dirāz nagardad*". ("On the exposition of the word *gandharb* and its meaning: anyone who knows perfectly and completely the *marga* and the *deshi* is called a *gandharb*… I do not write anything about the reason of the meaning [of this word], so that the book does not become too long"); 'Umar Sama' Yahya al-Kabuli (2001), see below for the definition of the *Ghunyat al-munyā*.

50 Regarding musicological literature and patronage in the Sultanate of Gujarat, see Delvoye (2000).

51 I suggest to read *ba* instead of *bar*.

52 *Ghunyatu'l-munya* (2003), Persian text, pp. 109-10, translation slightly modified from that given by Sarmadee (1978), pp. 130-31.

> *He is the conductor of music,*[53] also called *gandharp*. The duties assigned to him are to inquire about the specific *raga*, the type of music and the type of dance the Master of the Assembly desires to have, and to tell the above mentioned group [of musicians and dancers]. In the course of song and dance when any tonal flourish or a beautiful dance-figure is accomplished, he approves it and specifies [what has been performed]. He is expected to know everything about all forms of song and all figures of dance.

Now let us come back to the excerpt of *Padmāvatī* quoted before. The poet says he will highlight some topics related to *sangita*, and in the verses that immediately follow he provides a detailed exposition of technical features related to the subject. The first thing he mentions is the organisation of a performance with its inaugural benediction and the invocation of Ganesha and other deities. He also indicates that the name of the musical mode should be pronounced (*rāga ucāriyā*) and the various things performed described by their name (*yateka sādhanā hena kahi nāma laiyā*).[54] One cannot fail to recognise here the figure of the *gandharp* defined in the fourteenth-century Persian treatise from Gujarat. This is not an isolated case: Alaol does a similar exposition regarding *sangita* in *Saptapaykara*. There again he uses the pretext of a dance performance in the narrated story to display his mastery of the subject and fulfill his function of *gandharp*.[55]

## Conclusion

Alaol's care in displaying his knowledge on *sangita* shows that the topic was an unavoidable part of the courtly culture of his time. In this essay I have argued that thanks to the context in which Alaol's poems were performed, the paradigm of performance and composition of his texts extended simultaneously towards greater textuality and increased attention to the lyrical parts. One of the consequences of this move was the insertion of scholarly comments by the author. The author acted as an intermediary between the audience and the text performed. This

53 The term *mu'arrif* usually means "herald". He was the individual in charge of announcing anyone who would come to the Sultan's court. See the article 'Mu'arrif', in Dihkhuda (2002).

54 Alaol (2002), p. 300.

55 Alaol (2007), pp. 252-53.

feature is salient in the scenes of *sangita* performances that occur inside the story Alaol is rendering into Bengali.

In the broader historical and cultural context, this interest in the technical aspects of *sangita* in a court milieu promoting vernacular literature was not restricted to Mrauk-U. Two leads have to be further explored in order to understand the cultural atmosphere in which this literature came into existence. The first one is the Jaunpur and Indo-Afghan courtly cultures of the fifteenth and sixteenth centuries. More than any other branch of Sanskrit knowledge, *sangita* was actively investigated by the scholars of this period who worked at royal and secondary courts. The *Lahjāt-i Sikandarshāhī* is a good example of the thorough scholarship of Indo-Persian authors in the field of lyrical arts. Similarly, Jaunpur became a major centre of patronage during this period. In the Awadhi romances from the same eastern region that were composed from the early sixteenth century, like Qutban's *Mirigāvatī* (1503), performance was an aspect of the poetry itself, and the authors frequently included passages in which the technical vocabulary of *sangita* was used.[56] Alaol testifies to the continuity and transformations of this literary tradition. He went further into the explanatory details and he cited his sources. The treatises mentioned by the Bengali poet of Mrauk-U are extremely relevant in the context of the courtly culture of the regional kingdoms of Northeast India. To mention just a few examples, Shubhankara was quoted very often by authors in Mithila, Nepal, Assam, and Bengal, and Narada's *Pañcamasārasaṃhitā* is said to have played a central role in the formation of the lyrical tradition at the court of Manipur in the late eighteenth century. The king of Orissa Sarvajna Jagannatha Narayanadeva (r.1648-1664) also quoted from both treatises in his *Saṅgītanārāyaṇa*.[57]

The next step will be to observe how the poets put the content of these technical texts into practice and combined the Sanskrit ethos with their regional tradition. The technical literature circulating in the regional courts was very specific, and it is possible to identify this corpus with great accuracy. In Alaol's case we saw how one can describe the pattern

56 See Miner in the present volume.

57 See Emie te Nijenhuis's comments in the introduction of Delvoye et al., eds. (2010), p. 40.

of composition of his poems with the technical vocabulary provided by the handbooks available to him. The complex relation between the content of the Sanskrit treatises, the fragments of Alaol's own technical texts, and the information provided by his poem still await further study.

# 17. The Musical Lives of Texts: Rhythms and Communal Relationships among the Nizamis and Some of Their Neighbours in South and West Asia[1]

*Richard K. Wolf*

*The audiovisual examples listed by number in this article may be heard and viewed on the author's website: richardkwolf.com/audio-visual.*

Every year during the first month of the Muslim calendar, members of a variety of religious communities—Hindu and Muslim—strike drums, sound trumpets, recite poetry, and participate in grand processions to observe Muharram at the shrine of the sufi saint Hazrat Nizamuddin Auliya in Delhi. These practices serve as a useful point of departure for exploring the artistic, symbolic, emotional, and political relationships between South Asian Shi'i and Sunni communities via the textual, musical, and ritual practices these two communities share. This article

1 This article draws from research presented in a different form in chapter 9 of *The Voice in the Drum: Music, Language and Emotion in Islamicate South Asia* (Urbana: University of Illinois Press, 2014). I conducted this field research initially in India and Pakistan over 27 months, 1996-99. Comments on Karachi use the ethnographic present of 1997. Information on Delhi was gleaned in 1998-99 and 2009-10. Shi'i will be used adjectivally while Shi'a will be used for the people themselves. Because most of the Muharram rituals are not conducted in Delhi at the Nizamuddin shrine itself, but rather in the neighbourhood and along processions routes, and because there is a parallel tradition celebrated in Karachi, I refer in this article to Muharram practices in the "Nizamuddin tradition" rather than at the shrine.

 http://dx.doi.org/10.11647/OBP.0062.17

explores a little-known facet of drumming in South Asia—its potential to communicate texts. In the context of the Nizamuddin tradition, participants share a knowledge of these texts to varying extents. The following case study of the Nizamuddin tradition in Delhi and Karachi, together with Iranian and Indo-Caribbean examples, suggests more generally that instrumental iterations of poetic and other texts may play a role in the way such texts have been passed down and transformed over time. These kinds of possible transformation ought to figure in our modern understandings of written texts that once lived in performance.

Muharram commemorates the battle of Karbala in 680 CE in which the henchmen of the Ummayyad Caliphate in Damascas mercilessly slaughtered Husain (the grandson of the Prophet Muhammad) and his small band of followers. Although Shi'as are known for emphasising mournful aspects of Muharram, the emotional texture of the occasion is more complex in diverse public gatherings such as those associated with the Nizamuddin tradition. For one thing, since Husain died upholding the principles of Islam and love for the Prophet's family, his death is also considered a moral victory. Shi'as and Sunnis generally share this sense, but those associated with the Nizamuddin tradition go so far as to celebrate Muharram as an *'urs*, the death day of a saint. Despite these nuances, differences between Shi'i and Sunni approaches to Muharram tend to be stereotyped. Shi'i Muharram practices are associated with mourning and those of Sunnis, with celebration. These differences are expressed in the communities' views on self-mortification, drumming, and many other matters. Some Shi'as object to drumming, especially on the shallow, bowl-shaped *tasha* (*tāshā*), citing its self-evidently celebratory qualities. The *tasha*'s crisp timbre, lack of bass resonance, and associated technique of rapid-fire strokes render it unsuitable for connoting seriousness or gravity. Views on the emotional and symbolic meanings of drumming vary according to region, however, and have been undergoing revision as relationships among Shi'as and Sunnis have continued to fluctuate.[2] Drumming and poetry are worthy of close consideration not only because of their mutual relations, but also because of the ways that they lend emotional ambiguity and nuance to Muharram observances.

2 Richard K. Wolf, 'Embodiment and Ambivalence: Emotion in South Asian Muharram Drumming', *Yearbook for Traditional Music* 32 (2000), 81-116.

In this chapter I explore the ways in which Shi'i, Sunni, and Hindu communities assign meaning to drumming and understand relationships to one another through co-participating in Muharram. How, I ask, is knowledge of instrument-associated texts linked to the social formations that transmit and preserve such knowledge? Reading the drum patterns closely, I create a typology for understanding drumming in the rituals of the Nizamuddin tradition and in the larger context of South and West Asia, where instruments articulate texts in a variety of ways. The verbally explicit dimensions of meaning in certain instrumental traditions distinguish those traditions from their more abstract (non-texted) counterparts and also create a field of potential insider knowledge to which listeners have differential access.

This chapter is organised in three parts. The first provides background on text-music relationships and those who perceive them in South and West Asia, the saint Nizamuddin Auliya and his followers in Delhi and Karachi, and basic principles of Shi'i and sufi devotionalism. The second part approaches Muharram ethnographically, focusing mainly on the Nizamuddin Muharram traditions of Delhi and Karachi and secondarily on Indo-Trinidadian observances in which failures in textual memory dissolve any specific links that might have existed between drummed and verbal phrases. Part III provides technical analyses of text-music relationships using parallel examples from the Nizamuddin tradition and Iran.

## Part I. Song, Text, and Instrument: Performing and Hearing

In South, Southeast, and West Asia, studies from several disciplines have explored how metre, vowel length, word division, and other textual matters constrain declaimed and sung performances of texts,[3] and how

3 Regula Burkhardt Qureshi, 'Tarannum: The Chanting of Urdu Poetry', *Ethnomusicology* 13.3 (1969), 425-68; 'Indo-Muslim Religious Music: An Overview', *Asian Music* 3.2 (1972), 15-22; 'Islamic Music in an Indian Environment: The Shi'a Majlis', *Ethnomusicology* 25.1 (1981), 41-71; 'Musical Gesture and Extra-Musical Meaning: Words and Music in the Urdu Ghazal', *Journal of the American Musicological Society* 43.3 (1990), 457-97; *Sufi Music in India and Pakistan* (Chicago: University of Chicago Press, 1995); also Gen'ichi Tsuge, 'Rhythmic Aspects of the Avaz in Persian Music', *Ethnomusicology* 14.2 (1970), 205-28; Owen Wright, *Touraj Kiaras and Persian Classical Music: An Analytical Perspective* (Aldershot: Ashgate, 2009); Harold Powers, 'Verbal

musical factors may shape the composition or forms of poems and narratives.[4] Less attention has been devoted to the rendering of texts on musical instruments, perhaps because South Asian languages are rarely associated with speech surrogates.[5] Although using instruments to mimic specific messages does not depend on fully developed speech-surrogate systems, the question of what an instrument most directly imitates is relevant both to the study of speech surrogates and to the use of instruments to articulate texts.

The story of how texts are articulated on instruments can be usefully directed to explore social implications, viz, what people are saying about themselves by making claims of textuality. The flip side of the poietic process of making instruments sound textual is the esthesic process of listeners making something out of what they hear.[6] Artful manipulation of texts in performance invites multiple kinds of possible reception: hearing the (musical) surface with little or no concern for semantic meaning; hearing with the general knowledge of text beyond the surface; and hearing with the knowledge of one or more specific texts. These different kinds of hearing might index the membership of listeners or performers in one or more social groups that are defined by such distinguishers as education, class, caste (*jati* or *qaum*), and placement in a religious hierarchy.

---

and Musical Rhythms in Dikshitar and Tyagaraja', Dr Raghavan Shastyabdhapurthy Endowed Lecture, Music Academy (Madras), Chennai, December 2001; Benjamin Brinner, *Music in Central Java: Experiencing Music, Expressing Culture* (New York: Oxford University Press, 2008), p. 76 ff; Richard Wallis, 'The Voice as a Mode of Cultural Expression in Bali' (PhD dissertation, University of Michigan, 1979), p. 140ff. and passim.

4 Lynn Ate, 'Literary Metre versus Rhythmic Beat in Tamil Alvar Literature', *Journal of South Asian Literature* 19.2 (1984): 1-7; Rupert Snell, *The Eighty-four Hymns of Hita Harivaṃśa: An Edition of the Caurāsī Pada* (Delhi: Motilal Banarsidass, 1991); John Smith, *The Epic of Pābūjī: A Study, Transcription and Translation* (Cambridge: Cambridge University Press, 1991), p. 30ff.

5 Speech surrogates are systems for encoding and transmitting speech using instruments, humming, whistling, and so forth. If scholarly treatment in Thomas A. Sebeok and Donna Jean Umiker-Sebeok, eds., *Speech Surrogates: Drum and Whistle Systems* (The Hague: Mouton, 1976) is any indication, Africa holds by far the largest range of speech surrogates (Oceania and the Americas run a distant second). South Asia was represented in that volume only in terms of the whistled languages of some Tibeto-Burman languages in Nepal; Sebeok and Sebeok (1976), pp. 993-1022.

6 On poiesis and esthesis, see Jean-Jacques Nattiez, *Music and Discourse: Towards a Semiology of Music*, trans. by Carolyn Abbate (Princeton: Princeton University Press, 1990); and Jean Molino, 'Fait musical et sémiologue de la musique', *Musique en Jeu* 17 (1975), 37-62.

Views on drumming may stem from the identity of participants as Sunnis, Shi'as, or Hindus and from their changing experiences after migrating across land or sea. Populations relocated, mainly from North India, for a variety of political and economic reasons. Many Muslims resettled in Pakistan (and Hindus in India) at the time of the Partition of India and Pakistan in 1947. Followers of Nizamuddin Auliya, who were among these Muslim resettlers, set up a system of ritual and musical practices in Karachi reproducing that of their kin in Delhi. Other Indians of many backgrounds had migrated to the British West Indies in the nineteenth century, at which time labourers were in high demand after the recent abolition of slavery. As these displaced populations established themselves culturally and socially in their new surroundings, their musical and ritual traditions developed and changed in ways that further complicated the relationships between drumming traditions and texts. Sometimes only the vaguest memories held on to traces of these texts.[7]

## Nizamis: Background

The Chishti sufi order is significant in South Asia for many reasons, including its support for music as a legitimate means for seeking spiritual closeness to god. Nizamuddin Auliya (1236-1325), the fourth in a line of succession of sufi saints in this order in South Asia, was known to have defended spiritual listening (*sama'*) against periodic attacks by orthodox theologians. Nizamuddin's shrine in New Delhi is currently the site of a range of celebrations, including the *'urses* of Nizamuddin and of Amir Khusrau. Nizamuddin's spiritual descendants form a *khandan* (lineage) consisting of a number of families, many of whom take the last name Nizami. (For simplicity here, Sunni Muslims formally affiliated with the shrine are being collectively termed Nizamis even if they do not use the surname.) Those in the upper rungs of the shrine's hierarchy are known as *pirzadas*. As of 2010 two men were holding competing claims for *sajjada-nishin*, the post at the top of the hierarchy.

Because they emphasise mystical love and support musical practices, sufi orders such as the Chishtiya tend to promote social and religious

7 Frank J. Korom, *Hosay Trinidad: Muharram Performances in an Indo-Caribbean Diaspora* (Philadelphia: University of Pennsylvania Press, 2002).

inclusiveness and attract a wide variety of devotees to their celebrations. Despite this philosophical catholicism, Nizamis in Delhi were quick to identify themselves as Sunni when I began to show interest in their Muharram practices and distanced themselves from Shi'as in a somewhat defensive manner. What appears here to be a hardening of religious boundaries needs to be understood in a contemporary global climate that pits Shi'as against Sunnis. Although Shi'i-Sunni differences have always been potential sources of conflict, it is not difference per se that engenders conflict but the social and political conditions under which some differences become politically charged (for example, in Iraq and Syria in recent decades). Some of the conditions that have informed the Nizami context developed in the aftermath of Partition in Delhi and Karachi. The point to keep in mind is that Nizamis draw distinctions between themselves and Shi'as while at the same time embracing much of what Shi'as do when they observe Muharram—honour the memory of Imam Husain (the Prophet's grandson) and the virtues for which he has come to stand.

Nizamis in Delhi—but not in Karachi—are particularly uncomfortable with signs of mourning during Muharram, particularly the Shi'i practice of *matam* (*mātam*). Literally "mourning", *matam* refers either to self-mortification, ranging from gentle strikes of the hand on the breast to more energetic and wound-inflicting activities, or to drum patterns with similar connotations. The reasons Shi'as emphasise mourning and Sunnis do not stem from their respective views about the historical events Muharram commemorates.

## Muharram, Shi'ism, Sufism, and Mimesis

The gruesome conflict in Karbala grew from a disagreement about who should succeed the Prophet Muhammad when he died in 632 CE. In the 680 CE battle, the small party of Husain faced the army of the Umayyad caliph Yazid, who had demanded that Husain abdicate his right of succession. The men in Husain's party were brutally dismembered and the women, children, and the ill marched to Damascus. Shi'i practice and theology worldwide is rooted in contemplating the details of the battle's narrative and the moral implications for Muslims of remaining on Husain's side. The battle's narrative is relevant to sequences of items played on musical instruments in some Muharram ceremonies.

Even when texts are largely forgotten, the idea of performing energetic, martial drumming followed by a sombre, mournful pattern (or some other kind of contrast) is maintained wherever Muharram drumming is found, including in Trinidad. Participants usually associate these patterns with moments in the battle of Karbala.

Muslims in South Asia embrace the moral righteousness of Husain but disagree on the ways in which acknowledgement of this should form part of religious practice. Nizamis in Delhi, along with other Sunnis, object to Shi'i shedding of blood and weeping because they view the ultimate result as a victory for Islam; Shi'as, by contrast, find spiritual merit in lamenting the loss of Husain and his party and dissolving their own personal pains and sorrows in the remembrance of the more profound suffering endured at Karbala. Devout Shi'as often see themselves as distinct from those involved actively in sufism, but both Shi'ism and sufism share an emphasis on love for the Prophet and, usually, 'Ali (his nephew and son-in-law).

Spiritual presences and key religious figures, in Shi'ism and sufism, can act as intermediaries between the individual and god. Drawing oneself closer to these intermediaries often involves replicating activities undertaken by such figures in the past. In shrine-based sufism, for example, the *'urs*, or death-day observance of a saint, celebrates the metaphorical "marriage" (the literal meaning of *'urs* in Arabic) of the saint's spirit to god. The ecstasy of participants in the *'urs* replicates to some extent the ecstasy of the saint; this in turn creates an experience of proximity to the saint and by extension to god. For many Shi'as, retelling and stylised reenactment of the Karbala narrative, and responding to these with heartfelt tears, are meritorious acts that have the potential to make participants experience connectedness with the martyrs and so-called pure and flawless ones, the *ma'sumin*, who can intercede with god on their behalf. For detractors, the idea of intermediaries, whether dead saints or living spiritual guides, suggests that some humans can compete with god's divinity and amounts to heresy.

Another way of engaging with the Karbala narrative is to participate in processions that recall aspects of the battle or those who were martyred in it. Both Shi'as and Sunnis in South Asia may participate in Muharram by carrying symbolic items in procession, the most impressive of which is the *ta'ziya*. Members of both communities have made the (historically unsubstantiated) claim that practices of carrying *ta'ziyas* date back to the Turkic-Mongol ruler Timur (Tamerlane ["Timur-the-lame"], 1336-1405), whom Shi'as believe was strongly attached to the Prophet's family. According to one oft-repeated story, Husain appeared to Timur in a dream and said (in reference to Timur's lame condition), "it is not necessary that you visit my mausoleum. Make a replica of my mausoleum and visit that instead". Timur heard the voice "Husain, Husain, Husain" in his dream and now, some say, the drums of Muharram project that voice (*sada*). In the view of many modern-day South Asian Muslims, drums, *ta'ziyas*, and other *ziyarat*s and replicas (*shabih*) continue to serve the similar functions of bringing the subject closer to Husain.

The relationship of certain types of ritual action and objects to historical actions and objects—such as that between the *ta'ziya* and a real mausoleum—is paralleled in the relationship between performances on musical instruments and the texts those performances are meant to express or evoke. Both involve kinds of mimesis, acts of forging and asserting resemblance, perhaps persuading others that today's actions recapitulate or otherwise set in motion practices motivated in the past, or reminding listeners that instrumental sounds are actually words.

The fact that mimesis is not merely a display of likeness, but an active effort to make perceivers recognise similarities, beckons us to look carefully at how actors choose their models, emulate those models, and argue about the potential significance of their actions. The drum patterns called *matam* in South Asia (and *mahatam* in Trinidad), for instance, nominally refer to "mourning" in general but also, more specifically, the act of self-mortification in which (mainly) Shi'as engage as part of their piety. Both the patterns and the Shi'i bodily practices refer back to battle scenes in which fighters received blows on their bodies, but in the case of the drums, it is as if the blows were now deflected onto the drums.[8] However, in concrete situations where both Shi'as and Sunnis are present observing Muharram after their own fashions, the two versions of *matam*—drumming and body percussion—have the potential to refer to one another as well.

In the Nizami case, *matam* involves three levels of textual reference. One is the chant "Husain, Husain" that Shi'as utter while executing

8 Richard K. Wolf, 'Doubleness, *Mātam*, and Muharram Drumming in South Asia', in *Pain and its Transformation*, ed. by Sarah Coakley and Kay Kaufman Shelemay (Cambridge, MA: Harvard University Press, 2007), pp. 331-50.

*matam*; one is a poetic text that almost no one remembers; and one is a song, now played on brass band instruments. The idea of using drums to encode texts directly related to the Muharram context is common to many parts of South Asia as well as Trinidad, and related uses of musical instruments extend to the Shi'i heartland of Iran.[9]

Outside of Muharram, in sufi shrines across Pakistan, and particularly in shrines that have come to be associated with Lal Shabaz Qalandar in Sindh, *faqirs*, drummers, and shrine-goers sometimes represent the drum pattern *dhamāl* by the mnemonics *"dam-ā-dam mast qalandar, 'alī dā pahlā 'number'"* (roughly: "with each and every breath, the qalandar asserts the primacy of 'Ali"), and listeners can be heard chanting these words at Thursday-evening shrine-gatherings at the Shah Jamal shrine in Lahore and elsewhere.[10] In Iran, patterns on the *dotār* and other instruments sometimes imitate other verbal formulas, called *zekrs* (*ẕekr*), the repetitions of which are meant to focus the devotee's whole being on god (Example 1).

The relationship between Iranian *dotar* examples and the texts (involving *zekrs*) sung in conjunction with them is probably obvious to most local listeners because of the opportunity to hear the rhythms superimposed during singing and sequentially before and after verses. The same holds true for the *dhamal* pattern, because so many of those in attendance have heard *"dam-ā-dam mast qalandar"* recited during drumming sessions. Participants' knowledge of Muharram-related texts associated with musical instruments in South Asia and Trinidad, by contrast, is scant, owing to, among other things, the lack of reinforcement during performance. South Asian drummers might verbalise Muharram drum patterns as texts for the purpose of teaching them, but there is no public ritual context in which anyone recites these texts. The texts themselves, when available, are merely phrases or a few stanzas, and are

9 In the Northern Iranian province of Gilan, trumpets are used to convey verbal formulas during Muharram, and were used historically to make announcements; Mohammad Reza Darvishi, *Haft awrang: marūrī bar mūsīqī sunnatī va maḥalī Irān* (Tehran, 1370/1991). In southern Iran, elaborate drumming traditions using instruments similar to the *dhol* and *tasha* of South Asia apparently continue to be used for Muharram processions although the linguistic implications, if any, of the drum rhythms have yet to be described in print. This was reported to me by several students and colleagues in Tehran in January 2006, when I presented my work on South Asian Muharram drumming, rituals, and music at the conference on the music of Khorasan and Transoxania.

10 See Wolf (2006) and (2014).

transmitted mainly among skilled musicians or among drummers who vary in their technical abilities.

# Part II. Case Studies

Table 17.1 is a typology of text-music relationships, focusing mainly on rhythm. This typology, while grounded in the musical examples discussed in this essay, points towards more general cross-cultural possibilities. In each case study, I have taken participants' claims to textuality seriously, but also noted their varying degrees of specific textual awareness and training. Each example discussed below is keyed by number to the typology; technical details will be explored in Part III.

Table 17.1: Typology of text-musical rhythmic pattern relationships

| | |
|---|---|
| Type 1 | Very general notions or beliefs such as, "our drumming tells the story of Karbala", oft heard in India, or the notion in Torbat-e Jam that *dotar* rhythms are related to *zekrs* (Example 1). |
| Type 2 | Associations at the level of a whole rhythmic pattern indicated by such statements as, "The sequence of these patterns corresponds to such and such structural points of the narrative". |
| Type 3 | Associations at the level of a specific pattern:<br>a) Asserted but analytically opaque connection that may or may not have historical validity (*matam* example) (equivalent to Type 1 but more specific as to pattern and meaning);<br>b) Association at the level of rhythmic emphasis, i.e. *wazn* (*kalma*, example 2); giving weight to certain beats in a sequence in accordance with the way they would be spoken or chanted;<br>c) Association at the level of poetic metre, such that:<br>i. at a minimum, distinctions between long and short syllables are maintained;<br>ii. *sequences* of long and short syllables as given in a particular metre are preserved ("*ran mēn̲ jis dam*" and *rūpak tal* example; "*hū hū*" and *dotar* pattern example—examples 3 and 1 respectively);<br>iii. sequences of rhythmic patterns (or vocable patterns in vocal music) derived from the poetic metre prepare singer for verses;[11] |

11 Thanks to Stephen Blum for suggesting this possibility.

| | |
|---|---|
| Type 3 cont. | d) Association at the level of hypermetre (*dhīma*, example 4);<br>e) Association via a melody as an intermediate layer (without any necessary memory of the original text) (drummers' memories of melodies for *matam* and *dhima*, examples 5 and 6). |
| Type 4 | Deformations:<br>a) Musical patterns, not only poetic metrical conventions, may impact upon recitation;<br>b) Distinctions between long and short syllables may be obscured by the many possible values of long syllables and the positions in which such syllables appear. |

# Indo-Caribbean Drumming

Indo-Caribbean Hosay (Muharram) drumming conveys text in generalised ways which correspond to Types 1 and 2 of Table 17.1. Indo-Caribbeans migrated mainly from Uttar Pradesh and Bihar in North India beginning in the mid-nineteenth century and carried with them the knowledge to perform Muharram ceremonies. They developed new designs for *tadjas* (*ta'ziyas*) and creatively modified other objects and practices. The *tassa*, the shallow, bowl-shaped drum in Trinidad that accompanies these processions, is wider in diameter than many of its Indian counterparts, which are called *tasha* and related names. The "bass" in Trinidad is also more massive than most of the *dhols* found in India that accompany the *tasha*. The name of the occasion, too, changed from Muharram to "Hosay", after Husain.

In 1995-1996 I conducted research in New York City with a group of Indo-Trinidadian drummers called US #1. Example 7 is excerpted from my video documentation of Hosay in Manhattan. The edits highlight the contrast, oft noted by participants in South Asia, between the excitement of battle and the sober mourning over the dead: 1) upbeat drumming (battle); 2) a view of the *tadja*; 3) a slow march played just after the *tadja* begins to be disassembled (the scene of death after the battle); and 4) a change of mood signaled/cued by the speeding up of the drumming and followed by joyous dancing. Both Hindus and Muslims participated in this celebration of Hosay and the Muslim participants did not distinguish themselves along Shi'i and Sunni lines.

According to Frank Korom, the first scholar to write about the issue of drum-encoded messages among Indo-Trinidadians, drummers in

Trinidad alluded to how Hosay drumming communicates a story, in part through the large-scale sequencing of drum patterns that they call "hands". The differences between the faster and slower patterns, and between the more rapid pattern at the beginning and the dancing pattern at the end, "convey the notions of marching or journey, war, death, sorrow and lamentation, and burial".[12] So, although the messages to which these consultants referred were not at equivalent levels of analysis, most conformed to Types 1 and 2 in Table 17.1. To put the macro level structure of these intrumental performances in context, it is important to keep in mind that the sequencing of rhythmic patterns on musical instruments is often important in South, Central, and West Asia, whether or not the sequences are accorded narrative significance.

Korom's informants reported that in an earlier era participants used to sing while drummers played one of the lamentational hands. Based on this evidence Korom suggested that over the past two generations the drums may have grown more important in their communicative function, while the singing practice gradually died out. Knowledge of the associated textual traditions has not been well preserved or creatively developed. Although Trinidadian drummers and those who hear them understand the drums to communicate texts in different ways, they do not currently locate that communication at the level of the syllabic utterance (Table 17.1: 3b and c). By contrast, in traditions associated with *zikr* (or *zekr*) in many parts of the Muslim world, text and instrumental rendition may correspond quite assiduously at the micro level.

## The Nizamuddin Tradition in Delhi and Karachi

The South Asian *tasha* and *dhol* traditions from which the Indo-Caribbean *tassa* and bass traditions evolved are diverse. The Nizamuddin drumming tradition is of interest because, as in the Indo-Caribbean tradition, knowledgable participants associate drum patterns with texts.

In 1997 some *dhol* and *tasha* players belonging to the Nizami *khandan* were living in the Jacob Lines neighbourhood of Karachi (and presumably continue to do so at the time of this writing). Communication between Nizamis in Karachi and Delhi had continued since Partition: relatives

12 Korom (2003), p. 165.

would travel to and from Delhi, sometimes bringing spare drum parts and also sharing musical and other kinds of information connected with the performance of Muharram rituals. The attitudes and practices associated with the Nizamis in Jacob Lines had emerged in response both to local circumstances and to ongoing developments in Delhi.

The *dhol* player Hashim 'Ali was an unschooled floor-maker, aged about 45 in 1997. A Shi'i neighbour and friend, who will be called Nasir, participated in a conversation about the practices associated with the Nizamuddin tradition in Karachi and specifically about the participation of Shi'as—a community the Nizamis of Karachi (but not those of Delhi) specified as important to the Nizamuddin Muharram rituals.[13] Nasir and the other Shi'as who participate in the Nizamuddin rituals in Karachi will be referred to as "partners" of the Nizamis to differentiate them from the many other Shi'i or Shi'i-related groups.

Hashim described the four main items of repertoire: *kalma*, *dhima*, *matam*, and *savari*. (The order in which they are played is somewhat variable in practice and will be addressed later.) *Savari* (*savārī*, meaning "ride"), is commonly found in names of *talas* for the *tabla* and *pakhavaj* as well as for the *dhol* in Panjab, although this pattern is musically unrelated.[14] In the Muharram context, participants view *savari* as the accompaniment for a royal cavalcade with Husain as the symbolic king. Hashim indicated that the drumming, in general, provides enjoyment (*maza*) for those listening and watching the procession; more specifically it informs them that the procession is connected with Muharram. Emphasising the role of text, he said that the Nizami drummers play "only *marsiyas*, within which a *lay* [rhythmic pattern on the drums] is built" ("*ṣirf* [...] *marṣiya, us ke andar ek lay banā'ī jātī hai*"). Nasir mentioned also that Shi'as chant "Husain, Husain" continuously with the *matam* pattern (see example 10). Hashim also emphasised (and this is fairly common among Muslim Muharram drummers) that they do not play patterns associated with happy occasions. This is a symbolic distinction

13 I was not asked to preserve anyone's anonymity, but this man did not provide his name or any personal information when I asked each man present his name, education level, job, and instrument. He described himself as a "friend". Only later in the conversation, through various hints, did it become clear he was a Shi'a.

14 James Kippen, *Gurudev's Drumming Legacy: Music, Theory and Nationalism in the Mṛdaṅg aur Tabla Vādanpaddhati of Gurudev Patwardhan* (Aldershot: Ashgate, 2006); Lowell Lybarger, 'The Tabla Solo Repertoire of Pakistani Panjab: An Ethnomusicological Perspective' (PhD dissertation, University of Toronto, 2003).

of social as well as religious importance because it marks the occasion as serious and it reduces the stigma of these drummers as musicians—that is, it suggests that they are serious religious functionaries and not merely providers of entertainment.

Sunnis and Shi'as conventionally differ in their emotional involvement in Muharram. How did such participants as Hashim represent their emotional understandings of drumming? Regarding *matam*, for example, Hashim said, "people are... in a languid state (*sust kaifīyat*); they listen, deeply immersed... and many begin weeping also; they shed tears; their hearts are moved". Different Muharram patterns have different emotional implications. "[Y]ou can feel what is [different] in" ("*āp ko maḥsūs hogā ki is mẽ kyā hai*") a particular pattern by listening to it, Hashim said. Those who know the textual details can conjure up a specific image of what each pattern encodes; others, such as Hashim, feel the emotional shades as aesthetic differences in the drumming itself. Hashim's description of the "state" or "condition" of the listener differed from Shi'i and Sunni stereotypes of Sunnis as those who celebrate rather than mourn the death of Husain. He used the term *sust*, which means slow, heavy, languid, and weak, thereby drawing a connection between slowness in time, weight, and bodily condition that contrasts strongly with the lack of gravity Shi'as predicate upon Sunni Muharram drummers. It is possible that Hashim's own bodily responses to drumming were conditioned by his specialisation on the *dhol*, which, as a bass drum with less frequent attacks, would indeed carry the physical connotation of weight and slowness.

According to Hashim, Shi'as had participated in Muharram drumming to a limited extent in the past (although he was very unclear on this point); at present, he said, drummers associated with his tradition were Sunni. Shi'i partners in the area would invite Sunni drummers to perform at their Muharram observances and both communities would attend one another's functions. Nasir also reported that his Shi'i sub-community did not participate as drummers in Muharram, only as performers of *matam*. However one of their relatives, the late Vajid Khurshid 'Ali (d. 1952), was a well-known *tabla* player who performed classical drums out of individual passion (*shauq*), not out of a ritual obligation connected with his religious affiliation; he didn't play *dhol* or *tasha*. The Sunni *tasha* player Muhammad Bakhsh described the one Shi'i *ta'ziya* that used to be taken out at Nizamuddin, the Khurshid *ta'ziya*, which was presumably sponsored by Vajid Khurshid 'Ali. He said that the Nizami Sunnis would play the drums on one side of the *ta'ziya* and the special group of Shi'as associated with it would do *sīna zanī* (breast beating) on the other side. Apparently there were a few Shi'as who also played *tasha* at that time in Delhi, including one man named Ansar Husain, but this was a matter of controversy among Shi'as. Many Shi'as view it as a sin (*gunah*) to play the drums, citing stories and poetry that describe Yazid's side playing the *tabal* drum to celebrate their victory every time they slayed a member of Husain's tribe.

Nasir went on to describe their mutual commitment to this joint tradition:

> [Since coming to Karachi] this practice of playing (*silsila*) has been going on. We have maintained that chain such that, for example, their father and grandfathers have died and now their descendants have started [playing]. That which was a family (*khandani*) practice has been made to continue. In the same connection, we also call them, so that that custom (*rasm*) which is going on should continue. We tell our children that this has to be done, that anyone might die at any time so if we die you [must continue this practice].

Although the Nizamis in Delhi in 2009-2010 did not acknowledge Shi'i involvement in their Muharram practices, the content of the two communities' practices overlapped significantly. Moreover, historical evidence suggests that the interaction between the communities may have been more extensive than that to which contemporary Nizamis in Delhi have admitted or perhaps remembered. It will be useful to describe parts of the Delhi ceremonies.

## Muharram in Delhi

At the Nizamuddin shrine in Delhi, several processions take place around the Nizamuddin *basti*, including one on the seventh of Muharram in which standards (*'alams*) are carried to houses of *pirzadas*, *salamis* (salutes) performed on the drums, and *marsiyas* recited; and one on the ninth, when small *ta'ziyas*, called *mehndi*s, are taken from individual homes. The *ta'ziya* in Nizamuddin *imambara* (the shrine for remembrance of Husain, which is located near the main shrine) is also brought around the neighbourhood in some of these processions. On the tenth of Muharram, this *ta'ziya* is carried to the Karbala in Jorbagh, the destination of a number of different *ta'ziya* float processions from around the city.

One of the notable features of drumming during the Delhi processions is the role of Hindus. A professional drumming group led by a man named Mamraj is in charge of Muharram drumming. Mamraj was unaware of whether his teacher—the Muslim formerly in charge of Muharram drumming at Nizamuddin—was Sunni or Shi'a and he himself was not interested in the demarcation of religions because for him it was "all one". Mamraj said that he plays in service (*sevā*) of Nizamuddin Auliya. Mamraj's son Bharat Singh likened Muharram to Ram Lila, where for some 12 days Hindus take out floats representing scenes from Hindu mythology. In Bharat Singh's view, Hindus believe in/attend to ("*mānte haiṉ*") the floats in a manner comparable to the ways Muslims focus attention on *ta'ziyas*.

The Census of India sponsored studies on Muharram in several Indian cities, which resulted in a number of monographs.[15] The Delhi study corroborates aspects of the story of cooperation told by the Sunnis and Shi'as in Karachi. The "notional place of Karbala ground, Ali Ganj, Delhi, and adjoining dargah shah-e-mardan, showing the places of various activities connected with the performance of moharram" illustrates clearly that most of the places for "burial of tazias by Sunnis on Ashra [sic] day (10 Moharram)'" are spatially segregated from those of the "burial of tazias by Shi'ahs on Chehellum day (10 Safar) and 8 Rabi-ul Awwal". The notable exception was one Sunni *ta'ziya*—that from the Nizamuddin *imambara*.[16] The study further notes that the "division of the ground for burial of tazias by Sunnis and Shi'ahs was effected during British rule some 30 years ago"[17]—i.e. in the mid-1930s, preceding the time of Partition by more than ten years. Although some might credit colonialism with exacerbating tensions between Shi'as and Sunnis, it is likely the burial places were ultimately segregated for the same reasons processions in Karachi were made to be separate by the Pakistani government: repeated outbreaks of violence. The fact that the Nizami processions were not kept separate would suggest that in

15 See especially Government of India, *Muharram in Two Cities: Lucknow and Delhi* (Delhi: Census of India, 1961 [1965?]) (despite the publication date of this volume, the study in Delhi was carried out in May 1964); Khaja Moinuddin, *A Monograph on Muharram in Hyderabad City* (Delhi: Census of India, 1971 [1977]).

16 Government of India (1961 [1965?]), pp. 57, 78.

17 Ibid, p. 57.

the 1930s there was no reason to keep the Nizami Sunnis and Shi'as separate. Indeed the closeness of the practices, and the involvement of both communities, would have been a good reason to keep the Nizami practices unsegregated on the Shi'i side. The Census description shows the active involvement of both communities, including the Shi'i chanting of "Husain, Husain" and performance of *matam*—precisely what Nasir described in Karachi with regard to Shi'i responses to the Sunni *matam* drum pattern.[18] According to the Census study, Nizami participation in the Shi'i procession occurred at one of the prominent halting points of the procession, the Jama Masjid, where a half-hour speech was delivered by Pir Zamin Nizami Syed Bukhari:

> He said that some might be surprised that he being a Sunni, was speaking in a gathering of the Shias. But there was nothing strange in that. The political, economic and religious condition of the country demanded that the Hindus, Muslims and Sikhs of all sects share in each other's joys and sorrows. There was a special need for the Shias and Sunnis to come closer to each other as both were based on some common principles.[19]

This historical evidence from the 1960s, the spatial organisation of the Karbala, and the oral evidence from the Nizami Sunnis and their Shi'i partners in Karachi seem to militate against the contemporary view of Nizamis in Delhi that their observance of Muharram has never involved Shi'as in a significant way, and that Shi'as did not do *matam* in their presence.

## Controversies and Political Obstacles

While it is not surprising, in the contemporary global climate of tension among Islamic factions, that Sunni-Shi'i relations in Nizamuddin are not as they once were (although one should be careful not to romanticise

18 Ibid, p. 77. The Delhi Census study was divided into two sections; the first follows processions and *majlises* of Shi'as, the second, of Sunnis (primarily the Nizamis). The Shi'i section mentioned the participation of non-Shi'as in a couple of instances as well; ibid, pp. 70-72.

19 Ibid, p. 73. Pir Zamin Nizami Syed Bukhari was a leading *pirzada* at Nizamuddin dargah and the father of one of the current *sajjada-nishins*, Pir Ahmed Nizami. According to his grandson Farid Ahmed Nizami, he took a special interest in Muharram and attempted to trace the history of Nizami Muharram practices. His search took him back only about 250 years.

these past relations), it is nevertheless useful to examine how in Karachi the actors involved have reacted to negative pressure.

At the time of my interview in 1997, some Shi'i *muhajirs* not connected with the Nizamuddin tradition had begun to object to the Nizami drumming tradition. Hashim described the changes:

> We lived in India, that is, we lived side by side, the two of us. Our relationships with them were good. There was chatting; that is, everything was there. They also believed in this thing [our drumming and so forth]. They came; they came in our procession as well. We went in their processions. In this manner, I mean, these chains [*silsile*] were going on. Now, having come here, they, having come to Karachi for some time, we continued together. Approximately eight, nine years, ten years, our processions walked together. After that, a change came such that [we] became separate. Their procession goes first; I mean a lot of changes have come. Those who were there in the old days, those who were coming with us [on procession], they still hold the same [relations] with us. But some other people from other places, they have completely parted ways.

Nasir pointed out that in each era (*har daur me<u>n</u>*), opponents (*mu<u>kh</u>ālifīn*) kept coming up to block their path—meaning literally the path of the procession, but also by implication the chain or custom pursued jointly by the Nizamis and their Shi'i partners. In particular, they mentioned the interference of the Sipah-e-Sabah, a now-outlawed, militant, anti-Shi'a group, and the Imamia Students Organization, which is pro-Shi'a but opposed to drumming and other aspects of the public observances supported by the Nizamis and their Shi'i partners. They said that members of groups like these would not intervene directly on their own behalf, but would rather, in the context of an occasion in which Shi'as and Sunnis were operating together, throw a stone, or tear the *dhol*, or hit one of the drummers, and then disappear into the crowd. After incidents of this sort, Shi'as and Sunnis in this locale began to keep their observances separate.

Anti-Shi'a groups would spread propaganda that Shi'as are not Muslims, but *kafirs* (unbelievers); the association with Shi'as would rub off on the Nizamis and these religious factions would tell the Nizamis that they were committing sins (*gunah*) by playing the drums and performing other Muharram rituals. Because of these local conflicts, the community was threatened against bringing their drums outdoors to demonstrate for me in 1997—even though, technically speaking, this was within the longer sixty-day period in which Muharram is observed in South Asia. The Nizamis had brokered a fragile deal with their local opponents such that they would play in public only on limited days, so long as they did not play during *namaz* time.

Drumming was disliked by the neighbours of the Nizamis in Karachi in part for the public vision of Islam it presented, one perhaps lacking decorum and sobriety and suggesting a love of music. It also drew attention to rituals involving *ta'ziyas* and blurred the distinctions between Shi'as and Sunnis. Over the centuries Chishti sufis (who are Sunnis) have suffered criticism from many kinds of orthodox or reactionary parties. The move from Delhi to Karachi changed the position of the Nizamis from a powerful, influential and firmly rooted presence in Delhi to a relatively weaker, economically depressed minority community in Karachi—although *muhajirs* were generally better educated and wealthier than their Sindhi and Pashtun counterparts. In the competition for economic and political resources in Pakistan, different *muhajir* groups vied with one another and with these other ethnic groups. The customs the Nizamis and their Shi'i partners so valued made them especially vulnerable to attack. In 1989 the Nizami Institute in Karachi published a pamphlet written in Urdu by Sayyad 'Ali Abbas Nizami called "The Constitution of the Faith of the Nizami Family for the *'Urses* of the Great Religious People".

This fifteen page constitution, or *dastūr-e 'amal*, is framed as a response to a *fatwa* against members of the Nizami *khandan* for engaging in unauthorised religious innovations (*bida't*). Defensive responses of this kind in this family date back to the time of Nizamuddin himself. The publication of this statement in 1989 suggests the extent to which the troubles discussed by Hashim and Nasir have had an impact on the larger communities of the Nizamis and their Shi'i partners in contemporary Karachi.

Among the criticisms to which the constitution responds are those against celebrating *'urses* and listening to musical instruments (*sāz*) as part of spiritual audition (*sama'*), including *qawwali* sessions. The Nizamis are also accused of acknowledging a plurality of divinities (*shirk*), by performing rituals connected with the *ta'ziya*. The responses of this Nizami group were that their Chishti sufi order is esteemed in many lands; that the practice of observing *'urses* and listening to pure, mystical poetry (*pākīza 'arfana kalām*) constitutes worship; and that denying this reality or truth (*haqīqat*) amounts to straying from the path. They deny that rituals with *ta'ziya*, which include drumming and recitation of poetry, are religious (*mazhabī*) actions at all because, they argue, no Muslim regards the *ta'ziya* as god.[20]

The Nizami defense of rituals involving the *ta'ziya* in the *dastur-e 'amal* makes reference to both attitudes and emotions: when members of that community take the *ta'ziya* on procession they adopt an attitude of respect and create impressions (*ta'ssurāt*) of happiness (*khūshī*) and sadness (*gham*) mixed (*mile jule*);[21] this intermediate view is also widely held with regard to the proceedings as a whole and drumming in particular. The following *marsiya* (example 3) illustrates the multivalent position of drumming. It is maintained as one of the texts associated with the Nizami tradition and is associated with both a tune and the *dhima* drum pattern (see part III):

*ran me͟n jis dam ṣubḥa 'āshūrā āyā͟n hone lagī*

At the moment the morning of Ashura first dawned in the battlefield

*lashkar-e shāh-e shahīdā͟n me͟n aẕān hone lagī*

the call to prayer started amidst the army of the king of martyrs,

*yāh namāze͟n aur kamar bandī vahā͟n hone lagī*

where prayers and preparations (for battle) were taking place

*is ṭaraf tadbīr qatl-e tishnegī hone lagī*

on the other side they were scheming to slay those thirsting ones[22]

*tāl o jangī kī sadāe͟n jā sunī ma'ṣūm nē*

Then that innocent (Husain) stood listening
to the sound of drums and battle

*tā lagī talvār bhī ḥaidar ka qabzā cūmne.*

until the swords themselves came close enough
to kiss the hilt of Haidar's sword (which Husain had).

(translation by Amy Bard)

20 Sayyid 'Ali Abbas Nizami, *Khāndān-e Niẓāmī kā 'aqīdah va dastūr-e 'amal: urās buzurgān-e dīn va dīgar* (Karachi: Idar-e Nizami, 1989).

21 Nizami (1989), p. 3.

22 Thirsty literally because of being blocked from getting water from the Euphrates, and thirsty metaphorically for battle, martyrdom, etc.

# Part III. Text-Music Relationships

Performers in Trinidad, and the best among them in India and Pakistan, play the *dhol* and *tasha* together in three distinct rhythmic strata: an ostinato pattern or a returning riff on the *dhol*, a duple or triple ostinato pattern on one or more *tashas*, and a rotating improvisatory part on *tasha*. The *dhol* part in general defines an item of *dhol-tasha* repertoire. In the Nizami tradition the *dhol* pattern holds what performers regard as the tune (*naghma*) and outlines texts. In addition to recapitulating the sound of Husain's voice that legendarily issued from the drums in Timur's time, it is also said to take the burden off *marsiya* reciters during the arduous days of ritual observance.

The following analysis shows how Nizami drum patterns in Karachi and Delhi relate to the poetic metre and stress patterns of verbal phrases said to underlie those drum patterns. Considering examples of chanted, sung, and instrumentally performed *zekr* from Iran provides a broader context for understanding the abstraction that takes place in moving from language to instrumental performance. In undertaking this analysis, I assume that there is a logic to Nizami claims that specific texts lie behind their drum patterns, even though many of the performers themselves have difficulty in articulating the mechanics of the system. It is also important to recognise that claims of textuality are claims to contextually relevant meaning. Such claims deflect possible criticisms of Muharram drumming as a form of music by suggesting that it communicates texts with religious significance. These texts, in the Nizamuddin drumming traditions of Delhi and/or Karachi consist of (a) two poems, a *marsiya* for *dhima* and a *salam* for *matam*; (b) the Muslim statement of faith, called the *kalma*, which serves as a returning phrase on the *dhol*; (c) a couplet whose recitation overlays the *kalma*; (d) the words "Husain, Husain" which accompany the performance of *matam*; (e) the words to a song played on brass instruments along with *matam/savari*; (f) and the words (as yet undetermined) to an alternate tune hummed by Mamraj as the underlying pattern for *dhima* (example 6). In what follows I will examine the textual implications of each repertorial item. The method of connecting text to drum pattern varies somewhat from pattern to pattern and there are intriguing ambiguities. Nevertheless, a general logic related to stress and syllable length pervades the whole.

Muhammad Bakhsh (Karachi) provided one of the most important clues to the textual basis of drumming when he said that the *dhol* stick (*cob*) falls (*paṛegī*) in the places of words. This does not mean the *dhol* stroke corresponds to each word. Rather the *dhol* indexes emphasised words—words given stress in recitation and/or words that have implied stress in the metre. The *tasha*, by contrast, keeps track of the intervening *mātras* (counts) and sometimes the words.

*Savari* is a faster version of *matam* and is based on the same text. The idea of building speed and intensity is intrinsic to this repertoire. According to Sarir Ahmed Nizami and Muhammad Bakhsh, the sequence begins with the *dhima* pattern, which is also very slow (the word itself means "slow"), followed by *matam*, *savari*, and optionally *kalma*. In practice (in Delhi at least), the order of performance depends more on the stopping and starting of the procession and the choices made by the drummers than on any fixed order.

The following describes the basic textual and contextual features of the four main pieces of repertoire, *kalma, dhima, matam/savari*, and then analyzes each of them along with their related secondary texts. The contextual discussion of *matam* and *savari* is followed directly by a technical analysis of poetic and other chanted texts, breast striking and drum strokes. This analysis relies on several conjectures about how the poetry is iterated on the drums. Principally, long syllables in the metre become bass strokes on the drum and short syllables are articulated as higher-pitched rim strokes. Following the analysis of *matam/savari* is a discussion of the distinction between metre (e.g. in the *'aruz* system) and weight or emphasis in the verbal performance of a text more generally. Musical renditions may draw from or emphasise aspects of poetic metre and/or weight, which may or may not differ significantly. To illustrate this idea, I return to examine the *kalma* more closely. Although it has metrical implications, the *kalma* is not in a particular poetic metre. The relationship of the *kalma* text to the drum pattern is readily apparent to anyone who hears it. Analytically, it is possible to speak of this relationship in terms of a hypermetre. This idea of hypermetre proves useful for analyzing the *dhima* pattern, whose relationship to its poetic text is not obvious. Finally I put the Nizami case study in a broader framework, with a brief excursion to Eastern Iran, suggesting that many of the examples discussed here may be fruitfully examined in terms of what Stephen Blum terms "rhythmic templates".[23]

## *Kalma*

*Kalma* (also called the *shahada*) is the Muslim declaration of the unity of god and the prophethood of Muhammad: "*lā illāha illa'llāh muḥammadur rasūl 'allāh*". In the Nizami context, musicians rather than ritual needs dictate when to play the *kalma* and for how long; it is not tied thematically to Muharram. According to Muhammad Bakhsh, drummers associated with Nizamuddin invented the *kalma* pattern to pass the time, for enjoyment (*shauq*) when they get "fed up" (*z̲ehn bhar jātā hai*). It provides a change of pace from playing the other patterns incessantly. Versions of this text are widespread in sufi *zikr*s and will be considered in Iranian contexts below. The Nizamis in Karachi (but not in Delhi) said that a second pattern, with its own text, is superimposed over the *kalma*. That pattern is called *'Alī kī ẓarben̲*, or the "strikes of 'Ali", the idea being that beating the drums constitutes calling out the name of 'Ali.

## *Dhima*

*Dhima* is played in open areas at moments when processioners can stand around and listen, thoughtfully. A single line from a *marsiya* is said to underlie *dhima* in rhythm and narrative import:

> *āj ṣughrā yūn̲ madīne men̲ hain̲ rotī bhar ke nain.*
>
> Today Sughra cries in Medina like this with eyes full of tears.

According to the performers, this drum pattern is supposed to give the effect/impression (*ta'ssur*) of the day in which Sughra, Husain's daughter, received the news of her father's martyrdom. Being ill, she had been left in Medina when her family traveled to Karbala. The *marsiya* associated with *dhima* continues with additional lines and stanzas, some of which were quoted earlier in connection with "drums and war" (*tal o jang*) on

23 M.A. Khalilian and Stephen Blum, 'Musical Ontology of the Naqhsbandi Order in Eastern Iran', unpublished paper (Society for Ethnomusicology Annual Meeting: 2007).

the day of battle. This scene is a good example of the subtle emotional modalities brought into play in Muharram rituals. The emotional effect of the battle, with its immediacy and bloodiness (the moment emphasised in the earlier quoted lines), is distinct from the shock, horror, and pain of loved ones when they receive word of the events at Karbala (the moment emphasised in the key line about Sughra).

## *Matam* and *Savari*

S.A. Nizami sang the following line of poetry in *salam* style and identified it as the text underlying both the *matam* and *savari* patterns (slower and faster versions of the same pattern respectively).[24]

> *jab Fāṭima firdaus se kahtī hu'ī ā'īn̲ maẓlūm Ḥusainā*
>
> When Fatima came from paradise saying "Oppressed Husain"

The words "oppressed Husain" (*maẓlūm Ḥusainā*) serve as a refrain in this poem, so if one continues to examine the next line, one encounters what Fatima actually "says" in this poem, namely, "because of your [Husain's] dying, all I [Fatima] had invested as a mother was plundered". Understanding that "oppressed Husain" is a refrain is important in interpreting the scansion and its drummed analogue.

The impression conveyed in this drum pattern is of Fatima, the mother of Husain, as a woman mourning the loss of her child. The image links this particular tone of mourning, which mixes love and loss, with the call to fight oppression—a universalist message that has been taken up beyond the confines of Muslims in South Asia. The link between the named item *matam*, the Shi'i action of breast beating, and the meanings behind *matam*, are made poetically concrete through reference to this text.

A second text is also associated with *matam* via the tune the brass instruments play in procession:

> *Karbalā men̲ mehndī voh, kar ga'ī savārī vakṛi ab bajāo Ḥusain kā mātam*
>
> That *mehndī* in Karbala has been completed, the procession is extraordinary; now play the *matam* of Husain.[25]

---

24 It is technically a *salam*, although participants called it *marsiya*.

25 *Mehndi* is henna and is traditionally applied as part of wedding celebrations.

This song describes the process of performing Muharram rituals and calls attention to spectacular and colourful features of the Nizami observance: the *mehndi* rituals, the procession (*savari*), and the *matam* drum pattern. It seems significant that both *savari* and *matam* are mentioned in a song that is associated with drum patterns of those very names.

Moving on to a more detailed consideration, *matam* and *savari* drum patterns are logically linked to both texts: both are the same number of beats, although they do not begin in exactly the same place. In "*jab Fāṭima*", the long ( – ) and short ( ⌣ ) syllables can be projected onto the resonant bass strokes and short-duration rim strokes of the *dhol* respectively. Each syllable is rendered on the drum with an equal duration, with differences in timbre and decay distinguishing long from short syllables. When this text is recited musically in *salam* style, however, little of its surface rhythm can be heard on the drums. Instead, the sung version sounds almost as if the poetry scanned – – ⌣ – /– – ⌣ – /– – ⌣ – / – – (– – ⌣ ⌣ – – ); i.e. every fourth syllable in the first twelve gets a melodic extension which pulls against the scansion of that syllable (which is short). S.A. Nizami's recognition of this apparent mismatch was implied by his explanation that, when the text is performed on the drums, it is rendered "quickly" (*jalad*; his pronunciation). The rhythmic patterning of the sung version is reconfigured to flatten out the syllabic durations, however, and not merely to speed them up proportionally.

The brass band song (which does not follow the *'aruz* metrical system) provides a better analogue of the surface rhythm, with the text as sung (example 8) providing primary and secondary accents in logical positions within the drumming pattern. Table 17.2 shows how "*jab Fāṭima*" correlates with the poetic metre, bass and rim strokes on the *dhol*, right and left hand strokes of the *tasha* ostinato (not the improvisation), *matam* strikes on the chest, the chanting of "Husain, Husain", and the text of the song associated with the brass band tune. The only text actually uttered during a performance, and only in Karachi (as of 1997), is "Husain, Husain". Each column of the table receives a count, logically grouped into fours based on the drum strokes. The doubled column

According to the lore of the Karbala battle, Husain's nephew Qasim was married to Husain's daughter Fatima Kubra on the battlefield just as Qasim was going off to battle (this fulfilled a promise of Husain to his brother Hasan). The *mehndi* ceremony is celebrated on the 7th of Muharram in some areas and, moreover, the small *ta'ziyas* carried in the Nizami neighbourhood are called *mehndis*.

marked "pause?" is a suggestion of how to account theoretically for the projection of the – – ˘ ˘ foot continuously from the main text of the poem into the refrain (which does not figure into the scansion). The first four syllables of the text provide a template for the entire drum pattern (Centre Centre Rim Rim on the *dhol*).

Table 17.2.

| | | | | | | | | | | | | | | | | | | | | | | |
|---|---|---|---|---|---|---|---|---|---|---|---|---|---|---|---|---|---|---|---|---|---|---|
| jab | fā | ṭi | ma | fir | dau | s | se | kah | tī | hu | 'ī | ā | 'īṉ | (pause?) | | maẓ | lū | m | ḥu | sai | nā | |
| – | – | ˘ | ˘ | – | – | ˘ | ˘ | – | – | ˘ | ˘ | – | – | (˘ ˘) | | – | – | ˘ | ˘ | – | – | |
| C | C | R | R | C | C | R | R | C | C | R | R | C | C | R | R | C | C | R | R | C | C | |
| rl | r. | rl | r. | rl | r. | rl | r. | rl | r. | rl | r. | rl | r. | rl | r. | rl | r. | rl | r. | rl | r. | |
| x | x | x | x | x | x | x | x | x | x | x | x | x | x | x | x | x | x | x | x | x | x | |
| .hss | .hss | .hss | .hss | .hss | .hss | .hss | .hss | .hss | .hss | .hss | .hss | .hss | .hss | .hss | .hss | .hss | .hss | .hss | .hss | .hss | .hss | |
| | **kar.** | ba | *lā* | meṉ | **mehn** | dī | *voh* | | **kar** | ga'ī sa | *vā* | ri | **va** | kṛi | | ab ba | **jāo** | hu | *sain* | kā | **mā** | tam |

| | |
|---|---|
| Row 1 | 1st line of *marsiya* for *matam* pattern according to S.A. Nizami (example 9); |
| Row 2 | Scansion of *marsiyas* (also taking into account the second line of the poem, provided by Ghulam Hasnain Nizami), with an added 2 short/ silent syllables between main poem and refrain "*maẓlūm Ḥusainā;*" |
| Row 3 | From demo of *savari*, June 8, 1997 (example 10): *Dhol* pattern by stick (*cob*) in right hand (left hand plays centre with bare hand bisecting each stick stroke). C = Centre, resonant stroke; R = Rim stroke; |
| Row 4 | From demo of *savari*, June 8, 1997: *Tasha* ostinato pattern; r = right hand; l = left hand; |
| Row 5 | From demo of *savari*: *sīna zanī* (breast beating): strikes on chest; |
| Row 6 | From demo of *savari*: chanting of Husain (not continuous); h = hu (almost silent) ss = sain (loud for two pulses); |
| Row 7 | From interview with Mamraj (example 8): text to song played on brass instruments, with primary accents bolded and secondary accents in italics. |

# *Wazn*, *'Aruz*, and Other Bases for Text-Music Relationships

The manner in which the drums follow the text in the Nizami tradition can be understood in terms that are also relevant to other instrumental and vocal treatments of texts. They may reproduce the general rhythmic feel, or *wazn* ("weight" or "measure"), of the text (Table 17.1: 3b); closely approximate a more specific pattern of literary metre, such as the

Perso-Arabic *'aruz* or the *matra*-based metres of Hindi (Table 17.1: 3c); and they may articulate a hypermetre, a metre abstracted from points of emphasis in the performance of a text (Table 17.1: 3d). In some cases, agogic stress is transformed into dynamic stress (i.e. length is translated into loudness on an instrument). Instrumental renditions may follow the groove of a melody that carries or once carried text (Table 17.1: 3e); or it may evoke text in spirit only, perhaps having once held a more analytically specifiable relationship (Table 17.1: 1 and 2). Many listeners who have been told a pattern is connected with a text do not know how to hear the connection.

Sometimes the instrumental rendition does more than one thing at the same time, as in the several examples which are associated with more than one text. Collectively these otherwise rather simple patterns involve a number of simultaneous operations: matching iterations of up to two texts, following an abstract model of the pattern (sequence of strokes separated by counts), and reacting to the cues of the lead *tasha* player.

The terms *'aruz* and *wazn* are often used interchangeably for poetic metre in languages that have adopted versions of the Arabic metric system.[26] But sometimes *wazn* can be used to describe a more general kind of emphasis or "weight"—the literal meaning of the term. For example, the *qawwali* singer Mehr 'Ali when he was in Boston in April 2008 pointed out that even poetry in so-called free metre, *azad nazm*, bore a *wazn* that he would articulate in singing *qawwali*. The reader superimposes measurement and stress to lend sense and aesthetic appeal to all poetry, whether or not it fits within a rigid system such as that of the Perso-Arabic *'aruz*. As Derek Attridge wrote of so-called free verse in English: "although verse always implies some principle of regularity of equivalence, it need not be based on the production of controlled numbers of beats by the disposition of stressed and unstressed syllables in certain syntactic and linear arrangements".[27]

26 L.P. Elwell-Sutton identifies *wazn* as the metres poets actually use, as opposed to the theoretical system of named feet in Arabic, the *buḥūr* (s. *baḥr*). By this he means, for example, the *baḥr* called *ramal*, – ᴗ – –, when actually used as a Persian metre, is combined with others (or more iterations of itself) and syllables might be omitted. In this article we come across the following metre, for example: – ᴗ – – /– ᴗ – – / – ᴗ – – /– ᴗ – . This is what Elwell-Sutton identifies as a *wazn*; *The Persian Metres* (Cambridge: Cambridge University Press, 1976), p. 42.

27 Derek Attridge, *Poetic Rhythm: An Introduction* (Cambridge: Cambridge University Press, 1995), p. 167.

The phrases *"lā illāha illa'llāh muḥammadur rasūl 'allāh"* which constitute the *kalma* do not fall within an *'aruz*-based metre, but they are durationally and dynamically patterned. In the *zekr "lā ellāhā illa'llāh"* as recorded by Stephen Blum among members of the Khaksar sufi order at a Khaneqah in Qazvin, Northwestern Iran (example 11), chanters provide equally spaced stresses on the syllables in bold: **lā** ell**ā**hā **el**la'll**ā**h.

## *Kalma*

Returning now to the *kalma* (example 2) for a closer look, the points of emphasis indicated in bold receive *cob* (stick) strokes on the *dhol*. The pattern is essentially the same as in the previous example, except that an additional stress bisects the last two (i.e. instead of the two points of emphasis in the chant "**e**lla'l**ā**h", the drummed version provides three points of emphasis, "**il la**' l**ā**h", with a stroke emphasising "**la**'" in the middle). The increased density of articulation provides energetic drive to the second half of the cycle in a manner much in keeping with Indic rhythmic organisation generally.

**lā** ill**ā**ha **illa**'ll**ā**h mu**ḥam**ma**dur** ras**ū**l **'allāh**

♩ ♩ ♪♪ ♩ ♩ ♩ ♪ ♪♩

Assigning a value of "1" for short syllables and "2" for long syllables, the rhythmic sequence would be roughly as follows ("/" indicates division between bolded letters, corresponding to divisions between drum strokes):

| | | | | | | | | | | | | | | | | |
|---|---|---|---|---|---|---|---|---|---|---|---|---|---|---|---|---|
| **lā** | il | /**lā** | ha | /**il** | /**la** 'l | /**lāh** | mu | /**ḥam** | ma | /**dur** | ra | /**sū** | /l **'al** | /**lāh** | | |
| **2** | 2 | /**2** | 1 | /**2** | /**2** | /**2** | 1 | /**2** | 1 | /**2** | 1 | /**2** | /**2** | /**2** | | |

Organised into a hypermetre of longs and shorts (with longs being units adding up to 4 or 3 and shorts being units adding up to 2), and dividing the phrase into two halves, this sequence would yield,

– – ᴗ ᴗ – , – – ᴗ ᴗ ᴗ

This is very close to the musical durations played on the drums.[28]

The *kalma* is performed in two ways: one is to insert a single iteration of the – – ᵕ ᵕ – phrase within the performance of another pattern. This was evident, for example, in some of the processional drumming performed at the Nizamuddin celebration of Muharram in 2009. Example 12 shows drummers in Delhi playing *savari* and then, as the drums change hands, playing *kalma* once. The other way is for performers to use this phrase as a refrain that the *tasha* players cue. In such instances, performers neither repeat the *kalma* phrase continuously nor do they return to it after a consistent number of beats or cycles (example 2).

## Metrical Puzzles: The Case of *Dhima*

Whereas the analytic device of specifying a hypermetre merely formalised the emphasis one can readily hear when the *kalma* is spoken, it would be difficult to account for the relationship of the spoken or sung text of *dhima* to the drum pattern by that name without recourse to the idea of a hypermetre. Neither the *tala* nor the surface rhythm resembled the drum rhythm as it was played for me in Karachi (1997) (example 13) and Delhi (1998 and 1999) (example 4). The poetic metre of the *dhima* poem (*ramal musamman mahzuf*) features a repeating foot: – ᵕ – – / – ᵕ – – / – ᵕ – – / – ᵕ – . Unlike the *salam* rendition associated with *matam*, which didn't seem to highlight the metrical conventions in the poetry, the tune for *dhima* follows it closely. The vocal renditions (examples 3, 14, 15) fit into the framework of the Hindustani *rūpak tāl* of seven counts. Textually, the poetic metre fits the musical rhythm (at the beginning of the sung version, but not later, where the syllables are more drawn out) by mapping short syllables onto one count and long syllables onto two counts.[29] The rhythm is not metronomic, however, and it is not clear

---

28 The extension of the final syllable "lāh" into a hypermetric "long" makes sense because it appears at the end of the phrase. Note the fourth unit in the first phrase, "lal", is only a hypermetric "short" because it is pronounced as a contraction. The way it is spelled in Arabic, *lā 'al*, would take more time to pronounce and would scan as 2 + 2.

29 Because of its 7 counts, *rupak* is an obvious choice for setting this poetic metre in the Hindustani *tal* system, but it is not the only possibility. Regula Qureshi provides examples of *qawwali* renditions of a *ramal* metre variant set to an 8 beat musical metre as well as one set to *rupak* (1995, 24 and 29).

whether each line should be analyzed in isolation, or whether a flexible metric framework is meant to hold continuously throughout.

**Rupak tal**: basic *theka*

0 = *k̲h̲ālī*, "empty" or section indicated by a hand wave
\+ = *tālī* (or *bharī*, "filled"), hand clap

| | | | | | | | | | |
|---|---|---|---|---|---|---|---|---|---|
| 0 | | | | + | | | | | |
| I | tin | tin | na | I | dhi | na | I | dhi | na |
| | 1 | 2 | 3 | | 4 | 5 | | 6 | 7 |

The distinctive feature in *dhima* is supposed to be the sequence of emphasised *dhol* strokes. In my first recording (example 13), Hashim and other junior drummers in Karachi performed a version of *dhima* that lacked clear periodicity. The number of beats separating the first 9 *dhol* strokes were 7, 7, 7, 5, 5, 6, 5, and 5. On a return visit, two senior drummers who had emigrated from India led the performance and the pattern was more regular (example 16), although technically not skillful. Each set of three *dhol* strokes fell into a pattern of 3 + 4 + 7 beats which was isomorphic with the number of counts in the *tala*. But *tala* alone didn't help me understand why the 7 was consistently broken up into 3 + 4. When I traveled to Delhi and recorded Mamraj's professional ensemble, they proved to be virtuosic and highly knowledgable regarding nearly all of their extensive repertoire. However, when they played *dhima* they too displayed inconsistency (example 4). Their *dhol* strokes were separated by the following number beats in sequence: 6, 4, 4, 4, 4, 8, followed by 8s through to the end. In considering all of these patterns, I thought that all the musicians had simply lost the knowledge to perform *dhima* correctly. Perhaps the text S.A. Nizami had cited, I thought, was a red herring.

However, in 2009 I had the opportunity to interview and videotape Ghulam Hasnain Nizami, a *pirzada* and an acknowledged master of the Nizamuddin drum tradition in Delhi. He sang the very same text that S.A. Nizami had demonstrated in Karachi and he showed me precisely where the *dhol* beats should fall in relation to the text (example 15). When I watched him perform the *dhol* while Mamraj played the *tasha* and the other players followed suit, I observed that the sequence of beats was again inconsistent (although the 3 + 4 + 7 pattern was evident in many of the repetitions) (example 17). Yet the surety with which he had shown me the way the *dhol* strokes were supposed to fall led me to seek an explanation that did not rely on the drummers holding a pattern with a consistent number of beats. Indeed I found that the *dhol* strokes are consistent at a hypermetric level. They articulate relations of short, long, and prolonged, after the syllables *yūn̲* (short, 7 units), *men̲* (long, 10 units), and *nain* (prolonged, 11 units), where the "units" are the syllable values of 1 (short) or 2 (long) added together.

**Dhima:** Hypermetre, metre, stressed syllables, and *dhol* strokes.

| | | | | | | | |
|---|---|---|---|---|---|---|---|
| | | short | | long | | | prolonged |
| Hyper metre: | | ᵕ (7) | | _ (10) | | | __ (11) |
| Poetic metre: | _ᵕ _ _ | /_ | ᵕ _ _ | /_ | ᵕ _ _ | /_ ᵕ | _(_)* |
| Stressed syllables: | *āj ṣughrā* | **yūn̲** | *madīne* | **men̲** | *hain̲ rotī* | *bhar ke* | **nain** |

The final syllable "nain" is longer than the penultimate stressed syllable "men̲" because the melodic rendition fills out the seven-count duration as if the final foot were – ᵕ – – and includes the pause provided in the sung rendition. The parenthetical numbers indicate quantifications of poetic meter where ᵕ = 1 and – = 2. The sequence of durations 7-10-11 corresponds to short-long- prolonged or ᵕ – —.

*(pause at line end)

Although this analysis rests on a number of assumptions,[30] it does account for the relative placement of the three *dhol* strokes in relation

30 My suggestion that the hypermetre of the text has been carried over on the drums is based on two assumptions. One is that the drummer (G.H. Nizami) is reciting the text in his head, somewhat flexibly so that the subdivisions between *ḍhol* strokes aren't exactly the same each cycle but the proportions are retained; the other is that the poetic metre retains a presence in the "mental" version that overrides the durations in the melody. The (musical) metric ambiguity of the singing complicates this analysis. A particular issue concerns the end of the third poetic foot, "*rotī*". "Tī" gets extended in such a way that, if one holds a strict seven-count *tala* like *rupak* during the melisma, the syllable *nain* in the last foot would line up with the *sam* (first beat) of the *tala*. If one allowed for extensive elasticity in the musical metre, corresponding to the poetic metre, *nain* would fall on the fourth count (shown in lines 3-4). Hearing *nain* on the *sam* would not be problematic—indeed one feels the sense of metric resolution on that syllable—were it not for the fact that the next line of text starts as if *nain* had fallen on count 4. If a continuously repeating seven-count *tala* had been maintained strictly, the singer would have had to wait until the completion of the *avarta* (*tala* cycle) before repeating or continuing (shown hypothetically in lines 5-6). Unless someone

to the text. Table 17.3 displays the *dhima* text in possible rhythmic relationships with *rupak tal*.

Table 17.3: The text of *dhima* in metric relations with *rupak tal*

| 1 | 2 | 3 | 4 | 5 | 6 | 7 | 1 | 2 | 3 | 4 | 5 | 6 | 7 | 1 | 2 | 3 | 4 | 5 | 6 | 7 | 1 | 2 | 3 | 4 | 5 | 6 | 7 |
|---|---|---|---|---|---|---|---|---|---|---|---|---|---|---|---|---|---|---|---|---|---|---|---|---|---|---|---|
| ā | | j | ṣu | gh | rā | | **yūn̲** | | ma | dī | | ne | | **men̲** | | hain | ro | | tī | | bhar | | ke | **nain** | | | |
| ā | | j | ṣu | gh | rā | | **yūn̲** | | ma | dī | | ne | | **men̲** | | hain | ro | | tī | | | | | | bhar | | ke |
| nain | | | | āj | etc | | | | | | | | | | | | | | | | | | | | | | |
| ā | | j | ṣu | gh | rā | | **yūn̲** | | ma | dī | | ne | | **men̲** | | hain | ro | | tī | | | | | | bhar | | ke |
| nain | | | | | | | āj | etc | | | | | | | | | | | | | | | | | | | |

| | |
|---|---|
| Row 1 | counts of *rupak tal;* |
| Row 2 | text lined up as if one "foot" corresponded to one iteration of *tal,* with an extra "long" added in the 4th foot to make a repeating structure, yielding hypermetric relations of 7, 10, 11; |
| Rows 3-4 | approximation of how text is actually sung with *rupak tal* superimposed, which yields hypermetric relations of 7, 14, 12; |
| Rows 5-6 | possible "correction" of return to first line on *sam* of *rupak tal,* which would yield hypermetric relations of 7, 14, 14. |

# Rhythmic Templates: *Zikr* in Comparative Perspective

The idea that poetic metres can both affect and be affected by rhythmic patterns in music leads us to consider what Stephen Blum has called rhythmic templates, "conventional combination[s] of features, including possible variants and substitutions" (pers. comm., 27 April 2009). Khalilian and Blum (2007) argued that performers in Torbat-e-Jam, Iran, render the *zekr "lā ellāha el l'allāh"* using such templates, which provide metric form and serve as models upon which *dotar* players may build their rhythms. The Muharram repertoire at Nizamuddin may be fruitfully described in terms of templates as well; most are derived from either one phrase or one complete iteration of a verbal utterance. The two examples of *"lā illāha illallāh"*, one chanted (example 8) and one

composed this *soz* with the idea of a 32 count *tala,* divided 3+4+3+4+3+4+7+4, the performer seems to combine two possible interpretations of the poetic metre in relation to 7 counts. In the sung versions, neither yields a hypermetric sequence of short-long-prolonged in terms of melodic durations.

drummed (*kalma*, example 2), are defined by a single four-beat sequence. The *matam/savari* example is defined by alternating sets of two strokes on the centre and rim of the *dhol*, corresponding to the first repeating unit in the poetic metre. *Dhima* is longer and more complicated in derivation, but nevertheless represents the application of two related templates; the vocal rendition makes use of – ˘ – – and the drummed version uses ˘ – ––.

As alluded to earlier, one difference between the Muharram drum patterns and the *dotar* patterns is that the latter are used to accompany vocal iterations of the *zekrs*. Like the incantation of "*dam-ā-dam mast qalandar*" in the Shah Jamal shrine of Lahore, the presence of chants side by side with the instrumental patterns serves to reinforce the verbal meanings of the latter.

My initial comparison of the drummed *kalma* with chanting of the same material in Qazvin, Iran (example 11), drew attention to their common emphasis on the syllables in bold, **lā** *el***lā***hā* **el***la'l***lāh**, organised into four equal beats. An excerpt of a song sung by Nur Mohammad Dorrpur and accompanied on *dotar* by Zolfeqar 'Askaripur (example 18) modifies this basic text to conform with the template ˘ – – – by adding the particle "ke". "Ke" here indicates that someone is uttering the words that follow. The text "*ke lā ellāha ella'llāh muḥammad yār rasūl allāh*" serves as a refrain:

| ˘ | – | – | – | ˘ | – | – | – | ˘ | – | – | –(˘) | ˘ | – | – | – |
|---|---|---|---|---|---|---|---|---|---|---|---|---|---|---|---|
| ke | lā | el | lā | ha | el | la'l | lāh | mu | ḥam | mad | yār | ra | sū | la'l | lāh |

The same template can be found in a performance by Torbat-e Jam musicians Habib Habibi (vocal) and Sarvar Ahmadi (*dotar*) at the "Conference on the Music of Khorasan and Transoxiana", Tehran, 4 January 2006 (example 1). The seven-pulse rhythmic pattern played on the *dotar* is related to the repeating foot of ˘ – – – in the poetry. Although it defies a simple transformation of quantified poetic metric units to musical ones, the germination of the instrumental pattern from the text is obvious even from a superficial listening.

"Hu hu"

˘ – – – /˘ – – – /˘ – – –/ ˘ – – –

*cho qomrī har zamān kū kū be har dam mī-zanam hū hū*

*qalandarwār o yā man hū na pūyam ghayr-e 'ellā hū*

Like the turtledove's incessant "ku ku",
with every breath I say "hu hu" [the name of god].
Oh! in the manner of a qalandar, I don't seek anyone other than Allah.[31]

While the performer could have applied the rhythmic template ⏑ – – – in a simple manner to generate a *dotar* rhythm emphasising the pattern ♪ ♩ ♩ ♩, his more interesting choice (roughly, ♪ ♪ ♪. ♩‿♪., but with the second eighth note slightly prolonged) creates a counterpoint between the rhythm embodied in the utterance of the poetry and the abstraction of that rhythm used as the seed of the instrumental pattern.

A similar process operates in the *soz* for *dhima*. In examples 14 and 15, sung in Karachi and Delhi, one may perceive the syllable "nain" falling on beat 1—the *sam* of the *tala*—by projecting the metric framework of 3+4 counts forward for a fourth cycle (Table 17.3, lines 3-4). In this way, the template – ⏑ – – remains active even though no instrument or hand motion is actually reiterating it. The drummed version operates at a more remote level of abstraction and perhaps for that reason remains elusive for most contemporary performers.

The Torbat-e Jam *dotar* examples and the *dhamal* pattern as played on *dhol* at Shah Jamal shrine in Lahore draw the listener's attention to the connection between the sound of the musical instrument and the copresent sound of text. Muharram drumming in the Nizami tradition, by contrast, creates a distance between the textual object, the verbal message, and the public proclamation. The drummers cannot make their instruments articulate vowels and consonants, so, in the absence of actual singers, drum patterns can only abstract the text. Drum patterns may further distance the text from the listener by only partially replicating its rhythmic emphasis or metre. Depending on the productive and receptive capabilities of the performers and listeners respectively, the sounds of the drums may in some cases not communicate the structure of the associated text at all—only the idea of text. Despite the distancing created between drumming and textual object, however, the drumming activates, or is supposed to activate, specific memories of texts and

31 Text adapted from Muhammad Taqi Massoudieh, *Mūsīqī-yi Torbat-i Jām* (Tehran, 1980), p. 70, translation by Richard Wolf. When the singer refers to saying (*zadan*) the name of God, he may also be referring to striking (*zadan*) the strings, since the rhythmic pattern of both this *zekr* and the *dotar* are the same.

through that, emotional ties to the events at Karbala. In this sense, the drumming is an insider's code.

Aspects of the relationship between Sunnis and Shi'i partners in the Nizamuddin tradition indicate that they together constitute a unified social entity while they also remain separate parts of a shared whole. This in-betweenness is one of the reasons the Nizami community is under pressure in the highly factionalised context of modern Karachi and one reason why Sayyad 'Ali Abbas Nizami would have been motivated to write a *dastur e 'amal*. It is noteworthy, in this context, that musical matters should play such a significant role in the definition of this unusual community.

One of the fundamental motivations to perform in the Nizami case, and arguably in many others, is the desire to express sentiments that are both general and specific. The general messages are "a procession is coming", "someone is celebrating something", and the like—the kinds of things suggested by number 1 in Table 17.1. As listeners draw near, they may be enticed to hear chanting, witness *matam*, ask questions, and be drawn into a world of poetry and music that operates outside that which is accessible to the public at large. The idea that drumming and music, like other forms of pageantry, mainly serve the function of attracting people, after which time the more serious business of teaching religion can take place, is a common apologia. Significant here is the way in which this hybrid, minority community of Muharram participants has both distanced and embraced musical performance. Such performances are among the practices that set this community apart in its post-Partition life in Pakistan, despite threats against them from factionalist political groups.

Mixed oral and written traditions such as those discussed here have the potential to communicate traces of relationships—of trade, conquest, spiritual transmission, and artistic production, among others—which are built on layers of prior relationships stretching back over long periods of time. Nizami drumming is both a conduit and a residue of relationships among special groups of Shi'as, Sunnis and Hindus. It is a reason for these groups to join: some Shi'as may value drumming rituals so long as they are not the drummers. In Delhi, Hindu professional musicians have little difficulty incorporating their service for Nizamuddin into their broader idea of appropriate social-religious behaviour, and their presence ensures at least a minimum level of artistic quality. Sunni community members participate as a matter of obligation, service, and personal pleasure—since they take turns, they are only responsible for the moments in which they play, not for the upkeep of the ritual drumming throughout.

The drum rhythms publicly reiterate the ongoing relationship of Nizamis in Karachi with their counterparts in Delhi, as well as their relationship with descendants of the Shi'as from the same area who now live in Karachi. The performance of the *zikr "lā illāha ill 'allāh"*, which is part of the *kalma*, also iterates relationships between the Nizamis and Muslim performers of other instrumental traditions, and with other orders or branches of Islamic practice; at the same time, it fits into a non-exclusivist world view of the Hindu participants—put in quasi-Advaita Vedantic terms, the notion of "one god" in the *kalma* implies that divinity itself is unitary, not that there is one true god and all the other (Hindu etc.) gods are false.

The relationships among these communities are ever changing. Perhaps the sense of Shi'i-Sunni community that those in Karachi remember and value was the product of a historical moment, born from the enthusiasm of Khurshid 'Ali and later to fizzle out in Delhi. Now Shi'i involvement is on the rise in a different way in Delhi and drumming and *matam* (performed on the body) are no longer intimately connected. Drumming and the idea of embodied texts remain important markers of the connection between Karachi and Delhi, just as Hosay drumming in Trinidad creates an aura of textuality connected with a period closer to the first arrival of the ancestors of today's Indo-Caribbeans from India. In both cases, the significance of text in drumming may be generalised, operating in the regions of Types 1 and 2 in Table 17.1. Drumming in this tradition can also convey contextually appropriate information to new or distantly familiar listeners, who might pick up on contrasts between fast and slow patterns and associate them with the heat of battle and death or woundedness respectively; at the same it provides deeper meaning to those who belong to the community, who would hear the relationship between drumming and text in the case of the *kalma*, and know that they should be associating the scene of Sughra with the *dhima* pattern; and finally a smaller group would be able to hook into the finer points of musical organisation and feel the connection with the specific poetic texts associated with *matam/savari* and *dhima*. Presumably those involved in hearing and performing the Indian traditions that took root in Trinidad over the generations went through a process of knowledge loss that corresponds roughly with moving from the bottom of Table 17.1 to the top; along the way, knowledge of the tradition must have been dispersed unevenly throughout the communities involved.

The fact that text-music relationships as laid out in Table 17.1 can operate at several levels at one time allows the meaning of drumming to be scalable. At the most intimate level, the Nizami drumming patterns imply a special connection between poets and the sphere of the *majlis* and the public sphere of Muharram processions. Perhaps it is in that connection, between narrow and broad, private and public, that we can best apprehend the scalability of meaning in this drumming and its significance in holding together this fragile community in Karachi.

Looking outward from these case studies, I hope to suggest that some of the transformations laid out in Table 17.1 are among the possible ways written texts from the past may be perpetuated through performance from generation to generation. Of particular interest are the roles of actual or imagined verbal performances that mediate instrumental iterations/interpretations of a text, the roles of pre-existing instrumental rhythms and other templates that affect the ways texts are delivered in performance, and the possibility that prosodic features of texts carry the seeds of their rhythmic expression in musical performances.

These transformations are socially coded: the nature of the music-text relationships, as well as the texts themselves, may say something about how the communities associated with those who perform wish to, or in effect do, position themselves with respect to others. These creative, social, and sometimes commemorative activities continue to unfold in time: they are remembered, forgotten, bolstered, overlaid with new material (such as the multiple texts for *dhima*), defended or rejected. In this process, these kinds of performative and social materials also document, or suggest, relationships among populations in the past.

## A Note on Transliterating Persian and Indic Terms from Persian

The short vowel called *kasre* in Persian is transliterated "e" in Persian language contexts and "i" in Indic contexts. The default, if unspecified, is "i". The short vowel *zamme* is likewise transliterated "o" for Persian and "u" for Indic languages.

## Examples for the Musical Lives

richardkwolf.com/audio-visual

1) "Hu Hu," Habib Habibi (vocal) and Sarvar Ahmadi (*dotar*), recorded by Richard K. Wolf, Tehran, Jan 4, 2006.
http://dx.doi.org/10.11647/OBP.0062.19

2) *Kalma* as performed by Mamraj's *tasha* group, March 13, 1999. Recorded by Richard K. Wolf.
http://dx.doi.org/10.11647/OBP.0062.20

3) "Ran meṉ jis dam"—alternate text for *dhima* sung in *soz* style by Sayyad Sarir Ahmed Nizami, June 8, 1997. Recorded by Richard K. Wolf.
http://dx.doi.org/10.11647/OBP.0062.21

4) "*Dhima*" performed by Mamraj's *tasha* group, March 13, 1999. Recorded by Richard K. Wolf.
http://dx.doi.org/10.11647/OBP.0062.22

5) Mamraj humming *matam* melody, March 13, 1999. Recorded by Richard K. Wolf.
http://dx.doi.org/10.11647/OBP.0062.23

6) Mamraj humming *dhima* melody, March 13, 1999. Recorded by Richard K. Wolf.
http://dx.doi.org/10.11647/OBP.0062.24

7) Indo-Trinidadian performance of *tassa* and bass during Hosay in Manhattan, Aug 31-Sept 1, 1996. Recorded by Richard K. Wolf.
http://dx.doi.org/10.11647/OBP.0062.25

8) Mamraj singing song associated with brass band melody for *matam/savari*, Aug 13, 1998. Recorded by Richard K. Wolf.
http://dx.doi.org/10.11647/OBP.0062.26

9) S. A. Nizami singing the *salam* text associated with the *matam* drum pattern. June 8, 1997. Recorded by Richard K. Wolf.
http://dx.doi.org/10.11647/OBP.0062.27

10) Demonstration of *savari* drum pattern with chanting of "Husain, Husain" and performance of *matam*, June 8, 1997, Jacob Lines, Karachi. Recorded by Richard K. Wolf.
http://dx.doi.org/10.11647/OBP.0062.28

11) *Zekr*, "lā ellāhe ellā'llāh," chanted by members of a *khaksar* Sufi brotherhood. Recorded by Stephen Blum at Khāneqāh-a La'me, Qazvin, Iran, Aug 10, 1995.
http://dx.doi.org/10.11647/OBP.0062.29

12) *Savari* pattern followed by one iteration of *kalma*. Mamraj's drum group performing during Muharram at the Nizamuddin shrine, late December 2009. Recorded by Richard K. Wolf.
http://dx.doi.org/10.11647/OBP.0062.30

13) *Dhima* performed by junior drummers, Jacob Lines, Karachi, June 2, 1997 (Hashim Ali, Akram Ali, Aslam Ali, M. Arsshad, M. Tanveer, M. Safdar). Recorded by Richard K. Wolf.
http://dx.doi.org/10.11647/OBP.0062.31

14) "Āj Sughrā"—text for *dhima* sung in *soz* style by Sayyad Sarir Ahmed Nizami, June 8, 1997, Jacob Lines, Karachi. Recorded by Richard K. Wolf.
http://dx.doi.org/10.11647/OBP.0062.32

15) "Āj Sughrā"—text for *dhima* sung in *soz* style by Ghulam Hasnain Nizami Dec 27, 2009, Delhi. Recorded by Richard K. Wolf.
http://dx.doi.org/10.11647/OBP.0062.33

16) *Dhima* drum pattern (and transition into *savari*) as demonstrated by expert drummers in Jacob lines, Karachi, June 8, 1997. Recorded by Richard K. Wolf.
http://dx.doi.org/10.11647/OBP.0062.34

17) *Dhima* as performed by Ghulam Hasnain Nizami during Muharram Dec 27, 2009, Delhi. Recorded by Richard K. Wolf.
http://dx.doi.org/10.11647/OBP.0062.35

18) *Zekr*, "lā ellāhe ellā'llāh," as part of a song. Nur Mohammad Dorrpur (voice) and Zolfekār 'Askaripur (dotār). *Musiqi-ye Khorasan*, 3, B:2. Iranian Music Association.
http://dx.doi.org/10.11647/OBP.0062.36

# Glossary

*abhang* Marathi devotional song
*acharya* religious master
*adhyay* chapter of a book
*advaita* non-dualistic
*ahl-e bait* the family of the Prophet Muhammad
*'alam* standard that is part of Muharram commemoration of Imam Husain's martyrdom
*alankara* figure of speech
*alankarashastra* lit. science of ornaments, rhetoric
*arilla* short poetical form in Brajbhasha
*arthav* exposition
*azan* call to prayer

*bada* notebook
*band baja* music with brass band
*bandijan* musician
*basti* neighbourhood
*batin* hidden, esoteric
*bayaz* poetic scrapbook
*bhajan* devotional song
*bhakha* lit. language, term for Hindi
*bhaktamal* biographical compilation of devotees and saints
*bhakti* lit. "sharing", devotion
*bhang* drink laced with marijuana
*bhanita* poet's signature line at the end of a poem
*bhattarak* head of Digambara Jain institution
*bhava* emotion
*bhramargit* lit. "songs of the bee", song-poems in which Krishna is compared to a bee which sucks nectar from many flowers
*bol* syllable, drum/dance mnemonic
*brahmachari* celibate
*brahman* the ultimate reality underlying all phenomena
*buzurg* elder, important man

*charan* panegyric singer and genealogist in the Rajput domains
*charya* Bengali sung poem
*chaumasa, chaturmasa* the four months of the rainy season, in which itinerant ascetics do not travel
*chaupai* quatrain

*daitya, dait* race of giants who fought against the gods; in Persian translations of Sanskrit texts usually assimilated to *asura*s and *rakshasa*s, demons
*dapha* genre of Newar devotional singing
*darbar court*
*dargah* lit. threshhold, sufi shrine, see also *khanqah*
*darshan* polysemic word, may mean ritual and mutual viewing of god/spiritual master and devotee or system of philosophy
*dastan* story
*devata* god
*dhadhi* musician specialising in drum and sarangi accompaniment and panegyric and martial singing
*dharma* religious duty
*dhatu* the melodic component of a song (as in *dhatu-matu*)
*dhrupad* (also *dhurpad*) preeminent courtly song genre in Braj language
*dhyana, ragadhyana* poetical description of the iconic form of a *raga* (see below)
*din* faith
*divan, diwan* book of poetry
*doha* verse couplet
*drishtant* example, verse used as an example
*dunya, duniya* the world

*gaddi* seat
*ghazal* Persian and Urdu lyrical poem
*gita* song
*goshti, goshthi* (religious) discussion
*gotra* clan lineage
*gunigana* knowledgeable audience
*guru* master, teacher
*guthi* voluntary society
*gyan goshti* knowledge discussion

*hadis* traditions of the Prophet
*hun kar* lit. "hmm", listener's assent that prompts a storyteller to continue

*'ibadat* worship
*imam* the twelve leaders of Shi'a Islam; leader of a mosque
*imambara, imambargah* Shi'a commemoration hall
*islah* critique and correction of poetry

*jati* caste, community (see also *qaum*)
*jawab* response (as in call and response, Q&A)

*jinn* spirits, lower than the angels, who appear in human and animal form

*kahani* story
*kalam* discourse
*kalawant* hereditary court musician of high status
*kalima, kalma* Muslim declaration of faith
*karamat* miracles performed by saints
*Karbala* location of a battle in 680 CE which gave rise to the split between Sunnis and Shi'is and which Shi'is commemorate every year during the month of Muharram
*karma* lit. action, and the consequences that each action has in one's past, present, or future existence
*katha* story
*kathak, kathakar, kathavachak* storyteller (*kathak* only began to designate a dance form in the twentieth century)
*kavi* poet
*kavitt, kavitta* poem, which may also be sung
*kavya* poetry
*Kayasth* professional scribal caste
*khanqah* sufi monastery, see also *dargah*
*khandan* family, hereditary lineage
*khatima* concluding section of a text
*Khatri* professional caste of scribes and merchants
*khayal* virtuosic courtly song genre
*kinnara* celestial musician in Buddhist and Hindu mythology
*kirtan* religious song form
*kirtankar* religious public performer of *kirtan*

*lazzat* taste, pleasure (see also *zauq*)
*lila* dance, play

*madrasa* school, teaching institution
*mahant* head of a monastery (*math*)
*mahatmya* text describing the greatness of a place, a god/goddess, or a sacred text
*mahfil, mehfil* assembly, gathering
*mahotsav* (devotional) festival
*maidan* public park
*majlis* (pl. *majalis*) assembly, gathering
*maktab* literary school or circle
*malfuz* (pl. *malfuzat*) sayings (of a sufi saint)
*manaqib* an Arabic biographical-hagiographic genre about the qualities of noble individuals
*mandali* small group
*mandir* temple
*mangalkabya* Bengali genre of narrative poetry about the relationship between gods, humans, and places

*mansabdar* Mughal officer
*marsiya* sung or recited Muharram elegy in poetical form
*marsiya-go* performer of *marsiya*
*ma'sumin* pure and flawless ones
*masjid* mosque
*masnavi* Persian or Urdu narrative poem
*matam* physical self-mortification during Muharram ritual
*math* monastery
*matu* the textual component of a song (as in *dhatu-matu*)
*maulvi, mawlawi* person who has completed full course of Arabic and Persian studies
*mazhab* belief
*mela* fair
*mo'jizat* miracle stories
*mohajir, muhajir* migrant to Pakistan from India, usually at Partition
*muktaka* independent verse
*musha'ira* Persian and Urdu poetry recital
*mushkil-kusha* resolver of difficulties

*naga* warrior ascetic
*nama* Persian narrative, chronicle
*namaz* prayer, one of the five mandatory Islamic prayers
*naqqal* actor, mime
*nayak* hero, protagonist
*nayika* heroine, protagonist
*nayika-bhed* poetic genre detailing the different types of heroines
*nazar* offering
*niqabposh* hidden, in disguise
*niti* lit. ethics or policy, genre of instructional texts
*nitya lila* lit. "eternal play", the notion that Krishna is eternally playing with the milkmaids of Braj in a higher sphere (*loka*)
*niyaz* ritual offering
*niyaz kahani* ritual stories
*nritya* dance

*ojas* martial spirit

*pakhawaj* double-headed barrel drum that accompanies *dhrupad* songs
*pan* digestive made of betel nut and leaves
*panchali* Bengali genre of performed poetry
*pande, pandit* educated Brahmin or (among Jains) temple ritual specialist; scholar
*parchai* biography
*parhna* to read
*paryushana* season of sermons given by Jain monks during the rainy season
*patur(a)* courtesan, female singer/dancer
*pir* sufi master

*pirzada* living descendent of a sufi saint
*pothi* manuscript book, often compilation
*prasad* offering received back with god's blessing
*prasang, prastav* context of an example
*pravachan* spiritual discourse
*prem-katha* love story
*Purana* lit. old, compilation of narratives about gods, communities, and places

*qasba* small town
*qasida* Arabic, Persian, or Urdu ode/praise poem
*qaum* caste, community (see also *jati*)
*qawwal, qavval* professional sufi musician who also performed at court
*qawwali* song performances of *qawwals*, usually at sufi shrines
*qiyamat, qayamat* the Day of Judgement in Islam
*qissa* story
*qissa-khwan* storyteller

*raga* melodic mode
*ragamala* lit. garland of *ragas*; 6 male *ragas* each with 5 wives called *raginis*
*raja* king (also *maharaja*, great king)
*rajguru* royal *guru*
*rakshas* demon
*ramat* itinerancy in a group of followers
*ramshala* place where Dadupanthi ascetics spend the rainy months
*ras lila* performance of Krishna's life
*rasa* juice, sentiment, one of nine affective essences
*rasika* connoisseur
*rishi* seer, sage
*riti* lit. style, courtly style of poetry in Brajbhasha
*ritigranth* manual of poetics

*sabad* lit. word, devotional song-poem
*sadhu* ascetic
*sadhvi* female ascetic
*sajjada-nishin* current head of a sufi shrine
*sakhi* poetic couplet, often gnomic in kind
*sakhi* the female confidante of the *nayika*
*salam* greeting; the first item in a series of performances
*sama'* lit. audition, sufi musical assembly
*samasyapurti* poetic game in which poets are given a word or part of a verse and have to complete it to a set metre
*sampradaya* religious group, association
*samskara* polysemic word which means life-ritual and ceremony, and the trace and influence that actions and thoughts leave
*sangita* music, dance, and drama; lyrical arts
*sangitashastra* musical science, music treatise

*sant* lit. "good man", holy person in a devotional context
*saqi-nama* poems addressed to the *saqi* or cup-bearer
*sarvangi* comprehensive compilation of devotional songs
*satsang* congregation of devotees with music and discourses
*savab* religious merit
*sayyid* descendant of the Prophet Muhammad
*seva* service
*shakti* the power of the goddess
*shauq* desire, pleasure
*shudra* lower caste
*silsila* lit. chain, lineage
*sipara* chapter of the Qur'an
*soz* Persian or Urdu elegy to commemorate the martyrdom of Imam Husain (the Prophet Mohammad's grandson) and his family at Karbala
*stotra* hymn
*sufi* mystical branch of Islam, based on observance of a path under the guide of a *pir*
*sukhan* speech, discourse
*sunna* to listen, to hear
*svadhyaya* self-study

*tabarruk* blessed food
*tabla* set of two drums that is the pre-eminent accompaniment to classical music genres
*takhyil* deception
*tala* rhythmic cycle
*tamasha* spectacle, and a Marathi performance genre
*tappa* courtly Panjabi song genre
*tarikh* chronogram
*tariqa* sufi path and organisation
*tasha* drum associated with Muharram
*ta'sir* effect, impact
*taza-gui* "fresh speech", new style of Persian poetry in Safavid and Mughal times
*ta'ziya, tazia* replica of a mausoleum used in Muharram processions
*tazkira* biographical dictionary, prosopography (usually of poets or sufi saints)
*tirthankara* one of the 24 founding Jinas

*'urs* lit. "marriage", death anniversary of a sufi saint.
*ustad* master

*vacana* speech
*vaggeyakar* song-poet
*vani* (also *bani*) lit. speech, collected sayings of a saint or poet
*varnashrama* the system of four major castes (*varna*) and four stages of life (*ashrama*)
*varta* story

*vira* heroic, the heroic sentiment (*rasa*)
*virah* the longing and pain of separation
*virahini* woman pining for her absent beloved
*virakt* renunciant, in the specific case, Dadupanthi itinerant *sadhu*
*virudavali* panegyric genre panegyric made of linked chain of epithets
*vistar* exposition (of a *raga*)
*vrat-katha* ritual story with vow and fast

*wazn* rhythmic emphasis in a poetical or musico-rhythmic cycle

*yuga* epoch

*zahir* apparent, exoteric
*zakir* one who remembers
*zauq* taste, pleasure, see also *lazzat*
*zikr*, *zekr* repetitive chanting in sufi ritual practice
*ziyarat* pilgrimage

# Bibliography


'Abbasi, Mustafa ibn Khaliqdad. 1997 [1954]. *Daryā-i asmār: Tarjuma-i Kathāsaritsāgar*. Ed. by Tara Chand and Amir Hasan Abidi. Aligarh: Aligarh Muslim University.

Abbott, Justin E., and Narhar R. Godbole, trans. 1996 [1933]. *Stories of Indian saints: English translation of Mahipati's Marathi Bhaktavijaya*. Delhi: Motilal Banarsidass.

'Abd al-Baqi Nihavandi. 1924-1931. *Ma'āṡir-i Raḥīmī*. Ed. by M. Hidayat Husain. 3 vols. Calcutta: Asiatic Society of Bengal.

'Abd al-Qadir Bada'uni. 2000-2001. *Muntakhab al-tavārīkh*. Ed. by Maulvi Ahmad 'Ali Sahib and Taufiq Subhani. Tehran: Anjuman-i Asar va Mafakhir-i Farhangi.

'Abd al-Sattar Lahori. 2006. *Majālis-i Jahāngīrī*. Ed. by Arif Naushahi and Muin Nizami. Tehran: Miras-i Maktub.

Abhayadatta. 2005. *La vie merveilleuse de 84 grands sages de l'Inde ancienne*. Trans. by Djamyang Khandro Ahni. Paris: Éditions du Seuil.

Abu'l Fazl "'Allami". 1873-1887. *Akbarnāma*. Ed. by Agha Ahmad Ali and Maulawi Abd-ur-Rahim. Calcutta: Asiatic Society of Bengal.

—. 2005. *Ā'īn-i Akbarī*. Ed. by Sir Sayyid Ahmad. Reprint Aligarh: Aligarh Muslim University.

—. 2008 [1868-1877]. *Ā'īn-i Akbarī*. Trans. by H. Blochmann and Col. H.S. Jarrett. New Delhi: Asiatic Society of Bengal and Baptist Mission Press. Reprint Delhi: Low Price Publications.

Agraval, Saroj. 1962. *Prabodhacandroday aur uskī hindī paramparā*. Allahabad: Hindi Sahitya Sammelan.

Ahmed, Wakil. 1994. *Madhyayuge bāṃlā kāvyera rūpa o bhāṣā*. Dhaka: Khan Brothers and Co.

Ahobala Pandit. 1971. *Saṅgītapārijāta*. Hathras: Sangit Karyalaya.

Aitken, Molly E. 2010. *The Intelligence of Tradition in Rajput Court Painting*. New Haven: Yale University Press.

Alam. 1982. *Ālamkṛt Mādhavānala Kāmakandalā*. Ed. by Rajkumari Misra. Allahabad: Ratnakumari Svadhyay Sansthan.

Alam, Muzaffar. 1998. 'The Pursuit of Persian: Language in Mughal Politics', *Modern Asian Studies* 32, 2: 317-49. http://dx.doi.org/10.1017/s0026749x98002947

—. 2009. 'The Mughals, the Sufi Shaikhs and the Formation of the Akbari Dispensation', *Modern Asian Studies* 39, 1: 135-74. http://dx.doi.org/10.1017/s0026749x07003253

—. 2011. 'The Debate Within: A Sufi Critique of Religious Law, *Tasawwuf* and Politics in Mughal India'. In *Religious Cultures in Early Modern India: New Perspectives*. Ed. by Rosalind O'Hanlon and David Washbrook. London: Routledge, pp. 8-39.

Alam, Muzaffar, and Sanjay Subrahmanyam. 2011. *Writing the Mughal World*. New York: Columbia University Press.

Al Deen, Selim. 1995. *Madhyayugera bāṃlā nāṭya*, Dhaka: Bangla Academy.

Alaol. 1992. *Satī-maynā Lora Candrāṇī*. Ed. by Muhammad Abdul Qayyum. Dhaka: Bangla Academy.

—. 2002. *Padmāvatī*. Ed. by Debnath Bandyopadhyay. Kolkata: Pashcimavanga Rajya Pustaka Parshat.

—. 2007. *Ālāol racanāvalī*. Ed. by Muhammad Abdul Qayyum and Razia Sultana. Dhaka: Bangla Academy.

Ali, Daud. 2004. *Courtly Culture and Political Life in Early Medieval India*. Cambridge: Cambridge University Press.

Allah Diya ibn Shaikh 'Abd al-Rahman Chishti, Shaikh. 2007. *Khvājagān-i Chisht, Siyar al-aqṭāb*. Ed. by Muhammad Sarvar Maulai. Tehran: 'Ilm.

Allen, Michael. 1996. 'Procession and Pilgrimage in Newar Religion'. In *Change and Continuity*. Ed. by S. Lienhard. Turin: Edizioni dell'Orso, pp. 209-22.

Alvi, Sajida S. 1989. 'Religion and State During the Reign of Mughal Emperor Jahăngĭr (1605-27): Nonjuristical Perspectives', *Studia Islamica* 69: 95-119. http://dx.doi.org/10.2307/1596069

Amin, Shahid. 2002. 'On Retelling the Muslim Conquest of Northern India'. In *History and the Present*. Ed. by Partha Chatterjee and Anjan Ghosh. New Delhi: Permanent Black, pp. 24-43.

—. 2005. 'Un saint guerrier: Sur la conquête de l'Inde du nord par les Turcs au XI siècle', *Annales: Histoire, Sciences Sociales* 60, 2: 265-93.

Amir-Moezzi, Mohammad Ali. 1994. *The Divine Guide in Early Shi'ism: The Sources of Esotericism in Islam*. Trans. by David Streight. Albany: State University of New York Press.

Amma, Visweswari. 1985. *Udayana and His Philosophy*. Delhi: Nag Publishers.

Amritachandra. 1964. *Samayasāra kalaśa*, with *Bālbodh* of Pande Raymall. Ed. by Pandit Phulchandra Siddhantashastri. Songarh: Digambar Jain Svadhyay Mandir Trust.

'Andalib, Khwaja Muhammad Nasir. 1984. *Nāla-i 'Andalīb*. Bhopal: Matba Shahjahani.

Andaya, Barbara Watson. 2011. 'Distant Drums and Thunderous Cannon: Authority in Traditional Malay Society', *International Journal of Asia Pacific Studies* 7, 2: 19-35.

Anderson, Benedict. 2006. *Imagined Communities: Reflections on the Origin and Spread of Nationalism*. Revised edn. London: Verso.

Anon. [n.d.]. *Ācārya Pravar Śrī Śrī 1008 Śrī Hari Rām jī Mahārāj: Pravacan (Śrī Dadu avatārotsav melā 1987)*. 1. CD.

Anon. [n.d.]. *Das bībiyon̲ kī kahānī*. Bombay: [n.p.].

Anon. [n.d.]. *Harbans purāna*. British Library, IO Islamic 1777.

Anon. [n.d.]. *Janāb-e Sayyida*. Karachi: [n.p.].

Anon. [n.d.]. *Janāb-e Sayyida kī kahānī*. Bombay: [n.p.].

Anon. [n.d.]. *Safīna-i bahr al-muhīt*, Ms. Orient Fol. 248, Staatsbibliothek zu Berlin.

Anon. 1978. *Ghunyat-ul-Munya: The Earliest Known Persian Work on Indian Music*. Trans. by Shahab Sarmadee. Bombay: Asian Publishing House.

Anon. 1979. *Mahābhārata*. Trans. by Mir Ghiyas al-Din 'Ali Qazvini, ed. by S.M. Reza and N.S. Shukla. Tehran: Kitabkhana-i Tahuri.

Anon. 1992. *Saṅgītaśiromaṇi: A Medieval Handbook of Indian Music*. Ed. and trans. by Emmie Te Nijenhuis. Leiden: Brill.

Anon. 2003. *Ghunyatu'l Munya: The Earliest Persian Work on Indian Classical Music*. New Delhi: Indian Council of Historical Research in association with Northern Book Centre.

Appadurai, Arjun. 1990. 'Disjuncture and Difference in the Global Cultural Economy', *Public Culture* 2, 2: 1-24. http://dx.doi.org/10.1215/08992363-2-2-1

Archer, W.G. 1958. *Central Indian Painting*. London: Faber & Faber.

Asadi Tusi. 1336/1957. *Lughat-i furs*. Ed. by M. Dabbirsiyaqi. Tehran: Tahuri.

Asani, Ali. 2002. *Ecstasy and Enlightment: The Ismaili Devotional Literature of South Asia*. London: Institute of Ismaili Studies.

Ashadhara, Pandit. 1954. *Jinasahasranāma stavana*, with Sanskrit *vivr̥ti* of Ashadhara and Sanskrit *ṭīkā* of Shrutasagara. Ed. by Hiralal Jain. Banaras: Bharatiya Jnanpith.

Ashadhara, Pandit, and Jinasena. 1929. *Jinasahasranāma stavana*, and *Bhāṣāsahasranām* of Banarsidas. Ed. by Nathuram Premi. 2nd edn. Bombay: Jain Granth Ratnakar.

Asher, Catherine B. 2006. 'Urban Growth and Decline: Housing the Moving Jina in Jaipur, Delhi and Lucknow', *Jinamañjari* 34, 2: 79-91.

Asher, Catherine B. and Cynthia Talbot. 2006. *India Before Europe*. Cambridge: Cambridge University Press.

Ashk, Khalil 'Ali Khan. 1863. *Dāstān-i Amīr Ḥamza*. Bombay: Matba'-i Haidari.

Ate, Lynn. 1984. 'Literary Metre Versus Rhythmic Beat in Tamil Alvar Literature', *Journal of South Asian Literature* 19, 2: 1-7.

'Attar, Farid al-Din. 2009. *Asrār nāma*. Ed. by Sadiq Gauharin. Tehran: Chap-e Sharq.

—. 1959. *Musībat nāma*. Ed. by Nurani Wisal. Tehran: Zawwar.

—. 1961. *Ushtūr nāma*. Ed. by Mahdi Muhaqqiq. Tehran: Chap-e Taban.

Attridge, Derek. 1995. *Poetic Rhythm: An Introduction*. Cambridge: Cambridge University Press.

—. 2004. *J.M. Coetzee and the Ethics of Reading: Literature in the Event*. Chicago and London: University of Chicago Press.

Aufrecht, Theodore. 1891. *Catalogus Catalogorum: An Alphabetical Register of Sanskrit Works and Authors*. Leipzig: F.A. Brockhaus.

Ayoub, Mahmoud. 1978. *Redemptive Suffering in Islam*. New York: Mouton. http://dx.doi.org/10.1515/9783110803310

Babar, S., et al. 1970. *Śrī Nāmdev gāthā*. Bombay: Maharashtra State Government Printing Press.

Bahura, Gopalnarayan. 1976. *Literary Heritage of the Rulers of Amber and Jaipur: (in the Maharaja Sawai Man Singh II Museum) with an Index to the Register of Manuscripts in the Pothikhana of Jaipur*. Jaipur: Maharaja Sawai Man Singh II Museum.

—, ed. 1990. *Māncaritāvalī: Amber ke suprasiddh rājā Mānsiṃh ke carit se sambandhit pāṃc rājasthānī racnāoṃ kā saṅkalan*. Jaipur: Maharaja Savai Man Singh II Sangrahalay.

Bakhana. [n.d.]. *Baṣanāṁ-vāṇī*. Ed. by Bhajandās Svami, commentary by Brajendrakumār Siṃhal. Jaipur: Śrī Svami Lakṣmīrām Trust.

Bakhle, Janaki. 2005. *Two Men and Music: Nationalism in the Making of an Indian Classical Tradition*. New York: Oxford University Press.

Bakhtin, Mikhail. 2004. *The Dialogic Imagination: Four Essays*. Trans. by Caryl Emerson and Michael Holquist. Austin: University of Texas Press.

Balkhi (al-), Abu-Zaid Ahmed bin Sahl. 1901. *Kitāb al-bada'a wa al-tārīkh*. Ed. by Marie-Clément Huart. Paris: Leroux.

Banarsidas. *Ardhakathānaka*. See Lath 1981.

—. 1970. Trans. by Ramesh Chandra Sharma. 'The Ardha-Kathānak: A Neglected Source of Mughal History', *Indica* 7, 1: 49-73; and 7, 2: 105-20.

—. 2009. *Ardhakathanak: A Half Story*. Trans. by Rohini Chowdhury. New Delhi: Penguin Books.

—. 2011. *Ardhakathānaka. Histoire à demi: autobiographie d'un marchand Jaina du XVIIe siècle*. Trans. by Jérôme Petit. Paris: Presses Sorbonne Nouvelle.

—. 1906. *Banārsī vilās*. Compiled by Jagjīvanrām. Ed. by Nathuram Premi. Bombay: Jain Granth Ratnākar Kāryālay.

—. 1954. *Banārsī vilās*. Ed. by Bhanvarlal Jain Nyaytirth and Kasturcand Kaslival. Jaipur: Vir Vani Press, Nanulal Smarak Granthmala, 1954 (first printing).

—. 1987. *Banārsī vilās*. 2nd edn. Jaipur: Akhil Bharatiya Jain Yuva Phedareshan.

—. 2010. *Dhyānabattīsī*. Trans. by Jérôme Petit. Mumbai: Hindi Granth Karyalay.

—. 2010. *Karma chattīsī*. Trans. by Jérôme Petit. In *Svasti: Essays in Honour of Prof. Hampa Nagarajaiah for his 75th Birthday*. Ed. by Nalini Balbir. Krishnapuradoddi: K.S. Muddappa Smaraka Trust, pp. 231-42.

—. 1941. *Nāmamālā*. Ed. by Jugalkishor Mukhtar. Sarsawa: Vir Seva Mandir.

—. 1971. *Samayasār nāṭak*, with Hindi *ṭīkā* of Pandit Buddhilal Shravak. Bhavnagar: Shri Vitrag Sat Sahitya Prasarak Trast.

Bangha, Imre. 2004. 'Dynamics of Textual Transmission in Premodern India: The *Kavitavali* of Tulsidas', *Comparative Studies of South Asia, Africa and the Middle East* 24, 2: 33-44. http://dx.doi.org/10.1215/1089201x-24-2-33

—. 2007. 'Courtly and Religious Communities as Centres of Literary Activity in Eighteenth-Century India: Ānandghan's Contacts with the Princely Court of Kishangarh-Rupnagar and with the Maṭh of the Nimbārka Sampradāy in Salemabad'. In *Indian Languages and Texts through the Ages: Essays of Hungarian Indologists in Honour of Prof. Csaba Tottossy*. Ed. by Csaba Dezso. Delhi: Manohar, pp. 307-54.

—. 2011. 'Writing Devotion: the Dynamics of Textual Transmission in the *Kavitāvalī* of *Tulsīdās*'. In *Forms of Knowledge in Early Modern Asia: Explorations in the Intellectual History of India and Tibet, 1500-1800*. Ed. by Sheldon Pollock. Durham: Duke University Press, pp. 257-332.

—. 2014. *Scorpion in the Hand: Brajbhāṣā Court Poetry from Central India around 1800: A Critical Edition of Ṭhākur's Kabittas*. Delhi: Manohar.

—. 2014. 'Early Hindi Epic Poetry in Gwalior'. In *After Timur Left: Culture and Circulation in Fifteenth-century North India*. Ed. by Francesca Orsini and Samira Sheikh. New Delhi: Oxford University Press, pp. 365-402.

Bangha, I., and D. Mistry, eds. (work in progress). *Omniscient Lepers, Hunchback Burglars and the Way to God: A Critical Edition of the Poetry of Vājīd*.

Bansat-Boudon, Lyne. 1992. *Poétique du théâtre indien*. Paris: École Française d'Extrême Orient.

Barber, Karin. 2007. *The Anthropology of Texts, Persons and Publics*. Cambridge: Cambridge University Press. http://dx.doi.org/10.1017/cbo9780511619656

Bard, Amy C. 2002. 'Desolate Victory: Shi'i Women and the Marsiyah Texts of Lucknow'. PhD dissertation, Columbia University.

—. 2011. 'Everyday Life in a Lucknow Locality: Histories, Stories, and Lies'. Paper delivered at South Asian Religion Symposium in Honor of Jack Hawley, University of California-Santa Barbara, 17 November.

Baru Chandidasa. 1361 BA. *Śrīkr̥ṣṇakīrtana*. Ed. by Vasantarañjan Ray Vidvadvallabh, Calcutta: Vangiya Sahitya Parishat.

—. 1984. *Singing the Glory of Lord Krishna: The Śrīkr̥ṣṇakīrtana*. Trans. by M.H. Klaiman. Chico: Scholars Press.

Bayly, C.A. 1996. *Empire and Information: Intelligence Gathering and Social Communication in India, 1780-1870*. Cambridge: Cambridge University Press. http://dx.doi.org/10.1017/cbo9780511583285

Bedil, Mirza 'Abd al-Qadir. 1965-1966 [1344 AH]. *Kulliyāt*. Vol. 4. Ed. by K. Khalili. Kabul: da Pahane wizarat, da Dar al-ta'lif riyasat.

Berlioz, Jacques. 1991. 'Les recherches en France sur les exemples médiévaux, 1968-1988'. In Haug and Wachinger 1991: 288-317.

Behl, Aditya. 2007. 'Presence and Absence in Bhakti: An Afterword', *International Journal of Hindu Studies* 11, 3: 321-22. http://dx.doi.org/10.1007/s11407-008-9051-2

—. 2007. English translation of the *Miragāvati* music passage, verses 246-52. Unpublished draft.

—. 2008. *Lecture II: "The Scent of the Invisible World" Allegory, Rasa and Ma'nī*. Unpublished.

—. 2009. '"The Path of True Feeling": On Translating Qutban's *Mirigāvatī*', published as the introduction to "Qutban, from *Mirigāvatī*". *Calque* 5: 68-113, http://calquezine.blogspot.co.uk [last accessed 11 October 2013].

—, trans. 2012a. *The Magic Doe: Qutban Suhravardī's Mirigāvatī*. Ed. by Wendy Doniger. New York: Oxford University Press. http://dx.doi.org/10.1093/acprof:osobl/9780199842926.001.0001

—. 2012b. *Love's Subtle Magic: An Indian Islamic Literary Tradition, 1379-1545*. Ed. by Wendy Doniger. New York: Oxford University Press. http://dx.doi.org/10.1093/acprof:oso/9780195146707.001.0001

Bellos, David. 2011. *Is that a Fish in Your Ear: Translation and the Meaning of Everything*. New York: Faber & Faber.

Benoît, Philippe. 1992. 'Quatre chansons de paṭuyā du Bengale sur le Rāmāyaṇa'. *Bulletin d'Études Indiennes* 10: 53-87.

*Bhagāvata-purāna*. Persian translation attributed to Faizi Fayyazi. British Library, IO Islamic 1544 and IO Islamic 452.

Bhagvandin, Lala. [n.d.]. 'None arjun siṃh kā saṃkṣipt hāl'. In *Padmākarkṛt himmatbahādurvirudāvalī*. Ed. by Lala Bhagvandin. Varanasi: Nagari Pracharini Sabha, pp. 31-2.

Bharata. 1992. *Nāṭyaśāstra*. Edited by K. Krishnamoorthy. Vol. 1. 4th (revised) edn. Baroda: Oriental Institute.

Bhatt, Bansidhar. 1974. 'Vyavahāra-naya and Niścaya-naya in Kundakunda's Works'. In *XVIII. Deutscher Orientalistentag vom 1. bis 5. Oktober 1972 in Lübeck, Vorträge. Zeitschrift der deutschen Morgenländischen Gesellschaft, Supplement II*. Ed. by Wolfgang Voigt. Wiesbaden: Franz Steiner Verlag, pp. 279-91.

—. 1994. 'On the Epithet: *Nāṭaka* for the *Samayasāra* of Kundakunda'. In *Jainism and Prakrit in Ancient and Medieval India: Essays for Prof. Jagdish Chandra Jain*. Ed. by N.N. Bhattacharyya. New Delhi: Manohar, pp. 431-62.

Bhattacharya, France. 1984. 'A propos d'une représentation du Caṇḍi Maṅgal au Bengale Occidental', *Adyatan "d'aujourd'hui"* 3: 7-26.

—. 1999. 'Hari the Prophet: An Islamic View of a Hindu God in Saiyid Sultan's *Nabi Vamsa*'. In *Essays in Memory of Mumtazur Rahman Tarafdar*. Ed. by Perween Hasan and Mufakharul Islam. Dhaka: Centre for Advanced Research in the Humanities, pp. 192-208.

Bhattacharya, Yatindramohan, 1984. *Bāṅgālāra vaiṣṇavabhāvāpanna musalmāna kavira padamañjuṣā*. Calcutta: Kalikata Vishvavidyalaya.

*Bhavishyapurāna*. 1967-1968. Trans. by Shri Ram Sharma. 2 vols. Bareilly, U.P.: Samskriti Samsthan.

Bhawalkar, Vanamala. 2002. *Eminent Women in the Mahābhārata*. Vol. 2. Delhi: Sharada Publishing House.

Bhikharidas. 1957. *Kāvyanirṇay*. In *Bhikhārīdāsgranthāvalī*. Vol 2. Ed. by Vishvanathprasad Mishra. Varanasi: Nagari Pracarini Sabha.

Bilgrami, 'Abdullah Husain, and Mirza Aman Allah Ghalib Lakhnawi. 2007. *The Adventures of Amir Hamza: Lord of the Auspicious Planetary Conjunction*. Trans. by Musharraf Ali Farooqi. 1st edn. New York: Modern Library.

Bilgrami, Mir 'Abd al-Wahid. 1957. *Haqā'iq-i Hindi*. Trans. by S.A.A. Rizvi. Kashi: Nagari Pracharini Sabha.

Bilgrami, Mir Ghulam 'Ali Azad. 1913. *Ma'āṣir al-kirām*. Ed. by Maulavi 'Abdul Haq. Hyderabad: Kutab Khanabi-i Asafiyah.

Biswas, Shailendra, comp. 1995. *Samsad Bengali-English Dictionary. Rev. 5th edn. Calcutta: Sahitya Samsad.*

Blackburn, Stuart. 2006. *Print, Folklore, and Nationalism in Colonial South India*. New Delhi: Permanent Black.

Blackburn, Stuart, Peter J. Claus, Joyce B. Flueckiger, and Susan S. Wadley, eds. 1989. *Oral Epics in India*. Berkeley: University of California Press.

Bladel, Kevin van. 2010. 'The Astrological Current in the Formation of Islamic Historiography', unpublished paper presented at the University of Chicago, 10 February.

Bonazzoli, Giorgio. 1983. 'Remarks on the Nature of the *Purāṇas*', *Purāṇa* 25, 1: 77-113.

—. 1983. 'Composition of the *Purāṇas*', *Purāṇa* 25, 2: 254-80.

Booth, W.C. 1961. *The Rhetoric of Fiction*. Chicago: University of Chicago Press.

Bor, Joep, Françoise "Nalini" Delvoye, Emmie te Nijenhuis, and Jane Harvey, eds. *Hindustani Music: Thirteenth to Twentieth Centuries*. New Delhi: Manohar.

Borges, Jorge Luis. 1962. 'Pierre Menard, Author of Don Quixote'. Trans. by Anthony Bonner. In *Ficciones*. Ed. by Anthony Kerrigan. New York: Grove Press, pp. 45-55.

—. 1964. 'Pierre Menard, Author of Don Quixote'. Trans. by James E. Irby. In *Labyrinths*. Ed. by Donald A. Yates and James E. Irby. New York: New Directions, pp. 36-44.

Bouillier, Véronique. 2009. 'Y'a-t-il des monastères dans l'Hindouisme? Quelques exemples shivaïtes'. In *La Vie monastique dans le miroir de la parenté*. Ed. by Adeline Herrou and Gisèle Krauskopff. Paris: L'Harmattan, pp. 25-35.

Bourdieu, Pierre. 1999. *Distinction: A Social Critique of the Judgment of Taste*. London: Routledge.

Boutcher, Warren. 2000. 'The Renaissance'. In *The Oxford Guide to Literature in English Translation*. Ed. by Peter France. Oxford: Oxford University Press, pp. 45-55. http://dx.doi.org/10.1093/acref/9780198183594.001.0001

Brac de la Perrière, Éloïse. 2008. *L'Art du livre dans l'Inde des sultanats*. Paris: Presses de l'Université Paris-Sorbonne.

Brinkhaus, H. 1987. *The Pradyumna-Prabhāvatī Legend in Nepal*. Stuttgart: Franz Steiner Verlag.

—. 2003. 'On the Transisiton from Bengali to Maithili in Nepalese Dramas of the 16th and 17th Centuries'. In *Maithili Studies: Papers Presented at the Stockholm Conference on Maithili Language and Literature*. Stockholm: Department of Indology, University of Stockholm, pp. 67-77.

Brinner, Benjamin. 2008. *Music in Central Java: Experiencing Music, Expressing Culture*. New York: Oxford University Press.

Brockington, J. 1998. 'Formulaic Expression in the Rāmāyaṇa: Evidence for Oral Composition?' In *The Epic: Oral and Written*. Ed. by L. Honko, J. Handoo, and J.M. Foley. Mysore: Central Institute of Indian Languages, pp. 128-38.

Brown [Schofield], Katherine Butler. 2006. 'Evidence of Indo-Persian Musical Synthesis? The *Tanbur* and *Rudra Vina* in Seventeenth-century Indo-Persian Treatises', *Journal of the Indian Musicological Society* 36-7: 89-103.

—. 2006. 'If Music be the Food of Love: Masculinity and Eroticism in the Mughal *mehfil*'. In *Love in South Asia: A Cultural History*. Ed. by Francesca Orsini. Cambridge: Cambridge University Press, pp. 61-83.

—. 2010. 'The Origins and Early Development of Khayal'. In *Hindustani Music: Thirteenth to Twentieth Centuries*. Ed. by Joep Bor, Francoise "Nalini" Delvoye, Jane Harvey, and Emmie te Nijenhuis. New Delhi: Manohar, pp. 159-94.

Brown, W. Norman. 1948. 'Some Early Rajasthani Raga Paintings', *Journal of the Indian Society of Oriental Art* 16: 1-10.

de Bruijn, J.T.P. 1983. *Of Piety and Poetry: The Interaction of Religion and Literature in the Life and Works of Ḥakīm Sanā'ī of Ghazna*. Leiden: Brill.

—. 1997. *Persian Sufi Poetry. Introduction to the Mystical Use of Classical Poems*. London: Routledge/Curzon. http://dx.doi.org/10.4324/9781315026237

—. 2010. 'Dialogism in a Medieval Genre: The Case of the Avadhi Epics'. In *Before the Divide: Hindi and Urdu Literary Culture*. Ed. by F. Orsini. New Delhi: Orient Blackswan, pp. 121-41.

Bryant, Kenneth E. 1978. *Poems to the Child-God: Structures and Strategies in the Poetry of Sūrdās*. Berkeley: University of California Press.

Busch, Allison. 2003. 'The Courtly Vernacular: The Transformation of Brajbhaṣa Literary Culture (1590-1690)'. PhD dissertation, University of Chicago.

—. 2004. 'The Anxiety of Innovation: The Practice of Literary Science in the Hindi/ *Riti* Tradition', *Comparative Studies of South Asia, Africa and Middle East* 24, 2: 45-59. http://dx.doi.org/10.1215/1089201x-24-2-45

—. 2005. 'Literary Responses to the Mughal Imperium: The Historical Poems of Keśavdās', *South Asia Research* 25: 31-54. http://dx.doi.org/10.1177/0262728005051606

—. 2010. 'Hidden in Plain View: Brajbhasha Poets at the Mughal Court', *Modern Asian Studies* 44, 2: 267-309. http://dx.doi.org/10.1017/s0026749x09990205

—. 2011. *Poetry of Kings: The Classical Hindi Literature of Mughal India*. New York: Oxford University Press. http://dx.doi.org/10.1093/acprof:oso/9780199765928.001.0001

Callewaert, Winand M. 1974-1977. 'The Anabhay-prabodha of the Dadupanthi Garībdās', *Orientalia Lovaniensia Periodica* 5: 163-85; 8: 309-30.

—. 1992. *The Life and Works of Raidās*. New Delhi: Manohar.

—. 1996. *Sri Guru Granth Sahib with complete index. Part II*. Delhi: Motilal Banarsidass.

Callewaert, Winand M., and Shilanand Hemraj. 1983. *Bhagavadgītānuvāda: A Study in Transcultural Translation*. Ranchi: Satya Bharati Publication.

Callewaert, Winand M., and Mukund Lath. 1989. *The Hindi Songs of Namdev*. Orientalia Lovaniensia Analecta 29. Leuven: Departement Orientalistiek.

Callewaert, Winand M., and Bart Op de Beeck. 1991. *Nirguṇa bhakti sāgara = Devotional Hindī Literature: A Critical Edition of the Pañc-Vāṇī* or *Five works of Dādū, Kābir, Nāmdev, Raidās, Hardās with the Hindī songs of Gorakhnāth and Sundardās, and a Complete Word-Index*, 2 vols. New Delhi: Manohar Publications.

Calmard, Jean. 2000. 'Safavid-Persia in Indo-Persian Sources and in Timurid-Mughal Perception'. In *The Making of Indo-Persian Culture: Indian and French Studies*. Ed. by Muzaffar Alam, Françoise "Nalini" Delvoye, and Marc Gaborieau. New Delhi: Manohar, pp. 351-92.

Caron, James. 2011. 'Reading the Power of Printed Orality in Afghanistan: Popular Pashto Literature as Historical Evidence and Public Intervention', *Journal of Social History* 45, 1: 172-194. http://dx.doi.org/10.1093/jsh/shr011

Certeau, Michel, de 1988. *The Writing of History*. New York: Columbia University Press.

Chandel, Umapati Rai. 1976. *Hindī sūfī kāvya meṃ paurāṇik ākhyān*. Delhi: Abhinav Prakashan.

Chatterjee, Chaya. 1996. *Śāstrīya Saṅgīta and Music Culture of Bengal through the Ages*. New Delhi: Sharada Publishing House.

Chatterjee, Indrani. 2013. 'Monastic Governmentality, Colonial Misogyny, and Postcolonial Amnesia in South Asia', *History of the Present* 3, 1: 57-98. http://dx.doi.org/10.1111/1468-0424.12082

Chaudhri, Gulab Chandra. 1973. *Jain sāhitya kā bṛhad itihās*, Vol. 6: *Kāvya sāhitya*. Varanasi: Parshvanath Vidyashram Shodh Sansthan.

Chaudhuri, Amiya Shankar. 1989. 'Kṛttivāsera puthi saṃvāda'. In *Kavi Kṛttivāsa saṃkalana grantha*. Phuliya: Kavi Krittivasa Smaraka Grantha Prakashaka Samiti, pp. 183-201.

Chaudhuri, Jatindrabimal. 2009 [1981]. *Muslim Patronage to Sanskritic Learning*. Delhi: Idarah-i Adabiyat-i Delli.

Chishti, 'Abd al-Rahman. *Mir'āt al-makhlūqāt*. MS Or. 1883, Asian and African Collections (formerly Oriental and India Office Collections), The British Library, London.

—. *Mir'āt al-makhlūqāt*. MS. *Fārsiyya Taṣawwuf*, 21/343, Habibganj Collection, Maulana Azad Library, Aligarh Muslim University, Aligarh.

—. *Mir'āt al-asrār*. British Library, MS Or. 216.

Chittick, William C. 1994. *Imaginal Worlds: Ibn 'Arabi and the Problem of Religious Diversity*. Albany: State University of New York Press.

Clayton, Martin. 2001. 'Introduction: Towards a Theory of Musical Meaning (in India and Elsewhere)', *Ethnomusicology Forum* 10, 1: 1-17. http://dx.doi.org/10.1080/09681220108567307

Clooney, Francis X. 1989. 'Evil, Divine Omnipotence and Human Freedom: Vedanta's Theology of Karma', *The Journal of Religion* 69, 4: 530-48. http://dx.doi.org/10.1086/488203

Cohen, Ralph. 1986. 'History and Genre', *New Literary History* 17, 2 (Winter): 203-218. http://dx.doi.org/10.2307/468885

Cort, John E. 1994. 'Translation, Indeterminacy, Meaning, Socks, and Moral Peril'. Paper presented at Annual Meeting of the Association for Asian Studies.

—. 2000. 'Defining Jainism: Reform in the Jain Tradition'. In *Jain Doctrine and Practice: Academic Perspectives*. Ed. by Joseph T. O'Connell. Toronto: University of Toronto, Centre for South Asian Studies, pp. 165-91.

—. 2002. 'A Tale of Two Cities: On the Origins of Digambar Sectarianism in North India'. In *Multiple Histories: Culture and Society in the Study of Rajasthan*. Ed. by Lawrence A. Babb, Varsha Joshi and Michael W. Meister. Jaipur: Rawat Publications, pp. 39-83.

—. 2004. 'Jains, Caste, and Hierarchy in North Gujarat'. In *Caste in Question: Identity or Hierarchy?* Ed. by Dipankar Gupta. New Delhi: Sage Publications, pp. 73-112.

—. 2005. 'Devotional Culture in Jainism: Mānatuṅga and His *Bhaktāmara Stotra*'. In *Incompatible Visions: South Asian Religions in History and Culture: Essays in Honor of David M. Knipe*. Ed. by James Blumenthal. Madison: Center for South Asia, University of Wisconsin, pp. 93-115.

—. 2006. 'A Spell against Snakes and other Calamities: The *Uvasaggahara Stotra* Attributed to Bhadrabāhu Svāmī', *Jinamañjari* 34, 2: 34-43.

Crane, R.S. ed. 1952. *Critics and Criticism: Ancient and Modern*. Chicago: University of Chicago Press.

d'Hubert, Thibaut, 2010. *Histoire culturelle et poétique de la traduction. Alaol et la tradition littéraire bengali au XVIIe siècle à Mrauk-U, capitale du royaume d'Arakan*. Paris: École Pratique des Hautes Études.

—. Forthcoming. 'Reading Persian Poetry in Seventeenth-Century Arakan: The Sāqī as a Guru and the Figure of the Patron in Alaol's Bengali Translation of Niẓāmī's Sharafnāma'. In *Patronage in Indo-Persian Culture*. New Delhi: Manohar.

Dadu. 1985. *ŚrīDadubāṇī (Śrīsvamī Dadudayāljī Mahārāj kī anbhai bāṇī)*. With Angbandhu commentary. Ed. by C. Tripathi. Banaras: Sant Sahitya Akadami.

—. 2004. *Śrī Daduvāṇī*. Ed. by Svami Narayandas. 6th edn. Jaipur: Shri Dadu Dayalu Mahasabha.

Dadu, Sukhdayal. 1976 (2033 VS). *Maharṣi Vāzidjī Mahārāj ke arill*. Delhi: Shri Dadudayal Trust.

Dahmen-Dallapiccola, Anna Libera. 1975. *Ragamala-Miniaturen von 1475 bis 1700*. Wiesbaden: Harrassowitz.

Damodara Mishra. *Saṅgītadarpaṇa*. Ms. Sanscrit n. 771, Paris: Bibliothèque Nationale de France.

—. 1985. *Saṅgītadarpaṇa. Damodara Paṇḍita viracita*. Ed. by Sridhar Ranganath Kulkarni. Mumbai: Maharastra Rajya Sahitya Sanskrti Mandal.

—. 1989. *Saṅgīta darpaṇam*. Ed. by K. Vasudeva Sastri. 2nd edn. Tanjore: Maharaj Serfoji's Sarasvati Mahal Library.

Dara Shukoh. 1929. *Majma'-ul-baḥrain*. Ed. by M. Mahfuz-ul-Haq. Calcutta: Asiatic Society.

Dargah Quli Khan. 1989. *Muraqqa'-e Dehli*. Trans. by Chander Shekhar and Shama Mitra Chenoy. Delhi: Deputy.

Darvishi, Mohammad Reza. 1991 [1370 AH]. *Haft awrang: marūrī bar mūsīqī sunnatī va maḥalī Irān*. Tehran: Art Centre.

Das, Kshudiram, 1994. *Bāṃlā kāvyera rūpa o rīti*. Calcutta: Deśa Publishing.

Dasa, Ramagopala and Pitambara Dasa. 1963. *Rāmagopāla Dāsa-viracita Rasakalpavallī o anyānya nibandha, Pītāmbara Dāsa-viracita Aṣṭarasavyākhyā o Rasamañjarī*. Ed. by Harekrishna Mukhopadhyay, Sukumar Sen, and Praphullacandra Pala. Calcutta: Kalikata Vishvavidyalaya.

Davis, Paul. 2008. *Translation and the Poet's Life: The Ethics of Translating in English Culture, 1646-1726*. Oxford: Oxford University Press. http://dx.doi.org/10.1093/acprof:oso/9780199297832.001.0001

De, Sushil Kumar. 1961. *Early History of the Vaiṣṇava Faith and Movement in Bengal*. Calcutta: Firma K.L. Mukhopadhyaya.

De Clercq, Eva. 2014. 'Apabhraṃśa as a Literary Medium in Fifteenth Century North India'. In *After Timur Left: Culture and Circulation in Fifteenth-century North India*. Ed. by Francesca Orsini and Samira Sheikh. New Delhi: Oxford University Press, pp. 339-64.

Dehejia, Harsha V. 2005. *Celebrating Krishna: Sacred Words and Sensuous Images, The Tenth Book of the Bhagavata Purana*. Ahmedabad: Mapin.

Dehlavi, Amir Hasan Sijzi. 1885. *Fawāid al-fu'ād,* Lucknow. Trans. by Bruce Lawrence. New York: Paulist Press, 1992.

Delvoye, Françoise "Nalini". 1990. *Tânsen et la tradition des chants dhrupad en langue braj, du XVIe siècle à nos jours*. Paris: Université de la Sorbonne Nouvelle Paris III.

—. 1990. 'The Verbal Content of Dhrupad Songs from the Earliest Collections, I: The *Hazar Dhurpad* or *Sahasras*', *Dhrupad Annual*: 93-109.

—. 1991. 'Les chants *dhrupad* en langue braj des poètes-musiciens de l'Inde Moghole'. In *Littératures médiévales de l'Inde du Nord*. Ed. by Françoise Mallison. Paris: École Française d'Extrême-Orient, pp. 139-85.

—. 1994. 'The Thematic Range of Dhrupad Songs Attributed to Tānsen, Foremost Court-Musician of the Mughal Emperor Akbar'. In *Studies in South Asian Devotional Literature*. Ed. by Alan W. Entwistle and Françoise Mallison. New Delhi: Manohar, pp. 406-29.

—. 2000a. 'The Image of Akbar as a Patron of Music in Indo-Persian and Vernacular Sources'. In *Akbar and His India*. Ed. by Irfan Habib. New Delhi: Oxford University Press, pp. 188-214.

—. 2000b. 'Indo-Persian Accounts on Music Patronage in the Sultanate of Gujarat'. In *The Making of Indo-Persian Culture: Indian and French Studies*. Ed. by Muzaffar Alam, Françoise "Nalini" Delvoye, and Marc Gaborieau. Delhi: Manohar and Centre de Sciences Humaines, pp. 253-80.

2010. 'Collections of Lyrics in Hindustani Music: The Case of Dhrupad.' In *Hindustani Music: Thirteenth to Twentieth Centuries*. Ed. by J. Bor, F. "Nalini" Delvoye, E. te Nijenhuis, and J. Harvey. New Delhi: Manohar, pp. 141-58.

Dempsey, Corinne. 2008. 'The Science of the Miraculous at an Upstate New York Hindu Temple'. In *Miracle as Modern Conundrum in South Asian Religious Traditions*. Ed. by Corinne G. Dempsey and Selva J. Raj. Albany: State University of New York Press, pp. 119-40.

Dhananjaya. 1950. *Nāmamālā*, with *bhāṣya* of Amarakirti. Ed. by Pandit Shambunath Tripathi. Varanasi: Bharatiya Jnanpith.

Dhanki, Madhusudan, and Jitendra Shah. 1999. *Mānatuṅgācārya aur unke stotra*. 2nd edn. Ahmedabad: Shardaben Cimanbhai Ejyukeshanal Risarch Sentar.

Digby, Simon. 1991. 'Mas'udi', *Encyclopedia of Islam*. Vol. 6. Leiden: Brill, pp. 783-84.

—. 2003. 'Two Captains of the Jawnpur Sultanate'. In *Circumambulations in South Asian History: Essays in Honour of Dirk H.A. Kolff*. Ed. by J. Gommans and O. Prakash. Leiden: Brill, pp. 159-78.

Dihkhuda, 'Ali Akbar. 2002. Mu'arrif. In *Lughatnāma-yi Dihkhudā*. Tehran: Intisharat-i Danishgah-i Tihran, CD.

Dillon, Emma. 2012. *The Sense of Sound: Musical Meaning in France, 1260-1330*. New York: Oxford University Press.

Dimock, Edward C. Jr. and Tony K. Stewart, eds. 1999. *Caitanya Caritāmṛta of Kṛṣṇadāsa Kavirāja: A Translation and Commentary*. Cambridge, MA: Harvard Oriental Series.

Dundas, Paul. 1996. 'Jain Attitudes towards the Sanskrit Language'. In *Ideology and Status of Sanskrit: Contributions to the History of the Sanskrit Language*. Ed. by Jan E.M. Houben. Leiden: Brill, pp. 137-56.

—. 1998. 'Becoming Gautama: Mantra and History in Śvetāmbara Jainism'. In *Open Boundaries: Jain Communities and Cultures in Indian History*. Ed. by John E. Cort. Albany: State University of New York Press, pp. 31-52.

—. 2007. *History, Scripture and Controversy in a Medieval Jain Sect*. London: Routledge.

Dunham, Mary Frances, 1997. *Jarigan: Muslim Epic Songs of Bangladesh*, Dhaka: The University Press Limited.

Dvijendra, Gaurishankar Mishra. 1975. *Hindī sāhitya kā chandovivecan*. Patna: Bihar Rashtrabhasha Parishad.

Eaton, Natasha. 2004. 'Between Mimesis and Alterity: Art, Gift, and Diplomacy in Colonial India, 1770-1800', *Comparative Studies in Society and History* 46, 40: 816-44. http://dx.doi.org/10.1017/s0010417504000374

Ebeling, Klaus. 1973. *Ragamala Painting*. Basel: Ravi Kumar.

Edgerton, Franklin 1924. *The Panchatantra Reconstructed: An Attempt to Establish the lost Original Sanskrit Text*. New Haven: American Oriental Society.

Ehnbom, Daniel J. 1984. 'An Analysis and Reconstruction of the Dispersed Bhāgavata Purāṇa from the Caurapañcāśikā Group'. PhD dissertation, University of Chicago.

Elkman, Stuart. 1986. *Jva Gosvāmin's Tattvasandarbha: A Study on the Philosophical and Sectarian Development of the Gauḍīya* Vaiṣṇava *Movement*. Delhi: Motilal Banarsidass.

Elwell-Sutton, L.P. 1976. *The Persian Metres*. Cambridge: Cambridge University Press.

Entwistle, Alan W. 1987. *Braj, Centre of Krishna Pilgrimage*. Groningen: Egbert Forsten.

Ernst, Carl W., and Bruce B. Lawrence. 2002. *Sufi Martyrs of Love: The Chishti Order in South Asia and Beyond*. New York: Palgrave Macmillan.

Ethé, Carl Hermann. 1903. *Catalogue of Persian Manuscripts in the Library of the India Office*. Oxford.

Fakhr al-Zamani Qazwini, 'Abd al-Nabi. 1983. *Tażkira-i maikhāna*. Ed. by Ahmad Gulcin-i Ma'ani. 3rd edn. Tehran: Iqbal.

Faqirullah, Saif Khan. 1996. *Tarjuma-i-Mānakutūhala & Risāla-i-Rāgadarpaṇa*. Ed. and trans. by Shahab Sarmadee. Kalāmūlasāstra Series 21. New Delhi: Indira Gandhi National Centre for the Arts and Motilal Banarsidass.

Farès, Bichr. 2009. 'Murū'a'. In *Encyclopaedia of Islam, Second Edition*. Ed. by P. Bearman, Th. Bianquis, C.E. Bosworth, E. van Donzel, and W.P. Heinrichs. Brill Online. http://www.brillonline.nl

Faruqi, Ziaul Hasan. 1996. *Fawaid Al-Fuad: Spiritual and Literary Discourses of Shaikh Nizamuddin Awliya*. New Delhi: D.K. Printworld.

Faruqi, Shamsur Rahman. 1999. *Sāḥirī, shāhī, sāḥib-qirānī: Dāstān-i Amīr Ḥamza kā mutāla'a*. Vol. 1. New Delhi: Qaumi Council bara'e furugh-i Urdu zaban.

Faruqui, N.R. 2006. *Medieval India: Essays on Sufism, Diplomacy and History*. Allahabad: Laburnum Press.

Feld, Steven. 1996. 'Waterfalls of Song: An Acoustemology of Place Resounding in Bosavi, Papua New Guinea.' In *Senses of Place*. Ed. by Steven Feld and Keith Basso. Santa Fe: School of American Research Press, pp. 91-135

Field, Claud, 1910. *Mystics and Saints of Islam*. London: F. Griffiths.

Finnegan, Ruth. 1989. *Literacy and Orality: Studies in the Technology of Communication*. Oxford: Blackwell.

Flatt, Emma. 2011. 'The Authorship and Significance of the Nujūm al-'Ulūm: A Sixteenth-Century Astrological Encyclopedia from Bijapur'. *Journal of the American Oriental Society* 131, 2: 223-44.

Flueckiger, Joyce. 2006. *In Amma's Healing Room: Gender and Vernacular Islam in South India*. Bloomington: Indiana University Press.

Flügel, Peter. 2006. 'Demographic Trends in Jaina Monasticism'. In *Studies in Jaina History and Culture: Disputes and Dialogues*. Ed. by Peter Flügel. London: Routledge, pp. 312-98. http://dx.doi.org/10.4324/9780203008539

Forbes, Duncan. 1830. *The Adventures of Hatim Taï: A Romance*. London: Oriental Translation Fund.

France, Peter, ed. 2000. *The Oxford Guide to Literature in English Translation*. Oxford: Oxford University Press. http://dx.doi.org/10.1093/acref/978019818 3594.001.0001

Gallego, María Angeles. 2003. 'The Languages of Medieval Iberia and their Religious Dimension', *Medieval Encounters* 9, 1: 107-39.

Gangoly, O.C. 1989. *Ragas and Raginis: A Pictorial and Iconographic Study of Indian Musical Modes based on Original Sources*. Vol. 1. Reprint New Delhi: Munshiram Manoharlal.

Gautam, Manmohan. 1958. 'Piṅgalnirūpak ācārya'. In *Hindī sāhitya kā bṛhat itihās: Rītikāl*. Ed. by Dr. Nagendra. Banaras: Kashi Nagaripracharini Sabha.

Gellner, David. 1995. 'Introduction'. In *Contested Hierarchies: A Collaborative Ethnography of Caste among the Newars of the Kathmandu Valley, Nepal*. Ed. by David N. Gellner and Declan Quigley. Oxford: Oxford University Press.

Gellner, David N., and Pradhan, Rajendra P. 1995. 'Urban Peasants: The Maharjans (Jyāpu) of Kathmandu and Lalitpur'. In *Contested Hierarchies: A Collaborative Ethnography of Caste among the Newars of the Kathmandu Valley, Nepal*. Ed. by David N. Gellner and Declan Quigley. Oxford: Oxford University Press.

Gerow, Edwin. 1971. *A Glossary of Indian Figures of Speech*. The Hague and Paris: Mouton. http://dx.doi.org/10.1515/9783110905250

Ghalib Lakhnawi, Mirza Aman 'Ali. 1855. *Tarjama-i dāstān-i Ṣāḥib-qirān*. Calcutta: Matba'-i Imdadiyya.

Ghani, Abdul. 1960. *Life and Works of Abdul Qadir Bedil*. Lahore: Publishers United.

Ghanimat, Muhammd Akram. 1962 [c.1690]. *Nairang-i 'ishq*. Ed. by 'Aziz, Ghulam Rabbani. Lahore: Panjabi Adabi Akademi.

al-Ghazzali, Abu Hamid. 1910 [c.1100]. *The Alchemy of Happiness* [*Kimīyā-yi sa'ādāt*]. Trans. by Claud Field. London: John Murray.

Ghoshal, Satyendranath. 1959. *Beginning of Secular Romance in Bengali Literature*. Santiniketan: Visva-Bharati.

Gilmont, Jean-François, and Alexandre Vanautgaerden, eds. 2010. *Les instruments de travail à la Renaissance* (Nugae humanisticae sub signo Erasmi). Turnhout: Brepols.

*Gītapañcāśika*. [Śāke 1550/1628], Nepal National Archives, MS no. 1-399.

Godlas, Alan. 2006. 'Sufism'. In *The Blackwell Companion to the Qur'ān*. Ed. by Andrew Rippin. Oxford: Blackwell, pp. 350-61. http://dx.doi.org/10.1002/9780470751428.ch23

Gold, Ann Grodzins. 1992. *A Carnival of Parting: The Tales of King Bharthari and King Gopi Chand As Sung and Told by Madhu Natisar Nath of Ghatiyali*. Berkeley: University of California Press.

—. 2008. 'Showing Miracles in Rajasthan: Proof and Grace'. In *Miracle as Modern Conundrum in South Asian Religious Traditions*. Ed. by Corinne G. Dempsey and Selva J. Raj. Albany: State University of New York Press.

Goody, J. and I. Watt. 1963. 'The Consequences of Literacy', *Comparative Studies in Society and History* 5, 3 (April): 304-45. http://dx.doi.org/10.1017/s0010417500001730

Gopaldas. 1993. *The* Sarvāṅgī *of Gopāldās: A 17th Century Anthology of Bhakti Literature*. Ed. by Winand M Callewaert. New Delhi: Manohar.

Gordon, Stewart, ed. 2003. *Robes of Honour: Khil'at in Pre-colonial and Colonial India*. New Delhi: Oxford University Press.

Gorekar, N.S. 1965. 'Persian Language and Sanskrit Lore', *Indics* 2: 107-19.

Goswami, C.L., trans. 1995 [1971]. *Śrīmad Bhāgavata Mahāpurāṇa (with Sanskrit Text and English Translation)*. Gorakhpur: Gita Press.

Grafton, Anthony, with April Shelford and Nancy Siraisi. 1992. *New Worlds, Ancient Texts: The Power of Tradition and the Shock of Discovery*. Cambridge, MA: Harvard University Press.

Grandin, Ingemar. 1989. *Music and Media in Local Life: Music Practice in a Newar Neighbourhood in Nepal*. Lingköping: Lingköping University.

Granoff, Phyllis. 1989-1990. 'The Biographies of Siddhasena: A Study in the Texture of Allusion and the Weaving of a Group-Image', *Journal of Indian Philosophy* 17, 4: 329-84 and 18, 4: 261-304. http://dx.doi.org/10.1007/bf00194175 http://dx.doi.org/10.1007/bf00160794

—. 1991. 'Buddhaghoṣa's Penance and Siddhasena's Crime: Remarks on Some Buddhist and Jain Attitudes Towards the Language of Religious Texts'. In *From Benares to Beijing: Essays on Buddhism and Chinese Religion*. Ed. by Koichi Shinohara and Phyllis Granoff. Oakville, Ont.: Mosaic Press, pp. 17-33.

—. [n.d.]. 'When is a Translation not a Translation, or Some Reflections on Attitudes towards Translation in Medieval India'. Unpublished manuscript.

Gross, Jo-Ann. 2012. 'Shrines of the Pamirs'. In *Tajikistan and the High Pamirs*. Ed. by Robert Middleton and Huw Thomas. Hong Kong: Airphoto International, p. 635.

Grubmüller, Klaus, L. Peter Johnson, and Hans-Hugo Steinhoff, eds. 1988. *Kleinere Erzählformen im Mittelalter: Paderborner Colloquium 1987* (Schriften der Universität-Gesamthochschule Paderborn, Reihe Sprach- und Literaturwissenschaft 10). Paderborn: Schöningh.

Gude, Tushara Bindu. 2009. 'Between Music and History: Rāgamāla Paintings and European Collectors in Late Eighteenth-Century Northern India'. PhD dissertation, University of California, Los Angeles.

Guha, Sumit. 2004. 'Transitions and Translations: Regional Power and Vernacular Identity in the Dakhan, 1500-1800', *Comparative Studies of South Asia, Africa and the Middle East* 24, 2: 23-31. http://dx.doi.org/10.1215/1089201x-24-2-23

Gulchin-i Ma'ani, Ahmad. 1969-1971. *Tārīkh-i taẕkirahā-yi fārsī*. 2 vols. Tehran: Intisharat-i Danishgah-i Tihran, 1348-50 AH.

Gupta, Dinadayalu. 1970. *Aṣṭachāp aur Vallabh-Sampradāy*. 2nd edn. Vol. 1. Allahabad: Hindi Sahitya Sammelan.

Gupta, Kiśorīlāl. 2007. *Iśk dariyāv*. Jhansi: Abhinav Prakashan.

Gupta, Parameshvarilal. 1981. *Malik Muhammad Jāyasī kṛt Kanhāvat*. Banaras: Vishvavidyalay Prakashan.

Hadi, Nabi. 1995. *Dictionary of Indo-Persian Literature*. New Delhi: Abhinav.

Hansen, Kathryn. 2010. 'Who Wants to be a Cosmopolitan? Readings from the Composite Culture', *Indian Economic and Social History Review* 47, 3: 291-308. http://dx.doi.org/10.1177/001946461004700301

Haravi, Amir Hasan. 1992. *Masnavī-hā-i 'irfānī*. Ed. by Sayyid Muhammad Turabi. Tehran: Mu'assasah-i Chap va Intisaharat-i Danishgah-i Tihran, 1371.

Harinarayanji, Purohit. 1961. *Vidyā-bhūṣaṇ-granth-saṃgrah-granth-sūcī* (Rajasthan Puratan Granthmala 55). Ed. by Gopalnarayan Bahura and Lakshminarayan Gosvami Diksit. Jodhpur: Rajasthan Oriental Research Institute.

Hariray. 1970. *Caurāsī vaiṣṇavan kī vārtā*. Ed. by Dv. Parikha and G. Shukla. Mathura: Shri Govardhana Granthamala Karyalaya.

Hasan, Qazi. [1664]. *Miftāḥ al-sarūd* [mistransliterated *Miṣbāḥ al-sorūr*]. Asiatic Society of Bengal, no. 1629 M136.

Hasrat, Bikrama Jit. 1953. *Dara Shikuh: Life and Works*. Calcutta: Visvabharati.

Hastings, James M. 2002. 'Poets, Saints and Warriors: The Dadu Panth, Religious Change and Identity Formation in Jaipur State. Circa 1562-1860 CE'. PhD dissertation, University of Wisconsin-Madison.

Hatcher, Brian A. 2010. 'Writing Sanskrit in the Vernacular: Vidyāsāgar, the Śāstras, and the Reading Public'. Paper presented at the Annual Meeting of the Association for Asian Studies. Philadelphia.

Haug, Walter. 1991. 'Exempelsamlungen im narrativen Rahmen: Von 'Pañcatantra' zum 'Dekamerone''. In: Haug and Wachinger, 264-87.

Haug, Walter and Burghart Wachinger, eds. 1991. *Exempel und Exempelsammlungen* (Fortuna vitrea 2). Tübingen: Niemeyer.

Hawley, John Stratton. 1984. *Sūr Dās: Poet, Singer, Saint*. Seattle: University of Washington Press, and Delhi: Oxford University Press.

—. 1988. 'Author and Authority in the Bhakti Poetry of North India', *The Journal of Asian Studies* 47, 2: 269-90. http://dx.doi.org/10.2307/2056168

—. 2005. *Three Bhakti Voices: Mirabai, Surdas, and Kabir in Their Times and Ours*. New Delhi: Oxford University Press.

—. 2009. 'The *Bhāgavata Māhātmya* in Context'. In *Patronage and Popularisation, Pilgrimage and Procession: Channels of Transcultural Translation and Transmission in Early Modern South Asia; Papers in Honour of Monika Horstmann*. Ed. by Heidi R.M. Pauwels. Wiesbaden: Harrassowitz, pp. 81-100.

—. 2009. *The Memory of Love: Sūrdās Sings to Krishna*. New York: Oxford University Press.

—. 2016. *Into Sūr's Ocean: Poetry, Context, and Commentary*. Cambridge, MA: Harvard Oriental Series.

Hayes, Richard D. 1974. *Svāmī Haridās and the Haridāsī Sampradāy*. Dissertation in South Asia Regional Studies, University of Pennsylvania.

Hazra, R.C. 1958. *Studies in the Upapurāṇas*, Vol. *I, Saura and Vaiṣṇava Upapurāṇas*. Calcutta: Sanskrit College.

Hein, Norvin. 1969. 'Guru Nanak's Comment on the Vaishnava Lila'. In *Perspectives on Guru Nanak*. Ed. by Harbans Singh. Patiala: Punjabi University, pp. 493-501.

—. 1972. *The Miracle Plays of Mathurā*. New Haven: Yale University Press.

Henry, E.O. 2002. 'The Rationalization of Intensity in Indian music', *Ethnomusicology* 46, 1: 33-55. http://dx.doi.org/10.2307/852807

Herman, A.L. 1971. 'Indian Theodicy: Samkara and Ramanuja on Brahmasutra II.1.32-36', *Philosophy East and West* 21, 3: 265-81. http://dx.doi.org/10.2307/1398356

Hermans, Theo. 1985. 'Metaphor and Imagery in the Renaissance Discourse on Translation'. In *The Manipulation of Literature: Studies in Translation*. Ed. by Theo Hermans. New York: St. Martin's Press, pp. 103-35.

Hermansen, M.K. 1997. 'Religious Literature and the Inscription of Identity: The Sufi Tazkira Tradition in Muslim South Asia', *The Muslim World* 87, 3/4 (Jul-Oct): 315-20. http://dx.doi.org/10.1111/j.1478-1913.1997.tb03642.x

Hermansen, M.K., and B.B. Lawrence. 2000. 'Indo-Persian *Tazkiras* as Memorative Communications'. In *Beyond Turk and Hindu. Rethinking Religious Identities in Islamicate South Asia*. Ed. by D. Gilmartin and B.B. Lawrence. Gainesville, FL: University Press of Florida, pp. 149-75.

Hertel, J. 1908. *The Panchatantra: A Collection of Ancient Hindu Tales in the Recension called Panchakhyanaka, and Dated 1199 A.D., of the Jaina Monk Purnabhadra*. Cambridge, MA: Harvard University Press.

Heyat, Mamud. 2000. *Kavi Heyāt Māmud*. Ed. by Mazharul Islam. Dhaka: Agami Prakashana.

Hiltebeitel, A. 2001. *Draupadī Among Rajputs, Muslims and Dalits: Rethinking India's Oral and Classical Epics*. New Delhi: Oxford University Press.

Hindi, Bhagvan Das. 1958. *Safīna-yi Hindī*. Ed. by S. Shah Md. Ataur Rahman. Patna: Institute of Post Graduate Studies and Research in Arabic and Persian.

Horstmann, Monika. 2000. 'The Flow of Grace: Food and Feast in the Hagiography and History of the Dādūpanth', *Zeitschrift der Deutschen Morgenländischen Gesellschaft* 150: 513-80.

—. 2006. 'Dadupanthi Anthologies of the Eighteenth and Nineteenth Centuries'. In *Bhakti in Current Research, 2001-2003*. New Delhi: Manohar, pp. 163-77.

—. 2008. 'An Indian Sacred Journey'. In *Prozessionen, Wallfahrten, Aufmärsche: Bewegung zwischen Religion und Politik in Europa und Asien seit dem Mittelalter*. Ed. by J. Gengnagel, M. Horstmann, and G. Schwedler. Köln, Weimar, Wien: Böhlau, pp. 336-60.

—. 2009. 'Texts and How to Practise Them'. In Écrire et transmettre an Inde classique (Études thématiques 23). Ed. by G. Colas and G. Gerschheimer. Paris: Ècole française d'Extrême-Orient, pp. 27-42.

Hyder, Syed Akbar. 2008. Reliving Karbala: Martyrdom in South Asian Memory. New York: Oxford University Press. http://dx.doi.org/10.1093/acprof:oso/9780195373028.001.0001

Ibbetson, Denzil and Edward Maclagan. 1911. *A Glossary of the Tribes and Castes of the Punjab and North-West Frontier Province*. Lahore: Superintendent, Govt. Printing.

Ibn 'Arabi, Muhyi al-Din. 1972. *al-Futūḥāt al-Makkīya*. Ed. by 'Othman Yahya; revised by Ibrahim Madkour. Cairo: Al-Hai'at al-Misriyya al-Amma, and Paris: Sorbonne.

Ibn Sina, Abu 'Ali al-Husain b. 'Abd Allah. 1973. 'Fann al-shi'r'. In *Fann al-shi'r*. Ed. by 'Abd al-Rahman Badawi. 2nd edn. Beirut: Dar al-thaqafa, pp. 159-98.

"Insha," Insha'allah Khan. 1925 [1803]. *Ranī Ketakī kī kahānī*. Ed. by Shyamsundardas. Kashi: Nagari Pracharini Sabha.

Iskandar Munshi. 1978. *History of Shah 'Abbas the Great, Tārīk-e Ālamārā-ye 'Abbāsī*. Vol. 1. Trans. by Roger M. Savory. Boulder: Westview Press.

Islam, Riazul. 2002. *Sufism in South Asia: Impact on Fourteenth Century Muslim Society*. Karachi: Oxford University Press.

Jacobi, Herman. 1989 [1895]. *Jaina Sūtras Part 2: Translation of the Uttarādhyanasūtra and Sūtrakṛtānga*. Oxford: Oxford University Press.

Jahanara. 1991. *Mūnis al-arvāḥ*, in *Princess Jahān Ārā Begam, Her Life and Works*. Ed. by Qamar Jahan Begam. Karachi: S.M. Hamid 'Ali.

Jahangir, Nur al-Din Muhammad. 1359 AH. *Jahāngīrnāma (Tūzuk-i Jahāngīrī)*. Ed. by Muhammad Hashim. Tehran: Bunyad-i Farhang-i Iran.

Jai Singh. 2002. *Kāvyaras*. Ed. by Devendra. Jodhpur: Rajasthan Oriental Research Institute.

Jain, Balbhadra, ed. 1974. *Bhārat ke digambar jain tīrth*, Vol. 1. Bombay: Bharatvarshiya Digambar Jain Tirthkshetra Kameti.

Jain, Kamtaprasad. 1947. *Hindī jain sāhitya kā saṅkṣipt itihās*. Banaras: Bharatiya Jnanpith.

Jain, Mulchand, "Vatsal". 1937. *Jain kaviyoṃ kā itihās yā prācīn hindī jain kavi*. Damoh: Subhchintak Press.

Jain Shastri, Paramanand. 1941. 'Prastāvnā'. In *Nāmamālā of Banārsīdās*. Ed. by Jugalkishor Mukhtar. Sarsawa: Vir Seva Mandir, pp. 5-16.

Jain, Ravindra Kumar. 1966. *Kavivar Banārsīdās (jīvan aur kṛtitva)*. Varanasi: Bharatiya Jnanpith Prakashan.

Jaini, Padmanabh S. 2004. '*Caurāsī Bol* of Hemrāj Pāṇḍe'. In *Jambū-jyoti (Munivara Jambūvijaya Festschrift)*. Ed. by M.A. Dhaky and J.B. Shah. Ahmedabad: Shreshthi Kasturbhai Lalbhai Smarak Nidhi, pp. 374-98.

—. 2007. 'Jain Sectarian Debates: Eighty-four Points of Contention (*Cauryāṁsī bol*) Between Śvetāmbaras and Digambaras (Text and Translation)', *Journal of Indian Philosophy* 36: 1-246. http://dx.doi.org/10.1007/s10781-007-9020-x

Jaipur state. VS 1863 and 1874. *Dastūr komvār* 31. Rajasthan State Archives, Bikaner.

Jameson, Fredric. 1981. *The Political Unconscious: Narrative as a Socially Symbolic Act*. Ithaca, N.Y.: Cornell University Press.

Jangopal. 1988. *The Hindī Biography of Dādū Dayāl*. Ed. and trans. by Winand M. Callewaert. Delhi: Motilal Banarsidass.

Jasanoff, Maya. 2006. *Edge of Empire: Conquest and Collecting in the East, 1750-1850*. London: Harper Perennial.

Jauss, Hans Robert. 1982. *Toward an Aesthetic of Reception*. Minneapolis: University of Minnesota Press.

Jayasi, Malik Muhammad. 1971. *Kanhāvat*. Ed. by Parameshwarilal Gupta. Banaras: Annapurna Prakashan.

—. 1973. *Padmāvat*. Ed. by Mata Prasad Gupta. 2nd edn. Allahabad: Bharati Bhandar.

—. 1981. *Kanhāvat*. Ed. by Shivsahay Pathak. Allahabad: Sahitya Bhawan.

Jenner, Gero. 1969. *Die poetischen Figuren der Inder von Bhāmaha bis Mammaṭa*. Hamburg: Ludwig Appel Verlag.

Jha, Sobhadra. 1954. *Vidyāpati-Gīt-Saṅgrah or The Songs of Vidyāpati*. Banaras: Motilal Banarsidass.

Jinasena. 1963-65. *Ādipurāṇa*. Ed. and trans. by Pandit Pannalal Jain. 2 vols. Varanasi: Bharatiya Jnanpith.

—. 1969. *Jinasahasranāma stavana*. Ed. by Mohanlal Shastri. Jabalpur: Saral Jain Granth Bhandar.

—. [n.d.]. *Jinasahasranāma stavana*. With Sanskrit *ṭīkā* of Amarakirti and Hindi translation of Brahmachari Pramila Jain. Giridih: Shri Digambar Jain Madhyalok Shodh Sasthan.

Johrapurkar, Vidyadhar. 1958. *Bhaṭṭārak sampradāy*. Sholapur: Jain Samskriti Samrakshak Sangh.

Jones, William and N. August Willard. 1962. *Music of India*. Calcutta: Susil Gupta.

Jnaneshvar. 1967. *Jñāneśvari (Bhāvārthadīpikā)*. Trans. by V.G. Pradhan; Ed. by H.M. Lambert. 2 vols. London: Allen and Unwin.

Kabi, Bhima. 1966 [1493]. *Ḍaṅgvai kathā*. Ed. by Shivgopal Misra. Allahabad: Hindi Sahitya Sammelan.

Kalidasa. 1993. *Raghuvaṃśa*. Ed. by Rewa Prasad Dwivedi. New Delhi: Sahitya Akademi.

Kamgar Husaini, Khvaja. 1978. *Ma'āṣir-i Jahāngīrī*. Ed. by Azra Alavi. New York: Asia Publishing House.

Kamilkhani, 'Ivaz Muhammad. 1668. *Risāla dar 'amal-i bīn o thātha-yi rāg-hā-yi Hindī*. Bodleian Library, Ouseley 158, ff. 123a-32b.

Kamphorst, Janet. 2008. 'In Praise of Death'. PhD dissertation, Leiden University.

Karim, Shaikh 'Abdul, bin Shaikh Farid Ansari al-Qadiri. c.1630. *Javāhir al-mūsīqāt-i Muḥammadī*. British Library, Or. 12,857.

Kashani, 'Izz al-Din Mahmud bin 'Ali. 2008. *Misbāh al-hidāya wa miftāha al-kifāya*. Ed. by 'Iffat Karbasi and Muhammad Riza Barzgar Khaliqi. Tehran: Zavvar.

Kashefi, Husain Va'ez. 1911. *Rawżat as-shohadā*. Kanpur: Naval Kishor.

Kashifi, Husayn Va'iz, 2000. *The Royal Book of Spiritual Chivalry (Futūwat nāmah-yi sulṭānī)*. Trans. by Jay R. Crook. Chicago: Great Books of the Islamic World.

Kaslival, Kasturchand. 1986. *Kavivar Bulākhīcand, Bulākīdās evaṃ Hemrāj*. Jaipur: Shri Mahavir Granth Akademi.

Kaslival, Kasturchand, and Anupchand Nyaytirth, eds. 1962. *Rājasthān ke jain śāstra bhaṇḍāroṃ kī granth-sūcī*, Vol. 4. Jaipur: Shri Digambar Jain Atishay Kshetra Shri Mahavirji.

—. 1972. *Rājasthān ke jain śāstra bhaṇḍāroṃ kī granth-sūcī*, Vol. 5. Mahavirji: Shri Digambar Jain Atishay Kshetra Shri Mahavirji.

Kaur, Madanjit. 1983. *The Golden Temple: Past and Present*. Amritsar: Department of Guru Nanak Studies, Guru Nanak Dev University.

Kavindra Parameshwar Das. 1999. *Kavīndra-Mahābhārata*. Ed. by Kalpana Bhowmik. Dhaka: Bangla Academy.

Kavindracharya Sarasvati. *Kavīndrakalpalatā*. Pothikhana, manuscript no. 1174, Maharaja Sawai Man Singh II Museum, Jaipur.

—. 1958. *Kavīndrakalpalatā*. Ed. by Rani Lakshmikumari Chundavat. Jaipur: Rajasthan Oriental Research Institute.

Kaviraj, Sudipta. 2003. 'The Two Histories of Literary Culture in Bengal'. In *Literary Cultures in History*. Ed. by Sheldon Pollock. Berkeley and Los Angeles: University of California Press.

Kay Kavus. 1951. *A Mirror for Princes, The Qābūs Nāma*. Trans. by Reuben Levy. New York: E.P. Dutton.

Keshavadas. 1954. *Kavipriyā*. In *Keśavgranthāvalī*, Vol 1. Ed. by Vishvanathprasad Mishra. 3 vols. Allahabad: Hindustani Academy.

—. 1954. *Rasikpriyā*. In *Keśavgranthāvalī*, Vol 1. Ed. by Vishvanathprasad Mishra. 3 vols. Allahabad: Hindustani Academy.

—. 1959. *Jahāngīrjascandrikā*. In *Keśavgranthāvalī*, Vol 3. Ed. by Vishvanathprasad Mishra. 3 vols. Allahabad: Hindustani Academy.

—. 1959. *Vīrsiṃhdevcarit*. In *Keśavgranthāvalī*, Vol 3. Ed. by Vishvanathprasad Mishra. 3 vols. Allahabad: Hindustani Academy.

—. 1994. *Jahāngīrjascandrikā*. Ed. by Kishorilal. Allahabad: Sahitya Bhavan.

—. 1997. *Vīrsiṃhdevcarit*. Ed. by Kishorilal. Allahabad: Hindi Sahitya Sammelan.

Keshava Mishra. 1926. *Alaṅkāraśekhara*. Ed. by Pandit Shivadatta and Kashinath Pandurang Parab. 2nd edn. Bombay: Nirnaya Sagar Press.

Keshavmurti, Prashant. 'Ḥaqīrī Kāšānī, *Maṯnawī-i mādhavānal-kāmakandalā mausūm ba maḥẓ-i i'jāz*', *Perso-Indica*, http://perso-indica.net/work.faces?idsec=16&idw=122

Ketakadas Kshemanand. 1384 BA. *Manasāmaṅgala*. Ed. by Akshaykumar Kayal and Citra Dev. Kolkata: Lekhapada.

Khalilian, M.A. and Stephen Blum. 2007. 'Musical Ontology of the Naqshbandi Order in Eastern Iran', unpublished paper. Society for Ethnomusicology Annual Meeting.

Khan, Karamatullah. 1908. *Isrār-e Karāmat*. Allahabad: Janaki Press.

Khan, Khushhal "Anup". [1800, Brajbhasha]. *Rāg darshan*. University of Pennsylvania Rare Book and Manuscript Library, Lawrence J Schoenberg Collection, LJS 63.

—. [1808, Persian]. *Rāg darshan*. Government Oriental Manuscripts Library, University of Madras, D1024 P Ms.

—. [1818-1834]. *Rāg-rāginī rōz o shab*. Salar Jung Museum Library, Urdu Mus 2.

Khan, Mirza, ibn Fakhruddin Muhammad. 1968 [c.1675]. *Tuḥfat al-Hind*. Vol. 1. Ed. by N.H. Ansari. Tehran: Bunyad-i Farhang-i Iran.

Khan, Muhammad Karam Imam. 1925 [1869]. *Ma'dan al-mūsīqī*. Ed. by Sayyid Wajid 'Ali. Lucknow: Hindustani Press.

Khan, Pasha M. 2009. 'Genre Identifications: Hatim-namas as Romance and Qissa'. Paper presented at the annual meeting of the Association for Asian Studies, 28 March, Chicago.

—. 2012. 'Marvelous Histories: Reading the *Shāhnāmah* in India', *Indian Economic and Social History Review* 49, 4: 527-56. http://dx.doi.org/10.1177/0019464612463807

Khan, Ras Baras. 2012 [1698]. *Shams al-aṣvāt*. Ed. and trans. by Mehrdad Fallahzadeh. Uppsala: Acta Universitatis Upsaliensis.

Khan, Nawwab Samsam-ud-daula Shah Nawaz and 'Abdul Hayy. 1952 [1747/1780]. *The Maāthir-ul-Umarā*. Vol. 2. Trans. by H. Beveridge. Calcutta: Oriental Press.

Khosla, Preeti. 2014. 'The Visual Languages of the North Indian Styles of Book Paintings during the Sultanate Period (1411-1525)'. PhD dissertation, School of Oriental and African Studies, London.

Khwushgu, Bindraban Das. 1959. *Safīna-yi Khwushgū*. Ed. by S. Shah Md. Ataur Rahman. Patna: Institute of Post Graduate Studies and Research in Arabic and Persian.

King, Christopher. 1994. *One Language, Two Scripts: The Hindi Movement in Nineteenth-Century North India*. Oxford: Oxford University Press.

Kippen, James. 2006. *Gurudev's Drumming Legacy: Music, Theory and Nationalism in the* Mṛdaṅg aur Tabla Vādanpaddhati *of Gurudev Patwardhan*. Aldershot: Ashgate.

Korom, Frank J. 2002. *Hosay Trinidad: Muharram Performances in an Indo-Caribbean Diaspora*. Philadelphia: University of Pennsylvania. http://dx.doi.org/10.9783/9780812202526

Kosambi, D.D. 1962. 'Urvasi and Pururavas'. In *Myth and Reality: Studies in the Formation of Indian Culture*. Bombay: Popular Prakashan.

Krittibas. 1936. *Mahākavi Kṛttivāsa viracita Rāmāyaṇa, Ādikāṇḍa*. Ed. by Nalinikantha Bhattashali. Dhaka: Shrinath Press.

—. 2002. *Kṛttivāsī Rāmāyaṇa*. Ed. by Harekrishna Mukhopadhyay. Kolkata: Sāhitya Saṃsad.

Kshemakarna. 2003. *Rāgamālā*. Ed. and trans. by Vinod Shastri and Rama Gupta. Jaipur: Rajasthan Sanskrit Academy.

Kumbha, Maharana. 1963. *Saṅgītarāja*. Vol. 1. Ed. by Premlata Sharma. Hindu Vishvavidyalaya Nepal Rajya Sanskrit Series Vol. 5. Varanasi: Hindu Vishvavidyalaya Sanskrit Publication Board.

Kumudachandra. 1974. *Kalyāṇamandira stotra*, with Sanskrit *ṭīkā* of Chandrakirti and Hindi translation of Banarsidas. Ed. by Pandit Pannalal Shastri "Vasant". Bombay: Virendrakumar Devendrakumar Jain.

Kundakunda. 1935. *Pravacanasāra*, with Sanskrit *ṭīkās* of Amritachandra and Jayasena and Hindi *Bālbodh* of Pande Hemraj. Ed. by A.N. Upadhye. Bombay: Parama Shruta Prabhavaka Mandala.

Lacrosse, Joachim. 2007. 'Some Remarks about a Meeting between Socrates and an Indian (Aristoxenus 53)', *Archiv für Geschichte der Philosophie* 89, 3: 247-63. http://dx.doi.org/10.1515/agph.2007.012

Lahori, 'Abd al-Sattar ibn Qasim. 1385 S. *Majālis-i Jahāngīrī. Majlis-hā-yi shabāna-yi sarbār-i Nūr al-Dīn Jahāngīr, az 24 rajab 1017 tā 19 ramaẓān 1020 h.q.* Ed. by Riza Allah Shah 'Arif Nawshahi and Mu'in Nizami. Tehran: Markaz-i Pizhuhishi-i Mirath-i Maktub.

Lath, Mukund. 1981. *Half a Tale: A Study in the Interrelationship between Autobiography and History*. Jaipur: Rajasthan Prakrit Bharati Sansthan.

Levy, R.I. 1990. *Mesocosm: Hinduism and the Organization of a Traditional Newar City in Nepal*, 2nd edn. Indian reprint 1992. Delhi: Motilal Banarsidass.

Lewis, Franklin. 2000. *Rumi, Past and Present, East and West: The Life, Teaching and Poetry of Jalāl al-Din Rumi*. Oxford: Oneworld.

Livingstone, David. 2008. *Adam's Ancestors: Race, Religion and the Politics of Human Origins*. Baltimore: The John Hopkins University Press.

Lodi, Sher 'Ali Khan. 1998 [1691]. *Tazkira-yi mir'āt al-khayāl*. Ed. by Hamid Hasani and Bihruz Safarzadah. Tehran: Rawzanah.

Lorenzen, David. 1996. 'Sain's *The Kabir-Raidas debate*'. In *Praises to a Formless God: Nirguṇī Texts from North India*. Albany: State University of New York Press, pp. 169-204.

Losensky, Paul E. 1993. *Welcoming Fighani: Imitation, Influence, and Literary Change in the Persian ghazal, 1480-1680*. Costa Mesa, CA: Mazda.

—. 1998. *Welcoming Fighāni: Imitation and Poetic Individuality in the Safavid-Mughal* Ghazal. Costa Mesa, CA: Mazda.

Lutgendorf, Philip. 1991. *The Life of a Text: Performing the* Rāmcaritmānas *of Tulsidas*. Berkeley: University of California Press.

Lybarger, Lowell. 2003. 'The Tabla Solo Repertoire of Pakistani Panjab: An Ethnomusicological Perspective'. PhD dissertation, University of Toronto.

Lyons, John D. 1989. *Exemplum: The Rhetoric of Example in Early Modern France and Italy*. Princeton: Princeton University Press.

Lynch, Jack. 1998. 'Political Ideology in Translations of the Iliad, 1660-1715'. *Translation and Literature* 7, 1: 23-41. http://dx.doi.org/10.3366/tal.1998.7.1.23

Maheshvari, Hiralal. 1980. *History of Rajasthani Literature*. New Delhi: Sahitya Academy.

Mahipati. 1890. *Bhaktavijay*. Bombay: Saka.

Mahjub, Muhammad Ja'far. 1991. 'Tahawwul-i Naqqali wa Qissa-khwani', *Irannama* 9: 186-211.

Majumdar, Bimanbehari. 1961. 'The *Bhāgavata Purāṇa* and its Influence in the Sixteenth Century', *Journal of the Bihar Research Society* 47, 1-4: 381-93.

Malik, Aditya ed. 2003. *Śrī Devnārāyaṇ Kathā: An Oral Narrative of Marwar* (South Asia Insitute, New Delhi Branch, Heidelberg University, South Asia Studies 52). New Delhi: D.K. Printworld.

Malik, Aditya. 2005. *Nectar Gaze and Poison Breath: An Analysis and Translation of the Rajasthani Oral Narrative of Devnārāyaṇ*. New York: Oxford University Press.

Malik, J. 2003. 'Muslim Culture and Reform in 18th Century South Asia', *Journal of the Royal Asiatic Society* 13, 2: 227-43. http://dx.doi.org/10.1017/s1356186303003080

Mallison, Françoise. 2011. 'The Teaching of Braj, Gujarati and Bardic Poetry at the Court of Kutch: The *Bhuj Braj-bhāṣā Pāṭhśālā* (1749-1948)'. In *Forms of Knowledge in Early Modern Asia: Explorations in the Intellectual History of India and Tibet, 1500-1800*. Ed. by Sheldon Pollock. Durham: Duke University Press.

Malviya, Lakshmidhar. 2008. *Bihārīdās kī satsaī*. Vol. 1. New Delhi: Aditya Prakashan.

Manatunga. 1907. *Ādināth̄a stotra arthāt Bhaktāmara stotra*, with *saral bhāṣāṭīkā* and *navīn padyānuvād*. Trans. by Nathuram Premi. Bombay: Jain Granth Ratnākar Kāryālay.

—. c.1990. *Bhaktāmarastotra*, with Hindi translations of Hemraj. Ed. by Pandit Girdhar Sharma and Nathuram Premi. Surat: Digambar Jain Pustakalay.

—. 2012. *Bhaktāmarastotra*. Hindi poetic trans. and gloss by Pandit Nathuram Premi, English trans. by Manish Modi. Mumbai: Hindi Granth Karyalay.

Mangaldas, Svami ed. 1948. *Pañcāmṛt*. Jaipur: Shri Svami Lakshmiram Trust.

Manjhan. 2000. *Madhumālatī*. Trans. by Aditya Behl and Simon Weightman with Shyam Manohar Pandey. Oxford: Oxford University Press.

Mann, Gurinder Singh. 2001. *The Making of Sikh Scripture*. Oxford: Oxford University Press.

Marcus, Scott L. 1989. 'The Rise of a Folk Music Genre: Biraha'. In *Culture and Power in Banaras: Community, Performance, and Environment, 1800-1980*. Ed. by Sandria B. Freitag. Berkeley: University of California Press, pp. 93-113.

Matilal, B.K. 1992. 'Samkara's Theodicy', *Journal of Indian Philosophy*, 20, 4: 363-76.

Matthee, Rudi. 2009. *The Pursuit of Pleasure: Drugs and Stimulants in Iranian History*. Princeton: Princeton University Press.

Matthiessen, F.O. 1931. *Translation: An Elizabethan Art*. Cambridge, MA: Harvard University Press.

McClish, Mark, and Patrick Olivelle. 2012. *The Arthaśāstra*. Indianapolis and Cambridge: Hackett Publishing Company.

McGregor, R.S. 1968. *The Language of Indrajit of Orcha*. Cambridge: Cambridge University Press.

—, trans. 1973. *Nanddas, The Round Dance of Krishna and Uddhav's Message*. London: Luzac and Company.

—. 1984. *Hindi Literature from its Beginnings to the Nineteenth Century*. Wiesbaden: Harrassowitz.

—. 1991. 'An Early Hindi (Brajbhāṣā) Version of the *Rāma* Story: The *Rāmāyaṇ-kathā* (A.D. 1442) of Viṣṇudās'. In *Devotion Divine: Bhakti Traditions from the Regions of India: Studies in Honour of Charlotte Vaudeville*. Ed. by Diana L. Eck and Françoise Mallison. Groningen: Egbert Forstein, and Paris: École Française D'Extrême-Orient, pp. 181-96.

—. 1993. *The Oxford Hindi-English Dictionary*. Delhi: Oxford University Press.

—. 1999. 'Viṣṇudās and his *Rāmāyan-kathā*'. In *Studies in Early Modern Indo-Aryan Languages, Literature and Culture*. Ed. by Alan W. Entwistle and Carol Salomon. Delhi: Manohar, pp. 239-47.

—. 2000. 'A Narrative Poet's View of his Material: Viṣṇudās's Introduction to his Brajbhāṣā *Pāṇḍav-carit* (AD 1435)'. In *The Banyan Tree: Essays on Early Literature in New Indo-Aryan Languages*. Ed. by Mariola Offredi. New Delhi: Manohar, pp. 335-42.

Mehta, Mohanlal, and Hiralal R. Kapadiya. 1968. *Jain sāhitya kā bṛhad itihās, Vol. 4, Karm-sāhitya va āgamik prakaraṇ*. Varanasi: Parshvanath Vidyashram Shodh Sansthan.

Meisami, Julie Scott. 1987. *Medieval Persian Court Poetry*. Princeton: Princeton University Press.

—. 2010. 'A Life in Poetry: Hafiz's First Ghazal', in *The Necklace of the Pleiades. 24 Essays on Persian Literature, Culture and Religion*. Ed. by F.D. Lewis and S. Sharma. Leiden: Leiden University Press, pp. 163-81.

Menariya, Motilal. 1999. *Rājasthānī bhāṣā aur sāhitya*. Reprint Jodhpur: Rajasthani Granthagar.

Miner, Allyn. 1997. *Sitar and Sarod in the 18th and 19th Centuries*. New Delhi: Motilal Banarsidas.

Mir Khvand, Mir Muhammad bin Siyid Burhan al-Din Khvandshah. 1959. *Tārīkh-i rawżat al-ṣafā'*. Tehran: Markazi Khayam Piroz, 1338 *shamsi*.

—. 1982. *The Rauzat-us-Safa, or, Garden of Purity: Containing the Histories of Prophets, Kings, and Khalifs*. Trans. by E. Rehatsek, ed. by F.F. Arbuthnot. Reprint Delhi: Idarah-i Adabiyat-i Delli.

Mishra, Shitikanth. 1994. *Hindī jain sāhitya kā br̥had itihās, bhāg 2, Sattrahvīṃ śatī*. Varanasi: Pujya Sohanlal Smarak Parshvanath Shodhpith.

Mishra, Surati. 1992. *Jorāvarprakāś*. Ed. by Yogendrapratap Singh. Allahabad: Hindi Sahitya Sammelan.

Mishra, Vishvanathprasad. 1959. 'Sampādakīya'. In *Padmākargranthāvalī*. Varanasi: Nagari Pracarini Sabha.

Misra, Rajkumari ed. 1982. *Ālamkr̥t Mādhavānala Kāmakandalā*. Allahabad: Ratnakumari Svadhyay Sansthan.

Misra, Shivgopal. 1958. *Satyavatī kathā tathā anya kr̥tiyāṃ*. Gwalior: Vidyamandir Prakashan.

—. 1966. *Ḍaṅgvai kathā tathā cakravyūha kathā*. Allahabad: Hindi Sahitya Sammelan.

Modi, Manish. 2007. 'Pandit Nathuram Premi: Jain Scholar and Publisher', *Jaina Studies: Newsletter of the Centre of Jaina Studies* 2: 42-44.

Mohanta, Sambaru Chandra. 2006. 'Panchali'. In *Banglapedia*. Ed. by Sirajul Islam. Dhaka: Asiatic Society of Bangladesh. CD.

Moinuddin, Khaja. 1971 [1977]. *A Monograph on Muharram in Hyderabad City*. Delhi: Census of India.

Molino, Jean. 1975. 'Fait musical et sémiologue de la musique', *Musique en Jeu* 17: 37-62.

Momen, Moojan. 1985. *An Introduction to Shi'i Islam*. New Haven: Yale University Press.

Monier-Williams, Monier. 1956 [1899]. *A Sanskrit-English Dictionary*. Oxford: Clarendon Press.

von Moos, Peter. 1988. *Geschichte der Topik. Das rhetorische Exemplum von der Antike zur Neuzeit und der Historiae im "Polycraticus" Johanns von Salisbury*. Hildesheim: Georg Olms.

Muhammad Salih Kanbo. 1967-1972. *'Amal-i Ṣāliḥ*. Ed. by Ghulam Yazdani and Vahid Quraishi. Lahore: Majlis-i Taraqqi-yi Adab.

Mukhopadhyay, Sukhmay. 2000. *Purātana bāṃlā sāhityera tathya o kālakrama*, Dhaka: Khan Brothers and Co.

Mutribi Samarqandi. 1977. *Khāṭirāt-i Muṭribī*. Ed. by 'Abd al-Ghani Mirzayif. Karachi: Mu'assasah-yi Tahqiqat-i Asiya-yi Miyanah va Gharbi, Danishgah.

Muttaqi (Al-), 'Ala al-Din 'Ali. 2004. *Kanz al-'ummāl fi sunan al-aqwāl wa al-af'āl*. Ed. by Shaykh Bakri Hayyani and Shaykh Safwat al-Saqa. Beirut: Dar al-Kutub al-'Ilmiyah.

Muqtadir, Khan Bahadur 'Abdul, ed. 1970. *Catalogue of Arabic and Persian Manuscripts in Khuda Bakhsh Oriental Public Library, Patna, Vol. XIV*. Reprint Patna.

Nahta, A., ed. 1965. *Rāghavdāskr̥t bhaktamāl*. Jodhpur: Rajasthan Oriental Research Institute.

Naim, C.M. 1991. 'Poet-Audience Interaction at Urdu Musha'iras'. In *Urdu and Muslim South Asia: Studies in honour of Ralph Russell*. Ed. by C. Shackle. Delhi: Oxford University Press, pp. 167-73.

Nainsi, Mumhata. 1960. *Naiṇsī rī khyāt*. Ed. by Badariprasad Sakariya. Jodhpur: Rajasthan Oriental Research Institute.

Nanddas. 1949. *Nanddās granthāvalī*. Ed. by Vrajratnadas. Banaras: Nagari Pracharini Sabha.

Narada, Damodara Sen. 1984. *Pañcamasārasaṃhitā and Saṅgītadāmodara*. Ed. by Guru Bipin Singh, trans. by Lalmani Tiwari. Calcutta: Manipuri Nartanalaya.

Narayandas, Swami. [2019 VS]. *Śrī Dṛṣṭānt-sudhā-sindhu*. 6 vols. Jaipur: [n.p.].

—. [2035-36 VS]. *Dadu panth paricay*. 3 vols. Jaipur: Shri Dadu Dayalu Mahasabha.

—. [2040 VS]. *Śrī Daduvāṇī pravacan paddhati*. Jaipur: Shri Dadu Mahasabha.

Narayandas, Swami, ed. 1969. *Rāghavdāskṛt bhaktamāl*. Jaipur: Shri Dadudayal Mahasabha.

—. 1985. *Sant pravar Dādūjī ke suyogya śiṣya Jagannāthjī āmer vālõ kā saṅgrah gratha Guṇgañjnāmā 37 aṅgõ kī ṭīkā śeṣ kī ṭippaṇī sahit*. Jaipur: Shri Dadudayal Mahasabha.

Nassakh, 'Abd al-Ghafur. 1982. *Sukhan-i shu'arā'*. Lucknow: Uttar Pradesh Urdu Academy.

Nattiez, Jean-Jacques. 1990. *Music and Discourse: Towards a Semiology of Music*. Trans. by Carolyn Abbate. Princeton: Princeton University Press.

Nawab, Sarabai M. 1956. *Masterpieces of the Kalpasutra Paintings*. Jain Art Publication Series no. 7, Ahmedabad: Sarabhai Manilal Nawab.

Nawab, Vidya Sarabhai. 1964. *419 Illustrations of Indian Music and Dance in Western Indian Style*. Ahmedabad: Sarabhai Manilal Nawab.

Nemichandra. 1978-1979. *Gommaṭasāra*. Ed. by Adinath Neminath Upadhye and Pandit Kailashchandra Shastri. 2 vols. Delhi: Bharatiya Jnanpithh Prakashan.

Nemichandrasuri, Acharya. 1962. *Ākhyānakamaṇikośa*, with *vṛtti* of Amradevasuri. Ed. by Muni Punyavijay. Varanasi: Prakrit Granth Parishad.

Niemann, Grahame. 1993. 'Bhūpati's *Bhāgavat* and the Hindi *Bhāgavat* Genre'. In *Bhakti in Current Research, 1979-82*. Ed. by Monika Thiel-Horstmann. Berlin: Dietrich Reiner Verlag, pp. 257-69.

Nijenhuis, Emmie te. 1977. *A history of Indian literature. Vol. VI, Scientific and technical literature*, Part III. Fasc. 1, Musicological literature. Wiesbaden: Harrassowitz.

Nijhawan, Michael. 2006. *Dhadi Darbar: Religion, Violence, and the Performance of Sikh History*. New Delhi: Oxford University Press.

Nizami, Sayyid 'Ali Abbas. 1989. *Khāndān-e Niẓāmī kā 'aqīdah va dastūr-e 'amal: urās buzurgān-e dīn va dīgar*. Karachi: Idar-e Nizami.

Novetzke, C. 2003. 'Divining an Author: The Idea of Authorship in an Indian Religious Tradition', *History of Religions* 42, 3 (February): 213-42. http://dx.doi.org/10.1086/375037

—. 2008. *Religion and Public Memory: A Cultural History of Saint Namdev in India.* New York: Columbia University Press.

O'Flaherty, Wendy Doniger. 1979. 'Sacred Cows and Profane Mares in Indian Mythology', *History of Religions* 19, 1: 1-26. http://dx.doi.org/10.1086/462833

—. 1980. *Women, Androgynes, and Other Mythical Beasts.* Chicago: University of Chicago Press.

Oldenburg, Veena Talwar. 1990. 'Lifestyle as Resistance: The Case of the Courtesans of Lucknow, India', *Feminist Studies* 16, 2 (Summer): 259-87. http://dx.doi.org/10.2307/3177850

Orsini, Francesca. 2002. *The Hindi Public Sphere 1920-1940.* New Delhi: Oxford University Press. http://dx.doi.org/10.1093/acprof:oso/9780198062202.001.0001

—. 2008. 'Jayasi's *Kanhāvat*: An Analysis', presented at the Department of Middle Eastern, South Asian and African Studies, Columbia University, New York, 11 April.

—. 2009. *Print and Pleasure: Popular Literature and Entertaining Fictions in Colonial North India.* Ranikhet: Permanent Black.

—. 2009. 'Kathās as Sites of Religious Interchange: Sufis and Krishna Bhaktas in Awadh', paper delivered at Oxford University, 5 June.

—, ed. 2010. *Before the Divide: Hindi and Urdu Literary Culture.* New Delhi: Orient Blackswan.

—. 2014a. '"Krishna is the Truth of Man": Mir 'Abdul Wahid Bilgrami's *Haqā'iq-i Hindī* (Indian Truths) and the Circulation of Dhrupad and Bishnupad'. In *Culture and Circulation: Literature in Motion in Early Modern India.* Ed. by Thomas de Bruijn and Allison Busch. Leiden: Brill, pp. 222-46.

—. 2014b. 'Inflected *Kathas*: Sufis and Krishna *Bhakta*s in Awadh'. In *Religious Interactions in Mughal India.* Ed. by Vasudha Dalmia and Munis Faruqui. New Delhi: Oxford University Press, pp. 195-232.

—. 2014c. 'Traces of a Multilingual World: Hindavi in Persian Texts'. In *After Timur Left: Culture and Circulation in Fifteenth-century North India.* Ed. by F. Orsini and S. Sheikh. New Delhi: Oxford University Press, pp. 403-36.

Osho. 1995. *Kahe Vājīd pukār*. Poona: Rebel Publishing House.

Padmakar. 1959. *Himmatbahādurvirudāvalī.* In *Padmākargranthāvalī.* Ed. by Vishvanathprasad Mishra. Varanasi: Nagari Pracarini Sabha.

—. 1959. *Pratāpsiṃhvirudāvalī.* In *Padmākargranthāvalī.* Ed. by Vishvanathprasad Mishra. Varanasi: Nagari Pracarini Sabha.

—. [n.d.]. *Padmākarkṛt himmatbahādurvirudāvalī.* Ed. by Lala Bhagvandin. Varanasi: Nagari Pracharini Sabha.

Pagden, Anthony. 1982. *The Fall of Natural Man: The American Indians and the Origins of Comparative Ethnology.* Cambridge: Cambridge University Press.

Page, Mary E. 1977. 'Naqqāli and Ferdowsi: Creativity in the Iranian National Tradition'. PhD dissertation, University of Pennsylvania.

Pandey, Shyam Manohar. 1982. *The Hindi Oral Epic Canainī (The Tale of Lorik and Candā)*. Allahabad: Sahitya Bhawan Ltd.

—. 1996-2005. *The Hindi Oral Epic Tradition: Bhojpurī Lorikī*. Allahabad: Sahitya Bhawan.

Panipati, Nizam. 1981. *Jūg bashist, dar falsafa wa 'irfān-i Hind*. Ed. by Muhammad Riza Jalali Naini and N.S. Shukla. Tehran: Iqbal.

Panipati, Qazi Sana-Allah. 1961. *Tafsīr-i maẓharī*. Trans. by Abd al-Dayim al-Jalali. Delhi: Nadvat al-Musannifin.

Patel, Deven. 2011. 'Source, Exegesis, and Translation: Sanskrit Commentary and Regional Language Translation in South Asia', *Journal of the American Oriental Society* 131: 245-66.

Patterson, Annabel. 1984. *Censorship and Interpretation: The Conditions of Writing and Reading in Early Modern England*. Madison: University of Wisconsin Press.

Pauwels, Heidi R.M. 1996. *Kr̥ṣṇā's Round Dance Reconsidered: Harirām Vyās's Hindi Rās-pañcādhyāyi*. Richmond: Curzon.

—. 2002. *In Praise of Holy Men: Hagiographic Poems by and about Harirām Vyās*. Groningen: Egbert Forsten.

—. 2012. 'Whose Satire? Gorakhnāth Confronts Krishna in *Kanhāvat*', in *Indian Satire in the Period of First Modernity*. Ed. by Monika Horstmann and Heidi Pauwels. Wiesbaden: Harrassowitz, pp. 35-64.

Payeur, Brittany. 2009. 'The Lilly Shamshir Khani in a Franco-Sikh Context: A Non-Islamic "Islamic" Manuscript'. In *The Islamic Manuscript Tradition: Ten Centuries of Book Arts in Indiana University Collections*. Ed. by Christiane Gruber. Bloomington: Indiana University Press, pp. 221-48.

Pellò, Stefano. 2007. 'Il ritratto e il suo doppio nel maṣnawī indo-persiano di Nāṣir 'Alī Sirhindī'. In *La mandorla e il mirabolano: Esotismi, contaminazioni, pittura e Oriente*. Ed. by R. Favaro. Venice: Cafoscarina, pp. 85-119.

—. 2014a. 'Persian as a Passe-Partout: The Case of Mirza 'Abd al-Qadir Bedil and his Hindu Disciples'. In *Culture and Circulation: Literature in Motion in Early Modern India*. Ed. by Thomas de Brujin and Allison Busch. Leiden: Brill, pp. 21-46.

—. 2014b. 'Drowned in the Sea of Mercy: The Textual Identification of Hindu Persian Poets from Shi'i Lucknow in the *Tazkira* of Bhagwān Dās Hindī'. In *Religious Interactions in Mughal India*. Ed. by V. Dalmia and M. Faruqi. New Delhi: Oxford University Press, pp. 135-58.

—. 2014c. 'Local Lexis? Provincializing Persian in Fifteenth-Century North India'. In *After Timur Left: Culture and Circulation in Fifteenth-century North India*. Ed. by F. Orsini and S. Sheikh. New Delhi: Oxford University Press, pp. 166-85.

Petit, Jérôme. 2013. 'De la convention à la conviction: Banārsīdās dans l'histoire de la pensée Digambara sur l'absolu'. PhD dissertation, Universite Sorbonne Nouvelle – Paris III.

Phukan, Shantanu. 1996. '"None Mad as a Hindu Woman": Contesting Communal Readings of *Padmavat*', *Comparative Studies of South Asia, Africa and the Middle East* 16, 1: 41-54. http://dx.doi.org/10.1215/1089201x-16-1-41

—. 2001. '"Through Throats Where Many Rivers Meet": The Ecology of Hindi in the World of Persian', *Indian Economic and Social History Review*, 38, 1: 33-58. http://dx.doi.org/10.1177/001946460103800102

Pinault, David. 1992. *The Shiites: Ritual and Popular Piety in the Muslim Community*. New York: St. Martin's Press.

—. 2001. *Horse of Karbala: Muslim Devotional Life in India*. New York: Palgrave.

Pindye, Jayarama. 1989 [1922]. *Rādhāmādhavavilāsacampū*. Ed. by V.K. Rajvade. Pune: Varda books.

Platts, John T. 1997 [1884]. *A Dictionary of Urdū, Classical Hindī, and English*. New Delhi: Munshiram Manoharlal.

Plukker, D.F. 1981. *The Miragāvatī of Kutubana: Avadhi text with critical notes* (thesis Amsterdam, 1981), http://gretil.sub.uni-goettingen.de/gretil/3_nia/hindi/kutmir_u.htm [Copies of the thesis available from the author: d.plukker@inter.nl.net]

Poddar, Neeraja. 2014. 'Krishna in his Myriad Forms: Narration, Translation, and Variation in Illustrated Manuscripts of the Latter Half of the Tenth Book of the *Bhāgavata Purāṇa*.' PhD dissertation, Columbia University.

Pollock, Sheldon. 1998. 'The Cosmopolitan Vernacular', *The Journal of Asian Studies* 57, 1: 6-37. http://dx.doi.org/10.2307/2659022

—, ed. 2002. 'Introduction: Working Papers on Sanskrit Knowledge-Systems on the Eve of Colonialism', *Journal of Indian Philosophy* 30: 431-39. http://dx.doi.org/10.1007/s10781-004-9050-6

—, ed. 2003. *Literary Cultures in History: Reconstructions from South Asia*. Berkeley: University of California Press.

—. 2006. *The Language of the Gods in the World of Men: Sanskrit, Culture, and Power in Premodern India*. Berkeley and Los Angeles: University of California Press.

—. 2007. 'Literary Culture and Manuscript Culture in Precolonial India'. In *Literary Cultures and the Material Book*. Ed. by Simon Eliot, Andrew Nash, and Ian Willison. London: British Library, pp. 77-94.

Powers, Harold. 1980. 'Illustrated Inventories of Indian Rāgamālā Painting'. Review article *Journal of the American Oriental Society* 100, 4: 473-93. http://dx.doi.org/10.2307/602092

—. 2001. 'Verbal and Musical Rhythms in Dikshitar and Tyagaraja', Dr Raghavan Shastyabdhapurthy Endowed Lecture, Music Academy (Madras), Chennai, December.

Premi, Nathuram. 1915. 'Digambar sampradāy ke saṅgh', *Jain Śvetāmbar Kānfarens Herald* 11, 9: 530-39.

—. 1956. *Jain sāhitya aur itihās*. Bombay: Hindi Granth Ratnakar.

—. 1957. *Kavivar Banārsīdās viracit ardha kathānak*. 2nd edn. Bombay: Hindi Granth Ratnakar.

Pritchett, Frances W. 1991. 'Introduction'. In *The Romance Tradition in Urdu: Adventures from the Dastan of Amir Hamza*. New York: Columbia University Press, pp. 1-58.

—. 2003. 'A Long History of Urdu Literary Culture, Part 2'. In *Literary Cultures in History: Reconstructions from South Asia*. Ed. by Sheldon Pollock. Berkeley: University of California Press, pp. 864-911.

Qureshi, Regula Burkhardt. 1969. 'Tarannum: The Chanting of Urdu Poetry', *Ethnomusicology* 13, 3: 425-68. http://dx.doi.org/10.2307/849999

—. 1972. 'Indo-Muslim Religious Music: An Overview', *Asian Music* 3, 2: 15-22. http://dx.doi.org/10.2307/833955

—. 1981. 'Islamic Music in an Indian Environment: The Shi'a Majlis', *Ethnomusicology* 25, 1: 41-71. http://dx.doi.org/10.2307/850974

—. 1990. 'Musical Gesture and Extra-Musical Meaning: Words and Music in the Urdu Ghazal', *Journal of the American Musicological Society* 43, 3: 457-97. http://dx.doi.org/10.2307/831743

—. 1995. *Sufi Music in India and Pakistan*. Chicago: University of Chicago Press.

Qutbjahani, Sufi Sharif. *Atwār fi hall al-asrār*, MS Or. 1883, British Library; also included in *Majmū'a-i rasā'il*, Lucknow, 1885.

Raghavan, V. 1940. 'Kavīndrācārya Sarasvatī'. In *D.R. Bhandarkar Volume*. Ed. by Bimala Churn Law. Calcutta: Indian Research Institute.

—. 1963. *Bhoja's Śṛṅgāra prakāśa*. Madras: Punarvasu.

Raghavdas. 1965. *Bhaktamāla* (Caturdās kṛt ṭīkā sahit). Ed. by Agarchand Nahta. (Rajasthan Puratan Granthmala 78). Jodhpur: Rajasthan Pracyavidya Pratishthan.

—. [n.d.]. *Bhaktamāla* (Caturdās jī kṛt padya ṭīkā tathā *Bhaktacaritra prakāśikā* gadya ṭīka sahit). Ed. by Sv. Narayandas. Jaipur: Shri Dadu Dayalu Mahasabha.

Raghunatha "Kavitarkika". 1997. *Kautukaratnākara*. Ed. and trans. by Dulal K. Bhowmik. Dhaka: Dhaka University.

Rajan, C. 1993. Viṣṇu Śarma: *The Pañcatantra*. London: Penguin.

Rajashekhara. 1934. *Kāvyamīmāṃsā*. Ed. by C.D. Dalal, R.A. Sastry; revised and enlarged by K.S. Ramaswami Sastri Siromani. 3rd edn. Baroda: Oriental Institute.

Rajashekharasuri. 1935. *Prabandhakośa*. Ed. by Muni Jinavijay. Shantiniketan: Singhi Jain Pith.

Rajnish, Govind. 2004. *Pañcāmṛt aur Pañcraṃg: Madhyakālīn sant-kaviyoṃ kā prāmāṇik pāṭh-sampādan*. Jaipur: Maya Prakashan Mandir.

Rajpurohit, Dalpat. 2013. 'Thematic Groupings of Bhakti Poets: The Dādūpanth and Sarvāṅgī literature'. In *Bhakti Beyond the Forest: Current Research on Early Modern Literatures in North India, 2003-2009*. Ed. by I. Bangha. New Delhi: Manohar, pp. 51-72.

Ramachandrudu, P.S. 2002. 'Introduction to the Second Edition'. In *Panditaraja kavya samgraha*. Ed. by K. Kamala. Hyderabad: Sanskrit Academy, Osmania University.

Ramanujan, A.K. 1970. 'Toward an Anthology of Indian City Images'. In *Urban India: Society, Space, and Image*, ed. by Richard G. Fox. Durham: Duke University, pp. 224-44.

—. 1991. 'Three Hundred *Rāmāyaṇas*: Five Examples and Three Thoughts on Translation'. In *Many Rāmāyaṇas: The Diversity of a Narrative Tradition in South Asia*. Ed. by Paula Richman. Berkeley: University of California Press, pp. 22-49. Reprint in *The Collected Essays of A.K. Ramanujan*. Ed. by Vinay Dharwadker. 1999. New Delhi: Oxford University Press, pp. 131-60.

Ramanujan, A.K. and Stuart H. Blackburn, eds. 1986. *Another Harmony: New Essays on the Folklore of India*. Berkeley: University of California Press.

Randles, W.G.L. 1991. '"Peuples sauvages" et "états despotiques": La pertinence, au XVIe siècle, de la grille aristotélicienne pour classer les nouvelles sociétés révélées par les Découvertes au Brésil, en Afrique et en Asie', *Mare Liberum* 3: 299-307.

Rao, Velcheru Narayana, and David Shulman. 1999. *A Poem at the Right Moment*. Delhi: Oxford University Press.

Ray Shivdas. *Sarasasāra*. Hindi Sahitya Sammelan, Allahabad, manuscript no. 2715/1492.

Razi, Najm al-Din. 1973. *Mirsād al-'ibād ila al-mabda' wa al-ma'ād*. Ed. by Muhammad Amin Riyahi. Tehran: Shirkat-i Intisharat-i 'Ilmi va Farhangi.

Rice, Timothy. 1994. *May it Fill Your Soul: Experiencing Bulgarian Music*. Chicago: Chicago University Press.

Richard, Yann. 1995. *Shi'ite Islam*. Trans. by Antonia Nevill. Cambridge, MA: Blackwell.

Rieu, Charles. 1883. *Catalogue of the Persian Manuscripts in the British Museum*. London: Gilbert and Rivington.

Rizvi, S.A.A. 1966. *Muslim Revivalist Movements in Northern India in the Sixteenth and Seventeenth Centuries*. Agra: Agra University.

—. 1982. *Shah Abd al-Aziz: Purtanism, Sectarian Polemics and Jihad*. Delhi/Canberra: Marifat Publishing House.

—. 1983. *A History of Sufism in India*. 2 vols. New Delhi: Munshiram Manoharlal.

Rocher, Ludo. 1983. 'Reflections on One Hundred and Fifty Years of *Purāna* Studies', *Purāna* 25, 1: 64-76.

—. 1986. *The Puranas*. Vol. 2, Fasc. 3. In *A History of Indian Literature*. Ed. Jan Gonda. Wiesbaden: Harrassowitz.

Roger, Henry ed. 1870. *The Poetical Works of Henry Marvell*. London: A. Murray.

Rowell, Lewis E. 1992. *Music and Musical Thought in Early India*. Chicago Studies in Ethnomusicology. Chicago: University of Chicago Press.

Roy, Asim. 1983. *The Islamic Syncretistic Tradition in Bengal*. Princeton: Princeton University Press.

Roy Chaudhuri, Vimalakant. 1998. *Bhāratīya saṅgītakośa*. New Delhi: Vani.

Rubanovich, Julia. 2011. 'Orality in Medieval Persian Literature'. In *Medieval Oral Literature*. Ed. by Karl Reichl. Berlin: De Gruyter, pp. 653-79.

—. 2012. 'Tracking the *Shahnama* Tradition in Medieval Persian Folk Prose'. In *Shahnama Studies II: The Reception of Firdausi's* Shahnama. Ed. by Charles Melville and Gabrielle van den Berg. Leiden: Brill, pp. 11-34.

Ruffle, Karen G. 2011. *Gender, Sainthood, and Everyday Practice in South Asian Shi'ism*. Chapel Hill: University of North Carolina Press.

Rührdanz, Karin. 1997. 'About a Group of Truncated *Shāhnāmas*: A Case Study in the Commercial Production of Illustrated Manuscripts in the Second Part of the Sixteenth Century', *Muqarnas* 14: 118-34. http://dx.doi.org/10.2307/1523240

Rumi, Jalaluddin. 1925. *The Mathnawí of Jalálu'ddín Rúmí, Edited from the Oldest Manuscripts Available, with Critical Notes, Translation and Commentary*. Ed. by R.A. Nicholson. London: Luzac and co.

Ryder, A.W. 1956. *The Pañcatantra*. Chicago: University of Chicago Press.

Sadriniya, Baqir. 2009. *Farhang-i māsūrāt-i mutūn-i 'irfānī*. Tehran: Surush.

Saeed, Mian Muhammad. 1972. *The Sharqi Sultanate of Jaunpur: A Political and Cultural History*. Karachi: University of Karachi.

Sakhawi (Al-), Shams al-Din Muhammad ibn 'Abd al-Rahman. 1997. *Al-ajwibāt al-murdīyya*. Ed. by Muhammad Ishaq Muhammad Ibrahim. Riyadh: Dar al-Rayah.

Samuels, David W., et al. 2010. 'Soundscapes: Towards a Sounded Anthropology', *Annual Review of Anthropology* 39: 329-45. http://dx.doi.org/10.1146/annurev-anthro-022510-132230

Sanyal, Ritwik, and Richard Widdess. 2004. *Dhrupad: Tradition and Performance in Indian Music*. SOAS Musicology Series. London: School of African and Oriental Studies.

Saraswati, Dayananad. 1970. *Satyārth prakāsh*. English trans. as *Light of Truth* by Shri Durga Prasad. Reprint New Delhi: Arya Prakashan, 2007.

Sarkhwush, Muhammad Afzal. 1951. *Kalīmāt al-shu'arā*. Ed. by M.H. Mahvi Lakhnawi. Madras: [n.p.].

Sastri, Vinod, ed. 2003. *Rāgamālā of Kṣemakarṇa*. Jaipur: Rajasthan Sanskrit Academy.

Sathyanarayana, R. 1994. 'Introduction'. In *Nartananirṇaya of Paṇḍarīka Viṭṭhala*. Vol. 1. Ed. by R. Sathyanarayana. 3 vols. Delhi: Indira Gandhi National Centre for the Arts and Motilal Banarsidass.

Schafer, Richard Murray. 1977. *The Soundscape: Our Sonic Environment and the Tuning of the World*. New York: Knopf.

Schimmel, Annemarie. 1993. *The Triumphal Sun: A Study of the Works of Jalaloddin Rumi*. Albany: State University of New York Press.

—. 2003 [1997]. *My Soul is a Woman: The Feminine in Islam*. New York: Continuum.

Schippers, Huib. 2007. 'The Guru Recontextualized? Perspectives on Learning North Indian Classical Music in Shifting Contexts for Professional Training', *Asian Music* 38, 1: 123-38. http://dx.doi.org/10.1353/amu.2007.0020

Schofield, Katherine Butler. 2010. 'Reviving the Golden Age Again: "Classicization", Hindustani Music, and the Mughals', *Ethnomusicology* 54, 3: 484-517. http://dx.doi.org/10.5406/ethnomusicology.54.3.0484

—. 2014. 'Indian Music in the Persian Collections: The Javahir al-Musiqat-i Muhammadi', parts 1 and 2, British Library Asian and African Studies Blog (October 2014), http://britishlibrary.typepad.co.uk/asian-and-african/

—. Forthcoming. 'Sense and Sensibility: The Domain of Pleasure and the Place of Music in Mughal Society'.

Schouten, G. 1708. *Voiage de Gautier Schouten aux Indes orientales. Commencé l'an 1658 et fini l'an 1665*. Amsterdam: Pierre Mortier.

Schubel, Vernon. 1993. *Religious Performance in Contemporary Islam: Shi'i Devotional Rituals in South Asia*. Columbia: University of South Carolina Press.

Sebeok, Thomas A., and Donna Jean Umiker-Sebeok, eds. 1976. *Speech Surrogates: Drum and Whistle Systems*. The Hague: Mouton.

Seeger, Charles. 1977. 'Speech, Music, and Speech About Music'. In *Studies in Musicology, 1935-1975*. Berkeley: University of California Press, pp. 16-30.

Sen, Sukumar. 1971. *An Etymological Dictionary of Bengali, c.1000-1800 A.D.* Calcutta : Eastern Publishers.

—. 2000. *Bāṅgālā sāhityera itihāsa*. Vol. 2, 6th edn. Kolkata: Ananda Publishers.

—. 2001. *Bāṅgālā sāhityera itihāsa*. Vol. 1, 3rd edn. Kolkata: Ananda Publishers.

Seyller, John. 2000. 'A Mughal Code of Connoisseurship', *Muqarnas* 17: 177-202. http://dx.doi.org/10.2307/1523297

—. 2002. *The Adventures of Hamza: Painting and Storytelling in Mughal India*. Washington, DC: Smithsonian Institution.

Shackle, Christopher. 1996. 'Settings of Panegyric: The Secular Qasida in Mughal and British India'. In *Qasida Poetry in Islamic Asia and Africa*. Ed. by Stefan Sperl and Christopher Shackle. Leiden: Brill, pp. 205-52.

—. 1999. 'Persian Poetry and Qadiri Sufism in Late Mughal India: Ghanimat Kunjahi and his Mathnawi Nayrang-i 'Ishq'. In *The Heritage of Sufism: III. Late Classical Persianate Sufism (1501-1750)*. Ed. by Leonard Lewisohn. Oxford: Oneworld, pp. 435-63.

Shafi'i-Kadkani, Muhammad Riza. 1381. 'Nigāhī ba Ṭirāz al-akhbār', *Nama-yi Baharistan* 1, 5 (Summer): 109-22.

Shafiq, Lacchmi Narayan. [n.d.]. *Tazkira-yi gul-i ra'nā*. Hyderabad: 'Ahd Afarin Barqi Press.

Shahnavaz Khan, 1888. *Ma'āthir al-umarā'*. Ed. by Maulvi 'Abd al-Rahim. Calcutta: Asiatic Society of Bengal.

*Shahr-i Masnavī-i Maulāna Rūm ma' dībācha-i 'Abd al-Latīf*, MS no. F. 1785, Nawwab Muzammilullah Library, Aligarh.

Sharar, 'Abd al-Halim. 2000. *Guzashta Lakhnau*. Ed. Rashid Hasan Khan. Delhi: Maktaba-i Jami'a.

Sharif, Ahmed, ed. 1967. *Madhyayugera rāga-tāla-nāmā*. Dhaka: Bangla Academy.

—, 1970. 'Rāgatālanāmā o padāvalī', *Sāhitya Patrikā* 7, 1: 1-48.

Sharma, Acharya Nalinavilocana, and Shriramanarayan Shastri, eds. 1963. *Lālacdās-racit Avadhī-kāvya Haricarit*. Patna: Bihar-Rashtrabhasha Parishad.

Sharma, Premlata. 1972. 'Sampādakīya bhūmikā'. In *Sahasras*. Ed. by Premlata Sharma. New Delhi: Sangit Natak Akademi.

—, ed. 1972. *Sahasras: Nāyak Bakhśū ke dhrupadoṃ kā saṅgrah*. New Delhi: Sangit Natak Academy.

Sharma, Ramesh Chandra. 1974. 'Life of a Middle-class Man in the Seventeenth Century', *Journal of Indian History* 52: 389-403.

Sharma, Rameshchandra. 2007. *Hindī kavitt-sāhitya kā vikās*. Jaipur: Aruna Prakashan.

Sharma, Swapna. [n.d.]. *Gadādhar Bhaṭṭ: paramparā aur sāhitya*. Vrindaban: Vrajagaurav Prakashan.

Sharma, Sunil. 2002. 'Amir Khusraw and the Genre of Historical Narratives in Verse', *Comparative Studies of South Asia, Africa and the Middle East* 22, 1: 112-18. http://dx.doi.org/10.1215/1089201x-22-1-2-112

—. 2004. 'The City of Beauties in the Indo-Persian Poetic Landscape', *Comparative Studies of South Asia, Africa and the Middle East* 24, 2: 73-81. http://dx.doi.org/10.1215/1089201x-24-2-73

—. 2005. *Amir Khusraw: The Poet of Sufis and Sultans*. Oxford: Oneworld.

—. 2009. 'Translating Gender: Āzād Bilgrāmī on the Poetics of the Love Lyric and Cultural Synthesis', *The Translator* 15, 1: 87-103. http://dx.doi.org/10.1080/13556509.2009.10799272

Sharngadeva. 1959. *The Saṅgītaratnākara of Śārṅgadeva with the Kalānidhi of Kallinātha and the Saṅgītasudhākara of Siṃhabhūpāla*. Ed. by S. Subrahmanyam Shastri and V. Krishnamacharya. Madras: The Adyar Library and Research Centre.

Shastri, Hirananda. 1925. *The Baghela Dynasty of Rewah: Memoirs of the Archaeological Survey of India*, no. 21. Calcutta: Govt. of India.

Shastri, Keshavram K. 1976. *Bṛhad gujarātī koś*. 2 vols. Ahmedabad: Yunivarsiti Granth Nirman Bord.

Shringy, R.K. and Prem Lata Sharma. 1989. *Saṅgītaratnākara of Śārngadeva: Text and English Translation*. Vol. 2. Delhi: Munshiram Manoharlal.

Shrotriya, Prannath. 'Basant kī khabari hai'. 398(4). Pothikhana, manuscript no. 3398(4). Jaipur: Maharaja Sawai Man Singh II Museum.

Shubhankara, 1960. *Saṅgītadāmodaraḥ*. Ed. by Gaurinath Sastri and Govindagopal Mukhopadhyay. Calcutta: Sanskrit College.

Shukla, Dayashankar. 1967. *Hindī kā samasyāpūrti kāvya*. Lucknow: Ganga Pustakmala Karyalay.

Shukla, N.S. 1974. 'Persian Translations of Sanskrit Works', *Indological Studies* 3, 1-2: 175-91.

Shulman, David. 2001. 'Poets and Patrons in Tamil Literary Legend'. In *The Wisdom of Poets: Studies in Tamil, Telugu, and Sanskrit*. New Delhi: Oxford University Press, pp. 63-102.

Shyamsundardas, Balakrishan Bhatt, Amir Singh and Ramchandra Shukla, eds. 1965. *Hindīśabdsāgar*. Varanasi: Nagari Pracharini Sabha.

Silk, Marc Reuel. 1982. 'Scientia Rerum: The Place of the Example in Later Medieval Thought'. PhD dissertation, Harvard University (Dissertation Abstract International 43A, 1982-83, 1639).

Simhal, Brajendrakumar. 2007. *Sant Bājīd granthāvalī I*. Delhi: Dharika Publications.

Simhal, Dharm Pal. 1990. *Sarvāṅgī: guṇ gañj-nāmā sahit*. Jalandhar: Dipak Publishers.

Simidchieva, Marta. 2003. 'Imitation and Innovation in Timurid Poetics: Kāshifī's *Badāyi' al-afkār* and its Predecessors, *al-Mu'jam* and *Ḥadā'iq al-siḥr*', *Iranian Studies* 36, 4: 509-30. http://dx.doi.org/10.1080/0210860032000139203

Singh, Gadadhar. 1994. *Hindī sāhitya ke vikās meṃ jain kaviyoṃ kī yogdān*. Muzaffarpur (Bihar): Prakrit, Jain-Shastra aur Ahimsa Shodh Sansthan.

Singh, Gurnam. 2001. *Sikh Musicology: Sri Guru Granth Sahib and Hymns of the Human Spirit*. New Delhi: Kanishka Publishers.

Singh, Nagendra and Abdul Mabud Khan, eds. 2004. *Encyclopaedia of the World Muslims: Tribes, Castes and Communities*. Delhi: Global Vision Publishing House.

Singh, Yogendrapratap. 1992. 'Bhūmikā'. In *Jorāvarprakāś*. Allahabad: Hindi Sahitya Sammelan.

Sirhindi, Shaikh Ahmad. 1873. *Maktūbāt-i Imām Rabbānī*. Ed. by 'Aziz al-Din Dehlavi. Delhi: Matba-i Ahmadi.

Skelton, Robert. 1970. 'Mughal Paintings from the Harivaṃśa Manuscript', *Victoria and Albert Museum Yearbook* 2: 41-54.

Smith, John D. 1991. *The Epic of Pābūjī*. Cambridge: Cambridge University Press.

Smith, Jonathan Z. 2001. 'A Twice-told Tale: The History of the History of Religions' History', *Numen* 48, 2: 131-46. http://dx.doi.org/10.1163/156852701750152636

Smith. Mark M., ed. 2004. *Hearing History: A Reader*. Athens, GA: University of Georgia Press.

Smith, William L. 1979. 'The Turkish Conquest and the Dark Age of Bengali Literature'. In *Ludwik Sternbach Felicitation Volume*. Ed. by J.P. Sinha. Vol. 2. Lucknow: Akhila Bharatiya Sanskrit Parishad, pp. 708-13.

Snell, Rupert. 1991. *The Eighty-four Hymns of Hita Harivaṃśa: An Edition of the Caurāsī Pada*. Delhi: Motilal Banarsidass.

—. 2005a. 'Confessions of a 17th-Century Jain Merchant: The *Ardhakathānak* of Banārsīdās', *South Asia Research* 25: 79-104. http://dx.doi.org/10.1177/0262728005051608

—. 2005b. 'Introduction: The Study of Pre-Modern Hindi Literature', *South Asia Research* 25: 5-11. http://dx.doi.org/10.1177/0262728005051604

—. 2009. 'Preface'. In Banarasidas, *Ardhakathanak: A Half Story*. Trans. by Rohini Chowdhury. New Delhi: Penguin Books, pp. vii-xxii.

Somadeva. 1924-1928. *The Ocean of Story, Being a Translation of Somadeva's Kathā Sarit Sāgara*. Ed. by N.M. Penzer, trans. by C.H. Tawney. London: Sawyer.

—. 1994. *Tales from the Kathāsaritsāgara*. Ed. and trans. by Arshiya Sattar. New Delhi: Penguin.

Somaprabha. 1981. *Sūktimuktāvalī*, with Hindi translation by Banarsidas. Mahavirji: Shri 108 Acharya Shivsagar Di. Jain Granthmala.

—. 1984. *Sindūraprakara* with Sanskrit *Vyākhyā* by Harshakirtisuri. Ed. and trans. by Pannyas Pradyumnavijaygani. Ahmedabad: Shrutajnan Sabha.

Sreenivasan, Ramya. 2006. 'Drudges, Dancing Girls, Concubines: Female Slaves in Rajput Polity, 1500-1850'. In *Slavery and South Asian History*. Ed. by Indrani Chatterjee and Richard M. Eaton. Bloomington and Indianapolis: Indiana University Press, pp. 136-61.

—. 2007. *The Many Lives of a Rajput Queen: Heroic pasts in India, c.1500-1900*. New Delhi: Permanent Black.

Steiner, George. 1992. *After Babel: Aspects of Language and Translation*. 2nd edn. Oxford: Oxford University Press.

Steingass, Francis Joseph. 1982. *A Comprehensive Persian-English Dictionary*. London: Routledge & Kegan Paul.

Stewart, Tony K. 2010. *The Final Word: The Caitanya Caritāmṛta and the Grammar of Religious Tradition*. New York: Oxford University Press.

Sudhakalasa. 1998. *The Saṅgītopaniṣatsāroddhārah. A Fourteenth-century Text on Music from Western India*. Ed. and trans. by Allyn Miner. Kalāmūlaśāstra Series. New Delhi: Indira Gandhi National Centre of the Arts and Motilal Banarsidass.

Sundar Kaviray. 2004. *Sundarśṛṅgār*. In *Sundar kavirāy granthāvalī*. Ed. by Ramanand Sharma. Delhi: Lok Vani Samsthan.

Surdas. 1972/1976. *Sūrsāgar*. Ed. by Jagannathdas "Ratnakar", Nandadulare Vajpeyi, et al. 2 vols. Varanasi: Kashi Nagaripracharini Sabha.

—. 2014. *Sur's Ocean: Poems from the Early Tradition.* Ed. by Kenneth E. Bryant, trans. by John Stratton Hawley. Harvard: Harvard University Press.

Surjandas, [Svami] ed. 2009 VS. *Śrī Dadu mahāyāvidyālay rajat-jayantī granth.* Jaipur: Sri Dadu Mahavidyalay Rajat-Jayanti Mahotsav Samiti.

Tabari (Al-), Muhammad bin Jarir. 1960. *Tārīkh al-rusul wa al-mulūk.* Ed. by Muhammad Abu al-Fazl Ibrahim. Cairo: Dar al-Ma'arif.

—. 2003. *Jāmī' al-bayān 'an ta'wīl āy al-Qur'ān.* Ed. by 'Abdullah bin 'Abd al-Muhsin al-Turki. Riyadh: Dar 'Alam al-Kutub.

Tarafdar, M.R. 1965. *Husain Shahi Bengal, 1494-1538 AD: A Socio-Political Study.* Dhaka: Asiatic Society of Pakistan.

Tavakoli-Targhi, Mohamed. 1996. 'Orientalism's Genesis Amnesia', *Comparative Studies of South Asia, Africa, and the Middle East* 16, 1: 1-14. http://dx.doi.org/10.1215/1089201x-16-1-1

—. 1999. 'Contested Memories of Pre-Islamic Iran', *The Medieval History Journal* 2, 2: 245-75. http://dx.doi.org/10.1177/097194589900200203

Temple, Richard C. 1884. *Legends of the Panjâb.* Bombay: Education Society's Press, and London: Trübner & Co.

Tessitori, Luigi Pio. 2000. 'Paramajotistotra: An Old Braja Metrical Version of Siddhasenadivākara's Kalyāṇamandirastotra', *Studi Gianici.* Udine: Società Indologica Luigi Pio Tessitori, pp. 307-15. Originally in *Indian Antiquary* 43 (1913): 42-46.

Thackston, Wheeler, trans. 2002. *Bāburnāma of Babur.* New York: The Modern Library.

Thiel-Horstmann, Monika. 1986. *Symbiotic Antinomy: The Social Organisation of a North Indian Sect* (The 1985 Basham Lecture). Canberra: Faculty of Asian Studies, Australian National University.

—. 1989. 'Dadupanthi Sermons', in association with Tilak Raj Chopra. In *Living Texts from India.* Ed. by Monika Thiel-Horstmann and Richard K. Barz. Wiesbaden: Harrassowitz, pp. 141-83.

—. 1999. *In Favour of Govinddevjī: Historical Documents Relating to a Deity of Vrindaban and Eastern Rajasthan.* Delhi: Indira Gandhi National Centre for the Arts in association with Manohar Publishers and Distributors.

Todorov, Tzvetan. 1990. *Genres in Discourse.* Cambridge: Cambridge University Press.

Toffin, G. 2007. *Newar Society: City, Village and Periphery.* Kathmandu: Social Science Baha.

Tomlinson, Gary. 2009. *The Singing of the New World: Indigenous Voice in the Era of European Contact.* Cambridge: Cambridge University Press.

Trivedi, Harish. 2006. 'In Our Own Time, On Our Own Terms: "Translation" in India'. In *Translating Others.* Vol. 1. Ed. by Theo Hermans. 2 vols. Manchester: St. Jerome Publishing, pp. 102-19.

Truschke, Audrey. 2011. 'The Mughal *Book of War*: A Persian Translation of the Sanskrit *Mahabharata*', *Comparative Studies of South Asia, Africa and the Middle East* 31, 2: 506-20. http://dx.doi.org/10.1215/1089201x-1264388

—. 2012. 'Cosmopolitan Encounters: Sanskrit and Persian at the Mughal Court'. PhD dissertation, Columbia University. http://academiccommons.columbia.edu/item/ac:145903

—. Forthcoming. *Culture of Encounters: Sanskrit at the Mughal Court*. New York: Columbia University Press.

Tsuge, Gen'ichi. 1970. 'Rhythmic Aspects of the Avaz in Persian Music', *Ethnomusicology* 14, 2: 205-28. http://dx.doi.org/10.2307/849797

Tulpule, Shankar Gopal. 1979. *Classical Marāṭhī Literature: From the Beginning to A.D. 1818*. Wiesbaden, Harrassowitz.

Tulsidas. 1969. *Rāmcaritmānas*. Ed. by Hanumanprasad Poddar. 15th edn. Gorakhpur: Gita Press.

—. 1990. *Rāmcaritmānas*. Ed. and trans. by R.C. Prasad. Delhi: Motilal Banarsidass.

'Umar Sama' Yahya al-Kabuli. 2001. *Lahjāt-i Sikandarshāhī wa laṭā'if-i nā-matnāhī*, ed. by Syeda Bilqis Fatema Husaini. 2 vols. Mumbai: Alhyat Research Center.

Upadhyaya, Ved Prakash. 1991. *Kalki avatār aur Muhammad Sāhib*. Trans. by 'Azizul Haq 'Umari Maunath Bhanjan. Hyderabad: Deendar Anjuman.

'Usmani, Shams Naved and S. 'Abdullah Tariq. 1989. *Agar ab bhī na jāge to (…)*. Delhi: Jaseem Book Depot.

Vallabhacharya. 1985. *Chaurasi Baithak: Eighty-four Seats of Shri Vallabhacharya*. Trans. by Sham Das. Baroda: Shri Vallabha Publications.

Valmiki. 2005. *Rāmāyaṇa: Ayodhyā (Book Two)*. Trans. by Sheldon Pollock. New York: New York University Press and JJC Foundation.

Vamshi, Baldev. 2002. *Smaraṇāñjali: Śrī 1008 Śrī Dadu sampradayācārya Śrī Svami Harirām jī Mahārāj (1917-2001)*. New Delhi: Akhil Bharatiya Shri Dadu Sevak Samaj.

Vanina, Eugenia. 1995. 'The *Ardhakathanaka* of Banarsi Das: A Socio-cultural Study', *Journal of the Royal Asiatic Society*, Third Series, 5: 211-24. http://dx.doi.org/10.1017/s1356186300015352

Varma, Dhirendra, ed. 1963. *Hindī sāhitya koś*. Two vols. Varanasi: Jnanmandal Limited.

Varma, Ved Prakash, 2005. 'Non-Theism in the *Mimamsa* Philosophy'. In *Philosophical Reflections: Essays on Socio-Ethical Philosophy and Philosophy of Religion*. Lucknow: Allied Publishers, pp. 179-91.

Vasari, Giorgio. 1880. *Le vite de' più eccellenti pittori, scultori, ed architettori*. Vol. 5. Ed. by G. Milanesi. Florence: G.C. Sansoni.

Vassie, Roderic. 1988. 'Persian Interpretations of the Bhagvadgita in the Mughal Period', PhD dissertation, School of Oriental and African Studies, London.

Venuti, Lawrence. 1995. *The Translator's Invisibility: A History of Translation*. London: Routledge.

Vergati, Anne. 1995. *Gods, Men and Territory: Society and Culture in Kathmandu Valley*. New Delhi: Manohar.

—. 2004. 'Gods and Monuments in Late Malla Period Paintings'. In *Nepal: Old Images, New Insights*. Ed. by Pratapaditya Pal. Mumbai: Marg Publications, pp. 92-106.

Vetta Mani. 1998. *Purānic Encyclopaedia*. Reprint Delhi: Motilal Bannarsidass.

Vinaysagar, Mahopadhyay. 2006. *Khartar gacch sāhitya koś*. Jaipur: Prakrit Bharati Akadami.

Wade, Bonnie. 1998. *Imaging Sound: An Ethnomusicological Study of Music, Art and Culture in Mughal India*. Chicago: University of Chicago Press.

Wadley, Susan S. 2004. *Raja Nal and the Goddess: The North Indian Epic* Dhola *in Performance*. Bloomington: Indiana University Press.

Wajid 'Ali Shah. 1987. *Bānī*. Lucknow: Sangit Natak Akademi.

Walbridge, John. 2001. *The Wisdom of the Mystic East: Suhrawadi and Platonic Orientalism*. Albany: State University of New York Press.

Waldschmidt, Ernst and Rose Leonore. 1975. *Miniatures of Musical Inspiration in the Collection of the Berlin Museum of Indian Art*, Part 11: *Ragamala Pictures from Northern India and the Deccan*. Berlin: Museum für Indische Kunst.

Walker, Paul E. 1991. 'The Doctrine of Metempsychosis in Islam'. In *Islamic Studies Presented to Charles J. Adams*. Ed. by Wael B. Hallaq and Donald B. Lille. Leiden: Brill, pp. 219-38.

Wallis, Richard. 1979. 'The Voice as a Mode of Cultural Expression in Bali', Ph.D. dissertation, University of Michigan.

WaThiong'o, Ngugi. 2007. 'Notes towards a Performance Theory of Orature', *Performance Research* 12, 3: 4-7. http://dx.doi.org/10.1080/13528160701771253

Wegner, Gert-Matthias and Richard Widdess. 2004. 'Musical Miniatures from Nepal: Two Newar Ragamalas'. In *Nepal: Old Images, New Insights*. Ed. by Pratapaditya Pal. Mumbai: Marg Publications, pp. 81-91.

Widdess, Richard. 1995. *The Rāgas of Early Indian Music: Modes, Melodies and Musical Notations from the Gupta Period to c.1250*. Oxford Monographs on Music. Oxford: Clarendon Press.

—. 2006. 'Musical Structure, Performance and Meaning: the Case of a Stick-Dance from Nepal', *Ethnomusicology Forum* 15, 2: 179-213. http://dx.doi.org/10.1080/17411910600917964

—. 2010. 'The Emergence of Dhrupad'. In *Hindustani Music: Thirteenth to Twentieth Centuries*. Ed. by Joep Bor, Françoise "Nalini" Delvoye, Emmie te Nijenhuis, and Jane Harvey. New Delhi: Manohar, pp. 117-40.

—. 2011. '*Dāphā*: Dancing Gods, Virtual Pilgrimage, and Sacred Singing in the Kathmandu Valley', *Musiké* 5, 6: 55-79.

—. 2013. *Dāphā: Sacred Singing in a South Asian City. Music, Performance and Meaning in Bhaktapur, Nepal.* SOAS Musicology Series. Aldershot: Ashgate. http://dx.doi.org/10.1093/ml/gcv025

Williams, R. 1963. *Jaina Yoga: A Survey of the Mediaeval Śrāvakācaras*. Oxford: Oxford University Press.

Woodward, Kenneth L. 2001. *The Book of Miracles: The Meaning of the Miracle Stories in Christianity, Judaism, Buddhism, Hinduism and Islam*. New York: Simon & Schuster.

Wolf, Michaela. 2007. 'Introduction: The Emergence of a Sociology of Translation'. In *Constructing a Sociology of Translation*. Ed. by Michaela Wolf and Alexandra Fukari. Amsterdam: John Benjamins Publishing Company, pp. 1-36.

Wolf, Richard K. 2000. 'Embodiment and Ambivalence: Emotion in South Asian Muharram Drumming', *Yearbook for Traditional Music* 32: 81-116. http://dx.doi.org/10.2307/3185244

—. 2007. 'Doubleness, *Mātam*, and Muharram Drumming in South Asia'. In *Pain and its Transformation*. Ed. by Sarah Coakley and Kay Kaufman Shelemay. Cambridge, MA: Harvard University Press, pp. 331-50.

—. 2014. *The Voice in the Drum: Music, Language and Emotion in Islamicate South Asia*. Urbana: University of Illinois Press.

Wright, Owen. 2009. *Touraj Kiaras and Persian Classical Music: An Analytical Perspective*. Aldershot: Ashgate.

—, ed. and trans. 2010. *Epistles of the Brethren of Purity: On Music*. Oxford: Oxford University Press and The Institute of Ismaili Studies.

Yamamoto, Kumiko. 2003. *The Oral Background of Persian Epics: Storytelling and Poetry*. Leiden: Brill.

Zadeh, Travis. 2007. 'Translation, Geography, and the Divine Word: Mediating Frontiers in Pre-Modern Islam'. PhD dissertation, Harvard University.

—. 2010. 'The Wiles of Creation: Philosophy, Fiction, and the 'Aja'ib Tradition', *Middle Eastern Literatures* 13, 1: 21-48. http://dx.doi.org/10.1080/14752620903566095

Zaidi, Ali Jawad. 1989. *Tārīkh-i mushā'ira*. Delhi: [n.p.].

Zakaria, Saymon. 2008. *Bāṃlādeśera lokanāṭaka: viṣaya o āṅgika-vaicitrya*. Dhaka: Bangla Academy.

Zaki, Mohammed. 1980. 'Mir'ātul Makhluqāt of Abdur Rehman Chishti'. In *Bias in Indian Historiography*. Ed. by D. Devahuti. Delhi: DK Publications, pp. 352-54.

Zamir, Mirza Raushan. [1666]. *Tarjuma-yi Pārijātak*. British Library, Egerton 793.

Zarqani (Al-), Muhammad ibn 'Abd al-Baqi. 1982. *Mukhtasar al-maqāsid al-Hasana fi bayān al-ahādis al-mushtahira 'ala al-Alsina*. Ed. by Muhammad al-Sabbagh. Beirut: Al-Maktab al-Islami.

Zarrinkub, A.H. 1992. *Zā'ir-i Hind*. In *Sā'ib va sabk-i hindī*. Ed. by M.R. Daryagasht. Tehran: Nashr-i Qatra, pp. 75-83.

Zelliot, Eleanor. 2003. 'A Medieval Encounter Between Hindu and Muslim: Eknath's Drama-Poem Hindu-Turk. Samvad'. In *India's Islamic Traditions, 711-1750*. Ed. by Richard Eaton. New Delhi: Oxford University Press, pp. 64-82.

Ziauddin. [late eighteenth century]. *Ḥayy al-arwāḥ*. John Rylands Library University of Manchester, Persian 346.

Ziegler, Norman. 1976. 'The Seventeenth-Century Chronicles of Mārvāṛa: A Study in the Evolution and Use of Oral Traditions in Western India', *History in Africa* 3: 127-53. http://dx.doi.org/10.2307/3171564

Zipoli, Riccardo. 1993. *The Technique of the Ǧawāb: Replies by Nawā'ī to Ḥāfiẓ and Ǧāmī*. Venice: Cafoscarina.

—. 1994. 'Oscenità poetiche neopersiane: due *tarjī'-band* sulla masturbazione', *Annali di Ca' Foscari* 33 (Serie orientale 25): 249-91.

—. 1996. 'Elementi osceni nella lessicografia neopersiana', *Annali di Ca' Foscari* 35: 249-89.

—. 2001. 'The Obscene Sanâ'î', *Persica* 17: 173-94. http://dx.doi.org/10.2143/pers.17.0.507

Zumthor, Paul, 1983. *Introduction à la poésie orale*. Paris: Éditions du Seuil.

# Index


*abhang* 171
*Ādigranth* 397, 399
*Afsānah-i Shāhān* (of Muhammad Kabir) 225
Agra 15, 69, 84, 95, 285, 287
*Ā'īn-i Akbarī* (of Abu'l Fazl) 286
Ajmer 192
*Akbarnāma* (of Abu'l Fazl) 288
*alankara* 369
*alankarashastra* 249, 265, 275, 279
Alaol 424, 430-431, 434, 437, 442
Allahabad 215
*'Amal-i Ṣāliḥ* (of Muhammad Salih Kanbo) 301
Amber 262, 364
Apabhramsha 89, 104, 365
Arabic 9, 129, 322
Arakan 424
*Ardhakathānak* (of Banarsidas) 70, 72, 75, 100
*Argalpur jinvandanā* (of Pandit Bhagavatidas) 69
*arilla* 16, 360
Assam 442
audience. *See* connoisseur, patron, etc.
  addressed in texts 380
  music attracting an 479
  participation in *kirtan* 172
  represented in texts 425
Auliya, Nizamuddin 107, 445, 449, 460, 463, 479
Avicennian classifications 195
Awadh 204
Awadhi 151, 354, 359, 424, 442
*badas* 174
Baghelas 337
*bahurupiya* (street performers) 420
Bajid 360
Bakhana 36, 44, 47, 437
Banaras 323, 336
Bangladesh 424
Bedil, Mirza 313, 314, 317, 321, 323
Bengal 25, 34, 245, 312, 389, 428, 442
Bengali 14, 68, 423, 429, 430, 436
*Bhāgavad gītā* 170
*Bhāgavata Māhātmya* 210, 217, 227, 230
  and performance standards 211
*Bhāgavata-purāṇa* 19, 22, 37, 90, 126, 209-210, 218, 220-221, 223, 226-227, 230, 355
  Brajbhasha versions 213
  exposition in Kannada 210
  literary activity in Sanskrit 214
  performances of 209, 216
  vernacular adaptations 214
*Bhaktamāl* (of Raghavdas) 37, 38, 45, 362, 363
*Bhaktāmara stotra* (of Manatunga) 88
Bhaktapur 232, 236, 238
*Bhaktavijay* (of Mahipati) 180
*bhakti* 5, 6, 8, 11, 23, 25, 170, 249, 280, 347, 373, 399, 405, 421, 485
  and disdain for writing 174
  as public experience 176, 184
  as superior to *dharma* 223
  poetry, and *raga* 396
*Bhāṣā dasamskandh* (of Bhupati) 213
*Bhāṣā dasamskandh* (of Nanddas) 96, 212, 229

Bhasha
grammatical and lexical flexibility compared to Sanskrit 273
*bhāva* 351
*Bhaviṣya-purāṇa* 10, 109
Bihar 193
*bishnupad* 274, 351
Biskah festival
and *dapha* 241
Bombay 147
Brajbhasha 7, 71, 249, 300, 359, 367, 370, 380, 408-411, 413, 419
as a language of refinement 229
translations from Sanskrit 78, 88, 94
Brindavan 210, 216
Buddhism 34, 64, 243
Bundelkhand 102
Burma. *See* Myanmar

*Candāyan* (of Daud) 354
*Caurāsī baiṭhak caritra* 217
*Caurāsī bol* (of Hemraj) 87
*Caurāsī vaiṣṇavan kī vārtā* 215, 224
censorship 101
*Chahār 'Unṣūr* (of Mirza Bedil) 324
chronology 112, 114, 120, 134
composite culture
music as constitutive of 11
connoisseur 412
connoisseurship 5, 347, 350
exclusive domains of 408
cosmopolitan local 308
court etiquette
partial reproduction in gatherings 424

Dadu Dayal 360
Dadupanth 172, 364, 368
fascination with writing 380
Dadupanthi 23
*Dādūvāṇī* 58
*Ḍaṅgvai kathā* (of Bhima Kabi) 328, 331, 335, 337, 346
*dapha* 15, 24, 231, 241
adoption by farming communities 237
groups as social networks 242
groups, initiation into 242
meanings generated through performance 244
origins of 233
*darud* 150
*Das bībiyoṉ kī kahānī* 149
*dastan* 185
Delhi 15, 285, 306, 312-313, 317, 319, 322, 324, 445, 457, 474, 479
*Dhammapada* 64
Dhar 287
*ḍhol* 455-456, 458, 462, 465, 469, 472, 474, 478
*dhrupad* 267, 274, 351, 393, 400, 419, 420
and Surdas 225
Dhundhari 367, 381
*Do sau bāvan vaiṣṇavan kī vārtā* (of Hariray) 228
*dotār* 453
*drishtant* 38-41, 43-44, 46
as exemplum 41
*drumming. See lalakhin, tasha*, etc.
and communication of texts 446
as sinful 459, 462
*Dṛṣṭānt-saṅgrah* (of Champaram) 46

elite tastes
for popular genres 16
English 171
epic-Puranic framing of tales 330

Farrukhabad 312
*Futuvvat-nāma-yi Sulṭānī* (of Husain Va'iz Kashifi) 285

*gandharva*
as knowledgeable intermediary 440
*Gañjanāmā* (of Jagannathdas) 366
*ghazal* 13, 298, 319
and performance in multiple contexts 294
performances, Jahangir's fondness for 296
*Gītagovinda* (of Jayadeva) 234
*Gītapañcāśika* (of Jagajjyoti) 234

*go'inda* (poet-musician) 393
Gokarn 209
Golconda 291
*Gommaṭasāra* (of Nemichandra) 71, 79
gossip 5, 315
  and storytelling 312
Gujarat 12, 34, 270, 291, 387, 440, 441
Gujarati 147
*gunigana*
  as knowledgable audience 432
Gwalior 12, 287, 393, 401

hagiography 303
*Haqā'iq-i Hindī* (of 'Abdul Wahid Bilgrami) 420
Haridas, Mandaleshwar 40
Hariram, Swami 40
Herat 287
heteroglossia
  in the *qissa* 205
*Himmatbahādurvirudāvalī*
  of Padmakar 264
Hindavi 8, 9, 14, 75, 93, 151, 300, 330, 354, 393, 395, 424
Hindi 9, 36, 39-40, 55, 57, 67, 77, 88-89, 92, 100, 147, 151, 153, 160, 177, 179, 209, 249, 279-280, 284, 290, 300-301, 309, 315, 322-324, 354, 359-361, 364-365, 367, 369, 381, 408, 471
  in Persian *tazkiras* 322
Hindi court culture
  aural landscape of 250
*Hindī sāhitya koś* (of Dhirendra Varma) 63
Hosay (Muharram) 455, 480
Husain
  as "Guru Husain" 161
hypermetre 466, 471, 473

interiority/exteriority 145
intermedial 12
intermediality 5
intertextuality
  and generic purity 204
Iraq 158

*Jahāngīrjascandrikā* (of Keshavdas) 256, 266, 281
Jainism 10, 15, 22, 32, 34, 35, 36, 62, 64, 69, 72, 74, 79, 81, 85, 88-92, 96-98, 100-102, 387, 392, 488
  Terapanth 102
Jaipur 16, 364
*Janāb-e sayyida kī kahānī* 149, 151, 153, 495
*jati* 448
Jats 55, 57
Jaunpur 13, 92, 317, 337, 385, 389, 402, 404, 442
*jhulna* 360
*Jinasahasranām* (of Banarsidas). *See Sahas Aṭhottar Nām* (of Banarsidas)
Jnaneshwar 170
*Jñāneśvarī* (of Jnaneshwar) 170
*Jorāvarprakāś* (of Surati Mishra) 278

Kabir 25, 53, 55-56, 58, 172, 234
*kahani* 137
  recitation 163
*kalawant* 20
*Kalimāt al-shu'arā* (of Mirza Afzal Sarkhush) 308-309
*Kālkī-purāṇa* 122
*kalma* 467, 472-473, 480
*Kalyāṇamandira stotra* (of Banarsidas) 84
*Kalyāṇamandira stotra* (of Kumudachandra)
  and *Banarsidas' Sivmandir* 79
*Kanhāvat* (of Malik Muhammad Jayasi) 212
Karachi 147, 446, 449, 457, 462-463, 469, 479
*karāmat* 155
Karbala 141, 154
Kashi. *See* Banaras
*katha* 17, 31, 33, 39, 41, 44, 109, 126, 330-335, 337, 344-345, 347, 351, 353-354, 437
  as a dialogic genre 333
  combination of instruction and entertainment in 328
  cyclical pattern of performance 355

*kathavachak* 228, 361
*Kaṭhiyārānāmau* (of Bajid) 361
Kathmandu Valley 232
*Kavīndrakalpalatā* (of Kavindracharya) 274
*Kavīndra-mahābhārata* (of "Kavindra" Parameshwar Dasa) 429
*Kavipriyā* (of Keshavdas) 44, 250, 252, 265, 278
*kavitt* 253, 274, 364
*kavya*
  in Sanskrit 250, 430
*Kāvyamīmāṃsā* (of Rajashekhara) 268
Keshavdas 250, 361
Khari Boli 367
*khayal* 13, 245, 363, 385, 402, 404
Khorasan 287, 312
*kirtan* 171, 334, 399
  at death ceremonies 173
*kirtankar* 6, 17, 23, 170, 238
*kirtankara* 371
*Kirtan mārgadarśikā* (of Lohiya, Krishnadas) 178
Krishna 12, 177, 340
  in sufi contexts 128
*kundaliya* 360

Lahore 144, 285, 453, 478
*lalakhin* (barrel drum) 233, 236, 242
listening 139
  as a feature of court life 283
  as a linguistic feature 153
  as meritorious 146, 331
literacy 180
  resistance to 170
literary activities
  as devotion 363
literary communities
  social broadening of in fifteenth and sixteenth centuries 294
Lucknow 15, 308, 312

*Ma'āṣir al-raḥīmī* (of 'Abd al-Baqi Nihavandi) 290
*Ma'āṣir al-'umarā* (of Shahnavaz Khan) 289
*Ma'dan al-mūsīqī* (of Muhammad Karam Imam Khan) 27
*Mādhavānala Kāmakandalā* (of Alam) 328
*Madhumālatī* (of Manjhan) 75, 91, 328
Madhya Pradesh 34
*Mahābhārata* 97, 109, 125, 220, 331, 335, 338, 343, 345
  logic of overturned in *katha* 344
Maharashtra 172
*mahfil* 250, 268, 281
  and assumed knowledge 279
Mahipati 180
*Mai-khāna* (of Fakhr al-Zamani) 193
Maithili 234, 238
*Majālis-i Jahāngīrī* (of 'Abd al-Sattar Qasim Lahori) 296, 298
*majlis* 138, 144, 296, 315, 322, 425, 481
  recreated in *tazkiras* 304
*maktab* 323
*malfuz* 107
Malwa 287
*Mānakutūhala* (attributed to Man Singh Tomar) 393, 405
*Māncarit* (of Amrit Rai) 258
manuals
  for preachers 59
Maratha Confederacy 176
Marathi 170, 177
*marsiya* 158, 465
*marsiya-go* 156
Mashhad 287, 310
*Masnavī-yi ma'navī* (of Jalaluddin Rumi) 13, 293, 321
*matam* 458
  musical practices associated with 450
Mathura 228
*melas* 1, 33, 56
Mewar 388
*Mir'āt al-asrār* (of 'Abd al-Rahman Chishti) 111
*Mir'āt al-makhlūqāt* (of 'Abd al-Rahman Chishti) 10, 108-110, 113, 124, 128-130, 134-136, 334
*Mirigāvatī* (of Qutban) 75, 91, 151, 328, 339, 350, 385, 390, 392, 396, 399, 404, 442

*mise en abyme*
as performance within text 430, 432, 438
Mithila 442
*mo'jizat* 137, 139, 148, 154, 160-161, 166
Mrauk-U 424, 431, 439, 442
Muharram 139, 142, 445, 453, 457, 459, 462, 467, 476, 478
*muktaka* (free-standing verses)
preference for 267
Multan 287
multilingualism 9, 11, 62, 328, 367
at the Mughal court 300
individual proficiency 271
multiple diglossias 9
*Mūnis al-arvāḥ* (of Jahanara) 299
*Muntakhab al-tavārikh* (of 'Abd al-Qadir Bada'uni) 287
*musha'ira* 488
non-courtly 307
music
as efficacious 417
musical accompaniment 171
musical exchange between court and sufi circles 402
musicians
in *kirtan* 172
Myanmar 424

Nagas 45
*Nairang-i 'ishq* (of Muhammad Akram Ghanimat) 420
*Nāmamālā* (of Banarsidas) 78, 80, 100
Namdev 172, 180, 234
*Nāṭyaśāstra* 234, 432
*Nawādir al-ḥikāyāt* (of Fakhr al-Zamani) 194
*nayika-bheda* 410, 412, 419
translation into Persian 410
Nepal 15, 442
Newar dance-drama 236
Newari 234
*nisani* 360
*nīti* (genre) 79, 94
*niyaz kahani* 7, 137, 155, 162, 164, 488
*Nuskha-yi zībā-yi Jahāngīrī* (of Mutribi Samarqandi) 297

ontologies
affinities between Persianate and Sanskritic 415
oral
circulation 136
culture
normative rules 284
exposition
of written tales 330
orality 170
as a site for experimentation 313
as public 174
in *tazkira* tellings 320
orality and literacy 5
as symbiotic 183
distinction between 169, 174
oral-literate 6, 20
oral transmission 6, 367
and shift to copying 361
of knowledge systems 256, 277
Orchha 14, 250, 254
Orissa 442

*pada* 226
*Padmāvatī* (of Alaol) 438
*Padmāvat* (of Malik Muhammad Jayasi) 328, 334, 425
painting 390
circulation of 392
*pakhavaj* 402
Pakistan 453, 463
*Pañcamasārasaṃhitā* (attributed to Narada) 442
Panchadan (Buddhist festival) 232
*panchali* 432, 434
as public performance 424
multiple performance styles 438
theatrical setting 430
*Panchatantra* 370, 376
Pande, Hemraj 87
Panjabi 155
*Param jyotī stotra* (of Banarsidas). *See Kalyāṇamandira stotra* (of Banarsidas)
paratextual elements
indicating performance 431

*pathshala*
as performance space 210
patron 14, 396
as *rasika* 414
in *kirtan* performances 172
royal, of *kirtankars* 176
patron-performer relationship 281
patrons 410
and their substitution in compositions 267
of *katha* 336
performance
and education 347
and improvisation 270, 278
and worldliness 186
as multivalent 244
as religious instruction 371
described in poetry 260
locations 232
religious performance 199
shaping composition and authorship 426
performance contexts 12
and transmission 427
of Surdas 225
travel of songs between 421
performances
and education 274, 277, 301
performative features
as clues to reception 252
as embedded in genres 250
Persian 7, 8, 9, 21, 129, 279, 284, 290, 303, 313, 319, 322, 361, 385, 395, 408, 411, 424, 440
versions of Hindi verses 301
pictures
as visual aids in storytelling 289
*pir*
as storyteller 108
pluralism
in Hinduism and Islam 135
poet. *See vaggeyakar*
as divinely inspired 19, 428
as performer 347, 428, 431
poetry
as performance 74, 84, 98
poets
and social mobility 291
as musicians, storytellers, and calligraphers 286
contrasts drawn between 313
itinerant 265
Pokhardas, Mahant 24, 40, 57
postmodernism
and power 169
Prakrit 65, 73, 81
*Pratāpsiṃhvirudāvalī* (of Padmakar) 262
*pravachan* 31
preacher 7, 23, 31-33, 36-37, 39-43, 48-49, 55, 57-59, 144, 149, 164
print culture
and changing literary tastes 360
*puja* 243
Pune 176
Punjab 2, 34, 401

*Qābūsnāma* (of Amir 'Unsur al-Ma'ali Kay Kavus) 284
*qasida* 283
replacement with *masnavi* 292
*qaum* 448
*qawwali* 299, 399, 463, 471
Qazvin 477
*qissa* 7, 24, 151, 185
and identification with English 194
and *qissa-khwani* 198, 289
as a master genre code 205
as a performative genre 186
as performative 198
endurance of "generic code" 186
genre codification 190
*qissa* recitation
benefits for the audience 201

*Rādhāmādhavavilāsacampū* (of Jayarama Pindye) 271
*raga* 5, 8, 13, 26, 59, 235, 241, 245, 385, 388, 393, 404, 417, 432
and Surdas 226

and Unani medicine 418
in Namdev's songs 179
*ragadhyana* 385, 387, 389-390, 404
*ragamala* 351, 385, 387, 390, 393, 414
as aggregation of courtly arts 392
musical meaning of 392
*Rāgamālā* (of Kshemakarna) 389, 393
*Rāgamālā* (of Pundarika Vitthala) 389
*Rāgatālanāmā* (of Alaol) 432
*Rāg darpan* (of Saif Khan "Faqirullah") 393, 414
Raghavdas 362
*ragini* 385
Rajasthan 32-35, 38, 49, 79, 360, 364, 366, 368, 399
*Rāmāyaṇa* 380
*Rāmāyaṇa* (of Krittibas) 429
*Rāmcaritmānas* (of Tulsidas) 17, 90, 329, 334, 355, 376
*Ranī Ketakī kī kahānī* (of Insha) 151
*rasa* 5, 26, 50, 52, 53, 77, 250, 327, 335, 346-347, 369, 408, 410-421, 430
theory of, at the Mughal court 410
*vira*, and martial spirit 262
*rasika* 5, 408-409, 411-413
as *nayak* 419
*Rasikapriyā* (of Keshavdas) 44
*ravi* (declaimer)
reciting others' poetry 283
readership
as central to literary culture 254
recitation
and war 264
in Persian literary culture 283
recitations
of religious texts 255
rekhta 323, 360
Rewa 13, 337
*Rigveda* 338
*riti* 10, 249, 268, 274, 408
*ritigranth* 24
*ritigranth* (poetry manual)
as signature genre 249
ritual storytelling 146
*sabha* 424, 430, 438
Sadhukkari 367
*Safīna-yi Hindī* (of Bhagvan Das Hindi) 308-309, 311, 318
*Safīna-yi Khwushgū* (of Bindraban Das Khwushgu) 308, 311, 314, 319, 323
*Sahas Aṭhottar Nām* (of Banarsidas) 81
*Sāhityadarpaṇa* (of Vishvanatha Kaviraja) 44
*sakhis* (as "testimonies") 44
*sama'* 449
*samasyapurti* 250, 265, 269, 272
as entertainment 271
*Samayasāra Kalaśa* (of Amritachandra) 82
*Samayasāra* (of Kundakunda) 72
*Samaysār Nāṭak* (of Banarsidas) 71, 74, 82, 86, 94
*sangita*
as "lyrical arts" 425, 432, 434, 441
*Saṅgīta-cintāmaṇi* (of Jagajjyoti) 235
*Saṅgītadāmodara* (of Shubankara) 389, 435
*Saṅgītadarpaṇa* (of Damodara Misra) 436
*Saṅgītapārijāta* (of Ahobala) 413
*Saṅgītarāja* (of Maharana Kumbha of Chitrakut) 388, 392
*Saṅgītaratnākara* 234, 392, 400-401, 440
*sangitashastra*
Sanskrit sources for 234
*Saṅgītopanisatsāroddhāra* (of Sudhakalasha) 387
Sanskrit 7-9, 14, 21-22, 37, 39, 43, 64-65, 67-68, 70, 72, 76, 78-80, 82-83, 89, 91, 94-98, 100, 102-104, 123, 126, 129, 130, 132-133, 175-177, 209, 218, 234, 249, 258, 271, 272, 354, 361, 380, 385, 389, 389-390, 395, 400, 409-410, 413, 424, 426, 429, 430, 434, 435, 436, 440
limits of comprehension 238
mixed with Newari 239
Sanskritic 16, 171, 230, 257, 361, 396, 400, 408, 409, 417
textual engagement with its past 280

sant 16, 19, 23, 32, 36, 41, 170-172, 175-177, 359, 365, 368, 371, 373
*Sarvāṅgī* (of Gopaldas) 369, 373
*satsang* 33, 490
*Satyavatī kathā* (of Isardas) 331, 335
*savaiya* 253
Sayyid 145, 157, 166
script and literacy 152-153
sermon 2, 5, 16, 20, 22-24, 31, 35-36, 39, 40-41, 57, 70, 73, 79, 87, 103, 115, 125, 145, 154, 163-165, 211, 256, 282, 488
  in poetry ("tattvajñān") 274
*Shāhnāma* (of Firdausi)
  in prosimetrum form 293
*shahr-ashub* 317-318
*Shams al-aṣwāt* (of Ras Baras Khan) 415
Shi'ism 138, 162
Sikhism 19, 399
Sindh 453
*Siyar al-aqṭāb* (of Shaikh Allah Diya) 300
social mobility
  and tension with lineage 295
songbook
  in *dapha* 233
*songs. See bishnupad, khayal, qawwali*, etc.
  multilingual 234
speech
  imitation by instruments 448, 452, 456, 465-466, 469, 471, 473, 478, 481
storyteller
  Akbar's enjoyment of 287
  and repertoire 354
  exposition of *kathas* 344
storytelling 10, 12
  and performance as validating the canon 288, 296
  as entertainment 360
  as sinful 197
*Subodhinī* (of Vallabhacharya) 215
sufism 8, 11, 19, 75, 93, 107, 112, 136, 151, 171, 285, 295, 297, 304, 313, 318-319, 327, 330, 349, 363, 402, 404, 406, 410-412, 417, 420-421, 445, 449, 451, 453, 463
*sukhan* 425
*Sūktimuktāvalī* (of Banarsidas and Kaunrpal) 84
Surdas 234
*Sūrsāgar* 223, 230

*tah* (cymbals) 233, 241
*tala* 235, 241, 245, 352, 401, 432, 473
Taleju (Tantric goddess)
  song in praise of 239
*tamasha* 176
Tansen 265, 287
*Tarjuma-i dāstān-i ṣāḥib-qirān* (of Mirza Aman 'Ali Khan) 187-188
*Tarjuma-yi pārijātak* (of Mirza Raushan Zamir) 413
*tasha* 446
*tazkira* 7, 307, 313, 317
  as catalogue and archive 303
territoriality 49, 59
texts
  as clues to meaning 244
  as evidence about performance 8, 271, 280
  as evidence for performance 284
  as evidence of performance 361
  as replicating performance 178
  as subordinate to performance 240
  bearing traces of orality 327
  oral traces in 380
textuality
  expansion of 21
Timurid
  influence of forms at Mughal court 283
  past in Mughal oral culture 299
*Ṭirāz al-akhbār* (of 'Abd al-Nabi Fakhr al-Zamani) 24, 186, 206
translation 61, 79, 93
  *anuvād* 67
  as a colonial concept 89
  as commentary 90, 94, 104
  as performance 62
  *bhāṣāntar* 68
  from Sanskrit, claims to be 130

in seventeenth-century England 95, 99
*tarjumo/tarjuma* 68
transmission 231
multiple technologies of 231
Trinidad 453, 465
Turki 290

Ujjain 353
Unani medicine 26
universalism 134
Urdu 7, 147, 151, 153, 164, 284, 408
*'urs* 451, 463
and Muharram 446
*ustad-shagird* 306
*Utpattināmau* (of Bajid) 368

*vachana* 425
*vaggeyakar* (poet-composer) 12, 264, 435, 436, 440
*vahis* 174
Varkari 170
*varnashrama dharma* 33, 123
verbal
limits of 25
vernacular 96
vernacularisation 90
*Vikramorvaśīya* (of Kalidasa) 338
*viraha* 50
*Vīrsiṃhdevcarit* (of Keshavdas) 253
*vrat kathas* 149
Vrindaban 12

women's religiosity 152

*yuga*. *See* chronology

# This book need not end here...

At Open Book Publishers, we are changing the nature of the traditional academic book. The title you have just read will not be left on a library shelf, but will be accessed online by hundreds of readers each month across the globe. We make all our books free to read online so that students, researchers and members of the public who can't afford a printed edition can still have access to the same ideas as you.

Our digital publishing model also allows us to produce online supplementary material, including extra chapters, reviews, links and other digital resources. Find *Tellings and Texts* on our website to access its online extras. Please check this page regularly for ongoing updates, and join the conversation by leaving your own comments:

http://www.openbookpublishers.com/isbn/9781783741021

If you enjoyed this book, and feel that research like this should be available to all readers, regardless of their income, please think about donating to us. Our company is run entirely by academics, and our publishing decisions are based on intellectual merit and public value rather than on commercial viability. We do not operate for profit and all donations, as with all other revenue we generate, will be used to finance new Open Access publications.

For further information about what we do, how to donate to OBP, additional digital material related to our titles or to order our books, please visit our website: http://www.openbookpublishers.com

www.ingramcontent.com/pod-product-compliance
Lightning Source LLC
Chambersburg PA
CBHW051331230426
43668CB00010B/1225
* 9 7 8 1 7 8 3 7 4 1 0 2 1 *